A REPORT

OF THE

RECORD COMMISSIONERS

OF THE

CITY OF BOSTON,

CONTAINING

BOSTON BIRTHS FROM A.D. 1700 TO A.D. 1800.

Notice

In many older books, foxing (or discoloration) occurs and, in some instances, print lightens with wear and age. Reprinted books, such as this, often duplicate these flaws, notwithstanding efforts to reduce or eliminate them. The pages of this reprint have been digitally enhanced and, where possible, the flaws eliminated in order to provide clarity of content and a pleasant reading experience.

A Report of the Commissioners of the City of Boston, Containing Boston Births From
A.D. 1700 to A.D. 1800.

Originally published
Boston
1894

Reprinted by:

Janaway Publishing, Inc.
732 Kelsey Ct.
Santa Maria, California 93454
(805) 925-1038
www.janawaygenealogy.com

2012

ISBN 13: 978-1-59641-177-7

Made in the United States of America

[DOCUMENT 43 — 1894.]

REPORT

OF THE

RECORD COMMISSIONERS.

This volume, the Twenty-fourth Report of the Record Commission, takes up the births in the town of Boston at the date reached in the Ninth Report, and contains all the births after 1699 recorded in two volumes of manuscript. It is needless to say that the record is approximately perfect only to 1745; after that date the number gradually diminishes till it becomes a small fraction of the births, which, of course, took place.

The Index has been made as exactly as possible on the same plan as those of the Ninth and Twenty-first Reports. The grouping of names is intended to be a convenience to the reader, but does not necessarily bring together all the different forms of spelling of every name.

The following birth ought to have been printed in the Ninth Report:

Sarah daughter of Ezekiel Cleasby and Sarah his wife born 20 September 1691.

The following entry also relates to the same report:

"Benjamin Son of Joseph & Esther Roberts born 30 April 1696.

N.B. Benjamin Roberts is Registered by the Name of *Samuel* in the Registry of Births within the Town of Boston by Mistake of the Name, and now Entred, from the Information of his Mother, Esther Roberts, this 27th April 1736 being Present in the Office with her said Son."

The editorial work of the present volume has been done by W. S. Appleton, of the original Record Commission.

The City Registrar, upon whom has devolved the duties of the Record Commissioners, desires to express his thanks to Mr. Appleton for his kindness in preparing this volume. It has seemed best to continue the old name of Reports of the Record Commission until the series is completed.

OLD COURT HOUSE, Nov. 1, 1894.

BOSTON TOWN RECORDS.

BIRTHS.

1700.

Ann Daughter of Jeremiah and Mary Allen,	Born	20 March.
Natha. Son of John and Elizabeth Alden,	"	6 July.
Ann Daughter of Joseph and Ann Allen,	"	28 Do.
Thomas Son of Matthew and Margaret Armstrong,	"	21 Do.
John Son of Samuel and Mary Avis,	"	14 October.
Lidia Daughter of William and Elizabeth Ambros,	"	25 February.
John son of John and Eliner Butler,	"	1 March.
Susanna Daughter of Newcomb and Mary Blaque,	"	19 Do.
Rebecca Daughter of William and Mary Brown,	"	5 April.
Henry son of Edward and Mary Brumfield,	"	13 Do.
John son of John and Deborah Burnet,	"	25 Do.
Samuel son of Samuel and Ann Brackinbury,	"	7 May.
John son of William and Ann Brown,	"	1 July.
Bethiah Daughter of Samuel and Christian Bridge,	"	6 Do.
John son of John and Rachel Barnes,	"	20 Do.
Susanna Daughter of Jacob and Thiadotia Bill,	"	7 August.
John son of Henry and Abiah Brightman,	"	10 Do.
Thomas son of Nicholas and Mary Buttolph,	"	12 Do.
John son of Stephen and Marcy Badger,	"	27 Do.
Thomas son of Joseph and Joanna Buckley,	"	7 October.
Eliza. Daughter of Thomas and Lidia Barnes,	"	16 November.
Samuel son of Adinah and Abigail Bulfinch,	"	20 Do.
Benja. son of James and Elizabeth Babbage,	"	8 December,
Thomas son of John and Elizabeth Bucannan,	"	27 Do.
Samuel son of Samuel and Sarah Barrett,	"	9 Do.
John son of William and Rebecca Briggs,	"	31 Do.
Nicholas son of Nicholas and Dorcus Bows,	"	4 January.
Thomas son of Edward and Mary Boylstone,	"	15 Do.
Benja. son of Benjamin and Elizabeth Brame,	"	24 Do.
Hannah Daughter of Joseph and Rebecca Brisco,	"	27 November.
William son of Thomas and Rooksby Creese,	"	24 March.
William son of Francis and Priscilla Castle,	"	30 April.
Keats son of Alexander and Sarah Chamberlin,	"	11 May.
Edward son of Edward and Mary Cox,	"	13 July.
John son of John and Ruth Cook,	"	21 Do.
Ann Daughter of John and Judeth Colman,	"	4 August.
Susanna Daughter of Ely and Susanna Crow,	"	24 September.
Sarah Daughter of Andrew and Sarh Cuningham,	"	16 Do.
Ezekiel son of Ezek. and Elizabeth Cravath,	"	2 October.
Benja. son of Jeremiah and Judeth Cushing,	"	15 November.
John son of Nathaniel and Elizabeth Coney,	"	14 January.
John son of William and Bethiah Clear,	"	2 February.

Abigail Daughter of John and Mary Coney,	Born	5 January.
Eliza. Daughter of Henry and Abigail Dason,	"	18 March.
Eliza. Daughter of Samuel and Elizabeth Drownd,	"	20 April.
Sarah Daughter of Charles and Sarah Demerry,	"	9 May.
John son of Stephen and Mercy Draper,	"	25 August.
John son of William and Dorothy Daniel,	"	6 November.
Benja. son of Benja. and Hannah Dyer,	"	27 Do.
Joseph son of Joseph and Ann Dowden,	"	23 Do.
Thomas son of Richard and Sarah Draper,	"	1 January.
Mary Daughter of John and Sybill Edwards,	"	8 March
Benja. son of Joseph and Sarah Eliot,	"	23 May.
Eliza. Daughter of Jonathan and Pnelope Everard,	"	17 June.
Samuel son of Benjamin and Elizabeth Emons,	"	27 Do
Mary Daughter of David and Rachel Eustis,	"	21 August.
John son of John and Katharin Eyres,	"	7 Do.
Mary Daughter of Obodiah and Judeth Emons,	"	2 September.
Margart. Daughter of Ned and Margaret Edwards Negros,	"	21 Do.
Mary Daughter of Nathaniel and Mary Emons,	"	29 October.
John son of John and Elizabeth Eustus,	"	16 November.
Jacob son of Joseph and Sylence Eliot,	"	14 Do.
Jonathon son of Jonathon and Sarah Eustis,	"	25 December.
Ebenezer son of William and Darcos Egglestone,	"	25 February.
Eliza. Daughter of James and Love English,	"	30 January.
William son of Robert and Elizabeth Ellis,	"	28 December.
Samuel son of Francis and Elizabeth Foxcroft,	"	5 June.
Richard son of Richard and Mary Fyfield,	"	20 July.
Joseph son of Benja. and Mary Fitch,	"	30 Do.
Joseph son of Joseph and Joanna Flood,	"	9 August.
Ann Daughter of Edward and Mary Gillings,	"	6 April.
Scarlot son of William and Elizabeth Gill,	"	10 Do.
Anna Daughter of Isaac and Anna Greenwood,	"	7 Do.
Margaret Daughter of Benja. and Hannah Gallop,	"	15 June.
Mary Daughter of Samuel and Elizabeth Gardner,	"	20 July.
Hannah Daughter of John and Sarah Gerrish,	"	14 August.
Barthol. son of Bartholomew and Mary Green,	"	29 Do.
Elias son of Samuel and Priscilla Grice,	"	1 September.
Thomas son of John and Mary Gyles,	"	8 October.
Richard son of James and Margaret Gooding,	"	18 Do.
Joseph son of James and Elizabeth Gooch,	"	18 November.
Hannah Daughter of Thomas and Experience Goold,	"	13 Do.
Benja. son of Benjamin and Mehitabell Gipson,	"	4 Do.
Eliza. Daughter of Nathaniel and Elizabeth Goodwin,	"	18 January.
David son of David and Martha Gwin,	"	17 Do.
John son of John and Mary Goodwin.	"	8 February.
Eliza. Daughter of Joseph and Mary Heath,	"	5 March.
Eliza. Daughter of Thomas and Mary Hunt,	"	2 April.
Priscilla Daughter of Atherton and Mary Haugh,	"	14 Do.
Nathaniel son of Nathaniel and Sarah Holmes,	"	22 July.
John son of Henry and Mary Hill,	"	7 August.
Sarah Daughter of Thomas and Sarah Huggins,	"	13 Do.
Joseph son of Samuel and Mary Hunting,	"	28 Do.
Richard son of Stephen and Mary Hunnowell,	"	9 September.
Abraham son of Abraham and Martha Hill,	"	5 October.
William son of Benja. and Mary Hollowell,	"	11 November.
Edward son of Edward and Mary Hill,	"	7 December.
Benja. son of Joseph and Elizabeth Hill,	"	28 Do.
Rebecca Daughter of Francis and Rebecca Holmes,	"	18 Do.
William son of William and Martha Hannah,	"	10 September.
David son of David and Mary Jesse,	"	18 April.
Mary Daughter of Mathew and Susanna Jones,	"	19 May.

BIRTHS — 1700. 3

Abigail Daughter of David and Mabell Jenners,	Born 19 September.
Susanna Daughter of John and Susanna Jackson,	" 6 December.
Zechary son of Daniel and Susanna Johonnot,	" 20 January.
Henry son of Nathaniel and Joanna Kittle,	" 31 March.
Halsey son of John and Lidia Kelton,	" 15 June.
Mary Daughter of Roger and Abigail Kilcup,	" 5 July.
John son of Joshua and Agnes Kent,	" 11 August.
Daniel son of Daniel and Priscilla Loring,	" 30 March.
Susanna Daughter of Nathaniel and Susanna Loring,	" 15 October.
Ann Daughter of John and Ann Lawson,	" 9 November.
Crumil son of Joseph and Elizabeth Lobdell,	" 3 December.
Ann Daughter of James and Ann Lablond,	" 12 Do.
William son of Isaac and Sarah Loring,	" 23 Do.
Abigail Daughter of Joseph and Mary Lowden,	" 2 October.
Elizabeth Daughter of Henry and Dinah Mattox,	" 10 March.
Thomas son of Thomas and Sarah Miller,	" 24 Do.
Mary Daughter of Dunkin and Mary Maycom,	" 15 Do.
Sarah Daughter of John and Sarah Marshall,	" 5 April.
Thomas son of Thomas and Sarah Molles,	" 4 May.
Mary Daughter of Christopher and Mary Monck,	" 20 Do.
Samuel son of Joseph and Hannah Maylem,	" 8 June.
Eliza. Daughter of Thomas and Mary Mollens,	" 25 August.
Joseph son of Samuel and Ruth Marshall,	" 4 October.
Mary Daughter of John and Mary Mountfort,	" 1 Do.
Ann Daughter of Thomas and Sarah Marbbell,	" 15 November.
Ezekiel son of Ezekiel and Priscilla Needham,	" 5 March.
Mary Daughter of Robert and Mary Noakes,	" 3 June.
John son of Natha. and Sarah Newdigate,	" 1 December.
Eliza. Daughter of George and Elizabeth Newel,	" 14 November.
Daniel son of Daniel and Elizabeth Oliver,	" 13 June.
Mary Daughter of Thomas and Remember Pirkins,	" 27 March.
Elizabeth Daughter of John and Mary Philips,	" 11 May.
Esther Daughter of Obediah and Margaret Procter,	" 25 June.
John son of James and Elizabeth Pitts,	" 9 July.
Elizabeth Daughter of John and Margaret Pratt,	" 24 August.
Hannah Daughter of Elias and Sarah Purington,	" 13 September.
Mary Daughter of Edward and Abiel Porter,	" 2 October.
James son of John and Sarah Parker,	" 28 Do.
Thomas son of Thomas and Hannah Platts,	" 1 February.
Abigail Daughter of Mark and Faith Pilkinson,	" 12 Do.
Mary Daughter of William and Mary Payne,	" 6 January.
John son of John and Margaret Richardson,	" 1 August.
William son of William and Elizabeth Randol,	" 26 October.
John son of John and Rebecca Ransford,	" 24 January.
Susanna Daughter of Humphry and Susanna Richards,	" 24 Do.
Ruth, Daughter of John and Martha Ruggles,	" 20 February.
Eliza } Mary } Twins of John and Grace Stephens,	" 21 March.
William son of William and Rachel Snoton,	" 26 Do.
Ruth Daughter of Richard and Margaret Stratton,	" 11 April.
Joshua son of Alexandr. and Sarah Sherrard,	" 7 Do.
Thomas son of Thomas and Eliza. Smith,	" 2 Do.
John son of John and Olive Smallpeace,	" 26 June.
Mary Daughter of Josiah and Rebecca Sanders,	" 5 July.
Sarah Daughter of Thomas and Sarah Stephens,	" 29 Do.
John son of William and Martha Shute,	" 3 August.
Francis son of Cyprian and Elizabeth Southack,	" 9 Do.
John son of Henry and Sarah Smith,	" 20 Do.
Mary Daughter of John and Mary Stephens,	" 8 Do.
Samuel son of Joseph and Hanna Simpson,	" 20 September.

Sarah Daughter of Jeremiah and Ann Smith,	Born	22 Do.
Thomas son of Thomas and Margat. Savage,	"	17 Do.
Eliza. Daughter of John and Rely Simpson,	"	30 November.
Thomas son of Nathaniel and Margaret Shaw,	"	19 Do.
Benja. son of Robert and Esther Sanderson,	"	22 December.
Thomas son of Richard and Sarah Sherren,	"	15 Do.
Rebecca Daughter of Wigglesworth and Nesly Switser,	"	10 Do.
Susanna Daughter of John and Lidia Solle,	"	25 Do.
Mary Daughter of Richard and Dorothy Smithson,	"	10 January.
Thomas son of John and Ann Smith,	"	19 February.
Abigail Daughter of Samuel and Abigail Torrey,	"	18 April.
John son of John and Deborah Tyler,	"	15 August.
James son of John and Martha Twing,	"	18 January.
Sarah Daughter of Anthony and Sarah Thorning,	"	14 June.
Samuel son of David and Mary Vaughan,	"	31 October.
Sarah Daughter of Andrew and Eliza. Veach,	"	20 Do.
Mercy Daughter of Thomas and Hanna Verin,	"	4 December.
Lidia Daughter of Samuel and Ann White,	"	5 March.
John son of John and Sarah Wharton,	"	27 Do.
Thadeus son of Edward and Sarah Watkins,	"	27 Do.
John son of Edward and Hanna Winslow,	"	14 April.
Mary Daughter of William and Mary Weber,	"	3 August.
Rebecca Daughter of Thomas and Rebecca Wells,	"	5 September.
Eliza. Daughter of Robert and Elizabeth White,	"	27 Do.
Daniel son of Daniel and Lidia Wier,	"	12 October.
Mary Daughter of James and Mary Wiborn,	"	27 Do.
Ruth Daughter of Eccabod and Dorothy Williston,	"	16 November.
Curnelius son of Jonathon and Hannah Woldo,	"	13 February.
Joseph Son of Soloman Kneeland and Mary his Wife,	"	14 December 1700.
John Son of Joseph Halsey and Eliza. his Wife,	"	3 February 1700.
John Son of Isaac Biscon and Ann his Wife,	"	16 November 1700.
Ralph Son of John Carter and Phillipie his Wife,	"	10 December 1700.
John Son of John Goff and Hannah his Wife,	"	16 March 1700.
Abigall Daughter of Nathaniel Green and Elizabeth his Wife,	"	9 February 1700.
Daughter of William Harwood and Phebee his Wife,	"	1 March 1700.
of Samuell Hood and Deborah his Wife,	"	8 May 1700.
Elizabeth Daughter of Andrew Knot and Susana his Wife,	"	21 March 1700.
James Son of Thomas Simkins and Margery his Wife,	"	15 February 1700.
Peter Son of Solomon Townsend and Elizabeth his Wife,	"	24 March 1700.
Joshua Son of James Townsend and Alice his Wife,	"	14 March 1700.
Mary Daughter of John Venteman and Eliza. his Wife,	"	14 March 1700.
Mary Daughter of William Way and Penelopee his Wife,	"	2 March 1700.
Mary Daughter of Thomas Winsor and Rachell his Wife,	"	24 March 1700.
Joseph Son of William Brown and Mercy his Wife,	"	11 March 1700.
Joseph Son of William Eustise and Sarah his Wife,	"	12 January 1700.
Jeremiah Son of a Negro Richard and Hager his Wife,	"	7 Aprill 1700.
Margaret daughter of Joseph Soper and Margaret his Wife,	"	14 October 1700.

BIRTHS — 1700-1.

Mercy daughter of James Taylor and Rebecca his Wife,	Born	13 November 1700.
Susana daughter of Daniel Willard and Mary his Wife,	"	15 November 1700.
Elizabeth daughter of Benja. Alford and Mary his Wife,	"	26 July 1700.
Abigall daughter of Elisha Audling and Mary his Wife,	"	1 January 1700.
Elizabeth daughter of James Ingles and Love his Wife,	"	30 January 1700.
Samuell Son of Samuell Meers and Mary his Wife,	"	10 April 1700.
James Son of Paul Collings and Mary his Wife,	"	26 September 1700.
Ann daughter of Peter Hauksworth and Eliza. his Wife,	"	13 December 1700.
William Son of Peter Townsend and Mary his Wife,	"	20 July 1700.
Benjamin Son of Benjamin Wheeler and Sarah his Wife,	"	17 November 1700.

1701.

Beginning ye year the 25th of March.

Josiah Son of Elisha Androse and Elinor his Wife,	Born	23 March 1700/1.
John Son of Silence Allen and Esther his Wife,	"	13 March 1700/1.
Thomas Son of John Adams and Hannah his Wife,	"	29 March 1701.
Joshua Son of John Atwood and Mary his Wife,	"	10 Aprill 1701.
Martha Daughter of Isaac Adams and Martha his Wife,	"	27 Aprill 1701.
Nathaniel Son of David Adams and Loice his Wife,	"	29 October 1701.
Thomas Son of John Alden and Elizabeth his Wife,	"	13 August 1701.
Samuell Son of Samuell Bason and Mary his Wife,	"	17 March 1700/1.
Joseph Son of Joseph Bridgham and Mercy his Wife,	"	16 Aprill 1701.
Samuell Son of Samuell Bow, a negro and Eliner his Wife,	"	7 July 1701.
Esther Daughter of John Brentall and Phebee his Wife,	"	5 July 1701.
Joseph Son of Joseph Burch and Elizabeth his Wife,	"	3 July 1701.
Sarah Daughter of Edward Belcher and Mary his Wife,	"	4 August 1701.
Samuell Son of Samuell Bayley and Deliverence his Wife,	"	26 July 1701.
Elizabeth Daughter of Henry Brightman and Abiel his Wife,	"	15 August 1701.
Elizabeth Daughter of Moses Bradford and Elizabeth his Wife,	"	21 September 1701.
Isabela Daughter of Samuell Burrell and Martha his Wife,	"	5 September 1701.
Sarah Daughter of Josiah Biles and Sarah his Wife,	"	24 September 1701.
Elizabeth Daughter of Samuell Brackenbery and Ann his Wife,	"	1 October 1701.
Mary Daughter of Richard Barnet and Katherine his Wife,	"	28 September 1701.
Damoras Daughter of Stephen Bruff and Damoras his Wife,	"	27 October 1701.
Allexander Son of Allexander Bulman and Margret his Wife,	"	26 October 1701.
Elizabeth Daughter of Gilbert Bant and Mercy his Wife,	"	11 July 1701.
John Son of John Bennet and Sarah his Wife,	"	14 May 1701.

Daniell Son of Daniell Berry and Mary his Wife,	Born	15 Novemoer 1701.
Jonathan Son of John Bennet and Ruth his Wife,	"	16 October 1701.
Edward Son of Lawrence Brown and Edite his Wife,	"	1 November 1701.
Jane Daughter of Negro Boston and Jane his Wife,	"	1 November 1701.
Jonathan Son of Jonathan Bill and Ann his Wife,	"	27 November 1701.
Elizabeth Daughter of Thomas Berry and Elizabeth his Wife,	"	27 March 1701.
Mary Daughter of William Bowen and Mary his Wife,	"	18 March 1700/1.
Jonathan Son of Thomas Cushing and Deberah his Wife,	"	13 March 1700/1.
Charles Son of Charles Chancey and Sarah his Wife,	"	30 March 1701.
Mary Daughter of William Crow and Elizabeth his Wife,	"	8 Aprill 1701.
Ruth Daughter of Ebenezer Chafen and Elizabeth his Wife,	"	28 May 1701.
David Son of David Crage and Deborah his Wife,	"	6 July 1701.
Susana Daughter of Samuell Clough and Ruth his Wife,	"	15 July 1701.
Samuell Son of Daniell Collins and Rebecca his Wife,	"	24 July 1701.
Sarah Daughter of Samuell Clark and Hannah his Wife,	"	15 August 1701.
Thomas Son of Thomas Carew and Anna his Wife,	"	12 August 1701.
Williams Son of Edward Collins and Sarah his Wife,	"	14 August 1701.
Joseph Son of Joseph Cowell and Elizabeth his Wife,	"	3 October 1701.
Thomas Son of Thomas Cox and Sarah his Wife,	"	6 October 1701.
William Son of Samuell Clark and Sarah his Wife,	"	26 October 1701.
Mehitabell Daughter of Thomas Cooper and Mehitabell his Wife,	"	24 August 1701.
Samuell Son of Mathias Cowdry and Sarah his Wife,	"	18 November 1701.
John Son of John Charnock and Mary his Wife,	"	11 December 1701.
Patience Daughter of David Copp and Patience his Wife,	"	25 December 1701.
James Son of Henry Chamlet and Elizabeth his Wife,	"	25 December 1701.
Still born: Son of John Conniball and Martha his Wife,	"	18 March 1701.
Jonathan Son of Eliazur Darbey and Mary his Wife,	"	11 March 1700/1.
Addington Son of Addington Davenport and Elizabeth his Wife,	"	16 May 1701.
William Son of Henry Dason and Abigall his Wife,	"	24 July 1701.
Elijah Son of Elijah Dubleday and Sarah his Wife,	"	12 August 1701.
Joshua Son of Joshua Davise and Rebecca his Wife,	"	11 September 1701.
Elizabeth Daughter of Mathew Delver and Elizabeth his Wife,	"	3 February.*
Ebenezer Son of Mathew Delver and Elizabeth his Wife,	"	16 April.*
Mary Daughter of Mathew Delver and Elizabeth his Wife,	"	2 September.*

* Of course these were not all born in 1701, but the edge of leaf is torn off.

Births — 1701.

Elizabeth Daughter of Joseph Dolbeer and Hannah his Wife,	Born	23.
William Son of Phillip Dillorock and Elizabeth his Wife,	"	1 J.
Bathsheba Daughter of Jonathan Evans and Mary his Wife,	"	1 March.
Lydia Daughter of Samuell Earl and Mary his Wife,	"	11 Aprill.
Thomas Son of Daniell Edwards and Martha his Wife,	"	30 March 1701.
Jacob Son of Jacob Emms and Mary his Wife,	"	16 May 1701.
Elizabeth Daughter of John Ela and Jane his Wife,	"	18 July 1701.
Elizabeth Daughter of John Foy and Sarah his Wife,	"	13th June 1701.
Samuell Son of Samuell Foster and Rebecca his Wife,	"	25 June 1701.
Sarah Daughter of John Foster and Sarah his Wife,	"	17 June 1701.
Abigall Daughter of Richard Frankling and Abigall his Wife,	"	13 July 1701.
Thomas Son of Thomas Freeman and Alice his Wife,	"	4 September 1701.
Mary Daughter of Benjamen Flood and Mary his Wife,	"	30 September 1701.
Ebenezer Son of Josiah Frankling and Abiah his Wife,	"	20 September 1701.
John Son of Richard Flood and Elizabeth his Wife,	"	7 December 1701.
Abigall Daughter of Richard Flood and Elizabeth his Wife,	"	7 December 1701.
Rachell Daughter of Henry Ferry and Susana his Wife,	"	12 December 1701.
Elizabeth Daughter of Azor Gale and Mary his Wife,	"	25 March 1701.
Joseph Son of Joseph Green and Mary his Wife,	"	22 June 1701.
Elizabeth Daughter of Thomas Godfrey and Esther his Wife,	"	12 June 1701.
Walter Son of Walter Gutrage and Anna his Wife,	"	9 July 1701.
Winsor Son of Winsor Golden and Elizabeth his Wife,	"	17 July 1701.
Bartholomew Son of Bartholomew Green and Mary his Wife,	"	22 October 1701.
Sarah Daughter of John Gibbs and Mary his Wife,	"	12 October 1701.
Harrison Son of Edward Gray and Susana his Wife,	"	22 November 1701.
Samuell Son of Robert Gibbs and Mary his Wife,	"	9 December 1701.
James Son of Briant Gilmore and Mercy his Wife,	"	1 December 1701.
Samuell Son of Samuell Gardener and Elizabeth his Wife,	"	17 December 1701.
Sarah Daughter of John Goldthwait and Sarah his Wife,	"	18 December 1701.
mas Son of William Gold and Mercy his Wife,	"	30 January 1701.
Daughter of Jonathan Gatchell and Martha his Wife,	"	3 March 1701.
beth Daughter of Nathaniell Gilbert and Elizabeth his Wife,	"	26 February 1701.
Daughter of Tarrence Henley and Elizabeth his Wife,	"	10 May 1701.
Daughter of Francis Hudson and Mary his Wife,	"	27 May 1701.

Son of John Homer and Margery his Wife,	Born	29 June 1701.
Son of Samuell Hewes and Hannah his Wife,	"	13 October 1701.
Sarah Daughter of Jacob Hallaway and Mary his Wife,	"	14 November 1701.
Elizabeth Daughter of John Hughs and Deliverence his Wife,	"	19 December 1701.
Daniell Son of Joshua Hensha and Mary his Wife,	"	3 December 1701.
William Son of Thomas Hay and Bridget his Wife,	"	8 February 1701.
Mary } Daughters of Joseph Hood and Judith his Sarah } Wife,	"	20 } 21 } February 1701.
Ruth Daughter of Thomas Hudson and Sarah his Wife,	"	13 March 1701.
Jonathan Son of Jonathan Jackson and Mary his Wife,	"	28 Aprill 1701.
John Son of John Jepson and Apthia his Wife,	"	26 March 1701.
Rebecca Daughter of Nathaniel Jarvise and Elizabeth his Wife,	"	11 December 1701.
Nathaniel Son of Stephen Johnson and Mary his Wife,	"	18 January 1701.
Hannah Daughter of Nathaniel Kettel and Johannah his Wife,	"	23 Aprill 1701.
Rebecca Daughter of Christopher Kelbey and Sarah his Wife,	"	27 December 1701.
Richard Son of Richard King and Abigall his Wife,	"	11 August 1701.
Joseph Son of Joseph Kemball and Elizabeth his Wife,	"	24 February 1701.
Ebenezer Son of Ebenezer Lowel and Elizabeth his Wife,	"	5 June 1701.
Mary Daughter of Edward Lyde and Deborah his Wife,	"	31 July 1701.
Martha Daughter of Thomas Lee and Deborah his Wife,	"	1 August 1701.
Sarah Daughter of Daniell Loreing and Priscilla his Wife,	"	15 November 1701.
Martha Daughter of David Langdon and Martha his Wife,	"	23 November 1701.
Mary Daughter of Thomas Leasonbee and Mercy his Wife,	"	14 November 1701.
Alice Daughter of Peter Leech and Hannah his Wife,	"	21 February 1701.
Sarah Daughter of Charles Morrise and Esther his Wife,	"	7 May 1701.
Joana Daughter of Samuell Marrion and Mary his Wife,	"	10 May 1701.
John Son of John More and Martha his Wife,	"	22 June 1701.
Sarah Daughter of Robert Mason and Moriah his Wife,	"	26 July 1701.
John Son of John Marshall and Sarah his Wife,	"	21 August 1701.
Deliverence Daughter of Robert Mogerage and Elizabeth his Wife,	"	23 July 1701.
Francis Son of Francis Marshall and Martha his Wife,	"	10 September 1701.
Hannah Daughter of Thomas Marshall and Dorcas his Wife,	"	5 September 1701.
Katherin Daughter of Samuell Miers and Mary Katherina his Wife,	"	25 September 1701.
Esther Daughter of Florence Mackartey and Sarah his Wife,	"	21 July 1701.

BIRTHS — 1701.

Hezekiah Son of Duncan Maicum and Mary his Wife,	Born	10 October 1701.
Joyce Daughter of Christopher Myngs and Joyce his Wife,	"	15 December 1701.
Jacob Son of Allexander Miller and Dorcas his Wife,	"	3 March 1701.
Sarah Daughter of John Noyes and Susana his Wife,	"	31 March 1701.
Mary Daughter of Ezekiel Needham and Priscilla his Wife,	"	8 April 1701.
Susana Daughter of Eley Orio and Ann his Wife,	"	3 May 1701.
John Son of John Plasteed and Sarah his Wife,	"	27 March 1701.
Joseph Son of Daniel Phippen and Elizabeth his Wife,	"	28 May 1701.
John Son of John Peirce and Mary his Wife,	"	9 July 1701.
Joseph Son of Jacob Peirce and Rachell his Wife,	"	17 August 1701.
Hamond Son of Thomas Pearson and Elizabeth his Wife,	"	7th September 1701.
Jacob Son of Jacob Parker and Ann his Wife,	"	29 August 1701.
Elizabeth Daughter of Edward Proctor and Elizabeth his Wife,	"	20 September 1701.
Joseph Son of Thomas Peck and Johanna his Wife,	"	27 August 1701.
Hannah Daughter of Mathew Pauling and Sarah his Wife,	"	16 October 1701.
Elizabeth Daughter of Thomas Perkins and Remember his Wife,	"	13 October 1701.
John Son of Obediah Proctor and Margaret his Wife,	"	19 November 1701.
Ann Daughter of Samuel Phillips and Hannah his Wife,	"	28 November 1701.
Sarah Daughter of Edward Porter and Abiel his Wife,	"	11 January 1701.
Sarah Daughter of John Paine and Bethia his Wife,	"	23 February 1701.
Elizabeth ⎫ Daughters of Allexander Prindle and Mary gem ⎬ Sarah his Wife,	" "	31 January 1701. 16 January 1701.
Peter Son of Peter Quakee and Hannah his Wife,	"	4 May 1701.
William Son of Thomas Russell and Ann his Wife,	"	1 July 1701.
James Son of Samuell Russell and Mary his Wife,	"	17 August 1701.
John Son of John Ruck and Hannah his Wife,		
Ebenezer Son of William Robie and Elizabeth his Wife,	"	29 September 1701.
Mehitabel Daughter of Joseph Russell and Mary his Wife,	"	27 September 1701.
Nicholas Son of Nicholas Roberts and Mary his Wife,	"	1 December 1701.
Samuell Son of James Seward and Edey his Wife,	"	7 Aprill 1701.
Joseph Son of Joseph Skinner and Elizabeth his Wife,	"	9 Aprill 1701.
Elizabeth Daughter of Joseph Simson and Elizabeth his Wife,	"	16 Aprill 1701.
Mary Daughter of Seth Smith and Mehitabel his Wife,	"	20 May 1701.
Elizabeth Daughter of John Sharp and Mary his Wife,	"	26 June 1701.
Allexander Son of Allexander Seers and Rebecca his Wife,	"	28 June 1701.
John Son of Joseph Snelling and Rebecca his Wife,	"	22 July 1701.

Mary Daughter of Winsor Sandey and Mehitabell his Wife,	Born	19 July 1701.
Richard Son of William Snowton and Rachell his Wife,	"	22 July 1701.
Ebenezer Son of Clement Sumner and Margaret his Wife,	"	1 September 1701.
Grace Daughter of John Stevens and Grace his Wife,	"	1 September 1701.
Thomas Son of William Simson and Susana his Wife,	"	5 September 1701.
Rebecca Daughter of Rowland Storey and Ann his Wife,	"	28 August 1701.
John Son of John Sables and Prissilla his Wife,	"	26 September 1701.
Elizabeth Daughter of John Smith and Jane his Wife,	"	2 September 1701.
James Son of James Smith and Elizabeth his Wife,	"	13 October 1701.
John Son of Joshua Scottow and Sarah his Wife,	"	15 November 1701.
Dorcas Daughter of Benjamen Snelling and Jamina his Wife,	"	13 December 1701.
Benjamen Son of Josiah Stone and Mary his Wife,	"	2 December 1701.
Winsor Son of Allexander Sherar and Sarah his Wife,	"	6 January 1701.
Sarah Daughter of William Smith and Mary his Wife,	"	1 January 1701
Lidia Daughter of James Studson and Susana his Wife,	"	1 January 1701.
Thomas Son of Thomas Stevens and Sarah his Wife,	"	31 December 1701.
Judeth Daughter of Samuell Sewall Esqr. and Hannah his Wife,	"	2 January 1701.
Mary Daughter of Thomas Savage and Mehitabel his Wife,	"	16 March 1701.
Ebenezer Son of Thomas Tyler and Meream his Wite,	"	31 March 1701.
Deborah Daughter of Samuell Torrey and Abigall his Wife,	"	2 August 1701.
Elizabeth Daughter of Samuell Tely and Sarah his Wife,	"	26 January 1701.
Ebenezer Son of Samuell Turell and Lidia his Wife,	"	5 February 1701.
Mary Daughter of Henry Tomson and Mary his Wife,	"	9 February 1701.
Mary Daughter of Richard Thomas and Mary his Wife,	"	25 January 1701.
George Son of John Viler and Mary his Wife.	"	17 May 1701
Jonathan Son of John Viall and Mary his Wife,	"	21 September 1701.
Daniell Son of James Updike and Elizabeth his Wife,	"	13 December 1701.
Elizabeth Daughter of Francis Whitman and Mary his Wife,	"	3 May 1701.
Jonathan Son of Jonathan Wardwell and Katherin his Wife,	"	11 May 1701
Nathaniell Son of Nathaniel Weeler and Mary his Wife,	"	25 May 1701.
Joseph Son of John Wakefeeld and Eliza: his Wife,	"	9 June 1701.
Rachell Daughter of Daniell Wormwell and Sarah his Wife,	"	21 June 1701.
Everill Son of James Waycomb and Elizabeth his Wife,	"	6 July 1701.
Abigall Daughter of Joseph Wadsworth and Hannah his Wife,	"	27 July 1701.

Births — 1701.

Mary Daughter of Jonathan Williams and Mary his Wife,	Born	4 August 1701.
Deborah Daughter of Andrew Waker and Elizabeth his Wife,	"	6 October 1701.
Christopher Son of John Wyate and Anna his Wife,	"	15 October 1701.
William Son of William White and Elizabeth his Wife,	"	16 October 1701.
Mary Daughter of Andrew Willet and Susana his Wife,	"	18 November 1701.
Mary Daughter of John Wharton and Sarah his Wife,	"	5 October 1701.
Sarah Daughter of Joseph Williams and Sarah his Wife,	"	6 December 1701.
Elisha Son of Elisha Webb and Lidia his Wife,	"	16 November 1701.
Nathaniell Son of Nathaniell Williams and Ann his Wife,	"	5 December 1701.
Thomas Son of Thomas Wells and Rebecca his Wife,	"	3 January 1701.
James Son of Mathew Watters and Jane his Wife,	"	17 February 1701.
Lydia daughter of William Alden and Mary his Wife,	"	22th December 1701.
Stillborn of Joseph Allen and Ann his Wife,	"	6 August 1701.
Enoch Son of Thomas Creese and Rooksbey his Wife,	"	5th March 1701.
Mary daughter of John Carpenter and Mary his Wife,	"	28 April 1701.
William Son of Ezekiel Carvat and Elizabeth his Wife,	"	20 March 1701.
Damaris daughter of Ebenezar Dennis and Damaris his Wife,	"	8 July 1701.
William Son of Robert Ellis and Elizabeth his Wife,	"	17 March 1701.
Lettice daughter of Henry Franckling and Sarah his Wife,	"	6 November 1701.
Jeremiah Son of Richard Gridley and Rebecca his Wife,	"	10 March 1701.
Hannah Daughter of Thomas Gyles and Martha his Wife,	"	4 February 1701.
Obediah Son of William Gill and Elizabeth his Wife,	"	3 March 1701.
Jane daughter of John Halsey and Jane his Wife,	"	10 March 1701.
Edward Son of John Hobbie and Ann his Wife,	"	13 July 1701.
Wilmat daughter of Samuell Mould and Mary his Wife,	"	5th July 1701.
Huldah Mounjoy daughter of William Normand and Huldah his Wife,	"	23 December 1701.
Ephraim Son of William Randoll and Eliza. his Wife,	"	18th March 1701.
Mary daughter of David Jesse and Mary his Wife,	"	20 May 1701.
Thomas Son of Thomas Smith and Mary his Wife,	"	10 March 1701.
Mellows Son of Richard Thornton and Sarah his Wife,	"	7 March 1701.
Thomas Son of Thomas Tomlin and Sarah his Wife.	"	11 August 1701
Sarah daughter of Thomas Wallise and Christian his Wife,	"	24 March 1701.
William Son of Daniell Willard and Mary his Wife,	"	1 February 1701.

William Son of Edward Winslow and Hannah his Wife,	Born	24 March 170'.
Mary daughter of Thomas Wright and Mary his Wife,	"	23 May 1701.
Joseph Son of John Wilkins and Eliza his Wife,	"	11 October 1701.
Ann daughter of George Worthylake and Ann his Wife,	"	14 October 1701.
Zacheriah Son of Zachry. Alden and Mary his Wife,	"	11 October 1701.
William Son of James Blyn and Margaret his Wife,	"	17 October 1701.
Mary daughter of William Webster and Mary his Wife,	"	3 July 1701.
Susanna daughter of James Webster and Mary his Wife,	"	30 September 1701.
Elizabeth daughter of Joseph Halsey and Eliza. his Wife,	"	23 July 1701.
Timothy Son of Timothy Coningham and Ruth his Wife,	"	22 September 1701.
Elizabeth daughter of Nicholas Cock and Eliza. his Wife,	"	23 May 1701.
Jane daughter of Benjamen Davise and Eliza. his Wife,	"	1 March 1701.
Benjamen Son of Benja. Gold and Mary his Wife,	"	5 December 1701.
Mary daughter of Thomas Gwin and Sarah his Wife,	"	26 July 1701.
Jane daughter of John German and Esther his Wife,	"	1 November 1701.
Margaret daughter of Samuell Haugh and Margaret his Wife,	"	10 March 1701.
Mary daughter of John Jenkins and Mary his Wife,	"	5 July 1701.
Benjamen Son of John Welch and Eliza. his Wife,	"	9 June 1701.
Phillip Son of Nathanll Rennolls and Ruth his Wife,	"	12 May 1701.
Joseph Son of Christor Capril and Tamzine his Wife,	"	25 September 1701.
William Son of John Greenough and Eliza. his Wife,	"	5 July 1701.
Thomas Son of Thomas Palmer Esq. and Abigal his Wife,	"	5 November 1701.

1702.

Nathaniel Son of Joseph Adams and Elizabeth his Wife,	Born	4 March 1701/2.
Mary Ann Daughter of Isaac Biscon and Ann his Wife,	"	21 February 1701/2.
William Son of Joseph Billings and Hannah his Wife,	"	3 January 1701/2.
Elizabeth Daughter of James Cock and Mary his Wife,	"	13 January 1701/2.
Divan Son of Thomas Berry and Elizabeth his Wife,	"	22 January 1701/2.
Thomas Son of John Edwards and Civell his Wife,	"	14 January 1701/2.
Abijah Son of John Adams and Hannah his Wife,	"	11 May 1702.
Thomas Son of Thomas Adkins and Ruth his Wife,	"	2 June 1702.
Hull Son of Moses Abbot and Rebecca his Wife,	"	15 June : 1702.
Jeremiah Son of Jeremiah Allen and Mary his Wife,	"	24 June 1702.
Elizabeth daughter of John Allen and Elizabeth his Wife,	"	31 August 1702.

BIRTHS — 1702.

Prissilla daughter of Eliah Adams and Prissilla his Wife,	Born	1 July 1702.
Mary daughter of Newcombe Blague and Mary his Wife,	"	19 March 1702.
Peter Son of John Beauchamp and Margt. his Wife,	"	17 April 1702.
Thomas Son of Thomas Barnes and Lydia his Wife,	"	20 May 1702.
Samuell Son of William Brown and Mercy his Wife,	"	16 May 1702.
Mary Daughter of John Butt and Mary his Wife,	"	2 July 1702.
Margaret daughter of George Barstow and Mercy his Wife,	"	10 July 1702.
William Son of Samuell Barrat and Sarah his Wife,	"	17 June 1702.
Mary daughter of David Buckland and Hannah his Wife,	"	19 July 1702.
Abiah daughter of John Barrell and Abiah his Wife,	"	13 July 1702.
Joanna daughter of Thomas Burrington and Lydia his Wife,	"	7 August 1702.
Ellen daughter of Samuell Bridge and Christian his Wife,	"	6 August 1702.
Sarah daughter of John Barret and Sarah his Wife,	"	15 September 1702.
Edward Son of Peter Barbour and Sarah his Wife,	"	25 September 1702.
Elizabeth daughter of Joseph Bridgham and Mercy his Wife,	"	27 September 1702.
George Son of George Ball and Katherine his Wife,	"	2 November 1702.
John Son of Timothy Batt and Sarah his Wife,	"	22 October 1702.
William Son of John Beer and Mary his Wife,	"	2 December 1702.
Mary daughter of Benjamen Brown and Mary his Wife,	"	12 December 1702.
Mary daughter of Daniel Bernardo and Mirian Milla his Wife,	"	30 December 1702.
Mary daughter of Anthony Bracket and Mary his Wife,	"	13 January 1702.
Samuel Son of Josiah Biles and Sarah his Wife,	"	30 January 1702.
William Son of Nicholas Bows and Dorcas his Wife,	"	28 January 1702.
Samuell Son of Joseph Birch and Elizabeth his Wife,	"	13 February 1702.
Huldah daughter of John Bucanan and Elizabeth his Wife,	"	2 March 1702.
Deborah daughter of John Burnet and Deborah his Wife,	"	17 February 1702.
Mercy daughter of Edward Cruff and Sarah his Wife,	"	1 Aprill 1702.
John Son of John Cotta and Sarah his Wife,	"	27 March 1702.
John Son of Andrew Cuningham and Sarah his Wife,	"	25 March 1702.
Ebenezar Son of John Clough and Mary his Wife,	"	5 Aprill 1702.
Hannah daughter of Richard Chever and Abigall his Wife,	"	5 July 1702.
Mary daughter of Francis Castle and Prissilla his Wife,	"	11 May 1702.
Mary daughter of John Carey and Sarah his Wife,	"	1 July 1702.
Sarah daughter of William Cotton and Anna his Wife,	"	11 August 1702.
Thomas Son of John Cerlile and Hannah his Wife,	"	10 June 1702.
Allexander Son of Allexr. Chamberlin: and Sarah his Wife,	"	28 August 1702.
Seth Son of Seth Cullever and Lydia his Wife,	"	23 September 1702.

James Son of Robert Calef and Margaret his Wife,	Born	21 December 1702.
Enoch Son of William Cleer and Bethia his Wife,	"	21 December 1702.
Hannah daughter of Thomas Cushing and Deborah his Wife,	"	12 January 1702.
Ebenezar Son of Ebenezar Clough and Thankfull his Wife,	"	27 January 1702.
Mary daughter of James Codner and Mary his Wife,	"	3 March 1702.
Sarah daughter of William Clark and Sarah his Wife,	"	17 February 1702.
Hannah daughter of Samuell Copp and Hannah his Wife,	"	11 July 1702.
Nathaniel Son of Nathaniel Draper and Elizabeth his Wife,	"	30 March 1702.
John Son of John Dolbeer and Sarah his Wife,	"	25 April 1702.
Abigall Daughter of Edward Durant and Ann his Wife,	"	15 May 1702.
John Son of Addington Davenport and Eliza. his Wife,	"	31 May 1702.
Margaret ⎫ daughters: of Edmund Dolbeer and Agnis ⎭ Sarah his Wife,	"	20 May 1702.
Samuell Son of Charles Demery and Sarah his Wife,	"	23 June 1702.
William Son of William Daniel and Dorothy his Wife,	"	16 September 1702.
Ann daughter of Samuel Durham and Eliza. his Wife,	"	14 September 1702.
Joseph Son of Benjamin Dyer and Hannah his Wife,	"	25 September 1702
Joseph Son of Joseph Dowding and Ann his Wife,	"	7 November 1702.
John Son of Richard Draper and Sarah his Wife,	"	29 October 1702.
Rebecca daughter of William Dinsdale and Martha his Wife,	"	10 January 1702.
William Son of William Dopson and Prudenc: his Wife,	"	27 October 1702.
Benjamen Son of William Endecot and Elizabeth his Wife,	"	10th Aprill 1702.
Joshua Son of David Eustise and Rachell his Wife,	"	11 February 1702.
Samuel Son of Samuell Engs and Annah his Wife,	"	2 October 1702.
John Son of Jonathan Everard and Penelopee his Wife,	"	3 February 1702.
Joanna daughter of Joseph Flood and Joanna his Wife,	"	26 December 1702.
William Son of Benjamen Gibson and Mehitabell his Wife,	"	6 Aprill 1702.
Mary daughter of John Goodwin and Mary his Wife,	"	21 Aprill 1702.
Ann daughter of William Gibson and Mary his Wife,	"	5 May 1702.
Isaac Son of Samuell Greenwood and Eliza. his Wife,	"	11 May 1702.
Rachell daughter of John Gerat and Susana his Wife,	"	27 May 1702.
Elizabeth daughter of Edward Gellings and Mary his Wife,	"	18 July 1702.
Sarah daughter of Samuell Grice and Prissila his Wife,	"	14 June 1702.
Sarah daughter of Noah Guille and Sarah his Wife,	"	8 November 1702.
Richard Son of John Gerrish and Sarah his Wife,	"	21 November 1702.
Orchard Son of John Guy and Anna his Wife,	"	11 November 1702.

BIRTHS — 1702.

Ebenezar Son of Joshua Gee and Elizabeth his Wife,	Born	22 December 1702.
Elizabeth daughter of William Gibbs and Eliza. his Wife,	"	20 January 1702.
Mary daughter of Tobias Green and Mary his Wife,	"	28 January 1702.
Elizabeth daughter of Thomas Gilbert and Lydia his Wife,	"	7 February 1702.
Susana daughter of Nathanll. Green and Eliza. his Wife,	"	3 September 1702.
Edward Son of Edward Gray and Susana his Wife,	"	20 March 1702.
John Son of Nathaniell Holmes and Sarah his Wife,	"	11 Aprill 1702.
Mary daughter of William Hannah and Martha his Wife,	"	28 Aprill 1702.
Esther daughter of Joseph Heath and Mary his Wife,	"	25 July 1702.
Thomas Son of Joseph Hubbert and Thankfull his Wife,	"	4 August 1702.
Daniell Son of James Habersham and Mary his Wife,	"	20 August 1702.
Elizabeth daughter of Joshua Hewes and Eliza. his Wife,	"	29 August 1702.
Joseph Son of Benjamen Hallaway and Mary his Wife,	"	22 November 1702.
Isaac Son of Francis Holmes and Rebecca his Wife,	"	1th January 1702.
Joseph Son of John Hobbie and Ann his Wife,	"	29 December 1702.
Tabitha daughter of Nathanll. Hodgdon and Susana his Wife,	"	4 January 1702.
William Son of William Hasey and Elizabeth his Wife,	"	4 February 1702.
Mary daughter of Charles Hobbie and Elizabeth his Wife,	"	19 February 1702.
Benjamen Son of William Indecot and Eliza. his Wife,	"	10 April 1702.
Mara daughter of John Jones and Margaret his Wife	"	6 May 1702.
Sarah daughter of John Ingram and Sarah his Wife,	"	20 July 1702.
Benjamen Son of Arthur Jeffry and Mary his Wife,	"	9 August 1702.
Prissilla daughter of Thomas Jackson and Prissilla his Wife,	"	27 August 1702.
Sarah daughter of William Ivory and Sarah his Wife,	"	28 October 1702.
Phinias Son of David Jesse and Mary his Wife,	"	24 December 1702.
Mercy daughter of John Jackson and Susana his Wife,	"	26 February 1702.
Rebecca daughter of John Kilbey and Rebecca his Wife,	"	30 March 1702.
Christopher Son of Christopher Kemball and Sarah his Wife,	"	2 September 1702.
Mary daughter of Solomon Kneeland and Mary his Wife,	"	15 October 1702.
Dudson Son of Roger Kilcup and Abigall his Wife,	"	28 December 1702.
Sarah daughter of John Lawson and Ann his Wife,	"	26 March 1702.
Richard Son of Richard Lax and Mary his Wife,	"	18 Aprill 1702.
John Son of John Lowrey and Mary his Wife,	"	28 May 1702.

Joseph Son of Joseph Lowden and Mary his Wife, Born 14 September 1702.
Knight Son of Thoms. Hudson Leverit and Rebecca
his Wife, " 1 January 1702.
Thomas Son of Thomas Lee and Deborah his Wife, " 17 December 1702.
Mary daughter of Isaac Loreing and Sarah his Wife, " 5 February 1702.
Margaret daughter of Florence Maccarty and Sarah
his Wife, " 29 March 1702.
Mary daughter of John Miles and Elizabeth his
Wife, " 5 Aprill 1702.
Arthur Son of Arthur Mason and Mary his Wife, " 14 May 1702.
John Son of Edward Martin and Sarah his Wife, " 21 June: 1702.
David Son of Timothy Mackue and Ann his Wife, " 21 June : 1702.
John Son of John Maxwel and Eliza. his Wife, " 12 July 1702.
Ann daughter of Samuell Mattock and Ann his
Wife, " 21 July 1702.
Ann daughter of Charles Morris and Esther his
Wife, " 23 September 1702.
Mary daughter of Benjamen Morss and Frances
his Wife, " 23 October 1702.
Benjamen Son of Thomas Mellens and Mary his
Wife, " 29 January 1702.
John Son of John Mountfort and Mary his Wife, " 24 February 1702.
Samuell Son of John Marshall and Sarah his Wife, " 18 February 1702.
Abigall daughter of Nathaniell Newell and Rest his
Wife, " 19 Aprill 1702.
Hannah daughter of Darbey Ofling and Hannah his
Wife, " 22 Aprill 1702.
Andrew Son of John Osborn and Mary his Wife, " 6 July 1702.
Abigall daughter of James Oborn and Abigall his
Wife, " 7 March 1702.
Abigall daughter of John Phillips and Mary his
Wife. " 26 Aprill 1702.
Sarah daughter of James Peirson and Eliza. his
Wife, " 8 July 1702.
John Son of John Petel and Rachell his Wife, " 14 September 1702.
Ann daughter of Joseph Pitman and Hannah his
Wife, " 3 September 1702.
Esther daughter of Obediah Parry and Mary his
Wife, " 22 September 1702.
Ebenezar Son of Ebenr. Pemberton and Mary his
Wife, " 12 Aprill 1702.
Mary daughter of John Plasteed and Sarah his
Wife, " 25 October 1702.
Hannah daughter of William Paine and Sarah his
Wife, " 27 January 1702.
George Son of George Peream and Mary his Wife, " 19 Aprill 1702.
Elizabeth daughter of Joseph Roberts and Esther
his Wife, " 27 September 1702.
Ann daughter of Thomas Russell and Ann his Wife, " 15 November 1702.
Hannah daughter of John Ruck and Hannah his
Wife, " 4 December 1702.
Mosly Son of John Ruggles and Martha his Wife, " 22 February 1702.
Thomas Son of Thomas Rowel and Dorothy his
Wife, " 9 February 1702.
Elizabeth daughter of John Richardson and Margaret his Wife, " 4 March 1702.
Mary daughter of Joseph Royall and Mary his
Wife, " 8 March 1702.
Mary daughter of Cyprian Southiack and Eliza. his
Wife, " 2 Aprill 1702.

Births — 1702.

Bartholomew Son of Daniell Stoddar and Eliza. his Wife,	Born	10 April 1702.
Grace daughter of Jeremiah Smith and Grace his Wife,	"	11 May 1702.
Grover Son of John Scolly and Lydia his Wife,	"	10 May 1702.
Elizabeth daughter of Thomas Sill and Agnis his Wife,	"	16 June 1702.
Jeremiah Son of Rowland Storey and Ann his Wife,	"	2 July 1702.
Joseph Son of Joseph Slegg and Ruth his Wife,	"	5 July 1702.
Josiah Son of Benjamen Stone and Joanna his Wife,	"	25 July 1702.
Gibbins Son of Gibbins Sharp and Sarah his Wife,	"	18 August 1702.
Mary daughter of Richard Stratton and Margaret his Wife,	"	7 September 1702.
Anna daughter of Isaac Spencer and Bethia his Wife,	"	9 October 1702.
John Son of John Simson and Rely his Wife,	"	24 October 1702.
Grace daughter of John Stevens and Grace his Wife,	"	18 December 1702.
Margaret daughter of Clemons Sumner and Margaret his Wife,	"	7 December 1702.
James Son of Joseph Simpson and Hannah his Wife,	"	8 January 1702.
Thomas Son of Thomas Simkins and Margry his Wife,	"	27 January 1702.
Susana daughter of Benjamen Swaine and Susana his Wife,	"	8 February 1702.
William Son of John Sharp and Mary his Wife,	"	25 February 1702.
Mary daughter of Joseph Soper and Margaret his Wife,	"	24 February 1702.
Nicholas Son of Nicholas Trarice and Hannah his Wife,	"	18 April 1702.
William Son of William Turner and Hannah his Wife,	"	20 Aprill 1702.
Mary daughter of Henry Too and Mary his Wife,	"	12 June 1702.
Mary daughter of James Taylor and Rebecca his Wife,	"	15 July 1702.
Moses Son of John Tiler and Deborah his Wife,	"	23 July 1702.
Elisha Son of James Townsend and Alice his Wife,	"	26 December 1702.
Elizabeth daughter of James Townsend and Rebecca his Wife,	"	25 January 1702.
Mary daughter of John Turner and Eliza. his Wife,	"	27 January 1702.
Abigall daughter of William Thomas and Abigall his Wife,	"	26 September 1702.
Samuell Son of John Vallentine and Mary his Wife,	"	28 December 1702.
Elizabeth daughter of Henry Wilson and Eliza. his Wife,	"	4 April 1702.
William Son of William Wire and Ellinor his Wife,	"	26 March 1702.
Joseph Son of Samuell White and Ann his Wife,	"	9 Aprill 1702.
Ezekiell Son of Ezekiel Walker and Ruth his Wife,	"	12 May 1702.
Joseph Son of Joseph Wheeler and Eliza his Wife,	"	27 April 1702.
Edward Son of George Wright and Margaret his Wife,	"	11 May 1702.

Mary daughter of Jonathan Williams and Mary his Wife,	Born	14 June 1702.
Howard Son of Daniel Wyborn and Sarah his Wife,	"	1 June 1702.
Sarah daughter of James Williams and Sarah his Wife,	"	5 July 1702.
John Son of Ichabod Williston and Dorothy his Wife,	"	7 September 1702.
Obediah Son of Obediah Wakefeeld and Rebecca his Wife,	"	17 December 1702.
John Son of John Williams and Humilis his Wife,	"	26 January 1702.
William Son of William Waters and Rebecca his Wife,	"	10 February 1702.
Samuel Son } of { Simon Willard and Eliza. Abigall daughter } of { his Wife,	"	19 January 1702.
John Son of John Wilson and Mary his Wife,	"	2 February 1702.
John Son of John Wells and Mary his Wife,	"	31 January 1702.
Robert Son of James Wacombe and Eliza. his Wife,	"	15 February 1702.
William Son of Anthony Young and Rachell his Wife,	"	13 February 1702.
Hannah daughter of John Clampit and Hannah his Wife,	"	23 November 1702.
Sarah daughter of Jonathan Eustice and Sarah his Wife,	"	18 March 1702.
David Son of David Faulkner and Eliza. his Wife,	"	12 March 1702.
William Son of Allexander Fullerton and Mary his Wife,	"	2 July 1702.
Mary daughter of Thomas Freeman and Alice his Wife,	"	1 June 1702.
Eliezur Son of John Flegg and Abiah his Wife,	"	12 February 1702.
Winsor Son of Winsor Golden and Elizabeth his Wife,	"	22 March 1702.
Elizabeth daughter of John Gill and Eliza. his Wife,	"	23 January 1702.
Mary daughter of Samuell Hood and Deborah his Wife,	"	11 March 1702.
Martha daughter of Peter Hauksworth and Eliza. his Wife,	"	23 December 1702.
Jennet daughter of David Johnson and Priscilla his Wife,	"	10 March 1702.
Mary daughter of Jonathan Jackson and Mary his Wife,	"	4 April 1702.
William Son of James Ingles and Love his Wife,	"	1 February 1702.
Christopher Son of Christor. Bridge and Eliza. his Wife,	"	21 February 1702.
Elizabeth daughter of William Cook and Eliza his Wife,	"	5 January 1702.
Johanna daughter of Benja. Alford and Mary his Wife,	"	24 May 1702.
Sarah daughter of Elisha Audling and Mary his Wife,	"	20 February 1702.
Ruth daughter of Joseph Belknap and Abigall his Wife,	"	2 March 1702.
Richard Son of John Broccus and Ann his Wife,	"	20 November 1702.
Agnis daughter of Joshua Kent and Agnis his Wife,	"	25 September 1702.
Richard Son of Richard Mortemore and Mary his Wife,	"	18 March 1702.

Edward Son of Josue Marriner and Hannah his Wife,	Born	20 November 1702.
Samuel Son of Samuel Mould and Mary his Wife,	"	10 January 1702.
Ann daughter of William Merret and Ann his Wife,	"	20 April 1702.
Susana daughter of Edward Merret and Susana his Wife,	"	12 May 1702.
Hannah daughter of Thomas Norrise and Hannah his Wife,	"	26 July 1702.
Agnis daughter of Jacob Pearce and Rachel his Wife,	"	8 March 1702
Robert Son of Robert Price and Hannah his Wife,	"	9 January 1702.
Thomas Son of Allexandr. Sherar and Sarah his Wife,	"	22 March 1702.
Elizabeth daughter of Samuell Shrimpton and Eliza. his Wife,	"	26 August 1702.
Sarah daughter of Joseph Smith and Mercey his Wife,	"	4 November 1702.
John Son of Sampson Shore and Mary his Wife,	"	2 December 1702.
Hannah daughter of Jonathan Waldo and Hannah his Wife,	"	23 January 1702.
Mary daughter of William White and Eliza. his Wife,	"	20 March 1702.
Margaret daughter of James Webster and Mary his Wife,	"	11 February 1702.
Ann daughter of Roger Earl and Lydia his Wife,	"	22 August 1702.
Samuel Son of John Elliston and Lucey his Wife,	"	28 Aprill 1702.
Katherine daughter of Benja. Gallop and Hannah his Wife,	"	22 July 1702.
Sarah daughter of Samuell Hurst and Sarah his Wife,	"	26 Aug. 1702.
Henry Son of William Robie and Eliza. his Wife,	"	18 February 1702.
Sarah daughter of John Ruggles and Tabitha his Wife,	"	28 November 1702.
Mehitabell daughter of Peter Townsend and Mary his Wife,	"	12 February 1702.
Dorothy daughter of George Thorold and Anna his Wife,	"	17 Aprill 1702.
Nathanll. Son of Nathanll. Williams and Ann his Wife,	"	12 February 1702.
Mary daughter of George Sirey and Jane his Wife,	"	12 September 1702.
Susanna daughter of Wentworth Paxton and Faith his Wife,	"	27 June 1702.
Andrew Son of Andr. Sigourney and Mary his Wife,	"	30 January 1702.
John Son of Thomas Hobbs and Katherine his Wife,	"	25 February 1702.
Samuel Son of Samuel Bill and Sarah his Wife,	"	21 May 1702.

1703.

Abigall daughter of Zachry Adams and Dinah his Wife,	Born	20 Aprill 1703.
Elizabeth daughter of Joseph Adams and Ann his Wife,	"	21 June 1703.
Ann daughter of Isaac Adams and Martha his Wife,	"	20 August 1703.
Samuell Son of Samuell Adams and Lydia his Wife,	"	7 November 1703.
Sarah daughter of John Baker and Mary his Wife,	"	31 March 1703.
James Son of Thomas Barnes and Lydia his Wife,	"	18 April 1703.
Anne daughter of Lewis Boucher and Sarah his Wife,	"	7 April 1703.

William Son of John Barnes and Rachel his Wife,	Born	29 Aprill 1703.
Mary daughter of Nicholas Buttolph and Mary his Wife,	"	8 May 1703.
Jeremiah Son of William Brown and Mary his Wife,	"	20 May 1703.
Elizabeth daughter of James Baynam and Bridget his Wife,	"	28 June: 1703.
Benjamen Son of William Brown and Ann his Wife,	"	2 July 1703.
William Son of William Briggs and Rebecca his Wife,	"	30 Aprill 1703.
Edward Son of Samuell Barrat and Sarah his Wife,	"	28 May 1703.
Richard Son of Samuell Bason and Mary his Wife,	"	21 January 1703.
John Son of Negro Boston and Jane his Wife,	"	22 August 1703.
William Son of Adinah Bulfinch and Abigal his Wife,	"	14 August 1703.
Nicholas Son of Nicholas Blatchford and Mary his Wife,	"	4 September 1703.
Elizabeth daughter of Henry Bridgham and Lydia his Wife,	"	1 October 1703.
Timothy Son of Timothy Burbanck and Rebecca his Wife,	"	13 October 1703.
Nathaniel Son of Joseph Belcher and Hannah his Wife,	"	5 October 1703.
Ebenezer Son of Daniell Berry and Mary his Wife,	"	15 December 1703.
Anna Daughter of Samuell Bayley and Deliverence his Wife,	"	6 January 1703.
Preserved daughter of Samll. Bayley and Deliveranc: his Wife,	"	
Anna daughter of John Barrel and Abiah his Wife,	"	26th January 1703.
Mary daughter of Thomas Berry and Elizabeth his Wife,	"	17 February 1703.
Simon Son of Daniel Barnardo and Marion his Wife,	"	5 March 1703.
Silvester Son of Mathew Carey and Mary his Wife,	"	18 June 1703.
John Son of Androse Cannon and Sarah his Wife,	"	21 August 1703.
Lydia daughter of Joseph Callender and Lydia his Wife,	"	16 August 1703.
Elizabeth daughter of Thomas Chubb and Eliza. his Wife,	"	27 September 1703.
David Son of David Cutler and Abigall his Wife,	"	28 September 1703.
John Son of David Craige and Deborah his Wife,	"	27 September 1703.
Elisha Son of Elisha Cook and Jane his Wife,	"	3 November 1703.
John Son of Samuell Clarke and Hannah his Wife,	"	22 November 1703.
Samuell Son of Ezekiel Carvat and Elizabeth his Wife,	"	15 December 1703.
Sarah daughter of Henry Chamlet and Eliza. his Wife,	"	17 December 1703.
Sarah daughter of John Clark and Sarah his Wife,	"	18 January 1703.
Mary daughter of Joseph Cowel and Eliza. his Wife,	"	1 February 1703.
Mary daughter of John Cunniball and Martha his Wife,	"	22 January 1703.
Peter Son of John Cotta and Sarah his Wife,	"	7 March 1703.
John Son of John Coleman and Judeth his Wife,	"	2 March 1703.
Barrat Son of Barrat Dyer and Hannah his Wife,	"	19 October 1703.

Births — 1703.

John Son of Addington Davenport and Eliza. his Wife,	Born	21 November 1703.
Sands Son of Joseph Dowding and Ann his Wife,	"	28 February 1703.
Francis Son of Eliezur Darbey and Mary his Wife,	"	16 March 1703.
William Son of William Egleston and Dorcas his Wife,	"	27 June 1703.
Connis Son of Anthony Eames and Naomi his Wife,	"	3 November 1703.
Ann daughter of John Edwards and Civill his Wife,	"	7 October 1703.
Samuell Son of Samuel Earl and Mary his Wife,	"	11 March 1703.
Lydia daughter of William Endecot and Eliza. his Wife,	"	19 June 1703.
Samuell Son of Thomas Fitch and Abiel his Wife,	"	31 August 1703.
Jacob Son of John Floyd and Rachel his Wife,	"	11 September 1703.
Martha daughter of Thomas Foster and Martha his Wife,	"	21 October 1703.
Thomas Son of Josiah Frankling and Abia his Wife,	"	7th December 1703.
Hannah daughter of Richard Flood and Elizabeth his Wife,	"	19 December 1703.
Richard Son of Richard Frankling and Abigall his Wife,	"	12 February 1703.
Ann daughter of Allexander Fullerton and Mary his Wife,	"	5 February 1703.
Benjamen Son of Benjamen Flood and Mary his Wife,	"	16 February 1703.
Mary daughter of James Gibson and Mary his Wife,	"	29 March 1703.
John Son of Samuel Gardener and Eliza. his Wife,	"	2 April 1703.
John Son of John Goldthwaite and Sarah his Wife,	"	24 May 1703.
Elizabeth daughter of Walter Gutradge and Anna his Wife,	"	14 July 1703.
Susanna daughter of Samuel Gray and Susanna his Wife,	"	8 July 1703.
Samuel Son of Bartholomw. Green and Mary his Wife,	"	2 November 1703.
John Son of Jonathan Gatchel and Martha his Wife,	"	15 December 1703.
Timothy Son of Timothy Green and Mary his Wife,	"	6 December 1703.
Martha daughter of John Goodwin and Mary his Wife,	"	19 December 1703.
Martha daughter of John Glass and Martha his Wife,	"	3 January 1703.
Mary daughter of John Gyles and Mary his Wife,	"	24 January 1703.
Isaac Son of Richard Gridley and Rebecca his Wife,	"	28 January 1703.
Katherine daughter of Noah Guille and Sarah his Wife,	"	11 February 1703.
Elizabeth daughter of Samuel Grice and Priscilla his Wife,	"	8 March 1703.
Elizabeth daughter of Allexandr. Hannah and Eliza. his Wife,	"	12 May 1703.
Mercey daughter of John Hisket and Dorcas his Wife,	"	29 Aprill 1703.
Joshua Son of Joshua Hencha and Mary his Wife,	"	2 August 1703.
Jannet daughter of Thomas Hay and Bridget his Wife,	"	16 August 1703.
Mercey daughter of Francis Hudson and Mary his Wife,	"	16 August 1703.

Ann daughter of William Harwood and Phebee his Wife,	Born	13 August 1703.
Michael Son of John Homer and Margery his Wife,	"	26 September 1703.
Benjamen Son of Samuell Hewes and Hannah his Wife,	"	15 November 1703.
Nathaniel Son of Nathanll. Holmes and Sarah his Wife,	"	29 December 1703.
Deborah daughter of Thomas Hetchbone and Frances his Wife,	"	25 January 1703.
Elizabeth daughter of John Holland and Elizabeth his Wife,	"	24 January 1703.
Elizabeth daughter of Thomas Jacobs and Mary his Wife,	"	21 May 1703.
Lydia daughter of William Indecot and Elizabeth his Wife,	"	19 June 1703.
Ebenezar Son of Mathew Joans and Susana his Wife,	"	11 November 1703.
Thomas Son of Timothy Kemball and Katherine his Wife,	"	29 May 1703.
Mary daughter of Joseph Kemball and Eliza. his Wife,	"	27 May 1703.
Abigall daughter of Christophr. Kimbal and Sarah his Wife,	"	28 January 1703.
Allexander Son of James Lablond and Ann his Wife,	"	31 March 1703.
Nicholas Son of Robert Lash and Elizabeth his Wife,	"	26 Aprill 1703.
Sarah daughter of Thomas Larkin and Sarah his Wife,	"	17 May 1703.
Mary daughter of Stephen Langley and Mary his Wife,	"	1 August 1703.
Bennet Son of John Love and Susana his Wife,	"	2 June 1703.
Daniel Son of Daniel Loreing and Priscilla his Wife,	"	25 October 1703.
Phillip Son of Phillip Lewis and Martha his Wife,	"	4 January 1703.
Mary daughter of Ezekiel Lewis and Mary his Wife,	"	21 January 1703.
Joseph Son of Joseph Lowden and Mary his Wife,	"	7 January 1703.
John Son of Ebenezar Lowle and Eliza. his Wife,	"	14 March 1703.
John Son of Samuel Marrion and Mary his Wife,	"	5 April 1703.
Joseph Son of Thomas Marshall and Dorcas his Wife,	"	19 June 1703.
Ebenezar Son of Duncan Maycome and Mary his Wife,	"	4 September 1703.
David Son of Arthur Mason and Mary his Wife,	"	2 July 1703.
Richard Son of Edward Martine and Sarah his Wife,	"	16 September 1703.
Hannah daughter of Joseph Maylem and Hannah his Wife,	"	8 July 1703.
Benjamen Son of Benja. Morss and Frances his Wife,	"	3th November 1703.
William Son of Lazurus Manley and Sarah his Wife,	"	30 January 1703.
James Son of Samuel Meers and Mary his Wife,	"	11 February 1703.
Sarah daughter of Henry Nicholson and Sarah his Wife,	"	29 March 1703.
Thomas Son of George Nowel and Eliza. his Wife,	"	30 March 1703.
Elizabeth daughter of Stephen Norwood and Eliza. his Wife,	"	7 May 1703.
John Son of John Northey and Sarah his Wife,	"	25 June 1703.
Mary daughter of John Noyse and Susana his Wife,	"	30 October 1703.

Births — 1703.

Abraham Son of Abraham Nicholls and Rebecca his wife,	Born	18 January 1703.
Stephen Son of Stephen North and Lydia his Wife,	"	6 March 1703.
Ebenezar Son of John Oliver and Sarah his Wife,	"	4 January 1703.
Daniel Son of Daniel Oliver and Eliza. his Wife,	"	14 January 1703.
Mary daughter of Ebenr. Pemberton and Mary his Wife,	"	14 Aprill 1703.
Mary daughter of John Pearse and Mary his Wife,	"	11 Aprill 1703.
Bridget daughter of William Phillips and Deborah his Wife,	"	31 May 1703.
Abraham Son of Nathanll. Perkins and Sarah his Wife,	"	21 June 1703.
John Son of Edward Proctor and Eliza. his Wife,	"	4 August 1703.
Ebenezar Son of William Parkman and Eliza. his Wife,	"	5 September 1703.
John Son of John Pitts and Hannah his Wife,	"	20 September 1703.
Rachel daughter of John Pettel and Rachel his Wife,	"	12 October 1703.
Joseph Son of Edward Porter and Abiel his Wife,	"	22 October 1703.
Rebecca daughter of Thomas Phillips and Rebecca his Wife,	"	1 November 1703.
Elizabeth daughter of Thomas Peck and Joanna his Wife,	"	24 October 1703.
Verrin Son of John Parker and Sarah his Wife,	"	26 May 1703.
John Son of Richard Proctor and Rachel his Wife,	"	29 December 1703.
James Son of James Pitts and Elizabeth his Wife,	"	13 December 1703.
John Son of Thomas Plats and Hannah his Wife,	"	19 December 1703.
Elizabeth daughter of Nathan Presbee and Eliza. his Wife,	"	12 January 1703.
Samuel Son of Thomas Prat and Mary his Wife,	"	27 January 1703.
Mehitabel daughter of Joseph Russell and Mary his Wife,	"	18th August 1703.
Mary daughter of Humphry Richards and Susana his Wife,	"	11 September 1703.
Alice daughter of William Reed and Alice his Wife,	"	19 October 1703.
Mary daughter of Thomas Robbinson and Rebecca his Wife,	"	29 December 1703.
John Son of John Radmore and Mary his Wife,	"	11 February 1703.
John Son of William Snoton and Rachel his Wife,	"	10 Aprill 1703.
John Son of John Spencer and Eliza. his Wife,	"	4 August 1703.
John Son of John Simpkins and Eliza. his Wife,	"	14 August 1703.
Abigall daughter of John Selly and Sarah his Wife,	"	23 August 1703.
Sarah daughter of Anthony Skeppell and Eliza. his Wife,	"	5 September 1703.
Elizabeth daughter of Jonathan Simpson and Eliza. his Wife,	"	13 September 1703.
Sarah daughter of Joseph Skinner and Eliza. his Wife,	"	1 October 1703.
Edward Son of Wigglesworth Swicher and Ursilla his Wife,	"	3 October 1703.
Thomas Son of Thomas Savage and Margaret his Wife,	"	9 September 1703.
Deliverence daughter of Allexandr. Seers and Rebecca his Wife,	"	13 October 1703.
Abigall daughter of William Shute and Martha his Wife,	"	9 August 1703.
Susana Daughter of Peter Stacey and Remember his Wife,	"	20 October 1703.
John Son of John Seacomb and Mehitabel his Wife,	"	19 November 1703.

Mehitabel daughter of John Sables and Priscilla his Wife,	Born	16 November 1703.
Peter Son of Peter Signac and Ann his Wife,	"	12 October 1703.
Susanna daughter of John Stevens and Grace his Wife,	"	16 January 1703.
Robert Son of Joseph Snelling and Rebecca his Wife,	"	10 January 1703.
Elizabeth daughter of John Smith and Jane his Wife,	"	4 November 1703.
John Son of Thomas Smith and Mary his Wife,	"	2 February 1703.
William ⟩ Sons of Samuell Torry and Abigall his Samuel ⟩ Wife,	"	29 May 1703.
Nathaniel Son of John Thwing and Martha his Wife,	"	17 August 1703.
Elizabeth daughter of Jonathan Townsend and Eliza. his Wife,	"	27 December 1703.
Thomas Son of Thomas Townsend and Sarah his Wife,	"	9 January 1703.
Mercey daughter of Jeremiah Tay and Mercey his Wife,	"	5 July 1703.
James Son of John Vickers and Sarah his Wife,	"	11 July 1703.
John Son of James Varney and Jane his Wife,	"	24 September 1703.
Elizabeth daughter of John Valentine and Mary his Wife,	"	22 February 1703.
Abigal daughter of James Williams and Abigal his Wife,	"	2th Aprill 1703.
Ann daughter of Adam Winthrop and Ann his Wife,	"	4 May 1703.
Sarah daughter of Thomas Wheeler and Sarah his Wife,	"	16 May 1703.
Mary daughter of Jonathan Williams and Mary his Wife,	"	8 June 1703.
Mary daughter of Nathanll. Wheeler and Mary his Wife,	"	7 June 1703.
Elizabeth Daughter of John Wakefeeld and Eliza. his Wife,	"	4 July 1703.
Elizabeth daughter of William Webber and Mary his Wife,	"	24 July 1703.
George Son of George Wadling and Rachel his Wife,	"	22 September 1703.
Joseph Son of Samuell White and Ann his Wife,	"	5 October 1703.
Sarah daughter of Daniell Willard and Mary his Wife,	"	12 June 1703.
Jonathan Son of Jonathn. Wardwel and Katherine his Wife,	"	19 October 1703.
Elizabeth daughter of John Wilkins and Eliza. his Wife,	"	16 January 1703.
William Son of William Webster and Mary his Wife,	"	2 December 1703.
Sarah daughter of William Wheeler and Eliza his Wife,	"	30 January 1703.
Edward Son of Edward Winslow and Hannah his Wife,	"	8 February 1703.
Ruth daughter of George Worthyleg and Ann his Wife,	"	6 March 1703.
Mercey daughter of Thomas Walker and Rebecca his Wife,	"	1 March 1703.
Judeth daughter of Paul Collings and Mary his Wife,	"	9 Aprill 1703.
William Son of Thomas Daws and Sarah his Wife,	"	4 December 1703.

BIRTHS — 1703.

Richard Son of Samuel Green and Ann his Wife,	Born	15 March 1703.
Rebecca daughter of Nathanll. Gilbert and Eliza. his Wife,	"	26 February 1703.
Isaac Son of Isaac Goose and Eliza. his Wife,	"	14 February 1703.
Jeremiah Son of Nathanll. Green and Eliza. his Wife,	"	21 March 1703.
Elizabeth daughter of Joseph Halsey and Eliza. his Wife,	"	12 July 1703.
John Son of John Hughs and Deliverence his Wife,	"	9 March 1703.
Samuell Son of Samll. Hurst and Sarah his Wife,	"	30 January 1703.
Mary daughter of Grove Hirst and Eliza. his Wife,	"	31 January 1703.
Samuell Son of Samuell Avise and Mary his Wife,	"	1 February 1703.
Ann daughter of John Broccus and Ann his Wife,	"	23 March 1703.
William Son of William Bowen and Mary his Wife,	"	1 March 1703.
Benjamen Son of Richard Barnerd and Katherine his Wife,	"	2 September 1703.
Samuel Son of David Copp and Patience his Wife,	"	8 March 1703.
Rooksbey daughter of Thomas Creese and Rooksby his Wife,	"	7 August 1703.
Margaret daughter of John Langdon and Eliza. his Wife,	"	10 August 1703.
Sarah daughter of Thomas Palmer Esq and Abigal his Wife,	"	15 October 1703.
Daniel Son of Phillip Marret and Mary his Wife,	"	16 June 1703.
Eliza. daughter of John Greenough and Eliza. his Wife,	"	7 July 1703.
Joanna daughter of Christor. Capril and Tamzine his Wife,	"	28 November 1703.
William Son of William Palfry and Abigall his Wife,	"	2 March 1703.
Elizabeth daughter of Ezekiel Carver and Eliza his Wife,	"	9 Aprill 1703.
Daniel Son of Daniel Johonot and Susana his Wife,	"	19 March 1703.
Gyles Son of William Goddard and Eliza. his Wife,	"	23 August 1703.
Thomas Son of William Eustice and Sarah his Wife,	"	16 November 1703.
Stutson Son of John Biles and Eliza. his Wife,	"	15 November 1703.
Samuel Son of Joseph Johnson and Anna his Wife,	"	8 March 1703.
Elizabeth daughter of Thomas Larkin and Sarah his Wife,	"	14 March 1703.
John Son of John Marlow and Eliza. his Wife,	"	4 March 1703.
George Son of Stephen Minot and Mary his Wife,	"	29 January 1703.
George Son of George Norton and Mary his Wife,	"	25 Aprill 1703.
Mary daughter of Robert Noaks and Mary his Wife,	"	29 Aprill 1703.
Mary daughter of Robert Orange and Hannah his Wife,	"	31 January 1703.
Isaac Son of Isaac Perkins and Mary his Wife,	"	9 March 1703.
Mary daughter of Benjamin Pemberton and Eliza. his Wife,	"	15 December 1703.
Ruth daughter of John Ruggles and Martha his Wife,	"	7 March 1703.
Mary daughter of Robert Sanderson and Esther his Wife,	"	25 November 1703.
Edward Son of John Sunderland and Mary his Wife,	"	7 November 1703.
Elizabeth daughter of John Venteman and Eliza. his Wife,	"	8 January 1703.
Isaac Son of Richard Woody and Sarah his Wife,	"	22 March 1703.
Thomas Son of Thomas Wallice and Grace his Wife,	"	9 February 1703.

1704.

Moses son of Moses Abbot and Rebecca his Wife,	Born	28 March 1704.
Eliah Son of Eliah Adams and Rebecca his Wife,	"	8 June 1704.
Elizabeth daughter of Thomas Adkins and Ruth his Wife,	"	19 July 1704.
Joseph Son of Joseph Allen and Ann his Wife,	"	7 August 1704
Joseph Son of Joseph Adams and Eliza his Wife,	"	10 December 1704.
Christian daughter of John Aspinall and Christian his Wife,	"	2 August 1704.
Katherine daughter of John Alden and Eliza his Wife,	"	17 February 1704.
Edward Son of Edward Ball and Hannah his Wife,	"	2 April 1704.
Susanna daughter of Thomas Bowman and Margaret his Wife,	"	3 Aprill 1704.
John Son of John Bennet and Hannah his Wife,	"	31 March 1704.
Samuell Son of Samuell Burrell and Martha his Wife,	"	17 Aprill 1704.
Mary daughter of Anthony Bracket and Mary his Wife,	"	8 May 1704.
Elizabeth daughter of Nicholas Boon and Mary his Wife,	"	5 July 1704.
Joseph Son of Samuel Bill and Sarah his Wife,	"	26 June 1704.
Mary daughter of John Bennet and Ruth his Wife,	"	5 July 1704.
Thomas Son of Thoms. Barbour and Eliza. his Wife,	"	12 July 1704.
Abigall daughter of Timothy Batt and Sarah his Wife,	"	25 July 1704.
Elizabeth daughter of John Brewer and Martha his Wife,	"	27 July 1704.
William Son of Willm. Butler and Mary his Wife,	"	21 September 1704.
Samuel Son of John Barr and Margaret his Wife,	"	2 October 1704.
Elizabeth daughter of Thomas Baker and Eliza. his Wife,	"	31 October 1704.
Mercy daughter of Joseph Bridgham and Mercy his Wife,	"	11 November 1704.
Robert Son of Alven Butcher and Eliza. his Wife,	"	27 November 1704.
Abigall daughter of Nicholas Buttolph and Mary his Wife,	"	23 November 1704.
Mary daughter of John Beer and Mary his Wife,	"	17 November 1704.
Martha daughter of William Bowen and Mary his Wife,	"	19 December 1704.
Peter Son of James Blyn and Margaret his Wife,	"	16 January 1704.
John Son of Timothy Burbank and Rebecca his Wife.	"	19 January 1704.
Clark Son of John Buccanan and Eliza. his Wife,	"	25 February 1704.
Sarah daughter of Thomas Bridge and Eliza. his Wife,	"	1 March 1704.
William Son of John Charnock and Mary his Wife,	"	28 March 1704.
Mary daughter of Samuell Clark and Sarah his Wife,	"	15 April 1704.
John Son of Thomas Cox and Sarah his Wife,	"	20 April 1704.
Thomas Son of John Clough and Mary his Wife,	"	20th April 1704.
Clement Son of Daniel Collins and Rebecca his Wife,	"	13 May 1704.

Births — 1704.

Elizabeth daughter of Robert Calef and Margaret his Wife,	Born	7 May 1704.
John Son of Ebenr. Clough and Thankful his Wife,	"	18 May 1704.
Ebenezar Son of Jeremiah Cushing and Judeth his Wife,	"	25 May 1704.
Elizabeth daughter of Edward Camden and Ruth his Wife,	"	18 June 1704.
Rebecca daughter of William Clark and Rebecca his Wife,	"	4 June 1704.
Phillip Son of Phillip Cooper and Sarah his Wife,	"	21 May 1704.
John Son of John Comer and Mary his Wife,	"	1 August 1704.
Mary daughter of John Campball and Mary his Wife,	"	23 July 1704.
Keats Son of Allexr. Chamberline and Sarah his Wife,	"	9 August 1704.
William Son of William Clark and Sarah his Wife,	"	19 July 1704.
Hannah daughter of Francis Clark and Deborah his Wife,	"	2 September 1704.
Benjamen Son of Benja. Coleman and Anne his Wife,	"	1 September 1704.
William Son of William Champlin and Martha his Wife,	"	2 September 1704.
Sarah daughter of Noah Champney and Sarah his Wife,	"	15 October 1704.
Samuell Son of Thomas Colworthy and Sarah his Wife,	"	25 October 1704.
Ephraim Son of Samuell Copp and Hannah his Wife,	"	25 October 1704.
James Son of James Codner and Mary his Wife,	"	7 November 1704.
Deliverence daughter of John Corser and Sarah his Wife,	"	14 October 1704.
Nathaniel Son of David Craige and Deborah his Wife	"	27 November 1704.
Abigall daughter of George Cabbot and Abigall his Wife.	"	4 December 1704.
Charles Son of Charles Chancey and Sarah his Wife.	"	1 January 1704.
Joanna daughter of Robert Cock and Agnis his Wife	"	1 January 1704.
Samuell Son of Thomas Cushing and Deborah his Wife,	"	11 January 1704.
James Son of James Cock and Mary his Wife,	"	12 August 1704.
John Son of Thomas Carew and Anna his Wife,	"	19 January 1704.
Martha daughter of Paul Collings and Mary his Wife,	"	1 February 1704.
Hannah daughter of John Dinley and Sarah his Wife.	"	18th May 1704.
Hannah daughter of Joseph Dolbeer and Hannah his Wife,	"	10 July 1704.
Samuel Son of Samuel Drown and Eliza. his Wife,	"	15 July 1704.
Mary daughter of Benjamen Dyer and Hannah his Wife.	"	14 November 1704.
Elizabeth daughter of Addington Davenport and Eliza. his Wife,	"	20 December 1704.
Mary daughter of James Denmark and Eliza. his Wife.	"	22 January 1704.
Mercey daughter of Joseph Dowding and Ann his Wife,	"	11 February 1704.

Still born ⎱ Sons of John Eastwick and Grizell his		
Still born ⎰ Wife,	Born	29 July 1704.
Mary daughter of Jonathan Eustice and Sarah his Wife,	"	1 January 1704.
Mary daughter of Samll. Eaton and Ruth his Wife,	"	1 May 1704.
John Son of Daniel Edwards and Martha his Wife,	"	9 February 1704.
Ann daughter of Benja. Fitch and Mary his Wife,	"	5 May 1704.
Hugh Son of Hugh Floyd and Eliner his Wife,	"	13 May 1704.
Margaret daughter of Henry Frankling and Margrt. his Wife,	"	19 June 1704.
Sarah daughter of Joseph Flood and Johanna his Wife,	"	8 August 1704.
Ann daughter of John Foster and Sarah his Wife,	"	21 February 1704.
Martha daughter of Thomas Fitch and Abiel his Wife,	"	25 September 1704.
Hannah daughter of Benja. Gold and Mary his Wife,	"	17 Aprill 1704.
Thomas Son of Thomas Godfrey and Esther his Wife,	"	15 Aprill 1704.
John Son of Samuel Gardener and Eliza. his Wife,	"	3 June 1704.
Elizabeth daughter of Joshua Gee and Eliza his Wife,	"	14 June 1704.
Anna daughter of John German and Esther his Wife,	"	11 June 1704.
William Son of Benja. Gibson and Mehitabell his Wife,	"	25 June 1704.
Martha daughter of Thomas Gyles and Martha his Wife,	"	9 July 1704.
Sarah daughter of Joseph Green and Mary his Wife,	"	1 July 1704.
Mary daughter of John Gerard and Susana his Wife,	"	16 July 1704.
Sarah daughter of John Gerrish and Sarah his Wife,	"	27 August 1704.
Thomas Son of Thomas Gwin and Sarah his Wife,	"	17 September 1704.
Windsor Son of Windsor Golding and Eliza. his Wife,	"	11 October 1704.
Benjamen Son of John Goldthwaite and Sarah his Wife,	"	25 November 1704.
Nathaniel Son of Edward Gellings and Mary his Wife,	"	12 December 1704.
Elizabeth daughter of Samll. Green and Eliza. his Wife,	"	10 December 1704.
John Son of John Gill and Eliza. his Wife,	"	12 February 1704.
John Son of John Hobbs and Susanna his Wife,	"	2 Aprill 1704.
Rose daughter of Jacob Hallaway and Mary his Wife,	"	2 May 1704.
Thomas Son of Henry Hill and Mary his Wife,	"	11 June 1704.
Hannah daughter of Joshua Hewes and Eliza. his Wife,	"	6 June 1704.
Joseph Son of Nathanll. Hodgsdon and Susanna his Wife,	"	5 June 1704.
Mary daughter of Robert Hannah and Hanna his Wife,	"	21 June 1704.
John Son of John Horton and Ann his Wife,	"	5 July 1704.
John Son of Nathanll. Harrise and Sarah his Wife,	"	17 August 1704.
John Son of Thomas Holland and Ann his Wife,	"	19 August 1704.
Thomas Son of Ephraim Hunt and Joanna his Wife,	"	10 August 1704.
John Son of John Hisket and Dorcas his Wife,	"	30 August 1704.

Births — 1704.

Foster Son of Thomas Hutchinson and Sarah his Wife,	Born	18 September 1704.
Benjamen Son of Arthur Hale and Mary his Wife,	"	13 October 1704.
Mary daughter of John Halsey and Jane his Wife,	"	29 December 1704.
John Son of John Herridge and Dorothy his Wife.	"	6 January 1704.
Thomas Son of Thomas Hobbs and Katherine his Wife,	"	14 February 1704.
Elizabeth daughter of Michael Hambleton and Mary his Wife,	"	4 March 1704.
Elizabeth daughter of David Jesse and Mary his Wife,	"	8 May 1704.
Jonathan Son of Jonathan Jackson and Mary his Wife,	"	14 June 1704.
Lydia daughter of William Indecot and Eliza. his Wife,	"	7 July 1704.
Ruth daughter of Abell Jones and Ruth his Wife,	"	18 September 1704.
John Son of John Ingram and Sarah his Wife,	"	23 January 1704.
Elizabeth daughter of John Ingolsbee and Sarah his Wife,	"	9 February 1704.
Phillipi daughter of James Lablond and Ann his Wife,	"	19 April 1704.
Joshua Son of Thomas Leveret and Rebecca his Wife,	"	4 May 1704.
Byfield Son of Edward Lyde and Deborah his Wife,	"	27 March 1704.
Janet daughter of Roger Lawson and Janet his Wife,	"	14 July 1704.
John } Savel } Sons of John Lawson and Anne his Wife,	"	10 July 1704.
Nathaniel Son of Nathanll. Loreing and Susana his Wife,	"	1 September 1704.
Elizabeth daughter of Jonathan Loreing and Eliza. his Wife,	"	13 September 1704.
Benjamen Son of Richard Lowden and Mary his Wife,	"	30 October 1704.
Edward Son of Samll. Lillie and Mehitabell his Wife,	"	20 November 1704.
Edward Son of Robert Lumley and Mary his Wife,	"	12 December 1704.
Elizabeth daughter of Nathaniel Lemon and Thankfull his Wife,	"	25 November 1704.
Deborah daughter of Thomas Lee and Deborah his Wife,	"	5 October 1704.
Sarah daughter of David Landon and Martha his Wife,	"	7 February 1704.
Joanna daughter of Jonathan Mountfort and Hannah his Wife,	"	2 June 1704.
Esther daughter of Charles Morrise and Esther his Wife,	"	30 June 1704.
Sarah daughter of Anthony Mannakin and Hannah his Wife,	"	12 July 1704.
Alice daughter of Francis Millar and Abigall his Wife,	"	25 July 1704.
Anne daughter of John Mortemore and Hephseba his Wife,	"	16 August 1704.
John Son of Samuel Mould and Mary his Wife,	"	7 August 1704.
John Son of Richard Mortemore and Mary his Wife,	"	3 September 1704.
Elizabeth daughter of Mr. Cotton Mather and Elizabeth his Wife,	"	13 July 1704.
James Son of John Meers and Ann his Wife,	"	31 October 1704.
Margaret daughter of Joseph Merefeeld and Margaret his Wife,	"	12 December 1704.

30   CITY DOCUMENT NO. 43.

Edward Son of Duncan Maycom and Mary his Wife,	Born	15 December 1704.
Susanna daughter of Thomas Mellens and Mary his Wife,	"	22 January 1704.
John Son of John Maxwell and Eliza. his Wife,	"	8 January 1704.
Anna daughter of Oliver Noyes and Anna his Wife,	"	17 Aprill 1704.
Zacheriah Son of George Nowell and Eliza his Wife,	"	20 August 1704.
John Son of Ezekiell Needham and Prissilla his Wife,	"	1 January 1704.
Sarah daughter of Walter Oglesbee and Sarah his Wife,	"	4 January 1704.
Randoll Son of Jacob Parker and Ann his Wife,	"	22 Aprill 1704.
Sarah daughter of William Paine and Margaret his Wife,	"	15 June 1704.
Mary daughter of Abraham Pullen and Mary his Wife,	"	16 August 1704.
Nathaniel Son of William Phillips and Deborah his Wife,	"	14 August 1704.
Joseph Son of Joseph Perram and Rebecca his Wife,	"	18 October 1704.
Hannah daughter of John Paine and Bethiah his Wife,	"	19 October 1704.
Thomas Son of Thomas Paine and Elizabeth his Wife,	"	25 December 1704.
Susanna daughter of John Petel and Rachel his Wife.	"	26 January 1704.
Sarah daughter of John Phelps and Sarah his Wife,	"	20 January 1704.
Rebecca daughter of John Plasteed and Sarah his Wife.	"	30 January 1704.
Henry Son of Samll. Phillips and Hannah his Wife,	"	21 February 1704.
Thomas Son of Thomas Phillips and Rebecca his Wife,	"	23 February 1704.
Mary daughter of George Peream and Mary his Wife,	"	25 February 1704.
Woodmansie Son of John Richardson and Margaret his Wife, .	"	17 July 1704.
Dorothy daughter of Thomas Rowell and Dorothy his Wife,	"	22 July 1704.
Sarah daughter of Joseph Rayner and Sarah his Wife,	"	25 July 1704.
Susanna daughter of James Rayner and Eliza. his Wife,	"	25 August 1704.
John Son of John Ruggles and Tabitha his Wife,	"	20 August 1704.
Ruth daughter of Nathanll. Rennolls and Ruth his Wife,	"	1 September 1704.
Gamaliel ⎫ Sons of Joseph Rogers and Eliza. his Benjamen ⎭ Wife,	"	19 September 1704.
Samuel Son of Samuel Rand and Sarah his Wife.	"	10 November 1704.
Nathaniel Son of Joseph Roberts and Esther his Wife,	"	29 November 1704.
Mercey daughter of William Robie and Eliza. his Wife,	"	29 August 1704.
Obediah Son of Humphry Richards and Susana his Wife,	"	14 January 1704.
Sarah daughter of William Shepreeve and Eliza. his Wife,	"	4 Aprill 1704.
Sarah daughter of Daniel Stoddard and Eliza. his Wife,	"	26 March 1704.
Martha daughter of Josiah Sanders and Rebecca his Wife,	"	22 Aprill 1704.

Births — 1704.

James Son of Benjamen Snelling and Jamina his Wife,	Born	23 April 1704.
William Son of James Stutson and Susana his Wife,	"	26 Aprill 1704.
Abigall daughter of Isaac Spencer and Bethiah his Wife,	"	24 May 1704.
Benjamen Son of Benjamen Swaine and Susana his Wife,	"	5 June 1704.
Hannah daughter of Joseph Soper and Margaret his Wife,	"	1 July 1704.
Mary daughter of Cyprian Southack and Eliza. his Wife.	"	7 June 1704.
Mary daughter of William Sargent and Mary his Wife,	"	21 June 1704.
Mary daughter of John Sharp and Mary his Wife,	"	21 August 1704.
Michael Son of Richard Shoot and Lydia his Wife,	"	16 September 1704.
John Son of Wigglesworth Sweetser and Ursilla his Wife,	"	12 September 1704.
Olive daughter of John Smalpeice and Olive his Wife,	"	2 October 1704.
Grover Son of John Scolley and Lydia his Wife,	"	12 October 1704.
William Son of Epaphras Shrimpton and Rebecca his Wife,	"	21 November 1704.
Nathaniel Son of John Sunderland and Mary his Wife,	"	10 November 1704.
Mary daughter of Richard Smith and Mary his Wife,	"	22 December 1704.
Rebecca daughter of Samuel Sewall and Rebecca his Wife,	"	30 December 1704.
Mary Ann daughter of Peter Signac and Ann his Wife,	"	26 January 1704.
Abigall daughter of John Simpson and Rely his Wife,	"	15 February 1704.
Habijah Son of Habijah Savage and Hannah his Wife,	"	17 February 1704.
Isaac Son of Isaac Townsend and Anna his Wife,	"	25 March 1704.
Lydia daughter of Soloman Townsend and Eliza. his Wife,	"	21 May 1704.
John Son of John Taylor and Anne his Wife,	"	30 August 1704.
Alice daughter of James Townsend and Alice his Wife,	"	23 October 1704.
John Son of John Tiler and Deborah his Wife,	"	4 October 1704.
Mary daughter of John Turner and Eliza his Wife,	"	11 October 1704.
Anna daughter of George Thorold and Anna his Wife,	"	21 December 1704.
Elizabeth daughter of Thomas Vering and Hannah Wife,	"	16 Aprill 1704.
Mary daughter of John Vriling and Mary his Wife,	"	10 Aprill 1704.
John Son of Anthony Underwood and Jane his Wife,	"	10 August 1704.
Thomas Son of Ambrose Vincent and Sarah his Wife,	"	19 October 1704.
Henry Son of Henry Wilson and Eliza. his Wife,	"	28 March 1704.
Joseph Son of Andrew Willet and Susana his Wife,	"	1 May 1704.
Mary daughter of William Wormwall and Sarah his Wife,	"	1 May 1704.
William Son of William Waine and Sarah his Wife,	"	15 May 1704.
Isaac Son of Ezekiel Walker and Ruth his Wife,	"	8 June 1704.
Sarah daughter of Joseph Williams and Sarah his Wife,	"	20 June 1704.
Nathaniel Son of Nathanll. Williams and Ann his Wife,	"	31 July 1704.

Sarah daughter of John Wilson and Sarah his Wife,	Born	12 June 1704.
Ann daughter of Adam Winthrop and Ann his Wife,	"	18 June 1704.
Ireland Son of Obediah Wakefeeld and Rebecca his Wife,	"	26 August 1704.
Elizabeth daughter of Francis Whitman and Mary his Wife,	"	8 September 1704.
Edward Son of Jonathan Waldo and Hannah his Wife,	"	23 August 1704.
Mary daughter of John Wilson and Mary his Wife,	"	8 November 1704.
Katherine daughter of Simon Willard and Eliza. his Wife,	"	20 December 1704.
Ebenezar Son of John Welch and Eliza his Wife,	"	27 January 1704.
Ann daughter of Edward Gray and Susana his Wife,	"	16 March 1704.
Mary daughter of Joseph Hood and Judeth his Wife,	"	10 March 1704.
Ebenezar Son of Francis Holmes and Rebecca his Wife,	"	6 November 1704.
Joseph Son of John Marshall and Sarah his Wife,	"	21 January 1704
Joseph Son of John Northey and Sarah his Wife,	"	15 March 1704.
Ebenezar Son of Ebenr. Pemberton and Mary his Wife,	"	6 February 1704.
Katherine daughter of Edward Weavor and Mary his Wife,	"	28 November 1704.
Elizabeth daughter of John Cronenshelt and Eliza. his Wife,	"	3 June 1704.
Obediah Son of Samuel Engs and Anna his Wife,	"	21 July 1704.
Samuel Son of Samll. Parker and Mary his Wife,	"	6 March 1704.
John Son of Edward Richards and Mary his Wife,	"	20 June 1704.
Elizabeth daughter of Samuel Barret and Sarah his Wife,	"	10 July 1704.
Peirses daughter of·Samuell Torrey and Abigall his Wife,	"	4 October 1704.
John Son of John Powell and Abigall his Wife,	"	2 January 1704.
Jane daughter of John Ela and Jane his Wife	"	25 February 1704.
Martha daughter of Thomas Palmer Esqr. and Abigal his Wife	"	21 January 1704.
Roger Son of Wentworth Paxton and Faith his Wife,	"	13 November 1704.
Eliza. daughter of Thomas Savage and Margaret his Wife,	"	29 September 1704.
Mary daughter of Richard Tyhurst and Mary his Wife,	"	2 November 1704.
Thomas Son of John Green and Bethiah his Wife,	"	27 July 1704.
Mary daughter of Robert Ellis and Eliza. his Wife,	"	9 July 1704.
Susanna daughter of Andr. Sigourney and Mary his Wife,	"	27 December 1704.

1705.

Hannah daughter of John Adams and Hannah his Wife,	Born	12 August 1705.
Joseph Son of Eliah Adams and Rebecca his Wife,	"	26 October 1705.
Mary daughter of Isaac Adams and Martha his Wife,	"	23 January 1705.
Abigall daughter of Joseph Allen and Ann his Wife,	"	11 February 1705.
Mary daughter of Henry Brightman and Abiel his Wife,	"	22 March 1704–5.

Births — 1705.

William Son of John Burnet and Deborah his Wife,	Born	22 April 1705.
Joseph Son of Moses Bradford and Eliza. his Wife,	"	14 May 1705.
Abraham Son of Joseph Belknap and Abigal his Wife,	"	2 May 1705.
John Son of John Barret and Sarah his Wife	"	17 May 1705.
Harborne ⎫ Sons of Thomas Bannister and Frances his Torshel ⎭ Wife,	"	4–5 June 1705.
John Son of William Brown and Mercy his Wife,	"	5 May 1705.
Thomas Son of John Baker and Mary his Wife,	"	24 May 1705.
Nathaniel Son of Adino Bulfinch and Abigall his Wife,	"	17 May 1705.
Alice daughter of Charles Bridger and Eliza. his Wife,	"	27 June 1705.
Robert Son of John Barnes and Rachel his Wife,	"	15 July 1705.
Mary daughter of Joseph Briscow and Mariah his Wife,	"	23 August 1705.
John Son of John Brick and Ann his Wife,	"	31 August 1705.
Soloman Son of Soloman Blake and Abigal his Wife,	"	12 September 1705.
Joseph Son of Thomas Barnes and Lydia his Wife,	"	20 September 1705.
John Son of John Ballentine and Mary his Wife,	"	1 October 1705.
Mary daughter of Samuel Bason and Mary his Wife,	"	27 September 1705.
George Son of George Brock and Mary his Wife,	"	8 October 1705,
Elizabeth daughter of Samuell Burnel and Eliza. his Wife,	"	8 November 1705.
Ann daughter of William Briggs and Ann his Wife,	"	22 November 1705.
Daniel Son of Daniel Ballard and Dorcas his Wife,	"	7 December 1705.
Deborah daughter of John Burnet and Johana his Wife,	"	12 December 1705.
James Son of Daniel Barnardo and Marian his Wife,	"	20 December 1705.
Elizabeth daughter of Jeremiah Bumsteed and Eliza. his Wife,	"	24 December 1705.
Elizabeth daughter of John Biles and Eliza. his Wife,	"	2 February 1705.
Abigall daughter of Benja. Brown and Mary his Wife,	"	4 February 1705.
Ruth daughter of Thomas Barbour and Eliza. his Wife,	"	15 February 1705.
Nicholas Son of Nicholas Boon and Mary his Wife,	"	8 February 1705.
John Son of Samuell Burrel and Martha his Wife,	"	16 March 1705.
Lydia daughter of Joseph Callender and Lydia his Wife,	"	7 Aprill 1705.
Jonathan Son of David Cutler and Abigall his Wife,	"	7 Aprill 1705.
Rachell daughter of John Cerlile and Hannah his Wife,	"	25 March 1705.
John Son of Jeremiah Cushing and Judeth his Wife,	"	4 July 1705.
Katherine daughter of William Crow and Eliza. his Wife,	"	2 July 1705.
Sands Son of Ezekial Carvat and Eliza. his Wife,	"	8 August 1705.
Lydia daughter of William Cook and Lydia his Wife,	"	21 August 1705.
Meddlecot Son of Elisha Cook and Jane his Wife,	"	13 August 1705.
Thomas Son of Thomas Cooper and Mehitabel his Wife,	"	20 August 1705.

John Son of David Coleson and Hannah his Wife,	Born	1 September 1705.
Richard Son of John Charnock and Mary his Wife,	"	2 November 1705.
Deborah daughter of Francis Clark and Deborah his Wife,	"	31 October 1705.
Rebecca daughter of Henry Chamlet and Eliza. his Wife,	"	8 November 1705.
Elizabeth daughter of Michael Coes and Rachel his Wife,	"	23 January 1705.
Margaret daughter of James Cook and Mary his Wife,	"	22 February 1705.
Masten Son of George Cabbot and Abigall his Wife,	"	20 February 1705.
John Son of Joseph Cowell and Eliza. his Wife,	"	13 March 1705.
Thomas Son of Paul Dudley Esqr. and Lucey his Wife,	"	13 Aprill 1705.
Thomas Son of Thomas Dawes and Sarah his Wife,	"	19 July 1705.
James Son of John Dolbeer and Sarah his Wife,	"	18 October 1705.
Edward Son of Richard Draper and Sarah his Wife,	"	9 September 1705.
Timothy Son of Seth Dwight and Abigall his Wife,	"	9 December 1705.
Samuel Son of David Eustice and Rachell his Wife,	"	23 Aprill 1705.
Edward Son of Edward Eades and Martha his Wife,	"	6 June, 1705.
Samuell Son of John Edwards and Sibell his Wife,	"	21 June 1705.
Richard Son of Joseph Emmons and Eliza. his Wife,	"	15 July 1705.
John Son of John Eastwick and Grizzel his Wife,	"	6 August, 1705.
Mary daughter of Samuel Earl and Mary his Wife,	"	9 September 1705.
Thomas Son of Thomas Freeman and Alice his Wife,	"	25 July 1705.
James Son of James Freeman and Rachel his Wife,	"	11 July 1705.
Abigall daughter of Richard Flood and Eliza. his Wife,	"	8 December 1705.
Mary daughter of Henry Frankling and Margart. his Wife,	"	20 February 1705.
Samuel Son of Samuell Frankling and Eliza. his Wife,	"	7 March 1705.
William Son of Nathanll. Gilbert and Eilza. his Wife,	"	9 March 1705.
Thomas Son of Nathaniel Green and Ann his Wife,	"	4 June 1705.
Mary daughter of John Gyles and Mary his wife,	"	9 June 1705.
Thomas Son of Nathanll Goodwin and Eliza. his Wife.	"	2 July 1705.
Margaret daughter of John Gerrish and Sarah his Wife,	"	30 August 1705.
George Son of Joseph Giddings and Eliza. his Wife,	"	3 November 1705.
Josiah Son of Samuel Grice and Prissilla his Wife,	"	18 August 1705
Benjamen Son Benjamen Gallop and Hannah his Wife.	"	22 November 1705.
Noyse Son of Thomas Godfrey and Esther his Wife,	"	10 December 1705.
Hannah daughter of John Goff and Hannah his Wife,	"	4 February 1705.
Mellows Son of Jonathan Gatchel and Martha his Wife.	"	12 February 1705.

BIRTHS — 1705.

Elias Son of John Garret and Susana his Wife,	Born	11 February 1705.
Bickford Son of David Greenliefe and Mary his Wife,	"	11 February 1705.
John Son of Joshua Hensha and Mary his Wife,	"	15 Aprill 1705.
Fortune Son of Ann Hartgrove Servt. of Savil Simpson,	"	19 May 1705.
Susana daughter of Nathanll Hodsdon and Susana his Wife,	"	8 July 1705.
Grigory Son of John Hobbs and Susana his Wife,	"	1 August 1705.
William Son of Francis Hudson and Mary his Wife,	"	31 August 1705.
Martha daughter of Joseph Hubbert and Thankful his Wife,	"	27 August 1705.
Margaret daughter of Peter Hauksworth and Eliza. his Wife,	"	7 September 1705.
Sarah daughter of Samnel Hood and Deborah his Wife,	"	14 September 1705.
Nathaniel Son of William Hasie and Eliza. his Wife,	"	14 October 1705.
Mary daughter of Hendrick Hurst and Mary his Wife,	"	10 October 1705.
Ann daughter of John Horton and Ann his Wife,	"	29 September 1705.
Samuel Son of Grove Hirst and Eliza. his Wife,	"	23 October 1705.
Nathanll. Son of Francis Holmes and Rebecca his Wife,	"	4 November 1705.
Ephraim Son of Ephraim Hunt and Johanna his Wife,	"	15 December 1705.
Ann daughter of Thomas Holland and Ann his Wife,	"	23 January 1705.
James Son of Thomas Hunt and Mary his Wife,	"	23 January 1705.
John Son of Joseph Hall and Blanch his Wife,	"	4 February 1705.
Ebenezar Son of Henry Hill and Mary his Wife,	"	15 February 1705.
Andrew Son of Daniell Johnnot and Susana his Wife,	"	20 June 1705.
Sarah daughter of William Indecot and Eliza his Wife,	"	21 August 1705.
Elizabeth daughter of John Jackson and Susana his Wife,	"	15 October 1705.
Elizabeth daughter of Jonathan Jackson and Mary his Wife,	"	26 November 1705.
Susana daughter of David Jesse and Mary his Wife	"	13 January 1705.
Christopher Son of John Kilbee and Rebecca his Wife,	"	25 May 1705.
Abigall daughter of Stephen Kingsley and Lydia his Wife,	"	16 November 1705.
James Son of Nathanll. Kettle and Johanna his Wife.	"	9 January 1705.
Abigall daughter of Samuell Kenney and Abigal his Wife,	"	4 January 1705.
John Son of John King and Eliza. his Wife,	"	2 January 1705.
Alice daughter of Peter Leech and Hannah his Wife,	"	26 Aprill 1705.
Thomas Son of Stephen Langley and Mary his Wife,	"	23 June 1705.
Robert Son of Robert Lumley and Mary his Wife,	"	3 November 1705.
John Son of John Love and Susana his Wife,	"	19 August 1705.
Isaac Son of Daniel Loreing and Prissilla his Wife.	"	30 November 1705.
Elizabeth daughter of Robert Lash and Eliza. his Wife,	"	9 January 1705.
Rebecca daughter of Thomas Leveret and Rebecca his Wife,	"	11 January 1705.
Samuel Son of Phillip Lewise and Martha his Wife.	"	10 February 1705.
Susanna daughter of John Mountfort and Mary his Wife,	"	1 Aprill 1705.

John Son of John Miles and Sarah his Wife,	Born	27 March 1705.
Elizabeth daughter of John Mason and Prudence his Wife,	"	18 Aprill 1705.
Hannah daughter of Josue Marriner and Hannah his Wife,	"	8 July 1705.
John Son of Debone Maison and Mary his Wife,	"	30 July 1705.
Sarah daughter of Joseph Marshall and Sarah his Wife,	"	21 August 1705.
Mary daughter of Benjamen Morss and Frances his Wife,	"	20 September 1705.
Elizabeth daughter of James Marshall and Sarah his Wife,	"	6 December 1705.
Sampson Son of Arthur Mason and Mary his Wife,	"	31 December 1705.
Katherine daughter of John Minzes and Eadey his Wife,	"	29 January 1705.
Joseph Son of Samuel Marrion and Mary his Wife,	"	22 July 1705.
Elizabeth daughter of Jonathan Mountfort and Hannah his Wife,	"	26 January 1705.
Powers Son of William Marriott and Ann his Wife,	"	25 March 1705.
Mary daughter of Daniel Needham and Mary his Wife,	"	6 Aprill 1705.
Susana daughter of John Noyes and Susana his Wife,	"	15 June 1705.
Oliver Son of Oliver Noyes and Anna his Wife,	"	4 July 1705.
Lydia daughter of George Nowel and Eliza. his Wife,	"	12 December 1705.
Thomas Son of Thomas Norrise and Martha his Wife,	"	24 September 1705.
John Son of Nathanll. Newel and Rest his Wife,	"	22 October 1705.
Jacob Son of Abraham Nicholls and Rebecca his Wife,	"	6 January 1705.
John Son of Jonah Perry and Susana his Wife,	"	15 Aprill 1705.
William Son of John Pitts and Hannah his Wife,	"	4 May 1705.
Thomas Son of John Parker and Sarah his Wife,	"	7 May 1705.
Josiah Son of John Pearce and Mary his Wife,	"	18 May 1705.
Mary daughter of James Pitts and Eliza. his Wife,	"	29 May 1705.
Elizabeth daughter of James Perry and Hannah his Wife,	"	28 May 1705.
Thomas Son of Edward Proctor and Eliza. his Wife,	"	16 June 1705.
John Son of John Peirse and Eliza. his Wife,	"	2 September 1705.
Hannah daughter of Edward Porter and Abiel his Wife,	"	4 September 1705.
Richard Son of Isaac Perkins and Mary his Wife,	"	12 September 1705.
Elizabeth daughter of James Pearson and Eliza. his Wife,	"	27 September 1705.
Susana daughter of Jacob Pearse and Rachel his Wife,	"	15 November 1705.
Abraham Son of Abraham Pullen and Mary his Wife,	"	9 December 1705.
Samuel Son of Joseph Prout and Mary his Wife,	"	31 January 1705.
William Son of Benjamen Pemberton and Eliza. his Wife,	"	15 January 1705.
Charles Son of Charles Packer and Mary his Wife.	"	15 June 1705.
Abigall daughter of Nathaniel Perkins and Sarah his Wife,	"	12 February 1705.
Sarah ⎱ daughters of William Randoll and Eliza. his Mary ⎰ Wife,	"	7 April 1705.
Rebecca daughter of William Russell and Eliza. his Wife.	"	9 April 1705.
Prissilla daughter of Samuell Royall and Hannah his Wife,	"	13 Aprill 1705.

BIRTHS — 1705.

Thomas Son of Thomas Robinson and Rebecca his Wife,	Born	11 May 1705.
Samuell Son of Thomas Rowell and Dorothy his Wife,	"	19 May 1705.
Susana daughter of John Russell and Mary his Wife,	"	13 June 1705.
Margaret daughter of Gyles Roberts and Margaret his Wife,	"	25 March 1705.
Thomas Son of Joseph Russell and Mary his Wife,	"	11 July 1705.
Clement Son of Charles Reneuf and Sarah his Wife,	"	20 August 1705.
Thomas Son of Thomas Russell and Ann his Wife,	"	1 September 1705.
Esther daughter of Richard Reed and Hannah his Wife,	"	15 February 1705.
Rebecca daughter of John Ransford and Rebecca his Wife,	"	4 March 1705.
Elizabeth daughter of John Spencer and Eliza. his Wife,	"	9 Aprill 1705.
Mary daughter of Joseph Simpson and Hannah his Wife,	"	1 Aprill 1705.
Mary daughter of James Seward and Edey his Wife,	"	1 May 1705.
Mary daughter of John Sables and Prissilla his Wife,	"	26 May 1705.
Rachel daughter of John Smith and Jane his Wife,	"	20 July 1705.
Simon Son of Simon Slocome and Abigall his Wife,	"	26 July 1705.
Margaret daughter of Clemons Sumner and Margaret his Wife,	"	18 July 1705.
Francis Son of Thomas Sargent and Ruth his Wife,	"	17 July 1705.
Dorothy ⎱ daughters of John Scott and Mary his Mary ⎰ Wife,	"	⎱ 22 ⎰ 25 July 1705.
Susana daughter of Joseph Shaw and Mercy his Wife,	"	4 September 1705.
James Son of James Scolley and Deborah his Wife,	"	8 August 1705.
Peter Son of Peter Stacey and Remember his Wife,	"	8 September 1705.
Mary daughter of Benjamen Simpson and Eliza. his Wife,	"	6 September 1705.
Margaret daughter of Richard Stratton and Margaret his Wife,	"	1 October 1705.
Hannah daughter of John Stevens and Grace his Wife,	"	12 October 1705.
Samuel Son of Benjamen Stone and Johanna his Wife,	"	20 October 1705.
Ebenezar Son of Wigglesworth Sweetser and Ursilla his Wife,	"	13 November 1705.
Abigall daughter of Josiah Stone and Mary his Wife,	"	29 January 1705.
William Son of Cyprian Southack and Eliza. his Wife,	"	12 January 1705.
William Son of William Shepreeve and Eliza. his Wife,	"	30 December 1705.
Elizabeth daughter of James Smith and Eliza. his Wife.	"	24 January 1705.
Agnis daughter of Thomas Sill and Agnis his Wife,	"	1 February 1705.
Samuel Son of Thomas Smith and Mary his Wife,	"	29 November 1705.
Rebecca daughter of Elias Townsend and Rebecca his Wife,	"	31 March 1705.
Mary daughter of Thomas Tomlin and Sarah his Wife,	"	12 June 1705.
George Son of Peter Thomas and Eliza. his Wife,	"	20 July 1705.

Sarah daughter of Miles Thompson and Abigal his Wife, Born 30 October 1705.
Mary daughter of Thomas Thurber and Mary his Wife, " 4 November 1705.
Soloman Son of Soloman Townsend and Eliza. his Wife, " 23 October 1705.
Andrew Son of Thomas Townsend and Eliza. his Wife, " 12 November 1705.
Hannah daughter of Benjamen Tolman and Ruth his Wife, " 30 October 1705.
William Son of Thomas Townsend and Sarah his Wife, " 20 December 1705.
Ebenezar Son of Isaac Townsend and Anna his Wife, " 2 January 1705.
Mehitabel daughter of Jabez Uter and Mary his Wife, " 12 September 1705.
Hennerina daughter of John Vryling and Mary his Wife, " 10 February 1705.
Ann daughter of Robert Wing and Mary his Wife, " 12 June 1705.
Mary daughter of William Webber and Mary his Wife, " 15 May 1705.
Henry Son of Henry Wakefeeld and Ann his Wife, " 8 July 1705.
Joshua Son of Joshua Wells and Sarah his Wife, " 18 July 1705.
James Son of James Williams and Abigall his Wife, " 20 August 1705.
Abigall daughter of Nathanll. Wheeler and Mary his Wife, " 29 July 1705.
Samuell Son of Edward Winslow and Hannah his Wife, " 29 May 1705.
Miles Son of John Wakefeeld and Eliza. his Wife, " 29 September 1705.
Robert Son of William White and Eliza. his Wife, " 6 October 1705.
Joseph Son of Samuel Willise and Eliza. his Wife " 26 November 1705.
Mehitable daughter of Daniel Willard and Mary his Wife, " 12 January 1705.
Nathaniel Son of Samuel White and Ann his Wife, " 12 January 1705.
Joseph Son of William Wheeler and Eliza. his Wife, " 30 January 1705.
Daniel Son of Daniel Wormwall and Hannah his Wife, " 2 February 1705.
Mary daughter of Zachry Wyre and Mary his Wife, " 16 December 1705.
Ann daughter of Nathaniel Williams and Ann his Wife, " 11 March 1705.
Joseph Son of Thomas Walker and Rebecca his Wife, " 18 February 1705.
Sarah daughter of Jacob Waters and Katherine his Wife, " 24 February 1705.
Sendall Son of Jonathan Williams and Mary his Wife, " 26 February 1705.
Mary daughter of Jonathan Waldo and Hannah his Wife, " 25 February 1705.
Sarah daughter of Thomas Bomer and Margaret his Wife, " 13 March 1705.
Joseph Son of Samuel Bill and Sarah his Wife. " 8 February 1705.
John Son of Joseph Bridgham and Mercy his Wife, " 23 February 1705.
Mary daughter of John Cotta and Sarah his Wife, " 29 December 1705.
Rebecca daughter of Samuel Eaton and Ruth his Wife. " 14 December 1705.
Mary daughter of Samuel Engs and Anna his Wife, " 21 February 1705.

BIRTHS — 1705–6. 39

Benjamen Son of John Jepson and Aphia his Wife,	Born	21 March 1705.
Sarah daughter of Edward Loyd Esq. and Deborah his Wife,	"	15 February 1705.
Mary Ann daughter of James Lablond and Ann his Wife,	"	4 March 1705.
Lazurus Son of Lazurus Manley and Sarah his Wife,	"	17 March 1705.
Mary daughter of Boston Negro and Jane his Wife,	"	18 March 1705.
James Son of James Robinson and Eliza. his Wife,	"	13 March 1705.
John Son of Thomas Webber and Mehitabel his Wife,	"	29 January 1705.
Mary daughter of William Willet and Mary his Wife,	"	15 March 1705.
James Son of Samuel Adams and Lydia his Wife,	"	14 November, 1705.
Samuel Son of Joseph Grant and Mary his Wife,	"	13 October 1705.
David Son of William Snowton and Rachel his Wife,	"	18 April 1705.
Mary daughter of Ambrose Vincent and Sarah his Wife,	"	10 February 1705.
Ebenezer Son of Ebenezer Williston and Judeth his Wife,	"	1 September 1705.
Sarah daughter of Benja. Hallaway and Mary his Wife,	"	1 September 1705.
Eliza. daughter of Henry Allen and Eliza. his Wife,	"	3 August 1705.
Nathaniel Son of Nathanll. Coney and Eliza. his Wife,	"	18 December 1705.
James Son of Gibbins Sharp and Sarah his Wife,	"	7 August 1705.
John Son of John Benning and Sarah his Wife,	"	24 November 1705.
Abigall daughter of John Greenough and Eliza. his Wife	"	8 August 1705.
Miles Son of Samll. Greenwood and Eliza. his Wife,	"	15 Aprill 1705.
Samuel Son of Samuel Keeling and Eliza. his Wife,	"	23 August 1705.
John Son of George Norton and Mary his Wife,	"	27 July 1705.
Christopher Son of Christopher Nicholson and Sarah his Wife,	"	22 December 1705.
Edward Son of Robert Orainge and Hannah his Wife,	"	24 January 1705.
Thomas Son of Paul Dudley Esqr. and Lucy his Wife,	"	13 Aprill 1705.
Mary daughter of Robert Fare and Sarah his Wife,	"	19 September 1705.
Sarah daughter of Jonathan Squire and Sarah his Wife,	"	15 May 1705.
Mary daughter of Samll. Deming and Hannah his Wife,	"	10 August 1705.
Gershom son of John Flagg and Abiel his Wife,	"	20 Aprill 1705.
Thomas Son of Robert Ellis and Eliza. his Wife,	"	23 January 1705.
Abigall daughter of Thomas Peirson and Eliza. his Wife,	"	20 September 1705.

1706.

Ebenezar Son of Ebenezar Ager and Abigal his Wife,	Born	23 Aprill 1706.
Hannah daughter of Mathew Armstrong and Margaret his Wife,	"	2 May 1706.
Mary daughter of Samuel Avise and Mary his Wife,	"	30 Aprill 1706.
Esther } Gimi of Thomas Androse and Esther his Martha } Wife,	"	9 June 1706.
William Son of William Antram and Abigal his Wife,	"	11 June 1706.

Mary daughter of William Alden and Mary his Wife,	Born	12 June 1706.
Samuel Son of Silence Allen and Esther his Wife,	"	7 September 1706.
Richard Son of Thomas Adkins and Ruth his Wife,	"	14 October 1706.
Elizabeth daughter of John Adams and Hannah his Wife,	"	13 January 1706.
Elizabeth daughter of Jeremiah Allen and Mary his Wife,	"	7 December 1706.
Elizabeth daughter of Moses Abbot and Rebecca his Wife,	"	10 March 1706.
Nicholas Son of Nicholas Buttolph and Mary his Wife,	"	13 May 1706.
Ann daughter of William Brown and Ann his Wife,	"	22 June 1706.
Ware Son of John Brewer and Martha his Wife,	"	20 July 1706.
Phillip Son of Newcombe Blague and Mary his Wife,	"	18 August 1706.
Hannah daughter of John Brewer and Ann his Wife,	"	19 August 1706.
John Son of John Ballard and Sarah his Wife,	"	10 September 1706.
John Son of Matthew Butler and Rachel his Wife,	"	20 September 1706.
Samuel Son of Timothy Burbank and Rebecca his Wife,	"	16 October 1706.
Henretta daughter of Thomas Bridgwater and Eliza. his Wife,	"	14 October 1706.
Joseph Son of Joseph Burch and Eliza. his Wife,	"	29 October 1706.
Elizabeth daughter of Edward Bickford and Eliza. his wife,	"	6 November 1706.
Nicholas Son of Nicholas Bowes and Dorcas his Wife,	"	4 November 1706.
Sarah daughter of Timothy Batt and Sarah his Wife,	"	21 November 1706.
Ephraim Son of Thomas Berry and Eliza. his Wife,	"	9 November 1706.
Jonathan Son of Henry Bridgham and Lydia his Wife,	"	10 December 1706.
Elizabeth daughter of Jeremiah Bumsteed and Eliza. his Wife,	"	16 December 1706.
Richard Son of Richard Bordman Negro and Ann his Wife,	"	18 January 1706.
Andrew Son of Jonathan Belcher and Mary his Wife,	"	7 November 1706.
Elizabeth daughter of James Barnerd and Eliza his Wife,	"	19 January 1706.
John Son of John Baker and Mary his Wife,	"	10 February 1706.
Zebdiel Son of Zebdiel Boylston and Jerusha his Wife,	"	10 February 1706.
Jane daughter of John Chamberline and Jane his Wife,	"	29 March 1706.
Samuel Son of Samuel Copp and Hannah his Wife,	"	18 Aprill 1706.
Elizabeth daughter of John Clough and Mary his Wife,	"	20 May 1706.
Benjamen Son of Thomas Chubb and Eliza. his Wife,	"	27 June 1706.
John Son of John Cookson and Rachel his Wife,	"	2 July 1706.
Mary daughter of John Cronenshelt and Eliza. his Wife,	"	2 July 1706.
Mary daughter of Thomas Creese and Rooksbee his Wife,	"	29 June 1706.
Martha daughter of John Clark Esqr. and Sarah his Wife,	"	26 June 1706.

BIRTHS — 1706.

Samuel Son of Daniel Collings and Rebecca his Wife,	Born	13 September 1706.
William Son of William Cleer and Bethia his Wife,	"	24 November 1706.
John Son of James Codner and Mary his Wife,	"	18 December 1706.
Jacob Son of Thomas Cox and Sarah his Wife,	"	23 December 1706.
Mary daughter of Charles Chauncey and Sarah his Wife,	"	19 December 1706.
Soloman Son of Samuel Drown and Eliza. his Wife,	"	26 March 1706.
Anna daughter of Robert Darbey and Martha his Wife,	"	11 November 1706.
Thomas Son of Thomas Dawes and Sarah his Wife,	"	25 January 1706.
Hannah daughter of John Emms and Hannah his Wife,	"	6 April 1706.
William Son of John Ellisit and Grace his Wife,	"	30 September 1706.
Andrew Son of Andrew Eliot and Ruth his Wife,	"	10 November 1706.
Hannah daughter of Jonathan Eustice and Sarah his Wife,	"	21 December 1706.
Susanna daughter of David Eustice and Rachel his Wife,	"	1 February 1706.
Nathaniel Son of Nathanll. Fadree and Isanna his Wife,	"	23 Aprill 1706.
Adam Son of Benjamen Flood and Mary his Wife,	"	19 May 1706.
Thomas Son of Thomas Foster and Martha his Wife,	"	26 May 1706.
Abigal daughter of Joseph Flood and Joanna his Wife,	"	29 May 1706.
Benjamen Son of Benja. Fitch and Mary his Wife,	"	25 September 1706.
Elizabeth daughter of John Fisher and Dorcas his Wife,	"	5 October 1706.
Mary daughter of Thomas Fitch and Abiel his Wife,	"	28 October 1706.
Thomas Son of Jabez Fox and Hannah his Wife,	"	7 December 1706.
Samuel Son of James Freeman and Rachel his Wife,	"	26 January 1706.
Mary daughter of Thomas Flagg and Esther his Wife,	"	20 February 1706.
Elizabeth daughter of Jeremiah Fenwick and Ann his Wife,	"	23 February 1706.
Mehitabel daughter of Benja. Gibson and Mehitabel his Wife,	"	5 August 1706.
James Son of James Gibson and Mary his Wife,	"	1 Aprill 1706.
Samuel Son of Timothy Green and Mary his Wife,	"	21 April 1706.
Sarah daughter of John Grant and Dorothy his Wife,	"	1 June 1706.
John Son of Robert Gutridge and Mary his Wife,	"	8 September 1706.
Samuel Son of James Goodwin and Margaret his Wife,	"	4 October 1706.
Mehitabel daughter of Benja. Goold and Mary his Wife,	"	5 October 1706.
Sarah daughter of Winsor Golding and Eliza. his Wife,	"	9 October 1706.
Daniel Son of William Goddard and Eliza. his Wife,	"	22 December 1706.
Robert Son of Robert Gutridge and Rebecca his Wife,	"	10 November 1706.
Joseph Son of John Goldthwait and Sarah his Wife,	"	11 November 1706.
Thomas Son of Walter Gutridge and Anna his Wife,	"	19 November 1706.
Deborah daughter of Bartholo Green and Mary his Wife,	"	9 November 1706.
Peirsis daughter of Edward Gray and Susanna his Wife,	"	10 January 1706.

Robert Son of John Homer and Margary his Wife,	Born	29 March 1706.
Frances daughter of Thomas Hetchbone and Frances his Wife,	"	16 May 1706.
George Son of William Hannah and Martha his Wife,	"	18 May 1706.
Hannah daughter of John Hughes and Deliverence his Wife,	"	18 July 1706.
Joseph Son of John Herridge and Dorothy his Wife,	"	16 August 1706.
Patience daughter of Nathanll. Hodsdon and Susana his Wife.	"	30 August 1706
Joseph Son of Stephen Hunewell and Mary his Wife,	"	26 August 1706.
Sarah daughter of Jacob Hasie and Hannah his Wife,	"	29 October 1706.
Abigall dautgher of Joseph Hasie and Elizabth. his Wife,	"	5 November 1706.
John Son of John How and Abigall his Wife,	"	7 November 1706.
Jack Son of Ann Hartgrove Servt. of Savil S:	"	13 December 1706.
Experience daughter of Michael Hamelton and Mary his Wife,	"	28 December 1706.
James Son of Joshua Hensha and Mary his Wife,	"	17 February 1706.
Eliza. daughter of John Heminway and Eliza. his Wife,	"	10 March 1706.
Broughton Son of William Johnson and Mary his Wife,	"	6 May 1706.
Marianna daughter of Daniel Johonot and Susanna his Wife,	"	17 August 1706.
Ephraim Son of Ephraim Jones and Hephseba his Wife,	"	20 September 1706.
Ruth daughter of Abel Jones and Ruth his Wife,	"	21 Obtober 1706.
Mary daughter of John Ireland and Eliner his Wife,	"	27 October 1706.
Sarah daughter of William Indecot and Eliza. his Wife,	"	6 November 1706.
Edward Son of Jonathan Jackson and Mary his Wife,	"	3 January 1706.
Jeremiah Son of Jeremi Jacksen and Hannah his Wife,	"	30 January 1706.
William Son of Soloman Kneeland and Mary his Wife,	"	30 March 1706.
Samuel Son of Christopher Kilbee and Sarah his Wife,	"	2 October 1706.
Thomas Son of Thomas Kempton and Margaret his Wife,	"	18 January 1706.
Daniel Son of Timothy Kembal and Katherine his Wife,	"	14 February 1706.
Abigal daughter of Samll. Lillie and Mehitabel his Wife,	"	26 April 1706.
Mary daughter of Jonathan Look and Eliza. his Wife,	"	8 May 1706.
John Son of Thomas Larkin and Sarah his Wife.	"	19 May 1706.
Abigal daughter of Ezekiel Lewise and Abigal his Wife,	"	12 June 1706.
Hannah daughter of John Lobdale and Hannah his Wife,	"	19 June 1706.
William Son of William Lee and Mercey his Wife,	"	27 June 1706.
George Son of Thomas Lee and Deborah his Wife,	"	21 July 1706.
Mary daughter of Joseph Lowden and Mary his Wife,	"	2 July 1706.
Mary Elizabeth } Gimmi of Timothy Lindall and Jane his Wife,	"	2 August 1706.

BIRTHS — 1706.

Joseph Son of Nathanll. Loreing and Susanna his Wife,	Born	23 October 1706.
Abigall daughter of Henry Lowder and Abigall his Wife,	"	5 August 1706.
John Son of John Love and Susanna his Wife,	"	18 December 1706.
John Son of Edward Martine and Sarah his Wife,	"	10 May 1706.
Mary daughter of Charles Morrise and Esther his Wife,	"	15 June 1706.
Mary daughter of Thomas Minner and Mary his Wife,	"	14 June 1706.
Mary daughter of Thomas Marshall and Mary his Wife,	"	11 October 1706.
Mary daughter of Daniel Mero and Frances his Wife,	"	16 September 1706.
Deborah daughter of Josue Marriner and Hannah his Wife,	"	28 October 1706.
Joshua Son of John Mountfort and Mary his Wife,	"	16 September 1706.
William Son of William Moor and Sarah his Wife,	"	21 January 1706.
Nicholas Son of John Miles and Sarah his Wife,	"	24 February 1706.
Henry Son of Henry Nicholson and Sarah his Wife,	"	25 May 1706.
Eunice daughter of David Norton and Sarah his Wife,	"	4 January 1706.
Daniel Son of Daniel Needham and Mary his Wife,	"	25 January 1706.
Andrew Son of Daniel Oliver and Eliza. his Wife,	"	28 March 1706.
Israel Son of Thomas Oliver and Bethia his Wife,	"	3 January 1706.
Elizabeth daughter of John Pitts and Sarah his Wife,	"	4 Aprill 1706.
Moses Son of William Paine and Sarah his Wife,	"	20 April 1706.
Abigall daughter of William Palfrey and Abigal his Wife,	"	1 July 1706.
Mary daughter of Samll. Parker and Mary his Wife,	"	26 June 1706.
Thomas Son of Thomas Porter and Prudence his Wife,	"	24 July 1706.
Rebecca daughter of John Plasteed and Sarah his Wife,	"	8 August 1706.
Jonathan Son of Samll. Pitcher and Eliza. his Wife,	"	22 August 1706.
Eliza. daughter of John Petel and Rachel his Wife,	"	27 September 1706.
Jacob Son of Jacob Parker and Ann his Wife,	"	24 September 1706.
William Son of William Paine and Margart. his Wife,	"	19 September 1706.
Mary daughter of George Peream and Mary his Wife,	"	15 December 1706.
Timothy Son of Edward Proctor and Eliza. his Wife,	"	12 January 1706.
Stephen Son of Stephen Parker and Margaret his Wife,	"	16 January 1706.
Mary daughter of John Pitts and Hannah his Wife,	"	24 January 1706.
Eliza. daughter of Samuel Robinson and Mary his Wife,	"	23 April 1706.
Rebecca daughter of David Ridley and Honour his Wife,	"	1 July 1706.
John Son of John Ruck and Hannah his Wife,	"	22 May 1706.
Joseph Son of William Rouse and Lydia his Wife,	"	14 July 1706.
Bethia daughter of Jeremiah Ruggles and Mehitabell his Wife,	"	18 July 1706.
Henry Son of Henry Rich and Eliza. his Wife,	"	18 September 1706.
Ann daughter of Thomas Rusnell and Ann his Wife,	"	7 October 1706.
Naomi daughter of Nathanll. Renolds and Ruth his Wife,	"	27 October 1706.
Mary daughter of Edward Richards and Mary his Wife,	"	16 November 1706.

44 CITY DOCUMENT NO. 43.

Mary daughter of John Richards and Mary his Wife,	Born	17 November 1706.
John Son of John Reed and Eliza. his Wife,	"	29 December 1706.
Samuel Son of John Ruggles and Tabitha his Wife,	"	25 December 1706.
Sarah daughter of Thomas Rowell and Dorothy his Wife,	"	26 February 1706.
James ⎱ Gimi: of Benja. Snelling and Jamina his Mary ⎰ Wife,	"	16 May 1706.
Joseph Son of John Seacom and Mehitabel his Wife,	"	14 June 1706.
Zacheriah Son of Rowland Storey and Ann his Wife,	"	27 June 1706.
William Son of John Savil and Prissilla his Wife,	"	8 June 1706.
Furnell Son of John Smalpeice and Olive his Wife,	"	3 May 1706.
Rebecca daughter of Robert Sharp and Mary his Wife,	"	16 July 1706.
Joshua Son of Allexr. Sherrar and Sarah his Wife,	"	22 July 1706.
Samuel Son of Samll. Smith and Sarah his Wife,	"	3 September 1706.
Nicholas Son of William Spencer and Mary his Wite,	"	6 September 1706.
Elizabeth daughter of Benja. Simpson and Eliza. his Wife,	"	8 August 1706.
Eliza. daughter of Thomas Short and Eliza. his Wife,	"	24 September 1706.
Ebenr. Son of John Simpson and Rely his Wife,	"	17 October 1706.
Deborah daughter of William Skinner and Deborah his Wife,	"	8 November 1706.
John Son of James Studson and Susana his Wife,	"	19 December 1706.
Susanna daughter of John Stevens and Grace his Wife,	"	29 January 1706.
Abigal daughter of John Sharp and Mary his Wife,	"	27 February 1706.
Mary daughter of Zachary Thare and Mary his Wife,	"	28 June 1706.
Deborah daughter of Joshua Thomas and Ann his Wife,	"	4 July 1706.
Susana daughter of James Townsend and Alice his Wife,	"	15 September 1706.
Elizabeth daughter of John Turner and Elizabeth his Wife,	"	15 October 1706.
William Son of William Thomas and Abigal his Wife,	"	21 January 1706.
Prudence daughter of John Viven and Prudence his Wife,	"	16 April 1706.
Mary daughter of John Venteman and Eliza. his Wife,	"	12 July 1706.
Sarah daughter of Mathew Vibert and Sarah his Wife,	"	20 August 1706.
James Son of James Varney and Jane his Wife,	"	8 August 1706.
Ann daughter of Ezekiel Walker and Ruth his Wife,	"	25 May 1706.
Joseph Son of Joseph Wadsworth and Hannah his Wife,	"	30 Aprill 1706.
Mary daughter of Joseph White and Sarah his Wife,	"	6 May 1706.
Lydia daughter of Joseph Williams and Sarah his Wife,	"	15 May 1706.
Christopher Son of George Wadling and Rachel his Wife,	"	13 July 1706.
Elizabeth daughter of Daniel Wyborn and Sarah his Wife,	"	29 July 1706.

BIRTHS — 1706.

Susana daughter of Henry Wilson and Eliza. his Wife,	Born	19 July 1706.
Hannah daughter of William Wright and Hannah Wife,	"	15 August 1706.
Ellis Son of John Wilson and Mary his Wife,	"	27 September 1706.
Mary daughter of Edward Weavor and Mary his Wife,	"	12 September 1706.
Seward Son of William Waters and Rebecca his Wife,	"	2 September 1706.
Mary daughter of John White and Mary his Wife,	"	2 November 1706.
Ann daughter of Henry Wakefeeld and Ann his Wife,	"	5 January 1706.
Elizabeth daughter of James Williams and Abigall his Wife,	"	12 January 1706.
Lydia daughter of Ebenr. Winburn and Lydia his Wife,	"	13 February 1706.
Rebecca daughter of William Webster and Mary his Wife,	"	2 March 1706.
James Son of John Allen and Elizabeth his Wife,	"	26 February 1706.
Lydia daughter of Thomas Barnes and Lydia his Wife,	"	1 March 1706.
Mather Son of Josiah Biles and Elizabeth his Wife,	"	15 March 1706.
Philip Son of George Brock and Mary his Wife,	"	18 February 1706.
Elizabeth Daughter of John Beer and Mary his Wife,	"	13 March 1706.
George Son of Samuell Barret and Sarah his Wife,	"	11 June 1706.
James Son of James Bridgham and Mercy his Wife,	"	21 March 1706.
William Son of Ebenezer Clough and Thankful his Wife,	"	21 February 1706.
Abigail Daughter of David Cutler and Abigail his Wife,	"	21 February 1706.
Elizabeth Daughter of William Clark and Rebecca his Wife,	"	7 March 1706.
William Son of David Copp and Patience his Wife,	"	24 March 1706.
Thomas Son of Thomas Gwin and Sarah his Wife,	"	10 June 1706.
John Son of Joshua Gee and Elizabeth his Wife,	"	23 March 1706.
Aaron Son of Moses Ingram and Mary his Wife,	"	17 March 1706.
Mary daughter of John Lorey and Mary his Wife,	"	6 March 1706.
Thomas Son of John May and Anna his Wife,	"	3 March 1706.
Mary daughter of Isaac Pirkins and Mary his Wife,	"	16 March 1706.
Elias Son of Timothy Robinson and Dorothy his Wife,	"	6 March 1706.
James Son of James Raymor and Eliza. his Wife,	"	8 March 1706.
Sarah daughter of Samuel Rand and Sarah his Wife,	"	4 November 1706.
Mary daughter of John Scot and Mary his Wife,	"	12 March 1706.
Elizabeth daughter of William Syms and Elizabeth his Wife,	"	20 March 1706.
William Son of Samuel Torrey and Abigall his Wife,	"	23 April 1706.
Patience daughter of Negro Exeter Turner and Lucey his Wife,	"	13 March 1706.
George Son of Symon Willard and Eliza. his Wife,	"	14 February 1706.
Eunice daughter of Thomas Wallis and Grace his Wife,	"	29 October 1706.
Ezekiel Son of Ezekiel Carver and Eliza. his Wife,	"	26 November 1706.

Benjamen Son of Josiah Frankling and Abiah his Wife, Born 6 January 1706.
Eliza. daughter of Samuel Green and Ann his Wife, " 10 Aprill 1706.
Eliza. daughter of Grove Hirst and Eliza. his Wife, " 20 October 1706.
Jane daughter of Ebenr Pemberton and Mary his Wife, " 15 November 1706.
Elizabeth daughter of John King and Eliza. his Wife, " 13 January 1706.
Hannah daughter of Richard Palfrey and Hannah his Wife, " 7 February 1706.
Thomas Son of Thomas Banister and Frances his Wife, " 2 June 1706.
Deliverence daughter of John Brewster and Deliverence his Wife, " 15 September 1706.
Eliazur Son of Christor. Capril and Tamzine his Wife, " 16 June 1706.
Rachel daughter of John Hurst and Rachell his Wife, " 7 March 1706.
Samll. Son of Mr. Cotton Mather and Eliza. his Wife, " 30 October 1706.
Susana daughter of Phillip Marret and Mary his Wife, " 9 Aprill 1706.
Eliza. daughter of Richard Tyhurst and Mary his Wife, " 13 April 1706.
Lucy daughter of Paul Dudley Esqr. and Lucy His Wife, " 5 May 1706.
Sarah daughter of Thomas Colsworthy and Sarah his Wife, " 26 September 1706.
Elias Son of Peter and Mary Sorien " 17 March 1706.

1707.

Eliza. daughter of Gibbins Sharp and Sarah his Wife, Born 3 March 1706-7.
Ebenr. Son of John Flagg and Abiel his Wife " 9 March 1706-7.
William Son of William Haley and Sarah his Wife " 17 March 1706-7.
Peter Son of Andr. and Sigourney and Mary his Wife, " 1 March 1706-7.
Ebenr. Son of Richard White and Abigall his Wife, " 7 March 1706-7.
Thomas Son of William Antram and Abigail his Wife, " 6 September 1707.
Hannah daughter of Joseph Allen and Ann his Wife, " 6 September 1707.
Mary daughter of John Aires and Elizabeth his Wife, " 14 September 1707.
Samuell Son of Samuell Avise and Mary his Wife, " 27 October 1707.
Jonathan Son of Samuell Adams and Lydia his Wife, " 20 November 1707.
Nathaniel Son of Nathaniel Adams and Joanna his Wife, " 9 March 1707.
Nicholas Son of Nicholas Blyth and Ann his Wife, " 14 May 1707.
Solomon) Gemni. of Solomon Blake and Abigail Abigaill) his Wife " 30 May 1707.
Susanna daughter of Hugh Babel and Sarah his Wife, " 23 May 1707.
Mary daughter of John Bennet and Hannah his Wife, " 23 June 1707.
Hannah daughter of Peter Butler and Mary his Wife, " 5 July 1707.

Births — 1707.

Lydia daughter of Samuell Barret and Sarah his Wife,	Born	25 May 1707.
John Son of John Barrel and Abiah his Wife,	"	9 August 1707.
Elizabeth daughter of Samuell Burnel and Elizabeth his Wife,	"	26 March 1707.
ne Daughter of John Buccanan and Eliza. his Wife,	"	12 July 1707.
...mes Son of Moses Bradford and Eliza. his Wife,	"	22 September 1707.
...hn Son of John Briggs and Katherine his Wife,	"	10 September 1707.
...ohn Son of Daniel Barnardo and Maryan his Wife,	"	27 September 1707.
Samuell Son of Samuel Belknap and Elizath. his Wife,	"	27 September 1707.
Hannah daughter of David Buckland and Hannah his Wife,	"	6 October 1707.
James Son of Joseph Belcher and Hannah his Wife,	"	30 October 1707.
Mary daughter of Josiah Biles and Abigail his Wife,	"	3 November 1707.
Jonathan Son of Jonathan Brown and Loise his Wife,	"	12 December 1707.
John Son of John Barret and Sarah his Wife,	"	17 December 1707.
Mary daughter of Thomas Bell and Mary his Wife,	"	31 December 1707.
Mary daughter of Richard Brooks and Mary his Wife,	"	1 November 1707.
Thomas Son of John Burnet and Deborah his Wife,	"	31 January 1707.
Thomas Son of Thomas Barnard and Silence his Wife,	"	11 February 1707.
Mary daughter of Daniel Berry and Mary his Wife,	"	23 February 1707.
Mary daughter of Thomas Baker and Thankfull his Wife,	"	17 February 1707.
Robert Son of John Brick and Ann his Wife,	"	16 July 1707.
John Son of Ezekiel Cravat and Elizath. his Wife,	"	28 April 1707.
Judeth daughter of John Colman and Judeth his Wife,	"	1 May 1707.
William Son of William Clark and Hannah his Wife,	"	14 June 1707.
Mary daughter of David Colson and Hannah his Wife,	"	25 May 1707.
John Son of William Cowel and Elizabeth his Wife,	"	1 July 1707.
Sarah daughter of John Coser and Sarah his Wife,	"	25 July 1707.
Nathaniel Son of Joseph Clough and Sarah his Wife,	"	20 August 1707.
Lydia daughter of William Cook and Lydia his Wife,	"	20 August 1707.
William Son of Jeremiah Condey and Susana his Wife,	"	15 August 1707.
Rachell daughter of John Cookson and Rachell his Wife,	"	10 September 1707.
Joseph Son of Noah Champney and Sarah his Wife,	"	12 September 1707.
Mathew Son of Mathew Collings and Dorcas his Wife,	"	8 September 1707.
Eliza. daughter of John Charnock and Mary his Wife,	"	8 September 1707.
John Son of John Cotta and Sarah his Wife,	"	18 September 1707.
Eliza. daughter of Peter Cutler and Ruth his Wife,	"	22 October 1707.
Elizath daughter of William Champlin and Martha his Wife,	"	25 January 1707.

William Son of James Cock and Mary his Wife,	Born	29 October 1707.
Phinias Son of Phinias Colefix and Jamina his Wife,	"	9 January 1707.
Abigail daughter of George Cabbot and Abigail his Wife,	"	29 January 1707.
Elisha Son of Benjamin Dyer and Hannah his Wife,	"	31 March 1707.
Abigail daughter of Thomas Dudley and Abigail his Wife,	"	3 April 1707.
Samll. Son of John Dolbeer and Sarah his Wife,	"	17 May 1707.
John Son of Eliezur Darby and Mary his Wife,	"	27 May 1707.
Ann daughter of Thomas Davise and Lydia his Wife,	"	27 May 1707.
Rebecca daughter of Addington Davenport and Eliza. his Wife,	"	18 May 1707.
Mehitabel daughter of John Downing and Eliza. his Wife,	"	9 July 1707.
Samuel Son of Richard Draper and Sarah his Wife,	"	1 June 1707.
Rebecca daughter of Joseph Dowding and Ann his Wife,	"	8 September 1707.
Joseph Son of John Edwards and Sivill his Wife,	"	11 June 1707.
Sarah daughter of Samuell Edwards and Katherine his Wife,	"	3 August 1707.
John Son of Edward Eades and Martha his Wife,	"	3 November 1707.
Samuell Son of William Eustice and Sarah his Wife,	"	2 January 1707.
Annah daughter of Samll. Engs and Annah his Wife,	"	2 February 1707.
Ruth daughter of Samuell Eaton and Ruth his Wife,	"	2 November 1707.
William Son of John Foster and Sarah his Wife,	"	5 Aprill 1707.
Mary daughter of Richard Flood and Elizabeth his Wife,	"	20 Aprill 1707.
Esther daughter: of Josiah Flynt and Mary his Wife,	"	13 May 1707.
John Son of Ephraim Fenno and Eliza. his Wife,	"	12 May 1707.
John Son of John Flood and Susana his Wife,	"	23 June 1707.
William Son of William Frathingham and Esther his Wife,	"	21 July 1707.
Elizabeth daughter of Hopestill Foster and Eliza. his Wife,	"	26 August 1707.
John Son of John Fisher and Dorcas his Wife,	"	7 February 1707.
Sarah daughter of Tobias Green and Mary his Wife,	"	2 April 1707.
Joseph Son of Joseph Gray and Rebecca his Wife,	"	9 April 1707.
Susanna daughter of Benjamin Gallop and Hannah his Wife,	"	19 April 1707.
John Son of William Goddard and Eliza. his Wife,	"	5 Aprill 1707.
Rufus Son of Nathaniel Green and Ann his Wife,	"	30 May 1707.
John Son of Thomas Gwin and Sarah his Wife,	"	4 June 1707.
Samuel Son of Samuel Goff and Hannah his Wife,	"	12 July 1707.
Lydia daughter of Thomas Gilbert and Lydia his Wife,	"	9 July 1707.
William Son of John Gerrish and Sarah his Wife,	"	21 July 1707.
Buttolph Son of Robert Gutridge and Mary his Wife,	"	16 September 1707.
Joseph Son of Joseph Giddings and Eliza. his Wife,	"	24 October 1707.
Mary daughter of Walter Gutridge and Anna his Wife,	"	26 October 1707.
Freelove daughter of Thomas Goodwin and Freelove his Wife,	"	3 November 1707.
Sarah daughter of Thomas Godfrey and Esther his Wife,	"	28 September 1707.
Nathaniel Son of Benjamin Gallop and Hannah his Wife,	"	19 March 1707.

Births — 1707.

William Son of William Holberton and Mary his Wife,	Born	3 April 1707.
Ann daughter of Arthur Head and Esther his Wife,	"	17 April 1707.
Sarah daughter of Joseph Hood and Judeth his Wife,	"	25 July 1707.
Samuel Son of Samuel Hurst and Sarah his Wife,	"	14 July 1707.
Joseph Son of William Hasie and Eliza. his Wife,	"	17 August 1707.
Mehitabel daughter of Henry Hurst and Mary his Wife,	"	30 August 1707.
Ann daughter of John Hook and Margaret his Wife,	"	29 August 1707.
Sarah daughter of John Horton and Ann his Wife,	"	9 November 1707.
Samuel Son of Benja. Halaway and Mary his Wife,	"	25 November 1707.
Mary daughter of Francis Hudson and Mary his Wife,	"	2 December 1707.
Hannah daughter of John Haies and Hannah his Wife,	"	15 December 1707.
Judeth daughter of Ephraim Hunt and Joanna his Wife,	"	29 December 1707.
Thomas Son of Thomas Holland and Ann his Wife,	"	24 February 1707.
Martha daughter of Joseph Hubbert and Thankful his Wife,	"	12 January 1707.
Mary daughter of John Haukins and Abigail his Wife,	"	23 August 1707.
Benjamin Son of John Ingram and Sarah his Wife,	"	13 April 1707.
John Son of John Jefferyes and Sarah his Wife,	"	13 August 1707.
John Son John Jent and Abigail his Wife,	"	16 August 1707.
Mary daughter of John Jarvise and Mary his Wife,	"	17 October 1707.
William Son of William Johnson and Mary his Wife,	"	12 December 1707.
Edward Son of Jonathan Jackson and Mary his Wife,	"	26 February 1707.
James Son of Natl. Kettle and Joanna his Wife,	"	13 April 1707.
Benja Son of Solomon Kneeland and Mary his Wife,	"	22 July 1707.
Elizabeth daughter of Roger Kilcup and Frances his Wife,	"	25 October 1707.
Mary daughter of Robert Lumley and Mary his Wife,	"	31 March 1707.
Lydia daughter of William Lowder and Lydia his Wife,	"	12 April 1707.
Eliza. daughter of Jonathan Loreing and Elizabeth his Wife,	"	21 April 1707.
Isaac Son of Isaac Lewise and Hannah his Wife,	"	1 July 1707.
Jane daughter of Timothy Lyndal and Jane his Wife,	"	19 August 1707.
William Son of Thomas Lee and Deborah his Wife,	"	24 September 1707.
William Son of Ezekiel Lewis and Abigall his Wife,	"	28 November 1707.
Ann daughter of Edward Lyde Esqr. and Deborah his Wife,	"	27 December 1707.
Susanah daughter of Peter Leech and Hannah his Wife,	"	11 January 1707.
Nathaniel Son of Nathaniel Lyndal and Elizabeth his Wife,	"	16 February 1707.
Abigall daughter of Thomas Lyndall and Abigall his Wife,	"	14 March 1707.
Thomas Son of Thomas Melladge and Mary his Wife,	"	4 April 1707.

Thomas Son of Joseph Merrefeeld and Margaret his Wife,	Born	29 March 1707.
Katherine Daughter of John Maxwell and Eliza. his Wife,	"	27 May 1707.
John Son of John Mason and Prudence his Wife,	"	26 May 1707.
William Son of Thomas Mellens and Mary his Wife,	"	13 June 1707.
Benja. Son of Benja. Marshall and Sarah his Wife,	"	19 June 1707.
James Son of James Marshall and Sarah his Wife,	"	28 May 1707.
Ephraim Son of Ephraim More and Elizabeth his Wife,	"	7 June 1707.
John Son of John Northey and Sarah his Wife,	"	4 April 1707.
Osborn Son of Henry Nicholson and Sarah his Wife,	"	28 July 1707.
Mary daughter of William Nicholson and Eliza. his Wife,	"	24 August 1707.
Oliver Son of Oliver Noyes and Anna his Wife,	"	1 September 1707.
Rebecca daughter of Abraham Nichols and Rebecca his Wife,	"	6 September 1707.
Jeffs Son of George Nowel and Eliza. his Wife,	"	4 October 1707.
Ezekiel Son of Ezekiel Needham and Prissilla his Wife,	"	24 September 1707.
Jane daughter of John Needham and Ann his Wife,	"	6 January 1707.
James Son of James Oborn and Abigall his Wife,	"	10 September 1707.
John Son of Richard Pitcher and Grace his Wife,	"	17 June 1707.
Mary daughter of James Pearson and Eliza. his Wife,	"	19 June 1707.
Hannah daughter of Thomas Plats and Hannah his Wife,	"	9 April 1707.
Sarah daughter of John Porter and Eliza. his Wife,	"	24 June 1707.
Lydia daughter of James Pits and Eliza. his Wife,	"	7 July 1707.
John Son of John Parker and Sarah his Wife,	"	5 July 1707.
Samuel Son of John Pain and Bethia his Wife,	"	29 June 1707.
Mary daughter of Thomas Pranket and Mary his Wife,	"	1 August 1707.
Abiel daughter of Edward Porter and Abiel his Wife,	"	22 June 1707.
Mary daughter of Benja. Pemberton and Eliza. his Wife,	"	10 August 1707.
Joseph Son of Thomas Pain and Eliza. his Wife,	"	9 August 1707.
Sarah daughter of Nathaniel Perkins and Sarah his Wife,	"	19 August 1707.
John Son of Richard Pitcher and Grace his Wife,	"	11 September 1707.
Joseph Son of Joseph Prout and Mary his Wife,	"	29 September 1707.
Samuel Son of Samuel Pike and Mary his Wife,	"	18 November 1707.
William Son of William Payne and Margaret his Wife,	"	26 January 1707.
Mary Susana daughter of Roger Pattenson and Judeth his Wife,	"	4 February 1707.
James Son of James Perry and Hannah his Wife,	"	19 January 1707.
Benjamen Son of Benjamin Pickman and Abigall his Wife,	"	28 January 1707.
Mary daughter of John Petail and Rachel his wife,	"	20 February 1707:
Hannah daughter of John Ruggles and Martha his Wife,	"	20 April 1707.
Abiel daughter of Fortune Redduck and Abiel his Wife,	"	5 June 1707.
John Son of Joseph Roberts and Esther his Wife,	"	25 June 1707.
Skinner Son of Joseph Russel and Mary his Wife,	"	29 September 1707.
William Son of William Rouse and Lydia his Wife,	"	8 November 1707.

BIRTHS — 1707.

Boylston Son of Rebecca Robinson	Born	21 November 1707.
Jeremiah Son of Jeremiah Ruggles and Mehitabel his Wife,	"	28 October 1707.
Elizabeth daughter of William Shepreeve and Eliza. his Wife,	"	11 April 1707.
Sarah daughter of John Smith and Jane his Wife,	"	5 May 1707.
Hannah daughter of John Sunderland and Mary his Wife,	"	11 May 1707.
John Son of John Shaw and Mercy his Wife,	"	3 June 1707.
Arthur Son of Daniel Stoddard and Eliza. his Wife,	"	7 June 1707.
Sarah daughter of John Staniford and Sarah his Wife,	"	12 June 1707.
Sarah daughter of Joseph Smith and Christian his Wife,	"	7 August 1707.
Mary daughter of John Salmon and Abiel his Wife,	"	11 August 1707.
Joseph Son of Thomas Savage and Margaret his Wife,	"	27 August 1707.
Elizabeth daughter of Clemans Sumner and Margaret his Wife,	"	8 October 1707.
Eliza. daughter of Edward Sanders and Eliza. his Wife,	"	21 October 1707.
Benjamin Son of Rowland Storey and Ann his Wife,	"	15 November 1707.
Eliza. daughter of Samuel Salter and Sarah his Wife,	"	9 December 1707.
Samuel Son of John Sables and Priscilla his Wife,	"	15 December 1707.
Abigall daughter of William Snowton and Rachel his Wife,	"	9 December 1707.
William Son of George Sirey and Jane his Wife,	"	27 December 1707.
William Son of William Skinner and Deborah his Wife,	"	10 January 1707.
Abigall daughter of Simon Slocome and Abigall his Wife,	"	14 January 1707.
Jonathan Son of Jonathan Simpson and Mary his Wife,	"	24 February 1707.
Elizabeth daughter of Thomas Townsend and Eliza. his Wife,	"	7 April 1707.
Edward Son of Edward Tuttle and Joanna his Wife,	"	21 July 1707.
Elizabeth daughter of Henry Tew and Mary his Wife,	"	20 August 1707.
John Son of John Thompson and Martha his Wife,	"	28 August 1707.
John Son of Samuel Torrey and Abigall his Wife,	"	29 November 1707.
Mary daughter of Zacheriah Thayer and Mary his Wife,	"	14 January 1707.
Hanna daughter of Negro Exeter Turner and Lucey Wife,	"	1 February 1707.
Lydia daughter of Cornelius Thayer and Lydia his Wife,	"	6 March 1707.
Ann daughter of Ambrose Vincent and Sarah his Wife,	"	10 April 1707.
Lydia daughter of Benja. Varney and Sarah his Wife,	"	14 August 1707.
Eliza. daughter of John Vryland and Mary his Wife,	"	12 October 1707.
Allen Son of Allen Wild and Eliza. his Wife,	"	28 March 1707.
William Son of William Watters and Loise his Wife,	"	10 April 1707.
John Son of Robert Wing and Mary his Wife,	"	5 May 1707.
Thomas Son of Thomas Webber and Mehitabel his Wife,	"	8 April 1707.

	Born	
Amey daughter of Nathaniel Wheeler and Mary his Wife,	Born	25 May 1707.
John Son of Thomas Walker and Rebecca his Wife,	"	2 July 1707.
William Son of William Willet and Mary his Wife,	"	9 July 1707.
Daniel Son of Isaac Webb and Abigall his Wife,	"	4 July 1707.
Samuel Son of John Wakefeild and Eliza. his Wife,	"	4 July 1707.
Rebecca daughter of Obadiah Wakefield and Rebecca his Wife,	"	27 August 1707.
Anne daughter of Adam Winthrop and Anne his Wife,	"	17 September 1707.
Lydia daughter of Daniel Wear and Mary his Wife,	"	9 September 1707.
Joseph Son of Joseph Webb and Deborah his Wife,	"	13 September 1707.
Dorothy daughter of Ichabod Williston and Dorothy his Wife,	"	11 September 1707.
William Son of Nathaniel Wardel and Hannah his Wife,	"	16 October 1707.
Daniel Son of Joseph Williams and Sarah his Wife,	"	6 November 1707.
Mary daughter of Nathll. Williams and Ann his Wife,	"	20 January 1707.
Hepzeba daughter of James Williams and Abigall his Wife,	"	2 January 1707.
Martha daughter of Ebenezer Williston and Judeth his Wife,	"	5 January 1707.
George Son of George Worthylake and Ann his Wife,	"	12 February 1707.
William Son of Edward Winslow and Hannah his Wife,	"	13 February 1707.
Eliza daughter of William Whetcomb and Rebecca his Wife,	"	20 December 1707.
John Son of John Wilson and Mary his Wife,	"	21 January 1707.
Nathll. Son of Isaac Adams and Martha his Wife,	"	25 February 1707.
Thomas Son of John Alden and Eliza. his Wife,	"	1 March 1707.
David Son of Phillip Britton and Eliza his Wife,	"	14 March 1707.
Japeth Son of Japeth Brown and Susanna his Wife,	"	22 March 1707.
James Son of James Bodwin and Sarah his Wife,	"	5 May 1707.
Anna daughter of Thomas Bridg and Eliza. his Wife,	"	14 October 1707.
Eliza. daughter of William Brown and Lydia his Wife,	"	5 November 1707.
Jane daughter of Benja. Colman and Jane his Wife,	"	25 February 1707.
Sarah daughter of Benjamen Edwards and Hannah Wife,	"	24 June 1707.
Abiah daughter of John Goodwin and Mary his Wife,	"	19 February 1707.
John Son of John Gibson and Mary his Wife,	"	12 October 1707.
Sarah daughter of Samuel Hood and Deborah his Wife,	"	6 March 1707
William Son of John Hobbie and Ann his Wife,	"	13 August 1707.
Samuel Son of Jeremiah Jackson and Hannah his Wife,	"	10 March 1707.
Joseph Son of Nathanll. Kettle and Joanna his Wife,	"	11 March 1707.
Samuel Son of Samuel Kenny and Abigall his Wife,	"	28 February 1707.

BIRTHS — 1707.

Joshua Son of Josue Marriner and Hannah his Wife,	Born	19 September 1707.
John Son of Milam Macklowd and Martha his Wife,	"	27 September 1707.
Hannah daughter of Jonathan Mountfort and Hanna his Wife,	"	22 October 1707.
James Son of James Manson and Joanna his Wife,	"	8 January 1707.
Robert Son of Robert Mires and Eliza. his Wife,	"	6 January 1707.
Eliza. daughter of Duncan Maycome and Mary his Wife,	"	13 October 1707.
Elizabeth daughter of John Plasteed and Sarah his Wife,	"	28 February 1707.
Samuel Son of Edward Proctor and Eliza. his Wife,	"	20 March 1707.
Mehitabel daughter of John Seacomb and Mehitabel his Wife,	"	21 February 1707.
William Son of Isaac Spencer and Bethia his Wife,	"	3 March 1707.
Mary daughter of Ambrose Vincent and Sarah his Wife,	"	22 March 1707.
Elizabeth daughter of William White and Eliza. his Wife,	"	15 March 1707.
Jonathan Son of William Wheeler and Eliza. his Wife,	"	8 March 1707.
Rebecca daughter of William Webster and Mary his Wife,	"	5 March 1707.
William Son of William Webber and Mary his Wife,	"	15 March 1707.
Hannah daughter of Peter Clark and Katherine his Wife,	"	8 August 1707.
John Son of Thomas Banister and Frances his Wife,	"	7 June 1707.
Still-born Son of Ebnr. Dennise and Susana his Wife,	"	17 September 1707.
Peirses daughter of Edward Gray and Susana his Wife,	"	14 December 1707.
Nathanll. Son of Samll. Greenwood and Eliza, his Wife,	"	27 March 1707.
Nathanll. Son of Mr. Cotton Mather and Eliza his Wife,	"	16 May 1707.
Abigall daughter of George Norton and Mary his Wife,	"	29 July 1707.
Abigal daughter of Robert Orainge and Hannah his Wife,	"	10 November 1707.
Charles Son of Wentworth Paxton and Faith his Wife,	"	28 February 1707.
Joseph Son of Paul Dudley Esqr. and Lucy his Wife,	"	14 October 1707.
Samll. Son of Samll. Bridgham and Mary his Wife,	"	7 July 1707.
Elias Son of Robert Cock and Agnis his Wife,	"	28 March 1707.
Thomas Son of Simon Record and Grace his Wife,	"	3 July 1707.
Bethiah daughter of John Green and Bethiah his Wife,	"	19 July 1707.
Eliza. daughter of John Lane and Prudence his Wife,	"	19 October 1707.
Daniel Son of Richard Tucker and Bethiah his Wife,	"	10 October 1707.
Ruth daughter of Zachry. Wire and Mary his Wife,	"	3 December 1707.
Christian daughter of Benja. Bridge and Christian his Wife,	"	12 October 1707.
Sarah daughter of Robert Ellis and Eliza. his Wife,	"	15 September 1707.
Joseph Son of Joseph Wakefeeld and Esther his Wife,	"	9 February 1707.
Thomas Son of Thomas Sargent and Ruth his Wife,	"	25 February 1707.
Mehitabel daughter of John Harrod and Mehitabel his Wife,	"	26 April 1707.

1708.

Jacob Son of Jacob Alley and Priscilla his Wife,	Born	3 May 1708.
David Son of Joseph Adams and Eliza. his Wife,	"	27 May 1708.
Mary daughter of John Adams and Hañah his Wife,	"	10 July 1708.
Susanna ⎱ Gimi. of William Antram and Abigal his Eliza. ⎰ Wife,	"	11 November 1708.
Drewry Son of William Alden and Mary his Wife,	"	12 May 1708.
Richard Son of Moses Abbot and Rebecca his Wife,	"	18 February 1708.
Rebecca daughter of Eliah Adams and Rebecca his Wife,	"	8 March 1708.
Jeremiah Son of Jer. Bumsted and Eliza. his Wife,	"	26 March 1708.
Eliza. daughter of Joseph Belknap and Abigal his Wife,	"	13 April 1708.
Benja. Son of Benjamen Brown and Mary his Wife,	"	27 May 1708.
Joseph Son of Joseph Briscow and Marya his Wife,	"	29 May 1708.
Peter Son of James Brown and Sarah his Wife,	"	4 June 1708.
Timothy Son of Timothy Batt and Sarah his Wife,	"	11 June 1708.
John Son of Samuel Barret and Sarah his Wife,	"	21 June 1708.
Mehitabel daughter of John Barr and Margaret his Wife,	"	10 June 1708.
John Son of John Brewer and Martha his Wife,	"	22 July 1708.
Susanna daughter of Hugh Babell and Sarah his Wife,	"	1 August 1708.
Hannah daughter of Thomas Boman and Margaret his Wife,	"	29 August 1708.
Eliza ⎱ Gimmi. of James Bodwin and Sarah his Mary ⎰ Wife,	"	27 June 1708. 31 August 1708.
Thomas Son of Thomas Berry and Eliza. his Wife,	"	14 August 1708.
Mary daughter of George Brock and Mary his Wife,	"	16 October 1708.
Timothy Son of William Brown and Ann his Wife,	"	1 November 1708.
Thomas Son of John Brentnel and Phebee his Wife,	"	17 October 1708.
Edward Son of John Buckley and Mary his Wife,	"	10 November 1708.
James Son of James Barnerd and Eliza. his Wife.	"	30 August 1708.
Benjamen Son of Benja. Briant and Abigall his Wife,	"	9 December 1708.
Richard Son of Samuel Bill and Sarah his Wife,	"	2 December 1708.
Ephraim Son of John Baker and Mary his Wife,	"	19 December 1708.
Sarah daughter of John Bucannan and Eliza. his Wife,	"	15 December 1708.
Marcy daughter of Benja. Bronsdon and Mary his Wife,	"	30 January 1708.
Peter Son of Peter Butler and Mary his Wife,	"	21 January 1708.
Anthony Son of Anthony Bracket and Mary his Wife,	"	25 January 1708.
Mary daughter of Joseph Burch and Eliza. his Wife,	"	20 January 1708.
Thomas Son of Thoms Baker and Thankfull his Wife,	"	17 February 1708.
Samuel Son of John Brick and Ann his Wife,	"	1 March 1708.
Rebeca daughter of Samuell Burnell and Eliza. his Wife,	"	10 February 1708.

BIRTHS — 1708.

Sarah daughter of John Clark and Sarah his Wife,	Born	11 May 1708.
Ann daughter of Robert Calef and Margaret his Wife,	"	7 July 1708.
Matha daughter of Ebenr. Chamberlin and Martha his Wife,	"	31 July 1708.
Eliza. daughter of John Cookson and Rachell his Wife,	"	10 October 1708.
Mary daughter of Joseph Callender and Lydia his Wife,	"	8 September 1708.
William Son of David Craig and Deborah his Wife,	"	18 October 1708.
Mary daughter of Peter Cutler and Ruth his Wife,	"	20 December 1708.
Mary daughter of Jonathn. Collings and Mary his Wife,	"	25 January 1708.
Deborah daughter of Francis Clark and Deborah his Wife,	"	31 January 1708.
Jeremiah Son of Jer. Condey and Susana his Wife,	"	9 February 1708.
Sarah daughter of John Colman and Judeth his Wife,	"	14 February 1708.
John Son of Samll. Copp and Hannah his Wife,	"	3 February 1708.
Rebecca daughter of William Clark and Rebecca his Wife,	"	28 January 1708.
Abigal daughter of Seth Dwight and Abigal his Wife,	"	8 August 1708.
Ambrose son of Thoms. Dawes and Sarah his Wife,	"	30 September 1708.
Susanna daughter of Ebenr. Dennis and Susana his Wife,	"	22 October 1708.
John Son of John Dorrel and Rachel his Wife,	"	6 September 1708.
Thomas Son of Thomas Diamond and Ann his Wife,	"	19 November 1708.
Sarah daughter of Benja. Dyer and Hannah his Wife,	"	13 December 1708.
Benjamin Son of John Dolbeer and Sarah his Wife,	"	4 December 1708.
Thomas Son of Samll. Drown and Eliza. his Wife,	"	23 December 1708.
Elizabeth daughter of Zebadiah Daniel and Eliza. his Wife,	"	18 January 1708.
James Son of Jona. Eustice and Sarah his Wife,	"	24 November 1708.
Ruth daughter of Andrew Eliot and Ruth his Wife.	"	29 September 1708.
Hopestill ⎱ Gimmi of Hopestill Foster and Eliza. his Eliza. ⎰ Wife,	"	28 June 1708.
Ephraim Son of Ephraim Fenno and Eliza. his Wife,	"	18 July 1708.
Katherine daughter of John Foster and Sarah his Wife,	"	10 August 1708.
Joseph Son of Joseph Flood and Joanna his Wife,	"	6 August 1708.
Lydia daughter of Josiah Frankling and Abiah his Wife,	"	8 August 1708.
James Son of Benja. Flood and Mary his Wife,	"	4 September 1708.
William Son of Henry Frankling and Margt. his Wife,	"	15 September 1708.
Mary daughter of Edward Gellings and Mary his Wife,	"	27 April 1708.
Newman Son of John Greenough and Eliza. his Wife,	"	6 May 1708.
Elizabeth daughter of Jonathan Gatchel and Martha his Wife,	"	5 June : 1708.
John Son of Timothy Green and Mary his Wife,	"	20 July 1708.
John Son of Stephen Greenliefe and Mary his Wife,	"	12 July 1708.
Elizabeth daughter of David Greenliefe and Mercy his Wife,	"	26 June 1708.

Ann daughter of Thomas Gwin and Sarah his Wife, Born 1 September 1708.
Hannah daughter of John Grant and Dorothy his Wife, " 27 July 1708.
Elizabeth daughter of Joseph Goff and Eliza. his Wife, " 15 August 1708.
Joseph Son of Joseph Gilbert and Mary his Wife, " 8 September 1708.
Samuel Son of Samuell Green and Ann his Wife, " 18 September 1708.
Thomas Son of John Gaud and Eliza. his Wife, " 20 October 1708.
Rebecca daughter of Richd. Gridly and Rebecca his Wife, " 2 November 1708.
Rebecca daughter of Joseph Gray and Rebecca his Wife, " 25 November 1708.
Sarah daughter of John Goldthwaite and Sarah his Wife, " 12 September 1708.
John Son of Samll. Grice and Priscilla his Wife, " 27 February 1708.
Robert Son of Nathanll. Holmes and Sarah his Wife, " 30 March 1708.
Samuell Son of Francis Holmes and Rebecca his Wife, " 13 Aprill 1708.
Thomas Son of Thoms. Hetchbon and Frances his Wife, " 30 June 1708.
Elizabeth daughter of Nathanll. Hodgdon and Susana his Wife, " 1 July 1708.
Samuel Son of Samuel Hurst and Sarah his Wife, " 3 July 1708.
Atherton Son of Samuel Haugh and Margaret his Wife, " 29 July 1708.
Abigall daughter of John How and Abigall his Wife, " 11 September 1708.
Jonathan Son of Jona. Hunlock and Abigall his Wife, " 31 October 1708.
William Son of Joshua Hensha and Mary his Wife, " 26 November 1708.
Hannah daughter of Grove Hirst and Eliza. his Wife, " 4 May 1708.
James Son of Michael Hamelton and Mary his Wife, " 28 January 1708.
John Son of John Holland and Susana his Wife, " 23 January 1708.
Elisha Son of Edward Hutchinson and Lydia his Wife, " 20 February 1708.
Eliza. daughter of Joseph Hall and Blanch his Wife, " 18 February 1708.
Eliza. daughter of John Jepson and Aphia his Wife, " 17 August 1708.
Joseph Son of Joseph Jewel and Mary his Wife, " 1 September 1708.
Grace daughter of Thoms. Jackson and Grace his Wife, " 30 August 1708.
Sarah daughter of John Jent and Abigall his Wife, " 21 December 1708.
Sarah daughter of John Ingram and Sarah his Wife, " 14 February 1708.
Samuel Son of John Jones and Margaret his Wife, " 9 February 1708.
Timothy Son of Timothy King and Sarah his Wife, " 18 August 1708.
Nicholas Son of John Kilbey and Rebecca his Wife, " 28 July 1708.
Sarah daughter of Christopher Kilbey and Sarah his Wife, " 10 July 1708.
Mary daughter of Peter King and Mary his Wife, " 17 February 1708.
Mary daughter of Thomas Larkin and Sarah his Wife, " 4 May 1708.
Mary daughter of Richard Lyne and Eliza. his Wife, " 3 September 1708.
John Son of Isaac Lewise and Hannah his Wife, " 10 January 1708.
Nathaniel Son of Daniel Loreing and Priscilla his Wife, " 19 February 1708.

BIRTHS — 1708.

Edey daughter of John Minzes and Edey his Wife, Born	9 April 1708.
John Son of John Milk and Mary his Wife, "	23 June 1708.
Amos Son of Amos Morrel and Rachel his Wife, "	26 July 1708.
Thomas Son of Joseph Merrefeeld and Margaret his Wife, "	8 August 1708.
Dorothy daughter of Charles Morrise and Esther his Wife, "	15 October 1708.
Lydia daughter of Joseph Morgan and Mercy his Wife, "	19 November 1708.
Abigal daughter of Francis Millar and Abigall his Wife, "	22 August 1708.
Thomas Son of Ephraim More and Eliza. his Wife, "	29 January 1708:
Susana daughter of Edward Martyn and Sarah his Wife, "	24 February 1708.
Ruth daughter of John Marshall and Martha his Wife, "	1 March 1708.
Elizabeth daughter of William Nicholson and Eliza. his Wife, "	3 August 1708.
Jane daughter of Boston Negro and Jane his Wife, "	8 August 1708.
John Son of George Nowell and Eliza. his Wife, "	7 December 1708.
David Son of David Pulsifer and Susana his Wife, "	7 May 1708.
Hannah daughter of Isaac Perkins and Mary his Wife, "	4 Aprill 1708.
Edward Son of Charles Pursley and Rachel his Wife, "	21 Aprill 1708.
Joseph Son of Stephen Parker and Margaret his Wife, "	29 Aprill 1708.
Joseph Son of William Palfrey and Abigal his Wife, "	23 May 1708.
James Son of Samuel Parker and Mary his Wife, "	13 July 1708.
Deborah daughter of Israel Phippeny and Sarah his Wife, "	30 August 1708.
William Son of Thomas Porter and Prudence his Wife, "	25 July 1708.
Mary daughter of William Perry and Hanna his Wife, "	30 September 1708.
Jeffs Son of William Peirse and Sarah his Wife, "	18 October 1708.
Abiel daughter of Edward Porter and Abiel his Wife, "	15 November 1708.
Rebecca daughter of Jacob Parker and Ursilla his Wife, "	25 February 1708.
John ⎱ Gimmi: of James Robinson and Eliza. his Grace ⎰ Wife, "	3 May 1708. 4 July 1708.
Peter Son of John Ruck and Hannah his Wife, "	29 July 1708.
Mary daughter of William Rolison and Eliza his Wife, "	26 August 1708.
Richard Son of Richard Reed and Hannah his Wife, "	14 August 1708.
Walter Son of Henry Rich and Eliza his Wlfe, "	24 June 1708.
Anna daughter of James Reed and Eliza. his Wife, "	1 July 1708.
William Son of William Ross and Eliza. his Wife, "	15 December 1708.
Elizabeth daughter of Samuel Rand and Sarah his Wife, "	20 December 1708.
Robert Son of John Ruggles and Tabitha his Wife, "	3 January 1708.
John Son of Fortune Reddock and Abiel his Wife, "	10 February 1708.
Mary daughter of Robert Rowles and Grace his Wife, "	9 February 1708.
Mosely Son of John Ruggles and Martha his Wife, "	5 Aprill 1708.
Sarah daughter of Joseph Snelling and Rebecca his Wife, "	9 May 1708.
Knight Son of Jeremi Sprague and Priscilla his Wife, "	

Mary daughter of Thomas Short and Eliza. his Wife,	Born	8 Aprill 1708.
Anna daughter of Robert Sanderson and Esther his Wife,	"	9 June 1708.
Mary daughter of Thomas Smith and Mary his Wife,	"	30 May 1708.
Mary daughter of William Spencer and Mary his Wife,	"	28 June 1708.
Deborah daughter of James Scolly and Deborah his Wife,	"	22 August 1708.
Richard Son of Richd. Smith and Mary his Wife,	"	25 August 1708.
Peirses daughter of Erasamus Stevens and Peirses his Wife,	"	20 October 1708.
William Son of John Smalpeice and Olive his Wife,	"	6 October 1708.
Benja. Son of James Seward and Eda his Wife,	"	6 January 1708.
Hannah daughter of Abijah Savage and Hanna his Wife,	"	29 January 1708.
William Son of Humphry Salsbury and Mary his Wife,	"	17 Aprill 1708.
John Son of Miles Thomson and Abigall his Wife	"	11 Aprill 1708.
Jeremiah Son of Soloman Townsend and Eliza. his Wife,	"	24 Aprill 1708
Davise Son of James Townsend and Agnis his Wife,	"	16 July 1708.
Lucee daughter of John Turner and Eliza. his Wife,	"	20 July 1708.
Joshua Son of Joshua Thomas and Ann his Wife,	"	12 August 1708.
Mary daughter of James Tileston and Mary his Wife,	"	20 December 1708.
Lydia daughter of Thomas Townsend and Sarah his Wife,	"	31 January 1708.
Samuel Son of Thomas Townsend and Eliza. his Wife,	"	12 March 1708.
Peter Son of Isaac Virgoose and Eliza. his Wife,	"	7 July 1708.
Joseph Son of Joseph White and Sarah his Wife,	"	8 Aprill 1708.
Ann daughter of Jonathan Waldo and Hannah his Wife,	"	13 Aprill 1708.
Ann daughter of John Williams and Humalis his Wife,	"	19 May 1708.
George Son of George Wadling and Rachel his Wife,	"	6 July 1708.
John Son of Thomas Wallise and Christian his Wife,	"	21 July 1708.
Michael Smith Son of Isaac Webb and Abigall his Wife,	"	31 August 1708.
Samuel Son of Ezekiel Walker and Ruth his Wife,	"	5 September 1708.
Mary daughter of John Winthrop and Ann his Wife,	"	18 September 1708.
Barnabas Son of Henry Wilson and Eliza. his Wife,	"	5 November 1708.
Samuel Son of Samuel Willise and Eliza. his Wife.	"	2 Aprill 1708.
Sarah daughter of John Willise and Sarah his Wife,	"	14 November 1708.
Nathanll. ⎱ Gimmi of Nathanall. Williams and Samll. ⎰ Ann his Wife,	"	1 January 1708.
Abigal daughter of John Wilson and Mary his Wife,	"	2 March 1708.
Abigall daughter of Adina Bulfinch and Abigall his Wife,	"	22 June 1708.
Peter Son of Paul Collings and Mary his Wife,	"	20 February 1708.
Hannah daughter of Samll. Goff and Hannah his Wife,	"	4 January 1708.

BIRTHS — 1708-9.

Sarah daughter of Thomas Hutchinson and Sarah his Wife,	Born	29 March 1708.
Jonathn Son of John Mountfort and Mary his Wife,	"	20 September 1708.
John Son of Ebenr. Pemberton and Mary his Wife,	"	25 January 1708.
William Son of Thoms. Payn and Eliza. his Wife,	"	23 February 1708.
Ebenr. Son of Ebenr. Tolman and Mary his Wife,	"	2 November 1708.
Welthen daughter of William Walter and Loise his Wife,	"	7 February 1708.
Sarah daughter of John Benning and Sarah his Wife,	"	1 November 1708.
Richard Son of John Cronenshilt and Eliza. his Wife,	"	28 December 1708.
Anna daughter of Christor. Capril and Tamzine his Wife,	"	22 October 1708.
Sarah daughter of Abram. Clark and Mary his Wife,	"	23 January 1708.
Nathanll. Son of Willm. Eustice and Sarah his Wife,	"	16 December 1708.
Benjamen Son of Benja. Glazier and Mary his Wife,	"	15 September 1708.
Edward Son of John Hobbie and Ann his Wife,	"	11 January 1708.
Benjamen Son of Willm. Indecot and Eliza. his Wife,	"	17 February 1708.
Eliza. daughter of Capt. Samll. Keeling and Eliza. his Wife,	"	23 August 1708.
Elisha Son of Elisha Odling and Mary his Wife,	"	2 February 1708.
Eliakim Son of Thomas Palmer Esqr. and Abigal his Wife,	"	22 March 1707/8.
Francis Son of William Skinner and Deborah his Wife,	"	14 February 1708.
James Son of James Carey and Sarah his Wife,	"	16 August 1708.
Lucy daughter of Paul Dudley Esqr. and Lucy his Wife,	"	12 March 1708.
Hannah daughter of Jabez Fox and Hannah his Wife,	"	27 June 1708.
Ruth daughter of Nathanll. Green and Eliza. his Wife,	"	2 August 1708.
Martha daughter of John Smith and Martha his Wife,	"	7 December 1708.
John Son of James Varney and Jane his Wife,	"	1 July 1708.
Mary daughter of Allexr. Baker and Hannah his Wife,	"	9 January 1708.
Hannah daughter of John Flagg and Abiel his Wife,	"	14 October 1708.
Eliza. daughter of Nathll. Harrise and Sarah his Wife,	"	6 September 1708.
Ruth daughter of Stephen Kempton and Ruth his Wife,	"	23 June 1708.
Thomas Son of Thomas Couverly and Mary his Wife,	"	30 May 1708.
Mary daur of William Haley and Sarah his Wife,	"	27 May 1708.
Sarah daur of Jonathan Belcher and Mary his Wife,	"	22 April 1708.

1709.

Maccarty Son of Ames Anger and Margaret his Wife,	Born	11 March 1708 /0.
Eliza. daughter of Jeremiah Allen and Mary his Wife,	"	31 March 1709.
Joseph Son of Silence Allen and Esther his Wife,	"	26 Aprill 1709.
William Son of Samuel Avise and Mary his Wife,	"	20 May 1709.
Jonathan Son of Joseph Allen and Anne his Wife,	"	20 September 1709.
Henry Son of Henry Allen and Eliza. his Wife,	"	21 December 1709.
Benjamen Son of Adam Bath and Mary his Wife,	"	15 March 1708/0

Bartholomew Son of Daniel Ballard and Dorcas his Wife,	Born	20 March 1708/0.
Dorcas daughter of Nicholas Bows and Dorcas his Wife,	"	19 May 1709.
Anna daughter of Stephen Boutineau and Mary his Wife,	"	24 Aprill 1709.
Abiah daughter of John Barrel and Abiah his Wife,	"	28 May 1709.
Katherine daughter of John Briggs and Katherine his Wife,	"	29 May 1709.
John Son of John Beal and Eliza. his Wife,	"	25 June 1709.
John Son of Zebdiel Boylston and Jerusha his Wife,	"	23 March 1708/9.
Eliza. daughter of Alwin Butcher and Eliza. his Wife,	"	14 July 1709.
Joseph Son of Soloman Blake and Abigall his Wife,	"	10 August 1709.
John Son of James Boudoin and Sarah his Wife,	"	22 August 1709.
Wife,	"	6 October 1709.
Hannah daughter of Barthol Barrat and Rebecca his Wife,	"	31 July 1709.
Joseph Son of Timothy Breed and Eunice his Wife,	"	24 September 1709.
Thomas Son of Thomas Barbour and Eliza. his Wife,	"	7 October 1709.
Susanna daughter of Jonathan Burnel and Susana his Wife,	"	25 October 1709.
Daniel Son of Daniel Blyn and Mercy his Wife,	"	9 November 1709.
Sarah daughter of John Beers and Mary his Wife,	"	24 October 1709.
Sarah daughter of Joshua Bill and Sarah his Wife,	"	11 November 1709.
Benja. Son of Samuel Bill and Sarah his Wife,	"	1 November 1709.
Thomas Son of ye Revd. Thoms. Bridge and Eliza. his Wife,	"	31 October 1709.
Esther daughter of James Barnerd and Eliza. his Wife,	"	26 August 1709.
Joanna daughter of Stephen Butler and Joanna his Wife,	"	11 December 1709.
George Son of George Brock and Mary his Wife,	"	17 December 1709.
Amose Son of James Ball and Mary his Wife,	"	20 January 1709.
Josiah Son of Nathanll. Breed and Sarah his Wife,	"	9 January 1709.
Josiah Son of Josiah Biles and Abigall his Wife,	"	14 January 1709.
Lydia daughter of Joseph Belknap and Abigal his Wife,	"	17 January 1709.
Ann daughter of Nicholas Blith and Ann his Wife,	"	20 February 1709.
David Son of David Colson and Hanah his Wife,	"	19 March 1708/9.
Jonathan Son of David Cutler and Abigall his Wife,	"	21 March 1708/9.
Rebecca daughter of Daniel Collings and Rebecca his Wife,	"	9 March 1708/9.
Peter Son of Peter Clarke and Katerine his Wife,	"	30 April 1709.
Mary daughter of William Champlin and Martha his Wife,	"	9 May 1709.
William Son of William Clark and Hannah his Wife,	"	17 May 1709.
Hannah daughter of William Cowel and Eliza. his Wife,	"	13 May 1709.
William Son of William Cook and Lydia his Wife,	"	9 July 1709.
William Son of James Codner and Mary his Wife.	"	24 July 1709.
Jonathan Son of David Copp and Patience his Wife,	"	5 August 1709.
Summers Son of Josiah Clark and Eliza. his Wife,	"	19 August 1709.
Gidian Son of James Cox and Mary his Wife.	"	15 August 1709.
Daniel Son of Nathanll. Coney and Eliza his Wife,	"	17 October 1709.
John Son of John Corser and Sarah his Wife,	"	29 October 1709.
Susana daughter of Ebenr. Clough and Thankfull his Wife,	"	23 August 1709.
Bethia daughter of John Cotta and Sarah his Wife,	"	13 January 1709.

BIRTHS — 1709.

Isaac Son of Charles Chauncey and Sarah his Wife	Born	1 December 1709.
Obadiah Son of John Cookson and Rachell his Wife,	"	1 February 1709.
Lucey daughter of Paul Dudley Esq. and Lucey his Wife,	"	12 March 1708/9.
John Son of John Draper and Joanna his Wife,	"	24 May 1709.
Eliza. daughter of Joseph Dowding and Ann his Wife,	"	29 September 1709.
Thomas Son of Robert Darbey and Martha his Wife,	"	20 November 1709.
Abraham Son of Isaac Decoster and Mary his Wife,	"	13 November 1709
Mary daughter of John Dixwell and Mary his Wife,	"	14 December 1709.
Eleazur Son of Addington Davenport Esq. and Eliza. his Wife,	"	21 November 1709.
Mary daughter of Zebadiah Daniel and Eliza. his Wife,	"	14 January 1709.
Mary daughter of Thomas Dawes and Sarah his Wife,	"	10 December 1709.
Benjamen Son of Eleazur Darbey and Mary his Wife,	"	18 March 1709.0
Jonathan Son of Edward Eades and Martha his Wife,	"	2 August 1709.
Joseph Son of Jonathan Evans and Mary his Wife,	"	25 August 1709.
Sarah daughter of Thomas Fax and Sarah his Wife,	"	14 Aprill 1709.
Jonathan Son of Jonathan Farnum and Ann his Wife,	"	2 July 1709.
Mary daughter of John Fisher and Dorcas his Wife,	"	24 September 1709.
James Son of Benja. Flood and Mary his Wife,	"	13 October 1709.
John Son of Thomas Fitch and Abiel his Wife,	"	19 October 1709.
Eliza. daughter of Robert Fethergill and Eliza. his Wife,	"	11 January 1709.
Samuel Son of Ephraim Fenno and Eliza his Wife,	"	1 March 1709/0.
Hannah daughter of Benja. Gibson and Mehitabel his Wife,	"	24 March 1708/9.
Nathanll. Son of Nathanll. Green and Ann his Wife,	"	14 May 1709.
Sarah daughter of Samll. Gardener and Eliza. his Wife,	"	27 May 1709.
Hannah daughter of Thomas Goodwin and Freelove his Wite,	"	18 June 1709.
James Son of Hill Green aud Hannah his Wife,	"	19 July 1709.
William Son of Edward Goddard and Susana his Wife,	"	22 March 1708/9.
Sarah daughter of John Goff and Hannah his Wife,	"	19 August 1709.
Joseph Son of John Gerrish and Sarah his Wife,	"	8 September 1709.
Benjamen Son of Benja. Goold and Mary his Wife,	"	11 September 1709.
Thomas Son of Thoms. Gyles and Martha his Wife,	"	29 September 1709.
Ephraim Son of Joseph Giddings and Eliza. his Wife,	"	3 November 1709.
Eliza. daughter of Bartholl. Gusier and Eliza. his Wife,	"	3 January 1709.
Joseph Son of Benja. Gallop and Hannah his Wife,	"	20 December 1709.
Hannah daughter of Samll. Greenliefe and Martha his Wife,	"	7 January 1709.
Eliza. daughter of Joshua Gee junior and Eliza. his Wife,	"	15 January 1709.
Mehitabel daughter of Henry Hurst and Mary his Wife,	"	26 May 1709.
Ann daughter of Arthur Hed and Esther his Wife,	"	15 May 1709.

Nathaniel Son of John Hobbs and Susana his Wife, Born		27 July 1709.
Abigall daughter of Thomas Hutchinson and Sarah his Wife,	"	2 August 1709.
Jacob Son of Jacob Hasie and Hannah his Wife,	"	24 August 1709.
John Son of Francise Hudson and Mary his Wife,	"	12 September 1709.
Nathanll. Son of Thomas Hetchbone and Frances his Wife,	"	28 October 1709.
John Son of John Hayes and Hannah his Wife,	"	12 January 1709.
Ann daughter of Joseph Hood and Judeth his Wife,	"	22 December 1709.
Abraham Son of Thomas Holland and Ann his Wife,	"	31 January 1709.
Katherine daughter of Nathan Howell and Kathern. his Wife,	"	10 January 1709.
Sarah daughter of Abell Jones and Ruth his Wife,	"	7 Mar : 1708/9
John Son of John Jeffers and Sarah his Wife,	"	25 Mar : 1709.
George Son of George Ingerson and Eliza. his Wife,	"	27 Aprill 1709.
William Son of Arthur Jeffery and Silence his Wife,	"	25 June 1709.
Elizabeth daughter of Jeremiah Jackson and Hannah his Wife,	"	14 July 1709.
Thomas Son of Mathew Jones and Sarah his Wife,	"	5 August 1709.
Thomas Son of Thomas Jackson and Grace his Wife,	"	15 February 1709.
James Son of Nathaniel Kettle and Joanna his Wife,	"	22 Mar. 1708/9.
Hannah daughter of Solomon Kneeland and Mary his Wife,	"	10 Aprill 1709.
Nathaniel Son of Nathanll. Kenny and Eliza. his Wife,	"	5 May 1709.
Henry Son of Henry Kelly and Eliza. his Wife,	"	13 May 1709.
Mary daughter of Timothy Kemball and Kathern. his Wife,	"	5 August 1709.
William Son of John King and Eliza. his Wife,	"	31 August 1709.
Mary daugi. te of Samuel Kenney and Abigall his Wife,	"	17 November 1709.
Mary daughter of Thomas Lowler and Eliza. his Wife,	"	1 March 1708/9.
Joseph Son of John Lothrop and Joanna his Wife,	"	28 May 1709.
Mercy daughter of Willm. Lee and Mercy his Wife,	"	9 July 1709.
Pool Son of Timothy Lendall and Jane his Wife,	"	10 August 1709.
Mary daughter of Stephen Labbe and Eliza. his Wife,	"	29 October 1709.
Thomas Son of Thomas Larkin and Sarah his Wife,	"	18 November 1709
Michael Son of Ebenr. Lowle and Eliza. his Wife,	"	22 December 1709.
Elizabeth daughter of Arthur Laughame and Rebecca his Wife,	"	22 January 1709.
Nicholas Son of Richard Morrise and Mary his Wife,	"	4 March 1708/9.
Jonn Son of Caesar Mitchell and Tabatha his Wife,	"	24 March 1708/9.
Eliza. daughter of Christopher Marvel and Jane his Wife,	"	10 Aprill 1709.
William Son of Willm Mallard and Abigal his Wife,	"	16 July 1709.
Thomas Son of Thomas Marshall and Mary his Wife,	"	8 September 1709.
Josue Son of Josue Marriner and Hanna his Wife,	"	10 October 1709
Susanna daughter of John Maxwell and Eliza. his Wife,	"	6 October 1709.
Prudence daughter of John Mason and Prudence his Wife,	"	10 October 1709.
Lydia daughter of Francise Moor and Mary his Wife,	"	10 October 1709.

BIRTHS — 1709.

Rebecca daughter of Duncan Maycome and Mary his Wife,	Born	23 November 1709.
Ruth daughter of Thomas Mellens and Mary his Wife,	"	10 January 1709.
Susanna daughter of John Needham and Mary his Wife,	"	16 March 1708/9.
David Son of John Northey and Sarah his Wife,	"	30 March 1709.
Mary daughter of Francis Nicholson and Abigll. his Wife,	"	9 June 1709.
Belcher Son of Oliver Noyes and Anna his Wife,	"	10 October 1709.
Jonathan Son of David Norton and Sarah his Wife,	"	4 November 1709.
Abraham Son of Abrm. Nicholls and Rebecca his Wife,	"	23 October 1709.
Bethiah daughter of Samuel Okes and Jamina his Wife,	"	14 September 1709.
John Son of John Orne and Eliza. his Wife,	"	16 February 1709.
Eliza. daughter of John Pearce and Eliza. his Wife,	"	13 Aprill 1709.
Isaac Son of Isaac Pearce and Grace his Wife,	"	12 Aprill 1709.
Edward Son of William Payn and Margaret his Wife,	"	17 March 1708/9.
Phillip Son of Samuel Pike and Mary his Wife,	"	27 March 1709.
Eliza. daughter of John Porter and Eliza. his Wife,	"	20 Aprill 1709.
Richard Son of Richd. Palfrey and Hannah his Wife,	"	23 Aprill 1709.
Susanna daughter of James Pecker and Susanna his Wife,	"	30 May 1709.
Moses Son of Moses Peirse and Eliza. his Wife,	"	23 May 1709.
Sarah daughter of James Pemberton and Hannah his Wife,	"	2 June 1709.
Sarah daughter of Jacob Parker and Ann his Wife,	"	17 August 1709.
Richard Son of John Pitts and Hannah his Wife,	"	30 August 1709.
Robert Son of Thomas Potts and Martha his Wife,	"	23 August 1709.
Benjamen Son of Joseph Prout and Mary his Wife,	"	24 September 1709.
Eliphalet Son of Stephen Parker and Margaret his Wife,	"	9 September 1709.
Nathanll. Son of Edward Proctor and Eliza. his Wife,	"	30 September 1709.
William Son of James Peirson and Eliza. his Wife.	"	22 October 1709.
Thomas Son of Thomas Plasteed and Mary his Wife,	"	9 December 1709.
Eliza. daughter of Timo. Prout and Lydia his Wife,	"	31 July 1709.
Samuel Son of John Reed and Eliza. his Wife,	"	1 Aprill 1709.
Budd Son of Timothy Robinson and Dorothy his Wife,	"	29 March 1709.
Iannah daughter of Thomas Rowell and Dorothy his Wife.	"	15 Aprill 1709.
Sarah daughter of Thomas Russell and Ann his Wife,	"	7 July 1709.
Jonathan Son of Joseph Russell and Mary his Wife,	"	9 August 1709.
James Son of Thomas Reed and Mary his Wife,	"	16 September 1709.
Eliza daughter of John Ruck and Hannah his Wife,	"	16 November 1709.
Love daughter of John Rawlings and Love his Wife,	"	29 July 1709.
Robert Son of Robert Rand and Eliza. his Wife,	"	29 January 1709.
Thomas Son of Thomas Ruck and Mary his Wife,	"	19 February 1709.

Sarah daughter of Gibbins Sharp and Sarah his Wife,	Born	15 March 1708/9.
Charles Son of Samuel Sanders and Eliza. his Wife,	"	1 April 1709.
Abigall daughter of Wigglesworth Sweetsir and Ursilla his Wife,	"	5 March 1708/9.
Samuel Son of John Shaw and Mercy his Wife,	"	17 May 1709.
Ann daughter of James Smith and Eliza. his Wife,	"	16 August 1709.
Samuel Son of Clemans Sumner and Margaret his Wife,	"	31 August 1709.
John Son of Simon Slocome and Eliza. his Wife,	"	22 September 1709.
Samuel Son of Samuel Soper and Mary his Wife,	"	1 November 1709.
Benjamen Son of Benja. Simpson and Eliza. his Wife,	"	6 June 1709.
Jacob Son of Jeremiah Sprague and Priscilla his Wife,	"	21 November 1709.
Sarah daughter of William Snoton and Rachell his Wife,	"	9 December 1709.
Samuel Son of Erasamus Stevens and Peirses his Wife,	"	15 December 1709.
Joseph Son of Joseph Shattuck and Mary his Wife,	"	22 December 1709.
Rebecca daughter of Thomas Smith and Mary his Wife,	"	24 January 1709.
Margaret daughter of William Thomas and Abigall his Wife,	"	4 March 1708/9.
Joanna daughter of Edward Tuttle and Joanna his Wife,	"	22 August 1709.
Sarah daughter of John Trask and Sarah his Wife,	"	8 February 1709.
Abraham Son of Abram. Townsend and Mary his Wife,	"	19 February 1709.
Samuel Son of Nathaniel Vial and Sarah his Wife,	"	12 May 1709.
Bethseda daughter of James Varney and Jane his Wife,	"	16 October 1709.
Mosely Son of Jonathan Williams and Rebecca his Wife,	"	15 March 1708/9.
Edward Son of William Waine and Sarah his Wife,	"	2 Aprill 1709.
Jacob Son of William Wormwall and Sarah his Wife,	"	11 March 1708/9.
Susanna daughter of Nathanll. Wheeler and Mary his Wife,	"	18 May 1709.
Mary daughter of Thomas Willet and Mary his Wife,	"	8 May 1709.
John Son of John Warrick and Susana his Wife,	"	25 June 1709.
Benjamen Son of John Wakefield and Eliza. his Wife,	"	23 June 1709.
Robert Son of James Williams and Abigall his Wife,	"	24 July 1709
Mary daughter of John Welch and Hannah his Wife,	"	1 August 1709.
John Son of John Wakefeeld and Ann his Wife,	"	4 August 1709.
Zedekiah Son of John Wiat and Sarah his Wife,	"	26 August 1709.
Isaac Son of Edward Winslow and Hanna his Wife,	"	2 May 1709.
Josiah Son of Jonathn. Waldo and Hannah his Wife,	"	13 August 1709.
Mary daughter of William Willet and Mary his Wife,	"	31 August 1709.
Mary daughter of Joseph Webb and Deborah his Wife,	"	3 October 1709.
Mary daughter of Daniel Wear and Mary his Wife,	"	11 October 1709.

BIRTHS — 1709.

Ann daughter of Adam Winthrop and Ann his Wife,	Born	9 August 1709.
Ann daughter of John Winthrop and Ann his Wife,	"	13 December 1709.
Laughton Son of Joseph Williams and Sarah his Wife,	"	13 July 1709.
William Son of Edward White and Sarah his Wife,	"	11 February 1709.
Ebenr. Son of Samuel White and Ann his Wife,	"	4 March 1709/0.
Mary daughter of William Young and Mary his Wife,	"	2 October 1709.
Ann daughter of John Brewster and Deliverence his Wife,	"	28 March 1709.
Susanna daughter of Mathew Butler and Sarah his Wife,	"	24 November 1709.
Eliza. daughter of William Cleer and Bethia his Wife,	"	2 April 1709.
John Son of Stephen Cross and Sarah his Wife,	"	24 June 1709.
Thomas Son of John Dorrel and Rachel his Wife,	"	8 January 1709.
William Son of Samll. Goff and Hannah his Wife,	"	28 February 1709.
Joseph Son of Samll. Greenwood and Eliza. his Wife,	"	5 June 1709.
Joseph Son of Joseph Hubbert and Thankfull his Wife,	"	8 January 1709.
Richard Son of Joseph Lowden and Hannah his Wife,	"	10 February 1709.
Allexander Son of James Lablond and Ann his Wife,	"	1 September 1709.
Archd.le Son of Thomas Palmer Esqr. and Abigll. his Wife,	"	3 July 1709.
James Son of James Reed and Eliza. his Wife,	"	24 November 1709.
Jane daughter of Thomas Steel and Jane his Wife.	"	20 April 1709.
Gamaliel Son of Thomas Wallice and Grace his Wife,	"	24 September 1709.
Eunice daughter of William Brown and Lydia his Wife,	"	11 May 1709.
Hannah daughter of John Jackson and Susana his Wife,	"	9 October 1709.
Susanna daughter of John Love and Susana his Wife,	"	8 March 1708/9.
Henry Son of Henry Lowder and Abigall his Wife,	"	20 May 1709.
Eliza. daughter of Thomas Phelps and Sarah his Wife,	"	1 July 1709.
Mary daughter of Samll. Bridgham and Mary his Wife,	"	16 November 1709.
Ruth daughter of Robert Cock and Agnis his Wife,	"	9 November 1709.
Hannah daughter of Samll. Deming and Hannah his Wife,	"	19 March 1708/9.
Susanna daughter of Edward Gray and Susanna his Wife,	"	9 December 1709.
John Son of Richard Tucker and Bethiah his Wife,	"	27 Septr 1709.
Robert Son of Robert Ellis and Eliza. his Wife,	"	13 June 1709.
Abigall dau^r of Thom^s Jenkins and Mary his Wife,	"	11 August 1709.
Mary dau^r of And^r Sigourney and Mary his Wife.	"	1 Aug. 1709.
Deliverance dau^r of Joseph Wakefeld and Esther his Wife,	"	23 Jan^{ry} 1709.
Thomas Son of Thomas and Hannah Moulin,	"	6 Sept. 1709.
Sarah dau^r of William and Ann Play,	"	5 Nov 1709.
John Son of Peter and Mary Sorien,	"	10 June 1709.

1710.

William Son of John Alden and Eliza. his Wife, Born	9 May 1710.
Eliza. daughter of Isaac Adams and Martha his Wife, "	19 May 1710.
Jeremiah Son of Jeremiah Allen and Mary his Wife, "	7 August 1710.
John Son of John Adams and Mary his Wife, "	10 October 1710.
Daniel Son of Benja. Alford and Rachel his Wife, "	9 February 1710.
Mercy daughter of John Alkin and Mercy his Wife, "	10 Aprill 1710.
Rebecca daughter of Thomas Bell and Mary his Wife, "	6 March 1709/0.
William Son of John Bennet and Hannah his Wife, "	19 March 1709/0.
Nathanll. Son of John Brewer and Martha his Wife, "	10 Aprill 1710.
Abigall daughter of Benjamen Brown and Mary his Wife, "	10 April 1710.
Eliza. daughter of John Barret and Sarah his Wife, "	13 May 1710.
Katherine daughter of James Berry and Susana his Wife, "	22 May 1710.
Mary daughter of George Boyd and Mary his Wife, "	25 May 1710.
Peter Son of John Buckley and Mary his Wife, "	21 May 1710.
John Son of Samuel Belknap and Eliza. his Wife, "	17 May 1710.
Elizabeth daughter of Zabdiel Boylston and Jerusha his Wife, "	29 June 1710.
Mary daughter of Joseph Briscow and Mariah his Wife, "	20 June 1710.
Sarah daughter of Thomas Banister and Frances his Wife, "	14 June 1710.
John Son of John Beech and Abigal his Wife. "	27 July 1710.
Huldah daughter of James Barnes and Mary his Wife, "	13 July 1710.
Mary daughter of Benja. Bronsdon and Mary his Wife, "	12 August 1710.
Ann daughter of John Brewster and Deliverence his Wife, "	17 May 1710.
Elizabeth daughter of Richard Bill and Sarah his Wife, "	8 September 1710.
Samuel Son of Samll. Bligh and Ann his Wife, "	12 March 1709/0.
Eliza. daughter of Jonathn. Bull and Eliza. his Wife, "	30 September 1710.
Mary daughter of John Baker and Mary his Wife, "	5 December 1710.
John Son of Mathew Butler and Sarah his Wife, "	29 December 1710.
Mary daughter of John Briggs and Kathern. his Wife, "	16 December 1710.
Susana daughter of Jer. Bumsted and Eliza. his Wife, "	7 December 1710.
Jonathn. Son of Jonathn. Belcher and Mary his Wife, "	23 July 1710.
Eliza. daughter of Thomas Barnerd and Silence his Wife, "	13 December 1710
Josiah Son of Jonathan Brown and Loise his Wife, "	23 April 1710.
Samuel Son of Peter Butler and Mary his Wife, "	12 January 1710.
James Son of Stephen Boutineau and Mary his Wife, "	27 January 1710.
Abigal daughter of James Butler and Abigal his Wife, "	26 January 1710.
Sarah daughter of Samuel Bill and Sarah his Wife, "	12 February 1710,
David Son of John Benning and Sarah his Wife, "	25 February 1710
Nathanll Son of Thomas Chubb and Eliza. his Wife, "	3 March 1709/0.
Mary daughter of John Charnock and Mary his Wife, "	9 March 1709/0.
Ebenr. Son of Jeremiah Cushing and Judeth his Wife, "	8 May 1710.

Births — 1710.

Eliza. daughter of Thomas Chamberlin and Sara his Wife,	Born	12 May 1710.
Abigal daughter of Samll. Clark and Sarah his Wife,	"	4 September 1710.
Margaret daughter of Robert Calef and Margaret his Wife.	"	4 October 1710.
Edward Son of Edward Cooper and Abigall his Wife,	"	16 October 1710.
Charles Son of William Champlin and Martha his Wife,	"	23 October 1710.
Eliza. daughter of Androse Cannon and Sarah his Wife,	"	26 October 1710.
Josiah Son of Josiah Clark and Priscilla his Wife,	"	29 November 1710.
Susanna daughter of Willm. Crouch and Susana his Wife,	"	9 November 1710.
Eliza. daughter of John Chamberlin and Anna his Wife,	"	26 September 1710.
Benjamen Son of John Colman and Judeth his Wife,	"	28 October 1710.
Henry Son of Thomas Crump and Anna his Wife,	"	19 January 1710.
Ruth daughter of John Center and Ruth his Wife,	"	19 January 1710.
Eliza. daughter of John Clark Esqr. and Sarah his Wife,	"	27 February 1710.
John Son of John Clough and Mehitabel his Wife,	"	13 March 1710/11.
Eliza. daughter of Stephen Cross and Sarah his Wife,	"	17 February 1710.
Mary daughter of John Dolbear and Sarah his Wife,	"	24 May 1710.
John Son of John Demery and Sarah his Wife,	"	27 December 1710.
John Son of Henry Dillaway and Abigall his Wife,	"	8 January 1710.
Mary daughter of Ebenr. Dennise and Susana his Wife,	"	18 January 1710.
Johanna daughter of Daniel Emorson and Jane his Wife,	"	2 October 1710.
Daniel Son of Daniel Epes and Hannah his Wife,	"	8 November 1710.
Abigall daughter of Jonathn. Eustice and Sarah his Wife,	"	24 January 1710.
James Son of Joseph Flood and Johanna his Wife,	"	27 April 1710.
Susana daughter of Gidian Florence and Susana his Wife,	"	20 August 1710.
John } Sons of John Foster and Sarah his Wife, William }	"	23 December 1710.
Abraham Son of Abram. Francise and Hanna his Wife,	"	16 January 1710.
Samll. Son of Richd. Flood and Eliza. his Wife,	"	11 February 1710.
Robert Son of Henry Franklin and Margart. his Wife,	"	21 January 1710.
Mary daughter of Joseph Goff and Eliza. his Wife,	"	17 March 1709/0.
Nathanll. Son of Timothy Green and Mary his Wife,	"	20 March 1709/0.
Stephen Son of Stephen Greenliefe and Mary his Wife,	"	17 March 1709/0.
Jonathn. Son of Jonathn. Gatchel and Martha his Wife,	"	13 August 1710.
John Son of James Gibson and Mary his Wife,	"	3 August 1710.
Thomas Son of John Greenough and Eliza. his Wife,	"	6 May 1710.
William Son of Willm. Grubb and Lydia his Wife,	"	19 August 1710.
Bethiah daughter of Edward Gray and Susana his Wife,	"	24 August 1710.
James Son of James Goold and Mary his Wife,	"	22 September 1710.
Jane daughter of Samll. Grice and Priscilla his Wife,	"	27 September 1710.

Joseph Son of Samll. Greenwood and Eliza. his
Wife, Born 18 August 1710.
Hannah daughter of Samll. Gerrish and Mary his
Wife, " 10 November 1710
Rebecca daughter of Samll. Green and Ann his
Wife, " 26 November 1710
Ruth daughter of Samll. Gardener and Eliza. his
Wife, " 13 December 1710.
Richd Son of Benja. Gallop and Hanna his Wife, " 17 December 1710.
Richard Son of Richd. Gridley and Rebecca his
Wife, " 3 January 1710
John Son of John Grant and Dorothy his Wife, " 4 December 1710.
Samll. Son of Joseph Gray and Rebecca his Wife, " 19 January 1710.
Lydia daughter of John Horton and Ann his Wife, " 4 March 1709/0.
Abigal daughter of Abram. Hasie and Abigal his
Wife, " 19 March 1709/0.
Mary daughter of Willm. Holberton and Mary his
Wife, " 22 Aprill 1710.
James Son of James Hill and Mary his Wife, " 9 Aprill 1710.
Anna daughter of Samll. Haugh and Margaret his
Wife, " 10 May 1710.
Susana daughter of John Holland and Susana his
Wife, " 4 June 1710.
John Son of Willm. Hasie and Sarah his Wife, " 21 July 1710.
Thomas Son of Thomas Hunt and Mary his Wife, " 2 August 1710.
Lydia daughter of Edward Hutchinson and Lydia
his Wife, " 26 July 1710.
Still-born Son of Nathanll. Henchman and Dorothy
his Wife, " 29 July 1710.
Phillip Son of Phillip Harley and Susana his Wife. " 2 September 1710.
James Son of James Habersham and Mehitabel his
Wife, " 28 October 1710.
Abigall daughter of James How and Abigall his
Wife, " 25 October 1710.
Susana daughter of Henry Howel and Martha his
Wife, " 28 September 1710.
Susana daughter of Benja. Haley and Susana his
Wife, " 21 November 1710.
Abigal daughter of Benja. Hart and Faith his
Wife, " 30 November 1710.
William Son of Willm. Heydon and Dinah his
Wife, " 13 December 1710.
Susana daughter of Samll. Hurst and Sarah his
Wife, " 29 December 1710.
Kathrn. daughter of William Haley and Sarah his
Wife, " 31 January 1710.
William Son of William Hutton and Ann his
Wife, " 5 February 1710.
Abigal daughter of John Jemeson and Abigal his
Wife, " 18 May 1710.
John Son of Richard Jenkins and Mary his Wife, " 15 July 1710.
Eliza. daughter of Thomas Jepson and Eliza. his
Wife, " 24 December 1710.
John Son of John Ireland and Elinor his Wife. " 14 December 1710.
Martha daughter of Soloman Kneeland and Mary his
Wife, " 19 March 1709/0.
John Son of Richd. Kemball and Hannah his
Wife. " 5 November 1710.
Edward Son of Nathanll. Kenney and Eliza. his
Wife, " 16 December 1710.

BIRTHS — 1710.

Nathanll. Son of Peter King and Mary his Wife,	Born	15 February 1710.
William Son of Joseph Leighton and Abigal his Wife,	"	21 March 1709/0.
John Son of John Lovel and Priscilla his Wife,	"	1 April 1710.
Sarah daughter of Ezekiel Lewise and Abigall his Wife,	"	21 May 1710.
John Son of John Lathrop and Johanna his Wife,	"	22 June 1710.
Sarah daughter of Peter Lamark and Sarah his Wife,	"	28 September 1710.
John Son of John Langley and Mary his Wife	"	12 October 1710.
Mary daughter of Timothy Lindall and Jane his Wife,	"	3 October 1710.
Sarah daughter of Samuel Lobdale and Sarah his Wife,	"	19 November 1710.
Mary daughter of James Lowell and Eliza. his Wife,	"	27 November 1710.
Hannah daughter of Isaac Lewise and Hannah his Wife,	"	19 October 1710.
Jane daughter of John Lorey and Mary his Wife,	"	9 January 1710.
Rachel daughter of Nathanll. Loreing and Susana his Wife,	"	14 December 1710.
Lucey daughter of Thomas Leechmer and Ann his Wife,	"	5 March 1710/11.
Thomas Son of Peter Mires and Mary his Wife,	"	29 May 1710.
Lydia daughter of Amos Morrel and Rachel his Wife,	"	15 June 1710.
Sarah daughter of Richard Morgan and Sarah his Wife,	"	13 July 1710.
Mary daughter of Joseph Meryfeeld and Margt. his Wife,	"	13 August 1710.
Joseph Son of James Marshall and Sarra his Wife,	"	6 September 1710.
Joseph Son of Joseph Morgan and Mercy his Wife,	"	7 October 1710.
Jonathan Son of Jona. Mountfort and Hanna his Wife,	"	20 November 1710.
Sarah daughter of Nathanll. Morss and Sarah his Wife,	"	17 December 1710.
Eliza. daughter of Joseph Marshal and Sarah his Wife,	"	29 September 1710.
Ann daughter of Daniel Mero and Frances his Wife,	"	7 January 1710.
John Son of Robert Mires and Eliza. his Wife,	"	8 January 1710.
Experience daughter of Phillip Marret and Mary his Wife,	"	27 January 1710.
James Son of John Milk and Mary his Wife,	"	31 January 1710.
Hannah daughter of John Mountfort and Mary his Wife,	"	14 January 1710.
Sarah daughter of Oliver Noyes and Anna his Wife,	"	21 October 1710.
Mehitabel daughter of Francis Nicholson and Abigal his Wife,	"	25 January 1710.
Burnel Son of Francis Norrise and Mary his Wife,	"	10 February 1710.
Robert Son of Robert Orainge and Hannah his Wife,	"	4 September 1710.
Mary daughter of Samuel Okes and Jamina his Wife,	"	11 February 1710.
Jerusha daughter of Peter Oliver and Jerusha his Wife,	"	17 December 1710.
James Son of Phillip Pereway and Hannah his Wife,	"	2 March 1709/0.

70   CITY DOCUMENT NO. 43.

Roger Son of Roger Patteson and Judeth his Wife,	Born	3 April 1710.
John Son of Obadiah Perry and Mary his Wife,	"	15 May 1710.
Beamsly Son of John 'Perkins and Mary his Wife,	"	27 April 1710.
Sarah daughter of Isaac Pearce and Grace his Wife,	"	22 May 1710.
Eliza. daughter of John Porter and Eliza. his Wife,	"	6 June 1710.
Joseph Son of Joseph Pulsefer and Mary his Wife,	"	19 June 1710.
Lydia daughter of William Palfrey and Abigal his Wife,	"	19 June 1710.
John Son of William Peirse and Sarah his Wife,	"	16 July 1710.
Sarah daughter of John Preston and Eliza. his Wife,	"	8 August 1710.
John Son of John Payn and Eliza. his Wife,	"	10 July 1710.
Elizabeth daughter of Thomas Palmer Esqr. and Abigal his Wife,	"	4 September 1710.
Ann daughter of John Pecker and Eliza. his Wife,	"	14 August 1710.
Susanna daughter of Edward Porter and Abiel his Wife,	"	22 September 1710.
Timothy Son of Timothy Prout and Lydia his Wife,	"	12 October 1710.
Eliazur Son of Eliazur Phillips and Lydia his Wife,	"	25 September 1710.
William Son of Benjamen Pickman and Abigal his Wife,	"	1 October 1710.
Susanna daughter of Stephen Payn and Mary his Wife,	"	7 December 1710.
Francis Son of Francis Plasteed and Hannah his Wife,	"	27 December 1710.
James Son of James Peneman and Mary his Wife,	"	10 January 1710.
Joseph Son of John Pitts and Hannah his Wife,	"	30 December 1710.
Hannah daughter of William Parkman and Hanna his Wife,	"	4 February 1710.
Ursilla daughter of Jacob Parker and Ursilla his Wife,	"	14 February 1710.
Daniel Son of Daniel Ross and Hannah his Wife,	"	20 March 1709/10.
Mercey daughter of John Rolston and Dorothy his Wife,	"	21 July 1710.
Francis Son of Francis Righton and Eliza. his Wife,	"	23 August 1710.
William Son of John Ripner and Ruth his Wife,	"	8 September 1710.
Martha daughter of James Raymer and Eliza. his Wife,	"	22 September 1710.
Mary daughter of Robert Rand and Susanna his Wife,	"	14 November 1710.
Samuel Son of Samuel Rand and Sarah his Wife,	"	29 November 1710.
John Son of Samuel Ramsdale and Abigal his Wife,	"	25 December 1710.
Susanna ⎱ Gimi. of William Rowlston and Eliza. his Abigal ⎰ Wife,	"	9 March 1710/11.
Gamaliel Son of Gamaliel Rogers and Mercy his Wife,	"	8 March 1710/11.
Nathaniel Son of John Simpson and Rely his Wife,	"	4 March 1709/10.
Samuel Son of Samuel Salter and Sarah his Wife,	"	25 Aprill 1710.
Lydia ⎱ Gimi. of John Strong and Lydia his Mary ⎰ Wife,	"	9 May 1710.
Mary daughter of John Smalpeice and Olive his Wife,	"	11 May 1710.
Benjamen Son of James Scolly and Deborah his Wife,	"	19 June 1710.
John Son of Jonathn. Simpson and Mary his Wife,	"	9 July 1710.
Gamon Son of John Stevens and Grace his Wife,	"	28 June 1710.
Joseph Son of Joseph Savill and Margaret his Wife,	"	15 Aprill 1710.

Births — 1710.

Eliza. daughter of Charles Shepreeve and Eliza. his Wife,	Born	26 June 1710.
Zachry. Son of William Skinner and Deborah his Wife,	"	10 July 1710.
Abraham Son of Abrm. Smith and Mary his Wife,	"	13 July 1710.
Mary daughter of Willm. Shepreeve and Eliza. his Wife,	"	26 July 1710.
Eliza. daughter of John Sharp and Mary his Wife,	"	16 August 1710.
Dorcas daughter of Sampson Shepcot and Dorcas his Wife,	"	1 August 1710.
Hannah daughter of Cyprian Southack and Eliza. his Wife,	"	31 July 1710.
Eliza. daughter of Benja. Snelling and Margt. his Wife,	"	10 September 1710.
William Son of William Spencer and Mary his Wife,	"	28 September 1710.
Abigall daughter of John Savill and Priscilla his Wife,	"	8 October 1710.
Thomas Son of John Simkins and Eliza. his Wife,	"	24 December 1710.
Thomas Son of Habijah Savage and Hannah his Wife,	"	5 January 1710.
William Son of William Smallage and Ruth his Wife,	"	1 January 1710.
James Son of Joseph Snelling and Rebecca his Wife,	"	19 January 1710.
Rebecca daughter of Joseph Shattuck and Mary his Wife,	"	20 January 1710.
Joseph Son of Joseph Savill and Margaret his Wife,	"	27 January 1710.
Rebecca daughter of George Thomas and Susanna his Wife,	"	7 April 1710.
James Son of James Townsend and Alice his Wife,	"	20 April 1710.
Elias Son of Peter Thomas and Eliza. his Wife,	"	4 June 1710.
Christopher Son of Joseph Thorn and Deborah his Wife,	"	6 July 1710.
Nathanll. Son of Cornelius Thayer and Lydia his Wife,	"	17 July 1710.
Elias Son of Elias Townsend and Rebecca his Wife,	"	27 October 1710.
Eliza. daughter of Joshua Thomas and Ann his Wife,	"	11 December 1710.
Henry Son of Henry Timberlake and Mary his Wife,	"	27 January 1710.
Thomas Son of Miles Thompson and Abigal his Wife,	"	4 March 1710/11.
Sarah daughter of John Vryling and Mary his Wife,	"	5 May 1710.
Thomas Son of Benja Varney and Sarah his Wife,	"	15 October 1710.
Ann daughter of Nathanll. Williams and Ann his Wife,	"	23 March 1709/0.
Thomas Son of Ebenr. Williston and Judeth his Wife,	"	21 April 1710.
Abigal daughter of Joseph White and Sarah his Wife,	"	6 July 1710.
George Son of George Worthylake and Ann his Wife,	"	5 July 1710.
Isaac Son of William White and Eliza his Wife.	"	27 July 1710.
Thomas Son of Ezekiell Walker and Ruth his Wife,	"	16 August 1710.
Thomas Son of Samuel Willise and Eliza. his Wife,	"	15 August 1710.
Susanna daughter of Henry Wakefeeld and Ann his Wife,	"	22 August 1710.
Eliza. daughter of John Welland and Eliza. his Wife,	"	27 August 1710.

Sarah daughter of Peter White and Sarah his Wife,	Born	6 October 1710.
Jane daughter of John Williams and Humilis his Wife,	"	5 December 1710.
Sarah daughter of Abrm. Wacome and Abigal his Wife,	"	9 December 1710.
Eliza. daughter of William Whetcomb and Mary his Wife,	"	18 December 1710.
Thomas Son of Thomas Walker and Jane his Wife,	"	1 January 1710.
Sarah daughter of William Webster and Mary his Wife,	"	15 January 1710.
Mary daughter of Cornelius Youngman and Mary his Wife,	"	3 August 1710.
Isabella daughter of Eliezur Armitage and Isabella his Wife,	"	6 November 1710.
Sarah daughter of James Cary and Sarah his Wife,	"	25 November 1710.
Lucy daughter of Paul Dudley Esqr. and Lucy his Wife,	"	6 December 1710.
John Son of Samuel Green and Eliza his Wife,	"	31 December 1710.
Ezekiel Son of John Goldthwaite and Sarah his Wife,	"	19 July 1710.
Palsgrove Son of Ephraim Hunt and Joanna his Wife,	"	23 February 1710.
William Son of Francis Holmes and Rebecca his Wife,	"	12 June 1710.
Johanna daughter of John Heminway and Eliza. his Wife,	"	10 March 1709/10.
Eliza. daughter of Daniel Morss and Amorill his Wife,	"	28 February 1710.
Cumby Son of Thomas Mires and Rebecca his Wife,	"	9 February 1710.
Ann daughter of Abrm. Nicholls and Rebecca his Wife,	"	26 February 1710.
Henry Son of Edmund Perkins and Mary his Wife,	"	20 August 1710.
Abigal daughter of Ebenr. Rand and Eliza. his Wife,	"	21 January 1710.
Mary daughter of John Ripner and Ruth his Wife,	"	5 December 1710.
Rebecca daughter of John Smith and Martha his Wife,	"	31 July 1710.
Mary daughter of William Sentall and Joanna his Wife,	"	29 September 1710.
Pool Son of James Varney and Jane his Wife,	"	8 January 1710.
Samuel Son of Samuel Bridgham and Mary his Wife,	"	7 September 1710.
William Son of William Dillaway and Sarah his Wife,	"	19 May 1710.
Ebenr. Son of John Flagg and Abiel his Wife,	"	27 October 1710.
Sarah daughter of Nathanll. Harrise and Sarah his Wife,	"	18 September 1710.
Abigall daughter of Stephen Kempton and Ruth his Wife,	"	18 October 1710.
Abigall daughter of Clement Norman and Abigal his Wife,	"	26 July 1710.
Martha daughter of Mathew Nazaro and Mary his Wife,	"	10 September 1710.

BIRTHS — 1710-11.

Cornelius Son of Simon Record and Grace his Wife,	Born	3 April 1710.
Simon Son of Simon Record and Grace his Wife,	"	29 Jan'y 1710.
Sarah dau' of Nathan'l Brick and Martha his Wife,	"	23 Nov' 1710.
Mary dau' of Thomas Couverly and Mary his Wife,	"	8 Jan'y 1710.
John Son of John Lane and Prudence his Wife,	"	12 May 1710.
Margaret dau' of Lewis Mallet and Margaret his Wife,	"	18 Jan'y 1710.
Lemuel Son of Thomas Trott and Zibiah his Wife,	"	30 March 1710.
Hannah dau' of Benj^a Bridge and Christian his Wife,	"	1 May 1710.
Jonathan Son of Jonath^n Kemball and Hannah his Wife,	"	9 Octo' 1710.
Mary dau' of John Jepson and Aphia his Wife	"	17 March 1710.
Mary dau' of Thomas Colsworthy and Sarah his Wife.	"	12 Sept'. 1710.
Eliza. dau' of William Payn and Hannah his Wife,	"	19 June 1710.
Hannah dau' of Thomas and Hannah Moulin,	"	20 Feb. 1710.
Richard Son of John and Sarah Merrett,	"	25 Feb. 1710.
Hannah dau' of Thomas and Hannah Walker,	"	5 July 1710.

1711.

Susanna daughter of John Allen and Eliza. his Wife,	Born	17 June 1711.
Robert Son of Robert Adams and Jane his Wife,	"	15 July 1711.
Moses Son of Moses Abbot and Rebecca his Wife,	"	3 August 1711.
Timothy Son of Thomas Adkins and Ruth his Wife,	"	19 December 1711.
John Son of William Alden and Mary his Wife,	"	22 January 1711.
Deborah daughter of Jeremiah Belknap and Sarah his Wife,	"	31 March 1711.
Mary daughter of Ebenr. Bridge and Mary his Wife,	"	15 March 1710/11.
Eliza. daughter of Ebenr Burges and Eliza his Wife,	"	23 March 1710/11.
Charles Son of Jonathn. Bill and Ann his Wife.	"	22 March 1710/11.
Jane daughter of Benja. Ballard and Jane his Wife,	"	31 March 1711.
Mary daughter of John Buttolph and Mehitabell his Wife,	"	5 May 1711.
Daniel Son of Daniel Bell and Abigall his Wife,	"	4 May 1711.
Hannah daughter of John Brett and Ann his Wife,	"	9 May 1711.
Edmund Son of John Brick and Ann his Wife,	"	17 June 1711.
John Son of John Bushnel and Mary his Wife,	"	7 June 1711.
Susanna daughter of Thomas Bomer and Margart. his Wife,	"	5 July 1711.
Eliza. daughter of Soloman Blake and Abigal his Wife,	"	16 July 1711.
Susanna daughter of Jonathn. Burnel and Susanna his Wife,	"	28 July 1711.
Eliza. daughter of John Barnes and Rachel his Wife,	"	30 July 1711.
Lydia daughter of William Brown and Lydia his Wife,	"	27 July 1711.
John Son of George Brock and Mary his Wife,	"	29 July 1711.
Phillip Son of Newcomb Blague and Mary his Wife.	"	8 September 1711.
Edward Son of John Beal and Eliza. his Wife,	"	11 August 1711.
John Son of Hugh Babell and Sarah his Wife,	"	23 August 1711.
Mary daughter of James Barnerd and Eliza. his Wife,	"	30 August 1711.
Samuel Son of Thomas Berry and Eliza. his Wife,	"	6 August 1711.
Joseph Son of Daniel Ballard and Dorcas his Wife,	"	11 June 1711.

Hannah daughter of Richd. Brooks and Mary his Wife,	Born	13 March 1710/11.
Katherine daughter of John Beers and Mary his Wife,	"	13 October 1711.
Samuel Son of William Brown and Ann his Wife,	"	20 October 1711.
Peter Son of James Bowdine and Sarah his Wife,	"	19 May 1711.
Lydia daughter of Henry Bridgham and Lydia his Wife,	"	18 January 1711.
Kellon Son of Nicholas Bly and Ann his Wife,	"	30 December 1711.
Bennet Son of Stephen Butler and Joanna his Wife,	"	4 January 1711.
Benjamen Son of Benja. Bramley and Dorcas his Wife,	"	15 January 1711
James Son of James Barnes and Mary his Wife,	"	17 February 1711
Mary daughter of John Brewster and Deliverence his Wife,	"	7 March 1711/12.
Mindwell daughter of Benja. Bird and Ann his Wife,	"	8 March 1711/12.
John Son of Abrm. Billins and Lydia his Wife,	"	9 March 1711/12.
Sarah daughter of Nathanll. Coney and Eliza. his Wife,	"	20 March 1710/11.
Eliza. daughter of Jeremiah Condey and Susana his Wife,	"	7 March 1710/11.
Joseph Son of Joseph Cluley and Mary his Wife,	"	12 Aprill 1711.
Gedny Son of Francis Clark and Deborah his Wife,	"	5 Aprill 1711.
Richard Son of William Clark and Hannah his Wife,	"	1 May 1711.
Reubin Son of John Cookson and Rachell his Wife,	"	10 May 1711.
John Son of Samll. Cunnibal and Abigall his Wife,	"	24 May 1711.
Mary daughter of Ebenr. Clough and Thankfull his Wife,	"	25 June 1711.
William Son of William Cowell and Eliza. his Wife,	"	6 August 1711
Mary daughter of William Clark and Rebecca his Wife,	"	20 August 1711
Ann daughter of John Cotta and Sarah his Wife,	"	6 September 1711.
Mary daughter of John Corser and Sarah his Wife,	"	1 October 1711.
Josiah Son of Mathew Collings and Dorcas his Wife,	"	19 October 1711.
Sarah daughter of James Cock and Mary his Wife,	"	4 November 1711.
Eliza daughter of James Codner and Mary his Wife,	"	9 February 1711.
James Son of Robert Calefe and Margaret his Wife,	"	24 February 1711.
Mary daughter of John Diamond and Mary his Wife,	"	19 March 1710/11.
William Son of Thomas Diamond and Ann his Wife,	"	23 March 1710/11.
Sarah daughter of James Davise and Sarah his Wife,	"	16 May 1711
Lydia daughter of Daniel Dupee and Lydia his Wife,	"	28 June 1711.
Sarah daughter of Thomas Dawes and Sarah his Wife,	"	24 July 1711.
Benja. Son of John Dolbear and Sarah his Wife,	"	23 July 1711.
John Son of Ralph Ditchfeeld and Margt. his Wife,	"	29 July 1711.
Hannah daughter of Rowland Dyke and Hannah his Wife,	"	1 September 1711.
Abigall daughter of Gasper Downing and Hannah his Wife,	"	7 December 1711.
Martha daughter of Robert Darby and Martha his Wife,	"	14 January 1711.

BIRTHS — 1711.

Martha daughter of Edward Eads and Martha his Wife,	Born	26 May 1711.
Ann daughter of John Ellet and Theodora his Wife,	"	18 September 1711.
Ruth daughter of Andrew Eliot and Ruth his Wife,	"	20 September 1711.
Henry Son of Thomas Freeman and Alice his Wife,	"	7 March 1710/11.
John Son of Robert Fare and Sarah his Wife,	"	21 March 1710/11.
Elisha Son of Hopestill Foster and Eliza. his Wife,	"	23 May 1711.
Susanna daughter of Jonathn. Farnum and Ann his Wife,	"	16 June 1711.
William Gimmi of William Fletcher and Margt. Margaret his Wife,	"	13 July 1711.
John Son of Thomas Fauks and Sarah his Wife,	"	8 August 1711.
Jerusha daughter of John Fairwether and Jerusha his Wife,	"	21 August 1711.
Judeth daughter of Jabez Fox and Hannah his Wife,	"	19 August 1711.
Miles Son of Benja. Flood and Mary his Wife,	"	13 January 1711.
William Son of Nathanll. Green and Ann his Wife,	"	3 May 1711.
Abigall daughter of Jacob Gale and Abigall his Wife,	"	5 May 1711.
Mary daughter of Edward Goddard and Susana his Wife,	"	4 June 1711.
Sarah daughter of Samll. Goff and Hannah his Wife,	"	25 May 1711.
Hannah daughter of Joseph Green and Eliza. his Wife,	"	15 June 1711.
Sarah daughter of John Gerrish and Sarah his Wife,	"	23 July 1711.
Mary daughter of John Glass and Martha his Wife,	"	2 August 1711.
Mercy daughter of David Greenlief and Mercy his Wife,	"	26 August 1711.
Eliza. daughter of Obadiah Gore and Sarah his Wife,	"	25 October 1711.
John Son of Samll. Grice and Priscilla his Wife,	"	20 December 1711.
Margaret daughter of John Goldthwaite and Sarah his Wife,	"	19 December 1711.
Jerusha daughter of John Greenough and Eliza. his Wife,	"	28 December 1711.
Samll Son of Benja. Gibson and Mehitabel his Wife,	"	31 October 1711.
Mary Anna daughter of Robert Guteridge and Mary his Wife,	"	2 September 1711.
Susanna daughter of Samuel Gardener and Eliza. his Wife,	"	7 March 1711/2.
Mary daughter of James Humphry and Judeth his Wife,	"	16 March 1710/11.
Richard Son of Thomas Hetchbon and Frances his Wife,	"	10 March 1710/11.
Ann daughter of John Hobbie and Ann his Wife,	"	27 March 1711.
Still-Born Son of Nathanll. Henchman and Dorothy his Wife,	"	11 July 1711.
Samuel Son of Joshua Hensha and Mary his Wife,	"	4 August 1711.
Thomas Son of John Holland and Susanna his Wife,	"	22 September 1711.
James Son of James Hincks and Eliza. his Wife,	"	13 September 1711.
Michael Son of Michael Hamelton and Mary his Wife,	"	2 October 1711.

John Son of Edward Hutchinson and Lydia his Wife,	Born	27 September 1711.
Joshua Son of James Hill and Mary his Wife,	"	21 October 1711.
Mary daughter of Francis Holmes and Rebecca his Wife,	"	17 June 1711.
Abigal daughter of Francis Hudson and Mary his Wife,	"	20 December 1711.
Charles Midlcot Son of Joseph Horsman and Esther his Wife,	"	12 January 1711.
Thomas Son of Capt. Thoms. Hutchinson and Sarah his Wife,	"	9 September 1711.
Mary daughter of John Heminway and Eliza. his Wife,	"	8 May 1711.
John Son of John Hayes and Hannah his Wife,	"	15 February 1711.
John Son of John Jent and Abigall his Wife,	"	11 May 1711.
Eliza. daughter of Joseph Jewel and Mary his Wife,	"	31 May 1711.
Abrm. Son of George Ingerson and Eliza. his Wife,	"	23 July 1711.
Samuell Son of Samll. Jones and Katherine his Wife,	"	29 September 1711.
Sarah daughter of John Jameson and Abigal his Wife,	"	8 October 1711.
John Son of Arthur Jeffery and Silence his Wife,	"	28 November 1711.
Eliza. daughter of Thomas Jackson and Grace his Wife,	"	7 December 1711.
Rebecca daughter of Thomas Jones and Bethiah his Wife,	"	12 December 1711.
John Son of John Jones and Margaret his Wife,	"	21 January 1711.
Ruth daughter of Abell Jones and Ruth his Wife,	"	5 March 1711/12.
Eliza. daughter of William Keen and Eliza. his Wife,	"	15 March 1710/11.
Ebenr. Son of John Kilby and Rebecca his Wife,	"	25 June 1711.
Stephen Son of Stephen Kingsly and Lydia his Wife,	"	23 July 1711.
Richard Son of John King and Eliza. his Wife,	"	25 October 1711.
Rebecca daughter of Samll. Kirby and Rebecca his Wife,	"	4 November 1711.
Henry Son of Henry King and Martha his Wife,	"	15 February 1711.
Edward Son of Nathanll. Kenny and Eliza. his Wife,	"	26 February 1711.
Joseph Son of Thomas Lee and Deborah his Wife,	"	23 March 1710/11.
Elizabeth daughter of Nathanll. Lyndall and Eliza. his Wife,	"	17 Aprill 1711.
William Son of William Lowder and Mary his Wife,	"	24 May 1711.
David Son of James Lenix and Mary his Wife,	"	20 August 1711.
William ⎱ Gimni of Henry Lowder and Abigall Mary ⎰ his Wife,	"	2 September 1711.
Katherine daughter of Kathrn. Long,	"	12 October 1711.
Mary daughter of John Legg and Martha his Wife.	"	16 October 1711.
Hannah daughter of Joseph Lowden and Hannah his Wife,	"	5 February 1711.
Stephen Son of John Mullens and Ann his Wife.	"	13 Aprill 1711.
Charles Son of Charles Morrise and Esther his Wife,	"	8 June 1711.
Nathanll. Son of Nathanll. Mason and Eliza his Wife,	"	28 July 1711.
Rebecca daughter of John Marshall and Martha his Wife.	"	28 August 1711.
John Son of John Maverick and Eliza. his Wife,	"	15 September 1711.

BIRTHS — 1711.

Ann daughter of Duncan Maycom and Mary his Wife,	Born	27 September 1711.
Mary daughter of Joseph Mason and Mary his Wife,	"	23 October 1711.
Ephraim Son of Ephraim More and Eliza his Wife,	"	28 November 1711.
Nathanll. Son of Edward Martyn and Sarah his Wife,	"	13 December 1711.
Jonathan Son of Samll. Mason and Abigall his Wife,	"	19 February 1711.
Spiller Son of Daniel Munden and Ann his Wife,	"	7 March 1711/12.
Samuel Son of Samll. Maxwel and Seferanna his Wife,	"	2 March 1711/12.
James Son of James Nash and Sarah his Wife,	"	27 October 1711.
Eliza. daughter of William Nicholson and Eliza. his Wife,	"	1 February 1711.
John Son of Francis Nicholson and Abigal his Wife,	"	4 March 1711/12.
Sarah daughter of John Oliver and Alice his Wife,	"	30 March 1711.
John Son of John Oliver and Martha his Wife,	"	6 June 1711.
Martha daughter of Nathanll. Oliver and Martha his Wife,	"	28 July 1711.
Peter Son of Daniel Oliver and Eliza. his Wife,	"	15 August 1711.
Eliza. daughter of John Orne and Eliza his Wife,	"	22 September 1711.
Hannah daughter of Robert Orrange and Hannah his Wife,	"	30 January 1711.
Dorcas daughter of Nathan Presbery and Eliza his Wife,	"	10 March 1710/11.
Mary daughter of Thoms. Plasted and Mary his Wife,	"	14 Aprill 1711.
Thomas Gimi. of Thomas Phillips and Mary his Howard Wife,	"	17 Aprill 1711.
Hannah daughter of James Pecker and Susanna his Wife,	"	21 July 1711.
John Son of John Perkins and Remembr his Wife,	"	4 August 1711.
Abiah Son of Joseph Pulsefer and Mary his Wife,	"	15 September 1711.
John Son of John Plasted and Sarah his Wife,	"	14 September 1711.
Samll. Son of Joseph Parsons and Eliza. his Wife,	"	13 September 1711.
Joseph Son of Joseph Peck and Mary his Wife,	"	16 September 1711.
Samll. Son of Abrm. Pullen and Mary his Wife,	"	30 September 1711.
Mary daughter of Samll. Pike and Mary his Wife,	"	15 October 1711.
Abigal daughter of Elias Purrington and Sarah his Wife,	"	28 November 1711.
Mary daughter of Joseph Perram and Rebecca his Wife,	"	15 December 1711.
Eliza. daughter of Bryant Parrot and Eliza. his Wife,	"	24 December 1711.
Rachel daughter of Ebenr. Prat and Rachel his Wife,	"	12 January 1711.
Abrm. Son of Phillip Perreway and Joanna his Wife,	"	13 January 1711.
Thoms. Son of Thomas Palmer Esqr. and Abigal his Wife,	"	2 December 1711.
Eliza. daughter of Henry Rich and Eliza. his Wife,	"	2 March 1710/11.
Margaret daughter of John Ruck and Hannah his Wife,	"	6 Aprill 1711.
Sarah daughter of Thomas Reed and Sarah his Wife,	"	12 May 1711.
Hannah daughter of Richd. Reed and Hannah his Wife,	"	17 June 1711.
Thomas Son of Robert Rand and Eliza. his Wife,	"	28 May 1711.
Hannah daughter of Thomas Rowel and Dorothy his Wife,	"	28 July 1711.
Sarah daughter of John Ruggles and Martha his Wife,	"	27 August 1711.

John Son of Daniel Rosey and Lydia his Wife,	Born	6 September 1711
Eliza. daughter of Edward Richards and Mary his Wife,	"	3 September 1711.
Mary daughter of Thomas Ruck and Mary his Wife,	"	11 September 1711.
Eliza. daughter of John Rouse and Martha his Wife,	"	18 September 1711.
Samuel Son of Humphry Richards and Susanna his Wife,	"	17 December 1711.
Hannah daughter of Joseph Russell and Mary his Wife,	"	8 September 1711.
James Son of James Robinson and Patience his Wife,	"	1 March 1711/12.
Mildred daughter of James Smith and Eliza. his Wife,	"	8 March 1710/11.
Richard Son of George Shore and Eliza. his Wife,	"	9 Aprill 1711.
John Son of John Salmon and Abiel his Wife,	"	15 April 1711.
Simmos Son of John Sacome and Mehitabel his Wife,	"	17 May 1711.
Benjamen Son of Clemons Sumner and Margt. his Wife,	"	28 May 1711.
Eliza. daughter of Simon Slocomb and Eliza. his Wife,	"	4 August 1711.
Elhanan Son of Samll. Soper and Mary his Wife,	"	3 October 1711.
Mehitabel daughter of Jacob Sheafe and Mary his Wife,	"	4 September 1711.
Joseph Son of John Savill and Priscilla his Wife,	"	3 October 1711.
Eliza. daughter of John Spike and Mary his Wife,	"	16 October 1711.
John Son of William Sanders and Bridget his Wife,	"	24 November 1711.
Peirses daughter of Erasamus Stevens and Peirses his Wife,	"	21 November 1711.
Joseph Son of William Seers and Eliza. his Wife,	"	29 November 1711.
Eliza. daughter of George Stewart and Mary his Wife,	"	14 December 1711.
Margaret daughter of Thomas Smith and Mary his Wife,	"	3 December 1711.
Elnathan Son of Elnathan Satly and Martha his Wife,	"	31 December 1711.
Abigall daughter of Joseph Scot and Deliverence his Wife,	"	12 January 1711.
Rebecca daughter of Thomas Smith and Rebecca his Wife,	"	11 December 1711.
Eneas Son of Samll. Salter and Sarah his Wife,	"	22 February 1711.
Samuel Son of Samll. Sarvice and Johanna his Wife,	"	4 February 1711.
Mary daughter of Robert Sharp and Mary his Wife,	"	16 February 1711.
William Son of Edward Tuttle and Joanna his Wife,	"	10 Aprill 1711.
Zachry Son of Zachry Thayer and Mary his Wife,	"	23 February 1711.
Nathanll. Son of Abraham Townsend and Mary his Wife,	"	31 May 1711.
David Son of John Trask and Sarah his wife.	"	23 May 1711.
Joseph Son of James Tileston and Mary his Wife,	"	12 August 1711.
Thomas Son of William Tyler and Sarah his Wife.	"	21 September 1711.
Benjamen Son of Benja. Thwing and Rebecca his Wife,	"	30 October 1711.
John Son of Noah Tucker and Mary his Wife,	"	20 November 1711.
Jeremiah Son of Isaac Townsend and Anna his Wife,	"	12 November 1711.
Samll. Son of Thomas Townsend and Eliza. his Wife,	"	8 February 1711.

BIRTHS — 1711.

Mary daughter of Nathanll. Vial and Sarah his Wife,	Born	23 August 1711.
Mary daughter of James Varney and Jane his Wife	"	14 January 1711.
Margaret daughter of John Vryling and Mary his Wife.	"	14 January 1711.
Katherine a third daughter of { John Winthrop and Ann his Wife,	"	9 March 1710/11.
Stephen Son of Stephen Willise and Martha his Wife,	"	8 March 1710/11.
Susanna daughter of John Wakefeeld and Eliza. his Wife,	"	15 March 1710/11.
John Son of John Wakefield and Ann his Wife.	"	9 Aprill 1711.
Hannah daughter of John Wilcot and Hannah his Wife,	"	6 April 1711.
Henry Son of William Welsteed and Eliza. his Wife,	"	3 April 1711.
Ebenr. Son of Jonathn. Williams and Rebecca his Wife,	"	25 May 1711.
Mary daughter of James Watson and Mary his Wife.	"	4 August 1711.
Ann daughter of Allexr. Williams and Ann his Wife.	"	8 August 1711.
John Son of John Welch and Hanna his Wife,	"	19 August 1711.
Abigall daughter of Jonathan Waldo and Hannah his Wife,	"	28 September 1711.
Eliza. daughter of Thomas Welch and Eliza. his Wife,	"	17 September 1711.
Francis Son of Jonathn. Wardwel and Frances his Wife,	"	12 October 1711.
John Son of Obadiah Wakefield and Rebecca his Wife,	"	8 October 1711.
Mary daughter of Thomas Worth and Mary his Wife,	"	29 October 1711.
Eliza. daughter of Nathanll. Woodward and Priscilla his Wife,	"	16 November 1711.
Eliza. daughter of John Warwick and Susanna his Wife,	"	25 November 1711.
John Son of Adam Winthrop and Ann his Wife,	"	11 December 1711.
Nathanll. Son of Nathanll. Wheeler and Mary his Wife,	"	17 December 1711.
John Son of John Welland and Eliza. his Wife,	"	12 January 1711.
Ann daughter of Edward White and Sarah his Wife,	"	24 January 1711.
Benja Son of John Waldo and Eliza his Wife,	"	21 February 1711.
Anne daughter of Samll. Burnel and Eliza. his Wife	"	6 June 1711.
sther daughter of Thomas Flagg and Esther his Wife,	"	12 March 1710/1.
Samuel Son of Samll. Greenwood and Philippi his Wife.	"	4 December 1711.
Eliza. daughter of Samll. Greenliefe and Martha his Wife.	"	8 August 1711.
Harrison Son of Edward Gray and Susanna his Wife.	"	24 February 1711.
Sarah daughter of Benja. Haley and Susanna his Wife,	"	23 February 1711.
Obadiah Son of Nathanll. Morss and Sarah his Wife,	"	29 February 1711.
Ephraim Son of Ephraim Marshall and Eliza. his Wife,	"	22 September 1711.

Ann dau^r of William Payn and Margaret his Wife, Born 8 June 1711.
Sarah dau^r of Daniel Ross and Hannah his Wife, " 26 Feb^{ry} 1711.
Eliza. dau^r of Benj^a Simpson and Eliza. his Wife, " 21 June 1711.
Wilmot Son of John Wass and Anne his Wife, " 9 Feb^{ry} 1711.
Sarah dau^r of Ab^{rm} Wacome and Abigall his Wife, " 9 Feb^{ry} 1711.
Mary dau^r of Thomas Webber and Mehitabel his Wife, " 27 Octo^r 1711.
Mary dau^r of Stephen Greenliefe and Mary his Wife, " 9 Jan^{ry} 1711.
Henry Son of Henry Howel and Martha his Wife, " 9 Octo^r 1711.
Mary dau^r of Thomas Hunt and Mary his Wife, " 3 Aug. 1711.
Eliakim Son of Willm Hutchinson and Eliza. his Wife, " 5 June 1711.
Edward Son of Edward Pell and Sarah his Wife, " 20 July 1711.
Thomas Son of Thomas Steel and Jane his Wife, " 4 May 1711.
Eliza. dau^r of Cornelius Waldo and Faith his Wife, " 17 Novr 1711.
Adam Son of David Colson and Hannah his Wife, " 7 April 1711.
Mary dau^r of Benj^a Gerrish and Mehitabel his Wife, " 12 Octo^r 1711.
Charles Son of And^r Sigourney and Mary his Wife, " 22 April 1711.
Sarah dau^r of Eben^r Scot and Sarah his Wife, " 2 May 1711.
William Son of William Short and Eliza. his Wife born at Road Island, " 13 July 1711.
Benonie Son of Samuel Eaton and Ruth his Wife, " 7 Aug. 1711.
Sarah dau^r of Samuel Kenney and Abigall his Wife, " 8 March 1711.
Jerusha daughter of Zabdiel Boylston and Jerusha his Wife, " 5 November 1711.
Robert Son of Robert and Rejoyce Lee, " 27 June 1711.

1712.

Abigall daughter of John Alkin and Mercy his Wife, Born 5 June 1712.
Edward Son of Edward Allexander and Lydia his Wife, " 17 June 1712.
Isaac Son of Samuel Avise and Mary his Wife, " 11 September 1712.
William Son of Jeremiah Allen and Mary his Wife, " 12 September 1712.
Sarah daughter of John Adams and Hannah his Wife, " 8 September 1712.
Mary daughter of Robert Anderson and Mary his Wife, " 19 October 1712.
Joseph Son of Oliver Atwood and Anna his Wife, " 22 October 1712.
Mercey daughter of Isaac Adams and Martha his Wife, " 26 November 1712.
Patience daughter of Milam Alcock and Mary his Wife, " 30 January 1712.
Eliza. daughter of James Butler and Abigall his Wife, " 3 March 1711/2.
Joseph Son of Thomas Baker and Thankfull his Wife, " 4 March 1711/2.
Ruth daughter of Sam^{ll}. Bill and Sarah his Wife, " 18 March 1711/2.
Eliza. daughter of Jonathan Bull and Eliza. his Wife, " 23 April 1712.
Eliza. daughter of John Baker and Mary his Wife, " 4 March 1711/2.
Robt. Son of Alvin Butcher and Eliza. his Wife, " 14 April 1712.
Margaret daughter of Richard Beaton and Marg^t. his Wife, " 15 June 1712.
William Son of William Bridgham and Tabatha his Wife, " 16 June 1712.

BIRTHS — 1712.

William Son of William Blare and Ann his Wife,	Born	14 July 1712.
Rebecca daughter of Benja. Bronsdon and Mary his Wife,	"	11 April 1712.
Mary daughter of Joseph Ballard and Mary his Wife,	"	31 July 1712.
Turfry Son of John Briggs and Katherine his Wife,	"	14 August 1712.
Ruth daughter of Phillip Bongarden and Ruth his Wife,	"	29 August 1712.
Hannah daughter of Robert Burgaine and Collet his Wife,	"	18 September 1712.
John Son of John Buttolph and Mehitabel his Wife,	"	23 September 1712.
Rebecca daughter of John Bushnel and Mary his Wife,	"	27 October 1712.
Hannah daughter of Thomas Barber and Eliza. his Wife,	"	31 August 1712.
Abigall daughter of Samll. Bligh and Anne his Wife,	"	4 October 1712.
Benjamen Son of Benja. Benson and Experience his Wife,	"	29 October 1712.
William Son of William Bill and Susana his Wife,	"	8 November 1712.
William Son of Benja. Bryant and Abigall his Wife,	"	30 October 1712.
John Son of Hugh Babell and Sarah his Wife,	"	9 November 1712.
Mary daughter of Cornelius Bennington and Mary his wife,	"	20 November, 1712.
Abigall daughter of Josiah Biles and Abigall his Wife,	"	17 November 1712.
Eliza. daughter of John Bulkley and Mary his Wife,	"	15 May 1712.
Hannah daughter of Benja. Brown and Mary his Wife,	"	27 May 1712.
Hannah daughter of Allexr. Baker and Hannah his Wife,	"	14 Aprill 1712.
Mary daughter of Collo. John Ballintine and Mary his Wife,	"	29 November 1712.
Ebenr. Son of Ebenr. Burges and Eliza. his Wife,	"	30 December 1712.
Mary daughter of Samll. Bridgham and Mary his Wife,	"	9 January 1712.
James Son of Samll. Belknap and Eliza. his Wife,	"	12 January 1712.
Eliza. daughter of Richd Bill and Sarah his Wife,	"	9 September 1712.
Hannah daughter of Joseph Belcher and Hannah his Wife,	"	20 February 1712.
Thomas Son of Thoms. Bell and Joanna his Wife,	"	18 February 1712.
Anne daughter of Joshua Bill and Sarah his Wife.	"	6 March 1712/3.
Abigall daughter of John Bulfinch and Jane his Wife,	"	14 February 1712.
Abigal daughter of Daniel Collings and Rebecca his Wife,	"	17 April 1712.
Samuel Son of Robert Cock and Agnis his Wife,	"	17 April 1712.
Abraham Son of Abrm. Clark and Anne his Wife,	"	19 May 1712.
Sands Son of Ezekiel Cravath and Eliza. his Wife,	"	27 July 1712.
Abigall daughter of Nathanll. Coney and Abigall his Wife,	"	28 July 1712.
Stephen Son of John Charnock and Mary his Wife,	"	3 September 1712.
Nathaniel ⎱ Gimi of Nathanll. Clark and Eliza. his Edward ⎰ Wife,	"	2 September 1712.
Thomas Son of Thomas Colesworthy and Sarah his Wife,	"	28 October 1712.

Bethiah daughter of William Clear and Bethiah his Wife,	Born	28 October 1712.
John Son of Joseph Cluley and Mary his Wife,	"	2 November 1712.
William Son of Saml. Clark and Sarah his Wife,	"	25 December 1712.
Hannah daughter of John Chamberlin and Hanna his Wife,	"	10 November 1712.
Abigall daughter of Saml. Cunneball and Abigall his Wife,	"	26 December 1712.
Phillip Son of William Champlin and Martha his Wife,	"	5 January 1712.
John Son of John Center and Ruth his Wife,	"	25 February 1712.
Mary daughter of Robert Calef and Margaret his Wife,	"	25 January 1712
Eliazur Son of Addington Davenport Esqr and Eliza. his Wife,	"	19 May 1712.
Sarah daughter of John Dolbear and Sarah his Wife,	"	25 July 1712.
Mary daughter of Edward Davise and Mary his Wife,	"	19 July 1712.
Sebella daughter of Joseph Dowding and Anne his Wife,	"	29 August 1712.
Harrise Son of John Dutch and Eliza. his Wife,	"	23 August 1712.
Benja. Son of William Dillaway and Sarah his Wife,	"	11 September 1712.
Storey Son of Thomas Dawes and Sarah his Wife,	"	9 October 1712.
Jane daughter of Saml. Deming and Hannah his Wife,	"	20 October 1712.
John Son of John Dinsdale and Eliza. his Wife,	"	16 October 1712.
Daniel Son of Daniel Dupee and Lydia his Wife,	"	22 October 1712.
John Son of John Demery and Sarah his Wife,	"	13 November 1712.
Samuel Son of Zebadiah Daniel and Eliz. his Wife,	"	28 December 1712.
Rebecca daughter of Benja. Edmunds and Rebecca his Wife,	"	26 March 1712.
Richard Son of John Edwards and Sivil his Wife,	"	3 May 1712.
Hannah daughter of Benja. Edwards and Hannah his Wife,	"	22 June 1712.
Timothy Son of Daniel Emorson and Jane his Wife,	"	10 October 1712.
John Son of Jonathn. Eustice and Sarah his Wife,	"	2 February 1712.
John Son of John Ellery and Jane his Wife,	"	19 February 1712.
Jane daughter of Josiah Franklin and Abiah his Wife,	"	27 March 1712.
Isanna daughter of Nathanll. Fadree and Isanna his Wife,	"	21 Aprill 1712.
Eliza. daughter of Ephraim Fenno and Eliza. his Wife,	"	23 June 1712.
Thomas Son of John Flagg and Abiel his Wife,	"	8 July 1712.
Richard Son of Thomas Freeman and Alice his Wife,	"	16 July 1712
Hannah daughter of Thomas Flagg and Esther his Wife,	"	6 December 171?
Hannah daughter of Daniel Floyd and Mary his Wife,	"	18 October 171?
William Son of John Fagen and Hannah his Wife,	"	15 December 1712.
William Son of William Flecher and Margaret his Wife,	"	14 January 1712.
Katherine daughter of Gidian Florence and Susanna his Wife,	"	22 January 1712.
Eliza. daughter of John Foster and Sarah his Wife,	"	12 February 1712.
Katherine daughter of Walter Gutridge and Anna his Wife,	"	21 March 1711/2.
Christopher Son of Daniel Goff and Eliza. his Wife,	"	13 March 1711/?.
Ann daughter of Joshua Gee and Eliza. his Wife,	"	4 March 1711/2.

BIRTHS — 1712.

Hannah daughter of Dean Grover and Martha his Wife,	Born	19 April 1712.
Eliza. daughter of Joseph Giddens and Eliza. his Wife,	"	17 March 1711/2.
Mary daughter of James Goold and Mary his Wife,	"	3 May 1712.
Sarah daughter of Thomas Goold and Sarah his Wife,	"	22 May 1712.
Sarah daughter of Elemuel Gowen and Sarah his Wife,	"	28 June 1712.
Rebecca daughter of Thomas Goodale and Rebecca his Wife,	"	28 July 1712.
Samuel Son of Samll. Greenliefe and Martha his Wife,	"	22 July 1712.
Susanna daughter of Robert Gribble and Susanna his Wife,	"	1 October 1712.
Samuel Son of Bartholl. Green and Jane his Wife,	"	4 October 1712.
Hill Son of Hill Green and Hannah his Wife,	"	6 October 1712.
Ebenr. Son of Edward Goddard and Susanna his Wife.	"	18 November 1712.
Jonas Son of Timothy Green and Mary his Wife,	"	24 December 1712.
Benja. Son of Nathanll. Green and Anne his Wife,	"	11 January 1712.
Jane daughter of Samll. Grice and Priscilla his Wife,	"	23 February 1712.
Prudence daughter of John Horton and Ann his Wife,	"	20 March 1711/2.
William Son of John Hook and Margaret his Wife,	"	29 March 1712.
Rebecca daughter of John Hunt and Rebecca his Wife,	"	22 March 1711/2.
Eliza. daughter of Anthony Haywood and Hanna his Wife,	"	27 May 1712.
Thomas Son of William Hoar and Susanna his Wife,	"	24 May 1712.
Sarah daughter of James How and Abigall his Wife,	"	24 May 1712.
Jacob Son of Jacob Hasie and Hannah his Wife,	"	3 July 1712.
Katherine daughter of Joseph Hall and Blanch his Wife,	"	20 July 1712.
John Son of William Holberton and Mary his Wife.	"	10 September 1712.
Richard Son of Richard Hall and Eliza. his Wife.	"	9 September 1712.
Ann daughter of Christor. Holland and Ann his Wife,	"	16 July 1712.
Eliza daughter of Wm. Hikinbotham and Anna his Wife,	"	21 September 1712.
Eunice daughter of Joseph Hubburd and Thankfull his Wife,	"	18 September 1712.
Johanna daughter of Ephraim Hunt and Johanna his Wife,	"	18 October 1712.
George Son of Nathan Howel and Katherine his Wife,	"	1 November 1712.
Mary daughter of Samll. Hunt and Mary his Wife,	"	26 January 1712.
Stil-born daughter of Nathanll. Henchman and Dorothy his Wife,	"	23 January 1712.
John Son of William Harrise and Anne his Wife,	"	30 January 1712.
Katherine daughter of William Healey and Sarah Wife,	"	9 February 1712.
Eliza. daughter of Charles Hudson and Sarah his Wife,	"	14 March 1712/3.

84   CITY DOCUMENT NO. 43.

Joseph Son of Joseph Hood and Judeth his Wife,	Born	2 March 1712/3.
Rebecca daughter of John Indecot and Rebecca his Wife,	"	14 March 1711/2.
Lydia daughter of John Jagger and Mary his Wife,	"	1 June 1712.
Josiah Son of Jeremlah Jackson and Hannah his Wife,	"	26 June 1712
Joseph Son of Joseph Jackson and Eliza. his Wife,	"	25 August 1712
Elinor daughter of John Ireland and Elinor his Wife,	"	22 October 1712.
Eliza. daughter of Henry Kally and Eliza. his Wife,	"	18 March 1711/2.
Elias Son of Elias Kingston and Martha his Wife,	"	13 July 1712.
Sarah daughter of Stephen Kempton and Ruth his Wife,	"	17 Aug. 1712.
Mary daughter of Christor Kilby and Sarah his Wife,	"	18 November 1712.
Abigall daughter of John Kent and Abigall his Wife,	"	11 January 1712.
Samuell Son of Samll. Kirby and Rebecca his Wife,	"	27 January 1712.
William Son of Willm. Letherbee and Lydia his Wife,	"	21 March 1711/2.
Nathanll. Son of John Langley and Mary his Wife,	"	25 May 1712.
Eliza. daughter of Peter Leech and Hannah his Wife,	"	7 June 1712.
Eliza. daughter of William Lee and Mercey his Wife,	"	14 July 1712.
Eliza. daughter of Ezekiel Lewise and Abigall his Wife,	"	22 August 1712.
Thomas Son of Thomas Leechmer and Anne his Wife,	"	23 October 1712.
James Son of John Lovell and Priscilla his Wife,	"	21 November 1712.
Abigall daughter of Joseph Leighton and Abigall his Wife,	"	7 November 1712.
Abigall daughter of Joshua Loreing and Hannah his Wife,	"	29 December 1712.
Allexandr. Son of Allexr. Miller and Eliza. his Wife,	"	15 April 1712.
Hannah daughter of John Minzes and Eadee his Wife,	"	9 May 1712.
Mary daughter of Daniel Macdaniel and Mary his Wife,	"	8 June 1712
Anne daughter of James Man and Priscilla his Wife,	"	2 September 1712.
Deborah daughter of John Man and Abigall his Wife,	"	8 September 1712.
Mary daughter of Ralph Maier and Martha his Wife,	"	6 October 1712.
John Son of Thomas Mellage and Mary his Wife,	"	28 August 1712.
Frances daughter of Francis Millar and Abigall his Wife,	"	19 October 1712.
Thomas Son of Michael Maclowd and Martha his Wife,	"	1 December 1712.
John Son of Francis Moor and Mary his Wife,	"	28 November 1712.
Joseph Son of Joseph Merrefeeld and Margt. his Wife.	"	9 December 1712.
Eliza. daughter of Ephraim Marshall and Eliza. his Wife.	"	12 January 1712.
Anna daughter of Joseph Marion and Ellen his Wife,	"	20 January 1712.

BIRTHS — 1712.

Eliza. daughter of John Neat and Eliza. his Wife,	Born	7 September 1712.
Sarah daughter of John Noyes and Susanna his Wife,	"	18 September 1712.
Clement Son of Clement Norman and Abigal his Wife,	"	19 December 1712.
Stephen Son of Mathew Nazaro and Mary his Wife,	"	18 December 1712.
James Son of James Newell and Mary his Wife,	"	9 January 1712.
Ruth daughter of Abraham Nicholls and Rebecca his Wife,	"	19 February 1712.
Eliza. daughter of John Orn and Eliza. his Wife,	"	29 November 1712.
Mary daughter of James Oliver and Rebecca his Wife,	"	21 November 1712.
William Son of Robert Orrange and Hannah his Wife,	"	2 February 1712.
Anna daughter of Eliazur Phillips and Lydia his Wife,	"	5 April 1712.
Eliza. daughter of Edward Porter and Abiel his Wife,	"	11 April 1712.
Ruth daughter of Edward Paige and Ruth his Wife,	"	27 April 1712.
Richard Son of William Palfrey and Abigall his Wife,	"	29 May 1712.
Jane daughter of Thomas Porter and Eliza. his Wife,	"	18 June 1712.
William Son of William Parteridge and Rachel his Wife,	"	4 July 1712.
Ebenezar Son of Edward Proctor and Eliza. his Wife,	"	12 August 1712.
Bozoon Son of James Peneman and Mary his Wife,	"	12 August 1712.
Lydia daughter of Isaac Peirse and Grace his Wife,	"	1 Septemter 1712.
William daughter (sic) of James Peek and Margaret his Wife,	"	29 August 1712.
James Son of James Peirson and Mary his Wife,	"	2 August 1712.
Martha daughter of Robert Patteshall and Jane his Wife,	"	7 September 1712.
Mary daughter of Stephen Payn and Mary his Wife,	"	9 October 1712.
Mary daughter of William Peirse and Sarah his Wife,	"	8 September 1712.
John Son of Indego Potter and Rebecca his Wife,	"	13 November 1712.
Mary daughter of Samuel Peck and Mary his Wife,	"	21 November 1712.
John Son of John Pumery and Lydia his Wife,	"	20 Nevember 1712.
Sarah daughter of Willian Parkman and Hanna his Wife,	"	11 November 1712.
Mary daughter of Richard Pitcher and Grace his Wife,	"	11 December 1712.
Eliza. daughter. of Timothy Prout and Lydia his Wife,	"	15 August 1712.
John Son of William Payn and Margaret his Wife,	"	9 February 1712.
Benj'a. Son of Stephen Parker and Margaret his Wife,	"	19 February 1712.
Samuel Son of Samuel Ramsdel and Abigall his Wife,	"	24 April 1712.
Robert Son of John Ruggles and Tabitha his Wife,	"	16 May 1712.
John Son of Fortune Ruddock and Abiel his Wife,	"	17 May 1712.
Joseph Son of Robert Randoll and Eliza. his Wife,	"	4 May 1712.
John Son of John Rolstone and Dorothy his Wife,	"	17 August 1712.
Mary daughter of John Ruck and Hannah his Wife,	"	20 September 1712.
Mary daughter of Henry Rich and Eliza. his Wife,	"	12 December 1712.
Lydia daughter of James Raymer and Eliza. his Wife,	"	21 December 1712.

Richard Son of Robert Rand and Susanna his Wife, Born 19 November 1712.
Mary daughter of Samuel Roberts and Sarah his Wife, " 20 January 1712.
Hannah daughter of Samll. Rand and Sarah his Wife, " 21 October 1712.
Thomas Son of John Smalpeice and Olive his Wife, " 9 March 1711/2.
David Son of Charles Shepreeve and Eliza. his Wife, " 20 March 1711/2.
Joseph Son of Joseph Savell and Margaret his Wife, " 7 April 1712.
John Son of James Scolly and Deborah his Wife, " 24 April 1712.
Martha daughter of John Smith and Martha his Wife, " 29 April 1712.
Jonathan Son of John Simpson and Rely his Wife, " 17 May 1712.
Jonathan Son of John Sharp and Mary his Wife, " 28 July 1712.
John Son of William Snoden and Rachel his Wife, " 16 July 1712
Joseph Son of Abraham Smith and Mary his Wife, " 18 September 1712.
Joseph Son of Joseph Shattuck and Mary his Wife, " 22 September 1712.
William Son of William Sentell and Johanna his Wife, " 25 September 1712.
Ann daughter of George Shore and Eliza. his Wife, " 31 October 1712.
Eliza. daughter of Benja. Snelling and Margaret his Wife, " 28 October 1712.
Jonathan Son of Jona. Simpson and Mary his Wife, " 30 October 1712.
John Son of John Strong and Lydia his Wife, " 22 November 1712.
Nathanll. Son of Joseph Snelling and Rebecca his Wife, " 25 December 1712.
Samuel Son of William Smallage and Ruth his Wife, " 31 December 1712.
Nathanll. Son of Nathnll. Storar and Margaret his Wife, " 23 December 1712.
Sarah daughter of Jabez Salter and Abagall his Wife, " 14 January 1712.
Benjamen Son of John Savill and Priscilla his Wife, " 2 February 1712.
Joseph Son of Edward Tuttle and Joanna his Wife, " 12 March 1711/2.
Sarah daughter of John Turner and Eliza. his Wife, " 15 April 1712.
Samll. Son of Samll. Tiley and Eliphal his Wife, " 27 April 1712.
John Son of John Turner and Rebecca his Wife, " 21 April 1712.
Robert Son of George Thomas and Susanna his Wife, " 8 April 1712.
Frances daughter of Henry Tew and Mary his Wife, " 2 July 1712.
Ruth daughter of James Townsend and Alice his Wife, " 26 December 1712.
Samuel Son of Cornelius Thayer and Lydia his Wife, " 30 December 1712.
John Son of John Trask and Sarah his Wife, " 18 February 1712.
Micall Son of Micael Thomas and Mary his Wife, " 4 August 1712.
Benjamen Son of Benja. Varney and Sarah his Wife, " 26 December 1712.
John Son of John Venteman and Mary his Wife, " 27 February 1712.
Eliza. daughter of John Watts and Eliza. his Wife, " 18 March 1711/2.
Abigail daughter of William Walter and Loise his Wife, " 2 April 1712.
Benja. Son of Benja. Williams and Eliza. his Wife, " 12 May 1712.
Grace daughter of Thomas Wallice and Grace his Wife. " 15 June 1712.
Sarah daughter of John Wilson and Mary his Wife, " 17 July 1712.
Abigall daughter of John Wakefield and Eliza. his Wife, " 25 June 1712,

Births — 1712.

Samuel } Gimi. of Jonathan Williams and Rebecca Rebecca } his Wife,	Born	4 August 1712.
Anne daughter of Joshua Williams and Anne his Wife,	"	24 July 1712.
Ephraim Son of Ephraim Weeler and Dorothy his Wife,	"	25 July 1712.
Isaac Son of Isaac White and Rebecca his Wife,	"	21 August 1712.
Lydia daughter of Daniel Wear and Mary his Wife,	"	16 September 1712.
Benja. Son of William Wheeler and Eliza. his Wife,	"	15 September 1712.
William Son of William Whitford and Eliza. his Wife,	"	29 July 1712.
Thomas } Gimi. of Thomas Willet and Mary his Martha } Wife,	"	7 October 1712.
Thomas Son of John Wyatt and Mary his Wife,	"	28 October 1712.
Thomas Son of Thoms. Welch and Eliza. his Wife,	"	17 October 1712.
Jeremiah Son of Joseph Williams and Sarah his Wife,	"	16 October 1712.
James Son of William Whetcomb and Mary his Wife,	"	7 December 1712.
John Son of Allen Wild and Eliza. his Wife,	"	12 December 1712.
Sarah daughter of Ebenr. Williston and Judee his Wife,	"	19 December 1712.
Stephen Son of Stephen Willise and Martha his Wife,	"	23 December 1712.
Benjamen Son of Joseph White and Sarah his Wife,	"	19 January 1712.
Frances daughter of Jonathn. Wardel and Frances his Wife,	"	20 January 1712.
William Son of William Young and Mary his Wife,	"	17 April 1712.
Isaiah Son of Samuel Barret and Sarah his Wife,	"	4 April 1712.
Mary daughter of John Cookson and Rachel his Wife,	"	23 February 1712.
Joseph Son of Joseph Callender and Lydia his Wife,	"	25 August 1712.
Francis Son of Daniel Epes and Hannah his Wife,	"	20 January 1712.
Martha daughter of Henry Howel and Martha his Wife.	"	28 February 1712.
Katherina daughter of Willm. Hutchinson and Eliza. his Wife,	"	6 September 1712.
Nathanll. Son of Nathanll. Harris and Sarah his Wife,	"	18 December 1712.
Rachel daughter of Amos Morrell and Rachel his Wife,	"	4 December 1712.
Sarah daughter of Edmund Morey and Sarah his Wife,	"	20 March 1711/2.
John Son of Anthony Oliver and Mary his Wife,	"	3 September 1712.
Samuel Son of Thomas Steel and Jane his Wife,	"	5 January 1712.
John Son of John Tuttle and Ruhama his Wife,	"	27 February 1712.
Eliz a. daughter of Edward Winslow and Eliza. his Wife,	"	16 February 1712.
Eliza. daughter of Samuel Willis and Eliza. his Wife,	"	9 February 1712.
Judeth daughter of Henry Allen and Eliza. his Wife,	"	26 September 1712.
Esther daughter of Benja. Bridge and Christian his Wife,	"	16 January 1712.
Hannah daughter of David Colson and Hannah his Wife,	"	14 July 1712.

88   CITY DOCUMENT No. 43.

John Son of John Oliver and Alice his Wife,	Born	28 February 1712.
Benjamen *Son of Benja. Gerrish and Mehitabel his Wife,	"	8 May 1712.
Mary daughter of Thomas Jenkins and Mary his Wife,	"	21 April 1712.
Elias Son of John Petail and Rachel his Wife,	"	7 July 1712.
William Son of Jonathan Belcher and Mary his Wife,	"	12 April 1712.
William Son of Grove Hirst and Eliza. his Wife,	"	9 July 1712.
Stephen Son of Stephen Labbee and Eliza. his Wife,	"	11 April 1712.
Judeth daughter of Phillip Rawlings and Hannah his Wife,	"	11 August 1712.
Thomas Son of John Vallentine and Mary his Wife,	"	3 August 1712.
Nathaniel Son of Nathaniel Wardel and Ruth his Wife,	"	30 April 1712.
William Son of William Payn and Hannah his Wife,	"	31 May 1712.
William Son of William and Elizabeth Keen,	"	19 September 1712.
Elizabeth daughter of Thomas and Hannah Moulin,	"	7 February 1712.
John Son of William and Margaret Payne,	"	9 February 1712.
Rebekah daughter of Thomas and Hannah Walker,	"	21 August 1712.
Samuel Son of Samuel and Martha Greenleaf,	"	22 July 1712.
Mary daughter of Richard and Mary Jenkins,	"	2 July 1712.
William Son of Joseph and Sarah Rayner,	"	23 July 1712.
William Son of Robert Ellis and Eliza. his Wife,	"	12 July 1712.

1713.

Mary daughter of Joseph Allen and Mary his Wife,	Born	8 August 1713.
Thomas Son of John Adams and Mary his Wife,	"	14 September 1713.
Benja. Son of Benja. Alford and Rachel his Wife,	"	9 December 1713.
John Son of Stephen Boutineau and Mary his Wife,	"	1 April 1713.
Isaac Son of John Beer and Mary his Wife,	"	12 April 1713.
Ruth daughter of Eliakim Blackman and Ruth his Wife,	"	25 April 1713.
Sarah daughter of Jeremiah Belknap and Sarah his Wife,	"	20 May 1713.
Nathanll. Son of Nathanll. Brick and Martha his Wife,	"	9 May 1713.
Mercey daughter of Samuel Barret and Sarah his Wife,	"	24 May 1713.
Hannah daughter of James Barnerd and Eliza. his Wife,	"	18 May 1713.
Hannah daughter of Ebenr. Bridge and Mary his Wife,	"	11 June 1713.
David Son of Daniel Bell and Abigall his Wife.	"	5 June 1713.
Mary daughter of Benja. Bird and Joanna his Wife,	"	4 July 1713.
Hannah daughter of Soloman Blake and Abigall his Wife,	"	17 June 1713.
Eliza. daughter of Thomas Barnerd and Silence his Wife,	"	9 July 1713.
Nathanll. Son of Nathanll. Breed and Sarah his Wife,	"	23 July 1713.
Thomas Son of Jonathn. Belcher and Mary his Wife,	"	14 May 1713.
John Son of Edward Ball and Rebecca his Wife,	"	29 August 1713.
Joseph Son of John Baker and Mary his Wife	"	21 August 1713.

*Born at Piscatiqua, as was also Mary of 1711.

BIRTHS — 1713.

Benja. Son of Benjamen Ballard and Anne his Wife,	Born	29 July 1713.
John Son of John Brett and Anne his Wife,	"	22 July 1713.
Eliza. daughter of Jonathn. Burnel and Susana his Wife,	"	6 September 1713.
Anne daughter of Samuel Burnel and Eliza. his Wife,	"	30 August 1713.
Benja. Son of John Bryant and Katherine his Wife,	"	15 September 1713.
Thomas Son of Richard Barrington and Sarah his Wife,	"	22 September 1713.
James Son of John Barton and Katherine his Wife,	"	16 October 1713.
James Son of William Brown and Lidia his Wife,	"	13 November 1713.
Sarah daughter of Daniel Ballard and Dorcas his Wife,	"	17 August 1713.
Eliza. daughter of Joseph Birch and Eliza. his Wife,	"	9 January 1713.
Eliza daughter of Samuel Bill and Sarah his Wife,	"	2 January 1713.
Peter Son of George Brock and Mary his Wife,	"	22 July 1713.
William Son of James Bodoin and Sarah his Wife,	"	14 June 1713.
James Son of James Butler and Abigall his Wife,	"	4 December 1713.
Thomas Son of John Beard and Mary his Wife,	"	26 January 1713.
Freeborn Son of Freeborn Balch and Susanna his Wife,	"	5 February 1713.
Rebecca daughter of Joseph Brisco and Mary his Wife,	"	13 February 1713.
Dorcas daughter of Noah Champney and Sarah his Wife.	"	10 March 1712/3.
Sarah daughter of Thomas Chamberline and Sarah his Wife.	"	13 March 1712/3.
William Son of William Condey and Joanna his Wife,	"	28 March 1713.
Anna daughter of John Coser and Sarah his Wife,	"	15 April 1713.
Hannah daughter of James Carey and Sarah his Wife,	"	22 April 1713.
Francis Son of Francis Clark and Deborah his Wife,	"	16 May 1713.
Dorcas daughter of Mathew Collings and Dorcas his Wife,	"	20 May 1713.
Richard Son of James Cock and Mary his Wife,	"	4 July 1713.
William Son of William Cowel and Eliza. his Wife,	"	19 July 1713.
Mary daughter of William Clark and Hannah his Wife,	"	1 August 1713.
William Son of John Colman and Judeth his Wife,	"	24 August 1713.
Mary daughter of Thomas Chute and Mary his Wife,	"	25 August 1713.
John Son of Thomas Couverly and Mary his Wife,	"	29 December 1713.
Eliza. daughter of William Cook and Rachel his Wife,	"	20 September 1713.
Richard Son of John Charnock and Mary his Wife,	"	5 February 1713.
John Son of John Cooledge and Hannah his Wife,	"	11 February 1713.
Samuel Son of Abrm. Clarke and Anne his Wife,	"	21 January 1713.
Anne daughter of John Clough and Mehitabel his Wife,	"	24 February 1713.
Mary daughter of Samll. Duncan and Mary his Wife,	"	14 June 1713.
Anne daughter of Nicholas Davis and Sarah his Wife,	"	25 July 1713.
John Son of Shem Drown and Katherine his Wife,	"	16 August 1713.
Ralph Son of Ralph Ditchfeeld and Margart. his Wife,	"	14 August 1713.
Eliza. daughter of Rowland Dike and Hannah his Wife,	"	2 September 1713.
John Son of Thomas Diamond and Anne his Wife,	"	18 Septmber 1713.

Thomas Son of Henry Dillaway and Abigall his Wife,	Born	22 September 1713.
Lydia daughter of Benja. Dresser and Lydia his Wife,	"	28 September 1713.
James Son of James Davis and Sarah his Wife,	"	12 October 1713.
Henry Son of Henry Dering and Eliza. his Wife,	"	22 November 1713.
Thomas Son of Thomas Debuke and Jamina his Wife,	"	14 December 1713.
David Son of John Dolbear and Sarah his Wife,	"	5 January 1713.
William Son of Thoms. Dawes and Sarah his Wife,	"	15 January 1713.
Eliza. daughter of John Dutch and Eliza. his Wife,	"	5 February 1713.
Ebenr. Son of Ebenr. Dennis and Susanna his Wife,	"	19 February 1713.
Benja. Son of Benja. Edmunds and Rebecca his Wife,	"	18 April 1713.
George Son of George East and Mary his Wife,	"	24 May 1713.
Samuel Son of Andrew Eliot and Ruth his Wife,	"	27 September 1713.
James & Susanna } Gimi. of Thomas Ellis and Sarah his Wife,	"	10 November 1713.
Sarah daughter of William Fisk and Mary his Wife,	"	19 April 1713.
John Son of John Foster and Mary his Wife,	"	10 April 1713.
Thomas Son of Thomas Foster and Ann his Wife,	"	15 July 1713.
Mary daughter of Joseph Farrindine and Mary his Wife,	"	9 October 1713.
Mary daughter of Robert Fethergill and Elíza. his Wife,	"	29 November 1713.
Sarah daughter of Samll. Gerrish and Sarah his Wife,	"	29 March 1713.
Joseph Son of Samuel Gardener and Eliza his Wife,	"	8 May 1713.
Mary daughter of Lately Gee and Sarah his Wife,	"	25 May 1713.
Margaret daughter of Bartholomew Gussire and Eliza. his Wife,	"	18 June 1713.
Anne daughter of Samuel Green and Anne his Wife,	"	25 June 1713.
John Son of Edward Gray and Susanna his Wife,	"	27 May 1713.
John Son of Samuel Green and Remember his Wife,	"	20 July 1713.
Eliza daughter of Lemuel Gowen and Sarah his Wife,	"	2 August 1713.
Rebecca daughter of Robert Gutridge and Rebecca his Wife,	"	12 November 1713.
Meriam daughter of Obadiah Gore and Sarah his Wife,	"	6 December 1713.
Ebenezer Son of Edward Goddard and Susanna his Wife,	"	17 January 1713.
William & Robert } Gimmi. of Phillip Harley and Susanna his Wife,	"	1 March 1712/3.
Mary daughter of Francis Holmes and Rebecca his Wife,	"	19 March 1712/3.
John Son of John Harwood and Mary his Wife,	"	10 March 1712/3.
Josiah Son of John Holland and Susanna his Wife,	"	18 March 1712/3.
George Son of George Hisket and Mary his Wife,	"	21 March 1712/3.
Eliza. daughter of John Hillier and Eliza. his Wife,	"	28 March 1713.
Anne daughter of John Hunt and Rebecca his Wife,	"	26 April 1713.
Sarah daughter of Thomas Holland and Anne his Wite,	"	22 March 1712/3.
Eliza. daughter of Edward Hutchinson and Lydia his Wife,	"	19 May 1713.
Abigall daughter of Ambrose Harrise and Abigall his Wife,	"	29 June 1713.
Ruth daughter of Samuel Hood and Deborah his Wife,	"	10 June 1713.
Samuel Son of William Hasie and Sarah his Wife,	"	18 September 1713.
Thomas Son of Samuel Hatch and Eliza. his Wife,	"	25 September 1713.
John Son of John Horton and Anne his Wife	"	5 October 1713.

BIRTHS — 1713.

Joseph Son of Richard Hall and Eliza. his Wife,	Born	3 December 1713.
Mary daughter of Thomas Hetchbone and Frances his Wife,	"	30 November 1713.
William Son of Willm. Hutchinson and Eliza. his Wife,	"	16 September 1713.
James Son of James How and Abigall his Wife,	"	22 December 1713.
William Son of James Humphryes and Judeth his Wife,	"	10 June 1713.
Richard Son of Richard Haisley and Tamozine his Wife,	"	30 January 1713.
Phillip Son of Phillip Howel and Sarah his Wife,	"	26 February 1713.
Ann daughter of Thomas Hunt and Mary his Wife,	"	18 February 1713.
Jamos Son of Jamas Haversham and Mehitall. his Wife,	"	6 August 1713.
Thomas Son of John Jent and Abigall his Wife,	"	18 July 1713.
John Son of John Jagor and Mary his Wife,	"	28 December 1713.
Eliza. daughter of Ebenezar Kemball and Eliza. his Wife,	"	19 March 1712/3.
George Son of George Kilcup and Mary his Wife,	"	3 August 1713.
Lydia daughter of John King and Eliza. his Wife,	"	19 January 1713.
John Son of John Letherbee and Eliza. his Wife,	"	19 April 1713.
Samuel Son of Samll. Langdon and Esther his Wife,	"	16 June 1713.
Nathanll. Son of Nathanl. Loring and Susanna his Wife,	"	11 June 1713.
Margaret daughter of Peter Lamarkin and Sarah his Wife,	"	22 July 1713.
Abigail daughter of Ebenr. Leadbetter and Abigall his Wife,	"	26 July 1713.
Mary daughter of James Lenix and Mary his Wife,	"	27 August 1713.
Martha daughter of John Legg and Martha his Wife,	"	16 September 1713.
Jonathan } Gimi. of William Lerabee and Lydia his Lydia } Wife,	"	7 October 1713.
Jonathan Son of William Lowder and Mary his Wife,	"	26 October 1713.
Michael Son of Michael Layton and Sarah his Wife,	"	8 November 1713.
William Son of Henry Lowder and Abigall his Wife,	"	1 December 1713.
Priscilla daughter of Daniel Loring and Priscilla his Wife,	"	15 January 1713.
Eliza. daughter of Lewis Mallet and Margaret his Wife,	"	7 March 1712/3.
Sarah daughter of Jonathan Mountfort and Hannah his Wife,	"	6 March 1712/3.
Sarah daughter of Joseph Morgan and Grace his Wife,	"	27 April 1713.
Ruth daughter of Thomas Mellens and Mary his Wife,	"	17 April 1713.
Martha daughter of Daniel Mero and Frances his Wife,	"	7 June 1713.
Mary daughter of Christopher Marvel and Jane his Wife,	"	6 June 1713.
John Son of John Mills and Eliza. his Wife,	"	1 June 1713.
John Son of John Mathews and Sarah his Wife,	"	6 June 1713.
John Son of William Mallerd and Abigall his Wife,	"	30 June 1713.
John Son of John Merefield and Bridget his Wife,	"	28 August 1713.
Richard Son of Richard Mayn and Sarah his Wife,	"	13 September 1713.
Eliza. daughter of Ephraim More and Eliza. his Wife,	"	6 September 1713.

Samuel Son of Samuel Mattock and Admonition his Wife,	Born	15 September 1713.
Mary daughter of Peter Mires and Mary his Wife,	"	23 September 1713.
James Son of Charles Morris and Esther his Wife,	"	30 September 1713.
John Son of John Milton and Mary his Wife,	"	2 October 1713.
Phebee daughter of William Marshall and Hannah his Wife,	"	14 November 1713.
Elijah Son of Allexander Millar and Eliza. his Wife,	"	8 January 1713.
Susanna daughter of Edmund Morey and Sarah his Wife,	"	21 December 1713
Ruth daughter of Daniel Macdaniel and Mary his Wife,	"	17 January 1713.
Thomas Son of William Man and Hannah his Wife,	"	11 March 1713/4.
Abraham Son of Charles Negro and Maudlin his Wife,	"	1 April 1713.
William Son of William Noyes and Hannah his Wife,	"	27 September 1713
John (Tertia) Son of Oliver Noyes and Anna his Wife,	"	12 August 1713.
Peter Son of Daniel Oliver and Eliza. his Wife,	"	26 March 1713.
Susanna daughter of Anthony Oliver and Mary his Wife,	"	12 July 1713.
Nathaniel Son of Nathaniel Oliver and Martha his Wife,	"	2 June 1713.
Hannah daughter of Francis Plasteed and Hannah his Wife,	"	19 March 1712/3.
ohn Son of Moses Peirse and Eliza. his Wife,	"	27 March 1713.
Rebecca daughter of Samuel Pearse and Mehitabel his Wife,	"	30 March 1713.
Joseph Son of John Pearse and Eliza. his Wife,	"	22 April 1713.
Stephen Son of John Payn and Bethiah his Wife,	"	1 March 1712/3.
Joshua Son of Joshua Pickman and Eliza. his Wife,	"	7 May 1713.
Thomas Son of George Pemberton and Susanna his Wife,	"	18 May 1713.
Lydia daughter of James Peneman and Mary his Wife,	"	16 June 1713.
Eliza. daughter of John Pecker and Eliza. his Wife,	"	12 July 1713.
Martha daughter of Elias Parkman and Martha his Wife,	"	22 July 1713.
William Son of William Price and Eliza. his Wife,	"	4 August 1713.
James Son of James Pecker and Susanna his Wife,	"	13 August 1713.
Sarah daughter of Edward Pell and Sarah his Wife,	"	1 September 1713.
Abraham Son of Phillip Pereway and Hannah his Wife.	"	30 May 1713.
Eliza daughter of Ebenr. Pratt and Rachell his Wife.	"	24 October 1713.
Sarah daughter of John Pettey and Eliza. his Wife,	"	10 October 1713.
Sarah daughter of Jacob Peirse and Rachel his Wife,	"	11 November 1713.
Mary daughter of Isaac Peirse and Grace his Wife,	"	7 December 1713.
William Son of Edward Paige and Ruth his Wife,	"	17 December 1713.
Abigall daughter of Bryant Parrot and Abigall his Wife,	"	3 January 1713.
Joseph Son of James Pitts and Eliza. his Wife,	"	6 March 1712/3.
Eliza. daughter of Thoms, Plasted and Abigall his Wife.	"	16 January 1713.
James Son of Thomas Porter and Eliza. his Wife,	"	31 January 1713.

BIRTHS — 1713.   93

Margaret daughter of John Ripener and Ruth his Wife,	Born	13 March 1712/3.
Mary daughter of Saml. Robinson and Mary his Wife,	"	3 May 1713.
Thomas Son of James Robinson and Patience his Wife,	"	15 September 1713.
John Son of Richard Richardson and Sarah his Wife,	"	29 August 1713.
Mary daughter of Henry Reading and Experience his Wife,	"	8 October 1713.
James Son of James Right and Mary his Wife,	"	6 December 1713.
Richard Son of Robert Rand and Susanna his Wife,	"	13 December 1713.
Ebenr. Son of Henry Rich and Eliza. his Wife,	"	28 December 1713.
Thomas ⟩ Gimi of William Skinner and Deborah his Mary ⟨ Wife,	"	8 March 1712/3.
Mary daughter of Samuel Sanders and Eliza. his Wife,	"	31 March 1713.
Mary daughter of Jacob Sheafe and Mary his Wife,	"	26 May 1713.
Joanna daughter of Bartholl. Spiller and Joanna his Wife,	"	11 June 1713.
James Son of Samuel Service and Joanna his Wife,	"	15 June 1713.
Mary daughter of John Sale and Anne his Wife,	"	3 July 1713.
William Son of James Smith and Eliza. his Wife,	"	24 July 1713.
Elisha Son of Elisha Storey and Lydia his Wife,	"	19 July 1713.
Thomas Son of Thomas Simpson and Christian his Wife,	"	6 July 1713.
John Son of Cyprian Southack and Eliza. his Wife,	"	12 July 1713.
John Son of Anthony Seers and Eliza. his Wife,	"	29 August 1713.
Erasamus Son of Erasamus Stevens and Peirses his Wife,	"	31 August 1713.
Deborah daughter of John Simpson and Rely his Wife,	"	15 September 1713.
Sarah daughter of John Salmon and Abiel his Wife.	"	24 September 1713.
John Son of Christian Snoman and Mary his Wife,	"	20 November 1713.
Hannah daughter of Thomas Smith and Mary his Wife.	"	26 October 1713.
William Son of William Seers and Eliza. his Wife,	"	6 December 1713.
Thomas Son of Samll. Salter and Sarah his Wife,	"	23 February 1713.
Robert Son of John Stevens and Grace his Wife,	"	21 February 1713.
Sarah daughter of John Sherlock and Sarah his Wife,	"	19 February 1713.
Stoughton Son of ye Honble. William Taylor Esqr. and Abigall his Wife,	"	30 April 1713.
Sarah daughter of Edward Tuttle and Joanna his Wife,	"	7 April 1713.
John Son of John Tuften and Susanna his Wife,	"	29 April 1713.
Thomas ⟩ Gimi. of Thomas Trott and Zibiah his Zibia ⟨ Wife,	"	26 April 1713.
John Son of Benjamen Thwing and Rebecca his Wife.	"	17 June 1713.
Robert Son of Henry Timberlake and Mary his Wife,	"	19 June 1713.
Miles Son of Miles Thompson and Abigall his Wife,	"	18 July 1713.
Mary daughter of William Tyler and Sarah his Wife,	"	2 August 1713.
Mary daughter of Michael Thomas and Mary his Wife,	"	24 August 1713.
Martha daughter of Thomas Townsend and Eliza. his Wife,	"	10 December 1713.
Mary daughter of Joseph Thorn and Deborah his Wife,	"	2 December 1713.

Eliphall daughter of Samuel Tyley and Eliphall his Wife,	Born	8 February 1713.
John Son of Collo. Adam Winthrop and Anne his Wife,	"	9 March 1712/3.
Thomas Son of Nathll. Wheeler and Mary his Wife,	"	8 March 1712/3.
John Son of Peter White and Sarah his Wife,	"	13 April 1713.
Phebee daughter of Allexr. Williams and Anne his Wife,	"	24 May 1713.
Rachel daughter of Adam Waters and Rachel his Wife,	"	16 May 1713.
Abraham Son of Abrm. Wacome and Abigall his Wife,	"	22 May 1713.
Ephraim Son of Zachry. Wire and Mary his Wife,	"	31 July 1713.
Sarah daughter of William Webber and Eliza. his Wife,	"	26 August 1713.
William Son of William Willis and Mary his Wife,	"	10 September 1713.
Ruth daughter of Ezekiel Walker and Ruth his Wife,	"	15 August 1713.
Mary daughter of Samll. White and Anne his Wife,	"	21 September 1713.
Lydia daughter of George Worthylake and Anne his Wife,	"	4 October 1713.
Eliza. daughter of Francis Wainright and Mary his Wife,	"	25 October 1713.
Nathanll. Son of Nathaniel Woodward and Priscilla his Wife,	"	16 October 1713.
Hannah daughter of Thoms. Warden and Hannah his Wife,	"	3 December 1713.
Susanna daughter of John Walker and Eliza. his Wife,	"	8 December 1713.
Susanna daughter of Edward Wildey and Agnis his Wife,	"	24 November 1713.
Rebecca daughter of Jonathn. Williams and Rebecca his Wife,	"	27 November 1713.
Jane daughter of John Williams and Humilis his Wife	"	18 December 1713.
Faith daughter of Cornelius Waldo and Faith his Wife,	"	1 January 1713.
William Son of John Waldo and Eliz. his Wife,	"	3 February 1713.
Benja. Son of William Waine and Sarah his Wife,	"	19 January 1713.
Joseph Son of Joseph Woodwel and Sarah his Wife,	"	16 January 1713.
James Son of Willlam Webster and Mary his Wife,	"	12 February 1713.
Thomas Son of John Warrick and Susanna his Wife,	"	13 February 1713.
John Son of David Webb and Jane his Wife,	"	18 February 1713.
John Son of Thoms. Welch and Eliza. his Wife,	"	16 January 1713.
Joseph Son of Mathew Butler and Sarah his Wife,	"	28 December 1713.
Mary daughter of Zabdiel Boylston and Jerusha his Wife,	"	28 July 1713.
Joseph Son of Benja. Brown and Mary his Wife,	"	29 January 1713.
Eliza. daughter of Jabez Crowel and Sarah his Wife,	"	17 January 1713.
James Son of John Channing and Mary his Wife,	"	20 June 1713.
John Son of John Dougles and Isabella his Wife,	"	18 February 1713.
Abigall daughter of Benja. Eliot and Susanna his Wife,	"	7 February 1713.
John Son of Benja. Gerrish and Mehitabel his Wife,	"	16 December 1713.
Joseph Son of Nathanll. Kenny and Eliza. his Wife.	"	16 February 1713.
Samll. Son of Jonathn. Kemball and Hannah his Wife,	"	5 April 1713.

BIRTHS — 1713-14.

William Son of Isaac Lewis and Hannah his Wife,	Born	31 January 1713.
James Son of James Pemberton and Hannah his Wife,	"	21 August 1713.
John Son of Fortune Ruddock and Abiel his Wife,	"	8 July 1713.
John Son of Thomas Ruck and Mary his Wife,	"	31 January 1713.
Eliza. daughter of Obadiah Reed and Jane his Wife,	"	1 January 1713.
Rachel daughter of Robert Sharp and Mary his Wife,	"	26 February 1713.
Charles Son of Benja. Simpson and Eliza. his Wife,	"	4 September 1713.
Anthony Son of Andr. Sigourney and Mary his Wife,	"	17 August 1713.
John Son of John Webster and Mary his Wife,	"	28 February 1713.
Jonathan Son of Jonathn. Wardel and Frances his Wife,	"	27 January 1713.
Mary daughter of Peter Butler and Mary his Wife,	"	28 July 1713.
John Son of Jonathn. Farnum and Anne his Wife,	"	24 September 1713.
Mary daughter of Joseph Lowden and Hannah his Wife,	"	24 December 1713.
Jonathn. Son of Jonathan Pickerin and Eliza. his Wife,	"	27 October 1713.
Nathaniel Son of Nathanll. Peirse and Abigall his Wife,	"	14 February 1713.
Samuel Son of Samll. Swasey and Amie his Wife,	"	5 July 1713.
Anna daughter of Ebenr. Scot and Sarah his Wife,	"	4 April 1713.
Eliza. daughter of Thomas Webber and Mehitabel his Wife,	"	11 November 1713.
John Son of John Child and Sarah his Wife,	"	4 February 1713.
Benjamen Son of Benja. Haley and Susana his Wife,	"	7 April 1713.
Mercy daughter of James Melven and Mercy his Wife,	"	10 June 1713.
Martha daughter of Elnathan Sautley and Martha his Wife,	"	12 January 1713.
John Son of John Butler and Hannah his Wife,	"	17 January 1713.
Anna daughter of Nicholas Dun and Deborah his Wife,	"	26 December 1713.
Mary daughter of Benja. Edey and Mary his Wife,	"	22 October 1713.
Sarah daughter of Samll. Haugh and Margaret his Wife,	"	15 October 1713.
Joseph Son of John Mountfort and Mary his Wife,	"	12 April 1713.
Josiah Son of Josiah Clark and Sarah his Wife,	"	1 January 1713.
Anne daughter of Thomas Loyd and Anne his Wife,	"	17 October 1713.
Mary daughter of Thomas Bostick and Abigall his Wife,	"	28 August 1713.
Robert Son of Benjamin and Mary Bronsdon,	"	6 July 1713.
James Son of James and Mehetabel Haversham,	"	6 August 1713.
John Son of John and Elizabeth Watts,	"	24 October 1713.

1714.

William Son of Ames Angier and Margaret his Wife,	Born	1 August 1714.
William Son of Henry Allen and Eliza. his Wife,	"	10 December 1714.
Mary daughter of Milam Alcock and Mary his Wife,	"	30 December 1714.
John Son of John Angier and Eliza. his Wife,	"	17 January 1714.
Silence daughter of John Adams and Hannah his Wife,	"	22 January 1714.

Lydia daughter of Edward Allexander and Lydia his Wife,	Born	20 February 1714.
Isaiah Son of James Barnes and Mary his Wife,	"	28 March 1714.
William Son of William Bill and Susanna his Wife,	"	27 March 1714.
Benjamen Son of John Brentnel and Phebee his Wife,	"	25 March 1714.
Joseph Son of John Briggs and Katherine his Wife,	"	8 May 1714.
Benjamen Son of Isarel Baley and Hannah his Wife,	"	9 June 1714.
John Son of John Belcher and Sarah his Wife,	"	2 June 1714.
Elizabeth daughter of John Buckley and Mary his Wife,	"	29 May 1714.
Eliza. daughter of Phillip Bongarden and Eliza. his Wife,	"	16 May 1714.
Lydia daughter of John Bradfield and Sarah his Wife,	"	15 March 1713/4.
Honnor daughter of Allexr. Baker and Hannah his Wife,	"	26 June 1714.
Henry Son of Henry Bridgham and Lydia his Wife,	"	4 July 1714.
John Son of Thomas Barber and Eliza. his Wife,	"	30 June 1714.
Joanna daughter of John Beer and Mary his Wife.	"	23 July 1714.
Ebenr. Son of John Buckley and Mary his Wife,	"	12 July 1714.
Mary daughter of Jonathan Bull and Eliza. his Wife,	"	13 July 1714.
William Son of John Barnes and Rachel his Wife,	"	10 August 1714.
Lydia daughter of Samuel Boyec and Abigall his Wife,	"	29 July 1714.
Nathaniel Son of William Brown and Anne his Wife,	"	7 September 1714.
Abigall daughter of Daniel Bell and Abigall his Wife,	"	10 October 1714.
John Son of Jonathn. Brown and Loise his Wife,	"	18 October 1714.
Jonathan Son of Jonathn. Burnel and Susanna his Wife,	"	9 November 1714.
Abigall daughter of Benjamen Bryant and Abigall his Wife,	"	30 October 1714.
Bill Son of Thoms. Bodely and Abigall his Wife,	"	11 November 1714.
Sarah daughter of Ebenr. Burges and Eliza. his Wife,	"	30 October 1714.
Dorothy daughter of William Brown and Lydia his Wife,	"	17 December 1714.
Mehitabel daughter of John Buttolph and Mehitabel his Wife,	"	4 December 1714.
Adinah Son of John Bulfinch and Jane his Wife,	"	27 December 1714.
Sarah daughter of Soloman Blake and Abigall his Wife,	"	30 December 1714.
Sarah daughter of John Bushnel and Mary his. Wife,	"	19 January 1714.
Mary daughter of Samuel Bill and Sarah his Wife,	"	24 January 1714.
Martha daughter of Edward Burbeck and Martha his Wife,	"	12 February 1714.
Hannah daughter of Nicholas Boon and Hannah his Wife,	"	10 February 1714.
Sarah daughter of Phillip Bargier and Mary his Wife,	"	25 December 1714.
Mary daughter of James Barnerd and Eliza. his Wife.	"	4 February 1714.
Eliza. daughter of Samuel Cunneball and Mary his Wife,	"	24 April 1714.
Robert Son of Henry Calley and Eliza. his Wife,	"	26 April 1714.

BIRTHS — 1714.

Thomas Son of Thomas Chamberlin and Sarah his Wife,	Born	14 May 1714.
Susanna daughter of Samuel Coverly and Susanna his Wife,	"	15 July 1714.
Thomas Son of Nathanll. Coney and Abigall his Wife,	"	2 July 1714.
Eliza. daughter of Ebenr. Clough and Thankfull his Wife,	"	23 September 1714.
David Son of David Copp and Patience his Wife,	"	25 October 1714.
Lydia daughter of David Colson and Hannah his Wife,	"	26 October 1714.
Androse Son of Androse Cannon and Sarah his Wife,	"	4 December 1714.
John Son of John Channing and Mary his Wife,	"	17 December 1714.
Hannah daughter of James Codner and Mary his Wife,	"	28 November 1714.
Susanna daughter of Jeremiah Condey and Susanna his Wife,	"	5 March 1713/4.
James Son of Thomas Chute and Mary his Wife,	"	1 January 1714.
Richard Son of John Cotta and Sarah his Wife,	"	13 January 1714.
Nathanll. Son of Job Coyt and Lydia his Wife,	"	18 January 1714.
James Son of John Clough and Mary his Wife,	"	25 January 1714.
Bethia daughter of Willm. Clear and Bethia his Wife,	"	2 February 1714.
Mary daughter of Josiah Clark and Priscilla his Wife,	"	1 February 1714.
Mary daughter of Joseph Cluley and Mary his Wife,	"	10 February 1714.
Andrew daughter of Robert Cock and Agnis his Wife,	"	7 February 1714.
Eliza daughter of John Dixwell and Mary his Wife,	"	17 March 1713/4.
Sarah daughter of John Demerry and Sarah his Wife,	"	12 April 1714.
Lydia daughter of Daniel Dupee and Lydia his Wife,	"	8 April 1714.
Lucey daughter of Addington Davenport Esq. and Eliza. his Wife,	"	11 June 1714.
John Son of Thomas Davise and Jane his Wife,	"	24 August 1714.
William Son of Shem Drown and Katherine his Wife,	"	22 September 1714.
Eliza. daughter of Zebadiah Daniel and Eliza. his Wife,	"	30 September 1714.
William Son of William Dillaway and Sarah his Wife,	"	1 December 1714.
Benja. Son of Benja. Eustice and Katherine his Wife,	"	19 December 1714.
John Son of John Eliot and Mariah his Wife,	"	25 February 1714.
William Son of Robert Ellis and Eliza. his Wife,	"	13 December 1714.
Jonathan Son of Jonathn. Eades and Joanna his Wife,	"	18 February 1714.
Hannah daughter of Benja. Flood and Mary his Wife,	"	15 March 1713/4.
Thomas Son of Thomas Freeman and Alice his Wife,	"	17 June 1714.
David Son of David Farnum and Dorothy his Wife,	"	30 June 1714.
Eliza. daughter of David Frankling and Eliza. his Wife,	"	15 June 1714.
William Son of William Fisk and Mary his Wife,	"	31 July 1714.
Thomas Son of Paul Farmer and Eliza. his Wife,	"	7 October 1714.
William Son of Nathanll. Fadroe and Isanna his Wife,	"	2 January 1714.
Margaret daughter of Francis Fredrick and Anne his Wife,	"	9 February 1714.

Gideon Son of Gidian Florence and Susanna his Wife,	Born	23 February 1714.
Mary daughter of John Foster and Mary his Wife,	"	16 February 1714.
Samuel Son of John Greenough and Eliza. his Wife,	"	26 June 1714.
Joseph Son of Samll. Gardener and Eliza. his Wife,	"	19 July 1714.
John Son of James Gibson and Mary his Wife,	"	8 July 1714.
Nathaniel } Gimi. of John Gerrish and Sarah his William } Wife,	"	11 October 1714.
John Son of Samuel Greenleaf and Martha his Wife.	"	10 December 1714.
Eliza. daughter of William Graham and Sarah his Wife,	"	11 December 1714.
Mary daughter of Thomas Gyles and Martha his Wife,	"	26 December 1714.
Thomas Son of Thomas Goodale and Rebecca his Wife,	"	1 January 1714.
Samuel Son of Samuel Grice and Priscilla his Wife,	"	5 January 1714.
John Son of Bartholl. Green and Jane his Wife,	"	20 January 1714.
Mary daughter of William Gurrin and Mary his Wife,	"	10 Febuary 1714.
Nathan Son of Nathan Howel and Katherine his Wife,	"	21 March 1713/4.
Mary daughter of Henry Harrise and Sarah his Wife.	"	20 April 1714.
Anne daughter of William Hutton and Anne his Wife,	"	20 May 1714.
Samuel Son of Samll. Holbrook and Hannah his Wife,	"	26 June 1714.
John Son of John Hunt and Rebecca his Wife,	"	18 April 1714.
Jane daughter of John Hobbs and Susanna his Wife,	"	1 September 1714.
Eliza. daughter of Francis Hudson and Mary his Wife,	"	10 September 1714.
Lydia daughter of Daniel Henchman and Eliza. his Wife,	"	4 October 1714.
Lydia daughter of Edward Hutchinson and Lydia his Wife,	"	30 September 1714.
Hannah daughter of Samuel Harris and Hannah his Wife,	"	10 October 1714.
Hannah daughter of Thomas Hutchinson Esq. and Sarah his Wife,	"	1 November 1714.
John Son of John Helyer and Eliza. his Wife,	"	7 December 1714.
Eliza. daughter of Israel How and Judeth his Wife,	"	23 June 1714.
Anne daughter of William Harris and Anne his Wife,	"	29 December 1714.
Christopher Son of John Holland and Susanna his Wife,	"	7 January 1714.
Benja. Son of John Harwood and Mary his Wife,	"	14 January 1714.
John Son of John Hayes and Hannah his Wife,	"	10 March 1714/5.
Mary daughter of John Jones and Eliza. his Wife,	"	15 March 1713/4.
Josiah Son of Jeremiah Jackson and Hannah his Wife,	"	27 March 1714.
Bethia daughter of Thomas Jones and Bethia his Wife,	"	21 May 1714.
Martha daughter of Joseph Jalla and Terasa his Wife,	"	7 July 1714.
Ephraim Son of John Jones and Margaret his Wife,	"	3 October 1714.
Mary daughter of John Jent and Abigall his Wife,	"	20 October 1714.
Thomas Son of Thomas Jenkins and Mary his Wife,	"	23 December 1714.

BIRTHS — 1714.

Hannah daughter of Joseph Jenkins and Hannah his Wife,	Born	11 February 1714.
Peter Son of Peter Joguet and Rebecca his Wife,	"	7 February 1714.
Rachel daughter of Jacob Key and Rachel his Wife,	"	8 March 1713/4.
Mehitabel daughter of Ebenr. Knight and Eliza. his Wife,	"	20 July 1714.
Stil-born daughter of Elijah Kenrick and Mary his Wife,	"	13 July 1714.
Josiah Son of Jonathan Loring and Eliza. his Wife,	"	17 April 1714.
Nicholas Winthrop Son of Thomas Leechmer and Anne his Wife,	"	13 June 1714.
Mary daughter of John Langdon and Mary his Wife,	"	20 June 1714.
John Son of George Lee and Eliza. his Wife,	"	12 October 1714.
Anne daughter of Nathan Lewis and Anne his Wife,	"	7 December 1714.
Daniel Son of Daniel Legeree and Ruth his Wife,	"	14 December 1714.
Hannah daughter of Ezekiel Lewis and Abigall his Wife,	"	14 September 1714.
Abigall daughter of William Lee and Mercey his Wife,	"	25 January 1714.
William Son of John Minzies and Edee his Wife,	"	9 March 1713/4.
Rachel daughter of Phillip Merrit and Mary his Wife,	"	22 March 1713/4.
Eliza. daughter of Capt. Edward Martyn and Sarah his Wife,	"	16 May 1714.
Abigall daughter of William Merchant and Abigall his Wife,	"	9 August 1714.
Paul Son of John Maverick and Eliza. his Wife,	"	10 April 1714.
Eliza. daughter of Samuel Mattox and Admonition his Wife,	"	13 November 1714.
James Son of James Man and Priscilla his Wife,	"	19 November 1714.
Ellen daughter of Joseph Marion and Ellen his Wife,	"	8 January 1714.
Jonathan Son of Jonathn. Mountfort and Hannah his Wife,	"	11 January 1714.
Edward Son of Edward Masters and Eliza. his Wife,	"	1 June 1714.
Sarah daughter of Joseph Merrifield and Margaret his Wife,	"	27 February 1714.
Theodora daughter of John Milton and Mary his Wife,	"	25 February 1714.
Mary daughter of Daniel North and Hannah his Wife,	"	1 June 1714.
Eliza. daughter of John Newton and Jane his Wife,	"	1 July 1714.
John Son of Clement Norman and Abigall his Wife,	"	13 November 1714.
Eliezur Son of Nathanll. Newel and Anne his Wife,	"	23 November 1714.
John Son of John Nicholls and Rebecca his Wife,	"	6 March 1714/5.
Benjamen Son of Robert Orange and Hannah his Wife,	"	24 March 1713/4.
Sarah daughter of John Orne and Eliza. his Wife,	"	23 September 1714.
Anthony Son of Anthony Oliver and Mary his Wife,	"	4 February 1714.
Mary daughter of David Porter and Mary his Wife,	"	17 March 1713/4.
Richard Son of John Pitts and Hannah his Wife,	"	29 March 1714.
Edward Son of Nathll. Payn of Bristoll and Sarah his Wife,	"	18 April 1714.
Allen Son of James Penneman and Mary his Wife,	"	10 June 1714.
Noah Son of John Petaile and Rachel his Wife,	"	8 July 1714.
John Son of William Palfrey and Abigall his Wife,	"	23 June 1714.
John Son of Stephen Parker and Margaret his Wife,	"	21 June 1714.
Richard Son of Robert Patteshall and Jane his Wife,	"	15 July 1714.

Remember daughter of John Pirkins and Remember his Wife,	Born	30 July 1714.
Peter Son of Edward Pell and Sarah his Wife,	"	17 September 1714.
Johanna daughter of Joseph Payson and Mehitabel his Wife,	"	25 September 1714.
Sarah daughter of Jonathan Peirse and Mary his Wife,	"	28 September 1714.
William Son of William Peirse and Sarah his Wife,	"	15 October 1714.
Eliza. daughter of Moses Peirse and Eliza. his Wife,	"	12 November 1714.
Eliza. daughter of Edward Proctor and Eliza. his Wife,	"	21 December 1714.
William Son of William Price and Eliza. his Wife,	"	18 December 1714.
William ⟩ Gimi. of William Parkman and Hannah Eliza. ⟩ his Wife,	"	7 January 1714.
Thomas Son of Indego Potter and Rebecca his Wife,	"	13 February 1714.
Hannah daughter of John Ruggles and Martha his Wife,	"	6 March 1713/4.
John Son of Joseph Russell and Mary his Wife,	"	5 May 1714.
Eliza. daughter of Samll. Robinson and Mary his Wife,	"	9 May 1714.
Sarah daughter of Richard Richardson and Sarah his Wife,	"	16 July 1714.
Mary daughter of Robert Randoll and Eliza. his Wife,	"	13 September 1714.
Rebecca daughter of Thomas Rowel and Dorothy his Wife,	"	15 July 1714.
Timothy Son of Timothy Robinson and Dorothy his Wife,	"	10 September 1714.
Judeth daughter of John Rawlings and Love his Wife,	"	5 October 1714.
Eliza. daughter of Francis Richbee and Eliza his Wife,	"	6 December 1714.
Deborah daughter of Samll. Rand and Sarah his Wife,	"	3 September 1714.
Mary daughter of John Shaw and Martha his Wife,	"	26 March 1714.
Jonathan Son of Malachy Salter and Sarah his Wife,	"	9 April 1714.
Eliza. daughter of Smalpeice and Olive his Wife,	"	5 May 1714.
Eliza. daughter of John Simkins and Eliza. his Wife,	"	25 May 1714.
Mary daughter of Simon Slocome and Eliza. his Wife,	"	19 May 1714.
David Son of Thomas Steel and Jane his Wife,	"	16 May 1714.
Samll. Son of Samll. Stebbins and Rachel his Wife,	"	10 July 1714.
Constantine Son of William Spencer and Mary his Wife,	"	23 July 1714.
Susanna daughter of Benja. Storar and Susanna his Wife,	"	5 August 1714.
Ruth daughter of William Smallage and Ruth his Wife,	"	3 September 1714.
Mary daughter of Jonathn. Simpson and Mary his Wife,	"	8 October 1714.
Sarah daughter of John Sale and Anne his Wife,	"	11 October 1714.
John Son of Nathanll. Storar and Margaret his Wife,	"	17 October 1714.
Abigall daughter of Eliezur Starr and Ruth his Wife,	"	1 November 1714.
Samll. Son of James Scolley and Deborah his Wife,	"	15 November 1714.

BIRTHS — 1714.

Mary daughter of Jonathn. Sharp and Deborah his Wife,	Born	8 December 1714.
Bridget daughter of William Sanders and Bridget his Wife,	"	14 December 1714.
Hannah daughter of Joseph Savil and Margaret his Wife,	"	25 November 1714.
Sarah daughter of John Savil and Priscilla his Wife,	"	16 January 1714.
Tregoweth Son of Roger Tilbort and Hannah his Wife,	"	1 April 1714.
Edward Son of Edward Tillet and Hannah his Wife,	"	7 April 1714.
Anna daughter of Issac Townsend and Anna his Wife,	"	27 June 1714.
Rachel daughter of James Townesend and Alice his Wife,	"	13 July 1714.
Joshua Son of Joshua Thomas and Anna his Wife,	"	16 August 1714.
Eliza. daughter of Peter Thomas and Eliza. his Wife,	"	18 August 1714.
Joseph Son of Noah Tucker and Mary his Wife,	"	19 August 1714.
Samuel Son of Edward Tuttle and Joanna his Wife,	"	10 February 1714.
Deborah daughter of Cornelius Thayer and Lydia his Wife,	"	27 January 1714.
John Son of Samll. Tuttle and Abigall his Wife,	"	14 February 1714.
Thomas Son of Benja. Varney and Sarah his Wife,	"	19 September 1714.
John Lewis Son of John Lewis Venteno and Eliza. his Wife,	"	17 January 1714.
John Son of John Vryland and Mary his Wife,	"	9 February 1714.
Sarah daughter of Thomas Willet and Mary his Wife,	"	21 April 1714.
Ebenr. Son of Samll. Willis and Eliza. his Wife,	"	27 April 1714.
Eliza. daughter of Benja. Williams and Eliza. his Wife,	"	4 May 1714.
John Son of John Whitemore and Eliza. his Wife,	"	8 May 1714.
Mary daughter of John Wyat and Mary his Wife,	"	19 May 1714.
Joseph Son of Joseph Webb aud Deborah his Wife,	"	29 July 1714.
Eliza daughter of Allen Wild and Eliza. his Wife,	"	10 July 1714.
John Son of John Willis and Sarah his Wife,	"	22 August 1714.
Prudence daughter of Edward White and Sarah his Wife,	"	21 August 1714.
Sarah daughter of Charles Wager and Sarah his Wife,	"	26 August 1714.
Joseph Son of Joseph White and Eliza. his Wife,	"	10 November 1714.
Samll. Son of Ebenr. Wentworth and Rebecca his Wife,	"	15 November 1714.
John Son of Collo. Adam Winthrop and Anne his Wife,	"	8 December 1714.
John Son of Isaac White and Rebecca his Wife,	"	7 December 1714
Sarah daughter of Samll. Whitehed and Mary his Wife,	"	1 January 1714.
Eliza. daughter of John Wood and Anne his Wife,	"	25 January 1714.
Sarah daughter of Nathll. Weeler and Mary his Wife,	"	13 May 1714.
Joseph Son of Thomas Welch and Eliza. his Wife,	"	29 January 1714.
Grace daughter of John Welland and Eliza his Wife,	"	28 January 1714.
Hannah daughter of Hannah Woodbery and Hannah his Wife,	"	15 February 1714.
Sarah daughter of Thomas Yates and Mary his Wife,	"	21 March 1713/4.
Ebenezer Son of Ebenr. Youngman and Mercy his Wife,	"	1 January 1714.

Thomas Son of Jabish Crowel and Sarah his Wife,	Born	18 January 1714.
Moses Son of Joshua Felt and Anne his Wife,	"	22 December 1714.
Eliza. daughter of James How and Abigall his Wife,	"	26 December 1714.
Joseph Son of Joseph Jackson and Eliza. his Wife,	"	20 November 1714.
David Son of David Jefferyes and Katherin his Wife,	"	23 October 1714.
Joseph Son of Joseph Ingraham and Mary his Wife,	"	7 July 1714.
Robert Son of Nathanll. Kenny and Eliza. his Wife,	"	'30 December 1714.
Mary daughter of Francis More and Mary his Wife,	"	25 February 1714.
Leveret Son of James Oliver and Rebecca his Wife,	"	23 February 1714.
Deborah daughter of John Oulton and Deborah his Wife,	"	23 November 1714.
Paige Son of Nathll. Oliver and Martha his Wife,	"	3 February 1714.
Jonathan Son of Jonathn. Pickerin and Eliza. his Wife,	"	14 January 1714.
Sarah daughter of Joshua Preble and Sarah his Wife,	"	9 October 1714.
Daniel Son of Joseph Turel and Joanna his Wife,	"	22 February 1714.
Joseph Son of John Royall and Eliza. his Wife,	"	23 January 1714.
Mary daughter of Joseph Treat and Mary his Wife,	"	3 May 1714.
Daniel Son of Henry Timberlake and Mary his Wife,	"	6 September 1714.
Elihu Son of Jonathan Wardel and Frances his Wife,	"	25 January 1714.
Joanna daughter of Ralph Wood and Mary his Wife,	"	19 July 1714.
John Son of James Barter and Eliza. his Wife,	"	13 June 1714.
Jane daughter of George Bethune and Mary his Wife,	"	15 June 1714.
James Son of Robert Calef and Margaret his Wife	"	7 November 1714.
William Son of Grove Hirst and Eliza. his Wife,	"	5 August 1714.
John Son of Daniel Munden and Anne his Wife,	"	7 November 1714.
Mary daughter of James Melven and Mercy his Wife,	"	5 November 1714.
James Son of James Packanet and Mary his Wife,	"	4 February 1714.
Anne daughter of Benja. Bird and Johanna his Wife,	"	27 November 1714.
Thomas surnamed Siûit Son of Thos. Quaquo Negro,	"	14 October 1714.
John Son of Joseph Urann and Sarah his Wife,	"	3 February 1714.
Hannah daughter of William Payn and Hannah his Wife,	"	10 March 1714.
Sarah daughter of Elisha Storey and Sarah his Wife,	"	8 September 1714.
Magdalin daughter of John Dupee and Naomi his Wife,	"	7 December 1714.
William Son of Samuel Whitwell and Eliza. his Wife,	"	25 September 1714.
Susanna daughter of Samuel Kenney and Abigall his Wife,	"	5 March 1714.
Joseph Son of John Russel and Eliza. his Wife,	"	31 March 1714.
Gilbert Son of Benjamin and Mary Bronsdon,	"	22 February 1714.
John Son of Thomas and Hannah Moulin,	"	8 October 1714.
Dean Son of Dean and Martha Grover,	"	5 February 1714.
Hannah daughter of Jonathan and Hannah Kemball,	"	1 December 1714.
Mary daughter of Joseph and Sarah Rayner,	"	3 July 1714.

1715.

	Born	
Winborn Son of Hugh Adams and Susanna his Wife,	Born	19 April 1715.
Richard Son of Moses Abbot and Rebecca his Wife,	"	29 May 1715.
Joseph Son of Joseph Arthur and Abigall his Wife,	"	2 July 1715.
Phillip Son of Oliver Atwood and Anne his Wife,	"	14 May 1715.
Mercy daughter of Isaac Anthony and Mercy his Wife,	"	4 November 1715.
John Son of John Adams and Mary his Wife,	"	27 November 1715.
Mary daughter of Benjamin Alford and Rachel his Wife,	"	27 November 1715.
Richard Son of Samll. Adams and Mary his Wife,	"	21 January 1715.
John Son of John Bushel and Rebecca his Wife,	"	18 March 1714/5.
Lydia daughter of Collo. John Ballentine and Mary his Wife,	"	31 March 1715.
Mary daughter of John Beard and Mary his Wife,	"	28 March 1715.
Thomas Son of George Brock and Mary his Wife.	"	5 April 1715.
Benjamen Son of Benjamen Bridge and Christian his Wife,	"	27 April 1715.
Mary daughter of Jeremiah Belknap and Sarah his Wife,	"	9 May 1715.
Jacob Son of Jacob Blanchard and Abigall his Wife.	"	25 May 1715.
Mary daughter of John Herculus Brilsford and Mary his Wife,	"	11 May 1715.
Mary daughter of Joseph Brightman and Mary his Wife,	"	7 July 1715.
Mary daughter of Thomas Beetle and Eliza. his Wife,	"	3 August 1715.
Thomas Son of Zabdiel Boylston and Jerusha his Wife,	"	30 July 1715.
John Son of John Bolderson and Sarah his Wife,	"	18 August 1715.
Anne daughter of Samuel Bligh and Anne his Wife,	"	31 July 1715.
Samuel Son of James Bodwain and Hannah his Wife,	"	25 July 1715.
Nathaniel Son of Thomas Baker and Thankfull his Wife,	"	9 August 1715.
Benjamen Son of John Baker and Mary his Wife,	"	12 August 1715.
Samuel Son of Jonathan Burnel and Susanna his Wife,	"	24 September 1715.
Solomon Son of John Beal and Eliza. his Wife,	"	30 September 1715.
Silence daughter of Thomas Barnerd and Silence his Wife,	"	12 October 1715.
Susanna daughter of Mathew Butler and Sarah his Wife,	"	12 October 1715.
Mary daughter of William Barnes and Mary his Wife,	"	23 October 1715.
Joseph Son of Adam Beath and Mary his Wife,	"	16 October 1715.
Mary daughter of Stephen Boutineau and Mary his Wife,	"	5 August 1715.
Sarah daughter of John Brewster and Deliverence his Wife,	"	16 November 1715.
Anne daughter of Peter Butler and Mary his Wife,	"	10 July 1715.
John Son of Benja. Ballard and Ann his Wife,	"	8 November 1715.
John Son of John Barton and Katherine his Wife,	"	26 August 1715.
Gardener Son of Daniel Ballard and Dorcas his Wife,	"	18 December 1715.

Eliza. daugnter of Jonathan Boman and Mary his Wife,	Born	8 January 1715.
John Son of Benja. Bramley and Dorcas his Wife,	"	6 January 1715.
Sarah daughter of Josiah Biles and Abigall his Wife,	"	16 January 1715.
Susanna daughter of Freeborn Balch and Susanna his Wife,	"	11 February 1715.
James Son of James Barnerd and Eliza. his Wife,	"	10 February 1715.
Mary daughter of John Chamberlin and Hanna his Wife,	"	5 March 1714/5.
Stephen Son of John Charnock and Mary his Wife,	"	14 April 1715.
Eliza. daughter of Samll. Clark and Sarah his Wife,	"	21 April 1715.
Mary daughter of Edward Carpinter and Eliza his Wife,	"	24 April 1715.
Eliza. daughter of Thomas Colsworthy and Sarah his Wife,	"	15 May 1715.
Joseph Son of Joseph Cooledge and Hannah his Wife,	"	24 May 1715.
Martha daughter of William Champlin and Martha his Wife,	"	4 July 1715.
Abigall daughter of Andrew Cunningham and Mary his Wife,	"	5 July 1715.
William Son of William Clagget and Mary his Wife,	"	22 June 1715.
Joseph Son of Benja. Clough and Faith his Wife,	"	13 July 1715.
Joseph Son of John Center and Ruth his Wife,	"	5 August 1715.
John Son of James Carey and Sarah his Wife,	"	12 October 1715.
Margaret daughter of Salmagrave Claxton and Margaret his Wife,	"	17 December 1715.
Ezekiel Son of Ezekiel Cleasby and Abigall his Wife,	"	11 December 1715.
John Charles Saint ⟩ Charles DeLatour and An-Estinne Son of ⟨ gelique his Wife,	"	20 March 1714/5.
Mehitabel daughter of John Done and Abiah his Wife,	"	4 April 1715.
John Son of Robert Darby and Martha his Wife,	"	4 May 1715.
Samll. Son of Samll. Davis and Katherin his Wife,	"	11 May 1715.
George Son of John Dolbear and Sarah his Wife,	"	1 June 1715.
Anne daughter of Samll. Durant and Eliza. his Wife,	"	5 May 1715.
David Son of Edward Durant and Mary his Wife,	"	22 March 1714/5.
Thomas Son of Thoms. Debuke and Jamina his Wife,	"	11 June 1715.
Mary daughter of Benja. Dresser and Lydia his Wife,	"	13 June 1715
Anne daughter of John Davis and Eliza. his Wife,	"	8 July 1715.
Jonathn. Son of Charles Deming and Sarah his Wife,	"	25 June 1715.
Hannah daughter of Samll. Duncan and Mary his Wife,	"	22 July 1715.
John Son of Ralph Ditchfeeld and Margaret his Wife,	"	30 July 1715.
Hannah daughter of Thomas Demery and Hannah his Wife,	"	3 August 1715.
John Son of John Dorothy and Eliza. his Wife,	"	7 September 1715.
Anna daughter of Thoms. Down and Anna his Wife,	"	4 September 1715.
Susanna daughter of Thomas Davis and Sarah his Wife,	"	14 August 1715.

Births — 1715.

Isaac Son of Daniel Dupee and Lydia his Wife, Born	17 October 1715.
James ⎫ Sons of Henry Dillaway and Abigall his	
John ⎭ Wife, "	8 November 1715.
Michael Son of Ebenr. Dennis and Susanna his Wife, "	11 December 1715.
Eliza. daughter of Henry Dering and Eliza. his Wife, "	20 November 1715.
Thomas Son of Shem Drown and Katherine his Wife, "	14 December 1715.
Lydia daughter of Thomas Dagget and Lydia his Wife, "	27 January 1715.
Hephsiba daughter of Samuel Emms and Hephsiba his Wife, "	31 May 1715.
Susanna daughter of Benja. Eliot and Susanna his Wife, "	5 June 1715.
William Son of Edward Enstone and Mary his Wife, "	11 June 1715.
Eliza. daughter of Nathanll. Emms and Hannah his Wife, "	26 October 1715.
William Son of William Eustas and Eliza. his Wife, "	7 February 1715.
Thomas Son of Thomas Flagg and Hannah his Wife, "	20 June 1715.
John Son of John Fairwether and Jerusha his Wife. "	24 July 1715.
Mary daughter of Robert Frost and Mary his Wife, "	24 August 1715.
Hannah daughter of Abraham Francis and Hannah his Wife, "	24 September 1715.
Mary daughter of Thomas Foster and Anne his Wife. '	26 October 1715.
Mary daughter of Hopestill Foster and Eliza his Wife, "	29 August 1715.
Nataniel ⎫ Sons of Ephraim Fenno and Eliza. his	
Barnes ⎭ Wife, "	31 December 1715.
William Son of Jonathan Farnum and Anne his Wife, "	12 January 1715.
Eliza. daughter of Thomas Fleming and Eliza. his Wife, "	1 March 1715/6.
Hannah daughter of Bartholomew Gussear and Eliza. his Wife. "	23 April 1715.
Samuel Son of Samuel Gerrish and Sarah his Wife, "	17 May 1715.
Sarah daughter of Lately Gee and Sarah his Wife, "	23 July 1715.
Robert Son of John Gill and Rebecca his Wife, "	22 August 1715.
Ellis Son of Edward Grey and Hannah his Wife, "	7 September 1715.
Sarah daughter of Obadiah Gore and Sarah his Wife, "	29 December 1715.
Simon Son of John Greenliefe and Eliza. his Wife, "	9 January 1715.
Daniel Son of Daniel Goffe and Eliza. his Wife, "	26 January 1715.
Eliza. daughter of John Goldthwait and Sarah his Wife. "	31 October 1715.
Richard Son of Richard Huges and Sarah his Wife, "	15 March 1714/5.
Abigall daughter of Henry Howel and Martha his Wife, "	14 April 1715.
Thomas Son of Joshua Hensha and Mary his Wife. "	1 April 1715.
Chanterlin Son of William Harrison and Mary his Wife, "	4 May 1715.
Mary daughter of Thomas Holland and Anne his Wife, "	21 May 1715.
Hannah daughter of Samll. Hewes and Hannah his Wife, "	19 May 1715.

Zacheriah Son of Joseph Hall and Blanch his Wife, Born		10 May 1715.
Samuel Son of Samuel Hunt and Mary his Wife,	"	25 July 1715.
Rebecca daughter of William Hart and Katherine his Wife,	"	25 August 1715.
James Son of John Hubbart and Eliza. his Wife,	"	14 August 1715.
Sarah daughter of Charles Howel and Sarah his Wife,	"	21 August 1715.
Samuel Son of William Healey and Sarah his Wife,	"	11 September 1715.
Mary daughter of Thomas Huddiball and Mary his Wife,	"	7 September 1715.
Samuel Son of Samuel Harris and Rachel his Wife,	"	4 October 1715.
Joseph Son of Asa Hasie and Mary his Wife,	"	7 October 1715.
William Son of William Hunstable and Sarah his Wife,	"	18 November 1715.
John Son of John Hunt and Rebecca his Wife,	"	13 November 1715.
John Son of Richard Hazely and Tamozine his Wife,	"	13 December 1715.
William } Gimmi of James Habersham and Mehitabel his Wife, Mary }	"	2 February 1715.
Edward Son of Edward Hutchinson Esq. and Lydia his Wife,	"	24 January 1715.
Elisha Son of Thomas Hutchinson Esqr. and Sarah his Wife,	"	6 February 1715.
Sarah daughter of Ephraim Hunt and Johanna his Wife,	"	1 March 1715/6·
Jabez Son of Jonathan Jackson and Mary his Wife,	"	25 March 1715.
Thomas Son of Abel Jones and Ruth his Wife,	"	25 April 1715.
Robert Son of Robert Ingolls and Anna his Wife,	"	16 July 1715.
Eliza. daughter of John Jones and Eliza. his Wife,	"	20 August 1715.
Faith daughter of Jeremiah Jackson and Hannah his Wife,	"	24 November 1715.
Frances daughter of Nathanll. Josling and Frances his Wife,	"	23 January 1715.
Mary daughter of Samuel Jones and Mary his Wife,	"	17 February 1715.
John Son of John Indecot and Rebecca his Wife,	"	18 March 1715/6.
John Son of Thomas Kilby and Mary his Wife,	"	25 March 1715.
Abigall daughter of John Kent and Abigall his Wife,	"	24 August 1715.
Mary daughter of Henry Kenner and Abigall his Wife,	"	14 October 1715.
Oliver Son of Oliver Luckis and Rebecca his Wife,	"	22 March 1714/5.
John Son of John Leech and Ruth his Wife,	"	16 March 1714/5.
Benjamen Son of Thomas Lee and Anna his Wife,	"	15 April 1715.
Esther daughter of Samll. Langdon and Esther his Wife,	"	12 May 1715.
Eliza. daughter of Thomas Lee and Deborah his Wife,	"	22 May 1715.
Caleb Son of Caleb Lymon and Susanna his Wife,	"	27 July 1715.
James Son of John Lovel and Priscilla his Wife,	"	24 August 1715.
Thomas Son of Nathanll. Loring and Susanna his Wife,	"	20 August 1715.
Isaac Son of Samll. Lobden and Sarah his Wife,	"	6 July 1715.
James Son of Joseph Lowden and Hannah his Wife,	"	21 September 1715.
Mary daughter of Henry Lowder and Abigall his Wife,	"	28 October 1715.
Samuell Son of William Letherbee and Lydia his Wife,	"	18 December 1715.
Isaac Son of Michael Leyton and Sarah his Wife,	"	28 December 1715.

Births — 1715.

Eliza. daughter of Peter Lamarkin and Sarah his Wife,	Born	24 January 1715.
Mary daughter of Joseph Landon and Joanna his Wife,	"	28 January 1715.
Eliza. daughter of John Letherbee and Eliza his Wife,	"	4 February 1715.
Henry Son of Ralph Maire and Martha his Wife,	"	8 March 1714/5.
Eleshaway daughter of John Man and Abigall his Wife,	"	8 March 1714/5.
Eliza. daughter of Lewis Mallet and Margaret his Wife,	"	6 April 1715.
Samuel Son of Samuel Marion and Mary his Wife,	"	2 June 1715.
Deborah daughter of Nathanll. Man and Abigall his Wife,	"	29 May 1715.
Eliza. daughter of John Meers and Sarah his Wife,	"	9 June 1715.
Sarah daughter of Joseph Morgan and Grace his Wife,	"	2 June 1715.
Peter Son of Peter Mires and Mary his Wife,	"	21 June 1715.
Samuel Son of John Merefield and Bridget his Wife,	"	15 September 1715.
Hannah daughter of William Man and Hannah his Wife,	"	17 November 1715.
Sarah daughter of Ellias Martyn and Eliza. his Wife,	"	26 November 1715.
John Son of Charles Morris and Esther his Wife,	"	8 December 1715.
William Son of William Marshall and Hannah his Wife,	"	13 November 1715.
Samuel Son of William Mallard and Abigall his Wife,	"	1 January 1715.
Eliza. daughter of Daniel Macdaniel and Mary his Wife,	"	16 February 1715.
James Son of James Nolan and Hannah his Wife,	"	20 April 1715.
Hager daughter of Nanney Negro of Mr. Wm. Harriss. —	"	12 August 1715.
Anne daughter of Abrm. Nicholls and Rebecca his Wife,	"	27 July 1715.
William Son of William Noyes and Hannah his Wife,	"	19 October 1715.
Robert Son of Robt. Soco Negro and Fidella his Wife,	"	24 December 1715.
Mehitabel daughter of Robert Orange and Hannah his Wife,	"	11 April 1715.
Nicholas Son of John Oliver and Alice his Wife,	"	8 August 1715.
Sarah daughter of John Osborn and Sarah his Wife,	"	22 September 1715.
Ann daughter of Brattle Oliver and Anne his Wife,	"	18 November 1715.
Margaret daughter of Patrick Oglesbee and Margaret his Wife,	"	18 October 1715.
Thoms. Son of John Pumery and Lydia his Wife,	"	5 April 1715,
Elizabeth daughter of Jonathn. Pickerin and Eliza. his Wife,	"	3 April 1715.
Sarah daughter of Daniel Pecker and Sarah his Wife,	"	19 April 1715.
William Son of William Preeson and Rachel his Wife,	"	29 May 1715.
Benja. Son of Benja. Phillips and Hannah his Wife,	"	3 June 1715.
Eliza. daughter of Richard Pitcher and Grace his Wife,	"	6 June 1715.
Amorel daughter of John Padon and Amorel his Wife,	"	9 April 1715.
Mary daughter of William Parteridg and Rachel his Wife,	"	5 June 1715.

James Son of Francis Plasted and Hannah his Wife, Born 7 July 1715.
Samuel Son of Samuel Proctor and Mary his Wife, " 20 July 1715.
Hannah daughter of James Pemberton and Hannah Wife, " 10 March 1714/5.
Barbary daughter of Thoms. Palmer Esq. and Abigall his Wife, " 24 July 1715.
Edward Son of Edward Paige and Ruth his Wife, " 11 September 1715.
Samuel Son of Samuel Pousley and Eliza. his Wife, " 13 September 1715.
Thoms. Son of Samll. Peck and Eliza. his Wife, " 17 October 1715.
Hannah daughter of Thoms. Plasteed and Mary his Wife, " 28 October 1715.
Ebenezer Son of Ebenr. Prat and Rachel his Wife, " 16 November 1715.
Hannah daughter of Bryant Parrot and Abigall his Wife, " 18 November 1715.
William Son of John Peak and Sarah his Wife, " 4 December 1715.
Sarah daughter of Henry Pereno and Desire his Wife, " 16 January 1715.
Eliza. daughter of Isaac Peirse and Grace his Wife, " 17 January 1715.
Lydia daughter of Timothy Prout and Lydia his Wife, " 13 March 1714/5.
Eliza. daughter of John Peirse and Eliza. his Wife, " 19 February 1715.
Joseph Son of Nathanll. Peirse and Abigall his Wife, " 16 February 1715.
Anne daughter of James Pecker and Susanna his Wife, " 13 March 1715/6.
Still-born Son of James Redworth and Lydia his Wife, " 13 May 1715.
Peter Son of Peter Roliston and Eliza. his Wife. " 6 June 1715.
Henry Son of Henry Reading and Experience his Wife, " 1 June 1715.
Abigall daughter of Thoms. Ruck and Mary his Wife, " 4 June 1715.
Samuel Son of Samuel Right and Mary his Wife, " 13 July 1715.
Eliza. daughter of Samuel Robinson and Mary his Wife, " 3 September 1715.
Jane daughter of Jonathn. Rouse and Martha his Wife, " 23 August 1715.
Susanna daughter of Robert Rand and Susanna his Wife, " 12 February 1715.
Eliza. daughter of Capt. Thoms. Smith and Mary his Wife, " 1 March 1714/5.
Hannah daughter of Abrm. Smith and Mary his Wife, " 17 March 1714/5.
Peter Son of Joseph Scot and Deliverence his Wife, " 13 March 1714/5.
Thomas Son of Thomas Salter and Margaret his Wife, " 5 April 1715.
Samuel Son of ye Rd. Joseph Sewel and Eliza. his Wife, " 2 May 1715.
James Son of John Strong and Lydia his Wife, " 6 May 1715.
Abigall daughter of Jacob Sheafe and Mary his Wife, " 28 June 1715.
Henry Son of Edward Stanbridge and Mildred his Wife, " 16 June 1715.
Thomas Son of Thoms. Staples and Eliza. his Wife, " 5 July 1715.
Arthur Son of Habijah Savage and Hannah his Wife, " 19 July 1715.

Mary daughter of David Sinkler and Mary his Wife, Born 18 September 1715.
Ruth daughter of William Smallage and Ruth his Wife, " 5 October 1715.
Mary daughter of Ebenr. Scot and Sarah his Wife, " 28 May 1715.
Mary daughter of Joseph Snelling and Rebecca his Wife, " 6 November 1715.
Mary daughter of David Stoddard and Eliza. his Wife, " 11 November 1715.
James Son of Samll. Salter and Sarah his Wife, " 29 July 1715.
Edward Son of Edward Samson and Lettice his Wife, " 22 November 1715.
William Son of Benja. Street and Mary his Wife, " 11 September 1715.
Sarah daughter of John Smalpeice and Olive his Wife, " 20 January 1715.
Martha daughter of John Shaw and Martha his Wife, " 26 January 1715.
John Son of William Seers and Eliza. his Wife, " 8 February 1715
Holmes Son of John Simpson and Rely his Wife, " 9 February 1715.
John Son of Erasamus Stevens and Peirses his Wife, " 8 November 1715.
Abigall daughter of ye Honble William Tayler Esqr. and Abigall his Wife, " 16 March 1714/5.
John Son of Benja. Thwing and Rebecca his Wife, " 6 May 1715.
Thomas Son of Thomas Townsend and Eliza. his Wife, " 6 August 1715.
Deborah daughter of Joseph Thorn and Deborah his Wife, " 2 August 1715.
Mary daughter of Abrm. Townsend and Mary his Wife, " 2 November 1715.
Susanna daughter of George Thomas and Susanna his Wife. " 19 October 1715.
John Son of John Thwing and Mary his Wife, " 8 January 1715.
Mary daughter of John Tucker and Mary his Wife, " 26 December 1715.
Gillam Son of ye Honble. Willm. Tayler Esq. and Abigall his Wife, " 23 January 1715.
Patience daughter of James Townsend and Alice his Wife, " 22 January 1715.
Soloman Son of Soloman Townsend and Esther his Wife, " 25 August 1715.
Moses Son of Peter Thomas and Eliza. his Wife, " 25 February 1715.
Mary daughter of Elhanan Winchister and Mary his Wife, " 4 April 1715.
Sarah daughter of David Webb and Jane his Wife, " 19 March 1714/5.
Edward Son of Edward Wilkinson and Rebecca his Wife, " 12 April 1715.
Judeth daughter of Ebenr. Williston and Judeth his Wife, " 25 April 1715.
Sarah daughter of Cord Wing and Sarah his Wife, " 12 June 1715.
Loise daughter of William Waters and Loise his Wife, " 17 June 1715.
Sarah daughter of Joseph Williams and Sarah his Wife, " 20 June 1715.
Cornelius Son of Cornelius Waldo and Faith his Wife, " 25 April 1715.
Peter Son of Peter White and Sarah his Wife, " 19 July 1715.
Ruth daughter of William Whetcomb and Mary his Wife, " 31 August 1715.
Benja. Son of Benja. White and Mary his Wife, " 4 September 1715.
Samuel Son of Nathanl. Woodward and Priscilla his Wife, " 15 September 1715.

John Son of John Willis and Sarah his Wife,	Born	30 September 1715.
Anna daughter of Thoms. Wardel and Anna his Wife,	"	6 October 1715.
John Son of Richard Woods and Hannah his Wife,	"	16 November 1715.
Sarah daughter of Robert Williams and Sarah his Wife,	"	17 November 1715.
Joseph Son of Joseph Williams and Sarah his Wife,	"	25 December 1715.
Peter Son of Abrm. Wacome and Abigall his Wife,	"	30 December 1715.
Hepsibah daughter of Jona. Williams and Rebecca his Wife,	"	19 February 1715.
Daniel Son of Daniel Whitemore and Mary his Wife,	"	2 February 1715.
Eliza. daughter of John Young and Mary his Wife,	"	22 July 1715.
Isaiah Son of Samll. Barret and Sarah his Wife,	"	8 November 1715.
Eliza. daughter of James Barter and Eliza. his Wife,	"	13 November 1715.
Nathaniel Son of George Bethune and Mary his Wife,	"	25 July 1715.
Benjamin Son of Benja. Bagnald and Eliz. his Wife,	"	17 March 1714/5.
Mary daughter of Jeremiah Condey and Susana his Wife,	"	5 December 1715.
Thomas Son of Edward Eades and Susana his Wife,	"	11 April 1715.
Aaron Son of Joshua Felt and Anne his Wife,	"	21 January 1715.
John Son of John Grainger and Mary his Wife,	"	27 October 1715.
Joseph Son of Joseph Hood and Judeth his Wife.	"	3 November 1715.
Margaret daughter of Benja. Haley and Susana his Wife,	"	2 March 1714/5.
Elizabeth daughter of Willm. Maccarty and Margt. his Wife,	"	8 December 1715.
John Son of William Nichols and Bethia his Wife,	"	29 February 1715.
Mary daughter of John Oulton and Deborah his Wife,	"	12 December 1715.
Thomas Son of Willm. Parker and Anna his Wife,	"	19 January 1715.
Barbery daughter of Thoms. Palmer Esqr. and Abigall his Wife,	"	28 July 1715.
William Son of William Rand and Sarah his Wife,	"	31 March 1715.
Malachy Son of Malachy Salter and Sarah his Wife,	"	28 February 1715.
Elizabeth daughter of Wm. Short and Eliza. his Wife,	"	27 February 1715.
William Son of Benja. Simpson and Eliza. his Wife,	"	6 August 1715.
Daniel Son of Andrew Sigorney and Mary his Wife,	"	17 Novemher 1715.
Elizabeth daughter of Peter Cross and Eliza. his Wife,	"	16 February 1715.
Samuel Son of Nicholas Dun and Deborah his Wife,	"	24 November 1715.
Anna daughter of Samuel Eaton and Ruth his Wife,	"	7 August 1715.
Mary daughter of Anthony Oliver and Mary his Wife,	"	16 February 1715.
Hannah daughter of Phillip Rawlings and Hannah his Wife,	"	5 July 1715.
Mary daughter of John Vallentine and Mary his Wife,	"	23 March 1714/5.
Jacob Son of Jacob Wendall and Sarah his Wife,	"	4 September 1715.
Eliza daughter of William Cowel and Eliza. his Wife,	"	27 December 1715.
Edward Son of Edward Durant and Judeth his Wife,	"	7 February 1715.
Samuel Son of Samuel Deming and Hannah his Wife,	born	22 September 1715.

Births — 1715-16.

Mary daughter of Thomas Frank and Rachel his Wife,	Born	16 August 1715.
Sarah daughter of William Payn and Hannah his Wife,	"	5 October 1715.
Thomas Son of John Stocker and Abigall his Wife,	"	25 March 1715.
Thomas Son of Thomas Bostick and Abigall his Wife,	"	17 April 1715.
John Son of Samson Jarvise and Mary his Wife,	"	8 November 1715.
Anne daughter of William Inggs and Anne his Wife,	"	2 October 1715.
Joseph Son of Joseph and Mary Balch,	"	13 January 1715.
Benjamin Son of Benjamin and Mary Bronsdon	"	28 February 1715.
Anna daughter of David and Elizabeth Franklyn,	"	18 September 1715.
William Son of William and Elizabeth Fairfield,	"	23 January 1715.
John Son of John and Prudence Grover,	"	27 July 1715.
Rebekah daughter of William and Elizabeth Keen,	"	17 October 1715.
Elizabeth daughter of Joseph and Elizabeth Ricks,	"	16 March 1715.
Elizabeth daughter of John and Elizabeth Watts,	"	11 October 1715.
William Son of Richard and Sarah Bill,	"	31 August 1715.
Jonathan Son of John and Dorcas Mason,	"	18 August 1715.

1716.

Edward Son of Francis Archbald and Huldah his Wife,	Born	24 March, 1715/6.
Eliza. daughter of Jeremiah Allen and Mary his Wife,	"	12 June 1716.
Joseph Son of Isaac Adams and Martha his Wife,	"	18 August 1716.
Mehetabel daughter of Samll. Avis and Mary his Wife,	"	3 December 1716.
Mary daughter of Edward Aires and Rebecca his Wife.	"	16 February 1716.
Rebecca daughter of Benja. Brown and Mary his Wife,	"	1 April 1716.
Joseph Son of Joseph Bean and Hannah his Wife,	"	16 April 1716.
Susana daughter of Willm. Bill and Susana his Wife,	"	8 May 1716.
Henry Son of Henry Bridgham and Lydia his Wife,	"	11 June 1716.
Sarah daughter of John Briggs and Katherine his Wife,	"	17 June 1716.
Mary daughter of Joseph Bissit and Mary his Wife,	"	28 June 1716
Eliza. daughter of John Braddick and Mary his Wife,	"	11 July 1716.
John Son of John Bolderson and Sarah his Wife,	"	22 July 1716.
John Son of John Buckley and Eliza. his Wife,	"	16 July 1716.
Willm. Son of Edward Burbeck and Martha his Wife,	"	22 July 1716.
Eliza. daughter of Nicholas Boon and Hannah his Wife,	"	11 September 1716.
Thomas Son of John Barnerd and Sarah his Wife.	"	17 August 1716
Ebenezar Son of Ebenr. Burges and Eliza. his Wife,	"	21 July 1716.
Solomon Son of Solomon Blake and Abigall his Wife,	"	1 September 1716.
Henry Son of Henry Brightman and Eliza. his Wife,	"	1 September 1716.
Margaret daughter of Willm. Brown and Lydia his Wife,	"	24 September 1716.
William Son of William Bearstow and Eliza. his Wife,	"	4 October 1716.
Benjamen Son of John Baley and Mehitabel his Wife,	"	4 October 1716.

John Son of John Ballentine and Mary his Wife,	Born	30 October 1716.
Sarah daughter of John Buttolph and Mehitabel his Wife,	"	28 September 1716.
Jonathan Son of Jonathn. Boman and Mary his Wife,	"	18 November 1716.
Eliakim Son of Eliakim Blackman and Ruth his Wife,	"	14 November 1716.
Ebenezar Son of Ebenr. Bridg and Mary his Wife,	"	. 4 March 1715/6.
William Son of Willm. Bushnel and Mehitabel his Wife,	"	2 December 1716.
Joseph Son of Joseph Bosworth and Mary his Wife,	"	11 December 1716.
Eliza daughter of Zabdiel Boylston and Jerusha his Wife,	"	4 January 1716.
John Son of John Burt and Abigall his Wife,	"	29 December 1716.
Eliza. daughter of Benja. Bagnald and Eliza. his Wife,	"	7 December 1716.
John Son of James Barnes and Mary his Wife,	"	16 February 1716.
Joseph Son of Joseph Brightman and Mary his Wife,	"	19 January 1716.
Joseph Son of Jeremiah Belknap and Sarah his Wife,	"	12 February 1716.
Mathew Son of Mathew Bedlington and Eunice his Wife,	"	24 February 1716.
Phillip Son of Phillip Bongarden and Eliza. his Wife,	"	21 February 1716.
Sarah daughter of Thomas Baker and Thankfull his Wife,	"	13 February 1716.
Eliza. daughter of Stephen Beuteno and Mary his Wife,	"	11 February 1716.
Samuel Son of Samuel Burnel and Eliza. his Wife,	"	6 February 1716.
Pouning Son of Samuel Bridgham and Mary his Wife,	"	15 September 1716.
Mary daughter of Phillip Crane and Eliza his Wife,	"	12 March 1715/6.
Ellis Son of John Callender and Priscilla his Wife,	"	6 March 1715/6.
Sarah daughter of John Child and Sarah his Wife,	"	6 March 1715/6.
William ⎫ Sons of Samuel Cunnaball and Mary his Samuell ⎭ Wife,	"	13 March 1715/6.
John Son of George Cole and Mary his Wife,	"	4 April 1716.
John Son of John Collis and Abigall his Wife.	"	19 May 1716.
Eliza daughter of Nathll. Coney and Abigall his Wife,	"	15 May 1716.
Jonathan Son of John Coser and Sarah his Wife,	"	30 June 1716.
Benja. Son of James Cock and Mary his Wife,	"	10 July 1716.
Mehitabel daughter of John Clough and Mehitabel his Wife,	"	17 April 1716.
Eliza. daughter of John Chanter and Mary his Wife,	"	30 July 1716.
Mary daughter of Edward Cooper and Abigall his Wife,	"	8 August 1716.
Edward Son of Edward Cruft and Abigall his Wife,	"	22 August 1716.
Joseph Son of Joseph Clark and Margaret his Wife,	"	19 August 1716.
John Son of John Corragall and Mary his Wife,	"	3 September 1716.
Mary daughter of Thomas Chute and Mary his Wife,	"	30 October 1716.
Eliza. daughter of Willm. Clark and Hannah his Wife.	"	13 November 1716.
David Son of Jonathan Cox and Jane his Wife,	"	22 November 1716.
Phillips Son of Thomas Chamberlin and Hana his Wife,	"	28 September 1716.
Johanna daughter of Willm. Condey and Johanna his Wife,	"	22 November 1716.

Births — 1716.

John Son of Clement Chick and Mary his Wife,	Born	3 December 1716.
William Son of Benja. Clough and Faith his Wife,	"	20 January 1716.
Abraham Son of Abrm. Clark and Anne his Wife,	"	24 December 1716.
Samuel Son of Ephraim Crafts and Hannah his Wife,	"	10 July 1716.
Samuel Son of John Cookson and Rachel his Wife,	"	29 January 1716.
Mary daughter of Jer. Condey and Susana his Wife,	"	19 January 1716.
Priscilla daughter of John Clough and Mary his Wife,	"	10 February 1716.
Ebenr. Son of Ebenr. Clough and Thankfull his Wife,	"	29 November 1716.
Abigall daughter of Thoms. Colsworthy and Sarah his Wife,	"	8 February 1716.
Samuel Son of Samll. Cauverly and Susana his Wife,	"	15 February 1716.
Robert Son of Robert Calef and Margaret his Wife,	"	24 February 1716.
John Son of John Chamberlin and Hana his Wife,	"	9 March 1716/7.
Eliza. daughter of Humphry Davie and Margaret his Wife,	"	6 March 1715/6.
Anthony Son of Nicholas Davis and Sarah his Wife.	"	8 March 1715/6.
Eliza. daughter of John Dixwel and Mary his Wife,	"	12 April 1716.
Rebecca daughter of Rowland Dike and Hannah his Wife,	"	3 May 1716.
Abigall daughter of John Dutch and Eliza. his Wife,	"	29 May 1716.
George Son of Edward Durant and Mary his Wife,	"	20 June 1716.
Anne daughter of Thoms. Davis and Jane his Wife,	"	28 August 1716.
Charles Son of John Demery and Sarah his Wife,	"	20 December 1716.
Hannah daughter of Thoms. Dawes and Sarah his Wife,	"	19 December 1716.
Katherin danghter of Mary Dunbarr	"	15 January 1716.
William Son of Thoms. Debuke and Jeminah his Wife,	"	21 February 1716.
Samuel Son of Samll. Durant and Eliza. his Wife,	"	11 February 1716.
Samuel Son of Caleb Eddey and Hannah his Wife,	"	5 April 1716.
Bartholl. Son of John Ellet and Maria his Wife	"	1 June 1716.
Mercy daughter of Andrew Ellet and Ruth his Wife, .	"	25 August 1716.
Nehemiah Son of Nehemiah Eles and Hannah his Wife,	"	21 September 1716.
Isabella daughter of William Ellet and Isabella his Wife,	"	22 September 1716.
Henry Son of Nathll. Emms. and Hannah his Wife,	"	2 January 1716.
Eliza. daughter of Robert Ellis and Eliza. his Wife,	"	27 January 1716.
Paul Son of Paul Falmouth and Eliza. his Wife,	"	16 April 1716.
Thomas Son of Thoms. Fleet and Eliza. his Wife.	"	4 August 1716.
Mary daughter of Allexr. Fullerton and Eliza. his Wife,	"	17 September 1716.
John Son of John Fairwether and Jerusha his Wife.	"	26 September 1716.
Hannah daughter of Robert Fare and Sarah his Wife.	"	9 November 1716.
Lydia daughter of Benja Flood and Mary his Wife,	"	14 November 1716.
William Son of William Foy and Eliza. his Wife,	"	1 November 1716.
Anna daughter of John Foster and Mary his Wife,	"	26 December 1716.
William Son of Samuel Gardener and Eliza his Wife,	"	6 March 1715/6.
Eliza. daughter of James Gibson and Mary his Wife,	"	26 March 1716.
Edward Son of Joseph Grey and Rebecca his Wife,	"	10 March 1715/6.
Samuel Son of Joseph Gunison and Lydia his Wife,	"	28 July 1716.
William Son of Willm. Greenleiffe and Mary his Wife,	"	1 September 1716.

Eliza. daughter of John Greecion and Eliza. his Wife, Born 23 September 1716.
Anne daughter of James Gilcrist and Anne his Wife, " 15 September 1716.
Jonathan Son of Samll. Greenlieffe and Martha his Wife, " 22 September 1716.
Bartolomew Son of Bartholl. Gussear and Eliza. his Wife, " 17 January 1716.
Samuel Son of John Goodwin and Lydia his Wife, " 27 January 1716.
Eliza. daughter of James Gooch and Eliza. his Wife, " 8 March 1716/7.
Mary daughter of John Horton and Anne his Wife, " 14 April 1716.
John Son of Richd. Hall and Eliza. his Wife, " 24 April 1716.
Nathaniel Son of Israel How and Judeth his Wife, " 17 May 1716.
Susana daughter of Thomas Hancock and Susana his Wife, " 21 May 1716.
Snell Son of John Harwood and Mary his Wife, " 19 May 1716.
William Son of Francis Hudson and Mary his Wife, " 7 August 1716.
Sarah daughter of James Humphryes and Judeth his Wife, " 7 August 1716.
Benjamen Son of Samll. Hood and Deborah his Wife, " 4 August 1716.
Anne daughter of John Hobbs and Susana his Wife, " 24 August 1716.
Samuel Son of Benja. Haley and Susana his Wife, " 19 August 1716.
Mary daughter of John Hutchins and Eliza. his Wife, " 6 October 1716.
Hannah daughter of Jacob Hasie and Hannah his Wife, " 20 October 1716.
John Son of Samll. Hunt and Mary his Wife, " 19 November 1716.
Hannah daughter of Asa Hasie and Mary his Wife, " 11 December 1716.
Margaret daughter of Richd. Hasely and Tamozine his Wife, " 29 December 1716.
Ambrose Son of Ambrose Harris and Abigall his Wife, " 31 July 1716.
Hannah daughter of John Holland and Susana his Wife, " 31 January 1716.
Hannah daughter of John Haise and Hannah his Wife, " 24 January 1716.
William Son of Robert Holmes and Mary his Wife, " 10 January 1716.
Sarah daughter of Benja. Harris and Sarah his Wife, " 26 January 1716.
Leech Son of Samll. Harris and Hannah his Wife, " 14 February 1716.
Sarah daughter of Joseph Jenkins and Hannah his Wife, " 16 March 1715/6.
John Son of David Jenkins and Sarah his Wife, " 13 April 1716.
Susana daughter of John Jager and Mary his Wife, " 4 May 1716.
Leonard Son of Nathanll. Jarvis and Eliza. his Wife, " 7 May 1716.
Michael Son of John Jepson and Mercy his Wife, " 21 August 1716.
Martha daughter of Elias Kingston and Martha his Wife, " 19 June 1716.
Hannah daughter of Soloman Kneeland and Mary his Wife, " 1 July 1716.
Samuel Son of George Kilcup and Mary his Wife, " 16 June 1716.
Mary daughter of Thomas Kilby and Mary his Wife. " 9 September 1716.
John Son of Daniel Katen and Mary his Wife, " 21 October 1716.
Eliza. daughter of Nathanll. Keney and Eliza. his Wife, " 5 November 1716.
William Son of Willm. Lyon and Exprience his Wife, " 10 April 1716.

Births — 1716.

Abia daughter of William Lee and Mercy his Wife,	Born	11 April 1716.
Susana daughter of Victorius Loobey and Susana his Wife,	"	10 May 1716.
Joshua Son of Joshua Loring and Hanna his Wife,	"	3 August 1716.
Oliver Son of Oliver Luckis and Rebecca his Wife,	"	10 October 1716.
Phebee daughter of William Leveret and Mary his Wife,	"	2 October 1716.
Abigall daughter of Thomas Lee and Deborah his Wife,	"	17 November 1716.
Sarah daughter of Nathan Lewis and Anne his Wife,	"	9 February 1716.
Eliza. daughter of John Maverick and Eliza. his Wife,	"	7 March 1715/6.
Janet daughter of James Maurice and Janet his Wife,	"	8 March 1715/6.
John Son of Edward Masters and Eliza. his Wife,	"	8 March 1715/6.
John Son of Ephraim Moor aud Eliza. his Wife,	"	23 March 1715/6.
Sarah daughter of John Mills and Sarah his Wife,	"	28 May 1716.
Elisha Son of Allexandr. Millar and Eliza. his Wife,	"	23 June 1716.
Thomas Son of Thomas Millar and Mary his Wife,	"	11 June 1716.
John Son of John Minzes and Edee his Wife,	"	18 August 1716.
Anne daughter of Daniel Munden and Anne his Wife,	"	16 August 1716.
Jonathan Son of John Mason and Dorcas his Wife,	"	18 August 1716.
Nathanll. Son of Nathanll. Mason and Eliza. his Wife,	"	20 September 1716.
Anne daughter of James Morton and Margaret his Wife,	"	11 October 1716.
Samuel Son of Nathanll. Martine and Hanna his Wife,	"	18 October 1716.
Eliza. daughter of William Merchant and Abigall his Wife,	"	25 December 1716.
Mary daughter of Richard Morgan and Sarah his Wife,	"	16 January 1716.
Rebecca daughter of James Melven and Mercy his Wife,	"	13 February 1716.
Eliza. daughter of Mathew Nazro and Mary his Wife,	"	15 April 1716.
Nathaniel Son of Nathll. Newell and Ann his Wife,	"	6 April 1716.
Abigall daughter of John Noyes and Susana his Wife,	"	21 May 1716.
Wanlip Son of Nancy Negro Servant of Justice Palmer,	"	15 April 1716.
Mary daughter of Francis Norris and Mary his Wife,	"	19 December 1716.
Eliza, daughter of John Orno and Eliza. his Wife,	"	9 April 1716.
Margery daughter of John Orn and Eliza. his Wife,	"	16 December 1716.
Thomas Son of Robert Orange and Hanna his Wife,	"	16 February 1716.
Martha daughter of Robert Patteshall and Jane his Wife,	"	20 March 1715/6.
William Son of mr. Joseph Parsons and Eliza. his Wife,	"	21 April 1716.
Allen Son of James Peneman and Mary his Wife,	"	14 May 1716.
Mary daughter of Caleb Prat and Mary his Wife,	"	24 June 1716.
Mary daughter of Elias Parkman and Martha his Wife,	"	23 June 1716.
Richard Son of Stephen Payn and Mary his Wife,		16 August 1716.

Hannah daughter of Thoms. Potts and Mary his Wife,	Born	21 September 1716.
Thomas Son of Indego Potter and Rebecca his Wife,	"	17 September 1716.
Eliza. daughter of William Pitman and Eliza. his Wife,	"	22 September 1716.
Joseph Son of Benja. Purrington and Mary his Wife,	"	20 October 1716.
Rebecca daughter of Willm. Palfrey and Abigall his Wife,	"	15 October 1716.
John Son of Willm. Parkman and Hannah his Wife,	"	19 November 1716.
Mehitabel daughter of Joseph Payson and Mehitabel his Wife,	"	18 November 1716.
Sarah daughter of John Pitts and Hannah his Wife,	"	13 November 1716.
Mary daughter of Joseph Prince and Mary his Wife,	"	1 December 1716.
Mary daughter of Samll. Plummer and Eliza. his Wife,	"	1 January 1716.
Eliza. daughter of Caleb Parker and Eliza. his Wife,	"	29 December 1716.
William Son of Edmund Pirkins and Mary his Wife,	"	19 November 1716.
Eliza. daughter of William Prat and Mehitabel his Wife,	"	6 January 1716.
Mary daughter of Jonathn. Peirse and Mary his Wife,	"	13 December 1716.
Mary daughter of James Packanet and Mary his Wife,	"	15 August 1716.
Mary daughter of Joseph Peirce and Mary his Wife,	"	24 February 1716.
Samuel Son of Samll. Roberts and Sarah his Wife,	"	21 July 1716.
Samuel Son of Samll. Roberts and Abigall his Wife,	"	23 August 1716.
Timothy Son of Timothy Robinson and Dorothy his Wife,	"	24 August 1716.
William Son of Samll. Rand and Sarah his Wife,	"	27 August 1716.
Sarah daughter of William Rand and Sarah his Wife,	"	22 September 1716.
John Son of Richard Richardson and Sarah his Wife,	"	11 October 1716.
John Son of Thomas Ruck and Mary his Wife,	"	17 November 1716.
Knight Son of Thomas Rowel and Dorothy his Wife,	"	27 December 1716.
Mary daughter of John Souther and Mary his Wife,	"	1 April 1716.
Eliza. daughter of John Sherlock and Sarah his Wife,	"	9 March 1715/6.
Margaret daughter of Thomas Salter and Margaret his Wife,	"	4 May 1716.
Joseph Son of Joseph Stevens and Anne his Wife,	"	31 May 1716.
Rebecca daughter of Thoms. Smith and Mary his Wife,	"	18 June 1716.
Samuel Son of Samll. Saxton and Margaret his Wife,	"	5 July 1716.
Benja. Son of Benjamen Storey and Susanna his Wife,	"	7 July 1716.
John Son of Samll. Sarvice and Joanna his Wife,	"	21 June 1716.
Rachel daughter of Samll. Stebbins and Rachel his Wife,	"	21 August 1716.
Mary daughter of James Scut and Eliza. his Wife,	"	7 September 1716.

Births — 1716.

Priscilla daughter of John Smith and Priscilla his Wife,	Born	6 September 1716.
Sarah daughter of Simon Slocume and Eliza. his Wife,	"	7 October 1716.
William Son of Patrick Swanton and Prudence his Wife,	"	21 November 1716.
John Son of William Smallage and Ruth his Wife,	"	11 December 1716.
William Son of Charles Shepreeve and Eliza. his Wife,	"	5 December 1716.
Nathaniel Son of Thomas Stevens and Mary his Wife,	"	24 January 1716.
William Son of Richard Stebbens and Martha his Wife,	"	3 February 1716.
John Son of John Steel and Mary his Wife,	"	5 February 1716.
William Son of Abrm. Smith and Mary his Wife,	"	20 February 1716.
John Son of George Stuart and Ruth his Wife,	"	8 June 1716.
Sarah daughter of Josiah Torey and Sarah his Wife,	"	14 March 1715/6.
Abigall daughter of Joseph Treat and Mary his Wife,	"	10 March 1715/6.
William Son of William Tyler and Sarah his Wife,	"	11 March 1715/6.
Abigall daughter of Samll. Thorn and Experience his Wife,	"	6 May 1716.
Sarah daughter of Samll. Tyley and Eliphall his Wife,	"	31 March 1716.
Robert Son of John Tuften and Susanna his Wife,	"	10 June 1716.
Richard Son of Noah Tucker and Mary his Wife,	"	14 June 1716.
Peter Son of Peirse Tekel and Jane his Wife,	"	9 June 1716.
John Son of John Turner and Eliza. his Wife,	"	12 September 1716.
Eliza. daughter of James Tileston and Mary his Wife,	"	15 October 1716.
Ebenezar Son of Isaac Townsend and Anna his Wife,	"	22 June 1716.
Robert Son of Richard Thomas and Abigall his Wife,	"	27 September 1716.
Faur Son of William Tolman and Lydia his Wife,	"	28 October 1716.
William Son of William Thwing and Eliza. his Wife,	"	19 November 1716.
John Son of Elias Townsend and Rebecca his Wife,	"	20 November 1716.
Meriam daughter of Andrew Tiler and Meriam his Wife,	"	30 December 1716.
Joseph Son of Edward Tuttle and Joanna his Wife,	"	10 January 1716.
Michael Son of James Trench and Phillipee his Wife,	"	30 December 1716.
James Son of James Thompson and Mary his Wife,	"	30 January 1716.
Eliza. daughter of Thomas Tiley and Katherin his Wife,	"	1 February 1716.
Savage Son of Zachry Triscot and Mary his Wife,	"	22 February 1716.
Thomas Son of John Taylor and Mary his Wife,	"	21 February 1716.
Miles Son of John Wakefeild and Eliza. his Wife,	"	17 March 1715/6.
Abigall daughter of Thoms. Waite and Abigall his Wife,	"	28 April 1716.
Thomas Son of Ezekial Walker and Ruth his Wife,	"	11 April 1716.
Charles Son of Charles Waker and Sarah his Wife,	"	24 April 1716.
Andrew Son of Andrew Woodbery and Hannah his Wife,	"	29 April 1716.
Jerusha daughter of John Waldo and Eliza. his Wife,	"	6 May 1716.
John Son of John Wakefield and Sarah his Wife,	"	21 May 1716.
Sarah daughter of Thomas Wallis and Grace his Wife,	"	27 May 1716.
Hannah daughter of Thoms. Wiborn and Hannah his Wife,	"	31 May 1716.

Eliza. daughter of John Whitemore and Eliza. his Wife,	Born	19 June 1716.
Huldah daughter of Thoms. Waters and Huldah his Wife,	"	18 June 1716.
Eliza. daughter of Samll. Willis and Eliza. his Wife,	"	8 July 1716.
Samll. Son of Adam Winthrop Esqr. and Anne his Wife,	"	13 June 1716.
William Son of James Wright and Mary his Wife,	"	22 July 1716.
Mary daughter of Joseph White and Sarah his Wife,	"	5 July 1716.
Benja. Son of George Worthylake and Anne his Wife,	"	3 September 1716.
John Son of Thomas Willet and Mary his Wife,	"	7 September 1716.
Samuel Son of William Webster and Mary his Wife,	"	11 September 1716.
Susanna daughter of John Warwick and Susana his Wife,	"	17 September 1716.
John Son of John Walley and Bethia his Wife,	"	6 October 1716.
William Son of William Winter and Martha his Wife,	"	30 September 1716.
Samuel Son of Christr. Webb and Anne his Wife,	"	5 October 1716.
David Son of Ebenr. Wentworth and Rebecca his Wife,	"	7 October 1716.
Mary daughter of Francis Wainright and Mary his Wife,	"	29 July 1716.
Rachel daughter of Moses Walker and Rachel his Wife,	"	29 October 1716.
John Son of William Walter and Lois his Wite,	"	4 November 1716.
Hannah daughter of Edward White and Sarah his Wife,	"	22 August 1716.
Mary daughter of Joshua Williams and Anne his Wife,	"	8 November 1716.
Eliza. daughter of Joseph White and Eliza. his Wife,	"	4 December 1716.
Joshua Son of Allen Wild and Eliza. his Wife,	"	10 December 1716.
John Son of Thomas Worth and Mary his Wife,	"	30 December 1716.
Francis Son of Francis Whitman and Eliza. his Wife,	"	24 December 1716.
Rachel daughter of Peter White and Sarah his Wife,	"	17 December 1716.
Anna daughter of Cord Wing and Sarah his Wife,	"	17 January 1716.
Eliza. daughter of Elhanan Winchister and Mary his Wife,	"	20 December 1716.
John Son of Benja. White and Mary his Wife,	"	28 December 1716.
Jeremiah Son of John Wheelwright and Mary his Wife,	"	11 January 1716.
John Son of Ephraim Wheler and Dorothy his Wife,	"	28 January 1716.
Joseph Son of Daniel Wire and Mary his Wife,	"	5 March 1716/7.
Allexandr. Son of William Young and Mary his Wife,	"	10 June 1716.
Charles Son of Thomas Yates and Mary his Wife,	"	10 February 1716.
Eliza. daughter of Jonathn. Bull and Eliza. his Wife,	"	23 February 1716.
Eliza. daughter of John Butler and Hannah his Wife,	"	6 August 1716.
Sarah daughter of Benja. Bird and Johanna his Wife,	"	4 October 1716.
Deborah daughter of Nicholas Dun and Deborah his Wife,	"	13 October 1716.
Thos. Son of John Hunt and Rebecca his Wife,	"	31 January 1716.
John Son of John Osborn and Ruth his Wife,	"	16 May 1716.
Eliza. daughter of Timothy Prout and Lidia his Wife,	"	13 November 1716.

Births — 1716-17.

Simon Son of Simon Rogers and Mary his Wife,	Born	21 March 1715/6.
Eliza. daughter of Thomas Steel and Jane his Wife,	"	17 July 1716.
Sarah daughter of Joseph Urann and Sarah his Wife,	"	16 December 1716.
Eliza. daughter of Cornelius Waldo and Faith his Wife,	"	14 October 1716.
Nathanll. Son of Benja. Williams and Eliza. his Wife,	"	26 July 1716.
Jane daughter of Lewis Boucher and Sarah his Wife,	"	6 June 1716.
Joseph Son of Joseph Grant and Dorothy his Wife,	"	7 June 1716.
Mary daughter of Samuel Narramore and Rachel his Wife,	"	6 July 1716.
William Son of Samuel Rand and Sarah his Wife,	"	27 August 1716.
Payn Son of James Striger and Mary his Wife,	"	3 February 1716.
Mercy daughter of Ebenr. Youngman and Mercy his Wife.	"	27 November 1716.
Eliza. daughter of David Colson and Hannah his Wife,	"	7 September 1716.
John Son of John Dupee and Naomi his Wife,	"	10 October 1716.
Joseph Son of Joseph Goff and Eliza. his Wife,	"	25 March 1716.
Experience daughter of John Hillier and Eliza. his Wife,	"	25 December 1716.
Phillip Son of Thomas Bostick and Abigall his Wife,	"	13 October 1716.
Abigall daughter of Capt. Edward Martyn and Sarah his Wife,	"	20 July 1716.
James Son of James Prindle and Eliza. his Wife,	"	2 June 1716.
Eliza daughter of John Russel and Eliza. his Wife,	"	2 July 1716.
Sarah daughter of Samson Salter and Martha his Wife,	"	21 March 1715/6.
Nicholas Son of Thomas and Sarah Boylston,	"	13 March 1716.
Sarah, daughter of James and Grace Davenport,	"	10 October 1716.
Aaron Son of John and Abigail Deall,	"	17 June 1716.
Simpson Son of Thomas and Deborah Eyre.	"	3 September 1716.
Sarah daughter of Nathanael and Sarah Morse,	"	5 February 1716.
Margaret daughter of William and Margaret Payne,	"	22 May 1716.
Peter Son of John and Rachel Petell.	"	15 July 1716.
Martha daughter of Jonathan and Martha Salter,	"	19 September 1716.
John Son of Henry and Experience Redin,	"	7 July 1716.
Elizabeth daughter of Richard and Elizabeth Waite,	"	4 February 1716.

1717.

Robert Son of John Angier and Eliza. his Wife,	Born	26 May 1717.
Temperance daughter of James Adams and Temerance his Wife,	"	5 July 1717.
Mary daughter of Samll. Adams and Mary his Wife,	"	30 July 1717.
Ruth daughter of Thomas Adkins and Ruth his Wife,	"	3 September 1717.
Mary daughter of John Adams and Mary his Wife,	"	8 January 1717.
John Son of Thoms. Bell and Hannah his Wife,	"	4 April 1717.
Hannah daughter of Daniel Bell and Abigall his Wife,	"	24 March 1716/7.
Phillip Son of Phillip Bargier and Mary his Wife,	"	23 April 1717.
Mary daughter of John Baker and Mary his Wife,	"	12 May 1717.
Mary daughter of Ebenr. Burges and Eliza. his Wife,	"	30 June 1717.
Eliza. daughter of Francis Beardmore and Eliza. his Wife,	"	26 June 1717.
Joseph Son of James Barter and Eliza. his Wife,	"	26 June 1717.
Ebenezar Son of Ebenr. Belcher and Ruth his Wife,	"	30 June 1717.
Mary daughter of Thoms. Bronton and Lydia his Wife,	"	25 June 1717,

120   CITY DOCUMENT NO. 43.

Susanna daughter of Jno. Herculus Brilsford and Mary his Wife,	Born	10 July 1717.
Mary daughter of George Bethune and Mary his Wife,	"	27 April 1717.
Allen ⎱ Gimi. of Nathll. Breed and Sarah his Sarah ⎰ Wife,	"	5 August 1717.
Daniel Son of Benja. Ballard and Anne his Wife,	"	1 September 1717.
Abigall daughter of Samuel Boyce and Abigall his Wife,	"	21 September 1717.
Jeremiah Son of Edward Ball and Rebecca his Wife,	"	6 October 1717.
Susanna daughter of Samll. Barrat and Sarah his Wife,	"	24 October 1717.
Samll. Son of John Barton and Katherine his Wife,	"	26 September 1717.
Abigall daughter of Jacob Blancherd and Abigall his Wife,	"	27 November 1717.
Eliza. daughter of Henry Butler and Hannah his Wife,	"	5 January 1717.
Benjamen Son of Benja. Bird and Johanna his Wife,	"	15 January 1717.
John Son of John Brewster and Deliverence his Wife,	"	25 January 1717.
Martha daughter of Mathew Butler and Sarah his Wife,	"	20 January 1717.
Eliza daughter of James Beighton and Eliza. his Wife,	"	21 February 1717.
Eliza. daughter of John Beard and Mary his Wife,	"	24 February 1717.
Eliza. daughter of John Beal and Eliza. his Wife,	"	20 February 1717.
Rebecca daughter of Josiah Biles and Abigall his Wife,	"	21 February 1717.
Eliza. daughter of Joseph Cluley and Mary his Wife,	"	5 March 1716/7.
Mathew Son of Robert Cock and Agnis his Wife,	"	23 March 1716/7.
Benjamen Son of John Coolidge and Hannah his Wife,	"	10 April 1717.
Jonathan Son of James Carey and Sarah his Wife,	"	30 April 1717.
Mary daughter of John Channing and Mary his Wife,	"	3 May 1717.
Priscilla daughter of John Chandler and Priscilla his Wife,	"	9 May 1717.
Johanna daughter of John Charnock and Mary his Wife,	"	13 May 1717.
Richard Son of Henry Canner and Abigall his Wife,	"	4 June 1717.
Samuel ⎱ Gimi. of John Center and Ruth his Soloman ⎰ Wife,	"	29 December 1717.
Mary daughter of Peter Cross and Eliza. his Wife,	"	9 February 1717.
John Son of William Champlin and Martha his Wife,	"	23 January 1717.
Jane daughter of John Chandler and Priscilla his Wife,	"	19 January 1717.
Rebecca daughter of Josiah Clark and Priscilla his Wife,	"	18 February 1717.
Mary daughter of Andrew Cuñingham and Mary his Wife,	"	2 March 1717/8.
William Son of William Cuñingham and Eliza. his Wife,	"	14 February 1717/8.
Thomas Son of George Cole and Mary his Wife,	"	28 February 1717.
Mary daughter of Daniel Dupee and Lydia his Wife,	"	3 April 1717.
Eliza. daughter of John Dorothy and Eliza. his Wife,	"	22 May 1717.
Charles Son of Charles Deming and Sarah his Wife,	"	25 July 1717.

Births — 1717.

Samll. Son of Samll. Duncan and Mary his Wife,	Born	6 August 1717.
Joshua Son of John Done and Abia his Wife,	"	22 September 1717.
Joseph Son of Samll. Davise and Katherin his Wife,	"	11 October 1717.
Gilbert Son of Evos Davise and Mary his Wife,	"	15 October 1717.
Joseph Son of Shem Drown and Katherin his Wife,	"	10 December 1717.
Robert Son of Robert Darby and Martha his Wife,	"	20 December 1717.
Dorcas daughter of Nicholas Dun and Deborah his Wife,	"	1 November 1717.
Mary daughter of Henry Dering and Eliza. his Wife,	"	· 7 February 1717.
Mary daughter of Samll. Emms and Hephsiba his Wife,	"	1 June 1717.
Benjamen Son of Benja. Edwards and Hanna his Wife,	"	10 June 1717.
Eliza. daughter of William Eustas and Eliza. his Wife,	"	22 September 1717.
John Son of Patrick Erskin and Sarah his Wife,	"	9 October 1717.
Mary daughter of John Ellery and Jane his Wife,	"	1 January 1717.
Nathanll. Son of Nathll. Emms and Hannah his Wife,	"	18 February 1717.
Timothy Son of Nehemiah Eales and Hannah his Wife,	"	23 February 1717.
Sarah ⎱ Gimi. of Ephraim Fenno and Eliza. his Nathaniel ⎰ Wife,	"	10 April 1717.
Peter Son of David Farnum and Dorothy his Wife,	"	13 May 1717.
Samuel Son of Samll. Foy and Eliza. his Wife,	"	31 May 1717.
Abigall daughter of John Fife and Abigall his Wife,	"	9. July 1717.
Danforth Son of Hopestil Foster and Eliza. his Wife,	"	27 July 1717.
Susanna daughter of Edward Freeman aad Mary his Wife,	"	6 October 1717.
John Son of William Foy and Eliza. his Wife,	"	14 November 1717.
Edward Son of Thomas Foster and Anne his Wife,	"	16 November 1717.
Abraham Son of Gidian Florence and Susanna his Wife,	"	8 January 1717.
Mary daughther of John Fairwether and Jerusha his Wife.	"	10 January 1717.
Mary daughter of John Farro and Mary his Wife,	"	5 February 1717.
Anna daughter of William Gill and Anna his Wife,	"	16 March 1716/7.
Rebecca daughter of Thomas Goodwill and Rebecca his Wife,	"	15 May 1717.
James Son of Thomas Gyles and Martha his Wife,	"	15 June 1717.
Benjamen Son of John Gerrish and Sarah his Wife,	"	19 October 1717.
Baxter Son of John Grangier and Mary his Wife,	"	22 October 1717.
Mary daughter of Edward Grey and Hannah his Wife,	"	15 December 1717.
Thomas Son of John Goldthwait and Jane his Wife,	"	15 January 1717.
Eliza. daughter of Nathll. Gardener and Mary his Wife,	"	23 January 1717.
Joseph Son of Joseph Gunnison and Lydia his Wife,	"	9 February 1717.
Abigall daughter of Nicholas George and Mary his Wife,	"	13 February 1717.
Eliza. daughter of Edward Hutchinson Esq. and Lydia his Wife,	"	3 March 1716/7.
Joseph Son of Samll. Holbrook and Hannah his Wife,	"	6 March 1716/7.
Mary daughter of Owen Harrise and Susanna his Wife,	"	12 March 1716/7.
Hannah daughter of Joshua Hewes and Hannah his Wife,	"	26 April 1717.
Jacob Son of John Homer and Anne his Wife,	"	26 April 1717.

Mary daughter of John Harwood and Mary his Wife,	Born	6 June 1717.
Lydia daughter of Thos. Hutchinson Esq. and Sarah his Wife,	"	30 May 1717.
Mary daughter of Samll. Hunting and Mary his Wife,	"	11 June 1717.
Eliza. daughter of Benj. Hillier and Eliza. his Wife,	"	24 June 1717.
Thoms. Son of John Hubbert and Eliza. his Wife,	"	1 July 1717.
Cumbey Son of Joseph Hood and Rebecca his Wife,	"	28 August 1717.
Nebery Son of Phillip Howel and Sarah his Wife,	"	23 September 1717.
Martha daughter of Francis Hudson and Mary his Wife,	"	30 September 1717.
Mary daughter of Ephraim Hunt and Johanna his Wife,	"	3 January 1717.
Mary daughter of Richard Hunt and Sarah his Wife,	"	19 December 1717.
Eliza. daughter of John Hunt and Rebecca his Wife,	"	9 January 1717.
Anne daughter of John Hobbs and Susanna his Wife,	"	18 October 1717.
Thomas Son of John Jent and Abigall his Wife,	"	5 March 1716/7.
Peter Son of Thomas Jenkins and Mary his Wife,	"	25 June 1717.
Abraham Son of Nathanll. Josling and Frances his Wife,	"	18 November 1717.
Sarah daughter of Thomas Jackson and Sarah his Wife,	"	10 February 1717.
Eliza. daughter of Ebenr. Knight and Eliza. his Wife,	"	28 March 1717.
Eliza. daughter of Samll. Knight and Eliza his Wife,	"	18 August 1717.
John Son of John Kent and Abigall his Wife,	"	25 November 1717.
Peter Son of Peter King and Eliza. his Wife,	"	17 February 1717.
Mary daughter of Samll. Langdon and Esther his Wife,	"	15 March 1716/7.
Sarah daughter of Ebenr. Lamson and Sarah his Wife,	"	15 March 1716/7.
Katherin daughter of Edward Lyd and Eliza. his Wife,	"	1 April 1717.
Ezekiel Son of Ezekiel Lewis and Abigall his Wife,	"	15 April 1717.
Israel Son of Nathll. Loring and Susanna his Wife,	"	25 May 1717.
Marian daughter of John Lawrence and Marian his Wife,	"	4 July 1717.
Anne daughter of Thoms. Leechmer and Anne his Wife,	"	21 August 1717.
Anne daughter of Henry Lowder and Abigall his Wife,	"	16 October 1717.
Lydia daughter of William Letherbee and Lydia his Wife,	"	9 December 1717.
Mary daughter of William Lyon and Experience his Wife,	"	16 December 1717.
Mary daughter of Nathll. Leman and Mary his Wife,	"	17 February 1717.
Abijah Son of Isaac Lewis and Hannah his Wife,	"	9 September 1717.
Ruth daughter of Ebenr. Leadbetter and Abigall his Wife,	"	11 February 1717.
Deborah daughter of Thoms. Mellens and Mary his Wife,	"	24 March 1716/7.
Anna daughter of Lewis Mallet and Margaret his Wife,	"	14 April 1717.
Margaret daughter of Willm. Maccarty and Margt. his Wife,	"	6 April 1717.
George Son of John Meers and Sarah his Wife,	"	28 May 1717.

BIRTHS — 1717.

Edmund Son of John Mountfort and Mary his Wife,	Born	20 May 1717.
Mary daughter of John Mireck and Hannah his Wife,	"	10 July 1717.
John Son of John Millar and Mary his Wife,	"	3 July 1717.
Eliza. daughter of John Paul Mascarane and Eliza. his Wife,	"	3 July 1717.
Mary daughter of Samll. Mould and Mary his Wife,	"	28 July 1717.
Jane daughter of Daniel Mero and Frances his Wife,	"	27 July 1717.
John Son of Samll. Marion and Mary his Wife,	"	7 August 1717.
Johanna daughter of Jonathn. Mountfort and Hanna his Wife,	"	12 August 1717.
Thomas Son of Francis Moor and Mary his Wife,	"	28 August 1717.
Rebecca daughter of Willm. Man and Hannah his Wife,	"	21 August 1717.
Abigall daughter of William Mallard and Abigall his Wife,	"	7 November 1717.
Thomas Son of John Merrifield and Bridget his Wife,	"	29 December 1717.
John Son of Allexandr. Miller and Eliza. his Wife,	"	18 January 1717.
James ⎰ Sons of James Maurice and Jannet his John ⎱ Wife,	"	8 February 1717.
Samuel Son of Ephraim Mair and Eliza. his Wife,	"	20 December 1717.
Moses Son of Moses Norman and Anne his Wife,	"	25 June 1717.
Jane daughter of John Newton and Jane his Wife,	"	3 September 1717.
Bethia daughter of William Nicholls and Bethia his Wife.	"	24 September 1717.
Jane daughter of Anthony Oliver and Mary his Wife,	"	16 April 1717.
Lazarus Son of Lazarus Oxman and Gartright his Wife,	"	29 August 1717.
Alice daughter of John Oliver and Alice his Wife,	"	3 October 1717.
Daniel Son of Daniel Pecker and Sarah his Wife,	"	8 March 1716/7.
Sarah daughter of Willm. Peirse and Sarah his Wife,	"	2 April 1717.
Charles ⎰ Gimi of Thomas Porter and Eliza. his Hannah ⎱ Wife,	"	18 April 1717.
Jonathn. Son of Jonathn. Pickering and Eliza. his Wife,	"	29 April 1717.
John Son of John Peak and Sarah his Wife,	"	9 May 1717.
John Son of Thomas Plasteed and Mary his Wife,	"	17 July 1717.
Sarah daughter of Bryant Parrot and Abigall his Wife,	"	24 July 1717.
John Son of Edward Paige and Ruth his Wife,	"	29 July 1717.
Sarah daughter of Joseph Price and Sarah his Wife,	"	18 August 1717.
Lydia daughter of John Pumery and Lydia his Wife,	"	25 August 1717.
Samuel Son of Samll. Peck and Eliza. his Wife,	"	9 September 1717.
Joseph Son of Joseph Prat and Sarah his Wife,	"	5 November 1717.
Nathll. Son of Nathanll. Peirse and Abigall his Wife,	"	2 November 1717.
Eliza. daughter of Samll. Pousley and Eliza. his Wife,	"	23 November 1717.
William Son of Wm. Parker and Anna his Wife,	"	26 November 1717.
Caleb Son of Caleb Prat and Mary his Wife,	"	17 December 1717.
Anna daughter of Caleb Parker and Eliza. his Wife,	"	30 December 1717.
John Son of James Packanet and Mary his Wife,	"	18 November 1717.
Thomas Son of Willm. Palfrey and Abigall his Wife,	"	13 January 1717.
Mary daughter of James Peat and Susanna his Wife,	"	22 January 1717.

Mary daughter of James Peneman and Mary his Wife, Born 23 September 1717.
Eliza. daughter of David Pulsifer and Susanna his Wife, " 11 February 1717.
Charity daughter of Benja. Ricks and Mary his Wife, " 13 March 1716/7.
Edward daughter of Edward Richards and Mary his Wife, " 16 May 1717.
Martha daughter of Samll. Robinson and Hannah his Wife, " 11 May 1717.
Cartwright Son of John Rawlings and Love his Wife, " 24 April 1717.
Mary daughter of Peter Row and Mary his Wife, " 8 July 1717.
Sarah daughter of John Richards and Mary his Wife, " 16 July 1717.
Robert Son of Richard Reeves and Anne his Wife, " 26 August 1717.
Thomas Son of Joseph Robinson and Rachel his Wife, " 27 September 1717.
Susanna daughter of Obadiah Reed and Jane his Wife, " 28 September 1717.
Mary daughter of Simon Rogers and Mary his Wife, " 1 December 1717.
Martha daughter of Jonathn. Rouse and Martha his Wife, " 11 January 1717.
Nathaniel Son of Nathll. Rogers and Eliza. his Wife, " 5 February 1717.
Samuel Son of Samuel Roberts and Abigall his Wife, " 11 February 1717.
Constantine Son of Willm. Spencer and Mary his Wife, " 20 March 1716/7.
John Son of Willm. Sentel and Johanna his Wife, " 28 March 1717.
Margaret daughter of Jacob Sheafe and Mary his Wife, " 7 May 1717.
John Son of Thomas Shaw and Sarah his Wife, " 6 May 1717.
Susanna daughter of Thomas Salter and Margaret his Wife, " 17 July 1717.
Jahleel Son of John Smith and Martha his Wife, " 30 March 1717.
Samuel Son of Samll. Sargent and Eliza. his Wife, " 22 June 1717.
John Son of John Stride and Jane his Wife, " 14 August 1717.
Robert Son of John Smalpeice and Olive his Wife, " 2 September 1717.
Hannah daughter of Willm. Sanders and Bridget his Wife, " 23 August 1717.
John Son of John Stocker and Abigall his Wife, " 1 October 1717.
William Son of James Scolley and Deborah his Wife, " 28 September 1717.
Michael Son of Michael Shaler and Meriam his Wife, " 6 November 1717.
Christian daughter of Thoms. Simpson and Christian his Wife, " 15 December 1717.
Lydia daughter of Barthll. Spiller and Johanna his Wife, " 17 December 1717.
Anthony Son of Anthony Stoddard Esq. and Martha his Wife, " 6 May 1717.
David Son of David Sinkler and Mary his Wife, " 18 December 1717.
Nathanll. Son of Malachy Salter and Sarah his Wife, " 28 December 1717.
Margaret daughter of Joseph Savill and Margaret his Wife, " 25 November 1717.
Peter Son of Joseph Scot and Deliverence his Wife, " 10 January 1717.
John Son of John Souther and Mary his Wife, " 23 January 1717.
Lydia } Gimi. of John Savil and Priscilla his Wife, " 23 January 1717.
Mary }

BIRTHS — 1717.

Samuel Son of Habijah Savage Esqr. and Hannah his Wife,	Born	16 July 1717.
Richard Son of Richard Stanney and Mary his Wife,	"	17 January 1717.
Rachel daughter of Andrew Segarnee and Mary his Wife,	"	5 March 1717/8.
Elisha Son of Elisha Storey and Sarah his Wife,	"	3 March 1717/8.
Mary daughter of Samll. Stebbins and Rachel his Wife,	"	24 February 1717.
Eliza. daughter of Oxenbridge Thatcher and Eliza. his Wife,	"	19 March 1716/7.
Jane daughter of Roger Talbut and Hannah his Wife,	"	16 March 1716/7.
Timothy Son of Timothy Thornton and Eliza. his Wife,	"	5 April 1717.
John Son of John Thompson and Hannah his Wife,	"	26 June 1717.
Rebecca daughter of Benja. Thwing and Rebecca his Wife,	"	24 July 1717.
Abraham Son of Abrm. Townsend and Mary his Wife,	"	5 November 1717.
Andrew Son of Andr. Tyler and Meriam his Wife,	"	30 January 1717.
Joseph Son of Joseph Thorn and Deborah his Wife,	"	11 February 1717.
John Son of Benja. Varney and Sarah his Wife,	"	11 March 1716/7.
Mary daughter of Charles Vaneps and Emme his Wife,	"	4 May 1717.
Eliza. daughter of Nathll. Vial and Sarah his Wife,	"	3 July 1717.
Sarah daughter of Thoms. Vering and Sarah his Wife,	"	1 December 1717.
Edmund Son of John Vallentine and Mary his Wife,	"	22 October 1717.
Joseph Son of Joseph Urann and Sarah his Wife,	"	14 February 1717.
Samuel Son of Samuel Watts and Eliza. his Wife,	"	28 March 1717.
Isaac Son of Jacob Waldering and Hannah his Wife,	"	2 April 1717.
Mary daughter of Joshua Williams and Mary his Wife,	"	14 May 1717.
William Son of Andrew Woodbery and Hannah his Wife,	"	27 May 1717.
John Son of John Welland and Eliza. his Wife,	"	10 June 1717.
Mercy daughter of Jacob Wendall and Sarah his Wife,	"	22 June 1717.
William Son of Adam Winthrop Esqr. and Anne his Wife,	"	3 July 1717.
Eliza. daughter of William Watson and Eliza. his Wife,	"	2 August 1717.
Samuel Son of Daniel Whitemore and Mary his Wife,	"	6 August 1717.
Katherin daughter of Daniel Willard and Abigall his Wife,	"	29 July 1717.
Thomas Son of Thomas Wharton and Eliza. his Wife,	"	20 August 1717.
Benja. Son of Michael Willis and Mary his Wife,	"	1 September 1717.
Willm. Son of William Walter and Mary his Wife,	"	6 September 1717.
Thomas Son of Richd. Woods and Hannah his Wife,	"	3 October 1717.
Rachel daughter of Benja. Williams and Eliza. his Wife,	"	14 September 1717.
Mary daughter of Ebenr. Williston and Judeth his Wife,	"	22 September 1717.
Sarah daughter of John Wiat and Mary his Wife,	"	2 October 1717.
Joseph Son of John Willis and Sarah his Wife.	"	23 October 1717.
Ebenr. Son of Joseph White and Sarah his Wife,	"	4 December 1717.

Thomas Son of Thomas Warden and Hannah his Wife,	Born	5 December 1717.
Sarah daughter of John Williams and Rebecca his Wife,	"	31 January 1717.
Samuel Son of Samll. Whitehead and Mary his Wife,	"	4 February 1717.
Gidion Son of John Young and Mary his Wife,	"	4 September 1717.
William Son of William Young and Martha his Wife,	"	30 December 1717.
William Son of John Buttolph and Mehitabel his Wife,	"	17 February 1717.
Jonathan Son of Joseph Belcher and Hannah his Wife,	"	27 February 1717.
Mercy daughter of Henry Coffin and Mercy his Wife,	"	27 February 1717.
Mary daughter of William Cowel and Eliza. his Wife,	"	6 January 1717.
Anne daughter of James Cock and Anne his Wife,	"	23 December 1717.
Daniel Son of Daniel Collings and Rebecca his Wife,	"	17 February 1717.
Thomas Son of Thomas Frank and Rachel his Wife.	"	14 January 1717.
Rebecca daughter of Stephen Kempton and Rebecca his Wife,	"	24 November 1717.
Margaret daughter of Thomas Lataile and Kathern his Wife,	"	26 October 1717.
John Son of John Lawson and Sarah his Wife,	"	4 October 1717.
Anthony Son of Nicholas Mitchel and Jane his Wife,	"	18 December 1717.
Mary daughter of John Osborn and Sarah his Wife,	"	26 February 1717.
Deborah daughter of James Prince and Deborah his Wife,	"	23 February 1717.
Margaret daughter of Nathanll. Storey and Margaret his Wife,	"	9 January 1717.
Eliza. daughter of Erasmus Stevens and Peirses his Wife,	"	15 August 1717.
Grant Son of John Webster and Mary his Wife,	"	31 January 1717.
Rebecca daughter of William Wilson and Mercy his Wife,	"	28 February 1717.
Joseph Son of John Wakefield and Sarah his Wife,	"	21 February 1717.
Job Son of Job Coyt and Lydia his Wife,	"	10 April 1717.
Naomi daughter of John Dupee and Naomi his Wife,	"	7 December 1717.
Henry Son of Thomas Down and Anna his Wife,	"	13 February 1717.
Benja. Son of ye Rd. mr. Henry Harrise and Sarah his Wife,	"	3 February 1717.
Anne daughter of Edward Rawson and Preserved his Wife,	"	15 July 1717.
Anna daughter of Isaac White and Rebecca his Wife,	"	9 April 1717.
Samuel Son of Samuel Whitwel and Eliza. his Wife,	"	30 December 1717.
Rebecca daughter of Thomas Dawes and Sarah his Wife,	"	9 March 1717.
Jane daughter of William Inggs and Anne his Wife,	"	2 January 1717.
Hannah daughter of Samuel Kenney and Abigall his Wife,	"	21 July 1717.
Eliner daughter of Thomas Velvin and Sarah his Wife,	"	25 January 1717.
William Son of Matthew and Mary Adams,	"	1 March 1717.
Sarah, daughter of Anthony and Amaritta (Free Negroes)	"	15 April 1717.

BIRTHS — 1717-18.

Mary, daughter of Joseph and Mary Balch,	Born	4 March 1717.
Thomas, Son of Thomas and Elizabeth Bedel,	"	24 December 1717.
Sarah daughter of Thomas and Sarah Boylston,	"	7 January 1717.
Robert Son of Benjamin and Mary Bronsdon,	"	9 Augugt 1717.
Joseph Son of Joseph and Susanna Candish,	"	12 May 1717.
Abraham Son of Jeremiah and Anna Clemans,	"	30 October 1717.
William Son of James and Grace Davenport.	"	19 October 1717.
Mary daughter of John and Prudence Grover,	"	31 July 1717.
James Son of James and Joanna Landman,	"	8 June 1717.
Dorcas daughter of Christopher and Elizabeth Marshall	"	17 September 1717.
Benjamin Son of Thomas and Hannah Moulin,	"	30 March 1717.
Mary daughter of James and Hannah Pemberton,	"	25 June 1717.
Joseph Son of Joseph and Elizabeth Ricks,	"	30 December 1717.

1718.

Thomas Son of William Allen and Mary his Wife,	Born	10 May 1718.
Mary daughter of Jonathan Adams and Mary his Wife,	"	28 May 1718.
Rebecca daughter of James Adams and Temperance his Wife	"	21 August 1718.
John Son of John Allen and Mary his Wife,	"	27 October 1718.
Eliza. daughter of Isaac Adams and Martha his Wife,	"	4 February 1718.
Sarah daughter of Ebenr. Bridge and Mary his Wife,	"	20 March 1717/8.
Abigall daughter of Freeborn Balch and Susanna his Wife,	"	9 March 1717/8.
Lydia daughter of Nicholas Boon and Hannah his Wife,	"	27 March 1718.
Elias Son of George Barter and Sarah his Wife,	"	15 March 1717/8.
John Son of John Bradford and Sarah his Wife,	"	21 March 1717/8.
John Son of Thomas Baker and Thankfull his Wife,	"	27 March 1718.
Abigall daughter of John Burt and Abigall his Wife,	"	28 March 1718.
John Son of Thomas Barnerd and Silence his Wife,	"	9 April 1718.
Lydia daughter of Samuel Bass and Christian his Wife,	"	24 April 1718.
Custine Son of John Bushnel and Mary his Wife,	"	11 May 1718.
John Son of Othniel Beal and Abigall his Wife,	"	25 May 1718.
George Son of William Bearstow and Eliza. his Wife,	"	25 May 1718.
Eliza. daughter of Benj. Brown and Mary his Wife,	"	28 June 1718.
John Son of Jonathan Bull and Eliza. his Wife,	"	6 July 1718.
Joshua Son of Joshua Blanchard and Sarah his Wife,	"	8 July 1718.
James Son of Ebenr. Burges and Eliza. his Wife,	"	10 July 1718.
Eliza. daughter of John Bolderson and Sarah his Wife,	"	4 August 1718.
Ebenr. Son of William Brown and Anne his Wife.	"	1 August 1718.
Sarah ⟩ Gimi. of John Baley and Mehitabel his John ⟨ Wife,	"	20 August 1718.
Hannah daughter of John Baker and Mary his Wife,	"	14 August 1718.
Thomas Son of Jonathan Boman and Mary his Wife,	"	2 September 1718.
Hannah daughter of Thomas Bamus and Hannah his Wife,	"	8 July 1718.

Susanna daughter of William Burrel and Johanna his Wife,	Born	14 September 1718.
George Son of George Butler and Mary his Wife,	"	26 September 1718.
Thomas Son of Thomas Brunton and Lydia his Wife,	"	15 September 1718.
Hannah daughter of Israel Baley and Hannah his Wife,	"	13 November 1718.
Margaret daughter of Mathew Bedlington and Eunise his Wife,	"	12 November 1718.
Edward Son of John Briggs and Katherin his Wife,	"	26 October 1718.
Rebecca daughter of Samuel Badcock and Martha his Wife,	"	25 November 1718.
Benja. Son of James Barnes and Mary his Wife,	"	26 November 1718.
Mary daughter of William Brown and Lydia his Wife,	"	24 November 1718.
Ruth daughter of Thomas Barer aud Eliza. his Wife,	"	25 December 1718.
Priscilla daughter of Hezekiah Butler and Priscilla his Wife,	"	7 December 1718.
Willm. Owen Son of Barthol. Barret and Rebecca his Wife,	"	1 February 1718.
Mary daughter of Stephen Boutineau and Mary his Wife,	"	18 January 1718.
William Son of Willm. Cook and Rachel his Wife,	"	9 March 1718.
Christopher Son of Christor. Capril and Mary his Wife,	"	2 May 1718.
Samuel Son of Samuel Clark and Patience his Wife,	"	24 May 1718.
Anne daughter of Abrm. Clark and Anne his Wife,	"	6 July 1718.
Daniel Son of Daniel Cole and Prudence his Wife,	"	11 August 1718.
James Son of John Christy and Eliza. his Wife,	"	9 October 1718.
Mary daughter of Clement Chick and Mary his Wife,	"	3 November 1718.
George Son of John Charnock and Mary his Wife,	"	4 January 1718.
Sarah daughter of Samuel Cunnaball and Mary his Wife,	"	22 February 1718,
Cornelius Son of Edward Durant and Judeth his Wife,	"	25 March 1718.
Frances daughter of James Dowel and Hannah his Wife,	"	17 July 1718.
Bethiah daughter of Willm. Daviss and Bethiah his Wife,	"	22 October 1718.
Elias Son of Daniel Dupee and Lydia his Wife,	"	31 December 1718.
Joseph Son of Samuel Deming and Hannah his Wife,	"	23 January 1718.
Abigall daughter of Robert Dickers and Abigall his Wife,	"	27 February 1718.
Mary daughter of Thomas Debuke and Jamina his Wife,	"	2 March 1718/9.
Joseph Son of Joseph Dyer and Lydia his Wife,	"	7 February 1718.
Joshua Son of Jonathn. Eustas and Sarah his Wife,	"	7 April 1718.
Georg Son of Benja. Eustas and Katherin his Wife,	"	24 April 1718.
Mary daughter of Edward Enstone and Mary his Wife,	"	21 April 1718.
Maria daughter of John Ellet and Maria his Wife.	"	5 May 1718.
Willm. Son of Edward Eades and Susanna his Wife,	"	8 March 1717/8.
Samuel Son of Samll. Eaton and Ruth his Wife,	"	20 May 1718.
Hannah daughter of Caleb Eddy and Hannah his Wife,	"	5 November 1718.

BIRTHS — 1718.

Thomas Son of Thomas Eyeres and Deborah his Wife,	Born	3 November 1718.
Henry Son of Samuel Emms and Hephzibah his Wife,	"	24 December 1718.
Andrew Son of Andrew Eliot and Ruth his Wife,	"	21 December 1718.
William Son of Francis Fredrick and Anne his Wife,	"	1 March 1717/8.
Allexander Son of Allexr. Fullerton and Eliza. his Wife,	"	3 April 1718.
Eliza. daughter of Paul Farmer and Eliza. his Wife,	"	16 April 1718.
David Son of Jonathan Farnum and Anne his Wife,	"	29 April 1718.
William Son of Willm. Fletcher and Margaret his Wife,	"	7 June 1718.
Sarah daughter of John Fator and Sarah his Wife,	"	21 June 1718.
Eliza. daughter of Thomas Fleming and Eliza. his Wife,	"	12 July 1718.
Eliza. daughter of Joseph Ferrington and Mary his Wife,	"	23 July 1718.
Barnes Son of Ephraim Fenno and Eliza. his Wife,	"	10 August 1718.
Eliza. daughter of Willm. Foy and Eliza. his Wife,	"	23 October 1718.
Anne daughter of John Fisher and Sarah his Wife,	"	29 October 1718.
Amie daughter of William Fletcher and Margaret his Wife,	"	4 December 1718.
Mary daughter of John Foster and Mary his Wife,	"	4 February 1718.
John Son of Joseph Grant and Dorothy his Wife,	"	5 March 1717/8.
Edward Son of Charles Gyles and Mary his Wife,	"	23 May 1718.
Joseph Son of John Gray and Eliza. his Wife,	"	20 June 1718.
Abigall daughter of Robert Grater and Abigall his Wife,	"	8 July 1718.
Lemuel Son of Lemuel Gowen and Sarah his Wife,	"	2 August 1718.
Joseph Son of Willm. Greenliefe and Mary his Wife,	"	14 September 1718.
Martha daughter of Samll. Greenliefe and Martha his Wife,	"	22 July 1718.
Samuel Son of Ebenr. Graves and Sarah his Wife,	"	22 December 1718.
Willm. Seuel Son of Bartholl. Gosears and Eliza. his Wife,	"	12 January 1718.
John Son of Obadiah Gore and Sarah his Wife,	"	29 December 1718.
Susanna daughter of Barnabas Gilbert and Susana his Wife,	"	22 July 1718.
Mathew Son of James Habersham and Mehitabel his Wife,	"	22 March 1717/8.
John Son of Phillip Hekew and Eliza. his Wiie,	"	19 March 1717/8.
James Son of James Halsey and Anne his Wife,	"	4 April 1718.
Blanch daughter of Joseph Hall and Blanch his Wife,	"	1 April 1718.
Grace daughter of Joseph Howard and Grace his Wife,	"	1 May 1718.
Abraham Son of Asa Hasie and Mary his Wife,	"	13 April 1718.
Susanna daughter of John Harwood and Mary his Wife,	"	30 April 1718.
Eliza. daughter of Richard Hall and Eliza. his Wife,	"	16 June 1718.
Abigall daughter of Willm. Harris and Abigall his Wife,	"	18 June 1718.
Tamozine daughter of Richard Hazely and Tamozin his Wife,	"	10 June 1718.
Mary daughter of Samuel Hunting and Mary his Wife,	"	29 June 1718.
Eliza. daughter of Phillip Hedman and Eliza. his Wife,	"	26 March 1718.
Abia Son of Abia Holbrook and Mary his Wife,	"	14 July 1718.

Roop Son of Ambrose Harris and Abigall his Wife, Born		7 July 1718.
Eliza. daughhter of Samll. Haley and Eliza. his Wife,	"	21 August 1718.
Mary daughter } of Edward Hutchinson Esq. and Clark Son } Lydia his Wife,	"	18 August 1718.
Samuel Son of Ebenr. Heath and Deborah his Wife,	"	5 November 1718.
William Son of John Hayes and Hannah his Wife,	"	18 October 1718.
Mary daughter of Samll. Hunt and Mary his Wife,	"	24 October 1718.
Sarah daughter of John Holland and Susana his Wife,	"	29 January 1718.
Sarah daughter of John Hubbert and Eliza. his Wife,	"	3 February 1718.
Joseph Son of Joseph Hines and Mary his Wife,	"	15 February 1718.
Mary daughter of William Henderson and Esther his Wife,	"	11 February 1718.
Joseph Son of John Johnson and Susana his Wife,	"	28 June 1718.
Francis } Sons of Edward Joyner and Eliza. his William } Wife,	"	24 July 1718.
Thomas Son of Thomas Inches and Rachel his Wife,	"	26 August 1718.
Eliza. daughter of John Jent and Abigall his Wife,	"	18 January 1718.
Sarah daughter of Ebenr. Knight and Eliza. his Wife,	"	21 November 1718.
Martha daughter of Thomas King and Martha his Wife,	"	11 March 1718/9.
Edward Son of Victorius Loobey and Susanna his Wife,	"	27 June 1718.
Martha daughter of Thomas Lee and Anna his Wife,	"	3 June 1718.
John Son of John Leath and Eliner his Wife,	"	1 July 1718.
Nathan Son of Nathan Lewis and Anne his Wife,	"	27 August 1718.
Anne daughter of Thomas Leechmer and Anne his Wife,	"	29 November 1718.
Mercy daughter of Thomas Lee and Deborah his Wife,	"	27 December 1718.
Eliza. daughter of James Lenix and Mary his Wife,	"	25 January 1718.
Sarah daughter of John Lawson and Sarah his Wife,	"	7 December 1718.
John Son of John Mills and Sarah his Wife,	"	13 March 1717/8.
Jane daughter of Thomas Millar and Mary his Wife,	"	1 April 1718.
Mary daaghter of Isaac Marion and Rebecca his Wife,	"	15 April 1718.
Jotham Son of John Maverik and Eliza. his Wife,	"	20 March 1717/8.
John Son of John Meers and Sarah his Wife,	"	12 June 1718.
Thomas Son of Caesar Mitchel and Tabitha his Wife,	"	25 July 1718.
Mary daughter of Jonathan Mountfort and Hannah his Wife,	"	2 August 1718.
Nathaniel Son of Nathll. Martain and Hannah his Wife,	"	29 July 1718.
William Son of William Merchant and Abigall his Wife,	"	23 October 1718.
Hannah daughter of Daniel Mundan and Anne his Wife,	"	3 November 1718
William Son of Ralph Maier and Martha his Wife,	"	25 November 1718.
Eliza. daughter of James Melvin and Mercy his Wife,	"	13 January 1718.
Eliza. daughter of Charles Morriss and Esther his Wife,	"	3 February 1718.
Sisley daughter of Dinah Negro Servt. of mr. Bongardon,	"	15 May 1718.
Patience daughter of Tobey Negro and Patience his Wife,	"	2 March 1717/8.

Births — 1718.

Rachel daughter of Clement Norman and Abigall his Wife,	Born	9 October 1718.
Fidella daughter of Robt. Socow Negro and Fidella his Wife,	"	18 December 1718.
John Son of Oliver Noyes Esqr. and Anna his Wife,	"	8 August 1718.
Frances daughter of John Osborn and Ruth his Wife,	"	26 April 1718.
Abigall daughter of John Orn and Eliza. his Wife,	"	6 January 1718.
Robert Son of Robert Pason and Jane his Wife,	"	16 March 1717/8.
Elias Son of Elias Parkman and Martha his Wife,	"	10 March 1717/8.
James Son of James Pitson and Hannah his Wife,	"	6 March 1717/8.
William Son of Willm. Pitman and Eliza. his Wife,	"	10 July 1718.
Nathaniel Son of Joshua Pickman and Eliza. his Wife,	"	28 July 1718.
Peter Son of Edward Pell and Sarah his Wife,	"	28 June 1718.
Benjam. Son of William Parkman and Hannah his Wife,	"	3 September 1718.
Mary daughter of Edmund Perkins and Mary his Wife,	"	25 October 1718.
Daniel Son of Thomas Porter and Eliza. his Wife,	"	1 November 1718.
Mary daughter of Steven Payn and Mary his Wife,	"	20 October 1718.
Thomas } Phillip } Sons of John Peck and Sarah his Wife,	"	9 November 1718.
Mary daughter of Samuel Proctor and Mary his Wife,	"	17 February 1718.
Mathew Son of Mathew Pool and Sarah his Wife,	"	21 March 1718/9.
Susanna daughter of Jonathan Peirse and Mary his Wife,	"	9 March 1718/9.
Nathaniel Son of Nathll. Renalls and Mary his Wife,	"	19 March 1717/8.
Hannah daughter of John Rachel and Hannah his Wife,	"	16 July 1718.
Johanna daughter of William Rand and Sarah his Wife,	"	28 April 1718.
Samuel Son of Samuel Robinson and Mary his Wife,	"	8 September 1718.
John Son of Ichabod Rogers and Hannah his Wife,	"	17 September 1718.
Mary daughter of Samuel Rand and Sarah his Wife,	"	25 September 1718.
Johanna daughter of John Rogers and Johanna his Wife,	"	27 November 1718.
Eliza. daughter of Peter Rollanson and Eliza. his Wife,	"	13 December 1718.
Joseph Son of Joseph Roberts and Rachel his Wife,	"	8 January 1718.
Thomas Son of Nathaniel Renalls and Mary his Wife,	"	25 February 1718.
Elizabeth daughter of John Seers and Eliza. his Wife,	"	3 March 1717/8.
Mary daughter of Richd. Shute and Lydia his Wife,	"	24 March 1717/8.
Lydia daughter of Elisha Storey and Sarah his Wife,	"	26 March 1718.
Lydia daughter of Thomas Studson and Mary his Wife,	"	6 April 1718.
Pen Townsend Son of John Sale and Anne his Wife,	"	9 April 1718.
Samll. Phillips Son of Arthur Savage and Faith his Wife,	"	27 April 1718.
Joseph Son of Abrm. Smith and Mary his Wife,	"	26 April 1718.
Ebenr. Son of John Shaw and Mercy his Wife,	"	3 June 1718.
Anthony Son of William Sears and Eliza. his Wife,	"	16 June 1718.

132   CITY DOCUMENT NO. 43.

Anne daughter of Jonathan Simpson and Mary his Wife,	Born	12 June 1718.
Benjamin Son of Benja. Street and Mary his Wife,	"	2 June 1718.
Sarah daughter of David Stoddard and Eliza. his Wife,	"	10 August 1718.
John Son of James Shaw and Rachel his Wife,	"	27 August 1718.
David Son of Samuel Service and Johanna his Wife,	"	18 August 1718.
John Son of John Sleeper and Sarah his Wife,	"	28 September 1718.
Sarah daughter of Thomas Smith and Sarah his Wife,	"	16 September 1718.
Prudence daughter of Patrick Swanton and Prudence his Wife,	"	3 October 1718.
Mary daughter of Joseph Snelling and Rebecca his Wife,	"	8 November 1718.
Mary daughter of Joseph Snelling and Mary his Wife,	"	23 December 1718.
William Son of William Scot and Sarah his Wife,	"	28 December 1718.
Sarah daughter of Thomas Shaw and Sarah his Wife,	"	13 January 1718.
Sarah daughter of Willlam Tiler and Sarah his Wife,	"	21 March 1717/8.
Mary daughter of Henry Timber Lake and Mary his Wife,	"	9 April 1718.
Thomas Son of John Tufton and Susanna his Wife,	"	12 June 1718.
Mary daughter of Edward Tuttle and Johanna his Wife,	"	23 June 1718.
Rebecca daughter of ye Honble. William Tayier Esqr. and Abigall his Wife,	"	3 July 1718.
Farr Son of William Tolman and Lydia his Wife,	"	24 June 1718.
Anne daughter of Francis Trebeo and Anne his Wife,	"	19 July 1718.
Eliza. daughter of Samuel Tiley and Eliphall his Wife,	"	31 July 1718.
William Son of William Thomas and Anne his Wife,	"	30 August 1718.
Anne daughter of Joseph Turel and Joanna his Wife,	"	13 September 1718.
Grigory Son of Soloman Townsend and Esther his Wife,	"	27 December 1718.
Danforth Son of Timothy Thornton and Eliza. his Wife,	"	25 February 1718.
Thomas Son of John Thompson and Hannah his Wife,	"	5 March 1718/9.
Mary daughter of Samuel Townsend and Mary his Wife,	"	25 February 1718.
Hannah daughter of Thomas Vamus and Hannah his Wife,	"	8 July 1718.
Ruth daughter of Elhanan Winchister and Mary his Wife,	"	19 March 1717/8.
Mary daughter of Benja. White and Mary his Wife,	"	15 April 1718.
Mercy daughter of William Webber and Mary his Wife,	"	24 May 1718.
Edward Son of Edward Watts and Anne his Wife,	"	27 Mary 1718.
Eliza. daughter of John Watkins and Rachel his Wife,	"	13 June 1718.
Peter Son of William Whetcomb and Mary his Wife,	"	10 June 1718.
William Son of Samuel Willis and Eliza. his Wife,	"	4 August 1718.

BIRTHS — 1718.

Experience daughter of Ebenr. Wakefield and Experience his Wife,	Born	28 July 1718.
Ebenr. Son of Allen Wild and Eliza. his Wife,	"	3 July 1718.
Thomas Son of Thomas Waters and Huldah his Wife,	"	18 August 1718.
Edward Son of John Whitemore and Eliza. his Wife,	"	17 August 1718.
Stephen Son of Thomas Willet and Mary his Wife,	"	21 August 1718.
Abigall daughter of Daniel Willard and Abigall his Wife,	"	27 October 1718.
Thomas Son of Cornelius Waldo and Faith his Wife,	"	8 September 1718.
James Son of Richard White and Abigall his Wife,	"	15 December 1718.
Rebecca daughter of Moses Walker and Rachel his Wife,	"	26 December 1718.
Eliza. daughter of Thomas Welch and Eliza. his Wife,	"	8 January 1718.
Richard Son of Samll. Watts and Eliza. his Wife,	"	23 January 1718.
Eliza. daughter of Jacob Wendall and Sarah his Wife,	"	20 January 1718.
Hannah daughter of Thomas Weems and Hannah his Wife,	"	8 July 1718.
Edmund Son of Joseph Whitemore and Eliza. his Wife,	"	17 January 1718.
Margaret daughter of Jonas Webber and Margaret Wife,	"	4 February 1718.
John Son of Timothy Yeals and Eliza. his Wife,	"	16 June 1718.
Obadiah Son of William Young and Mary his Wife,	"	27 September 1718.
Susanna daughter of Ebenr. Youngman and Mercy his Wife,	"	14 October 1718.
Anne daughter of Joseph Bisset and Mary his Wife,	"	17 March 1718.
Joseph Son of Abrm. Billings and Lydia his Wife,	"	7 February 1718.
John Son of Daniel Bell and Abigall his Wife,	"	7 March 1718.
Mehitabell daughter of Caleb Blanchard and Alice his Wife,	"	16 March 1718.
Thomas Son of Henry Brightman and Eliza. his Wife,	"	5 March 1718.
Eliza. daughter of George Betune and Mary his Wife,	"	1 June 1718.
Samuel Son of Benja. Bagnald and Eliza. his Wife,	"	16 December 1718.
Abigall daughter of James Carey and Sarah his Wife,	"	5 March 1718.
Joseph Son of Joseph Clough and Mehitabel his Wife,	"	9 April 1718.
David Son of David Crouch and Susanna his Wife,	"	3 March 1718.
Samuel Son of Zabdiel Daniel and Eliza. his Wife,	"	16 February 1718.
Thomas Son of Thomas Down and Anna his Wife,	"	30 January 1718.
Anne daughter of Thomas Grecian and Anne his Wife,	"	7 March 1718.
Mary daughter of Samll. Greenwood and Mary his Wife,	"	31 October 1718.
Scarlet Son of William Gill and Hannah his Wife,	"	25 January 1718.
Israel Son of Israel How and Judeth his Wife,	"	17 February 1718.
John Son of John Jenkins and Mary his Wife,	"	22 March 1718.
Mary daughter of Stephen Kempton and Rebecca his Wife,	"	6 March 1718.
Lydia daughter of William Mackinley and Lydia his Wife,	"	12 March 1718.
Daniel Son of Anthony Oliver and Mary his Wife,	"	20 March 1718.
Joseph Son of William Peirse and Sarah his Wife,	"	28 February 1718.

Joseph Son of Joseph Payson and Mehitabel his Wife,	Born	3 February 1718.
Joanna daughter of Humphry Richards and Joanna his Wife,	"	16 March 1718.
Mary daughter of Joseph Rogers and Eliza. his Wife,	"	8 July 1718.
Margaret daughter of Jacob Sheafe and Mary his Wife,	"	12 February 1718.
Eliza. daughter of John Smith and Priscilla his Wife,	"	28 December 1718.
Anne daughter of John Warwick and Susanna his Wife,	"	28 February 1718.
Anna daughter of Nathaniel Wardel and Anna his Wife,	"	12 December 1718.
Samuel Son of Nathanl. Coney and Abigall his Wife,	"	15 April 1718.
Joseph Son of John Coolidge and Hannah his Wife,	"	10 February 1718.
Lydia daughter of William Forbish and Sarah his Wife,	"	12 March 1718.
Lydia daughter of Timothy Prout and Lydia his Wife,	"	12 May 1718.
Rebecca daughter of James Scolley and Deborah his Wife,	"	29 December 1718.
Charles and Henry } Gem. Sons of Henry and Hannah Butler,	"	9 March 1718.
Katharine daughter of Matthew and Mary Adams,	"	12 March 1718.
Elizabeth daughter of Thomas and Elizabeth Fleet,	"	21 October 1718.
William Son of William and Elizabeth Fairfield,	"	27 March 1718.
Mary daughter of Samuel and Mary Greenwood,	"	31 October 1718.
Esther daughter of Nathanael and Sarah Harris,	"	12 August 1718.
Elizabeth daughter of Jacob and Abigail Hasey,	"	18 October 1718.
Mary daughter of Richard and Mary Hubbard,	"	16 December 1718.
Mary daughter of James and Joanna Landman,	"	12 March 1713.
Yelverton Son of John and Abigail Man	"	20 October 1718.
Anna daughter of Nathanael and Sarah Morse,	"	3 April 1718.
William Son of William and Ann Noble,	"	12 July 1718.
Richard Son of William and Margaret Payne,	"	4 April 1718.
Sarah daughter of Jonathan and Martha Salter,	"	20 February 1718.
William Son of Elijah and Elizabeth Vinall,	"	20 May 1718.

1719.

Eliza. daughter of John Angeir and Eliza. his Wife,	Born	3 April 1719.
Sarah daughter of Thomas Armstrong and Sarah his Wife,	"	10 April 1719.
John Son of Henry Allen and Mary his Wife,	"	14 May 1719.
John Son of Benja. Andrews and Katherine his Wife,	"	28 August 1719.
John Son of John Alden and Anna his Wife,	"	29 November 1719.
Rebecca daughter of Jonathan Adams and Mary his Wife,	"	15 December 1719.
Anna daughter of Jeremiah Belknap and Sarah his Wife,	"	19 April 1719.
William Son of Nathanll. Bread and Sarah his Wife,	"	20 May 1719.
John Son of John Barber and Eliza. his Wife,	"	14 June 1719.
Mary daughter of Nicholas Boon and Hannah his Wife,	"	7 July 1719.
Loise daughter of Samuel Bligh and Anne his Wife,	"	23 June 1719.

Births — 1719.

Sarah Daughter of John Bonner and Sarah his Wife,	Born	3 July 1719.
Edward Son of Soloman Blake and Abigall his Wife,	"	10 August 1719.
Sarah daughter of John Bradford and Sarah his Wife	"	10 August 1719.
Abigall daughter of John Bulfinch and Jannet his Wife,	"	22 August 1719.
Robert Son of John Buckley and Mary his Wife,	"	27 October 1719.
George Son of George Bethune and Mary his Wife,	"	24 June 1719.
Katherine daughter of John Barton and Katherine his Wife,	"	30 September 1719.
Sarah daughter of Thomas Brooks and Sarah his Wife,	"	2 May 1719.
Samuel Son of James Beighton and Eliza. his Wife,	"	22 November 1719.
Ebenezar Son of Ebenr. Belcher and Ruth his Wife,	"	1 June 1719.
Mercy daughter of Ebenr. Burges and Eliza. his Wife,	"	19 July 1719.
Martha daughter of Israel Baily and Hannah his Wife,	"	15 December 1719.
Elizabeth daughter of Jonathan Burnel and Susanna his Wife,	"	7 January 1719.
William Son of Robert Burgone and Collet his Wife,	"	14 January 1719.
Peter Son of James Barnes and Mary his Wife,	"	11 January 1719.
Mercy daughter of Joseph Birsell and Mercy his Wife,	"	12 January 1719.
Dorcas daughter of John Bancks and Eliza. his Wife,	"	21 January 1719.
Thomas Son of John Buttolph and Mehitabel his Wife,	"	27 November 1719.
Hephsiba daughter of John Baker and Mary his Wife,	"	14 January 1719.
William Son of John Brett and Anne his Wife,	"	20 January 1719.
Mary daughter of Phillip Bargier and Mary his Wife,	"	7 February 1719.
Rebecca daughter of William Brown and Lydia his Wife,	"	15 February 1719.
Charles Son of William Burrel and Joanna his Wife,	"	21 February 1719.
Elisha Son of Josiah Biles and Abigall his Wife,	"	25 February 1719.
Sarah daughter of Jonas Clark and Grace his Wife,	"	30 March 1719.
Isaac Son of Isaac Calwel and Rebecca his Wife,	"	13 April 1719.
Sarah daughter of Samuel Clark and Patience his Wife,	"	12 May 1719.
Mary } Gimi. of Samuell Cook and Eliza. his Elizabeth } Wife,	"	16 June 1719.
Phillip Son of Thomas Chamberline and Hannah his Wife,	"	2 June 1719.
Edward Son of Josiah Chace and Sarah his Wife,	"	27 May 1719.
Lydia daughter of Benja. Clough and Faith his Wife,	"	1 July 1719.
John Son of Job Coyt and Lydia his Wife,	"	11 June 1719.
Thomas Son of Thomas Colesworthy and Sarah his Wife,	"	10 July 1719.
Alice daughter of James Cock and Alice his Wife,	"	15 August 1719.
Margaret daughter of Joseph Clark and Margaret his Wife,	"	5 August 1719.
James Son of John Collegall and Mary his Wife,	"	15 September 1719.
Richard Son of Richard Crocker and Mary his Wife,	"	21 September 1719.
Adam Son of David Colson and Hannah his Wife,	"	3 September 1719.
James Son of James Cock and Anne his Wife,	"	20 December 1719.
Eliza. daughter of Abrm. Clark and Anne his Wife,	"	7 March 1719.
Meriam daughter of John Dupee and Naomi his Wife,	"	17 April 1719.

William Son of William Doke and Lydia his Wife,	Born	29 April 1719.
William Son of William Down and Sarah his Wife,	"	16 May 1719.
John Son of John Doan and Abiah his Wife,	"	1 September 1719.
Rebecca daughter of Thomas Dagget and Lydia his Wife,	"	24 September 1719.
Charles Son of Thomas Demery and Hannah his Wife,	"	23 October 1719.
Mary daughter of James Dason and Mary his Wife,	"	21 October 1719.
Samuel Son of Shem Drown and Katherine his Wife,	"	18 December 1719.
Elizabeth daughter of Charles Demming and Sarah his Wife,	"	11 December 1719.
Faith daughter of John Durant and Rachel his Wife,	"	19 January 1719.
Thomas Son of Thomas Down and Anna his Wife,	"	30 January 1719.
James Son of Henry Dilloway and Abigall his Wife,	"	23 February 1719.
Samuel Son of William Eustice and Eliza. his Wife,	"	12 June 1719.
Mary daughter of Charles Forrist and Mary his Wife,	"	28 April 1719.
David Son of David Frankling and Eliza. his Wife,	"	24 May 1719.
Jonathan Son of Jonathn. Fuller and Anne his Wife,	"	17 July 1719.
Anne daughter of Paul Farmer and Eliza. his Wife,	"	19 July 1719.
Thomas Son of Thomas Fairwether and Hanna his Wife,	"	19 June 1719.
Hannah daughter of John Fife and Abigall his Wife,	"	10 August 1719.
Rebecca daughter of Richard Foster and Rebecca his Wife,	"	26 September 1719.
Benjamon Son of Ephraim Fenno and Eliza. his Wife,	"	3 November 1719.
Margaret daughter of Joseph Fitch and Margaret his Wife,	"	5 December 1719.
Bossenger Son of Thomas Foster and Anne his Wife,	"	21 January 1719.
Sarah daughter of James Goold and Mary his Wife,	"	14 May 1719.
James Son of James Gooch and Eliza. his Wife,	"	17 June 1719.
Stephen Son of Samuel Greenliefe and Martha his Wife,	"	22 July 1719.
Eliza. daughter of James Goodwin and Eliza. his Wife,	"	24 August 1719.
John Son of John Grey and Eliza. his Wife,	"	4 September 1719.
Nathaniel Son of Nathll. Gardener and Mary his Wife,	"	11 October 1719.
Mary daughter of Samuell Gerrish and Sarah his Wife,	"	11 September 1719.
Edward Son of Joseph Grant and Dorothy his Wife,	"	11 December 1719.
Anne daughter of John Gainger and Mary his Wife,	"	20 January 1719.
Mary daughter of Nicholas George and Mary his Wife,	"	13 February 1719.
Eliza. daughter of Franis Hudson and Mary his Wife,	"	26 March 1719.
Eliza. daughter of ye Rd. mr. Henry Harrise and his Wife,	"	29 March 1719.
Jonathan Son of John Hillier and Eliza. his Wife,	"	19 April 1719.
Hephsibah daughter of Nathaniel Howard and Hepsiah his Wife,	"	30 May 1719.

BIRTHS — 1719.

Sarah daughter of Samuel Haley and Eliza. his Wife,	Born	24 July 1719.
Nathaniel Son of Allexandr. Harper and Sarah his Wife,	"	28 July 1719.
Mercy daughter of Samuel Harrise and Hannah his Wife,	"	1 September 1719.
Lydia daughter of Elias Hart and Lydia his Wife.	"	12 September 1719.
Jeremiah Son of Jeremiah Hart and Miriam his Wife,	"	18 September 1719.
John Son of John Humble and Susanna his Wife,	"	11 October 1719.
Sarah daughter of Joseph Harrise and Eliza. his Wife,	"	8 October 1719.
Rachel daughter of John Henderson and Rachel his Wife,	"	11 October 1719.
Anna daughter of James Halsey and Anna his Wife,	"	13 November 1719.
Eliza. daughter of Richard Huges and Sarah his Wife,	"	21 December 1719.
Anne daughter of John Jefferyes and Anne his Wife,	"	25 June 1719.
Eliza. daughter of John Jenkins and Mary his Wife,	"	15 July 1719.
Mary daughter of Thomas Jenkins and Mary his Wife,	"	1 July 1719.
Rachel daughter of Thomas Inches and Rachel his Wife,	"	9 September 1719
Abigall daughter of Thomas Jones and Bethia his Wife,	"	10 October 1719
Benjamen Son of Nathaniel Kenny and Eliza. his Wife,	"	17 September 1719.
William Son of Elias Kingston and Martha his Wife,	"	31 September 1719.
Mary daughter of John King and Mary his Wife,	"	8 June 1719.
Ruth daughter of John Leech and Ruth his Wife,	"	5 June 1719.
John Son of John Lawrence and Mary Ann his Wife,	"	11 June 1719.
William Son of William Livermore and Eliza. his Wife,	"	1 July 1719.
Sarah daughter of John Letherbee and Eliza. his Wife,	"	12 July 1719.
Edward Son of Edward Lisk and Isabella his Wife,	"	25 July 1719.
Mary daughter of Ebenr. Lamson and Sarah his Wife,	"	12 August 1719.
Anne daughter of Edward Lyde and Eliza. his Wife,	"	22 July 1719.
Hannah daughter of David Linfield and Hannah his Wife,	"	18 October 1719.
Benja. Son of Oliver Luckey and Rebecca his Wife,	"	16 October 1719.
John Son of Jonathan Lambert and Mary his Wife,	"	26 October 1719.
William Son of John Lawson and Sarah his Wife,	"	27 March 1720.
Robert Son of John Logan and Mary his Wife,	"	10 November 1719.
Mary daughter of Isaac Lewise and Hannah his Wife,	"	9 October 1719.
Stephen Son of William Leatherbee and Lydia his Wife,	"	8 December 1719.
Eliza. daughter of Paul Lanksford and Eliza. his Wife,	"	10 January 1719.
Thomas Son of Richard Langdon and Thankfull his Wife,	"	19 February 1719.
Joseph Son of Joseph Leasonbee and Mary his Wife,	"	6 February 1719.
Hannah daughter of Samuel Langdon and Esther his Wife,	"	8 August 1719.
Matthew Son of Nathaniel Loring and Susanna his Wife,	"	14 February 1719.

Eliza daughter of Edward Low and Eliza. his Wife, Born 15 February 1719.
Mary daughter of Thadeus Maccarty and Mary his Wife, " 29 March 1719.
Thomas Son of William Maccarty and Margaret his Wife, " 22 May 1719.
Andrew Henry Son of Andrew Le Mercier and Margaret his Wife, " 4 August 1719.
Mary daughter of John Mellecan and Sarah his Wife, " 11 August 1719.
Abigall daughter of Jonathan Mountfor and Hannah his Wife, " 24 September 1719.
Mary daughter of Lewis Mallet and Margaret his Wife, " 4 September 1719.
Samuel Son of Samuel Moulds and Mary his Wife, " 16 September 1719.
Thomas Son of John Minzes and Eddee his Wife, " 22 September 1719.
Joanna daughter of Ephriam More and Eliza. his Wife, " 22 November 1719.
Nathaniel Son of Nathaniel Martyn and Hannah his Wife, " 26 November 1719.
Isabella daughter of Allexandr. Miller and Eliza. his Wife, " 23 December 1719.
George Son of John Mills and Sarah his Wife, " 13 February 1719.
Thomas Son of Thomas Nowel and Mary his Wife, " 5 May 1719.
Sarah daughter of Phillip Nowel and Anne his Wife, " 22 June 1719.
Sarah daughter of John Oliver and Alice his Wife, " 26 October 1719.
Edward Brattle Son of Brattle Oliver and Anne his Wife, " 20 November 1719.
Samuel Son of Isaac Peirse and Grace his Wife, " 11 April 1719.
Eliza daughter of David Prince and Eliza. his Wife, " 2 April 1719.
Sarah daughter of George Pemberton and Susanna his Wife, " 2 July 1719.
Hannah daughter of Thomas Plasteed and Mary his Wife, " 24 June 1719.
Isaac Son of William Parker and Anna his Wife, " 2 July 1719.
Abiel daughter of Edward Paige and Ruth his Wife, " 16 July 1719.
William Son of William Phillips and Anne his Wife, " 19 August 1719.
Mary daughter of Samuel Peck and Eliza. his Wife, " 22 August 1719.
John Son of Richard Pitcher and Grace his Wife, " 25 August 1719.
Joseph Son of James Peneman and Mary his Wife, " 27 August 1719.
Rebecca daughter of Indego Potter and Rebecca his Wife, " 28 September 1719.
Eliza. daughter of William Palfrey and Abigall his Wife. " 11 November 1719.
Mercy daughter of Peter Papillion and Kathern. his Wife, " 20 January 1719.
Sarah daughter of Simon Rogers and Mary his Wife, " 21 April 1719.
Joseph Son of Timothy Robinson and Dorothy his Wife, " 6 June 1719.
Preserved daughter of Edward Rawson and Preserved his Wife, " 27 June 1719.
Ruth daughter of John Renalds and Anna his Wife, " 16 October 1719.
Robert Son of Robert Rand and Susanna his Wife, " 8 November 1719.
Elias Son of Samuel Roberts and Abigall his Wife, " 21 August 1719.

BIRTHS — 1719.

William Son of Joseph Robie and Priscilla his Wife,	Born	12 January 1719.
Thomas Son of John Stocker and Abigall his Wife,	"	25 March 1719.
Allen Son of Thomas Steel and Jane his Wife,	"	3 April 1719.
Charles Son of Christopher Souther and Deborah his Wife,	"	16 April 1719.
William Son of William Starling and Grace his Wife,	"	18 April 1719.
Mary daughter of Richard Stebbens and Martha his Wife,	"	15 May 1719.
Mary daughter of John Sale and Anne his Wife,	"	21 May 1719.
Frances daughter of James Stringer and Mary his Wife,	"	19 June 1719.
Richard Son of John Steel and Mary his Wife,	"	26 June 1719.
Mehitabel daughter of David Stoddard and Eliza. his Wife,	"	5 July 1719.
Thomas Son of Thomas Studson and Mary his Wife,	"	25 July 1719.
George Son of Simon Slocome and Eliza. his Wife,	"	11 October 1719.
Frances daughter of Gravingham Salter and Abiel his Wife,	"	19 November 1719.
Anne ⎱ daughters of Thomas Smith and Sarah Bethia ⎰ his Wife,	"	3 November 1719.
Susanna daughter of Robert Sanders and Anne his Wife,	"	20 November 1719.
Mary daughter of Humphry Scarlet and Mehitabel his Wife,	"	23 November 1719.
Samuel Son of Samuel Stebbens and Rachel his Wife,	"	23 November 1719.
Sarah daughter of John Smith and Martha his Wife,	"	9 April 1719
Eliza. daughter of Robert Starkie and Walter his Wife,	"	29 November 1719.
Benjamen Son of Joseph Scot and Deliverence his Wife,	"	7 December 1719.
Erasamus Son of Erasamus Stephens and Peirces his Wife,	"	20 December 1719.
Eliza. daughter of Daniel Storey and Eliza. his Wife,	"	8 January 1719.
Sarah daughter of Mallachy Salter and Sarah his Wife,	"	17 February 1719.
Hannah daughter of Andrew Sigernee and Mary his Wife,	"	27 February 1719.
Joseph Son of Joseph Snelling and Mary his Wife,	"	8 March 1719.
Eliza. daughter of John Stride and Jane his Wife,	"	1 March 1719.
Mary daughter of Phinias Thomas and Anne his Wife,	"	4 May 1719.
James Son of James Trench and Phillippi his Wife,	"	26 April 1719.
Sarah daughter of Thomas Taylor and Sarah his Wife,	"	15 May 1719.
Hannah daughter of Michael Tapper and Submit his Wife,	"	30 June 1719.
Andrew Son of Andrew Tiler and Meriam his Wife,	"	20 August 1719.
Eliza. daughter of John Thomas and Eliza. his Wife,	"	23 August 1719.
Eliza. daughter of John Tiley and Eliza. his Wife,	"	5 November 1719.
Oxenbridge Son of Oxenbridge Thatcher and Eliza. his Wife,	"	29 December 1719.
James Son of James Trout and Abigall his Wife,	"	25 January 1719.
Mary daughter of Peter Townsend and Mary his Wife,	"	26 January 1719.
Royall Son of William Tyler and Sarah his Wife,	"	29 January 1719.
Jonathan Son of Silvanus Vickers and Anna his Wife,	"	6 September 1719.

William Son of Joseph Uran and Sarah his Wife,	Born	16 August 1719.
John Son of David Webb and Jane his Wife,	"	1 May 1719.
Hannah daughter of Ezekiel Walker and Ruth his Wife,	"	2 May 1719.
Anne daughter of John Waldo and Eliza. his Wife,	"	15 July 1719.
Mary daughter of John Welland and Eliza. his Wife,	"	13 July 1719.
James Son of Ephraim Wheeler and Dorothy his Wife,	"	20 August 1719.
Edward Son of Edward Wilkinson and Rebecca his Wife,	"	12 September 1719.
Eliza. daughter of Cord Wing and Sarah his Wife,	"	20 September 1719.
John Son of Richard Woods and Hannah his Wife,	"	16 October 1719.
John Son of John Wheelwright and Eliza. his Wife,	"	18 October 1719.
Thomas Son of Francis Warden and Eliza. his Wife,	"	5 October 1719.
Henry Son of Benja. White and Mary his Wife,	"	28 October 1719.
Mary daughter of James Wright and Mary his Wife,	"	5 November 1719.
John Son of Isaac White and Rebecca his Wife,	"	21 November 1719.
Nathaniel Son of Nathaniel Whitell and Eliza. his Wife,	"	3 December 1719.
Eliza. daughter of Ebenezar Wakefield and Experience his Wife,	"	26 November 1719.
Sarah daughter of Joshua Williams and Anne his Wife,	"	1 January 1719.
Thomas Son of Thomas Warden and Anna his Wife,	"	8 January 1719.
Thomas Son of Thomas Wallice and Grace his Wife,	"	1 February 1719.
Eliza. daughter of Samuel Whitwell and Eliza. his Wife,	"	23 October 1719.
Dorcas daughter of John Williss and Sarah his Wife,	"	20 March 1719.
James Son of Robert Williams and Sarah his Wife,	"	13 March 1719.
John Son of John Young and Mary his Wife,	"	10 October 1719.
Meriam daughter of Freeborn Balch and Susanna his Wife,	"	18 March 1719.
John Son of Ebenr. Clough and Thankfull his Wife,	"	9 February 1719
Samuel Son of John Clough and Mehitabel his Wife,	"	9 February 1719.
Sarah daughter of Joseph Calef and Hannah his Wife,	"	13 November 1719.
Sarah daughter of William Daviss and Hannah his Wife,	"	28 February 1719.
William Son of Thomas Dawes and Sarah his Wife,	"	2 October 1719.
Eliza. daughter of Jonathan Eustise and Sarah his Wife,	"	29 August 1719.
Peter Son of Gidian Florence and Susanna his Wife,	"	19 February 1719.
Thomas Son of ye Rd. Thomas Foxcroft and Anna his Wife,	"	3 January 1719.
Eliza. daughter of Allexander Fullerton and Eliza. his Wife,	"	17 March 1719.
Joseph Son of Samuel Holbrook and Hannah his Wife,	"	3 June 1719.
John Son of Charles Henley and Martha his Wife,	"	23 September 1719.
Lydia daughter of Samuel Kenney and Abigall his Wife,	"	6 May 1719.

BIRTHS — 1719.

Experience daughter of William Lyon and Experience his Wife,	Born	8 March 1719.
Margaret daughter of Thomas Leechmer and Anne his Wife,	"	4 March 1719.
Ebenezar Son of Ebenr. Leadbetter and Abigall his Wife,	"	17 March 1719.
Isaac Son of Isaac Marion and Eliza. his Wife,	"	4 March 1719.
Sarah daughter of John Meers and Sarah his Wife,	"	5 March 1719.
Eliza. daughter of Richard Morgan and Sarah his Wife,	"	5 March 1719.
Nathaniel Son Nathll. Mason and Eliza. his Wife,		14 March 1719.
James Son of James Melvin and Mercy his Wife,	"	11 April 1719.
Jamina daughter of John Maverick and Eliza. his Wife,	"	11 February 1719.
Timothy Son of Bryant Parrot and Abigall his Wife,	"	1 March 7119.
Benjamen Son of Benja. Pool and Sarah his Wife,	"	7 March 1719.
Ebenezar Son of Timothy Prout and Lydia his Wife,	"	8 October 1719.
Joseph Son of ye Rd. Joseph Sewall and Eliza. his Wife,	"	13 July 1719.
Mary daughter of Daniel Willard and Abigall his Wife,	"	29 February 1719.
Martha daughter of William Winter and Martha his Wife,	"	24 November 1719.
Katherine daughter of John Walley and Bethia his Wife,	"	5 October 1719.
John Son of Ebenr. Williston and Judeth his Wife,	"	10 March 1719.
Elizabeth daughter of Francise Whitman and Eliza. his Wife,	"	29 December 1719.
Deborah daughter of Joseph and Mary Balch,	"	8 September 1719.
Anna daughter of Thomas and Sarah Boylston,	"	8 January 1719.
William Son of Benjamin and Mary Bronsdon,	"	6 April 1719.
Thomas Son of Joseph and Mary Clewley,	"	21 June 1719.
Thomas, Son of Thomas and Elizabeth Cock,	"	31 August 1719.
Henry Son of Henry and Mercy Coffin,	"	31 December 1719.
Andrew Son of Andrew and Mary Cunningham,	"	2 October 1719.
Sarah daughter of James and Grace Davenport,	"	2 January 1719.
George Son of Samuel and Elizabeth Durant,	"	17 November 1719.
Joshua Son of Nathanael and Hannah Emmes,	"	17 November 1719.
Elizabeth daughter of William and Elizabeth Fairfield,	"	1 November 1719.
Mary daughter of Thomas and Mary Goodwin,	"	14 September 1719.
Mary daughter of Heman and Mary Henderson,	"	8 February 1719.
Susanna daughter of Benjamin and Elizabeth Hillier,	"	20 May 1719.
Samuel Son of John and Elizabeth Kneeland,	"	2 February 1719.
Elizabeth daughter of Samuel and Elizabeth Kneeland,	"	17 February 1719.
Rebekah daughter of Thomas and Mary Kilby,	"	17 September 1719.
Elizabeth Son of Samuel and Admonition Mattock,	"	14 October 1719.
Thomas Son of Christopher and Elizabeth Marshall,	"	21 July 1719.
Mary daughter of Samuel and Mary Marion,	"	18 April 1719.
Charles Son of Thomas and Hannah Moulin,	"	16 April 1719.
Thomas Son of Michael and Martha Mack,	"	24 August 1719.
Joseph Son of Nathanael and Abigail Pearse,	"	20 November 1719.
Sarah daughter of James and Hannah Pemberton,	"	11 December 1719.
John Son of Joseph and Elizabeth Ricks,	"	30 September 1719.
Mary daughter of John and Elizabeth Smith,	"	31 January 1719.
Ann daughter of Elijah and Elizabeth Vinall,	"	29 February 1719.
John Son of Joseph and Elizabeth White,	"	24 May 1719.
Mary daughter of Benjamin and Elizabeth Williams	"	26 September 1719.

1720.

Ruth daughter of James Arnall and Ruth his Wife,	Born	6 April 1720.
Joseph Son of John Adams and Mary his Wife,	"	1 June 1720.
John Son of Thomas Adkins and Ruth his Wife,	"	8 July 1720.
Thomas Son of John Allen and Mary his Wife,	"	5 August 1720.
Ebenezar Son of Ebenr. Allen and Eliza. his Wife,	"	26 August 1720.
Hannah daughter of Elnathan Aires and Mercey his Wife,	"	21 September 1720.
Hannah daughter of Samuel Adams and Mary his Wife,	"	6 November 1720.
Huldah daughter of Francis Archbald and Huldah his Wife,	"	25 December 1720.
Edward Son of Edward Aires and Rebecca his Wife,	"	26 December 1720.
Eliza. daughter of Phillip Alman and Jane his Wife,	"	14 January 1720.
Jonathan Son of John Bailey and Sarah his Wife,	"	8 April 1720.
Samuel Son of Samuel Bass and Christian his Wife,	"	28 April 1720.
Mary daughter of Andrew Brown and Mary his Wife,	"	25 May 1720.
Elizabeth daughter of William Bearstow and Eliza. his Wife,	"	29 May 1720.
Martha daughter of William Beal and Martha his Wife,	"	25 June 1720.
Hannah daughter of John Briant and Katherine his Wife,	"	14 June 1720.
Walter Son of Walter Baker and Ruth his Wife,	"	30 June 1720.
Hannah daughter of John Brewster and Deliverence his Wife,	"	26 July 1720.
Mary daughter of George Butler and Mary his Wife,	"	18 July 1720.
Abigall daughter of Joseph Brown and Hannah his Wife,	"	16 July 1720.
Josiah Son of Zabdiel Boylston and Jerusha his Wife,	"	11 July 1720.
Mary daughter of Thomas Barnerd and Silence his Wife,	"	27 July 1720.
Mary daughter of John Ballentine and Mary his Wife,	"	3 August 1720.
Elizabeth daughter of John Beaudry and Eliza. his Wife,	"	13 August 1720.
William Son of William Baker and Sarah his Wife,	"	11 August 1720.
Mary daughter of Daniel Ballard and Mary his Wife,	"	25 August 1720.
George Son of John Briggs and Katherine his Wife,	"	6 September 1720.
Elizabeth daughter of Thomas Brunton and Lydia his Wife,	"	26 September 1720.
Ebenr. Son of Benjamen Brown and Mary his Wife,	"	27 September 1720.
Rachel daughter of Ebenr. Burges and Eliza. his Wife,	"	22 September 1720.
Samuel Son of Samuel Badcock and Martha his Wife,	"	30 November 1720.
Sarah daugnter of John Burt and Abigall his Wife,	"	25 November 1720.
Jonathan Son of Jacob Blanchard and Abigall his Wife,	"	2 February 1720.
Sarah daughter of John Banks and Sarah his Wife,	"	31 January 1720.
Martha daughter of Benjamen Bagnald and Eliza. his Wife,	"	23 January 1720.
Abraham Son of Abraham Billins and Lydia his Wife,	"	22 February 1720.

BIRTHS — 1720.

Mercy daughter of Thomas Brooks and Sarah his Wife,	Born	27 January 1720.
Jeremiah Son of Jeremiah Belknap and Sarah his Wife,	"	10 February 1720.
Mary daughter of Nathll. Coney and Abigall his Wife,	"	18 March 1719/0.
Christopher Son of Christopher Capril and Mary his Wife,	"	18 March 1719/0.
David Son of David Cunningham and Sarah his Wife,	"	5 April 1720.
Willm. Down Son of Daniel Cheever and Mary his Wife,	"	18 July 1720.
Hannah daughter of Josiah Carter and Hannah his Wife,	"	21 July 1720.
James Son of James Cranston and Lydia his Wife,	"	22 July 1720.
John Son of Edward Cruff and Abigall his Wife,	"	8 August 1720.
William Son of William Cock and Eliza. his Wife,	"	28 August 1720.
John Son of John Compton and Rebecca his Wife,	"	29 September 1720.
John Son of William Cooper and Sarah his Wife,	"	31 October 1720.
William Son of Jeremiah Condey and Susanna his Wife,	"	16 September 1720.
Allexander Son of Robert Cummins and Elen his Wife,	"	31 December 1720.
Samuel Son of James Cock and Alice his Wife,	"	3 January 1720.
Benjamen Son of David Crouch and Susanna his Wife,	"	27 January 1720.
Hannah daughter of Samuel Clark and Patience his Wife,	"	2 February 1720.
Katherine daughter of Samuel Daviss and Katherine his Wife,	"	14 March 1719/20.
Mary daughter of Berton Denizot and Martha his Wife,	"	17 April 1720.
Elizabeth daughter of William Daviss and Bathsheba his Wife,	"	1 May 1720.
Thomas Son of James Daviss and Sarah his Wife,	"	14 May 1720.
Samuel Son of John Dupee and Naomie his Wife,	"	26 June 1720.
Abigall daughter of Andrew Durgee and Abigall his Wife,	"	19 June 1720.
Thomas Son of Henry Dering and Eliza. his Wife,	"	16 May 1720.
Lydia daughter of Benjamen Dresser and Lydia his Wife,	"	21 August 1720.
James Son of James Dowel and Hannah his Wife,	"	29 September 1720.
Mary daughter of John Dixwel and Mary his Wife,	"	1 November 1720.
Richard Son of Evan Daviss and Anne his Wife,	"	17 December 1720.
Butcher Son of Samuel Dyer and Lucey his Wife,	"	11 December 1720.
Anna daughter of Daniel Dupee and Lydia his Wife,	"	26 December 1720.
Abigall daughter of Thomas Dawes and Sarah his Wife,	"	14 January 1720.
Elizabeth daughter of Joseph Douglas and Eliza. his Wife,	"	14 April 1720.
Lydia daughter of William Dokes and Lydia his Wife,	"	13 February 1720.
Benjamen Son of Benja. Eustise and Katherine his Wife,	"	16 April 1720.
Nathaniel Son of John Ellery and Jane his Wife,	"	1 August 1720.
William Henry Son of Patrick Erskine and Sarah his Wife,	"	14 March 1719/20.
Sarah daughter of John Earl and Mary his Wife,	"	17 September 1720.
Elizabeth daughter of Samll. Emms and Hephsiba his Wife,	"	25 January 1720.

John Son of Nehemiah Eals and Hannah his Wife,	Born	18 February 1720.
Zacheriah Son of Zachry. Fitch and Abigall his Wife,	"	9 March 1719/20.
Thomas Son of Thomas Fleming and Eliza. his Wife,	"	12 March 1719/20.
David Son of Jonathn. Farnum and Anne his Wife,	"	3 April 1720.
George Son of George Folliss and Mary his Wife,	"	9 May 1720.
Thomas Grose Son of John Fairwether and Jerusha his Wife,	"	11 April 1720.
Mary daughter of William Foy and Eliza. his Wife,	"	7 June 1720.
Mary daughter of Samuel Foy and Eliza. his Wife,	"	20 August 1720.
John Son of William Fletcher and Margaret his Wife,	"	18 August 1720.
John Son of John Farmer and Eliza. his Wife,	"	1 October 1720.
Margaret daughter of Allexandr. Fife and Eliza. his Wife,	"	25 November 1720.
Margaret daughter of William Fletcher and Margaret his Wife,	"	6 January 1720.
Jonathan Son of David Frankling and Eliza. his Wife,	"	21 January 1720.
Peter Son of Peter Frazier and Mary his Wife,	"	30 October 1720.
Mary daughter of Charles Gyles and Mary his Wife,	"	26 March 1720.
Rachel daughter of William Goold and Rachel his Wife,	"	10 May 1720.
John Son of John Gaud and Anne his Wife,	"	6 June 1720.
Jane daughter of Alexandr. Grimes and Eliza. his Wife,	"	17 September 1720.
Mary daughter of William Gill and Anna his Wife,	"	18 October 1720.
Joseph Son of William Greenliefe and Mary his Wife,	"	10 November 1720.
Joseph Son of Samuel Gerrish and Sarah his Wife,	"	2 January 1720.
Eliza. daughter of William Garret and Grace his Wife,	"	13 January 1720.
Abigall daughter of Daniel Goffe and Elizabeth his Wife,	"	25 December 1720.
Eliza. daughter of James Garret and Eliza. his Wife,	"	27 January 1720.
Samuel Son of Samuel Greenwood and Mary his Wile,	"	18 May 1720.
Jane daughter of John Ireland and Jane his Wife,	"	15 May 1720.
Samuel Son of Samuel Jenkins and Eliza. his Wife,	"	15 June 1720.
Mary daughter of John Jenkins and Mary his Wife,	"	26 June 1720.
William } Gimi. of William Inngs and Anne his Avise } Wife,	"	24 August 1720.
David Son of David Jenkins and Sarah his Wife,	"	14 February 1720.
Edward Son of Richard Hazely and Tamozine his Wife,	"	18 April 1720.
Susanna daughter of Samuel Hill and Susanna his Wife,	"	23 April 1720.
Hannah daughter of John Harwood and Mary his Wife,	"	27 April 1720.
John Son of John Hooton and Sarah his Wife,	"	28 May 1720.
Mary daughter of John Holland and Susanna his Wife,	"	17 January 1720.
Samuel Son of Samll. Hunt and Mary his Wife,	"	18 January 1720.
Elizabeth daughter of John Harriss and Katherine his Wife,	"	14 January 1720.

Births — 1720.

John Son of John Hopkins and Susanna his Wife,	Born	1 February 1720.
Sarah daughter of James Humphryes and Judeth his Wife,	"	10 February 1720.
John Son of John Hurst and Mary his Wife,	"	14 June 1720.
George Son of George Henchlee and Mehitable his Wife,	"	4 July 1720.
Benjamen Son of Phillip Hedman and Eliza. his Wife,	"	20 March 1719/20.
Hannah daughter of Nathaniel Haywood and Hephsiba his Wife,	"	26 August 1720.
Elisha Son of Abiel Holbrook and Mary his Wife,	"	19 August 1720.
Sarah daughter of Arthur Hill and Rebecca his Wife,	"	29 September 1720.
Henaritta daughter of William Hender and Esther his Wife,	"	23 September 1720.
Haukins Son of Thomas Hutchinson Esqr. and Sarah his Wife,	"	12 February 1720.
Samuel Son of Samuel Healy and Eliza. his Wife,	"	9 March 1720.
Samuel Son of Samuel Knight and Eliza. his Wife,	"	27 August 1720.
Mary daughter of Elias Kingston and Martha his Wife,	"	22 December 1720.
Robert Son of Robert Kelder and Hannah his Wife,	"	27 December 1720.
William Son of Daniel Katen and Mary his Wife,	"	6 February 1720.
Thomas Son of Thomas Lawler and Eliza. his Wife,	"	28 March 1720.
Samuel Son of Henry Lowder and Abigall his Wife,	"	13 April 1720.
William Richee Son of Riche Love and Copia his Wife,	"	12 September 1720.
Samuel Son of John Leath and Eliner his Wife,	"	26 September 1720.
James Andrew Son of Andrew Lemercer and Margaret his Wife,		17 June 1720.
Mary daughter of Thomas Mauer and Mary his Wife.	"	7 June 1720.
Mary daughter of Richard Meda and Martha his Wife,	"	4 July 1720.
Sarah daughter of Charles Mossen and Eliner his Wife,	"	22 February 1720.
Sarah daughter of John Merrefield and Bridget his Wife,	"	9 August 1720.
Johanna daughter of Major Paul Mascareen and Eliza. his Wife,	"	19 August 1720.
Elizabeth daughter of Daniel Mundan and Anne his Wife,	"	16 August 1720.
John Son of Thomas Mitchel and Eliza. his Wife,	"	31 October 1720.
Mary daughter of Ralph Mayer and Martha his Wife,	"	31 October 1720.
Martha daughter of William Merchant and Abigall his Wife,	"	7 December 1720.
Joanna daughter of John Melling and Honour his Wife,	"	27 December 1720.
Rachel daughter of Samuell Narramore and Rachel his Wife,	"	22 June 1720.
Elizabeth daughter of Joseph Nowel and Eliza. his Wife,	"	28 August 1720.
Robert Son of Robert Nowel and Mary his Wife,	"	3 September 1720.
Woodbery Son of John Osborn and Sarah his Wife,	"	25 March 1720.
William Son of William Pitman and Eliza. his Wife,	"	10 April 1720.
Elizabeth daughter of Caleb Prat and Mary his Wife,	"	10 May 1720.
Sarah daughter of Peter Pritchet and Sarah his Wife,	"	2 June 1720.

William Son of William Pike and Susanna his Wife, Born 18 June 1720.
Elizabeth daughter of Joseph Prince and Mary his Wife, " 16 June 1720.
Aaron Son of Thomas Porter and Eliza. his Wife, " 14 July 1720.
Nathaniel Son of Nathll. Pulman and Susanna his Wife, " 7 August 1720.
Frizzel Son of Francis Parnel and Eliza. his Wife, " 28 July 1720.
Abigall daughter of Jonathan Parrot and Abigall his Wife, " 24 August 1720.
Nathaniel Son of William Parkman and Hannah his Wife, " 25 August 1720.
Eliza. daughter of Caleb Parker and Eliza. his Wife, " 9 September 1720.
Mary daughter of James Peeker and Susanna his Wife, " 15 September 1720.
Susanna daughter of James Peet and Susanna his Wife, " 4 September 1720.
Samuel Son of Stephen Payn and Mary his Wife, " 23 October 1720.
Thomas Son of Thomas Parker and Eliza. his Wife, " 1 November 1720.
Katherine daughter of Samuel Powsley and Eliza. his Wife, " 8 November 1720.
Dorcas daughter of James Prindle and Eliza. his Wife, " 31 August 1720.
Rebecca daughter of Richard Phillips and Rebecca. his Wife, " 25 December 1720.
Mary daughter of Joseph Payson and Mehitabel his Wife, " 30 December 1720.
Mary daughter of Robert Patteshall and Jane his Wife, " 24 December 1720.
Gill Son of William Prat and Mehitabel his Wife, " 12 January 1720.
Jonathan Son of James Peneman and Mary his Wife, " 3 December 1720.
Wheelwright Son of Thomas Pearson and Eunice his Wife, " 1 March 1720.
Susanna daughter of Joseph Russel and Abigall his Wife, " 29 April 1720.
Samuel Son of Samuel Robinson and Mary his Wife, " 27 April 1720.
Peleg Son of Jeremiah Rodes and Lydia his Wife, " 24 May 1720.
Rachel daughter of Joseph Roberts and Rachel his Wife, " 29 June 1720.
Edward Son of Edward Rumbley and Eliza. his Wife, " 19 August 1720.
Edward Son of Timothy Robinson and Dorothy his Wife. " 3 September 1720.
Abraham Son of Simon Rogers and Mary his Wife, " 10 November 1720.
Jonathan Son of Jonathan Rouse and Martha his Wife, " 20 October 1720.
Sarah daughter of John Rachel and Hannah his Wife, " 6 December 1720.
Spencer Son of Caleb Rayman and Mary his Wife, " 4 January 1720.
Sarah daughter of John Russel and Eliza. his Wife, " 20 June 1720.
Samuel Son of James Scolley and Deborah his Wife, " 26 March 1720.
William Son of John Seers and Eliza. his Wife, " 28 April 1720.
William Son of Elisha Storey and Sarah his Wife, " 25 April 1720.
Johanna daughter of Bartholomw. Spiller and Joanna his Wife, " 12 June 1720.
John Son of Stephen Sims and Eliza. his Wife, " 22 June 1720.
Martha daughter of David Stoddard and Eliza. his Wife, " 20 July 1720.
Thomas Son of Thomas Smith and Mary his Wife, " 2 August 1720.

Births — 1720.

Mary daughter of Patrick Swanton and Prudence his Wife,	Born	16 September 1720.
Samuel Son of William Smallage and Ruth his Wife,	"	16 September 1720.
Eliza. daughter of Jonathan Sewall and Eliza, his Wife,	"	13 September 1720.
Susauna daughter of Jonathan Simpson and Mary his Wife,	"	30 September 1720.
Joseph Son of Joseph Scot and Mehitabel his Wife,	"	20 October 1720.
Samuel Son of Samual Smith and Mary his Wife,	"	3 November 1720.
Elizabeth daughter of Elisha Salter and Katherine his Wife,	"	3 October 1720.
Edward Ladd Son of William Sanders and Bridget his Wife,	"	9 November 1720.
Sarah daughter of Michael Shaler and Meriam his Wife,	"	7 September 1720.
John Son of Thomas Steel and Jane his Wife,	"	24 November 1720.
John Son of Thomas Stesson and Mary his Wife,	"	12 January 1720.
Barthll. Gosier Son of Bartholomew Seers and Eliza. his Wife,	"	26 January 1720.
Mary daughter of William Steel and Mary his Wife,	"	12 February 1720.
Mary daughter of Joseph Turel and Joanna his Wife,	"	17 April 1720.
Anne daughter of William Thomas and Anne his Wife,	"	15 June 1720.
Robert Son of Robert Temlet and Mary his Wife.	"	20 June 1720.
Hannah daughter of Thomas Townsend and Eliza. his Wife,	"	15 July 1720.
Francis Son of Francis Trebou and Anne his Wife,	"	20 July 1720.
James Son of Henry Timberlake and Mary his Wife.	"	28 July 1720.
Joseph Son of Benja. Thwing and Bathsheba his Wife,	"	24 July 1720.
Nathaniel Son of James Trench and Phillippi his Wife,	"	17 October 1720.
Lewise Son of Samuel Tiley and Elliphall his Wife,	"	28 October 1720.
Joseph Son of Joseph Treat and Mary his Wife,	"	21 October 1720.
Rebecca daughter of William Tolman and Lydia his Wife,	"	13 December 1720.
James Son of Maverick Thomas and Joanna his Wife,	"	5 October 1720.
William Son of Andrew Tyler and Meriam his Wife,	"	28 January 1720.
Thomas Son of Thomas Velvin and Sarah his Wife,	"	25 April 1720.
Rachel daughter of John Vaughan and Rachel his Wife,	"	15 May 1720.
Mary-Anna daughter of Edward Vittery and Anna his Wife,	"	25 July 1720.
Mary daughter of Samuel Wright and Mary his Wife,	"	31 March 1720.
William Son of William Wilson and Eliza. his Wife,	"	26 April 1720.
Mary daughter of Samuel Whitehead and Mary his Wife,	"	4 May 1720.
Thomas Son of Joshua Williams and Mary his Wife,	"	27 April 1720.
Henry Son of John Webster and Mary his Wife,	"	12 May 1720.

Elizabeth daughter of Allen Wild and Eliza. his Wife,	Born	28 June 1720.
James Son of Peter Wooden and Joanna his Wife,	"	19 July 1720.
John ⎰ Gimi. of Henry Woolfe and Rachel his Mary ⎱ Wife,	"	12 August 1720.
Susanna daughter of James Wright and Susanna his Wife,	"	30 August 1720.
Hannah daughter of Ezekiel Walker and Ruth his Wife,	"	11 August 1720.
Cord Son of Cord Wing and Sarah his Wife,	"	23 September 1720.
Issabella daughter of Thomas Wems and Hannah his Wife,	"	20 October 1720.
Elizabeth daughter of Joseph Wadsworth and Eliza. his Wife,	"	19 September 1720.
Elizabeth daughter of Peleg Wiswall and Eliza. his Wife,	"	4 November 1720.
Joseph Son of John Wakefield and Sarah his Wife,	"	13 November 1720.
Elizabeth daughter of Samuel Watts and Eliza. his Wife,	"	25 November 1720.
Sarah daughter of Benja. White and Mary his Wife,	"	21 December 1720.
Susanna daughter of Thomas Welch and Eliza. his Wife,	"	6 January 1720.
Timothy son of Timothy Yeals and Eliza. his Wife,	"	31 May 1720
Susanna daughter of William Young and Mary his Wife,	"	13 November 1720.
Matthew Son of Matthew and Mary Adams,	"	22 February 1720.
William Son of Benjamin and Mary Bronsdon,	"	2 May 1720.
John Son of John and Sarah Bradford,	"	8 March 1720.
Mercy daughter of James and Elizabeth Barnard,	"	8 March 1720.
Isabella daughter of Henry and Elizabeth Brightman,	"	20 March 1720.
Elizabeth daughter of Thomas and Elizabeth Bedel,	"	9 May 1720.
George Son of George and Mary Bethune,	"	7 December 1720.
Mary daughter of John and Mary Beer,	"	6 August 1720.
Daniel Son of Daniel and Prudence Cole,	"	5 March 1720.
Richard Son of William and Elizabeth Cowell,	"	1 June 1720.
William Son of William and Hannah Everden,	"	2 March 1720.
Ann daughter of Thomas and Deborah Eyre,	"	13 October 1720.
William Son of Thomas and Elizabeth Fleet.	"	20 March 1720.
Thomas Son of Thomas and Hannah Fairweather,	"	6 March 1720.
Edward Son of John and Mary Foster,	"	20 September 1720.
Benjamin Son of William and Elizabeth Fairfield,	"	7 March 1720.
Sarah daughter of Edward and Hannah Gray,	"	27 May 1720.
Tuttle Son of John and Elizabeth Hubbart,	"	23 July 1720.
Heman Son of Heman and Mary Henderson,	"	8 March 1720.
Elizabeth daughter of Samuel and Elizabeth Hood,	"	14 March 1720.
Mary daughter of William and Abigail Harris,	"	19 March 1720.
Sarah daughter of John and Mary King,	"	27 February 1720.
Priscilla daughter of Stephen and Rebecca Kempton,	"	24 March 1720.
Elizabeth daughter of William and Elizabeth Lowder,	"	13 August 1720.
John Son of John and Abigail Man,	"	19 February 1720.
Nathanael Son of Nathanael and Sarah Morse,	"	29 April 1720.
Samuel Son of Samuel and Mary May,	"	30 April 1720.
Oliver Son of Oliver and Katharine Noyes,	"	8 December 1720.
Thomas Son of Thomas and Sarah Peck,	"	6 March 1720.
Mary daughter of John and Martha Prout,	"	13 March 1720.
Thomas Son of William and Margaret Payne,	"	23 April 1720.
Elizabeth daughter of Benjamin and Elizabeth Rolfe,	"	30 October 1720.
Mary daughter of John and Joanna Rogers,	"	16 March 1720.
Elizabeth daughter of Jacob and Mary Sheaf,	"	15 March 1720.

BIRTHS — 1720-21. 149

John Son of James and Ann Shipman,	Born	6 July 1720.
John Son of John and Martha Smith,	"	4 November 1720.
Ammi daughter of John and Mary Taylor,	"	28 November 1720.
Sarah daughter of Jacob and Sarah Wendell,	"	3 March 1720.
John Son of Cornelius and Faith Waldo,	"	30 October 1720.
John Son of Joseph and Elizabeth White,	"	27 February 1720.
Sarah daughter of John and Bethiah Walley,	"	18 January 1720.
Sarah daughter of John and Elizabeth Whittemore,	"	3 March 1720.
John Son of Nathanael and Ann Wardall,	"	3 October 1720.
Cornelius Son of Ebenezer and Mercy Youngman,	"	10 August 1720.
William Son of William Robie and Lois his Wife,	"	16 February 1720

1721.

Peter Son of Henry and Mary Allin,	Born	19 April 1721.
Mary daughter of John and Mary Allin,	"	30 December 1721.
Jonathan Son of Jonathn. and Mary Adams,	"	15 January 1721.
Experience daughter of Ebenezer and Mary Bridge,	"	10 July 1721.
Elias } Gem. Sons of Jeremiah and Susanna Ball, Philip }	"	1 July 1721.
Benjamin Son of John and Elizabeth Barber,	"	1 August 1721.
Elizabeth daughter of John and Elizabeth Banks,	"	18 August 1721.
Allin Son of Nathanael and Sarah Breed,	"	23 August 1721.
Daniel Son of Daniel and Abigail Bell,	"	17 August 1721.
Mary daughter of John and Mary Baker,	"	3 August 1721.
Jonathan Son of Jonathan and Bull,	"	30 October 1721.
Thomas Son of John and Katharine Barton,	"	30 August 1721.
Thomas Son of William and Lydia Brown,	"	29 July 1721.
Rachel daughter of William and Rachel Brown,	"	23 July 1721.
Matthew Son of John and Deliverance Brewster,	"	12 January 1721.
Elizabeth daughter of Nicholas and Elizabeth Belknap,	"	24 January 1721.
Sarah daughter of Thornton and Hephzibah Barret,	"	22 April 1721.
Samuel Son of John and Mehetabel Bailey,	"	24 May 1721.
Mary daughter of John and Mary Bulkley,	"	26 May 1721.
Stephen Son of Stephen and Mary Boutineau,	"	22 May 1721.
Jonathan Son of Solomon and Abigail Blake,	"	2 June 1721.
John Son of Nicholas and Hannah Boon,	"	24 June 1721.
William Son of John and Sarah Bolderson,	"	9 June 1721.
Joseph Son of Jonathan and Mary Bowman,	"	28 June 1721.
Sarah daughter of Joseph and Hannah Belcher,	"	6 July 1721.
Lydia daughter of Bartholomew and Rebekah Barret,	"	31 March 1721.
Custin Son of John and Mary Bushnel,	"	29 March 1721.
Thomas Son of Thomas and Sarah Boylston,	"	17 October 1721.
Elizabeth daughter of John and Sarah Beacham,	"	3 September 1721.
Bant Son of Benjamin and Mary Bronsdon,	"	23 October 1721.
Zechariah Son of Walter and Ruth Baker,	"	9 February 1721.
Thomas Son of Thomas and Hannah Chamberlain,	"	21 May 1721.
Gilbert Son of Thomas and Sarah Coleworthy,	"	16 June 1721.
Bethiah daughter of Benjamin and Faith Clough,	"	6 July 1721.
Ann daughter of Joseph and Mary Clewley,	"	31 May 1721.
Joseph Son of Job and Lydia Coit,	"	23 October 1721.
William Son of William and Judith Cooper,	"	1 October 1721.
Elizabeth daughter of Elisha and Elizabeth Callender,	"	5 July 1721.
Mary daughter of Ebenezer and Ann Clough,	"	27 July 1721.
Mary daughter of Thomas and Mary Coverly,	"	8 August 1721.
Ralph Son of George and Mary Cradock,	"	3 March 1721.
Hannah daughter of John and Hannah Coolidge,	"	11 August 1721.

Bethiah daughter of Abraham and Hannah Cornwall, Born		1 May 1721.
John Son of Thomas and Elizabeth Cock,	"	11 December 1721.
John Son of John and Bridget Clough,	"	3 September 1721.
Jane daughter of William and Jane Covell,	"	10 September 1721.
Mary daughter of Samuel and Elizabeth Checkley,	"	11 November 1721.
Sarah daughter of David and Sarah Cunningham,	"	21 December 1721.
Hannah daughter of Jonathan and Martha Clark,	"	5 February 1721.
Abigail daughter of Edward and Abigail Cruff,	"	19 January 1721.
Lydia daughter of David and Margaret Chapin,	"	14 May 1721.
James Son of William and Elizabeth Cunningham,	"	24 April 1721.
Patience daughter of Isaac and Sarah Clark,	"	20 May 1721.
Nathanael Son of Jeremiah and Anna Clemans,	"	20 May 1721.
Freelove James and Sarah Carey,	"	12 December 1721.
John Son of John and Hannah Cobbett,	"	8 January 1721.
Valentine Dery Son of John and Elizabeth Dorothy,	"	29 December 1721.
Elisha Son of John and Abiah Doane,	"	27 November 1721.
James Son of James and Mary Dawson,	"	4 September 1721.
Katharine daughter of Shem and Katharine Drowne,	"	22 March 1721.
Sarah daughter of John and Sarah Demerry,	"	2 December 1721.
Sarah daughter of Charles and Sarah Deming,	"	7 May 1721.
Katharine daughter of Thomas and Jemima Debuke,	"	12 December 1721.
John Son of John and Rachel Durant,	"	14 August 1721.
William Son of William and Lydia Dyer,	"	12 April 1721.
Samuel Son of Andrew and Abigail Durgy,	"	28 July 1721.
Elizabeth daughter of Zebediah and Elizabeth Daniel,	"	21 July 1721.
Samuel Son of William and Sarah Downe,	"	14 October 1721.
Susanna daughter of Thomas and Lydia Daggett,	"	9 October 1721.
Benjamin Son of John and Rachel Dorrell,	"	29 September 1721.
Rachel daughter of John and Rachel Dorrell,	"	25 December 1721.
John Son of John and Maria Eliot,	"	5 June 1721.
John Son of John and Mary Edmonds,	"	23 July 1721.
Jacob Son of Jonathan and Sarah Eustis,	"	23 September 1721.
Caleb Son of Caleb and Hannah Eddy,	"	30 March 1721.
William Son of John and Sarah Eliot,	"	7 April 1721.
Benjamin Son of Benjamin and Mary Eddy,	"	15 March 1721.
Sarah daughter of Joseph and Lydia Eaton,	"	8 February 1721.
Ann daughter of Francis and Ann Frederick,	"	8 April 1721.
Joseph Son of Joseph and Mary Farrington,	"	1 July 1721.
Elizabeth daughter of Samuel and Elizabeth Foye,	"	13 August 1721.
Alexander Son of Alexander and Elizabeth Forsyth,	"	20 October 1721.
Joseph Son of Joseph and Margaret Fitch,	"	21 August 1721.
Ann daughter of Thomas and Ann Foster,	"	19 December 1721.
Mary daughter of Zechariah and Abigail Fitch,	"	29 August 1721.
Elizabeth daughter of Thomas and Anna Foxcroft,	"	22 September 1721.
Charles Son of Charles and Mary Forest,	"	12 September 1721.
Mary daughter of William and Elizabeth Foye,	"	8 September 1721.
Samuel Son of Samuel and Hannah Franklyn,	"	21 October 1721.
William Son of William and Sarah Grayham,	"	6 May 1721.
Susanna daughter of Bartholomew and Abigail Gedney,	"	13 June 1721.
William Son of Thomas and Mary Goodwin,	"	22 May 1721.
William Son of William and Mary Giles,	"	14 July 1721.
Giles Son of Giles and Hannah Goddard,	"	22 December 1721.
Mary daughter of Robert and Abigail Grater,	"	16 September 1721.
John Son of James and Sarah Green,	"	23 January 1721.
Mary daughter of Thomas and Rebekah Goodwill,	"	11 November 1721.
Thomas Son of Edward and Hannah Gray,	"	12 November 1721.
Elizabeth daughter of Elias and Elizabeth Gerrish,	"	1 March 1721.
Joseph Son of Joseph and Elizabeth Harris,	"	13 July 1721.

Births — 1721.

Christopher Gregory Son of John and Susanna Hobbs,	Born	18 June 1721.
Joseph Son of Benjamin and Elizabeth Hillier,	"	1 June 1721.
Ebenezer Son of William and Sarah Hasey,	"	6 July 1721.
Ebenezer Son of Ebenezer and Deborah Heath,	"	28 April 1721.
John Son of Richard and Sarah Hunt,	"	13 July 1721.
Ames Son of Ames and Judith Howard,	"	25 November 1721.
Sarah daughter of Israel and Judith How,	"	8 August 1721.
Ann daughter of John and Ann Homer,	"	15 October 1721.
Martha daughter of Charles and Martha Henley,	"	19 April 1721.
Ann daughter of Richard and Mary Hubbard,	"	2 September 1721.
Elizabeth daughter of Richard and Thomazin Hasley,	"	30 June 1721.
John Son of John and Sarah Hooton,	"	12 December 1721.
George Son of George and Rebekah Hanners,	"	2 September 1721.
Samuel Son of Samuel and Mary Hunting,	"	14 October 1721.
Deborah daughter of Samuel and Elizabeth Hood,	"	16 July 1721.
Nathanael Son of Nathanael and Hephzibah Harwood,	"	13 October 1721.
Sarah daughter of Robert and Sarah Harris,	"	27 January 1721.
Susanna daughter of John and Susanna Johnson,	"	25 March 1721.
Matthias Son of John and Mary Jenkins,	"	16 February 1721.
Ann daughter of Samuel and Abigail Kenny,	"	28 March 1721.
William Son of Samuel and Elizabeth Kneeland,	"	3 October 1721.
John Son of William and Elizabeth Lowder,	"	9 January 1721.
Samuel Son of James and Joanna Landman,	"	9 July 1721.
Nathan Son of Isaac and Hannah Lewis,	"	6 December 1721.
Elizabeth daughter of Josiah and Elizabeth Langdon,	"	1 July 1721.
John Son of John and Ruth Leach,	"	31 April 1721.
Rebekah daughter of Josiah and Rebekah Lupton,	"	15 July 1721.
Mary daughter of Joseph and Mary Leasenby,	"	26 May 1721.
Hannah daughter of Joshua and Hannah Loring,	"	1 June 1721.
Philip Son of Samuel and Esther Langdon,	"	9 June 1721.
Abigail daughter of David and Hannah Linfield,	"	12 August 1721.
Margaret daughter of John and Sarah Lawson,	"	9 September 1721.
Margaret daughter of Andrew and Margaret Le Mercier,	"	10 December 1721.
Elizabeth daughter of Christopher and Elizabeth Marshall,	"	31 July 1721.
James Son of Samuel and Hannah Maxwell,	"	23 June 1721.
George Son of John and Sarah Mills,	"	5 August 1721.
Lydia daughter of William and Lydia Maxwell,	"	6 July 1721.
James Son of Thomas and Susanna Melling,	"	15 August 1721.
Hannah daughter of Nathanael and Hannah Martin,	"	18 September 1721.
Elizabeth daughter of Joseph and Ellen Marion,	"	22 September 1721.
Ann Sarah daughter of Samuel and Admonition Mattock,	"	12 April 1721.
Thomas Son of Robert and Joyce Marvel,	"	3 September 1721.
Martha daughter of Michael and Martha Mack,	"	27 November 1721.
Thaddeus Son of Thaddeus and Mary Maccarty,	"	18 July 1721.
Thomas Son of Thomas and Mary Millner,	"	28 March 1721.
James Son of Alexander and Elizabeth Miller,	"	2 December 1721.
Rebekah daughter of Ebenezer and Rebekah Messinger,	"	26 June 1721.
Susanna daughter of Thomas and Susanna Martin,	"	20 January 1721.
Ann daughter of John and Elizabeth Maverick,	"	6 December 1721.
Sarah daughter of Benjamin and Elizabeth Mason,	"	17 March 1721.
Hannah daughter of Edmund and Mary Newcomb,	"	18 June 1721.
Mary daughter of John and Elizebeth Orne,	"	5 April 1721.

Rebekah daughter of James and Rebekah Oliver,	Born	3 July 1721.
John Son of Philip and Jane Ormond,	"	10 January 1721.
David Son of David and Elizabeth Prince,	"	2 April 1721.
Thomas Son of Thomas and Martha Powel,	"	11 April 1721.
Hannah daughter of Thomas and Mary Pemberton,	"	2 May 1721.
Timothy Son of Timothy and Lydia Prout,	"	12 September 1721.
Sarah daughter of Daniel and Sarah Pecker,	"	16 May 1721.
Jane daughter of Samuel and Mary Procter,	"	8 June 1721.
Jonathan Son of Jonathan and Mary Peirce,	"	17 July 1721.
Nathanael Son of William and Ann Phillips,	"	11 August 1721.
Elizabeth daughter of William and Sarah Pearse,	"	5 July 1721.
Edward Son of William and Margaret Payne,	"	4 February 1721.
Joseph Son of Joseph and Mary Pearse,	"	21 September 1721.
Elizabeth daughter of Joseph and Mary Prince,	"	2 June 1721.
John Son of John and Margaret Peck,	"	23 July 1721.
Samuel Son of Peter and Katherine Papillon,	"	11 September 1721.
Peter Son of Peter and Elizabeth Peirce,	"	8 November 1721.
Daniel Son of Thomas and Mary Plaisted,	"	1721.
Ruth daughter of Richard and Rebekah Phillips,	"	8 January 1721.
Timothy Son of Timothy and Lydia Prout,	"	22 September 1721.
Susanna daughter of William and Abigail Palfrey,	"	13 February 1721.
Thomas Son of Thomas and Deborah Prince,	"	27 February 1721.
Elizabeth daughter of William and Hannah Parkman,	"	13 March 1721.
John Son of Edward and Ruth Page,	"	30 September 1721.
Benjamin Son of Joseph and Rachel Roberts,	"	14 September 1721.
Mary daughter of Joseph and Elizabeth Ricks,	"	15 August 1721.
Elizabeth daughter of Edward and Elizabeth Rumley,	"	24 February 1721.
Abigail daughter of Joseph and Abigail Russel,	"	20 February 1721.
Priscilla daughter of Jeremiah and Lydia Rhodes,	"	13 March 1721.
Joseph Son of Joseph and Priscilla Roby,	"	28 March 1721.
Humphrey Son of Humphrey and Joanna Richards,	"	4 April 1721.
Samuel Son of Samuel and Abigail Roberts,	"	6 April 1721.
Mary daughter of Samuel and Priscilla Royal,	"	21 May 1721.
Anna daughter of John and Anna Reynolds,	"	17 May 1721.
Thomas Son of Samuel and Mary Robinson,	"	18 June 1721.
Benjamin Son of Benjamin and Elizabeth Rolfe,	"	2 December 1721.
James Son of John and Elizabeth Rubey,	"	5 July 1721.
Thomas Son of Samuel and Sarah Rand,	"	24 May 1721.
Timothy Son of Thomas and Mary Ruck,	"	27 July 1721.
Samuel Son of John and Martha Steel,	"	13 April 1721.
Susanna daughter of Thomas and Abigail Stacey,	"	11 April 1721.
Mary daughter of George and Elizabeth Shore,	"	11 April 1721.
Mary daughter of Daniel and Elizabeth Story,	"	20 April 1721.
Ann daughter of Thomas and Sarah Smith,	"	29 April 1721.
Josiah Son of Luke and Margaret Stone,	"	16 May 1721.
Ann daughter of John and Mary Souther,	"	1 July 1721.
James Son of William and Mary Scott,	"	23 July 1721.
John Son of Joseph and Elizabeth Scott,	"	18 July 1721.
Richard Son of John and Abigail Salter,	"	31 July 1721.
Francis Son of Thomas and Sarah Shaw,	"	29 March 1721.
Stephen Son of Stephen and Elizabeth Sims,	"	11 July 1721.
Elizabeth daughter of John and Elizabeth Smith,	"	18 October 1721.
Abraham Son of Abraham and Hannah Snelling,	"	26 September 1721.
Mary daughter of Jonathan and Martha Salter,	"	9 February 1721.
Elias Son of Robert and Ann Sanders,	"	18 October 1721.
Abigail daughter of John and Abigail Stocker,	"	29 March 1721.
Samuel Son of Samuel and Hannah Sprague,	"	7 November 1721.
Erasmus Son of Erasmus and Persis Stevens,	"	18 December 1721.

BIRTHS — 1721-22.

James Son of James and Elizabeth Scutt,	Born	2 February 1721.
Jane daughter of John and Hannah Thompson,	"	19 May 1721.
Benjamin Son of Edward and Joanna Tuttle,	"	31 March 1721.
Nathanael Son of Nathanael and Sarah Tuttle,	"	24 December 1721.
Elizabeth daughter of Peter and Mary Thomas,	"	31 May 1721.
Abigail daughter of Alexander and Elizabeth Todd,	"	14 November 1721.
Ann daughter of William and Ann Thomas,	"	23 October 1721.
Hannah daughter of Benjamin and Bethiah Thwing,	"	2 December 1721.
Joseph Son of Joseph and Joanna Turell,	"	31 October 1721.
Mary daughter of Cornelius and Lydia Thayer,	"	16 December 1721.
Samuel Son of Timothy and Elizabeth Thornton,	"	25 March 1721.
Benjamin-Brame Son of John and Sarah Tyler,	"	29 March 1721.
Barnard Son of Barnard and Susanna Tuell,	"	7 May 1721.
Mary daughter of Joseph and Sarah Uran,	"	4 September 1721.
Mary daughter of Obadiah and Mary Wakefield,	"	16 September 1721.
Resign daughter of Daniel and Abigail Willard,	"	17 September 1721.
Elizabeth daughter of Francis and Elizabeth Warden,	"	5 March 1721.
Elizabeth daughter of John and Sarah Willis,	"	12 October 1721.
George Son of George and Mary Wilson,	"	10 June 1721.
Elizabeth daughter of Nathanael and Elizabeth White,	"	23 January 1721.
Aaron Son of Christopher and Sarah Webb,	"	25 April 1721.
Abigail daughter of Ephraim and Dorothy Wheeler,	"	2 February 1721.
Mary daughter of Gilbert and Sarah Warner,	"	3 May 1721.
Thomas Son of Thomas and Anna Warden,	"	7 February 1721.
Sarah daughter of Henry and Sarah Wheeler,	"	28 November 1721.
Abigail daughter of David and Jane Webber,	"	17 February 1721.
Lucy daughter of Adam and Ann Winthrop,	"	22 August 1721.
Mary daughter of John and Mary Webster,	"	9 November 1721.
Hannah daughter of John and Elizabeth Welland,	"	22 September 1721.
Nathanael Son of John and Elizabeth Wheelwright,	"	25 October 1721.
William-Wait Son of Thomas and Grace Wallis,	"	14 January 1721.
John Son of Robert and Martha Waite,	"	13 March 1721.
John Son of John and Rebekah Whittemore,	"	26 August 1721.
Mary daughter of John and Mary Young,	"	20 December 1721.
Martha daughter of Anthony and Rachel Young,	"	20 January 1721.
Sarah daughter of Ebenezer and Mercy Youngman,	"	13 February 1721.
Shute Shrimpton Son of John and Elizabeth Yeamans,	"	20 August 1721.
Abigail daughter of John Blowers and Abigail his Wife,	"	11 December 1721.

1722.

Thomas Son of Thomas and Rebekah Amory,	Born	23 April 1722.
Ebenezer Son of Ebenr. and Elizabeth Allin	"	28 May 1722.
Sarah daughter of John and Sarah Akin,	"	10 December 1722.
Anna daughter of John and Anna Alden,	"	29 January 1722.
Samuel Son of Benj. and Katharine Andrews,	"	21 January 1722.
David Son of John and Elisabeth Adams,	"	23 March 1722.
Mary daughter of John and Mary Adams,	"	16 August 1722.
Nathanael Son of Elnathan and Mercy Ayres,	"	5 January 1722.
Nathanael Son of William and Sarah Baker,	"	11 September 1722.
Thomas Son of Thomas and Susanna Belcher,	"	4 November 1722.
Blish Son of Robert and Martha Brown,	"	29 January 1722.
John Son of John and Sarah Banks,	"	26 May 1722.
John Son of Joseph and Dorothy Brown,	"	27 August 1722.
Lois daughter of Jonathan and Mary Brown,	"	25 December 1722.
Susanna daughter of George and Mary Bethune,	"	17 December 1722.

Rebekah daughter of Samuel and Ann Bleigh,	Born	10 September 1722.
Sarah daughter of John and Sarah Bolderson,	"	4 January 1722.
Ann daughter of Abraham and Lydia Billings,	"	6 January 1722.
Mehetabel daughter of John and Mehetabel Buttolph,	"	24 January 1722.
Martha daughter of Daniel and Abigail Bell,	"	23 January 1722.
Mary daughter of William and Mary Bucker,	"	24 January 1722.
Nathanael Son of John and Mary Baker,	"	7 February 1722.
John Son of Freeborn and Susanna Balch,	"	8 September 1722.
Robert Son of Benjamin and Mary Bronsdon,	"	10 March 1722.
Elizabeth daughter of John and Mary Beer,	"	12 May 1722.
Mary daughter of Thomas and Sarah Boylston,	"	19 February 1722.
Dorothy daughter of William and Lydia Brown,	"	12 September 1722.
Rebekah daughter of Thomas and Lydia Bronton,	"	7 June 1722.
Sarah daughter of John and Elizabeth Beaudri,	"	17 June 1722.
John Son of Thomas and Silence Barnard,	"	8 June 1722.
Abigail daughter of Jacob and Abigail Blanchard,	"	20 May 1722.
Samuel Son of Thornton and Hephzibah Barret,	"	28 June 1722.
Rebekah daughter of Jeremiah and Sarah Belknap,	"	18 August 1722.
Rachel daughter of George and Mary Butler,	"	2 August 1722.
Samuel Son of Samuel and Sarah Barber,	"	12 August 1722.
Mary daughter of Josiah and Mary Bacon,	"	28 September 1722.
Ruth daughter of Ebenezer and Ruth Belcher,	"	30 August 1722.
Elizabeth daughter of John and Abigail Burt,	"	26 July 1722.
Susanna daughter of Ebenezer and Elizabeth Burges,	"	2 December 1722.
Nathanael Son of John and Sarah Bradford,	"	11 February 1722.
Walker Son of William and Elizabeth Beairsto,	"	11 February 1722.
John Son of John and Ann Bish,	"	31 January 1722.
Peter Son of Stephen and Mary Boutineau,	"	11 December 1722.
Christian daughter of Samuel and Christian Bass,	"	19 December 1722
Abigail daughter of Nicholas and Hannah Boon,	"	18 March 1722.
Mary daughter of Jonathan and Mary Bowman,	"	18 March 1722.
Samuel Son of Joseph and Hannah Calef,	"	22 July 1722.
Jane daughter of Jonathan and Mary Clark,	"	9 September 1722.
Sarah daughter of William and Elizabeth Cowell,	"	14 October 1722.
Elizabeth daughter of James and Elizabeth Collings,	"	14 November 1722.
Clement Son of Clement and Mary Chick,	"	25 March 1722.
Abigail daughter of Samuel and Mary Conibal,	"	22 September 1722.
William Son of William and Jane Covell,	"	31 December 1722.
William Son of Joseph and Elizabeth Clewley,	"	19 January 1722.
Samuel Son of Richard-Carter and Jane Cowell,	"	23 January 1722.
Isaac Son of Isaac and Sarah Clark,	"	22 January 1722.
Priscilla daughter of Nathaniel and Abigail Coney at Sudbury,	"	2 April 1722.
William Son of John and Hannah Charnock,	"	15 February 1722.
John Son of Andrew and Mary Cunningham,	"	3 March 1722.
William Son of David and Susanna Crouch,	"	1 March 1722.
Mary daughter of Elisha and Elizabeth Callender,	"	4 March 1722.
Anna daughter of Jeremiah and Anna Clemans,	"	29 August 1722.
Abigail daughter of Daniel and Mary Cheever,	"	4 October 1722.
Rebekah daughter of John and Rebekah Compton,	"	17 September 1722.
William Son of William and Elizabeth Cunningham,	"	28 September 1722.
Timothy Son of Jonas and Grace Clark,	"	1 November 1722.
Samuel Son of Samuel and Elizabeth Checkley,	"	16 December 1722.
Nathan Son of Nathan and Hannah Cheever,	"	15 January 1722.
Caleb Son of David and Sarah Cunningham,	"	13 December 1722.
John Son of John and Abigail Deall,	"	23 August 1722.
Henry Son of Henry and Elizabeth Dering,	"	30 August 1722.
Elizabeth daughter of James and Sarah Davenport,	"	8 March 1722.

BIRTHS — 1722.   155

Elizabeth daughter of Thomas and Sarah Dawes,	Born	28 February 1722.
Hannah daughter of William and Hannah Davis,	"	16 February 1722.
Joseph Son of Samuel and Katherine Davis,	"	23 December 1722.
Eleazer Son of Eleazer and Mary Dorby,	"	31 March 1722.
John Son of John and Elizabeth Decoster,	"	18 January 1722.
Thomas Son of Samuel and Mary Duncan,	"	13 May 1722.
Mary daughter of Thomas and Mary Ellis,	"	1 July 1722.
Deborah daughter of Thomas and Deborah Eyre,	"	20 December 1722.
Rebekah daughter of John and Sarah Eliot,	"	22 August 1722.
Charles Son of Anthony and Hannah Ennes,	"	8 September 1722.
Lydia daugnter of Joseph and Lydia Eaton,	"	8 June 1722.
William Son of William and Jane Eustus,	"	7 May 1722.
Samuel Son of William and Ann Engs,	"	3 April 1722.
John Son of John and Rebekah Endicott,	"	23 June 1722.
John Son of Walter and Jane Edmonds,	"	11 March 1722.
Andrew Son of Gideon and Susanna Florence,	"	7 April 1722.
Daniel Son of William and Margaret Fletcher,	"	14 May 1722.
Jennet daughter of Charles and Mary Forest,	"	2 September 1722.
Mary daughter of Patrick and Prudence Flyn,	"	17 June 1722.
Samuel Son of Samuel and Mary Fyfield,	"	16 September 1722.
Ann daughter of Jonathan and Ann Farnam,	"	4 December 1722.
Lewis Son of George and Mary Follis,	"	25 November 1722.
Timothy Son of Thomas and Ann Foster,	"	1 February 1722.
Margaret daughter of William and Margaret Fletcher,	"	20 January 1722.
John Son of William and Elizabeth Foye,	"	8 February 1722.
Jonathan Son of Thomas and Hannah Fairweather,	"	9 March 1722.
Margaret daughter of Joseph and Margaret Fitch,	"	14 March 1722.
Mary daughter of William and Mary Greenleaf,	"	9 May 1722.
Charles Son of Charles and Mary Giles,	"	1 May 1722.
Benjamin Son of Samuel and Mary Greenwood,	"	30 May 1722.
Mary daughter of James and Elizabeth Gerreck,	"	10 May 1722.
Katharine daughter of Obadiah and Sarah Gore,	"	26 June 1722.
John Son of Nathanael and Mary Gardner,	"	5 May 1722.
Mary daughter of Samuel and Sarah Gerrish,	"	30 July 1722.
Francis Son of Francis and Rachel Gatcombe,	"	4 May 1722.
Nicholas Son of Nicholas and Mary George,	"	10 January 1722.
Thomas Son of Thomas and Mary Goodwin	"	25 May 1722.
Abigail daughter of Francis and Rachel Gatcombe,	"	12 March 1722.
James Son of James and Elizabeth Goodwin,	"	4 October 1722.
Mary daughter of William and Mary Giles,	"	15 March 1722.
Elizabeth daughter of Samuel and Mary Hunt,	"	23 August 1722.
Thomas Son of Samuel and Elizabeth Haley,	"	26 September 1722.
Phebe daughter of John and Susanna Hopkins,	"	4 September 1722.
Alexander Son of Arthur and Rebekah Hill,	"	23 August 1722.
Shrimpton Son of John and Rebekah Hunt,	"	17 October 1722.
Mary daughter of John and Kezia Harvey,	"	4 January 1722.
Ebenezer Son of Ebenezer and Deborah Heath,	"	12 February 1722.
Rebekah daughter of George and Rebekah Hanners,	"	25 January 1722.
Mary daughter of John and Elizabeth Hill,	"	20 February 1722.
Samuel Son of John and Elizabeth Helyer,	"	20 August 1722.
John Son of Gabriel and Ruth Hubbard,	"	8 May 1722.
John Son of John and Elizabeth Hubbard,	"	18 May 1722.
Samuel Son of Samuel and Judith Hill,	"	16 July 1722.
Mary daughter of Zechariah and Mary Hubbard,	"	5 March 1722.
Silvester Son of Richard and Thomazin Hasley,	"	11 February 1722.
Mary daughter of Richard and Mary Hern,	"	25 November 1722.
Sarah daughter of Edward and Lydia Hutchinson,	"	12 May 1722.
Abigail daughter of North and Abigail Ingham,	"	26 May 1722.
John Son of John and Rebekah Indicott,	"	23 June 1722.

Mary daughter of Elias and Mary Jarvis,	Born	10 May 1722.
Samuel Son of John and Susanna Johnson,	"	8 September 1722.
Ann daughter of John and Mary Jagger,	"	26 December 1722.
Mary daughter of Samuel and Elizabeth Kneeland,	"	2 October 1722.
John Son of John and Elizabeth Kneeland,	"	6 August 1722.
Katharine daughter of John and Lydia Kelton,	"	14 October 1722.
Mary daughter of Samuel and Mary Kneeland,	"	19 November 1722.
Matthew Son of William and Elizabeth Killworth,	"	6 September 1722.
Sarah daughter of Thomas and Mary Kilby,	"	12 May 1722.
Mary daughter of Robert and Susanna Kenton,	"	30 March 1722.
Elijah Son of John and Eleanor Lathe,	"	4 October 1722.
John Son of James and Mary Lenox,	"	22 June 1722.
Benjamin Son of Henry and Abigail Lowder,	"	28 May 1722.
Rachel daughter of Thomas and Rachel Lark,	"	11 November 1722.
Paul Son of Elias and Hannah Langsford,	"	29 May 1722.
William Son of William and Ruth Lee,	"	4 December 1722.
Thomas Son of Oliver and Rebekah Luckis,	"	26 June 1722.
Lydia daughter of William and Lydia Larraby.	"	5 January 1722.
Abigail daughter of Nathan and Ann Lewis,	"	27 July 1722.
John Son of Edward and Susanna Langdon,	"	17 January 1722.
Mary daughter of Joseph and Mary Leasenby,	"	29 December 1722.
William Son of William and Abigail Langdon,	"	16 July 1722.
Samuel Son of Samuel and Esther Langdon,	"	12 January 1722.
Thomas Son of Richard and Thankful Langdon,	"	26 August 1722.
Jonathan Son of Jonathan and Mary Lambert,	"	9 June 1722.
Nicholas Son of Thomas and Ann Lechmere,	"	29 July 1722.
Mary daughter of Ephraim and Elizabeth Moore,	"	12 February 1722.
Abigail daughter of Peter and Abigail Miers,	"	1 March 1722.
William Son of William and Abigail Merchant,	"	8 August 1722.
Thomas Son of Thomas and Elizabeth Mitchell,	"	19 October 1722.
Sarah daughter of Samuel and Ann Marion,	"	12 November 1722.
Nathanael Son of Jonathan and Hannah Mountfort,	"	13 November 1722.
Samuel Son of Hugh and Mary Markes,	"	20 November 1722.
Samuel Son of John and Eddy Menzies,	"	31 July 1722.
Elizabeth daughter of James and Mercy Melvel,	"	21 August 1722.
William Son of Isaac and Rebekah Marion,	"	12 September 1722.
Isaac Son of Daniel and Ann Mundan,	"	20 September 1722.
Elizabeth daughter of Thaddeus and Mary Maccarty,	"	7 October 1722.
William Son of William and Diana Milburn,	"	5 June 1722.
John Son of John and Mary Miller,	"	24 December 1722.
Deborah daughter of Nathanael and Sarah Morse,	"	1 December 1722.
Mary daughter of John and Susanna McLean,	"	12 December 1722.
Ann daughter of John and and Elizabeth Maverick,	"	6 December 1722.
Elizabeth daughter of Thomas and Mary Millner,	"	23 December 1722.
John Son of Samuel and Rachel Narramore,	"	20 August 1722.
George Son of Joseph and Elizabeth Nowell,	"	1 August 1722.
Henry Son of Henry and Elizabeth Neal,	"	26 January 1722.
Edmund Son of Edmund and Mary Newcomb,	"	26 December 1722.
William Son of William and Bethiah Nichols,	"	29 December 1722.
Mary daughter of Eliezer and Mary Newell,	"	5 January 1722.
William Son of William and Mary Neatby,	'	6 March 1722.
Katharine daughter of John and Sarah Osborne,	"	6 November 1722.
Ann daughter of Henry and Ann Palmer,	"	19 June 1722.
Mary daughter of Peter and Sarah Pritchard,	"	30 July 1722.
Mary daughter of John and Lydia Poumery,	"	16 August 1722.
Joseph Son of Joseph and Thankful Peirce,	"	2 September 1722.
Mary daughter of Peter and Katherine Papillon,	"	25 October 1722.
Robert Son of Robert and Jane Patishall,	"	8 November 1722
William Son of William and Mary Pike,	"	18 November 1722.
Mary daughter of James and Mary Penniman,	"	30 August 1722.

Births — 1722.

Isaac Peirce Son of Isaac and Grace Peirce,	Born	11 October 1722.
Benjamin Son of Benjamin and Margaret Procter,	"	17 November 1722.
John Son of Samuel and Mary Procter,	"	25 February 1722.
Mary daughter of John and Mary Potwine,	"	1 May 1722.
Edward Son of Edward and Elizabeth Potter,	"	10 June 1722.
John Symmes Son of John and Mary Pitts,	"	14 June 1722.
Henry Son of Joseph and Priscilla Roby,	"	3 October 1722.
Nicholas Son of Nicholas and Hannah Roach,	"	4 November 1722.
Elizabeth daughter of Simon and Thomazin Rogers,	"	27 November 1722.
Elizabeth daughter of Thomas and Elizabeth Rogers,	"	24 May 1722.
Matthew Son of James and Mary Roberts,	"	15 November 1722.
Abigail daughter of Samuel and Abigail Roberts,	"	22 November 1722.
Benjamin Son of Benjamin and Priscilla Roberts,	"	6 October 1722.
John Son of Samuel and Mary Robinson,	"	25 November 1722.
Thomas Son of Thomas and Mary Studson,	"	23 April 1722.
Rebekah daughter of John and Ann Sale,	"	26 May 1722.
Jonathan Son of Robert and Rachel Scrivener,	"	10 March 1722.
Joshua Son of Joseph and Mehetabel Scott,	"	17 August 1722.
Martha daughter of John and Martha Steel,	"	16 February 1722.
Mary daughter of Luke and Margaret Stone,	"	8 September 1722.
Martha daughter of Benjamin and Rebekah Smallege,	"	2 December 1722.
Rebekah daughter of Robert and Walter Starkey,	"	1 September 1722.
Samuel Son of Benjamin and Susanna Storer,	"	6 December 1722.
Thomas Son of Thomas and Sarah Shaw,	"	17 October 1722.
Mary daughter of Richard and Mary Stanney,	"	20 March 1722.
Henry Son of Ralph and Huldah Smith,	"	16 October 1722.
Ann daughter of Robert and Ann Sanders,	"	6 January 1722.
John Son of Simon and Elizabeth Slocum,	"	28 October 1722.
Lydia daughter of John and Lydia Simpson,	"	7 February 1722.
Lydia daughter of Jacob and Mary Sheafe,	"	1 October 1722.
Elizabeth daughter of Stephen and Elizabeth Sims,	"	1 December 1722.
Zechariah Son of Zechariah and Elizabeth Sims,	"	28 February 1722.
Sarah daughter of John and Sarah Tyler,	"	12 July 1722.
Sarah daughter of Henry and Mary Timberlake,	"	7 April 1722.
Joseph Son of William and Mary Thorn,	"	26 August 1722.
Mary daughter of William and Sarah Tyler,	"	14 June 1722.
John Son of John and Mary Taylor,	"	24 August 1722.
William Son of Andrew and Miriam Tyler,	"	10 October 1722.
Rebekah daughter of John and Rebekah Tenny,	"	8 October 1722.
Elizabeth daughter of Timothy and Elizabeth Thornton,	"	1 October 1722.
Elijah Son of Edward and Joanna Tuttle,	"	4 October 1722.
Cunningham Son of John and Katharine Temple,	"	14 November 1722.
Mary daughter of Joshua and Martha Thornton.	"	1 January 1722.
English Son of Maverick and Joanna Thomas.	"	4 January 1722.
William Son of William and Mary Trout,	"	1 February 1722.
William Son of Samuel and Eliphal Tyley,	"	17 January 1722.
Elizabeth daughter of Ebenezer and Elizabeth Thornton,	"	4 March 1722.
Daniel Son of Daniel and Sarah Teer,	"	22 March 1722.
Benjamin Son of Joseph and Sarah Uran,	"	15 January 1722.
John Son of John and Rachel Vaughan,	"	2 June 1722.
Samuel Son of Samuel and Elizabeth White,	"	17 August 1722.
Piercy Son of William and Mary Walter,	"	23 August 1722.
William Son of Samuel and Mary Wright,	"	18 March 1722.
Mary daughter of William and Mary Wilson,	"	5 September 1722.
William Son of John and Ann Waldo,	"	23 February 1722.
Mercy daughter of Jacob and Sarah Wendell,	"	10 April 1722.
Daniel Son of Peleg and Elizabeth Wiswall,	"	13 February 1722.

Sarah daughter of John and Sarah Wakefield,	Born	1 September 1722.
Elizabeth daughter of William and Elizabeth Waldron,	"	28 September 1722.
Joseph Son of Joseph and Abigail Webb,	"	19 July 1722.
Mary daughter of Davis and Susanna Whitman,	"	23 September 1722.
Elizabeth daughter of Allen and Elizabeth Wild,	"	3 November 1722.
James Son of James and Susanna Wright,	"	2 May 1722.
Abraham Son of Abraham and Dorothy White,	"	2 April 1722.
James Son of Isaac and Rebekah White,	"	6 April 1722.
Judith daughter of Ebenezer and Judith Williston,	"	15 March 1722.
Edward Son of Joshua and Elizabeth Winslow,	"	8 November 1722.
Joseph Son of Cornelius and Faith Waldo,	"	11 January 1722.
Benjamin Son of John and Susanna Warwick,	"	10 November 1722.
Sarah daughter of John and Bethiah Walley,	"	8 November 1722.
Thomas Son of Thomas and Huldah Walter,	"	11 November 1722.
Joseph Son of Joseph and Abigail Webb,	"	19 July 1722.
Abigail daughter of Benjamin and Abigail Walcott,	"	22 November 1722.
Rachel daughter of Thomas and Elizabeth Welch,	"	24 July 1722.
William Son of John and Esther Waters,	"	20 November 1722.
Joshua Son of Joshua and Ann Williams,	"	8 April 1722.
Mary daughter of Samuel and Sarah Warden,	"	26 January 1722.
Benjamin Son of Joseph and Elizabeth White,	"	18 May 1722.
Sarah daughter of Robert and Sarah Williams,	"	28 February 1722.
Mary daughter of Jonathan and Susanna Waldo,	"	22 February 1722.

1723.

Mary daughter of Henry and Mary Allen,	Born	7 April 1723.
Huldah daughter of Francis and Huldah Archibald,	"	13 June 1723.
Nicholas Son of Nicholas and Rachel Anthony,	"	21 June 1723.
Sarah daughter of John and Mary Allen,	"	15 August 1723.
Sarah daughter of Jer. and Rebekah Allen,	"	10 September 1723.
Elisabeth daughter of James and Elisabeth Audlington,	"	19 December 1723.
Mary daughter of Joshua and Elisabeth Atwood,	"	26 December 1723.
Mary daughter of Tho. and Rebekah Amory,	"	9 December 1723.
Samuel Son of Benj. and Katharine Andrews,	"	18 February 1723.
Moses Son of Moses and Hannah Ayres,	"	12 July 1723.
Ebenezer Son of Josiah and Abigail Byles,	"	26 March 1723.
William Son of William and Rachel Brown,	"	28 March 1723.
Ferdinando Son of Ferdinando and Hannah Bowd,	"	8 May 1723.
William Son of John and Elizabeth Banks,	"	4 April 1723.
Isaac Son of Isaac and Elizabeth Boynton,	"	31 March 1723.
John Son of Solomon and Elizabeth Blake,	"	1 May 1723.
Ebenezer Son of Joseph and Mary Balch,	"	14 May 1723.
Samuel Son of Jonathan and Elizabeth Bull,	"	13 May 1723.
Thomas Son of Thomas and Abigail Bradford,	"	17 June 1723.
Sarah and Elizabeth Gem. } daughters of Nathanael and Sarah Breed,	"	28 June 1723.
William Son of William and Mary Beal,	"	5 August 1723.
James Son of William and Lydia Brown,	"	28 October 1723.
John Son of Comfort and Rachel Bird,	"	30 October 1723.
Sarah daughter of John and Elizabeth Beal,	"	23 August 1723.
Joseph Son of Joseph and Abigail Bridgham,	"	22 November 1723.
William Son of Gideon and Martha Ball,	"	26 November 1723.
Thomas Son of Thomas and Elizabeth Betterly,	"	17 November 1723.
Bailey Son of Nathanael and Rebekah Belknap,	"	24 July 1723.
John Son of Ebenezer and Mary Bridge,	"	21 July 1723.
Dorothy daughter of Nathanael and Dorothy Barber,	"	26 August 1723.

BIRTHS — 1723.

Ann daughter of John and Ann Britt,	Born	27 August 1723.
Thomas Son of Thomas and Sarah Brooks,	"	11 September 1723.
William Son of John and Abigail Burt,	"	1 September 1723.
John Son of John and Hannah Brown,	"	2 October 1723.
Mary daughter of Hercules and Mary Brilsford,	"	29 September 1723.
Sarah daughter of John and Mary Beer,	"	5 February 1723.
Edward Son of Edward and Abigail Bromfield,	"	30 January 1723.
Mehetabel daughter of John and Sarah Banks,	"	14 February 1723.
John Son of Samuel and Sarah Barber,	"	1 March 1723.
Josiah Son of Josiah and Mary Bacon,	"	24 February 1723.
John Son of Thomas and Lydia Brunton,	"	16 March 1723.
Abigail daughter of Thomas and Ruth Bill,	"	10 December 1723.
Edward Son of Edward and Martha Burbeck,	"	18 December 1723.
Elizabeth daughter of John and Elizabeth Blanchard,	"	22 June 1723.
Elizabeth daughter of Thornton and Hephzibah Barret,	"	13 March 1723.
Mary daughter of James and Sarah Barrell,	"	9 May 1723.
Bathsheba daughter of Benjamin and Ruth Babbridge,	"	14 February 1723.
Joseph Son of Fleming and Hannah Barnard,	"	23 December 1723.
Richard Son of Richard and Sarah Barrington,	"	24 July 1723.
Esther daughter of John and Sarah Beacham,	"	9 March 1723.
Sarah daughter of Benjamin and Elizabeth Bagnall,	"	13 January 1723.
John Son of Thomas and Elizabeth Bedel,	"	30 March 1723.
Margaret daughter of Joseph and Margaret Clark,	"	16 August 1723.
Richard Son of Richard and Ammi Coleworthy,	"	23 July 1723.
Sarah daughter of William and Sarah Cooper,	"	1 September 1723.
Mary daughter of George and Mary Cradock,	"	18 May 1723.
Gibson Son of Ebenezer and Ann Clough,	"	28 September 1723.
James Son of Thomas and Elizabeth Cock,	"	20 January 1723.
John Son of William and Martha Champlin,	"	23 September 1723.
Mary daughter of John and Bridget Clough,	"	13 October 1723.
Samuel Son of Samuel and Elizabeth Checkley,	"	27 December 1723.
John Son of James and Lydia Cranston,	"	21 December 1723.
John Son of James and Mehetabel Cranston,	"	21 December 1723.
Sarah daughter of Samuel and Mary Carey,	"	5 February 1723.
John Son of John and Sarah Carnes,	"	11 July 1723.
Samuel Son of Samuel and Patience Clark,	"	1 August 1723.
William Son of William and Ann Coffin,	"	11 April 1723.
Bethiah daughter of Benjamin and Faith Clough,	"	25 April 1723.
Abigail daughter of James and Sarah Carey,	"	24 February 1723.
Cornelius Son of David and Sarah Cunningham,	"	21 November 1723.
William Son of Samuel and Mary Conibal,	"	4 March 1723.
Rebekah daughter of William and Rebekah Copp,	"	17 February 1723.
Samuel Son of Samuel and Sarah Cowdry,	"	1 September 1723.
Elizabeth daughter of James and Hannah Dowel,	"	19 April 1723.
Judith daughter of Edward and Judith Durant,	"	27 May 1723.
Elizabeth daughter of Isaac and Rebekah Dawbt,	"	29 August 1723.
David Son of Shem and Katharine Drowne,	"	6 October 1723.
John Son of Thomas and Anna Downe,	"	7 October 1723.
John Son of Robert and Elizabeth Daubigny,	"	17 August 1723.
Ruth daughter of Thomas and Jemima Debuke,	"	11 November 1723.
Thomas Son of Ebenezer and Sarah Dunton,	"	1 November 1723.
Samuel Son of James and Mary Dawson,	"	14 February 1723.
Abigail daughter of Andrew and Abigail Durgee,	"	17 February 1723.
Jonathan Son of Charles and Sarah Deming,	"	27 January 1723.
Ebenezer Son of Thomas and Anna Downe,	"	9 October 1723.
Mary daughter of Henry and Abigail Delaway,	"	23 April 1723.
Nathanael Son of Benjamin and Mary Eddy,	"	22 August 1723.

John Son of John and Ann Eyre,	Born	14 September 1723.
Robert Son of John and Abigail Earle,	"	15 October 1723.
Joseph Son of John and Rebekah Endicott,	"	9 June 1723.
John Son of William and Jane Eustus,	"	26 November 1723.
Mary daughter of John and Sarah Eliot,	"	14 February 1723.
John Son of John and Sarah Eliot,	"	5 February 1723.
Joseph Son of Joseph and Mary Farrington,	"	8 May 1723.
Robert Son of Alexander and Elizabeth Forsyth,	"	18 August 1723.
Martha daughter of Patrick and Prudence Flyn,	"	30 December 1723.
Joseph Son of Samuel and Elizabeth Foye,	"	11 September 1723.
Abigail daughter of Zechariah and Abigail Fitch,	"	6 September 1723.
Katharine daughter of William and Elizabeth Fine,	"	6 October 1723.
Ann daughter of Francis and Sarah Fowle,	"	17 December 1723.
John Son of Richard and Diana Flood,	"	7 October 1723.
Thomas Son of William and Margaret Fletcher,	"	4 February 1723.
James Son of John and Mary Foster,	"	14 February 1723.
Jonathan Armitage Son of Abraham and Mary Fyfield,	"	22 March 1723.
William Son of Edward and Hannah Gray,	"	28 January 1723.
Dorcas daughter of Francis and Rachel Gatcombe,	"	23 February 1723.
David Son of James and Elizabeth Gerreck,	"	1 March 1723.
John Son of John and Elizabeth Galpin,	"	23 September 1723.
William Son of William and Rachel Gould,	"	23 November 1723.
Sarah daughter of James and Sarah Green,	"	8 December 1723.
Joseph Son of Samuel and Sarah Gerrish,	"	25 October 1723.
Francis Son of Thomas and Elizabeth Gouge,	"	5 June 1723.
Eliza daughter of Elias and Eliza Gerrish,	"	12 November 1723.
John Son of John and Lydia Gendall,	"	31 December 1723.
Katharine daughter of William and Mary Greenleaf,	"	29 November 1723.
Benjamin Son of Benjamin and Elizabeth Hillier,	"	14 January 1723.
Jacob Son of Jacob and Martha Hartshorn,	"	7 March 1723.
Elizabeth daughter of James and Elizabeth Harris,	"	22 October 1723.
John Son of Nathanael and Hephzibah Hayward,	"	12 December 1723.
Martha daughter of Heman and Mary Henderson.	"	8 August 1723.
Thomas Son of John and Sarah Hooton,	"	10 September 1723.
Mary daughter of John and Mary Harley,	"	1 July 1723.
Rachel daughter of Thomas and Rachel Hogg,	"	10 October 1723.
Mary daughter of Charles and Martha Henley,	"	18 June 1723.
Rebekah daughter of Benjamin and Rebekah Hallowell,	"	29 June 1723.
Elizabeth daughter of Thomas and Sarah Hutchinson,	"	14 May 1723.
Richard Son of Joseph and Elizabeth Harris,	"	5 April 1723.
Judith daughter of Ames and Judith Howard,	"	18 November 1723.
Thomas Son of John and Rebekah Hunt,	"	21 November 1723.
Abigail daughter of John and Susanna Hopkins,	"	8 January 1723.
Lydia daughter of Edward and Lydia Hutchinson,	"	2 February 1723.
William Son of Samuel and Hannah Harris,	"	15 January 1723.
Joseph Son of Samuel and Mary Hunting,	"	22 January 1723
John Son of Robert and Elizabeth Jenkins,	"	18 May 1723.
Hannah daughter of Samuel and Ruth Jackson,	"	25 June 1723.
Mehetabel daughter of North and Abigail Ingham,	"	1 September 1723.
Abigail daughter of Nathanael and Abigail Jarvis,	"	23 March 1723.
Elizabeth daughter of William and Elizabeth Killworth,	"	12 December 1723.
John Son of John and Bathsheba Kent,	"	23 June 1723.
Henry Son of Henry and Mary Killigrew,	"	27 July 1723.
Sarah daughter of Richard and Hannah Kent,	"	29 May 1723.
Joseph Son of Joseph and Elizabeth Kneeland,	"	22 August 1723.
James Son of James and Elizabeth Kittyng,	"	17 June 1723

Births — 1723.

Andrew Son of Andrew and Martha Knox,	Born	20 September 1723.
William Son of John and Elizabeth Kneeland,	"	1 January 1723.
Joshua Son of Joshua and Margaret Kent,	"	7 November 1723.
Mary daughter of Elias and Martha Kingston,	"	6 December 1723.
David Son of John and Sarah Lawson,	"	28 March 1723.
Hannah daughter of Elias and Hannah Langsford,	"	8 January 1723.
Joseph Son of Isaac and Hannah Lewis,	"	11 January 1723.
Peter Son of Andrew and Margaret LeMercier,	"	7 August 1723.
Benjamin Son of James and Mary Lenox,	"	6 February 1723.
Peter } Isaac } Gem Sons of Peter and Elizabeth Luce,	"	15 May 1723.
Elizabeth daughter of William and Mary Lillo,	"	8 May 1723.
Thomas Son of Thomas and Lydia Leworthy,	"	29 May 1723.
Hannah daughter of John and Ruth Leach,	"	26 September 1723.
Elizabeth daughter of Alexander and Elizabeth Miller,	"	14 January 1723.
Elizabeth daughter of Benjamin and Elizabeth Mason,	"	24 September 1723.
William Son of William and Lydia Maxwell,	"	10 March 1723.
John Son of Nathanael and Elizabeth Mason,	"	25 September 1723.
Susanna daughter of Thomas and Susanna Melling,	"	18 June 1723.
James Son of John and Sarah Mills,	"	6 October 1723.
Elizabeth daughter of William and Elizabeth Maycock,	"	26 October 1723.
John Son of John and Elizabeth Maverick,	"	9 January 1723.
Robert Son of Robert and Joyce Marvel,	"	29 April 1723.
Hannah daughter of Samuel and Hannah Maxwell,	"	18 May 1723.
Sarah daughter of John and Jane Marshall,	"	21 June 1723.
John Son of Michael and Mehetabel Martin,	"	19 July 1723.
Abigail daughter of Thomas and Mary Moore,	"	30 July 1723.
Rebekah daughter of Antipas and Rebekah Marshall,	"	1 September 1723.
Ann daughter of Hugh and Mary Markes,	"	19 February 1723.
Dorcas daughter of Christopher and Elizabeth Marshall,	"	27 August 1723.
Ebenezer Son of Ebenezer and Rebekah Messinger,	"	25 November 1723.
Henry Son of Henry and Susanna Newell,	"	16 September 1723.
Samuel Son of William and Bethiah Nichols,	"	10 February 1723.
Frances daughter of John and Ruth Osborne,	"	28 May 1723.
Elizabeth daughter of James and Rebekah Oliver,	"	23 July 1723.
Jeremiah Son of John and Sarah Osborne,	"	28 December 1723.
Elizabeth daughter of Joseph and Mary Procter,	"	6 June 1723.
James Son of Daniel and Sarah Pecker,	"	1 March 1723.
David Son of David and Elizabeth Prince,	"	28 September 1723.
Joshua Son of Joshua and Mary Pratt,	"	20 February 1723.
Phebe daughter of Thomas and Phebe Pemberton,	"	26 September 1723.
Ann daughter of John and Margaret Pitts,	"	10 May 1723.
Jonathan Son of Edward and Ruth Page,	"	23 July 1723.
Luke Greenough Son of Nathanael and Abigail Pearse,	"	16 March 1723.
John Son of Edmund and Esther Perkins,	"	17 December 1723.
Samuel Son of James and Hannah Pemberton,	"	21 December 1723.
Ann daughter of William and Ann Phillips,	"	6 January 1723.
Joseph Son of Timothy and Lydia Prout,	"	1 September 1723.
Elizabeth daughter of Elias and Elizabeth Parkman,	"	4 August 1723.
Sarah daughter of Joseph and Thankful Peirce,	"	16 February 1723.
Hannah daughter of David and Hannah Powell,	"	23 November 1723.
Elias Son of Elias and Jane Pico,	"	5 June 1723.
Deborah daughter of Thomas and Deborah Prince,	"	23 December 1723.
Benjamin Son of Samuel and Mary Procter,	"	29 February 1723.

	Born	
William Son of William and Mehetabel Pratt,		30 March 1723.
Joseph Son of Joseph and Mary Prince,	"	12 April 1723.
Isaac Son of Isaac and Agnis Peirce,	"	3 April 1723.
Jane daughter of William and Margaret Payne,	"	17 February 1723.
Mary daughter of Samuel and Margaret Pousley,	"	10 April 1723.
Susanna daughter of George and Susanna Pemberton,	"	12 May 1723.
Charity daughter of Joseph and Elizabeth Ricks,	"	20 January 1723.
David Son of Edward and Elizabeth Rumley,	"	14 November 1723.
Ann daughter of John and Elizabeth Rubey,	"	15 February 1723.
Bartholomew Son of Robert and Susanna Rand,	"	30 July 1723.
Mary daughter of John and Hannah Rachel,	"	25 March 1723.
William Son of Robert and Elizabeth Rand,	"	6 July 1723.
Anna daughter of Ichabod and Anna Rogers,	"	21 May 1723.
Francis Son of Benjamin and Elizabeth Rolfe,	"	18 January 1723.
Mary daughter of Samuel and Priscilla Royal,	"	1 August 1723.
Sarah ⎱ Gem. daughters of John and Elizabeth		
Hannah ⎰ Smith,	"	31 December 1723.
Elizabeth daughter of James and Elizabeth Scutt,	"	5 February 1723.
John Son of John and Ann Sale,	"	17 March 1723.
Abigail daughter of John and Abigail Salter,	"	31 July 1723.
Katharine daughter of Elisha and Katharine Salter,	"	24 July 1723.
Hannah daughter of Benjamin and Hannah Snelling,	"	18 June 1723.
Thomas Son of Thomas and Abigail Stacey,	"	17 June 1723.
Elizabeth daughter of David and Elizabeth Stoddard,	"	27 June 1723.
Simeon Son of William and Sarah Stoddard,	"	16 June 1723.
John Son of Bartholomew and Elizabeth Sears,	"	4 May 1723.
Samuel Son of Joseph and Mary Snelling,	"	22 May 1723.
Mehetabel daughter of Joseph and Mehetabel Scott,	"	19 September 1723.
Mary daughter of Jonathan and Elizabeth Sewall,	"	5 September 1723.
William Son of William and Elizabeth Smith,	"	9 September 1723.
Edward Son of Edward and Mildred Stanbridge,	"	1 April 1723.
Mary daughter of John and Mary Steel,	"	15 October 1723.
Hannah daughter of Samuel and Hannah Sprague,	"	10 April 1723.
John Son of John and Mary Souther,	"	16 November 1723.
Sarah daughter of John and Abigail Stocker,	"	1 December 1723.
Martha daughter of John and Martha Smith,	"	21 April 1723.
Jabez Son of Jabez and Elizabeth Tuttle,	"	28 May 1723.
Sarah daughter of John and Sarah Teague,	"	10 June 1723.
William Blair Son of James and Elizabeth Townsend	"	6 July 1723.
Bathsheba daughter of Benjamin and Bathsheba Thwing,	"	9 April 1723.
Prince Son of William and Mary Thorald,	"	25 July 1723.
Elizabeth daughter of Alexander and Elizabeth Todd,	"	23 September 1723.
John Son of John and Elizabeth Tyley,	"	2 December 1723.
Mary daughter of John and Rebekah Tenney,	"	2 February 1723.
Mercy daughter of William and Mary Thorn,	"	16 January 1723.
Margery daughter of Andrew and Miriam Tyler,	"	12 February 1723.
Samuel Son of Joseph and Joanna Turell,	"	12 March 1723.
William Son of Joshua and Martha Thornton,	"	28 February 1723.
Thomas Son of Joseph and Sarah Uran,	"	3 February 1723.
John Son of John and Elizabeth Vail,	"	7 December 1723.
Nathanael Son of Nathanael and Mary Viall,	"	21 March 1723.
Mary daughter of Jacob and Sarah Wendell,	"	14 January 1723.
William Son of Adam and Ann Winthrop,	"	29 November 1723.
Elizabeth daughter of Samuel and Elizabeth White,	"	23 January 1723.
Samuel Son of Joseph and Abigail Webb,	"	31 July 1723.
Joshua Son of Joshua and Ann Wroe,	"	30 January 1723.
John Son of John and Rachel Watkins,	"	10 August 1723.

Births — 1723-24.

Susanna daughter of Davis and Susanna Whitman,	Born	15 December 1723.
Jacob Son of Jacob and Hannah Walden,	"	25 April 1723.
Esther daughter of John and Mary Webster,	"	19 March 1723.
Samuel Son of Joseph and Abigail Webb,	"	31 July 1723.
Joshua Son of Joshua and Ann Williams,	"	24 March 1723.
Bethiah daughter of John and Bethiah Walley,	"	3 March 1723.
John Son of Cord and Sarah Wing,	"	18 November 1723.
Joshua Son of William and Martha Winter,	"	5 December 1723.
Hannah daughter of Andrew and Hannah Woodberry,	"	5 June 1723.
Piercy Son of William and Mary Walter,	"	3 December 1723.
Sarah daughter of Robert and Martha Waite,	"	8 January 1723.
John Son of Thomas and Elizabeth Welch,	"	6 July 1723.
Nathan Son of John and Rebekah Whittemore,	"	5 August 1723.
Samuel Son of Samuel and Lucy Waldo,	"	7 May 1723.
Jeremiah Son of Jeremiah and Patience Whittemore,	"	16 August 1723.
William Son of William and Abigail White,	"	29 May 1723.
Ann daughter of Daniel and Ann Willard,	"	22 May 1723.
Elizabeth daughter of William and Susanna Young,	"	13 June 1723.
Nicholas Son of Ebenezer and Mercy Youngman,	"	18 October 1723.
Stedman Son of Nathanael and Esther Young,	"	23 July 1723.
Ann daughter of John and Mary Young,	"	21 March 1723.

1724.

John Son of John and Elizabeth Adams,	Born	9 January 1724.
John Son of John and Sarah Akin,	"	13 February 1724.
James Son of Jonathan and Mary Adams,	"	25 February 1724.
Francis Son of Francis and Huldah Archibald,	"	5 February 1724.
John Son of Samuel and Mary Adams,	"	4 September 1724.
Benjamin Son of John and Anna Alden,	"	18 September 1724.
Isaiah Son of Philip and Rene Benine Audebart,	"	6 December 1724.
John Son of James and Agnes Addison,	"	15 May 1724.
Sarah daughter of John and Mary Adams,	"	20 July 1724.
William Son of Moses and Hannah Ayres,	"	7 February 1724.
John Son of John and Margaret Brock,	"	13 June 1724.
Charles Son of John and Mary Brown,	"	23 June 1724.
John Son of Thomas and Abigail Bradford,	"	12 August 1724.
Kimbal Son of Philip and Mary Bass,	"	26 July 1724.
John Son of John and Mary Bulkley,	"	18 July 1724.
Isaac Son of Joshua and Sarah Blanchard,	"	30 July 1724.
Henry Son of George and Mary Bethune,	"	18 August 1724.
Samuel Son of John and Abigail Burt,	"	4 September 1724.
Elizabeth daughter of John and Elizabeth Barber,	"	9 September 1724.
Mary daughter of William and Jane Brewer,	"	24 August 1724.
Bridget daughter of Nicholas and Elizabeth Belknap,	"	29 September 1724.
Thomas Son of Stephen and Mary Boutineau,	"	11 October 1724.
Priscilla daughter of John and Sarah Bradford,	"	19 October 1724.
William Son of John and Mary Ballantine,	"	26 October 1724.
Augustus Son of James and Elizabeth Beauchamp,	"	18 November 1724.
Rebecca daughter of Ebenezer and Elizabeth Burges,	"	2 November 1724.
Abigail daughter of Joseph and Abigail Bridgham,	"	21 November 1724.
Mary daughter of Job and Alice Brown,	"	24 December 1724.
William Son of William and Elizabeth Bricksey,	"	5 January 1724.
Margaret daughter of John and Katharine Barton,	"	23 December 1724.
Sarah daughter of John and Elizabeth Barkes,	"	31 January 1724.
Esther daughter of Daniel and Mary Ballard,	"	31 January 1724.

Daniel Son of Samuel and Christian Bass,	Born	12 February 1724.
Eleanor daughter of James and Mary Best,	"	25 August 1724.
Benjamin Son of Joseph and Martha Brandon,	"	27 November 1724
Nathanael Son of Thomas and Sarah Boylston,	"	21 March 1724.
Elizabeth daughter of John and Elizabeth Bouve,	"	21 May 1724.
Eunice daughter of Anthony and Eunice Brownsoley,	"	19 March 1724.
Ebenezer Son of Freeborn and Susanna Balch,	"	16 January 1724.
Judith daughter of Thomas and Judith Bulfinch,	"	22 March 1724.
Sarah daughter of George and Sarah Barker,	"	28 March 1724.
Elizabeth daughter of Edward and Elizabeth Bray,	"	2 March 1724.
William Son of William and Elizabeth Blin,	"	1 March 1724.
Mary daughter of James and Elizabeth Beighton,	"	23 May 1724.
Elizabeth daughter of Richard and Hannah Barnard,	"	27 December 1724.
Katherine daughter of Daniel and Abigail Bell,	"	15 February 1724.
Sarah daughter of Elisha and Elizabeth Callender,	"	25 November 1724.
Richard Son of Samuel and Elizabeth Checkley,	"	14 December 1724.
Deborah daughter of George and Mary Cradock,	"	1 July 1724.
Martha daughter of John and Hannah Crawley,	"	30 November 1724.
Miriam daughter of Samuel and Miriam Clark,	"	27 December 1724.
Joseph Son of Nathaniel and Abigail Coney, born at Rehoboth	"	8 May 1724.
Samuel Son of James and Mary Clough,	"	29 January 1724.
Susanna daughter of David and Susanna Crouch,	"	24 January 1724.
Sarah daughter of John and Sarah Carnes,	"	11 February 1724.
John Son of William and Elizabeth Cox,	"	13 April 1724.
Lydia daughter of Josiah and Lydia Carter,	"	16 April 1724.
Mary daughter of Josiah and Priscilla Clark,	"	4 July 1724.
Hannah daughter of Ephraim and Mercy Copeland,	"	1 July 1724.
Sarah daughter of Joseph and Elizabeth Clewley,	"	1 July 1724.
Joanna daughter of Thomas and Patience Cleley,	"	1 October 1724.
Elizabeth daughter of William and Joanna Condy,	"	6 October 1724.
Richard ⎱ Gem. Children of Daniel and Mary Bartholomew ⎰ Cheever,	"	30 October 1724.
Samuel Son of Joseph and Hannah Calef,	"	4 November 1724.
Elizabeth daughter of William and Elizabeth Cunningham,	"	31 October 1724.
James Son of Samuel and Patience Clark,	"	8 November 1724.
Samuel Son of James and Alice Cox,	"	26 November 1724.
Richard Son of Richard-Carter and Jane Cowell,	"	22 December 1724.
Foreland Son of John and Susanna Coombs,	"	13 March 1724.
John Son of Andrew and Mary Cunningham,	"	5 December 1724.
Thomas Son of Thomas and Mary Cushing,	"	24 March 1724.
Mary daughter of John and Mary Cox,	"	11 October 1724.
John Son of Samuel and Sarah Cowdry,	"	28 February 1724.
Nanny daughter of Job and Lydia Coit,	"	23 April 1724.
William Son of William and Damaris Dorrington,	"	1 May 1724.
Cornelius Son of Edward and Judith Durant,	"	17 May 1724.
Hannah daughter of Thomas and Sarah Dawes,	"	7 July 1724.
James Son of James and Mary Dean,	"	1 August 1724.
Mary daughter of John and Abigail Deall,	"	15 August 1724.
John Son of Roger and Ann Dench,	"	7 September 1724.
Joseph Son of William and Lydia Doke,	"	13 September 1724.
James Son of James and Hannah Dowel,	"	24 September 1724.
Dorcas daughter of James and Sarah Davenport,	"	26 August 1724.
Thomas Son of John and Rachel Durant,	"	7 September 1724.
Sarah daughter of William and Sarah Downe,	"	25 September 1724.
Ann daughter of Henry and Elizabeth Dering,	"	6 October 1724.
Elizabeth daughter of Claudius and Ruth Delis,	"	14 January 1724.
Joseph Son of Joseph and Elizabeth Douglas,	"	21 January 1724.

BIRTHS — 1724.

Jane daughter of Nehemiah and Jane Doane,	Born	9 February 1724.
Isaac son of Charles and Sarah Deming,	"	31 August 1724.
Dorcas daughter of James and Sarah Davenport,	"	26 August 1724.
Joshua Son of Joshua and Elizabeth Dodge,	"	11 May 1724.
Isaac Son of Charles and Sarah Deming,	"	31 August 1724.
Ann daughter of John and Naomi Dupee,	"	22 March 1724.
John Son of Thomas and Mary Ellis,	"	7 March 1724.
Sarah daughter of Thomas and Sarah Edwards,	"	11 December 1724.
Thomas Son of Thomas and Deborah Eyre,	"	20 September 1724.
Ann daughter of Thomas and Ann Foster,	"	29 April 1724.
Giles Son of John and Martha Fifield,	"	27 April 1724.
Sarah daughter of Francis and Sarah Fletcher,	"	19 June 1724.
Isaac Son of Thomas and Elizabeth Fleet,	"	13 July 1724.
Isaac Son of Isaac and Ellen Fowle,	"	28 August 1724.
Prudence daughter of Joseph and Margaret Fitch	"	18 August 1724.
William Son of Jonathan and Ann Farnam,	"	2 December 1724.
Samuel Son of Thomas and Hannah Fairweather,	"	3 February 1724.
Mary daughter of Thomas and Anna Foxcroft,	"	4 September 1724.
Hannah daughter of James and Elizabeth Gooch,	"	14 November 1724.
Elizabeth daughter of William and Mary Giles,	"	25 December 1724.
Mary daughter of Jonathan and Judith Gatchell,	"	3 January 1724.
Anna daughter of William and Joanna Grozier,	"	15 December 1724.
Miles Son of Miles and Hannah Gale,	"	8 July 1724.
Jane daughter of Philip and Jane Godfrey,	"	10 September 1724.
Elizabeth daughter of Thomas and Elizabeth Gouge,	"	27 August 1724.
Joseph Son of Joseph and Elizabeth Grouard,	"	1 October 1724.
John Son of John and Sarah Greenough,	"	6 April 1724.
Elizabeth daughter of Daniel and Elizabeth Goffe,	"	13 April 1724.
Nathaniel Son of John and Mercy Goodwin,	"	14 May 1724.
Mary daughter of John and Hannah Giles,	"	11 May 1724.
Mary daughter of Bartholomew and Mary Gedney,	"	28 May 1724.
Mary daughter of Joshua and Sarah Gee,	"	23 May 1724.
John Son of Charles and Mary Giles,	"	4 June 1724.
Elizabeth daughter of Samuel and Mary Hunt,	"	22 September 1724.
Andrew Son of Andrew and Dorcas Hall,	"	13 October 1724.
Foster Son of Thomas and Sarah Hutchinson,	"	7 September 1724.
William Son of George and Rebekah Hanners,	"	28 October 1724.
Mary daughter of William and Mary Hallowell,	"	24 August 1724.
John Son of John and Kezia Harvey,	"	9 November 1724.
Elizabeth daughter of John and Elizabeth Helyer,	"	6 October 1724.
Hannah daughter of James and Anna Halsey,	"	1 February 1724.
Benjamin Son of Samuel and Elizabeth Hood,	"	28 October 1724.
John Son of Abiah and Mary Holbrook,	"	30 January 1724.
Isaac Son of Isaac and Abigail Hall,	"	31 January 1724.
Joseph Son of John and Elizabeth Hubbard,	"	16 January 1724.
Benjamin Son of Benjamin and Rebekah Hallowell,	"	2 February 1724.
Margaret daughter of John and Hannah Hayes,	"	29 April 1724.
Samuel Son of Samuel and Elizabeth Haley,	"	22 June 1724.
Zephaniah Son of Ralph and Mary Hart,	"	19 December 1724.
Mary daughter of David and Mary Huston,	"	19 June 1724.
Hannah daughter of Samuel and Mary Heath,	"	1 December 1724.
Ebenezer Son of Ebenezer and Hannah Hough,	"	28 June 1724.
Daniel Son of Daniel and Elizabeth Henshaw,	"	13 February 1724.
Elizabeth daughter of John and Elizabeth Hill,	"	28 June 1724.
Martha daughter of Robert and Martha Harley,	"	1 September 1724.
Joseph Son of Thomas and Hannah Inches	"	8 January 1724.
Elias Son of Elias and Mary Jarvis,	"	23 July 1724.
Elizabeth daughter of Samuel and Ruth Jackson,	"	14 August 1724.
Rachel daughter of John and Abigail Jent,	"	8 November 1724.
Daniel Son of Zechariah and Elizabeth Johonnott,	"	25 July 1724.

166   CITY DOCUMENT No. 43.

Katharine daughter of Thomas and Mary Kilby,	Born	26 March 1724.
Samuel Son of Samuel and Mary Kneeland,	"	15 March 1724.
William Son of Samuel and Elizabeth Kneeland,	"	21 July 1724.
Sarah daughter of Richard and Sarah Kent,	"	19 August 1724.
John Son of Robert and Susanna Kenton,	"	11 December 1724.
Sarah daughter of John and Bathsheba Kent,	"	25 December 1724.
Elizabeth daughter of Joseph and Elizabeth Kneeland,	"	17 February 1724.
Elizabeth daughter of Peter and Elizabeth Luce,	"	23 May 1724.
Edward Son of Edward and Susanna Langdon.	"	10 June 1724.
Rebekah daughter of David and Rebekah Lupton,	"	1 April 1724.
Benjamin Son of Joseph and Mary Leasenby,	"	10 June 1724.
Joseph Son of Joseph and Katharine Linton,	"	18 July 1724.
Thomas Son of Joseph and Elizabeth Lewis,	"	15 July 1724.
Thomas Son of William and Ruth Lee,	"	9 October 1724.
Mary daughter of Jonathan and Mary Lambert,	"	8 September 1724.
Zechariah Andrew Son of Andrew and Margaret Le Mercier,	"	24 October 1724.
Rebekah daughter of Oliver and Rebekah Luckis,	"	26 October 1724.
Mary daughter of Richard and Thankful Langdon,	"	25 November 1724.
Anthony Son of Thomas and Ann Lechmere,	"	10 February 1724.
William Son of William and Elizabeth Maycock,	"	2 December 1724.
Hannah daughter of Jonathan and Hannah Mountfort,	"	5 February 1724
Lydia daughter of Nathaniel and Sarah Morse,	"	10 March 1724.
John Son of Richard and Lydia Mortimer,	"	16 March 1724.
Daniel Son of Daniel and Ann Mundan,	"	10 January 1724.
Martha daughter of Hugh and Mary Markes,	"	18 March 1724.
Jane daughter of Edward and Jane Moberly,	"	14 March 1724.
Mary daughter of Peter and Abigail Miers,	"	18 March 1724.
James Son of John and Eddy Menzies,	"	6 May 1724.
Mary daughter of Samuel and Mary May,	"	26 April 1724.
Samuel Son of Samuel and Ann Marion,	"	17 May 1724.
Ignatius Son of Isaac and Rebekah Marion,	"	15 August 1724.
John Son of Thaddeus and Mary Maccarty,	"	15 August 1724.
Thomas Son of Thomas and Mary Melvel,	"	8 November 1724.
John Son of John and Elizabeth Maverick,	"	9 January 1724.
Mary daughter of Edmund and Mary Newcomb,	"	26 September 1724.
Susanna daughter of Henry and Susanna Newell,	"	10 November 1724.
Rebekah daughter of Eleazer and Mary Newell,	"	15 July 1724.
Thomas Son of Thomas and Hannah Newman,	"	30 September 1724.
William Son of William and Mary Nicholson,	"	8 April 1724.
Joseph Son of Joseph and Elizabeth Nowell,	"	8 July 1724.
John Son of John and Jane Newton,	"	5 June 1724.
Mary daughter of Thomas and Mary Nowell,	"	9 July 1724.
Sarah daughter of John and Ruth Osborne,	"	5 October 1724.
Mercy daughter of John and Sarah Osborne,	"	13 December 1724.
Samuel Son of Robert and Jane Pateshall,	"	13 October 1724.
Mary daughter of Thomas and Phebe Pemberton,	"	11 November 1724.
Thomas Son of Thomas and Martha Powell,	"	5 December 1724.
Agnes daughter of Isaac and Agnes Peirce,	"	17 March 1724.
Mary daughter of Joseph and Mary Procter,	"	6 May 1724.
Martha daughter of William and Hannah Parkman,	"	21 April 1724.
Richard Son of William and Abigail Palfrey,	"	9 June 1724
Thomas Son of Thomas and Eunice Pearson,	"	12 June 1724.
Sarah daughter of John and Mary Potwine,	"	10 July 1724.
Elizabeth daughter of Benjamin and Margaret Procter,	"	15 July 1724.
Thomas Son of John and Mary Payne,	"	30 August 1724.
Rachel daughter of Joseph and Rachel Roberts,	"	14 April 1724.
Abigail daughter of Joseph and Abigail Russell,	"	17 April 1724.

BIRTHS — 1724.

Joseph Son of Joseph and Priscilla Robey,	Born	12 May 1724.
John Son of Gamaliel and Mercy Rogers,	"	9 May 1724.
Mary daughter of Thomas and Mary Rogers,	"	29 July 1724.
Jonathan Son of Ichabod and Anna Rogers,	"	22 July 1724.
Elizabeth daughter of Simon and Thomazin Rogers,	"	16 August 1724.
Rebekah daughter of Samuel and Mary Robinson,	"	4 August 1724.
Priscilla daughter of Benjamin and Priscilla Roberts,	"	10 September 1724.
Sarah daughter of Peter and Elizabeth Rolandson,	"	3 January 1724.
Eliah Son of Samuel and Priscilla Royall,	"	28 February 1724.
William Son of William and Mary Richardson,	"	24 February 1724.
Joseph Son of Ebenezer and Mary Storer,	"	25 April 1724
Mildred daughter of Edward and Mildred Stanbridge,	"	27 January 1724.
Mary daughter of Stephen and Elizabeth Sims,	"	4 May 1724.
John Son of Ralph and Huldah Smith,	"	27 February 1724.
Sarah daughter of Thomas and Sarah Smith,	"	13 May 1724.
Ann daughter of John and Lydia Simpson,	"	21 December 1724.
Ebenezer Son of Thomas and Mary Studson,	"	20 May 1724.
Thomas Son of Jonathan and Martha Salter,	"	7 September 1724.
Sarah daughter of Nathanael and Sarah Story,	"	12 November 1724.
Mary daughter of James and Deborah Stratton,	"	2 May 1724.
Nathanael Son of Thomas and Tabitha Stoddard,	"	25 April 1724.
William Son of Thomas and Sarah Shaw,	"	20 October 1724.
Mary daughter of George and Ruth Stuart,	"	13 December 1724.
Elizabeth daughter of Ebenezer and Elizabeth Sumner,	"	11 October 1724.
William Son of William and Sarah Stoddard,	"	20 September 1724.
William Son of William and Elizabeth Snoden,	"	2 November 1724.
John Son of John and Susanna Stevens,	"	10 November 1724.
Robert Son of Robert and Ann Sanders,	"	11 February 1724.
Sarah daughter of Thomas and Katharine Tyley,	"	20 August 1724.
John Son of Michael and Submit Tapper,	"	14 April 1724.
Royall Son of William and Sarah Tyler,	"	8 September 1724.
Damaris daughter of Edward and Joanna Tuttle,	"	27 May 1724.
William Son of John and Mary Taylor,	"	11 September 1724.
Katharine daughter of John and Sarah Tyler,	"	15 June 1724.
Philippe daughter of James and Philippe Trench,	"	26 September 1724.
William Son of Benjamin and Bathsheba Thwing,	"	2 August 1724.
Elizabeth daughter of Joshua and Elizabeth Townsend,	"	7 October 1724.
Richard Son of John and Bethiah Taylor,	"	31 March 1724.
Mary daughter of Jonathan and Mary Tarbox,	"	1 December 1724.
Samuel Son of Timothy and Elizabeth Thornton,	"	6 December 1724.
Hannah daughter of Mark and Hannah Trecothick,	"	2 December 1724.
Mary daughter of Peter and Mary Thomas,	"	23 December 1724.
Experience daughter of Ebenezer and Elizabeth Thornton,	"	6 February 1724.
Ann daughter of Robert and Ann Thompson,	"	20 May 1724.
Joseph Son of Joseph and Joanna Turell,	"	4 March 1724.
John Son of Richard and Abigail Thomas,	"	1 March 1724.
Elizabeth daughter of John and Elizabeth Thomas,	"	5 March 1724.
Mary daughter of Joseph and Sarah Uran,	"	23 March 1724.
Susanna daughter of John and Sarah Wakefield,	"	8 August 1724.
Daniel Son of Cornelius and Faith Waldo,	"	29 October 1724.
Benjamin Son of Benjamin and Sarah Whittimore,	"	9 October 1724.
Thomas Son of Thomas and Jane Williston,	"	2 December 1724.
James Son of James and Rebekah Wimble,	"	20 December 1724.
Lucy daughter of Samuel and Lucy Waldo,	"	23 January 1724.
Ichabod Son of Ebenezer and Judith Williston,	"	5 February 1724.

168   CITY DOCUMENT NO. 43.

Parnell and ⎱ Gem. children of Wm. and Elizabeth		
Eleanor ⎰ Waldron,	Born	2 March 1724.
James Son of John and Mary Whitaker,	"	9 March 1724.
Susanna daughter of Andrew and Matthew Willet,	"	18 October 1724.
Mary daughter of Adam and Ann Winthrop,	"	22 March 1724.
John Son of John and Christian Wainwright,	"	8 December 1724.
Samuel Son of Samuel and Hannah Welles,	"	5 March 1724.
Margaret daughter of Joshua and Elizabeth Winslow,	"	28 April 1724.
William Son of Francis and Elizabeth Whitman,	"	9 June 1724.
Benjamin Son of Thomas and Anna Warden,	"	10 July 1724.
Edward Son of Samuel and Elizabeth Watts,	"	1 August 1724.
Mary daughter of John and Esther Waters,	"	3 April 1724.
William Son of William and Mary Warner,	"	10 April 1724.
Elizabeth daughter of Henry and Sarah Wheeler,	"	12 April 1724.
George Son of John and Elizabeth Welland,	"	17 May 1724.
Lydia daughter of Joseph and Abigail Webb,	"	11 February 1724.
William Son of William and Elizabeth Webster,	"	16 February 1724.
Lydia daughter of Joseph and Abigail Webb,	"	11 February 1724.
John Son of John and Sarah Winslow,	"	5 March 1724.
Elizabeth ⎱ Gem. daughters of Samuel and Mary		
and Mary ⎰ Wright,	"	24 January 1724.
Jonathan Son of Jonathan and Susanna Waldo,	"	18 August 1724.
Ruth daughter of Joseph and Ruth Whittimore,	"	19 February 1724.
Hannah daughter of Anthony and Rachel Young,	"	4 July 1724.
Ann daughter of William Beartell and Elizabeth his Wife,	"	23 October 1724.
Mary daughter of John Blowers and Abigail his Wife,	"	16 November 1724.

1725.

Kinsman Son of John and Mary Avis,	Born	26 June 1725.
Benjamin Son of John and Mary Adams,	"	9 August 1725.
Edward Son of Edward and Hannah Ayres,	"	19 August 1725.
Samuel Son of Benj. and Katherine Andrews,	"	12 August 1725.
Sarah daughter of James and Elisabeth Audlington,	"	20 August 1725.
Mary daughter of John and Mary Allin,	"	30 October 1725.
Deliverance daughter of Henry and Deliverance Atkins,	"	24 October 1725.
Joshua Son of Joshua and Elisabeth Atwood,	"	1 January 1725.
Elisabeth daughter of Jer. and Rebekah Allen,	"	22 April 1725.
Rebekah daughter of Thomas and Rebekah Amory,	"	12 June 1725.
Mary daughter of Zechr. and Jemima Alden,	"	8 March 1725.
Thomas Son of Thomas and Jane Alden,	"	10 June 1725.
John Son of Matthew and Katherine Adams,	"	19 June, 1725.
Mary daughter of James and Mary Barnes,	"	13 January 1725.
Mercy daughter of Joseph and Abigail Bridgham,	"	27 December 1725.
Ruth daughter of Benjamin and Ruth Babbidge,	"	3 February 1725.
Abigail daughter of Edward and Abigail Bromfield,	"	9 January 1725.
Susanna daughter of John and Susanna Brown,	"	10 February 1725.
John Son of John and Sarah Barnes,	"	11 September 1725.
Ann daughter of William Bowen and Ann his Wife,	"	4 January 1725.
Jonathan Son of Jonathan and Mary Blake,	"	23 February 1725.
Elizabeth daughter of John and Jennet Bulfinch,	"	6 March 1725.
James Son of William and Elizabeth Blin.	"	14 February 1725.
Elizabeth daughter of Amos and Elizabeth Breed,	"	16 March 1725.
William Son of Solomon and Abigail Blake,	"	26 March 1725.
Sarah daughter of John and Sarah Bolderson,	"	27 March 1725
John Son of John and Sarah Bowen,	"	8 April, 1725.

Births — 1725.

Elizabeth daughter of Jeremiah and Sarah Belknap,	Born	12 April 1725.
William Son of Gideon and Martha Ball,	"	24 April 1725.
Rebecca daughter of William and Elizabeth Beairsto	"	8 April 1725.
Ann daughter of Increase and Ann Blake,	"	8 May 1725.
Ann daughter of Wm. and Rachel Brown,	"	2 May 1725.
Nathanael Son of Nathanael and Dorothy Barber,	"	16 May 1725.
Joseph Son of Joseph and Susanna Burrell,	"	31 May 1725.
Samuel Son of Jonathan and Mary Bowman,	"	13 September 1725.
Rebecca daughter of Nathanael and Rebecca Belknap,	"	18 July 1725.
Katharine daughter of John and Katharine Berry,	"	2 October 1725.
Sarah daughter of Joshua and Sarah Blanchard,	"	29 September 1725.
Thomas and ⎫ Gem. Sons of Thomas and Susanna James ⎭ Bentley,	"	2 November 1725.
Mary daughter of Joseph and Jane Bissell,	"	7 October 1725.
Joseph Son of Josiah and Mary Bacon,	"	25 October 1725.
Mary daughter of Benjamin and Abigail Baxter,	"	28 July 1725.
Sarah daughter of Comfort and Rachel Bird,	"	15 November 1725.
John Son of John and Mary Beer,	"	25 November 1725.
William Son of Wm. and Abigail Brown,	"	15 December 1725.
Elizabeth daughter of Thomas and Esther Buchannon,	"	10 November 1725.
Waite Son of William and Lydia Brown,	"	28 November 1725.
William Son of John and Mehetabel Buttolph,	"	7 May 1725.
Hephzibah daughter of John and Mary Baker,	"	19 July 1725.
James Son of James and Elizabeth Beighton,	"	14 July 1725.
Jeremiah Son of Jeremiah and Mary Barto,	"	12 February 1725.
Jacob Son of John and Sarah Brewer,	"	20 September 1725.
Lucy daughter of Thomas and Sarah Boylston,	"	28 September 1725.
Mary daughter of Timothy and Mary Barron,	"	20 September 1725.
Elizabeth daughter of John and Elizabeth Bovey,	"	21 May 1725.
Jacob Son of Thomas and Ruth Bill,	"	24 May 1725.
Timothy Son of Joseph and Mary Balch,	"	28 May 1725.
James Son of Nicholas and Hannah Boon,	"	21 June 1725.
John Son of Thomas and Susanna Belcher,	"	29 June 1725.
Elisha and ⎫ Gem. Children of Ellis and Sarah Bennet, Sarah ⎭	"	10 June 1725.
James Son of James and Damaris Collins,	"	6 August 1725.
John Son of Samuel and Mary Conibal,	"	10 August 1725.
Thomas Son of William and Jane Covell,	"	27 July 1725.
William Son of William and Sarah Cooper,	"	29 September 1725.
Ebenezer Son of Ebenezer and Rachel Clough,	"	20 February 1725.
Sarah daughter of Henry and Sarah Carnel,	"	12 December 1725.
Elizabeth daughter of Samuel and Elizabeth Checkley,	"	15 March 1725.
Benjamin Son of William and Elizabeth Cunningham,	"	9 January 1725.
John Son of Robert and Jane Cole,	"	8 January 1725.
Nathanael Son of Daniel and Mary Capen,	"	21 December 1725.
Elizabeth daughter of George and Mary Cradock,	"	5 July 1725.
Samuel Son of Samuel and Sarah Clark,	"	12 January 1725.
Joseph and ⎫ Gem. Sons of Wm. and Elizabeth Christopher ⎭ Cowell,	"	10 July 1725.
Nathanael Son of Nathanael and Ann Cunningham,	"	26 April 1725.
Elizabeth daughter of Nathanael and Martha Cobbett,	"	23 July 1725.
Mary daughter of Jeremiah and Susanna Condy,	"	2 July 1725.
Samuel Son of Charles and Mary Coffin,	"	12 May 1725.
John Son of John and Rebekah Compton,	"	7 May 1725.

Elizabeth daughter of Jonathan and Elizabeth Chandler, Born 15 May 1725.
Mary daughter of James and Elizabeth Collings, " 26 March 1725.
Sarah daughter of Edward and Abigail Cruft, " 5 April 1725.
Jane daughter of John-Michael and Mary Chenevard, " 8 July 1725.
Josiah Son of Josiah and Lydia Carter, " 29 August 1725.
Nathaniel Son of William and Ann Coffin, " 24 July 1725.
Hannah daughter of Josiah and Lydia Carter, " 3 July 1725.
Elizabeth daughter of Henry and Abigail Deliway, " 6 May 1725.
Hannah daughter of Thomas and Lydia Dagget, " 22 July 1725.
Mary daughter of William and Damaris Dorrington, " 15 August 1725.
Sarah daughter of Shem and Katharine Drowne, " 19 September 1725.
Isaac ⎫ Gem. Children of Isaac and Rebekah
Elizabeth ⎭ Dawbt, " 30 October 1725.
Ebenezer Son of James and Hannah Dowell, " 19 November 1725.
Elizabeth daughter of James and Mary Day, " 5 April 1725.
William Son of Zebadiah and Elizabeth Daniel, " 5 February 1725.
Mary daughter of Thomas and Anna Downe, " January 1725.
Mary daughter of James and Sarah Davenport, " 7 March 1725.
Ezekiel Son of John and Elizabeth Decoster, " 30 June 1725.
John Son of James and Mary Dean, " 6 March 1725.
Jane daughter of Walter and Jane Edmonds, " 15 August 1725.
Susanna daughter of David and Susanna Eustus, " 16 September 1725.
David Son of David and Mary Evans, " 3 October 1725.
Sarah daughter of John and Sarah Eliot, " 28 October 1725.
John Son of John and Mary Edwards, " 15 June 1725.
Rebekah daughter of John and Rebekah Endicot, " 9 July 1725.
Abigail daughter of John and Abigail Earle, " 10 February 1725.
John Son of David and Elizabeth Franklyn, " 6 May 1725.
Joseph Son of Robert and Sarah Fothergill, " 12 July 1725.
James Son of William and Elizabeth Fine, " 19 July 1725.
Ruth daughter of Ebenezer and Elizabeth Fisher, " 9 August 1725.
Eleazar Son of Eleazer and Mary Flagg, " 6 November 1725.
Jacob Son of Zechariah and Abigail Fitch, " 3 September 1725.
John Son of John and Martha Fyfield, " 6 October 1725.
Thomas Son of William and Margaret Fletcher, " 9 October 1725.
Timothy Son of Joseph and Margaret Fitch, " 23 October 1725.
John Son of Patrick and Prudence Flyn, " 8 November 1725.
Timothy Son of Thomas and Ann Foster, " 30 November 1725.
Thomas Son of William and Margaret Fletcher, " 23 April 1725.
Sarah daughter of Hopestill and Sarah Foster, " 3 October 1725.
Dorothy daughter of Samuel and Elizabeth Foye, " 26 May 1725.
Dorothy daughter of Jonathan and Ann Farnam, " 12 February 1725.
John Son of Giles and Hannah Goddard, " 10 December 1725.
Joseph Son of John and Lydia Gendall " 9 December 1725.
Thomas Son of Thomas and Ann Green, " 19 October 1725.
Mary daughter of Bartholomew and Hannah Green, " 24 December 1725.
John Son of Peter and Elizabeth Gibbins, " 18 February 1725.
Abigail daughter of Thomas and Mary Goodwin, " 22 November 1725.
Mary daughter of Francis and Rachel Gatcombe, " 21 February 1725.
Shove Son of Joseph and Susanna Gunnison, " 12 March 1725.
James Son of James and Sarah Green, " 8 June 1725.
William Son of Bartholomew and Mary Gedney, " 24 October 1725.
Ebenezer Son of Robert and Abigail Grater, " 25 March 1725.
Nicholas Son of Philip and Hannah Gray, " 26 March 1725.
Joseph Son of James and Elizabeth Goodwin, " 30 April 1725.
Elizabeth daughter of Nicholas and Mary George, " 21 May 1725.
Joshua Son of Joshua and Sarah Gee, " 6 June 1725.
Dixe Son of Daniel and Elizabeth Goffe, " 22 June 1725.

BIRTHS — 1725.

Elizabeth daughter of John and Elizabeth Galpin,	Born	21 August 1725.
Sarah daughter of John and Elizabeth Greenleaf,	"	5 August 1725.
James Son of James and Elizabeth Gerreck,	"	9 September 1725.
John Son of Charles and Mary Giles,	"	29 August 1725.
Susanna daughter of William and Mary Greenleaf,	"	1 September 1725.
Ann daughter of Samuel and Ann Graiton,	"	5 September 1725.
Sarah daughter of William and Sarah Grayham,	"	20 September 1725.
Joseph Son of Richard and Elizabeth Hall,	"	11 July 1725.
Thomas Son of Thomas and Mary Hubbard,	"	9 July 1725.
Samuel Son of Ames and Judith Howard,	"	15 July 1725.
Elizabeth daughter of Samuel and Elizabeth Holyoke,	"	25 July 1725.
Rachel daughter of John and Mary Harey,	"	4 June 1725.
Elizabeth daughter of Joseph and Elizabeth Harris,	"	12 September 1725.
Arthur Son of Arthur and Rebekah Hill.	"	12 June 1725.
Benjamin Son of Heman and Mary Henderson,	"	5 September 1725.
Zechariah Son of Alexander and Mary Hunt,	"	18 September 1725.
Elizabeth daughter of Zechariah and Mary Hubbard,	"	26 September 1725.
Hannah daughter of Jeremiah and Margaret Hall,	"	2 October 1725.
Timothy Son of William and Margery Hodgdon,	"	25 November 1725.
Anna daughter of John and Elizabeth Hill,	"	17 December 1725.
Hannah daughter of Eleanor sic and Hannah Hough,	"	26 December 1725.
Tabitha daughter of Richard and Hannah Hayward,	"	18 January 1725.
Mary daughter of Samuel and Mary Hastings,	"	23 January 1725.
Ann daughter of David and Mary Huston,	"	12 February 1725.
Jacob Son of Jacob and Elizabeth Hurd,	"	1 March 1725.
Elizabeth daughter of Israel and Judith How,	"	1 May 1725.
Sarah daughter of John and Sarah Hooton,	"	14 April 1725.
Sarah daughter of John and Rachel Howard,	"	20 December 1725.
Thomas Son of Thomas and Bathsheba Harwood,	"	10 May 1725.
Elizabeth daughter of Ebenezer and Deborah Heath,	"	17 August 1725.
Elizabeth daughter of Samuel and Elizabeth Holland,	"	28 June 1725.
Charles Son of Charles and Martha Henley,	"	1 June 1725.
Zechariah Son of Zechariah and Elizabeth Johonnott,	"	17 January 1725.
Robert Son of Robert and Elizabeth Jenkins,	"	6 April 1725.
John Son of John and Lydia Kelton,	"	27 March 1725.
Mary daughter of Henry and Mary Killigrew,	"	11 July 1725.
Bartholomew Son of John and Elizabeth Kneeland,	"	11 November 1725.
Daniel Son of Samuel and Mary Kneeland,	"	11 November 1725.
Thomas Son of Thomas and Zeruiah Leasenby,	"	31 March 1725.
Paul Son of Elias and Hannah Langsford,	"	11 April 1725.
James Son of William and Lydia Larraby,	"	1 May 1725.
Abigail daughter of Ebenezer and Abigail Leadbetter,	"	8 July 1725.
Thomas Son of Joseph and Mary Leasenby,	"	10 October 1725.
Jemima daughter of Nathan and Ann Lewis,	"	15 January 1725.
Rebekah daughter of David and Rebekah Lupton,	"	13 October 1725.
Edward Son of Edward and Elizabeth Lyde,	"	29 December 1725.
William Son of James and Mary Lenox,	"	4 March 1725.
George Son of William and Lydia Maxwell,	"	1 May 1725.
David Son of David and Rachel Matthews,	"	6 September 1725.
Jonathan Son of Benjamin and Elizabeth Mason,	"	16 May 1725.
Christopher Son of Christopher and Eliza. Marshall,	"	15 September 1725.
Samuel Son of John and Eddy Menzies,	"	17 May 1725.
Martha daughter of William and Abigail Merchant,	"	13 October 1725.
Elizabeth daughter of Thomas and Mary Millner,	"	16 July 1725.

	Born	
Sarah daughter of John and Sarah Mills,		15 December 1725.
John Son of John and Martha Marshall,	"	20 August 1725.
Mary daughter of John and Elizabeth Maverick,	"	10 December 1725.
Mary daughter of William and Hannah Marshall,	"	9 September 1725.
Susanna daughter of Benjamin and Ann Mulbery,	"	9 January 1725.
William Son of Isaac and Rebekah Marion,	"	24 January 1725.
James Son of James and Susanna Melling,	"	10 March 1725.
Jane daughter of Edward and Jane Moberly,	"	18 March 1725.
Elizabeth daughter of Eleazer and Mary Newell,	"	14 August 1725.
Anna daughter of William and Mary Neatby,	"	5 March 1725.
Samuel Son of Samuel and Sarah Norton,	"	23 October 1725.
James Son of James and Rebekah Oliver,	"	16 April 1725.
Philip Son of Philip and Jane Ormond,	"	6 October 1725.
Mary daughter of Philip and Mary Obins,	"	25 December 1725.
Mary daughter of George and Susanna Pemberton,	"	27 August 1725.
John Son of William and Mehetabel Pratt,	"	6 August 1725.
John Son of John and Mary Papoon,	"	22 September 1725.
Mary daughter of John and Mary Phillips,	"	22 September 1725.
Mary daughter of Edward and Ruth Page,	"	13 July 1725.
Ann daughter of Moses and Elizabeth Pearse,	"	26 September 1725.
Elizabeth daughter of John and Esther Pitts,	"	7 November 172˙.
William Son of Samuel and Mary Procter,	"	29 November 1725.
John Son of Joseph and Mehetabel Payson,	"	2 May 1725.
Mary daughter of William and Abigail Palfrey,	"	12 November 1725.
Mercy daughter of Thomas and Deborah Prince,	"	6 December 1725.
Dorothy daughter of Elias and Elizabeth Parkman,	"	8 February 1725.
Samuel Son of William and Hannah Parkman,	"	3 March 1725.
William ⎱ Gem. Sons of William and Ann Zechariah ⎰ Phillips,	"	16 March 1725.
Moses Son of Nathanael and Abigail Pearse,	"	21 July 1725.
Thomas Son of Thomas and Mary Plaisted,	"	29 July 1725.
Isaac Son of Joseph and Mary Prince,	"	26 March 1725.
Rachel daughter of Joseph and Mary Procter,	"	7 April 1725.
William Son of David and Elizabeth Prince,	"	4 April 1725.
John Son of Henry and Walter Pigeon,	"	17 March 1725.
Mary daughter of Timothy and Lydia Prout,	"	22 July 1725.
Elizabeth daughter of Robert and Jane Pateshall	"	24 March 1725.
John Son of William and Mary Peck,	"	12 June 1725.
David Son of David and Hannah Powell.	"	28 February 1725.
Edmund Son of Edmund and Elizabeth Quincy,	"	6 February 1725.
James Son of Thomas and Elizabeth Rogers,	"	19 August 1725.
John Son of John and Hopestill Russell,	"	15 August 1725.
James Son of James and Mehetabel Ridgaway,	"	4 January 1725.
John Son of Samuel and Mary Robinson,	"	16 September 1725.
Zechariah Son of Robert and Susanna Rand,	"	22 October 1725.
John Son of Arthur and Lydia Rawlings,	"	9 May 1725.
Joseph Son of Joseph and Hannah Ranger,	"	7 December 1725.
John Son of Edward and Elizabeth Rumley,	"	21 July 1725.
Hannah daughter of Joseph and Priscilla Roby,	"	9 January 1725.
John Son of Samuel and Sarah Rand,	"	26 April 1725.
Benjamin Son of Simon and Thomazin Rogers,	"	3 March 1725.
Stephen Son of William and Mary Rillow,	"	13 September 1725.
Hannah daughter of Nicholas and Hannah Roach,	"	19 July 1725.
Sarah daughter of John and Sarah Skinner,	"	16 May 1725.
Mary daughter of Ebenezer and Mary Storer,	"	21 June 1725.
John Son of John and Abigail Salter.	"	25 June 1725.
Benjamin Son of Bartholomew and Elizabeth Sears,	"	10 July 1725.
Elizabeth daughter of Thomas and Tabitha Stoddard,	"	24 July 1725.
Mary daughter of John and Mary Simpson,	"	1 August 1725.

BIRTHS — 1725.

Elizabeth daughter of Joseph and Mehetabel Scott,	Born	2 August 1725.
Ruth daughter of Luke and Margaret Stone,	"	13 September 1725.
Margaret daughter of Jonathan and Mary Sewall,	"	14 October 1725.
Sarah daughter of Samuel and Hannah Sprague,	"	27 August 1725.
Grace daughter of Jonathan and Martha Salter,	"	10 November 1725.
John Son of William and Sarah Stoddard	"	1 March 1725.
Mary daughter of Jonathan and Mary Snelling,	"	22 December 1725.
John Son of Nicholas and Martha Salisbury,	"	28 January 1725.
Sarah daughter of Thomas and Mary Studson,	"	13 February 1725.
Jonathan Son of Benjamin and Susanna Storer,	"	16 February 1725.
Elizabeth daughter of Isaac and Mehetabel Stearns,	"	12 February 1725.
Joseph Son of William and Dorcas Somers,	"	15 November 1725.
John Son of Andrew and Miriam Tyler,	"	5 May 1725.
William Son of Phinehas and Ann Thomas,	"	5 November 1725.
William Son of William and Elizabeth Trow,	"	16 August 1725.
Lydia daughter of John and Sarah Teague,	"	30 May 1725.
Sarah daughter of John and Elizabeth Tyley,	"	4 September 1725.
Rebekah daughter of James and Elizabeth Townsend,	"	12 April 1725.
Mary daughter of William and Mary Thorn,	"	15 October 1725.
Persis daughter of Gershom and Priscilla Tenney,	"	27 October 1725.
John Son of Jabez and Elizabeth Tuttle,	"	5 November 1725.
Bathsheba daughter of Benjamin and Bathsheba Thwing,	"	18 January 1725.
John Son of John and Susanna Tinkum,	"	11 February 1725.
John Son of John and Sarah Tyler,	"	6 February 1725.
Love daughter of Maverick and Joanna Thomas,	"	19 March 1725.
Turell Son of Cornelius and Lydia Thayer,	"	13 March 1725.
Samuel Son of Nathanael and Mary Vial,	"	1 October 1725.
Ebenezer Son of John and Elizabeth Vail,	"	30 January 1725.
Mary daughter of Elijah and Elizabeth Vinall,	"	15 December 1725.
Rebekah daughter of John and Rebekah Whittemore,	"	3 May 1725.
Ann daughter of Jonathan and Martha Williams,	"	28 May 1725.
William Son of Samuel and Sarah Warden,	"	28 March 1725.
Hannah daughter of Oliver and Hannah Williams,	"	11 June 1725.
Mary daughter of Robert and Sarah Williams,	"	18 June 1725.
Sarah daughter of John and Elizabeth Wise,	"	17 June 1725
Samuel Son of Davis and Susanna Whitman,	"	24 June 1725.
Abigail daughter of William and Abigail White,	"	20 July 1725.
Martha daughter of Joseph and Elizabeth White,	"	28 July 1725.
Benjamin Son of Thomas and Elizabeth Welch,	"	23 August 1725.
Elizabeth daughter of Francis and Elizabeth Whitman,	"	12 October 1725.
Anna daughter of Joshua and Mary Winnock,	"	13 August 1725.
Jacob Son of Jacob and Elizabeth Wendell,	"	23 November 1725.
Mary daughter of William and Abigail Watson,	"	4 October 1725.
Andrew Son of Andrew and Martha Willet,	"	16 October 1725.
Elizabeth daughter of Henry and Sarah Williams,	"	16 September 1725.
Mary daughter of William and Mary Wheeler,	"	18 October 1725.
Rebekah daughter of Richard and Ann Walter,	"	6 November 1725.
Thomas Son of John and Bethiah Walley,	"	1 November 1725.
Priscilla daughter of Peleg and Elizabeth Wiswall,	"	17 December 1725.
Sarah daughter of Benjamin and Sarah Whittemore,	"	21 November 1725.
Moses Son of Nathanael and Susanna Wardall,	"	26 January 1725.
Mary daughter of William and Mary Warner,	"	29 January 1725.
Jacob Son of John and Elizabeth Wendell,	"	23 November 1725.
Sarah daughter of Ezekiel and Sarah Walker,	"	8 March 1725.
Hannah daughter of Joshua and Elizabeth Winslow,	"	8 March 1725.
Ann daughter of James and Margaret Webber,	"	8 March 1725.

Thomas Son of Ebenezer and Mercy Youngman,	Born	5 June 1725.
Margaret daughter of Anthony and Rachel Young,	"	7 June 1725.

1726.

James Son of James and Agnes Addison,	Born	4 April 1726.
Nicholas Son of Nicholas and Rachel Anthony,	"	18 June 1726.
Samuel Son of Samuel and Anna Appleton,	"	15 August 1726.
Joseph Son of Nathl. and Elisabeth Ayres,	"	24 January 1726.
Martha daughter of James and Elisabeth Audlington,	"	15 October 1726.
John Son of Samuel and Mary Adams,	"	28 October 1726.
Martha daughter of John and Mary Allen,	"	15 November 1726.
Jonathan Son of Thomas and Rebekah Amory,	"	19 December 1726.
John Son of Moses and Hannah Ayres,	"	20 November 1726.
William Son of John and Mary Adams,	"	28 December 1726.
Abigail daughter of Thomas and Abigail Bradford,	"	26 December 1726.
John Son of William and Rachel Brown,	"	9 December 1726.
Mary daughter of Benjamin and Abigail Baxter,	"	22 December 1726.
John Son of Jonathan and Mary Bowman,	"	19 January 1726.
Philip Son of Philip and Mary Bass,	"	22 January 1726.
Elizabeth daughter of Freeborn and Susanna Balch,	"	2 March 1726.
Hannah daughter of Richard and Hannah Barnard,	"	2 July 1726.
Elizabeth daughter of Shearjashub and Abigail Brown,	"	11 July 1726.
John Son of Nathanael and Sarah Breed,	"	24 August 1726.
Samuel Son of Ebenezer and Mary Bridge,	"	10 August 1726.
Sarah daughter of Edward and Alice Barret,	"	13 August 1726.
Sarah daughter of Jonathan and Ann Barnard,	"	15 September 1726.
Elizabeth daughter of Thomas and Elizabeth Barwick,	"	16 August 1726.
William and Sarah } Gem. Children of John and Abigail Burt,	"	6 September 1726.
Mary daughter of David and Rely Belcher,	"	29 August 1726.
Jane daughter of John and Elizabeth Banks,	"	19 October 1726.
Increase Son of Increase and Ann Blake,	"	28 October 1726.
Elizabeth daughter of John and Sarah Bradford,	"	24 October 1726.
Isabella daughter of Thomas and Lydia Brunton,	"	25 May 1726.
Isaac Son of Stephen and Mary Boutineau,	"	22 June 1726.
John Son of Benjamin and Elizabeth Bagnall,	"	21 July 1726.
Joshua Son of Thomas and Susanna Bentley,	"	16 January 1726.
Elizabeth daughter of Thomas and Sarah Brooks,	"	24 February 1726.
James Son of James and Hannah Bowdoin,	"	7 August 1726.
Sarah daughter of William and Hannah Bond,	"	28 December 1726.
Thornton Son of Thornton and Hephzibah Barret,	"	14 March 1726.
Samuel Son of John and Katharine Barton,	"	9 October 1726.
Peter Son of James and Mary Boyer,	"	11 July 1726.
Mary daughter of John and Mary Belitho,	"	14 May 1726.
John Son of John and Mary Bennet,	"	18 April 1726.
John Son of Job and Alice Brown,	"	1 May 1726.
Thomas Son of John and Sarah Banks,	"	2 May 1726.
Bartholomew Son of Daniel and Mary Cheever,	"	25 January 1726.
Ephraim Son of Ephraim and Mercy Copeland,	"	5 February 1726.
Richard Son of Samuel and Elizabeth Checkley,	"	20 February 1726.
Josiah Son of Josiah and Lydia Carter,	"	31 August 1726.
Elisha Son of Elisha and Elizabeth Callender,	"	10 May 1726.
Elizabeth daughter of John and Mary Cox,	"	14 March 1726.
Joshua Son of Joseph and Mary Cowell,	"	10 November 1726.
Lydia daughter of Job and Lydia Coit,	"	8 January 1726.

BIRTHS — 1726.

Ann daughter of Jeremiah and Ann Cushing,	Born	17 November 1726.
John Son of John and Emma Charnock,	"	6 June 1726.
Charles Son of Charles and Mary Coffin,	"	13 May 1726.
Eliza. ⎱ Gem. daughters of John and Sarah Mary ⎰ Carnes,	"	15 April 1726.
Sarah daughter of Benjamin and Miriam Clark,	"	28 July 1726.
Mary daughter of Thomas and Elizabeth Cock,	"	15 August 1726.
Jonas Son of Joseph and Margaret Clark,	"	1 August 1726.
William Son of Nathaniel and Abigail Coney, born at Rehoboth	"	29 March 1726.
Judith daughter of Benjamin and Elizabeth Cushing,	"	5 August 1726.
James Son of James and Sarah Clark,	"	4 September 1726.
Sarah daughter of Andrew and Mary Cunningham,	"	13 October 1726.
Benjamin Son of Joseph and Elizabeth Clewley,	"	3 August 1726.
Margaret daughter of John Michael and Margaret Chenevard,	"	· 13 October 1726.
Sarah daughter of James and Alice Cox,	"	29 October 1726.
Philip Son of Clement and Mary Chick,	"	14 November 1726.
William Son of Richard and Ammi Coleworthy,	"	22 November 1726.
Thomas Son of Harry and Abigail Deliway,	"	13 July 1726.
Mitchelson Son of Henry and Elizabeth Dering,	"	23 May 1726.
Mary daughter of Andrew and Abigail Durgee,	"	28 July 1726.
Dorcas daughter of Elijah and Dorcas Doubleday,	"	6 August 1726.
Benjamin Son of Benjamin and Margaret Dyer,	"	22 September 1726.
Jonathan Son of Eleazer and Mary Dorby,	"	14 September 1726.
William Son of William and Lydia Docke,	"	12 September 1726.
Caleb Son of Joshua and Elizabeth Dodge,	"	14 December 1726.
Thomas Son of William and Sarah Downe,	"	23 January 1726.
Mary daughter of Thomas and Anna Downe,	"	3 February 1726.
Mary daughter of Shem and Katharine Drowne,	"	10 February 1726.
Elizabeth daughter of Thomas and Jemima Debuke,	"	25 March 1726.
Margaret daughter of Francis and Margaret Duray,	"	21 May 1726.
Rachel daughter of John and Rachel Durant,	"	15 June 1726.
William Son of William and Hannah Davis,	"	17 March 1726.
Bethiah daughter of Benjamin and Bethiah Deming,	"	19 August 1726.
Elias Son of Elias and Mary Dupee,	"	25 April 1726.
Deborah daughter of Thomas and Deborah Eyre,	"	24 July 1726.
Hannah daughter of John and Ann Eastwicke,	"	29 September 1726.
Mary daughter of David and Mary Evans,	"	19 December 1726.
Richard Son of Benjamin and Ruth Eastabrook,	"	8 January 1726.
John Son of John and Hannah Ellis,	"	2 March 1726.
Hannah daughter of Nathanael and Hannah Emmes,	"	25 May 1726.
Hannah daughter of Samuel and Elizabeth Foye,	"	30 April 1726.
Ellen daughter of Isaac and Ellen Fowle,	"	11 June 1726.
Sarah daughter of Charles and Mary Forest,	"	3 July 1726.
Jonathan Son of Ephraim and Martha Fenno,	"	26 August 1726.
Martha daughter of Thomas and Anna Foxcroft,	"	5 August 1726.
John Son of William and Margaret Fletcher,	"	15 November 1726.
Thomas Son of Joseph and Margaret Fitch,	"	12 January 1726.
William Son of David and Elizabeth Franklyn,	"	7 February 1726.
William Son of Ebenezer and Elizabeth Fisher,	"	21 February 1726.
Abigail daughter of John and Mary Foster,	"	14 March 1726.
Hannah daughter of Thomas and Hannah Fairweather,	"	- 25 February 1726.
John Son of John and Mercy Goodwin,	"	13 May 1726.
Sarah daughter of John and Sarah Greenough,	"	11 July 1726.
Elizabeth daughter of Philip and Jane Godfrey,	"	27 October 1726.
Joseph Son of Joseph and Mercy Glydden,	"	20 July 1726.

Elizabeth daughter of William and Rebekah Goodwin,	Born	6 August 1726.
Sarah daughter of Joshua and Sarah Gee,	"	3 September 1726.
Hannah daughter of Nathanael and Elizabeth Greenwood,	"	14 September 1726.
Mary daughter of Richard and Elizabeth Goodwin,	"	3 January 1726.
Elizabeth daughter of James and Elizabeth Goodwin,	"	21 January 1726.
Anna daughter of Azor and Anna Gale,	"	4 April 1726.
Benjamin Son of Edward and Hannah Gray,	"	28 March 1726.
Edward Son of Thomas and Elizabeth Gouge,	"	6 May 1726.
Peter Son of Peter and Elizabeth Gibbons,	"	25 February 1726.
William Son of Bartholomew and Mary Gedney,	"	1 December 1726.
Abigail daughter of William and Mary Greenleaf,	"	29 October 1726.
William Son of William and Joanna Grozier,	"	13 December 1726.
Mary daughter of Samuel and Mary Heath,	"	3 August 1726.
William Son of George and Rebekah Hopkins,	"	20 August 1726.
Mary daughter of John and Mary Henderson,	"	4 September 1726.
John Son of Thomas and Ann Holland,	"	11 September 1726.
Sarah daughter of Ebenezer and Abigail Howard,	"	8 October 1726.
Thomas Son of John and Elizabeth Helyer,	"	14 October 1726.
Mary daughter of Joshua and Hannah Hubbard,	"	19 February 1726.
John Son of John and Mary Heaton,	"	6 October 1726.
Mary daughter of William and Elizabeth Healy,	"	15 May 1726.
Samuel Son of Samuel and Elizabeth Holyoke,	"	25 September 1726.
Joseph Son of Samuel and Elizabeth Hood,	"	4 November 1726.
Henry Son of Henry and Sarah Harris,	"	28 October 1726.
Benjamin Son of George and Elizabeth Hanners,	"	6 January 1726.
Sarah daughter of Thomas and Sarah Hillier,	"	16 November 1726.
Mary daughter of James and Ann Halsey,	"	24 March 1726.
Sarah daughter of Peter and Katharine Harratt,	"	1 August 1726.
Elizabeth daughter of Samuel and Hannah Harris,	"	24 July 1726.
Sarah daughter of John and Mary Hill,	"	5 April 1726.
Edward Son of Thomas and Sarah Hutchinson,	"	27 March 1726.
Mary daughter of Samuel and Elizabeth Haley,	"	30 March 1726.
Thomas Son of Thomas and Bathsheba Harwood,	"	24 December 1726.
Sarah daughter of Benjamin and Rebekah Hallowell,	"	24 February 1726.
Mary daughter of Joseph and Martha Harley,	"	22 May 1726.
Mary daughter of Thomas and Mary Hubbard,	"	16 June 1726.
John Son of Samuel and Mary Hunting,	"	26 June 1726.
Ann daughter of William and Mary Hallowell,	"	14 July 1726.
Joshua Son of Daniel and Elizabeth Henshaw,	"	21 July 1726.
Mary daughter of John and Mary Hawke,	"	23 July 1726.
Elizabeth daughter of John and Kezia Harvey,	"	7 July 1726.
Mary daughter of Ralph and Mary Hart,	"	31 July 1726.
Susanna daughter of John and Elizabeth Hubbard,	"	13 July 1726.
Henderson Son of Thomas and Hannah Inches,	"	31 May 1726.
Susanna daughter of North and Abigail Ingham,	"	6 July 1726.
John Son of Elias and Mary Jarvis,	"	28 May, 1726.
Mary daughter of William and Mary Jarvis,	"	20 September 1726.
Elizabeth daughter of Nathanael and Abigail Jarvis,	"	15 November 1726.
Mary daughter of John and Mary Jones,	"	8 January 1726.
Edmund Son of William and Elizabeth Killworth,	"	17 August 1726.
Elizabeth daughter of Thomas and Mary Kilby,	"	8 August 1726.
William Son of Elias and Martha Kingston,	"	2 September 1726.
Richard Son of Richard and Sarah Kent,	"	18 August 1726.
Sarah daughter of James and Mehetabel King,	"	30 October 1726.
Robert Son of Samuel and Elizabeth Kneeland,	"	10 April 1726

Births — 1726.

Susanna daughter of Robert and Susanna Kenton,	Born	14 December 1726.
Mary daughter of Joseph and Elizabeth Kneeland,	"	7 February 1726.
John Son of John and Esther Lansted,	"	21 April 1726.
Ann daughter of William and Ann Loring,	"	29 May 1726.
Mary daughter of John and Mary Little,	"	31 May 1726.
Mary daughter of John and Dorothy Lawrence,	"	1 July 1726.
John Son of Joseph and Katharine Linton,	"	1 August 1726
John Son of Thomas and Rachel Lillie,	"	17 July 1726.
Michael Son of Philip and Martha Lewis,	"	16 July 1726.
Sarah daughter of Ebenezer and Sarah Lampson,	"	25 July 1726.
Hannah daughter of Oliver and Rebekah Luckis,	"	16 November 1726.
Elizabeth daughter of Phillip and Elizabeth Lewis,	"	14 September 1726.
John Son of Knight and Abigail Leverett,	"	28 January 1726.
Sarah daughter of John and Mercy Late,	"	16 February 1726.
Eleanor daughter of John and Eleanor Leathe,	"	29 March 1726.
Benjamin Son of Joseph and Mary Leasenby,	"	26 March 1726.
Samuel Son of Theophilus and Hannah Lillie,	"	26 April 1726.
Hannah daughter of Samuel and Elizabeth Lugar,	"	2 October 1726.
Benjamin Son of William and Lydia Larraby,	"	4 August 1726.
Hannah daughter of William and Hannah Lynch,	"	17 March 1726.
Jane daughter of Andrew and Margaret LeMercier,	"	6 May 1726.
Mary daughter of Hugh and Mary Markes,	"	4 December 1726.
Thomas Son of Thomas and Mary Moore,	"	27 August 1726.
Ann daughter of Alexander and Eliza. Miller,	"	8 December 1726.
Ephraim Son of Ephraim and Elizabeth Moore,	"	14 February 1726.
Samuel Son of Samuel and Susanna Martin,	"	10 June 1726.
Thomas Son of Alexander and Mary Marten,	"	5 February 1726.
Lydia daughter of Joseph and Sarah Mather,	"	23 October 1726.
Mary daughter of Richard and Lydia Mortimer,	"	17 January 1726.
David Son of David and Susanna Mason,	"	19 March 1726.
Margaret daughter of Thomas and Margaret Mitchell,	"	10 March 1726.
Frances daughter of John and Ann Maylem,	"	13 March 1726.
James Son of William and Lydia Maxfield,	"	10 March 1726.
Esther daughter of Edmund and Mary Mountfort,	"	22 April 1726.
Lydia daughter of Jonathan and Hannah Mountfort,	"	6 June 1726.
Sarah daughter of John and Sarah Mills,	"	7 July 1726.
Elizabeth daughter of William and Elizabeth Maycock,	"	7 September 1726.
Abigail daughter of Christopher and Eliza. Marshall,	"	27 October 1726.
Henry Son of William and Mary Nicholson,	"	13 April 1726.
Sarah daughter of Edmund and Mary Newcomb,	"	23 November 1726.
Elizabeth daughter of William and Hannah Neal,	"	25 July 1726.
Elizabeth daughter of Joseph and Elizabeth Nowell,	"	11 September 1726.
James Son of William and Bethiah Nichols,	"	9 August 1726.
Mary daughter of William and Mary Owen,	"	14 September 1726.
Elizabeth daughter of Samuel and Margaret Pousley,	"	24 May 1726.
Elizabeth daughter of John and Mary Potwine,	"	25 May 1726.
Sarah daughter of John and Sarah Plaisted,	"	23 January 1726.
Esther daughter of Alexander and Esther Parkman,	"	29 June 1726.
Susanna daughter of Ezekiel and Susanna Perigo,	"	25 January 1726.
Mercy daughter of Robert and Mercy Peat.	"	1 September 1726.
Frances daughter of John and Elizabeth Pinckney,	"	22 September 1726.
Ruth daughter of Briantt and Ruth Parott,	"	26 December 1726.
Susanna daughter of Joseph and Mary Pearse,	"	1 June 1726.
John Son of John and Mary Phillips,	"	29 November 1726.
John Son of Benjamin and Margaret Procter,	"	29 January 1726.
John Son of John and Lydia Procter,	"	31 December 1726.
John Son of Moses and Elizabeth Pearse,	"	4 March 1726.

Samuel Son of Samuel and Rebekah Pratt,	Born	22 September 1726.
Garner Son of Edward and Ruth Page,	"	11 March 1726.
Henry Son of Edmund and Elizabeth Quincy,	"	20 January 1726.
Samuel Son of Samuel and Ruth Russell,	"	19 April 1726.
Mary daughter of Bridges and Mary Read,	"	12 May 1726.
Margaret daughter of Jeremiah and Lydia Rhodes,	"	17 July 1726.
Ruth daughter of Ichabod and Anna Rogers,	"	29 September 1726.
Thomas Son of Joseph and Rachel Roberts,	"	14 December 1726.
Samuel Son of Samuel and Naomi Ridgaway,	"	2 January 1726.
Ezekiel Son of Joseph and Abigail Russell,	"	27 March 1726.
Jacob Son of Samuel and Priscilla Royal,	"	26 January 1726.
James Son of Samuel and Mary Robinson,	"	14 February 1726.
Charles Son of Clement and Elizabeth Reneauf,	"	2 March 1726.
John Son of Abraham and Hannah Snelling,	"	26 July 1726.
Elizabeth daughter of William and Elizabeth Stone,	"	31 March 1726.
William Son of John and Abigail Stocker,	"	30 July 1726.
Rachel daughter of John and Mary Steel,	"	8 September 1726.
Susanna daughter of Ebenezer and Elizabeth Sumner,	"	13 September 1726
John Son of John and Sarah Sweetser,	"	7 October 1726.
Rebekah, daughter of Joseph and Mary Shead,	"	10 October 1726.
Elizabeth daughter of Ebenezer and Mary Storer,	"	24 December 1726.
Elizabeth daughter of William and Dorcas Sumner,	"	24 November 1726.
Elizabeth daughter of Richard and Mary Stanney,	"	8 January 1726.
Elizabeth daughter of Charles and Ann Sanders,	"	6 January 1726.
John Son of John and Elizabeth Scottow,	"	9 January 1726.
Elizabeth daughter of William and Elizabeth Simpkins,	"	7 January 1726.
Elizabeth daughter of Joseph and Elizabeth Snelling,	"	23 January 1726.
John Son of John and Lydia Stringer,	"	17 April 1726.
Mary daughter of William and Jerusha Salter,	"	4 July 1726.
Sarah daughter of John and Mary Souther,	"	27 March 1726.
Hannah daughter of John and Lydia Strong,	"	25 April 1726.
Hannah daughter of Bartholomew and Mary Sutton,	"	12 May 1726.
Samuel Son of Samuel and Elizabeth Seward,	"	10 June 1726.
Benjamin } Gem. Sons of Erasmus and Persis Stevens, Ebenezer	"	21 October 1726.
Mary daughter of Robert and Ann Sanders,	"	27 February 1726.
Joseph Son of Joseph and Sarah Stroud,	"	27 February 1726.
Joseph Son of Nathanael and Sarah Story,	"	12 November 1726.
William Son of Michael and Elizabeth Shaller,	"	12 January 1726.
Joanna daughter of Joseph and Joanna Turell,	"	18 June 1726.
Hannah daughter of Timothy and Elizabeth Thornton,	"	7 November 1726.
Edward Son of Edward and Thomazin Tyler,	"	28 November 1726.
Andrew Son of William and Sarah Tyler,	"	23 December 1726.
Ebenezer Son of Edward and Joanna Tuttle,	"	27 January 1726.
Timothy Son of Ebenezer and Elizabeth Thornton,	"	2 February 1726.
Mary daughter of John and Mary Taylor,	"	12 July 1726.
Timothy Son of Elias and Sarah Towzer,	"	9 July 1726.
Submit daughter of Michael and Submit Tapper,	"	4 August 1726.
Desire daughter of Robert and Ann Thompson,	"	28 February 1726.
Katharine daughter of Andrew and Miriam Tyler,	"	8 September 1726.
Jonathan Son of Jonathan and Mary Tarbox,	"	18 September 1726.
Ann daughter of Joshua and Elizabeth Townsend,	"	23 October 1726.
Joshua Son of Joshua and Martha Underwood,	"	6 February 1726.
Abigail daughter of Joseph and Sarah Uran,	"	8 January 1726.
Charles Son of Henry and Sarah Venner,	"	29 November 1726.
Charles Son of Charles and Martha Warham,	"	28 October 1726.
Joseph Son of Joseph and Ruth Whittemore,	"	19 November 1726.
Hannah daughter of Samuel and Lucy Waldo,	"	21 November 1726.
Anna daughter of John and Mary West,	"	25 November 1726.

BIRTHS — 1726-27.

Mary daughter of Nathan and Mary Wheeler,	Born	19 September 1726.
Elizabeth daughter of Oliver and Hannah Williams,	"	27 November 1726.
Mary daughter of Jonathan and Martha Williams,	"	5 October 1726.
Sarah daughter of Richard and Ann Walter,	"	26 December 1726.
John Son of Thomas and Anna Warden,	"	27 January 1726.
William Son of James and Rebekah Wimble,	"	28 January 1726.
Ann daughter of Samuel and Elizabeth Watts,	"	9 March 1726.
John Son of John and Lucy Wincoll,	"	23 June 1726.
John Son of Joseph and Susanna Warwick,	"	30 June 1726.
Abigail daughter of Thomas and Abigail Wheeler,	"	11 May 1726.
Francis Parnel Son of William and Elizabeth Waldron,	"	4 April 1726.
Thomas Son of Thomas and Hannah Windsor,	"	26 May 1726.
Abigail daughter of Joshua and Ann Williams,	"	26 July 1726.
Joanna daughter of John and Mary Webster,	"	23 June 1726.
Mary daughter of William and Mary Walter,	"	5 August 1726.
Ann daughter of Benjamin and Abigail Wolcut,	"	1 August 1726.
Thomas Son of Daniel and Sarah Weyman,	"	11 October 1726.
Mary daughter of Joshua and Mary Winnock,	"	19 August 1726.
Jane daughter of Thomas and Jane Williston,	"	29 March 1726.
John Son of Joseph and Elizabeth White,	"	8 August 1726.
Elizabeth daughter of John and Elizabeth Wheelwright,	"	2 April 1726.
Katharine daughter of Jacob and Sarah Wendell,	"	17 June 1726.
Rebekah daughter of Isaac and Rebekah White,	"	8 September 1726.
Butler Son of John and Elizabeth Welland,	"	8 September 1726.
Elisha Son of Joseph and Abigail Webb,	"	28 August 1726.
John Son of Ebenezer and Mercy Youngman,	"	20 July 1726.
James Son of John and Mary Young,	"	7 October 1726.
Abraham Son of Abraham and Amiable York,	"	29 November 1726.
Joseph Son of Andrew and Martha Willet,	"	3 February 1726.
Elizabeth daughter of William Beartell and Elizabeth his Wife,	"	25 September 1726.

1727.

Rebekah daughter of Henry and Deliverance Atkins,	Born	24 October 1727.
Mary daughter of Thomas and Rooksby Aston,	"	1 October 1727.
Jeremiah Son of Jeremiah and Rebekah Allen,	"	10 February 1727.
Elizabeth daughter of Joshua and Elizabeth Atwood,	"	18 February 1727.
Ammi daughter of Elnathan and Mercy Ayres,	"	29 February 1727.
Abijah Son of Abijah and Deborah Adams,	"	6 April 1727.
Hannah daughter of Edward and Hannah Ayres,	"	15 May 1727.
Katharine daughter of Benjamin and Katharine Andrews,	"	5 October 1727.
William Son of Thomas and Jane Alden,	"	26 October 1727.
Solomon Son of Moses and Hannah Ayres,	"	6 February 1727.
Mary daughter of John and Mary Avis,	"	25 August 1727.
Abigail daughter of Jeremiah and Sarah Belknap,	"	5 May 1727.
John Son of Josiah and Mary Bacon,	"	9 April 1727.
Thomas Son of Daniel and Abigail Bell,	"	18 April 1727.
Elizabeth daughter of William and Elizabeth Bricksey,	"	26 March 1727.
Susanna daughter of Thomas and Susanna Belcher,	"	20 April 1727.
John Son of Isaac and Elizabeth Beauchamp,	"	3 May 1727.
Susanna daughter of Huxtable and Susanna Baker,	"	7 May 1727.
Thomas Son of Thomas and Eunice Barnes,	"	15 May 1727.
Sarah daughter of Richard and Sarah Bill,	"	15 April 1727.
James Son of James and Mary Best,	"	30 September 1727.
Eddy daughter of John and Katharine Beney,	"	11 October 1727.

Sarah daughter of John and Mary Bennet,	Born	7 November 1727.
Mary daughter of John and Elizabeth Beal,	"	28 November 1727.
Thomas Son of Joshua and Sarah Blanchard,	"	29 May 1727.
Katharine daughter of John and Mary Beer,	"	14 December 1727.
Rebekah daughter of Samuel and Christian Bass,	"	27 December 1727.
Andrew Son of Martin and Susanna Brimmer,	"	28 December 1727.
Henry Son of Edward and Abigail Bromfield,	"	12 November 1727.
James Son of James and Mary Brown,	"	13 March 1727.
Sarah daughter of John and Sarah Bowen,	"	24 July 1727.
Margaret daughter of John and Margaret Breck,	"	7 August 1727.
John Son of John and Elizabeth Bulfinch,	"	17 July 1727.
Hannah daughter of William and Hannah Bond,	"	14 July 1727.
Susanna daughter of James and Mary Boyer,	"	16 March 1727.
Elizabeth daughter of Joseph and Elizabeth Belcher,	"	13 October 1727.
Daniel Son of Henry and Elizabeth Berry	"	3 June 1727.
Sarah daughter of Nathanael and Rebekah Belknap,	"	7 July 1727.
Thomas Son of Jeremiah and Mary Barto,	"	11 April 1727.
Rebekah daughter of Joshua and Rebekah Balch,	"	19 September 1727.
Esther daughter of Thomas and Esther Buchannon	"	18 March 1727.
William Son of John and Sarah Bolderson,	"	5 September 1727.
Franklyn Son of Gideon and Martha Ball,	"	16 February 1727.
Rebekah daughter of Thomas and Sarah Boylston,	"	7 December 1727.
Sarah daughter of John and Sarah Billings,	"	2 January 1727.
John Son of John and Elizabeth Bouve,	"	1 August 1727.
Edward Son of Thomas and Mary Cushing,	"	29 November 1727.
Ann daughter of James and Anna Cox,	"	20 January 1727.
John Son of William and Elizabeth Cunningham,	"	8 February 1727.
Rebekah daughter of Joseph and Elizabeth Clewley,	"	4 March 1727.
Jane daughter of Robert and Jane Cole,	"	15 June 1727.
Elizabeth daughter of William and Mary Clough,	"	8 March 1727.
Christiana daughter of George and Mary Cradock,	"	22 April 1727.
Richard Son of Richard and Ammi Coleworthy,	"	1 March 1727.
Ann daughter of John and Ann Chambers,	"	9 August 1727.
George Son of George and Hannah Cross,	"	11 March 1727.
Sarah daughter of John and Sarah Cushing,	"	21 March 1727.
John Son of John and Susanna Coombs,	"	28 March 1727.
Samuel Son of Jonathan and Hannah Chandler,	"	29 March 1727.
Sarah daughter of John and Hannah Coolidge,	"	30 March 1727.
Mary daughter of William and Joanna Condy,	"	9 April 1727.
Sarah daughter of Samuel and Sarah Cowdry,	"	3 May 1727.
Rebekah daughter of William and Elizabeth Cowell,	"	18 May 1727.
John Son of William and Ann Coffin,	"	2 June 1727.
Elias Son of Nicholas and Mary Cutting,	"	16 July 1727.
James Son of James and Elizabeth Collings,	"	1 August 1727.
Ann daughter of John and Ann Chambers,	"	3 August 1727.
Rachel daughter of Ebenezer and Rachel Clough,	"	12 May 1727.
Mary daughter of Charles and Mary Coffin,	"	16 May 1727.
Mary daughter of George and Judith Coleworthy,	"	29 December 1727.
Preserved Son of Samuel and Mary Conibal,	"	29 October 1727.
Anna daughter of Isaac and Hannah Cusno,	"	4 September 1727.
Richard Son of John and Rebekah Compton,	"	25 September 1727.
John Son of Benjamin and Ruhamah Crehore,	"	1 July 1727.
John Son of Thomas and Mary Carlisle,	"	14 October 1727.
Thomas Son of John and Emma Charnock,	"	8 November 1727.
William Son of Ebenezer and Ann Clough,	"	3 November 1727.
John Son of James and Elizabeth Cutts,	"	10 December 1727.
Abigail daughter of William and Sarah Cooper.	"	15 August 1727.
Joseph Son of Joseph and Martha Cook,	"	4 December 1727.
Rebekah daughter of Matthias and Mary Cussens,	"	3 February 1727.
Richard Son of John and Deborah Draper,	"	24 February 1726/7.

BIRTHS — 1727.

Samuel Son of Thomas and Jemima Debuke,	Born	23 July 1727.
William Son of Charles and Sarah Deming,	"	2 July 1727.
Mary daughter of James and Mary Day,	"	3 September 1727.
Henry Son of James and Mary Dawson,	"	25 March 1727.
Niot Son of Isaac and Rebekah Dawbt,	"	17 July 1727.
Josiah Son of James and Sarah Davenport,	"	18 December 1727.
Mary daughter of Elias and Mary Dupee,	"	25 July 1727.
Elizabeth daughter of John and Elizabeth Daniel,	"	9 October 1727.
Nicholas Son of Nicholas and Katharine Dear,	"	2 November 1727.
Elizabeth daughter of James and Hannah Dowell,	"	13 December 1727.
Thomas Son of Thomas and Hannah Emmes,	"	12 June 1727.
Mary daughter of David and Susanna Eustus,	"	6 July 1727.
John Son of John and Abigail Erving,	"	26 January 1727.
Thomas Son of Morgan and Elizabeth Edwards,	"	25 September 1727.
Joseph Son of John and Sarah Eliot,	"	9 March 1727.
Jane daughter of John and Jane Ellery,	"	20 October 1727.
Samuel Son of Samuel and Ruth Ellis,	"	28 November 1727.
Joseph Son of Benjamin and Mary Eddy,	"	24 October 1727.
Robert Son of Walter and Jane Edmands,	"	4 November 1727.
Mary daughter of Ephraim and Martha Fenno,	"	9 February 1727.
John Son of John and Ann Friend,	"	25 January 1727.
Benjamin Son of Zechariah and Abigail Fitch,	"	9 February 1727.
Rebekah doughter of Isaac and Ellen Fowle,	"	21 November 1727.
Deborah daughter of William and Margaret Fletcher,	"	29 January 1727.
William Son of William and Mary Fullarton,	"	30 November 1727.
Joshua Son of Thomas and Anna Foster,	"	16 February 1727.
Mary daughter of Benjamin and Sarah Flood,	"	14 February 1727.
Nathan Son of Patrick and Prudence Flyn,	"	15 September 1727.
Caleb ⎱ Gem. Sons of Jonathan and Ann Joseph ⎰ Farnam,	"	1 May 1727.
Benjamin Son of Hopestill and Sarah Foster,	"	27 May 1727.
William Son of Percival and Sarah-Mary Farmer,	"	16 June 1727.
Ann daughter of Thomas and Elizabeth Fleet,	"	11 September 1727.
Margaret daughter of Thomas and Ann Green,	"	3 May 1727.
Elizabeth daughter of William and Mary Greenleaf,	"	7 October 1727.
Elizabeth daughter of Joseph and Elizabeth Gooch,	"	29 October 1727.
Jacob Son of Jacob and Susanna Griggs,	"	2 June 1727.
Sarah daughter of Charles and Mary Giles,	"	15 November 1727.
Elizabeth daughter of Robert and Abigail Grater,	"	28 June 1727.
Mary daughter of John and Mary Greenough,	"	2 December 1727.
Sarah daughter of Miles and Hannah Gale,	"	24 August 1727.
Abigail daughter of Daniel and Elizabeth Goffe,	"	10 December 1727.
John Son of Samuel and Mary Greenwood,	"	7 December 1727.
Mercy daughter of Samuel and Elizabeth Holiand,	"	15 January 1727.
Joseph Son of Daniel and Elizabeth Henshaw,	"	20 December 1727.
Rachel daughter of John and Rachel Howard,	"	23 January 1727.
Sarah daughter of Samuel and Mary Hastings,	"	4 March 1727.
Abigail daughter of Ralph and Mary Hart,	"	8 December 1727.
John Son of David and Mary Huston,	"	14 December 1727.
John Son of Jacob and Elizabeth Hurd,	"	9 December 1727.
John Son of John and Ann Homer,	"	23 December 1727.
Christian daughter of John and Elizabeth Hill,	"	6 January 1727.
Dorcas daughter of Andrew and Dorcas Hall,	"	9 January 1727.
Mary daughter of Thomas and Mary Hubbard,	"	28 January 1727.
William Son of William and Hannah Hasey,	"	29 February 1727.
Sarah daughter of William and Elizabeth Healy,	"	5 December 1727.
Enoch Son of Ames and Judith Howard,	"	2 March 1727.
Katharine daughter of Thomas and Rachel Hogg,	"	17 May 1727.
John Son of Arthur and Grace Head,	"	27 February 1727.

John Son of John and Sarah Hyer,	Born	5 August 1727.
Elizabeth daughter of John and Kezia Harvey,	"	7 September 1727.
Stephen Son of Stephen and Elizabeth Honiwell,	"	18 September 1727.
Hephzibah daughter of Nathaniel and Hephzibah Howard,	"	28 May 1727.
James Son of James and Elizabeth Harris,	"	8 May 1727.
Sarah daughter of Ebenezer and Hannah Hough,	"	13 June 1727.
Nathanael Son of Isaac and Abigail Hall,	"	16 October 1727.
Mary daughter of Peter and Katharine Harratt,	"	27 October 1727.
Richard Son of John and Sarah Hooton,	"	23 May 1727.
William Son of Michael and Sarah Homer,	"	30 March 1727.
William Son of William and Hannah Hasey,	"	29 April 1727.
Joseph Son of Richard and Hannah Hayward,	"	1 May 1727.
Hannah daughter of Samuel and Ruth Jackson,	"	21 May 1727.
Susanna daughter of Zechariah and Elizabeth Johonnott,	"	20 December 1727.
John Son of Robert and Elizabeth Jenkins,	"	31 May 1727.
William Son of William and Margaret Jepson,	"	2 January 1727.
Mary daughter of George and Susanna Janvering,	"	13 August 1727.
Christopher Son of Thomas and Sarah Kilby,	"	16 October 1727.
Mary daughter of Samuel and Mary Kneeland,	"	2 August 1727.
Dorcas daughter of John and Elizabeth Kneeland,	"	21 October 1727.
James Son of Andrew and Martha Knox,	"	27 September 1727.
Lydia daughter of Solomon and Lydia Kneeland,	"	18 March 1727.
Elizabeth daughter of Nicholas and Elizabeth Lash,	"	2 March 1727.
Francis Son of William and Ruth Lee,	"	6 September 1727.
Stephen Bartholomew Son of Andrew and Margaret Le Mercier,	"	4 December 1727.
Susanna daughter of Edward and Susanna Langdon,	"	3 May 1727.
Elizabeth daughter of Joseph and Mary Leasenby,	"	3 June 1727.
Sarah daughter of John and Eleanor Leathe,	"	6 March 1727.
Thomas Son of Thomas and Mary Lake,	"	10 May 1727.
Elizabeth daughter of Joseph and Elizabeth Lewis,	"	22 December 1727.
Ann daughter of Alexander and Judith Leonard,	"	29 July 1727.
Daniel Son of Daniel and Eunice Merrett,	"	17 July 1727.
Hannah daughter of Benjamin and Elizabeth Mason,	"	5 June 1727.
Mercy daughter of William and Abigail Merchant,	"	25 August 1727.
Thomas Son of John and Katharine Morris,	"	18 November 1727.
Mary daughter of Nathanael and Sarah Morse,	"	16 October 1727.
John Son of John and Letitia Mark,	"	29 December 1727.
James Son of Edward and Elizabeth Masters,	"	6 March 1727.
Prudence daughter of Joseph and Ellen Marion,	"	15 October 1727.
Sarah daughter of Benjamin and Ann Mulbery,	"	31 December 1727.
Bridget daughter of Thomas and Dorothy Manning,	"	9 May 1727.
Joseph Son of John and Mary Miller,	"	5 December 1727.
Sarah daughter of James and Sarah Mattock,	"	15 January 1727.
Joanna daughter of John and Sarah Mills,	"	5 March 1727.
Mary daughter of William and Mary Neatby,	"	12 May 1727.
Eleazer Son of Eleazer and Mary Newell,	"	3 June 1727.
Edward Son of William and Bethiah Nichols,	"	24 August 1727.
Elizabeth daughter of Henry and Elizabeth Neal,	"	23 August 1727.
Mary daughter of George and Sarah Norton,	"	25 September 1727.
William Son of Samuel and Sarah Norton,	"	27 August 1727.
Mary daughter of John and Mary Nicholson,	"	8 February 1727.
Mary daughter of William and Mary Owen,	"	19 October 1727.
Elizabeth daughter of John and Sarah Osborne,	"	29 December 1727.
John Son of Daniel and Sarah Pecker,	"	11 September 1727.
Elizabeth daughter of Joseph and Mary Prince,	"	13 August 1727.
Samuel Son of William and Mary Peck.	"	25 October 1727
Samuel Son of Nathanael and Abigail Pearse.	"	9 November 1727.

BIRTHS — 1727.

Caleb Son of Samuel and Rebekah Pratt,	Born	11 March 1727.
James Son of John and Mary Pitts,	"	26 November 1727.
Lydia daughter of Robert and Lydia Price,	"	5 December 1727.
Susanna daughter of William and Susanna Parkman,	"	14 December 1727.
Joanna daughter of Isaac and Agnes Peirce,	"	6 April 1727.
Alexander Son of William and Ann Phillips,	"	8 February 1727.
David Son of David and Hannah Powell,	"	24 March 1727.
William Son of William and Susanna Pell,	"	28 March 1727.
Priscilla daughter of Joseph and Mehetabel Payson,	"	11 April 1727.
Elizabeth daughter of David and Elizabeth Prince,	"	20 April 1727.
Webb Son of Hammond and Esther Pearson,	"	28 April 1727.
Benjamin Son of Robert and Lydia Price,	"	14 May 1727.
Frances daughter of Robert and Jane Pateshall,	"	22 July 1727.
Ezekiel Son of Thomas and Elizabeth Price,	"	9 September 1727.
Elizabeth daughter of Edmund and Elizabeth Quincy,	"	15 October 1727.
Mary daughter of Henry and Experience Readin,	"	26 March 1727.
Abigail daughter of Samuel and Sarah Rand,	"	28 April 1727.
Jonathan Son of John and Esther Ransted,	"	20 January 1727.
Mary daughter of Gamaliel and Sarah Rogers,	"	4 April 1727.
John Son of Thomas and Elizabeth Rogers,	"	5 August 1727.
William Son of Joseph and Priscilla Robey,	"	5 June 1727.
Mehetabel daughter of James and Mehetabel Ridgaway,	"	30 December 1727.
Hannah daughter of Joseph and Abigail Russell,	"	22 June 1727.
Hannah daughter of Samuel and Hannah Russell,	"	9 June 1727.
Jeremiah Son of Jeremiah and Lydia Rhodes,	"	10 July 1727.
Samuel Son of William and Mary Richardson,	"	31 August 1727.
Samuel Son of Edward and Elizabeth Ramme,	"	21 August 1727.
Hannah daughter of John and Hannah Ranger,	"	6 October 1727.
Susanna daughter of Simon and Thomazin Rogers,	"	31 October 1727.
Edward Son of Edward and Hannah Richards,	"	8 November 1727.
Ann daughter of John and Ann Ruggles,	"	24 July 1727.
Bartholomew Son of Bartholomew and Elizabeth Sears,	"	6 September 1727.
William Son of Bartholomew and Mary Sutton,	"	26 November 1727.
Jeremiah Son of William and Ruth Smallege,	"	8 October 1727.
Thomas Son of Ralph and Huldah Smith,	"	7 February 1727.
Thomas Son of Jonathan and Mary Simpson,	"	1 November 1727.
Sarah daughter of Joshua and Mary Sherrer,	"	29 January 1727.
Richard Son of William and Elizabeth Snoden,	"	8 October 1727.
Elizabeth daughter of William and Sarah Stoddard,	"	24 October 1727.
Olive daughter of John and Olive Sturges,	"	19 December 1727.
Elizabeth daughter of John and Mary Simpson,	"	14 May 1727.
Jacob Son of Jacob and Mary Sheafe,	"	21 January 1727.
John Son of John and Ann Sale,	"	3 March 1727.
William Allen Son of William and Ann Scott,	"	5 November 1727.
Margaret daughter of Luke and Margaret Stone,	"	26 April 1727.
John Son of Edward and Mildred Stanbridge,	"	26 April 1727.
Martha daughter of Nicholas and Martha Salisbury,	"	6 April 1727.
Elizabeth daughter of Robert and Rachel Saunders,	"	28 April 1727.
Thomas Son of Jonathan and Martha Salter,	"	27 April 1727.
Susannah daughter of Thomas and Tabitha Stoddard,	"	23 August 1727.
Joseph Son of John and Sarah Skinner,	"	22 May 1727.
Robert Son of Robert and Lydia Snelling,	"	30 June 1727.
John Son of Joseph and Mehetabel Scott,	"	17 July 1727.
Mary daughter of Joseph and Margaret Savell,	"	31 October 1727.
Mary daughter of John and Elizabeth Thomas,	"	8 October 1727.
Mary daughter of Joseph and Joanna Turell,	"	19 October 1727.

184   CITY DOCUMENT NO. 43.

Daniel Son of Daniel and Sarah Tuttle,	Born	30 November 1727.
John Son of John and Sarah Tyler,	"	31 January 1727.
George Son of William and Elizabeth Trow,	"	10 January 1727.
Abigail daughter of Jonathan and Mary Tarbox,	"	21 January 1727.
William Son of Benjamin and Bathsheba Thwing,	"	20 May 1727.
George Son of George and Elizabeth Tilley,	"	16 February 1727.
Elizabeth daughter of Jabez and Elizabeth Tuttle,	"	14 March 1727.
Abigail daughter of Samuel and Abigail Torrey,	"	26 December 1727.
Samuel Son of Samuel and Ruth Trott,	"	2 July 1727.
Thomas Son of William and Mary Trout,	"	12 July 1727.
Martha daughter of Benjamin and Jane Tout,	"	19 July 1727.
Ann daughter of Phinehas and Ann Thomas,	"	18 May 1727.
Lydia daughter of John and Elizabeth Tyley,	"	11 April 1727.
Mary daughter of Andrew and Miriam Tyler,	"	9 August 1727.
Martha daughter of Joshua and Martha Thornton,	"	30 August 1727.
Mary daughter of Nathanael and Mary Vial,	"	23 May 1727.
Sarah daughter of John and Parthenia Vingus,	"	23 November 1727.
Elizabeth daughter of Henry and Sarah Venner,	"	14 December 1727.
John Son of Hugh and Mary Vans,	"	18 February 1727.
Mary daughter of John and Mary Whitaker,	"	13 June 1727.
Sarah daughter of Isaac and Sarah Walker,	"	4 July 1727.
Sarah daughter of Samuel and Mary Wheeler,	"	2 July 1727.
Nathanael Son of Nathanael and Elizabeth Welch,	"	24 June 1727.
Ezekiel Son of Ezekiel and Sarah Walker,	"	30 June 1727.
Jacob Son of Benjamin and Sarah Whittemore,	"	31 August 1727.
Thomas Son of John and Sarah Wakefield,	"	21 August 1727.
Lydia daughter of Cornelius and Faith Waldo,	"	22 June 1727.
Ann daughter of John and Mary Webster,	"	15 September 1727.
Benjamin Son of Benjamin and Rachel Wheeler,	"	27 August 1727.
Abraham Son of John and Elizabeth Wendell,	"	23 September 1727.
Robert Son of Robert and Sarah Williams,	"	1 September 1727.
Rebekah daughter of James and Elizabeth Watts,	"	17 April 1727.
Phebe daughter of John and Rebekah Whittemore,	"	26 October 1727.
William Son of Francis and Elizabeth Whitman,	"	1 November 1727
Sarah daughter of William and Sarah Wadland,	"	13 November 1727.
William Son of William and Abigail White,	"	16 November 1727.
Andrew Son of Andrew and Hannah Woodbery,	"	13 December 1727.
Abigail daughter of Thomas and Jane Williston,	"	31 December 1727.
Arnold Son of Samuel and Hannah Welles,	"	25 December 1727.
Ebenezer Son of Ebenezer and Jane Way,	"	14 March 1727.
Benjamin Son of William and Mary Warner,	"	31 January 1727.
James Son of John and Elizabeth Welland,	"	29 February 1727.
Abigail daughter of Joseph and Abigail Webb,	"	16 February 1727.
Samuel Son of Thomas and Mary Webb,	"	15 May 1727.
Joseph Son of Ebenezer and Judith Williston,	"	12 December 1727.
Joshua Son of Joshua and Mary Winnock,	"	3 January 1727.
Rachel daughter of William and Hannah Young,	"	17 March 1727.

1728.

John Son of Nicholas and Rachel Anthony,	Born	30 March 1728.
George Son of John and Mary Anderson,	"	23 July 1728.
John Son of Thomas and Rebekah Amory,	"	29 August 1728.
Elizabeth daughter of Nathanael and Elizabeth Adams,	"	3 October 1728.
Abigail daughter of Henry and Abigail Adams,	"	12 August 1728.
Joseph Son of Samuel and Mary Adams,	"	29 December 1728.
Nathanael Son of Matthew and Katharine Adams,	"	6 October 1728.
Lydia daughter of Benjamin and Lydia Barnard,	"	8 January 1727/8.

BIRTHS — 1728.

Adino ⎱ Gem. Sons of Adino and Susanna Bul-		
Nathanl. ⎰ finch,	Born	2 August 1728.
Benjamin Son of Benjamin and Mary Brown,	"	5 August 1728.
Simon Son of Jeremiah and Mary Barter,	"	11 August 1728.
Mary daughter of John and Sarah Barbeteau,	"	23 August 1728.
Mary daughter of John and Susanna Brown,	"	23 August 1728.
George Son of George and Mary Bedson,	"	3 September 1728.
Thomas Son of Thomas and Abigail Bradford,	"	27 September 1728.
Mary daughter of John and Sarah Bradford,	"	15 September 1728.
David son of Jonathan and Mary Bowman,	"	9 September 1728.
John Son of Francis and Jane Borland,	"	5 September 1728.
Hannah daughter of Jeremiah and Hannah Bill,	"	23 September 1728.
John Son of John and Sarah Beacham,	"	15 November 1728.
John Son of Thornton and Hephzibah Barret,	"	6 November 1728.
Hannah daughter of Solomon and Abigail Blake,	"	4 December 1728
Peter Son of William and Elizabeth Blin,	"	28 November 1728.
Mary daughter of Alden and Mercy Bass,	"	2 December 1728.
Abigail daughter of Benjamin and Christian Bridge,	"	13 December 1728.
Elizabeth daughter of Daniel and Phebe Ballard,	"	20 December 1728.
Thomas Son of Benjamin and Elizabeth Bagnall,	"	12 January 1728.
Elisha Son of Philip and Mary Bass,	"	2 February 1728.
Thomas Son of Thomas and Elizabeth Barrick,	"	26 March 1728.
Mary daughter of John and Mary Brown,	"	12 April 1728.
Sarah daughter of Joseph and Mary Balch,	"	13 April 1728.
John Son of William and Hannah Bond,	"	18 March 1728.
Elizabeth daughter of John and Elizabeth Bulfinch,	"	24 March 1728.
Nathanael Son of Nathanael and Dorothy Barber,	"	18 March 1723.
Joseph Son of Joseph and Martha Brandon,	"	2 August 1728.
James Son of Jonathan and Mary Black,	"	24 March 1728.
William Son of Caleb and Deliverance Bean,	"	25 January 1728.
Susanna daughter of William and Elizabeth Brick-		
sey,	"	9 February 1728.
Ann daughter of John and Margaret Breck,	"	23 October 1728.
Alice daughter of Job and Alice Brown,	"	16 April 1728.
Thomas Son of William and Elizabeth Beairsto,	"	16 April 1728.
John Son of Richard and Hannah Barnard,	"	27 April 1728.
John Son of John and Sarah Barnes,	"	5 June 1728.
Edward Son of Increase and Ann Blake,	"	9 July 1728.
Sarah daughter of George and Mary Bethune,	"	27 June 1728.
David Son of David and Rely Belcher,	"	1 August 1728.
Michael Son of John and Katharine Barton,	"	5 February 1728.
Susanna daughter of John and Susanna Blake,	"	18 February 1728.
Mary daughter of Ebenezer and Mary Berry,	"	7 March 1728.
Thomas Son of Thomas and Susanna Bentley,	"	1 March 1728.
James Son of James and Mary Brintnall,	"	15 March 1728.
Nathanael Son of Josiah and Lydia Carter,	"	1 October 1728.
Nathanael Son of Charles and Mary Coffin,	"	30 September 1728.
Joseph Son of Clement and Mary Chick,	"	19 October 1728.
George Son of George and Mary Cradock,	"	18 August 1728.
Susanna daughter of Andrew and Mary Cunning-		
ham,	"	30 November 1728.
Phebe daughter of Jacob and Abiel Chamberlain,	"	4 September 1728.
Joseph Son of Samuel and Sarah Cawdry,	"	21 December 1728.
Mary daughter of Ebenezer and Rachel Clough,	"	3 January 1728.
William Son of William and Deborah Corbin,	"	22 January 1728.
William Son of Thomas and Elizabeth Cock,	"	11 November 1728.
Benjamin Son of Benjamin and Faith Clough,	"	23 January 1728.
Mary daughter of Thomas and Mary Cushing,	"	18 October 1728.
Anna daughter of Nathaniel and Abigail Coney,	"	
at Stoughton,	"	23 September 1728.

John Son of James and Mary Carter,	Born	29 July 1728.
Mary daughter of Benjamin and Miriam Clark,	"	19 August 1728.
Sarah daughter of John and Mary Crocker,	"	28 August 1728.
Jeremiah Son of Jeremiah and Ann Cushing,	"	21 July 1728.
Hannah daughter of Samuel and Hannah Cutt,	"	3 April 1728.
Jonathan Son of David and Susanna Crouch.	"	22 April 1728.
Elizabeth daughter of Job and Lydia Coit,	"	17 April 1728.
Hannah daughter of Elisha and Elizabeth Callender,	"	26 May 1728.
Hannah daughter of James and Alice Cox,	"	15 June 1728.
Mehetabel daughter of Samuel and Elizabeth Checkley,	"	10 July 1728.
Mary daughter of John and Hannah Coolidge,	"	6 March 1728.
John Son of John and Mary Cannon,	"	2 June 1728.
Sarah daughter of Joseph and Mary Cowell,	"	12 May 1728.
Ann daughter of John and Sarah Carnes,	"	3 July 1728.
Henry Son of James and Mary Dawson,	"	25 January 1728.
Isaac Son of John and Elizabeth Decoster,	"	2 April 1728.
Joanna daughter of William and Lydia Doke,	"	2 June 1728.
Elijah Son of Elijah and Dorcas Doubleday,	"	8 July 1728.
John Son of Elias and Mary Dupee,	"	10 July 1728.
Mary daughter of Eleazer and Mary Dorby,	"	4 September 1728.
Jemima daughter of Thomas and Jemima Debuke,	"	5 December 1728.
Elizabeth daughter of Shem and Katharine Drowne,	"	16 January 1728.
John Son of John and Naomi Dupee,	"	10 January 1728.
Sarah daughter of Henry and Elizabeth Dering,	"	28 October 1728.
Mary daughter of William and Sarah Downe,	"	25 January 1728.
Andrew Son of Andrew and Abigail Durgee,	"	19 January 1728.
Elizabeth daughter of Edward and Judith Durant,	"	8 June 1728.
Elizabeth daughter of Philip and Elizabeth Dodd,	"	24 June 1728.
Thomas Son of Harbottle and Dorothy Dorr,	"	28 April 1728.
Nathanael Son of Nathanael and Mary Doubleday,	"	30 May 1728.
Stephen Son of William and Damaris Dorrington,	"	15 February 1728.
Mary daughter of Jacob and Mary Emmons,	"	6 April 1728.
Eleanor daughter of David and Mary Evans,	"	6 April 1728.
Sarah daughter of John and Abigail Earle,	"	3 July 1728.
Rebekah daughter of John and Rebekah Endicott,	"	27 July 1728.
Benjamin Son of Benjamin and Ruth Eastabrook	"	9 August 1728.
Thomas Son of Thomas and Deborah Eyre,	"	31 March 1728.
Elizabeth daughter of Joseph and Elizabeth Eliot,	"	24 September 1728.
Mary daughter of Nathanael and Hannah Emmes,	"	17 January 1728.
Sarah daughter of Thomas and Anna Foxcroft,	"	13 May 1728.
Sarah daughter of Benjamin and Elizabeth Fisher,	"	26 April 1728.
Jonas Son of Joseph and Margaret Fitch,	"	1 June 1728.
Grafton Son of Grafton and Sarah Feveryear,	"	1 August 1728.
Mary daughter of Eleazer and Mary Flagg,	"	18 March 1728.
William Son of Thomas and Hannah Fairweather,	"	28 September 1728.
Elizabeth daughter of William and Elizabeth Fairfield,	"	16 December 1728.
Ammi daughter of William and Margaret Fletcher,	"	30 October 1728.
Joshua Son of Nicholas and Elizabeth George.	"	3 August 1728.
Elizabeth daughter of Bartholomew and Mary Gedney,	"	9 August 1728.
Nathanael Son of Jeremiah and Sarah Green,	"	1 August 1728.
Anna daughter of Joseph and Anna Grigg.	"	4 October 1728.
Thomas Son of Peter and Elizabeth Gibbons,	"	14 August 1728.
Joseph Son of Joseph and Elizabeth Gooch,	"	27 November 1728.
William Son of Joseph and Dorothy Grant,	"	2 April 1728.
Mary daughter of Giles and Hannah Goddard,	"	15 November 1728.
Thomas Son of Stephen and Eunice Greenleaf,	"	17 July 1728.
Thomas Son of William and Hannah Grozier,	"	18 December 1728.

BIRTHS — 1728.

Anna daughter of Joseph and Anna Green,	Born	4 October 1728.
Mary daughter of Joseph and Mary Glydden,	"	16 December 1728.
Samuel Son of William and Anna Giles,	"	20 February 1728.
Rachel and ⎰ Gem. daughters of Francis and Rachel		
Elizabeth ⎱ Gatcombe,	"	21 December 1728.
Elizabeth daughter of Peter and Elizabeth Gibbons,	"	30 January 1728.
Samuel Son of Samuel and Sarah Gandy,	"	22 March 1728.
Ann daughter of Thomas and Ann Green,	"	27 February 1728.
Edward Son of Edward and Hannah Gray,	"	8 March 1728.
John Son of Samuel and Sarah Gerrish,	"	20 January 1728.
Edmund Son of John and Prudence Grover,	"	18 February 1728.
Henry Son of Thomas and Hannah Hill,	"	25 July 1728.
Hannah daughter of Ebenezer and Abigail Howard,	"	31 July 1728.
Joseph Son of Joseph and Martha Harley,	"	9 August 1728.
Jane daughter of John and Mary Hill,	"	11 September 1728.
William ⎰ Gem. Sons of William and Elizabeth		
Simmons ⎱ Healy,	"	5 March 1728.
Nathanael Son of Samuel and Mary Hunting,	"	1 October 1728.
Martha daughter of Samuel and Elizabeth Hood,	"	8 February 1728.
Sarah daughter of Samuel and Mary Heath,	"	6 October 1728.
Elizabeth daughter of Thomas and Sarah Hillier,	"	18 November 1728.
Elizabeth daughter of Nathanael and Hephzibah Howard,	"	3 November 1728.
Rachel daughter of Samuel and Elizabeth Haley,	"	8 June 1728.
Mary daughter of Ebenezer and Hannah Hough,	"	8 June 1728.
Zechariah Son of Zechariah and Mary Hubbart,	"	24 June 1728.
Samuel Son of Samuel and Elizabeth Holland,	"	16 December 1728.
Mary daughter of Peter and Mary Hopkins,	"	23 March 1728.
Elisha Son of Elisha and Martha Hedge,	"	14 February 1728.
Mercy daughter of Samuel and Elizabeth Holyoke,	"	7 February 1728.
Mary daughter of Daniel and Elizabeth Henshaw,	"	3 February 1728.
Calvin Son of James and Katharine Hodges,	"	26 March 1728.
Elizabeth daughter of John and Elizabeth Hubbart,	"	16 June 1728.
Richard Son of Joseph and Elizabeth Harris,	"	9 October 1728.
Mary daughter of Richard and Hannah Hayward,	"	23 December 1728.
Rebekah daughter of George and Rebekah Hanners,	"	3 December 1728.
Briggs Son of Benjamin and Rebekah Hallowell,	"	25 December 1728.
William Son of William and Susanna Jackson,	"	27 September 1728.
Samuel Son of Robert and Elizabeth Jenkins,	"	17 March 1728.
Ruth daughter of Samuel and Ruth Jackson,	"	28 January 1728.
William Son of William and Mary Jarvis,	"	2 March 1728.
John Son of William and Margaret Jepson,	"	18 February 1728.
William Son of Richard and Sarah Kent,	"	11 July 1728.
Abigail daughter of Dudson and Lois Kilcup,	"	8 September 1728.
Sarah daughter of Thomas and Sarah Kilby,	"	9 December 1728.
John Son of Elias and Martha Kingston,	"	20 March 1728.
Henry Son of William and Elizabeth Lowder,	"	24 March 1728.
Philip Son of Philip and Lydia Lewis,	"	14 March 1728.
Abigail daughter of William and Lydia Larraby,	"	25 March 1728.
Elizabeth daughter of Thomas and Elizabeth Lothrop,	"	28 November 1728.
Benjamin Son of John and Dorothy Lawrence,	"	13 September 1728.
John Son of Theophilus and Hannah Lillie,	"	8 August 1728.
Samuel Son of Joseph and Mary Leasenby,	"	19 June 1728.
William Son of William and Elizabeth Livermore,	"	7 October 1728.
Elizabeth daughter of George and Elizabeth Lamoth,	"	8 August 1728.
Rebekah daughter of Knight and Abigail Leveret,	"	5 December 1728.
John Son of John and Mercy Late,	"	17 January 1728.

Charles Son of James and Mary Lenox,	Born	1 February 1728.
Frances daughter of Robert and Elizabeth Lambert,	"	28 February 1728.
Jemima daughter of Thomas and Alice Landen,	"	13 February 1728.
Joseph Son of Joseph and Elizabeth Lewis,	"	12 April 1728.
Sarah daughter of Byfield and Sarah Lyde,	"	3 May 1728.
Martha daughter of Thomas and Elizabeth Lee,	"	27 May 1728,
Charles Son of Charles and Elizabeth Lebrit,	"	30 May 1728.
Mary daughter of William and Lydia Maxwell,	"	11 March 1728.
Elizabeth daughter of Robert and Elizabeth More,	"	23 November 1728.
Benjamin Son of Benjamin and Elizabeth Mason,	"	7 December 1728.
Elizabeth daughter of Ebenezer and Rebekah Messinger,	"	16 July 1728.
Mary daughter of John and Sarah Mills,	"	9 January 1728.
Mary daughter of David and Rachel Matthews,	"	4 February 1728.
Abigail daughter of Edward and Jane Moberly,	"	7 October 1728.
Sarah daughter of George and Jane McChune,	"	21 October 1728.
Christopher Son of Christopher and Elizabeth Marshall,	"	19 November 1728.
Hannah daughter of Ralph and Martha Meyer,	"	27 March 1728.
John Son of Alexander and Mary Marten,	"	10 May 1728.
Andrew Son of John and Elizabeth Maverick,	"	4 February 1728.
Edward Son of Isaac and Rebekah Marion,	"	10 May 1728.
Elias Son of John and Elisabeth Maverick,	"	4 February 1728.
Thomas Son of John and Mary Mellington,	"	25 June 1728.
John Son of John and Rebekah Masters,	"	21 July 1728.
Love daughter of Hugh and Mary Markes,	"	7 August 1728.
John Son of James and Susanna Melling,	"	16 August 1728.
Mary daughter of David and Susanna Mason,	"	20 September 1728.
John Son of William and Mary Nicholson,	"	26 June 1728.
John Son of Philip and Judith Norman,	"	4 September 1728.
Sarah daughter of Christopher and Mary Nicholson,	"	29 August 1728.
John Son of Thomas and Mary Nowell,	"	4 August 1728.
Joseph Son of William and Mary Neatby,	"	15 November 1728.
Susanna daughter of William and Bethiah Nichols,	"	4 January 1728.
William Son of William and Mary Owen,	"	9 December 1728.
Ann daughter of George and Ann Oxenden,	"	29 April 1728.
Edward Son of David and Sarah Orrock,	"	17 September 1728.
Ephraim Son of Benjamin and Margaret Procter,	"	8 October 1728.
Daniel Son of John and Mary Papoon,	"	24 March 1728.
John Son of William and Susanna Pell,	"	15 October 1728.
Esther daughter of Hammond and Esther Pearson,	"	10 March 1728.
Edward Son of Moses and Elizabeth Peirce,	"	10 October 1728.
John Son of John and Mary Perry,	"	22 March 1728.
Thomas Son of Thomas and Phebe Pemberton,	"	8 November 1728.
Mary daughter of Caleb and Mary Parker,	"	7 March 1728.
John Son of John and Mary Potwine,	"	7 May 1728.
Joseph Son of William and Elizabeth Pitman,	"	27 June 1728.
Anna daughter of Samuel and Margaret Pousley,	"	6 August 1728.
Abraham Son of Edmund and Elizabeth Quincy,	"	25 July 1728.
Ann daughter of Richard and Ann Richardson,	"	3 May 1728.
Elizabeth daughter of Simon and Elizabeth Rogers,	"	14 March 1728.
Abigail daughter of Robert and Susanna Rand,	"	12 June 1728.
Rebekah daughter of Thomas and Rebekah Ransford,	"	1 February 1728.
Ebenezer Son of Joseph and Priscilla Robey,	"	29 June 1728.
Samuel Son of Samuel and Hannah Russell,	"	3 January 1728.
Hannah daughter of Samuel and Mary Robinson,	"	26 June 1728.
John Son of Joseph and Hannah Ranger,	"	5 January 1728.
Mary daughter of Nathanael and Mary Roberts,	"	20 August 1728.
Benjamin Son of Benjamin and Elizabeth Russell,	"	16 September 1728.

BIRTHS — 1728.

John Son of Benjamin and Priscilla Roberts,		Born	16 November 1728.
Hayward Son of Nathanael and Sarah Story,		"	5 December 1728.
John Son of John and Elizabeth Spooner,		"	18 December 1728.
Mary daughter of William and Elizabeth Stone,		"	12 August 1728.
Margaret daughter of Luke and Margaret Stone,		"	22 December 1728.
Rebekah ⎫ Gem. daughters of Joseph and Eliza- and Hannah ⎭ beth Snelling,		"	25 November 1728.
Katharine daughter of Joseph and Susanna Shead,		"	27 December 1728.
Joseph Son of Richard and Mary Stanney		"	23 January 1728.
Mary daughter of Thomas and Elizabeth Simpkins,		"	9 March 1728.
Elizabeth daughter of John and Sarah Skinner,		"	27 July 1728.
Stephen Son of Stephen and Elizabeth Sims,		"	23 May 1728.
George Son of Robert and Rachel Sanders,		"	6 August 1728.
Elizabeth daughter of Alexander and Rebekah Sampson,		"	29 April 1728.
Thomas Son of Thomas and Mary Studson,		"	5 August 1728.
William Son of William and Dorcas Sumner,		"	10 August 1728.
William Son of John and Rachel Sowersby,		"	11 August 1728.
Mary daughter of Isaac and Mehetabel Sterns,		"	20 September 1728.
Sarah daughter of Joseph and Mehetabel Scott,		"	15 September 1728.
Huldah daughter of Ralph and Huldah Smith,		"	23 September 1728.
Elizabeth daughter of John and Sarah Sweetser,		"	17 August 1728.
Rebekah daughter of Jonathan and Mary Snelling,		"	11 November 1728.
William Son of John and Abigail Stringer,		"	25 July 1728.
Elizabeth daughter of William and Ruth Smallege,		"	5 November 1728.
Thomas Barton Son of William and Elizabeth Simpkins,		"	4 November 1728.
Mary daughter of Samuel and Elizabeth Seward,		"	11 November 1728.
Daniel Son of Joseph and Joanna Turell,		"	18 September 1728.
Thomas Son of Thomas and Waitstill Trott,		"	28 October 1728.
Katharine daughter of Andrew and Miriam Tyler,		"	12 August 1728.
Ruth daughter of Robert and Ruth Thompson, ·		"	26 August 1728.
Elizabeth daughter of William and Sarah Tyler,		"	1 November 1728.
Mary daughter of Nathanael and Joanna Thwing,		"	18 December 1728.
William Son of William and Mary Trout,		"	19 December 1728.
Mary daughter of Joshua and Elizabath Townsend,		"	17 June 1728.
Sarah daughter of Joshua and Martha Thornton,		"	28 March 1728.
William Son of Samuel and Elliphall Tyley,		"	10 April 1728.
Edward Son of George and Mary Treludia,		"	24 May 1728.
Eunice daughter of Edward and Joanna Tuttle,		"	30 April 1728.
Lydia daughter of Ebenezer and Elizabeth Thornton,		"	3 September 1728.
John Son of Nathanael an l Mary Vial,		"	6 December 1728.
Elizabeth daughter of Elijah and Elizabeth Vinall,		"	9 April 1728.
Michael Son of John and Elizabeth Ventinon,		"	29 December 1728.
Frances daughter of Samuel and Lucy Waldo,		"	13 June 1728.
Henry Son of William and Mary Walter,		"	11 July 1728.
William Son of William and Mary Wheeler,		"	18 May 1728.
Elias Son of Thomas and Magdalen Wroe,		"	28 July 1728.
Jane daughter of Abraham and Jane Wendell,		"	3 June 1728.
Sarah daughter of John and Elizabeth Whitney,		"	14 August 1728.
Elizabeth daughter of John and Elizabeth Wheelwright,		"	7 August 1728.
Isaac Son of Isaac and Sarah Walker,		"	13 March 1728.
Rachel daughter of John and Rachel Watkins,		"	22 October 1728.
Margt. daughter of Edward and Margaret Whitaker,		"	28 November 1728.
Hannah daughter of Joseph and Ruth Whittemore,		"	20 September 1728.
Charles Son of Charles and Anna Willis,		"	21 August 1728.
Martha daughter of Jonathan and Martha Williams,		"	1 September 1728.
John Mico Son of Jacob and Sarah Wendell,		"	31 May 1728.
Elizabeth daughter of Isaac and Rebekah White,		"	26 January 1728.

190　　　　　　　City Document No. 43.

Mary daughter of John and Sarah Wakefield,	Born	12 October 1728.
Elizabeth daughter of Samuel and Elizabeth Wood,	"	24 February 1728.
John Son of William and Abigail Ware,	"	4 March 1728.
John Son of William and Mary Warner,	"	14 March 1728.
Elizabeth daughter of Samuel and Elizabeth White,	"	27 January 1728.
Samuel Son of Samuel and Mary Waterhouse,	"	27 January 1728.
Experience daughter of John and Sarah Willis,	"	2 February 1728.
Samuel Son of Samuel and Mary Wheeler,	"	2 December 1728.
John Son of Thomas and Anna Warden,	"	12 December 1728.
Martha daughter of Charles and Martha Warham,	"	3 December 1728.
John Son of Abraham and Amiable York,	"	8 December 1728.
Abigail daughter of James and Jane Young,	"	12 January 1728.
William Son of Onesimus and Hagar his Wife, Free Negroes,	"	4 December 1728.
Sarah daughter of Samuel Torrey and Silence his Wife,	"	1 August 1728.

1729.

James Son of John and Sarah Aekin,	Born	16 April 1729.
John Son of Joshua and Elizabeth Atwood,	"	22 April 1729.
Margaret daughter of Nathaniel and Elizabeth Ayres,	"	11 June 1729.
Hannah daughter of Abijah and Hannah Adams,	"	1 July 1729.
Deliverance daughter of Henry and Deliverance Atkins,	"	19 July 1729.
Elizabeth daughter of John and Mary Avis,	"	5 July 1729.
Sarah daughter of Edward and Hannah Ayres,	"	2 October 1729.
John Son of Thomas and Jane Alden,	"	30 October 1729.
Mary daughter of Stephen and Elizabeth Avery,	"	30 September 1729.
William Son of John and Mary Allen,	"	30 November 1729.
John Son of Jeremiah and Rebekah Allen,	"	24 December 1729.
John Son of Jeremiah and Hannah Bill,	"	25 October 1729.
William Son of William and Ann Beath,	"	3 December 1729.
Jacob Son of Isaac and Elizabeth Boynton,	"	20 November 1729.
Benjamin Son of William and Lydia Brown,	"	25 December 1729.
Thomas Son of Thomas and Ruth Bill,	"	29 December 1729.
Caleb Son of Joshua and Sarah Blanchard,	"	2 January 1729.
Elizabeth daughter of John and Elizabeth Bennet,	"	9 January 1729.
John Son of Edward and Abigail Bromfield,	"	25 April 1729.
Samuel Son of William and Katharine Bulfinch,	"	23 January 1729.
Benjamin Son of John and Abigail Burt,	"	29 December 1729.
Anthony Son of Edward and Elizabeth Briggs,	"	11 March 1729.
John Son of John and Ruth Barrell,	"	17 March 1729.
Mary daughter of George and Mary Bedson,	"	11 March 1729.
Ignatius Son of William and Mary Brown,	"	17 June 1729.
Alexander Son of Huxtabel and Susanna Baker,	"	17 July 1729.
Charles Son of Charles and Hannah Busso,	"	10 May 1729.
Mary daughter of Richard and Mary Buckley,	"	7 June 1729.
Mary daughter of John and Susanna Blake,	"	17 March 1729.
John Son of John and Sarah Billings,	"	24 September 1729.
Timothy Son of Timothy and Mary Barron,	"	9 January 1729.
Richard Son of Richard and Mary Billings,	"	13 August 1729.
Dorothy daughter of Ellis and Sarah Bennet,	"	6 August 1729.
James Son of James and Mary Boyer,	"	31 July 1729.
Sarah daughter of William and Susanna Butler,	"	16 August 1729.
John Son of Joseph and Abigail Bridgham,	"	27 August 1729.
Mary daughter of Martin and Susanna Brimmer,	"	7 September 1729.
Caleb Son of Joshua and Rebekah Balch,	"	2 October 1729.
Simon Son of Jeremiah and Mary Barto,	"	23 September 1729.

BIRTHS — 1729.

Mary daughter of Thomas and Abigail Bradford,	Born	18 October 1729.
Abigail daughter of William and Abigail Brown,	"	8 November 1729.
Elizabeth daughter of John and Sarah Banks,	"	31 October 1729.
Jonathan Son of Richard and Hannah Barnard,	"	25 November 1729.
Joseph Son of Joseph and Elizabeth Belcher,	"	13 April 1729.
Joseph Son of Joseph and Mary Birch,	"	1 April 1729.
Samuel Son of Daniel and Abigail Bell,	"	4 May 1729.
Mary daughter of Jonathan and Martha Bridgham,	"	28 April 1729.
John Son of Edward and Abigail Bromfield,	"	25 April 1729.
Hugh Son of John and Susanna Coombs,	"	16 April 1729.
Mercy daughter of Edward and Abigail Cruft,	"	30 April 1729.
Charles Son of Charles and Elizabeth Chauncy,	"	16 May 1729.
Rebekah daughter of Daniel and Mary Cheever,	"	28 May 1729.
Hannah daughter of Samuel and Hannah Coleworthy,	"	8 June 1729.
Sarah daughter of Thomas and Ann Crafts,	"	17 June 1729.
Benjamin Son of William and Elizabeth Cowell,	"	29 June 1729.
Anna daughter of Nathanael and Martha Cobbit,	"	29 July 1729.
Isaac Son of Isaac and Hannah Casno,	"	2 July 1729.
Anne daughter of Robert and Jane Cole,	"	11 December 1729.
Mehetabel daughter of Samuel and Elizabeth Checkley,	"	8 July 1729.
Elizabeth daughter of James and Elizabeth Codner,	"	21 July 1729.
Ann daughter of Daniel and Mary Coffin,	"	15 July 1729.
James Son of James and Mary Carter,	"	5 September 1729.
James Son of Charles and Mary Coffin,	"	28 August 1729.
Hannah daughter of Samuel and Mary Conibal,	"	13 October 1729.
John Son of William and Ann Coffin,	"	19 August 1729.
Abraham) Sons of Joseph and Elizabeth Clewley, Isaac)	"	15 December 1729.
Mary daughter of William and Sarah Cooper,	"	26 December 1729.
Elizaboth daughter of Obadiah and Elizabeth Colbey,	"	28 December 1729.
John Son of John and Ann Chambers,	"	3 February 1729.
Ann daughter of William and Rebekah Copp,	"	31 January 1729.
Benjamin Son of James and Alice Cox,	"	28 February 1729.
John Son of John and Elizabeth Clark,	"	15 February 1729.
Benjamin Son of John and Mehetabel Clough,	"	20 January 1729.
James Son of James and Mary Clough,	"	11 March 1729.
William Son of Thomas and Abigail Cannington,	"	3 March 1729.
Mary daughter of John and Mary Cannon,	"	26 January 1729.
Benjamin Son of Benjamin and Elizabeth Cushing,	"	27 February 1729.
Elizabeth daughter of William and Elizabeth Cunningham,	"	7 March 1729.
Joanna daughter of George and Judith Coleworthy,	"	3 April 1729.
Ruth daughter of Nathanael and Ann Cunningham,	"	June 1729.
Ellis Son of John and Rebekah Compton,	"	28 September 1729.
Frances daughter of Richard and Ammi Coleworthy,	"	8 September 1729.
Hannah daughter of John and Sarah Carnes,	"	8 July 1729.
Thomas Son of Isaac and Rebekah Dawbt,	"	11 October 1729.
Deborah daughter of John and Elizabeth Daniel,	"	1 October 1729.
Abia daughter of James and Sarah Davenport,	"	2 October 1729.
John Son of John and Naomi Dupee,	"	18 February 1729.
Sarah daughter of Joseph and Sarah Davis,	"	10 February 1729.
Sarah daughter of James and Mary Day,	"	19 November 1729.
Mary daughter of Nathanael and Mary Doubleday,	"	3 August 1729.
John Son of John and Deborah Dyer,	"	30 March 1729.
Israel Son of James and Bathsheba Deverage,	"	31 March 1729.
Jonathan Son of Jonathan and Sarah Dacon,	"	14 June 1729.
Mary daughter of Nathanael and Mary Doubleday,	"	2 August 1729.

James Son of James and Hannah Dowel,	Born	13 September 1729.
Hannah daughter of Thomas and Hannah Emmons,	"	30 March 1729.
Abigail daughter of John and Abigail Erving,	"	16 May 1729.
Sarah daughter of Edward and Sarah Edes,	"	17 April 1729.
Mary daughter of Jacob and Mary Emmons,	"	25 July 1729.
Edward Son of David and Mary Evans,	"	10 August 1729.
Brice Son of Brice and Mary Eccles,	"	28 November 1729.
Elizabeth daughter of Thomas and Sarah Edwards,	"	17 October 1729.
David Son of David and Susanna Eustes,	"	22 February 1729.
David Son of Morgan and Elizabeth Edwards,	"	27 February 1729.
Elizabeth daughter of Gideon and Susanna Florence,	"	27 April 1729.
John Son of David and Elizabeth Franklyn,	"	2 June 1729.
Susanna daughter of Nathan and Margaret Foster,	"	24 July 1729.
Ebenezer Son of John and Mary Foster,	"	30 August 1729.
Sarah daughter of Benjamin and Sarah Floyd,	"	3 October 1729.
Isaac Son of Isaac and Ellen Fowle,	"	28 July 1729.
Thomas Son of Grafton and Sarah Feveryear,	"	25 August 1729.
David Son of David and Joanna Fowle,	"	30 August 1729.
Percival Son of Percival and Sarah-Mary Farmer,	"	9 September 1729.
Esther daughter of William and Elizabeth Fairfield, at Wenham,	"	5 February 1729.
Mary daughter of William and Mary Fullarton,	"	1 October 1729.
Mercy daughter of Thomas and Elizabeth Fleet,	"	3 October 1729.
Ann daughter of Hopestill and Sarah Foster,	"	3 October 1729.
Jeremiah Son of Joseph and Margaret Fitch,	"	10 November 1729.
Nathanael Son of Nathanael and Priscilla Fowle,	"	22 December 1729.
Thomas Son of William and Margaret Fletcher,	"	30 January 1729.
John Son of John and Mary Foster,	"	21 January 1729.
Anna daughter of Zechariah and Abigail Fitch,	"	20 March 1729.
Ann daughter of Rufus and Katharine Green,	"	16 December 1729.
Robert Son of Charles and Mary Giles,	"	6 December 1729.
James Son of Francis and Judith Gruzlier,	"	5 January 1729.
Elizabeth daughter of Jeremiah and Sarah Green,	"	31 December 1729.
Abigail daughter of Samuel and Sarah Goffe,	"	16 January 1729.
Stillborn daughter of Samuel and Mary Greenwood,	"	24 August 1729.
Joseph Son of Joseph and Ann Grigg,	"	7 February 1729.
Samuel Son of James and Elizabeth Goodwin,	"	18 February 1729.
Joseph Son of Joseph and Anna Green,	"	7 February 1729.
Lettice daughter of James and Elizabeth Gerreck,	"	1 February 1729.
Thomas Son of Thomas and Elizabeth Green,	"	18 February 1729.
Thomas Son of Thomas and Elizabeth Gouge,	"	3 February 1729.
Francis Son of Daniel and Elizabeth Goffe,	'	30 December 1729.
Thomas Son of Stephen and Eunice Greenleaf,	"	10 September 1729.
Sarah daughter of Richard and Elizabeth Goodwin,	"	5 December 1729.
Nathanael Son of Nathanael and Elizabeth Greenwood,	"	29 June 1729.
Joseph Son of Joseph and Rebekah Gray,	"	19 July 1729.
Henry Son of Henry and Elizabeth Gibbon,	"	26 April 1729.
Susanna daughter of Jacob and Susanna Griggs,	"	18 December 1729.
William Son of William and Alice Griffith,	"	29 January 1729.
Stephen Son of Stephen and Elizabeth Harris,	"	15 May 1729.
Mary daughter of Samuel and Mary Harding,	"	29 April 1729.
George Son of George and Rebekah Hopkins,	"	20 May 1729.
Nathanael Son of John and Anna Harris,	"	9 March 1729.
Katharine daughter of John and Jane Hobbs,	"	28 May 1729.
Thomas Son of Thomas and Eleanor Hartley,	"	25 May 1729.
Priscilla daughter of Joseph and Priscilla Hill,	"	23 June 1729.
Samuel Son of Samuel and Sarah Harsum,	"	15 May 1729.
Katharine daughter of James and Katharine Hodges,	"	4 July 1729.
John Son of John and Elizabeth Hubbart,	"	8 June 1729.

BIRTHS — 1729.

Robert Son of Robert and Sarah Harris,	Born	8 August 1729.
Martha daughter of John and Kezia Harvey,	"	16 August 1729.
Sarah daughter of Samuel and Elizabeth Hood,	"	5 April 1729.
Samuel Son of Samuel and Hannah Harris,	"	8 September 1729.
Elizabeth daughter of Stephen and Elizabeth Honiwell,	"	13 September 1729.
Samuel Son of Samuel and Deborah Hewes,	"	6 August 1729.
Hannah daughter of Samuel and Elizabeth Haley,	"	8 December 1729.
Edward Son of Edward and Lydia Hutchinson,	"	18 December 1729.
Mary daughter of Nathanael and Hepzibah Howard,	"	27 December 1729.
Samuel Son of Roger and Elizabeth Hardcastle,	"	4 April 1729.
William Son of John and Abigail Harper,	"	14 September 1729.
Joseph Son of John and Elizabeth Helyer,	"	29 March 1729.
Samuel Son of Samuel and Susanna Hill,	"	24 December 1729.
Rebekah daughter of Ralph and Mary Hart,	"	21 April 1729.
Benjamin Son of Daniel and Elizabeth Henshaw,	"	12 January 1729.
Vincent Son of John and Sarah Hyer,	"	11 January 1729.
Elizabeth daughter of David and Mary Huston,	"	20 February 1729.
William Son of John and Mary Hooton,	"	26 February 1729.
Sarah daughter of John and Elizabeth Hill,	"	16 March 1729.
John Son of Ebenezer and Hannah Hough,	"	13 March 1729.
Nathanael Son of Jacob and Elizabeth Hurd,	"	13 February 1729.
Benjamin Son of Benjamin and Abigail Jeffry,	"	19 June 1729.
John Son of John and Elizabeth Jandine,	"	11 June 1729.
Charles Son of Charles and Mary Jones,	"	29 September 1729.
Margaret daughter of Elias and Mary Jarvis,	"	18 October 1729.
Mary daughter of Nathaniel and Abigail Jarvis,	"	29 April 1729.
Peter Son of Zechariah and Elizabeth Johonnott,	"	23 September 1729.
Mary daughter of James and Ann Jeffs,	"	20 March 1729.
Jerusha daughter of John and Abigail Jent,	"	7 January 1729.
Susanna daughter of Vincent and Susanna Jerros,	"	23 February 1729.
Nathanaël Son of Joseph and Elizabeth Kneeland,	"	31 May 1729.
William Son of Christopher and Sarah Kilby,	"	23 September 1729.
James Son of Andrew and Martha Knox,	"	8 October 1729.
Joseph Son of Joseph and Mary Kneeland,	"	15 February 1729.
John Son of John and Abigail Low,	"	22 April 1729.
George Son of George and Mary Le Dane,	"	26 November 1729.
Jonathan Son of Israel and Mehetabel Look,	"	28 July 1729.
John Son of William and Mary Liswell,	"	18 February 1729.
Mary daughter of Joseph and Mary Leasenby,	"	11 August 1729.
Elizabeth daughter of Thomas and Elizabeth Lee,	"	19 February 1729.
John Son of Oliver and Rebekah Luckis,	"	2 September 1729.
Richard Son of Isaac and Margaret Lowry,	"	23 January 1729.
John Son of John and Mary Lappington,	"	10 September 1729.
Sarah daughter of William and Mary More,	"	26 March 1729.
Elizabeth daughter of Samuel and Martha Mellikin,	"	26 March 1729.
Sarah daughter of Joseph and Sarah Mather,	"	13 April 1729.
Elizabeth daughter of Thomas and Margaret Mitchell,	"	4 July 1729.
John Son of John and Dorothy Marion,	"	24 July 1729.
Lydia daughter of Thomas and Lydia Mellendy,	"	16 September 1729.
Mary daughter of Alexander and Mary Marten,	"	1 November 1729.
John Son of George and Jane McChune,	"	24 November 1729.
Samuel Son of Samuel and Margaret Mellish,	"	14 May 1729.
Esther daughter of John and Elizabeth McLean,	"	1 June 1729.
Mary daughter of William and Elizabeth Maycock,	"	29 May 1729.
Henry Son of Henry and Elizabeth Neal,	"	24 August 1729.
Josiah Son of Eleazar and Mary Newhall,	"	22 February 1729.
David Son of Samuel and Sarah Norton,	"	19 September 1729.

Mary daughter of Samuel and Mary Nutt,	Born	5 October 1729.
William Son of William and Hannah Neal,	"	17 October 1729.
Daniel Son of Andrew and Mary Oliver,	"	7 May 1729.
Richard Son of Richard and Hannah Peircy,	"	23 September, 1729.
Ann daughter of John and Mary Potwine,	"	20 December 1729.
Andrew Faneuil Son of Gillam and Mary Phillips,	"	1 October 1729.
William, Son of Peter and Martha Pelham,	"	22 February 1729.
Jane daughter of Samuel and Mary Procter,	"	11 November 1729.
John Son of John and Hannah Pepple,	"	16 July 1729.
Mary daughter of William and Hannah Parkman,	"	26 November 1729.
John Son of Isaac and Agnes Peirce,	"	23 June 1729.
Mary daughter of Samuel and Rebekah Phillips,	"	9 November 1729.
Martha daughter of William and Abigail Paltrey,	"	18 December 1729.
Jonathan Son of Joseph and Mary Peirce,	"	6 April 1729.
Abigail daughter of Edward and Abigail Pell,	"	1 March 1729.
Mary daughter of John and Elizabeth Pinckney,	"	7 March 1729.
Samuel Son of John and Mary Phillips,	"	15 March 1729.
Esther daughter of Alexander and Esther Parkman,	"	14 June 1729.
Hannah daughter of John and Hannah Procter,	"	21 June 1729.
Mary daughter of William and Mehetabel Pratt,	"	8 September 1729.
Ebenezer Son of Samuel and Rebekah Pratt,	"	13 March 1729.
Elizabeth daughter of Edmund and Elizabeth Quincy,	"	15 October 1729.
Susanna daughter of Simon and Thomazin Rogers,	"	27 October 1729.
John Son of James and Mehetabel Ridgaway,	"	12 March 1729.
Sarah daughter of Stephen and Sarah Randall,	"	16 October 1729.
Joseph Son of Edward and Elizabeth Rumley,	"	26 December 1729.
Joseph Son of Gamaliel and Sarah Rogers,	"	4 April 1729.
Nathanael Son of Nathanael and Mary Roberts,	"	28 January 1729.
Abigail daughter of Richard and Sarah Randall,	"	28 February 1729.
Nathanael Son of Samuel and Naomi Ridgaway	"	10 May 1729.
Joseph Son of John and Esther Ransted,	"	28 May 1729.
Nathanael Son of Nathanael and Martha Richardson,	"	11 June 1729.
Elizabeth daughter of Aaron and Mary Read,	"	10 August 1729.
Jonathan Son of Joseph and Rachel Roberts,	"	5 August 1729.
Mehetabel daughter of Benjamin and Elizabeth Rolfe,	"	16 June 1729.
William Son of William and Mary Richardson,	"	29 August 1729.
Stephen Son of Stephen and Elizabeth Sims,	"	23 January 1729.
Abraham Son of Nathanael and Sarah Story,	"	24 November 1729.
Joseph Son of William and Ruth Smallege,	"	11 March 1729.
Mary daughter of John and Mercy Smith,	"	29 December 1729.
Elizabeth daughter of John and Olive Sturges,	"	17 January 1729.
Ebenezer Son of Ebenezer and Mary Storer,	"	27 January 1729.
Alexander, Son of Alexander and Rebekah Sampson,	"	19 February, 1729.
Susanna daughter of Benjamin and Susanna Swain,	"	2 January 1729.
John Son of John and Abigail Salter,	"	20 July 1729.
John Elbridge Son of Nicholas and Martha Salisbury,	"	12 August 1729.
Thomas Son of John and Martha Symmes,	"	8 September 1729.
Anna daughter of Thomas and Elizabeth Sargent,	"	8 October 1729.
Lydia daughter of Robert and Lydia Snelling,	"	20 October 1729.
John Son of John and Mary Smallpeice,	"	2 November 1729.
Mary daughter of Bartholomew and Mary Sutton,	"	10 November 1729.
Edward-Bray Son of John and Elizabeth Scottow,	"	13 April 1729.
Sarah daughter of Jacob and Mary Sheafe,	"	7 June 1729.
Hannah daughter of Bartholomew and Elizabeth Seares,	"	9 June 1729.
Benjamin Son of Benjamin and Anna Sanders,	"	25 June 1729.
William Son of William and Sarah Stoddard,	"	6 August 1729.
Thomas Son of Thomas and Tabitha Stoddard,	"	11 July 1729.
John Son of John and Mary Simpson,	"	8 March 1729.

BIRTHS — 1730.   195

Elizabeth daughter of John and Mary Souther,	Born	29 June 1729.
Thomas Son of Timothy and Elizabeth Thornton,	"	13 June 1729.
Jonathan Son of Ambrose and Mary Tower,	"	4 June 1729.
William Son of William and Bethiah Torrey,	"	7 June 1729.
Joseph Son of Benjamin and Sarah Thompson,	"	16 June 1729.
Benjamin Son of Jonathan and Mary Tarbox,	"	26 June 1729.
Deborah daughter of Gershom and Priscilla Tenney,	"	14 August 1729.
Mary daughter of George and Elizabeth Tilley,	"	12 September 1729.
Samuel Son of Samuel and Ruth Trott,	"	25 May 1729.
Mary daughter of Samuel and Abigail Torrey,	"	31 August 1729.
Mary daughter of Edward and Elizabeth Tothill,	"	10 September 1729
Ebenezer Son of Ebenezer and Elizabeth Thornton,	"	27 October 1729.
Samuel Son of Ebenezer and Jane Turell,	"	2 February 1729
Elizabeth daughter of John and Sarah Tyler,	"	13 December 1729.
George Son of Maverick and Joanna Thomas,	"	9 July 1729
Thomas Son of Andrew and Miriam Tyler,	"	21 January 1729.
Elizabeth daughter of Alexander and Elizabeth Thorp,	"	9 August 1729
Sarah daughter of Nathanael and Joanna Thwing,	"	17 March 1729.
Martha daughter of Joshua and Martha Underwood,	"	24 May 1729
Sarah daughter of Henry and Sarah Venner,	"	2 September 1729.
Ebenezer Son of Hugh and Mary Vans,	"	21 April 1729
Elizabeth daughter of John and Elizabeth Whitney,	"	30 August 1729.
Hannah daughter of Thomas and Hannah Windsor,	"	18 July 1729.
Nathanael Son of Joshua and Ann Williams,	"	5 September 1729.
Elizabeth daughter of Joshua and Elizabeth Winslow,	"	29 April 1729.
Esther daughter of Benjamin and Sarah Whittemore,	"	30 September 1729.
Elizabeth daughter of John and Elizabeth Wendell,	"	16 October 1729.
Joanna daughter of John and Mercy Webster,	"	2 October 1729.
Edward Son of James and Elizabeth Watts,	"	18 May 1729.
Grace daughter of Joseph and Abigail Webb,	"	27 September 1729.
Joseph Son of John and Elizabeth Wheelwright,	"	9 November 1729.
Samuel Son of Samuel and Sarah Warden,	"	17 May 1729.
Oliver Son of Oliver and Hannah Williams,	"	25 May 1729.
Mary daughter of John and Mary West,	"	4 July 1729.
Abraham Son of Abraham and Jane Wendell,	"	17 July 1729.
Mary daughter of Robert and Martha Waite,	"	31 May 1729.
Joseph Son of Nathanael and Sarah Welch,	"	25 May 1729.
Jacob Son of Ebenezer and Jane Way,	"	7 September 1729.
Mary daughter of Francis and Elizabeth Whittemore,	"	28 December 1729.
Sarah daughter of William and Abigail White.	"	16 January 1729.
Elizabeth daughter of John and Elizabeth Webb,	"	13 February 1729.
Henry Son of William and Sarah Wedford,	"	10 February 1729.
Ann daughter of Thomas and Magdalen Wroe,	"	9 February 1729.
Joseph Son of William and Susanna Young,	"	12 February 1729.
Rebekah daughter of William and Hannah Young,	"	10 October 1729.
Ebenezer Son of Ebenezer Hayward and Rachel his Wife,	"	23 September 1729.
These two births are imperfectly recorded:		
Daniel Son of James and Mary Boyer,	"	14 June 172 .
Ann daughter of Henry and Sarah Venner,	"	14 May 172 .

1730.

Abigail daughter of Samuel and Mary Adams,	"	20 July 1730.
Elizabeth daughter of Nathanael and Mary Allen,	"	3 August 1730.

Nathanael Son of Nathanael and Elizabeth Adams,	Born	4 August 1730.
Ammi daughter of John and Mary Adams,	"	16 August 1730.
John-Bredger Son of Thomas and Elizabeth Allen,	"	17 February 1730.
Hannah daughter of Benjamin and Lydia Barnard,	"	19 February 1729/30.
Abigail daughter of Nathanael and Rebekah Belknap,	"	2 May 1730.
Ebenezer Son of Jonathan and Mary Bowman,	"	7 May 1730.
Joan daughter of John and Katharine Beney,	"	23 May 1730.
Thomas Son of Thomas and Jane Button,	"	1 July 1730.
Abigail daughter of Benjamin and Martha Bunker,	"	29 July 1730.
Hephzibah daughter of James and Hephzibah Bradford,	"	22 August 1730.
Joseph Son of Joseph and Jane Burrell,	"	23 August 1730.
Joseph Son of Joseph and Ruth Bradford,	"	12 August 1730.
Isaac Son of John and Sarah Beacham,	"	18 August 1730.
Hannah daughter of Joseph and Abigail Bridgham,	"	2 August 1730.
Margaret daughter of John and Margaret Breck,	"	18 August 1730.
Susanna daughter of Richard and Mary Buckley,	"	5 June 1730.
Mary daughter of Philip and Mary Bass,	"	24 August 1730.
William Son of Ebenezer and Mary Berry,	"	14 September 1730.
Mary daughter of George and Mary Bethune,	"	7 October 1730.
Mary daughter of Benjamin and Ann Babbidge,	"	20 September 1730.
Ann daughter of Caleb and Deliverance Bean,	"	27 October 1730.
Ann daughter of Alden and Mercy Bass,	"	28 February 1730.
Moses Son of William and Elizabeth Bearsto,	"	21 October 1730.
Ann daughter of William and Ann Beer,	"	19 January 1730.
Ebenezer Son of Samuel and Christian Bass,	"	6 November 1730.
Margaret daughter of William and Lydia Brown,	"	21 February 1730.
Robert Son of James and Mary Brown,	"	11 November 1730.
Rachel daughter of Henry and Rachel Barlow,	"	4 February 1730.
Sarah daughter of Belthazer and Mary Bayard,	"	16 November 1730.
Robert Son of William and Susanna Butler,	"	13 September 1730.
Elizabeth daughter of John and Elizabeth Bulfinch,	"	10 December 1730.
James Son of Increase and Ann Blake,	"	30 March 1730.
Abiel daughter of William and Hannah Bond,	"	10 November 1730.
Mary daughter of Edward and Abigail Bromfield,	"	15 September 1730.
Susanna daughter of Thomas and Susanna Bentley,	"	20 December 1730.
Jonathan Howkins Son of Jonathan and Ann Barnard,	"	19 July 1730.
Sarah daughter of John and Susanna Brown,	"	31 December 1730.
Susanna daughter of John and Susanna Bruno,	"	2 January 1730.
Hannah daughter of John and Sarah Billings,	"	11 January 1730.
Dorcas daughter of John and Mary Brown,	"	5 March 1730.
John Son of Benjamin and Mary Brown,	"	7 September 1730.
Hannah daughter of Nathanael and Hannah Balston,	"	2 October 1730.
Martha daughter of Joseph and Elizabeth Belcher,	"	20 July 1730.
Edward Son of John and Sarah Carnes,	"	8 September 1730.
William Son of William and Deborah Corbin,	"	18 October 1730.
Lydia daughter of Job and Lydia Coit,	"	12 December 1730.
John Son of Matthias and Mary Cussens,	"	15 December 1730.
Ann daughter of William and Ann Coffin,	"	15 December 1730.
William Son of Josiah and Lydia Carter,	"	17 December 1730.
Samuel Son of Joseph and Margaret Clark,	"	22 July 1730.
Abigail daughter of Isaac and Patience Clark,	"	24 December 1730.
Elizabeth daughter of John and Mary Cowell,	"	4 June 1730.
Benjamin Son of Benjamin and Miriam Clark,	"	30 December 1730.
Hephzibah daughter of Jeremiah and Ann Cushing,	"	6 August 1730.
William Son of John and Hannah Coolidge,	"	5 January 1730.
Nathaniel Son of George and Mary Cradock,	"	16 November 1730.
John Son of John and Mary Crocker,	"	15 January 1730.

Edmund Son of Jacob and Abiel Chamberlain,	Born	11 October 1730.
Ebenezer Son of Ebenezer and Ann Clough,	"	30 January 1730.
Isaac Son of Isaac and Susanna Cowdery,	"	20 February 1730.
Elisha Son of Elisha and Elizabeth Callender,	"	27 April 1730.
John Son of Clement and Sarah Collings,	"	19 September 1730.
Elizabeth daughter of Ebenezer and Rachel Clough,	"	1 May 1730.
Hannah daughter of Edward and Mary Cooper,	"	19 May 1730.
Hannah daughter of Edward and Mary Cooper,	"	29 May 1730.
Sarah daughter of James and Sarah Clarke,	"	29 June 1730.
Mary daughter of Lambert and Elizabeth Cox,	"	23 July 1730.
Susanna daughter of Thomas and Susanna Child,	"	10 July 1730.
Elizabeth daughter of James and Elizabeth Codner,	"	23 August 1730.
Lydia daughter of Samuel and Elizabeth Checkley,	"	7 September 1730.
Ann daughter of Elias and Mary Dupee,	"	13 May 1730.
Thomas Son of Edward and Judith Durant,	"	22 August 1730.
John Son of Benjamin and Margaret Dyer,	"	25 August 1730.
Elizabeth daughter of James and Mary Dawson,	"	13 March 1730.
Sarah daughter of Thomas and Anna Downe,	"	21 March 1730.
Elizabeth daughter of Thomas and Elizabeth Dawes,	"	16 April 1730.
John Son of Samuel and Katharine Davis,	"	4 February 1730.
Willard Son of Benjamin and Ruth Eastabrook,	"	25 March 1730.
Mercy daughter of Nathanael and Hannah Emmes,	"	17 July 1730.
Mary daughter of Samuel and Ruth Ellis,	"	6 June 1730.
Mary daughter of John and Abigail Erving,	"	19 June 1730.
Maria daughter of Edward and Mary Ellis,	"	1 May 1730.
Joseph Son of Joseph and Mary Eustus,	"	10 September 1730.
Nathanael Son of Brice and Mary Eccles,	"	17 November 1730.
Silence daughter of John and Sarah Eliot,	"	1 February 1730.
Benjamin Son of Benjamin and Bathsheba Edwards,	"	22 February 1730.
Savell Son of Thomas and Deborah Eyre,	"	18 May 1730.
John Son of John and Mary Earle,	"	24 March 1730.
Nathan Son of Nathan and Margaret Foster,	"	20 February 1730.
James Son of Neal and Mary Forbes,	"	23 March 1730.
Mary daughter of William and Margaret Fletcher,	"	20 June 1730.
Abigail daughter of Thomas and Anna Foxcroft,	"	29 September 1730.
Ann daughter of Thomas and Hannah Fairweather,	"	4 September 1730.
Gershom Son of Eleazer and Mary Flagg,	"	10 June 1730.
William Son of Thomas and Ann Foster,	"	9 May 1730.
John Son of James and Hannah Fosdick,	"	9 June 1730.
Mercy daughter of Bickford and Judith Greenleaf,	"	29 April 1730.
Mary daughter of Jacob and Mary Green,	"	31 May 1730.
Abigail daughter of Thomas and Abigail Goodwin,	"	5 September 1730.
Jonathan Son of John and Mary Gatchell,	"	16 October 1730.
Joseph Son of Joseph and Martha Goldthwait,	"	5 October 1730.
Abigail daughter of John and Sarah Greenough,	"	8 April 1730.
Benjamin Son of William and Anna Giles,	"	14 October 1730.
John Son of Henry and Elizabeth Gibbon,	"	25 February 1730.
Judith daughter of Joseph and Mary Glydden,	"	16 October 1730.
John Son of Elias and Sarah Girott,	"	17 February 1730.
Bartholomew Son of Bartholomew and Hannah Gedney,	"	5 September 1730.
Rebekah daughter of Nathanael and Rebekah Goodwin,	"	17 September 1730.
Hannah daughter of Samuel and Ann Grafton,	"	28 November 1730.
Bethiah daughter of Thomas and Anna Greene,	"	4 July 1730.
Richard Son of Samuel and Mary Green,	"	13 December 1730.
Ann daughter of Samuel and Abigail Green,	"	7 January 1730.
Caleb Son of John and Mary Griffin,	"	26 January 1730.
Joseph Son of Caleb Joseph and Mary Gray,	"	17 February 1730.
Stephen Son of Stephen and Eunice Greenleaf,	"	14 February 1730.

Elizabeth daughter of Charles and Martha Henley,	Born	30 August 1730.
Jonathan Son of Samuel and Mary Hunting,	"	16 September 1730.
Samuel Son of Samuel and Mary Heath,	"	10 August 1730.
Elizabeth daughter of Joseph and Martha Harley,	"	10 September 1730.
William Son of George and Rebekah Hanners,	"	19 April 1730.
Hannah daughter of Thomas and Hannah Hill,	"	8 June 1730.
Abraham Son of Abraham and Hannah How,	"	10 June 1730.
Ebenezer Son of Ames and Judith Howard,	"	12 October 1730.
William Son of William and Elizabeth Healy,	"	27 May 1730.
Joseph Son of Elias and Frances Hammond,	"	8 October 1730.
Samuel Son of George and Abigail Hewes,	"	12 July 1730.
James Son of James and Katharine Hodges,	"	21 October 1730.
Samuel Son of Ralph and Mary Hart,	"	12 December 1730.
Sarah daughter of Thomas and Mary Hubbard,	"	1 December 1730.
Samuel Jackson Son of Joseph and Elizabeth Harris,	"	9 December 1730.
Thomas Son of Richard and Hannah Hayward,	"	27 April 1730.
Peter Son of Peter and Katharine Harratt,	"	15 January 1730.
Susanna daughter of Andrew and Dorcas Hall,	"	18 April 1730.
Joseph Son of Benjamin and Rebekah Hallowell,	"	26 December 1730.
John Son of John and Mary Henshaw,	"	3 March 1730.
Lydia daughter of Samuel and Elizabeth Holland,	"	26 February 1730.
John Son of John and Mary Haro,	"	19 March 1730.
Elizabeth daughter of Jacob and Elizabeth Hurd,	"	17 March 1730.
Mary daughter of John and Mary Hill,	"	18 March 1730.
Charles Hobby Son of Zechariah and Mary Hubbart,	"	16 October 1730.
Elizabeth daughter of Robert and Elizabeth Jenkins,	"	16 August 1730.
Elizabeth daughter of Jeremiah and Rebekah Jackson,	"	5 January 1730.
Mary daughter of William and Mary Jarvis,	"	19 February 1730.
Margaret daughter of William and Margaret Jepson,	"	9 February 1730.
Christopher Son of Edward and Elizabeth Kelly,	"	10 February 1730.
Prudence daughter of Joseph and Elizabeth Kneeland,	"	23 February 1730.
Elizabeth daughter of William and Hannah Lynch,	"	14 September 1730.
Edward Son of John and Mercy Late,	"	20 February 1730.
John Son of John and Mary Lander,	"	15 December 1730.
Thomas Son of Knight and Abigail Leverett,	"	3 April 1730.
Hannah daughter of John and Hannah Ludgate,	"	24 December 1730.
James Son of John and Ruth Leach,	"	3 April 1730.
Sarah daughter of Joseph and Elizabeth Lewis,	"	7 April 1730.
Lydia daughter of Phillip and Lydia Lewis,	"	1 May 1730.
Joseph Son of Joseph and Rebekah Lowden,	"	2 July 1730.
Mary daughter of Nicholas and Elizabeth Lash,	"	15 September 1730.
Elizabeth daughter of Jonathan and Mary Lambert,	"	1 July 1730.
Deborah daughter of Byfield and Sarah Lyde,	"	9 February 1730.
Theophilus Son of Theophilus and Hannah Lillie,	"	18 August 1730.
Eunice daughter of Daniel and Eunice Merrett,	"	11 May 1730.
William Son of William and Mary More,	"	9 May 1730.
Letitia daughter of John and Letitia Mark,	"	21 April 1730.
Susanna daughter of James and Susanna Melling,	"	24 June 1730.
John Son of Peter and Priscilla Morrison,	"	30 July 1730.
William Son of William and Elizabeth Maycock,	"	27 August 1730.
Rebekah daughter of John and Dorothy Marion,	"	2 October 1730.
Rebekah daughter of Isaac and Rebekah Marion,	"	18 October 1730.
William Son of John and Mary Milton,	"	20 January 1730.
Ann daughter of Robert and Elizabeth Moore,	"	22 January 1730.
Samuel Son of John and Elizabeth Maverick,	"	19 January 1730.

BIRTHS — 1730.   199

James Son of Benjamin and Eliza. Mason,	Born	10 March 1730.
Deborah daughter of William and Deborah Mason,	"	15 March 1730.
Joseph Son of Alexander and Mary Marten,	"	16 March 1730.
Henry Son of Eleazar and Mary Newhall,	"	27 August 1730.
Samuel Son of Edmund and Mary Newcomb,	"	3 May 1730.
Samuel Son of John and Sarah Osborne,	"	16 April 1730.
Abigail daughter of William and Mary Owen,	"	31 January 1730.
Elizabeth daughter of Andrew and Mary Oliver,	"	7 June 1730.
Katharine daughter of Samuel and Margaret Pousley,	"	21 August 1730.
Benjamin Son of Briantt and Ruth Parott,	"	12 June 1730.
Samuel Son of John and Lydia Poumery,	"	4 August 1730.
John Son of David and Hannah Powell,	"	28 June 1730.
Hannah daughter of Joseph and Mary Procter,	"	22 September 1730.
John Son of John and Hannah Procter,	"	27 February 1730.
Samuel Son of Benjamin and Margaret Procter,	"	13 September 1730.
Sarah daughter of Joseph and Mehetabel Payson,	"	5 November 1730.
Elizabeth daughter of Moses and Elizabeth Peirce,	"	30 March 1730.
Dorcas daughter of Samuel and Dorcas Parkman,	"	13 November 1730.
Ruth daughter of Joseph and Mary Peirce.	"	20 December 1730.
Abigail daughter of Nathanael and Abigail Pearse,	"	1 December 1730.
Benjamin Son of Edward and Ruth Paige,	"	14 June 1730.
Mary daughter of John and Mary Papoon,	"	31 December 1730.
Robert Treat Son of Thomas and Eunice Paine,	"	12 March 1730.
Samuel Son of William and Ann Phillips,	"	21 January 1730.
Abigail daughter of Skinner and Elizabeth Russell,	"	31 December 1730.
Joseph Son of Benjamin and Elizabeth Russell,	"	11 May 1730.
Naomi daughter of Samuel and Naomi Ridgaway,	"	7 January 1730.
Jeremiah Son of Jeremiah and Lydia Rhodes,	"	31 October 1730.
Thomas Son of Thomas and Elizabeth Russell, at Sudbury,	"	4 July 1730.
Joseph Son of Benjamin and Priscilla Roberts,	"	8 February 1730.
John Son of Nathanael and Mary Roberts,	"	11 March 1730.
Abigail daughter of Stephen and Sarah Randall,	"	20 March 1730.
Mary daughter of James and Mary Read,	"	5 October 1730.
Elizabeth daughter of Simon and Elizabeth Rogers,	"	19 February 1730.
Sarah daughter of John and Abigail Ruggles,	"	6 May 1730.
John Son of William and Sarah Russell,	"	5 December 1730.
Caleb Son of Caleb and Deborah Ray,	"	12 September 1730.
Thomas Son of Thomas and Mary Stevens,	"	4 April 1730.
Thomas Son of Samuel and Elizabeth Seward,	"	1 May 1730.
John Son of John and Lydia Strong,	"	17 May 1730.
Edward Son of Joseph and Mehetabel Scott,	"	18 October 1730.
Thomas Son of Thomas and Sarah Shaw,	"	21 June 1730.
Sarah daughter of John and Sarah Sweetser,	"	31 August 1730.
William Son of William and Mary Sims,	"	30 July 1730.
John Son of John and Lydia Simpson,	"	29 January 1730.
Abigail daughter of John and Abigail Salter,	"	28 August 1730.
Sarah daughter of William and Sarah Stoddard,	"	24 September 1730.
Tabitha daughter of Thomas and Tabitha Stoddard,	"	15 September 1730.
Mary daughter of Samuel and Mary Smith,	"	31 October 1730.
Henry Son of Ralph and Huldah Smith,	"	5 September 1730.
Elizabeth daughter of William and Elizabeth Snoden,	"	20 July 1730.
Abigail daughter of Luke and Margaret Stone,	"	6 October 1730.
James Son of John and Elizabeth Spooner,	"	4 November 1730.
Peter Son of Benjamin and Ann Sanderson,	"	3 November 1730.
Lydia daughter of Joseph and Susanna Shead,	"	6 August 1730.
Margery daughter of William and Elizabeth Simpkins,	"	1 December 1730.
Hannah daughter of Abraham and Hannah Snelling,	"	26 December 1730.
Mary daughter of Nathan and Mary Sargent,	"	2 January 1730.

Samuel Son of Ebenezer and Elizabeth Sumner,	Born	22 December 1730.
Martha daughter of Elisha and Martha Townsend,	"	29 June 1730.
Samuel Son of William and Bethiah Torrey,	"	15 June 1730.
Sarah daughter of Joseph and Joanna Turell,	"	17 August 1730.
Richard Son of Richard and Abigail Trew,	"	9 August 1730.
Joseph Son of William and Sarah Tyler,	"	20 September 1730.
William Son of Thomas and Waitstill Trott,	"	1 November 1730.
Elizabeth daughter of George and Elizabeth Tilley,	"	1 December 1730.
Daniel Son of Daniel and Hannah Tucker,	"	15 December 1730.
Samuel Son of Jonathan and Mary Tarbox,	"	13 March 1730.
William Son of Hugh and Mary Vans,	"	10 April 1730.
John Son of John and Bethiah Vardy,	"	21 October 1730.
Moses Son of John and Elizabeth Ventinon,	"	30 January 1730.
Daniel Son of Samuel and Mary Waterhouse,	"	3 October 1730.
Martha daughter of Jonathan and Martha Williams,	"	7 October 1730.
Thomas Son of John and Sarah Wakefield,	"	25 February 1730.
Abigail daughter of Joseph and Ruth Whittemore,	"	27 July 1730.
John Son of John and Elizabeth Whitney,	"	24 March 1730.
Mary daughter of George and Mary Wadlin,	"	17 September 1730.
Ann daughter of Jacob and Sarah Wendell,	"	7 December 1730.
Charles Son of William and Mary Walter,	"	3 December 1730.
Mary daughter of Charles and Martha Warham.	"	4 November 1730.
Cord Son of Cord and Sarah Wing,	"	25 November 1730.
Mary Green daughter of Edward and Margaret Whitaker,	"	30 January 1730.
Abigail daughter of Samuel and Hannah Welles,	"	2 December 1730.
Ann daughter of Jacob and Sarah Wendell,	"	7 December 1730.
Hezekiah Son of Benjamin and Sarah Whittemore,	"	2 February 1730.
Nathanael Son of William and Mary Warner,	"	27 March 1730
John Son of Thomas and Jane Williston,	"	13 April 1730.
Samuel Son of Benjamin and Ruth Wheeler,	"	2 May 1730.
Susanna daughter of Joshua and Elizabeth Winslow,	"	25 February 1730.
Martha daughter of Owen and Martha Williams,	"	28 April 1730.
Isaac Son of Samuel and Mary Wheeler,	"	10 May 1730.
Ruth daughter of Isaac and Sarah Walker,	"	20 August 1730.
James Son of William and Mary Young,	"	9 April 1730.
James Son of James and Jane Young,	"	21 December 1730.
Joseph Son of Abraham and Amiable York,	"	5 February 1730.
Samuel Read Son of William Beartell and Elizabeth his Wife,	"	9 May 1730.
Mary daughter of John Gardner and Mary his Wife,	"	3 February 1730.
John Son of John Scot and Lydia his Wife,	"	13 October 1730.
John Son of Samuel Torrey and Silence his Wife,	"	22 September 1730.

1731.

Samuel Son of John and Sarah Aekin,	Born	17 July 1731.
Elizabeth daughter of Joshua and Elizabeth Atwood,	"	21 August 1731.
Zechariah Son of Zechariah and Lydia Alden,	"	20 July 1731.
Thomas Son of Samuel and Mary Adams,	"	23 December 1731.
Eleanor daughter of Henry and Deliverance Atkins.	"	5 December 1731.
John Son of John and Susanna Adams,	"	15 May 1731.
John Son of John and Mary Avis,	"	11 July 1731.
William Son of Daniel and Abigail Bell,	"	7 April 1731.
Abigail daughter of Ebenezer and Mary Bridge,	"	7 May 1731.
William Son of William and Katharine Bulfinch,	"	1 July 1731.
Martha daughter of John and Mary Beer,	"	2 January 1731.
Samuel Son of Thomas and Susanna Belcher,	"	4 July 1731.

Births — 1731.

Richard Son of John and Katharine Beny,	Born	18 February 1731.
Edward Son of Edward and Alice Barret,	"	25 July 1731.
John Son of John and Jerusha Baker,	"	17 June 1731.
Susanna daughter of John and Abigail Burt,	"	15 August 1731.
Susanna daughter of Martin and Susanna Brimmer,	"	8 August 1731.
Moses-Belcher Son of Moses and Hannah Bass,	"	27 August 1731.
Harrison Son of Increase and Ann Blake,	"	10 September 1731.
Ephraim Son of Ephraim and Mary Baker,	"	8 October 1731.
Mary daughter of John and Sarah Banks,	"	8 October 1731.
Sarah daughter of David and Rely Belcher,	"	30 November 1731.
Peter Son of James and Miriam Boyer,	"	2 November 1731.
John Son of John and Rebekah Barret,	"	7 December 1731.
Mary daughter of John and Elizabeth Beaudri,	"	6 December 1731.
Benja. Chamberlain Son of Benja. and Martha Bunker,	"	5 January 1731.
Sarah daughter of Tho. and Ruth Bill,	"	11 December 1731.
Ruth daughter of John and Sarah Bonner,	"	12 March 1731.
Richard Son of John and Katharine Binny,	"	18 February 1731.
Joseph Son of John and Sarah Bradford,	"	13 March 1731.
Mary daughter of Timothy and Mary Barron,	"	4 December 1731.
Jane daughter of Thomas and Sarah Brooks,	"	29 November 1731.
Ruth daughter of Joseph and Ruth Bradford,	"	28 August 1731.
Joseph Son of Richard and Mary Buckley,	"	10 January 1731.
James Son of Thomas and Elizabeth Barrick,	"	9 April 1731.
Sarah daughter of John and Susanna Blake,	"	24 January 1731.
Joseph Son of Richard and Mary Billings,	"	28 March 1731.
Elizabeth daughter of Thomas and Abigail Cannington,	"	9 April 1731.
Mary daughter of Jeremiah and Ann Cushing,	"	19 March 1731.
William Son of John and Elizabeth Clark,	"	9 April 1731.
Elizabeth daughter of Charles and Elizabeth Chauncy,	"	12 November 1731.
Hannah daughter of John and Hannah Coverly,	"	18 April 1731.
Nathanael Son of Nathanael and Martha Cobbit,	"	28 July 1731.
Benjamin Son of Benjamin and Lydia Chub,	"	16 May 1731.
Patience daughter of Henry and Elizabeth Coulton,	"	17 July 1731.
Ann daughter of James and Hannah Cox,	"	27 May 1731.
John Son of Nicholas and Mary Cutting,	"	20 June 1731.
Jane daughter of John and Ann Chambers,	"	11 July 1731.
Ames Son of Ames and Mary Cartwright,	"	2 July 1731.
Samuel Son of Isaac and Hannah Casno,	"	4 August 1731.
Nathanael Son of Ebenezer and Rachel Clough,	"	26 July 1731.
Ann daughter of William and Ann Currier,	"	18 November 1731.
Hannah daughter of Thomas and Ann Crafts,	"	22 August 1731.
John Son of Josiah and Lydia Carter,	"	19 November 1731.
John Son of Andrew and Mary Cunningham,	"	8 October 1731.
Joseph Son of Thomas and Elizabeth Cock,	"	24 January 1731.
Oliver Son of Jonathan and Hannah Chandler,	"	20 September 1731.
Nathanael Son of Benjamin and Elizabeth Cushing,	"	3 October 1731.
Sarah daughter of Clement and Sarah Collings,	"	24 November 1731.
James Son of James and Elizabeth Codner,	"	3 December 1731.
Moses Son of Moses and Mary Chaille,	"	11 September 1731.
Mary daughter of John and Abigail Colson,	"	6 March 1731.
Edward Son of Edward and Mary Cooper,	"	19 March 1731.
Richard Son of John and Rebekah Compton,	"	30 July 1731.
Robert Son of Joseph and Hannah Calef,	"	27 December 1731.
John Son of John and Elizabeth Dring,	"	22 May 1731.
William Son of William and Lydia Doke,	"	11 October 1731.
Mary daughter of Benjamin and Abigail Darling,	"	3 June 1731.
Isaac Son of John and Naomi Dupee,	"	27 December 1731.

Sarah daughter of Nathanael and Mary Doubleday,	Born	21 July 1731.
Frances daughter of Joseph and Frances Douglas,	"	29 December 1731.
Elizabeth daughter of John and Elizabeth Daniel,	"	3 August 1731.
Ann daughter of John and Deborah Dyer,	"	8 January 1731.
James Son of James and Mary Day,	"	18 August 1731.
Thomas Son of Thomas and Elizabeth Dawes,	"	5 August 1731.
Mary daughter of Jonathan and Mary Dwight,	"	6 February 1731.
Ann daughter of Eleazer and Mary Dorby,	"	30 March 1731.
Elizabeth daughter of Elias and Mary Dupee,	"	4 April 1731.
Elizabeth daughter of William and Damaris Dorrington,	"	12 April 1731.
James Son of George and Susanna Ducker,	"	19 April 1731.
Samuel Son of Brice and Mary Eccles,	"	2 December 1731.
Mary daughter of Thomas and Sarah Edgar,	"	22 August 1731.
Elizabeth daughter of Benjamin and Elizabeth Egglestone,	"	27 November 1731.
Nathanael Son of Jacob and Mary Emmons,	"	15 April 1731.
Sarah daughter of Thomas and Abigail Eustus,	"	17 May 1731.
Ann daughter of David and Mary Evans,	"	10 March 1731.
Peter Son of Samuel and Ruth Ellis,	"	12 September 1731.
Edward Son of Edward and Sarah Edes,	"	3 October 1731.
Joseph Son of Edward and Hannah Emerson,	"	13 September 1731.
William Son of John and Rebekah Endicott,	"	6 July 1731.
Elizabeth daughter of John and Abigail Erving,	"	14 September 1731.
John Son of Grafton and Sarah Feveryear,	"	28 March 1731.
Benjamin Son of Benjamin and Sarah Floyd,	"	4 April 1731.
Benjamin Son of William and Elizabeth Fairfield,	"	10 September 1731.
Stephen Son of William and Mary Fullerton,	"	19 September 1731.
Sarah daughter of Joseph and Margaret Fitch,	"	8 May 1731.
Prudence daughter of Thomas and Ann Foster,	"	28 June 1731.
John Son of Alexander and Deborah Forsyth,	"	5 November 1731.
Mary daughter of John and Mary Foster,	"	30 August 1731.
Mary daughter of Hopestill and Sarah Foster.	"	19 December 1731
Elizabeth daughter of Zechariah and Abigail Fitch,	"	31 January 1731.
James Son of James and Hannah Fosdick,	"	26 February 1731.
Mary daughter of Percival and Mary Farmer,	"	16 February 1731.
Elizabeth daughter of Edward and Elizabeth Fullerton.	"	24 February 1731.
Joseph Son of Emanuel and Mary Grace,	"	17 August 1731.
Samuel Son of Samuel and Elizabeth Grant.	"	9 September 1731.
Jerusha daughter of John and Sarah Greenough,	"	17 November 1731.
David Son of Bickford and Judith Greenleaf,	"	9 November 1731.
John Son of Thomas and Elizabeth Green,	"	24 December 1731.
Nathanael Son of Jeremiah and Sarah Green,	"	7 December 1731.
Joshua Son of Joseph and Anna Green,	"	17 May 1731.
Abigail daughter of Thomas and Abigail Goodwin,	"	19 December 1731.
Ebenezer Son of Samuel and Sarah Goffe,	"	1 November 1731.
Mary daughter of John and Martha Gibbs,	"	5 January 1731.
Mary daughter of Samuel and Mary Greenwood,	"	1 April 1731.
Eunice daughter of Stephen and Eunice Greenleaf,	"	2 February 1731.
Katharine daughter of Rufus and Katharine Green,	"	22 November 1731.
Judith daughter of Joseph and Mary Glydden,	"	15 March 1731.
Rebekah daughter of Joseph and Rebekah Gray,	"	2 January 1731.
Ann daughter of Joshua and Ann Gill,	"	28 June 1731.
Rachel daughter of Daniel and Elizabeth Goffe,	"	23 June 1731.
Richard Son of Richard and Hannah Gridley,	"	12 July 1731.
John Son of Joseph and Martha Goldthwait,	"	31 December 1731.
Elizabeth daughter of Newman and Elizabeth Greenough,	"	13 June 1731.
Ann daughter of Nathanael and Elizabeth Green,	"	5 August 1731.

Births — 1731.

Thomas Son of James and Sarah Green,	Born	17 June 1731.
Richard Son of James and Elizabeth Goodwin,	"	26 March 1731.
Sarah daughter of Samuel and Sarah Harsum,	"	15 July 1731.
Ann daughter of William and Wilhelmina Haslip,	"	13 August 1731.
John Son of Nathanael and Hephzibah Howard,	"	4 August 1731.
William Son of Samuel and Elizabeth Haley,	"	30 August 1731.
Jacob Son of Jacob and Susanna Holyoke,	"	26 June 1731.
William Son of William and Sarah Hanserd,	"	26 October 1731.
Charles Son of Robert and Sarah Harris,	"	27 February 1731.
Alice daughter of Abraham and Sarah Harris,	"	27 April 1731.
Anna daughter of John and Anna Harris,	"	24 August 1731.
Elizabeth daughter of Thomas and Hannah Hill,	"	3 November 1731.
Sarah daughter of John and Abigail Hasey,	"	1 February 1731.
Mehetabel daughter of Henry and Martha Howell,	"	19 June 1731.
Eleazer Son of Samuel and Elizabeth Holyoke,	"	11 May 1731.
Esther daughter of Thomas and Eleanor Hartley,	"	10 May 1731.
Mary daughter of John and Kezia Harvey,	"	1 June 1731.
Rachel daughter of Richard and Hannah Hayward,	"	20 June 1731.
Samuel Son of Samuel and Mary Harding,	"	28 August 1731.
Joan daughter of John and Sarah Hooton,	"	1 September 1731.
Ann daughter of Nathanael and Ann Hodgdon,	"	27 September 1731.
Charles Son of Robert and Sarah Harris,	"	27 February 1731.
Sarah daughter of John and Sarah Hyer,	"	15 September 1731.
Sarah daughter of Samuel and Mary Hunt,	"	19 July 1731.
Peter Son of George and Rebekah Hopkins,	"	22 October 1731.
Richard Son of Stephen and Elizabeth Hunniwell,	"	25 October 1731.
John Son of John and Jane Hobbs,	"	12 November 1731.
John Son of John and Elizabeth Hubbart,	"	21 June 1731.
Elizabeth daughter of Edward and Lydia Hutchinson,	"	1 December 1731.
Jane daughter of George and Sarah Jones,	"	26 May 1731.
Thomas Son of Thomas and Rachel Johnson,	"	4 July 1731.
Abigail daughter of Samuel and Ruth Jackson,	"	26 April 1731.
Sarah daughter of Thomas and Sarah Jenkins,	"	28 June 1731.
Elizabeth daughter of Thomas and Sarah Jackson,	"	21 October 1731.
Elizabeth daughter of Zechariah and Elizabeth Johonnott,	"	9 September 1731.
William Son of James and Mary Jackson,	"	13 June 1731.
Mary daughter of James and Jane Johnson,	"	16 November 1731.
Nathanael Son of Nathanael and Abigail Jarvis,	"	25 December 1731.
Edward Son of Elias and Mary Jarvis,	"	22 January 1731.
Dudson Son of Dudson and Lois Kilcup,	"	11 February 1731.
Robert Ellis Son of Thomas and Sarah Kilby,	"	16 May 1731.
Thomas Son of Thomas and Elizabeth Kemboll,	"	19 July 1731.
Prudence daughter of John and Prudence Kneeland,	"	2 January 1731.
Mercy daughter of Richard and Sarah Kent,	"	19 November 1731.
Mary daughter of Joseph and Mary Kneeland,	"	3 January 1731.
John Son of Israel and Mehetabel Look,	"	7 April 1731.
Elizabeth daughter of David and Abigail Lenox,	"	17 May 1731
Joanna daughter of John and Miriam Lupton,	"	5 April 1731
David Son of David and Rebekah Lupton,	"	8 June 1731.
Susanna daughter of Joseph and Elizabeth Lewis	"	5 July 1731.
Samuel Son of Phillip and Lydia Lewis,	"	20 November 1731.
Mary daughter of George and Mary Le Dane,	"	20 August 1731.
Elizabeth daughter of John and Margaret Le Cras,	"	25 August 1731.
Isaac Son of Isaac and Margaret Lowry,	"	4 February 1731.
Richard Son of John and Mary Lander,	"	25 November 1731.
Rebekah daughter of James and Mary Lenox,	"	4 February 1731.
Abigail daughter of Knight and Abigail Leveret,	"	25 February 1731.
Sarah daughter of John and Sarah Marine,	"	27 January 1731.

204 CITY DOCUMENT NO. 43.

Ann daughter of Samuel and Ann Moor,	Born	18 August 1731.
Richard Son of John and Sarah Mills,	"	29 June 1731.
Parsons Son of John and Sarah Morehead,	"	18 May 1731.
Thomas Son of William and Elizabeth Maycock,	"	17 August 1731.
John Son of Samuel and Margaret Mellish,	"	8 April 1731.
Martha daughter of Samuel and Martha Melikin,	"	16 September 1731.
Isabella daughter of Thomas and Abigail McCuloch,	"	11 April 1731.
Ann daughter of James and Sarah Mattock,	"	12 October 1731.
Margaret daughter of Thomas and Mary Maccollo,	"	31 December 1731
Mary daughter of John and Sarah Mortimer,	"	15 October 1731.
Arthur Son of David and Susanna Mason,	"	30 October 1731.
Sarah daughter of Richard and Lydia Mortimer,	"	10 January 1731.
Ammi daughter of Robert and Rachel Meyer,	"	5 February 1731.
John Son of Daniel and Eunice Merrett,	"	24 February 1731.
Thomas Son of James and Jane More,	"	10 June 1731.
Sarah daughter of Henry and Elizabeth Neal,	"	15 April 1731.
Thomas Son of Thomas and Elizabeth Nowell,	"	15 May 1731.
Mary daughter of Lewis and Abigail Nason,	"	13 May 1731.
John Son of William and Mary Neatby,	"	17 June 1731.
Joseph Son of Joseph and Lydia Norman,	"	6 May 1731.
John Son of John and Mary Norvell,	"	23 July 1731.
Andrew Son of Andrew and Mary Oliver,	"	13 November 1731.
Samuel Son of Samuel and Rebekah Pain,	"	16 June 1731.
Bartholomew Son of Daniel and Sarah Pecker,	"	16 June 1731.
Elizabeth daughter of Samuel and Rebekah Phillips,	"	21 June 1731.
Mary daughter of John and Mary Phillips,	"	12 August 1731.
Thomas Son of Thomas and Bethiah Phillips,	"	29 August 1731.
Abigail daughter of Robert and Mercy Peat,	"	9 April 1731.
Caleb Son of Joseph and Mary Prince,	"	6 October 1731.
Mary daughter of Hammond and Esther Pearson,	"	21 April 1731.
John Son of John and Elizabeth Pinckney,	"	30 December 1731.
Moses Paul Son of Jonathan and Mary Payson,	"	9 May 1731.
Thomazin daughter of Isaac and Agnes Peirce,	"	8 January 1731.
Caleb Son of Caleb and Mary Parker,	"	2 February 1731.
John Son of Robert and Lydia Price,	"	18 February 1731.
Thomas Son of John and Mary Potwine,	"	3 October 1731.
Benjamin Son of Benjamin and Elizabeth Russell,	"	20 June 1731.
John Son of James and Sarah Raimer,	"	22 June 1731.
Mary daughter of James and Mehetabel Ridgaway,	"	24 June 1731.
Esther daughter of Joseph and Rachel Roberts,	"	28 July 1731.
John Son of Richard and Ann Richardson,	"	24 December 1731.
Simon Son of Simon and Thomazin Rogers,	"	6 November 1731.
John Son of Samuel and Hannah Russell,	"	7 May 1731.
Deborah daughter of Paul and Deborah Rivoire,	"	21 February 1731.
Benjamin Son of Gamaliel and Sarah Rogers,	"	14 September 1731.
Benjamin Son of Joseph and Margaret Savell,	"	5 April 1731.
Philippe daughter of Josiah and Phillippe Snelling,	"	31 July 1731.
John Son of John and Abigail Salter,	"	8 August 1731.
Elizabeth daughter of James and Mary Sharp,	"	27 August 1731.
Samuel Son of John and Mary Simpson,	"	21 July 1731.
Sarah daughter of John and Sarah Smallpiece,	"	12 October 1731.
Arthur Son of Arthur and Faith Savage,	"	9 October 1731.
Hannah daughter of Benjamin and Hannah Simpson,	"	24 September 1731.
Elizabeth daughter of Jahn and Elizabeth Scottow,	"	21 November 1731.
Elizabeth daughter of Jacob and Mary Sheafe,	"	3 February 1731.
John Son of Alexander and Rebekah Sampson,	"	28 February 1731.
Katharine daughter of Richard and Mary Stanney,	"	9 April 1731.
John Son of John and Mercy Smith,	"	29 May 1731.
Philip Son of William and Dorcas Sumner,	"	3 April 1731.

Births — 1731.

Allison daughter of John and Mary Smibert	Born	14 May 1731.
Jonathan Son of Joseph and Elizabeth Snelling,	"	22 April 1731.
Rebekah daughter of Nicholas and Martha Salisbury,	"	27 March 1731.
Elizabeth daughter of Thomas and Elizabeth Simpkins,	"	7 July 1731.
Sarah daughter of Robert and Lydia Snelling,	"	17 July 1731.
Jane daughter of Jonathan and Mary Snelling,	"	20 July 1731.
Benjamin Son of John and Sarah Tyler,	"	27 October 1731.
Jeremiah Son of Edward and Elizabeth Tothill,	"	21 October 1731.
Samuel Son of Timothy and Elizabeth Thornton,	"	25 October 1731.
Joshua Son of Joshua and Elizabeth Townsend,	"	23 July 1731.
Samuel Son of Samuel and Abigail Torrey,	"	24 May 1731.
John Son of Joseph and Joanna Turell,	"	21 August 1731.
John Son of Moses and Hannah Tyler,	"	29 November 1731.
Bethiah daughter of William and Bethiah Torrey,	"	30 December 1731.
Joshua Son of Joshua and Martha Thornton,	"	15 January 1731.
Elizabeth daughter of William and Ann Thompson,	"	22 April 1731.
Mary daughter of Alexander and Elizabeth Thorp,	"	3 April 1731.
William Son of John and Susanna Tinkum,	"	11 May 1731.
Pepperrell Son of Andrew and Miriam Tyler,	"	12 April 1731.
Nathanael Son of Nathanael and Joanna Thwing,	"	26 June 1731.
Henry Son of Joshua and Martha Underwood,	"	5 July 1731.
John Son of Luke and Mary Vardy,	"	5 February 1731.
Elizabeth daughter of Isaac and Sarah Walker,	"	2 September 1731.
Elizabeth daughter of James and Elizabeth Watts,	"	5 March 1731.
Martha daughter of Owen and Mary Williams,	"	16 November 1731.
John Son of Peleg and Elizabeth Wiswall,	"	15 April 1731.
David Son of David and Alice Whittemore,	"	13 November 1731.
Mary daughter of John and Mary West,	"	7 June 1731.
Elias Son of Elias and Rhoda Whittemore,	"	22 January 1731.
Phebe daughter of Benjamin and Sarah Whittemore,	"	27 January 1731.
John Son of John and Elizabeth Wendell,	"	10 September 1731.
Abigail daughter of William and Mary Warner,	"	16 January 1731.
Rebekah daughter of Ebenezer and Rebekah Williston,	"	19 July 1731.
John Son of John and Elizabeth Webb	"	30 January 1731.
William Son of William and Elizabeth Wingfield,	"	15 April 1731.
Deborah daughter of John and Rebekah Wootton,	"	26 January 1731.
Sarah daughter of Sendell and Mehetabel Williams,	"	17 December 1731.
Samuel Son of Joseph and Ruth Whittemore,	"	20 March 1731.
Mary daughter of Isaac and Rebekah White,	"	20 June 1731.
John Son of John and Isabella Wyer,	"	27 June 1731.
Benjamin Son of Benjamin and Abigail Wolcut,	"	1 July 1731.
Mary daughter of Oliver and Hannah Williams,	"	10 July 1731.
William Son of Samuel and Mary Wright,	"	3 May 1731.
Joseph Son of Richard and Eunice Walker,	"	4 October 1731.
Thomas Son of Samuel and Mary Wheeler,	"	8 October 1731.
Matthew Son of Thomas and Magdalen Wroe,	"	26 October 1731.
Joseph Son of Thomas and Jane Williston,	"	11 November 1731.
Hannah daughter of William and Mary Whittemore,	"	9 January 1731.
Joseph Son of William and Hannah Young,	"	25 August 1731.
Margaret daughter of William Blin and Elizabeth his Wife,	"	3 October 1731.
Thomas Son of John Carnes and Sarah his Wife,	"	16 September 1731.
John Son of James Gooch and Hester his Wife,	"	8 June 1731.
Elizabeth daughter of William Maxwell and Lydia his Wife,	"	20 October 1731.
Anna daughter of Charles Willis and Anna his Wife,	"	29 December 1731.

John Son of Onesimus and Hagar his Wife, free
Negroes, Born 7 September 1731.
Nathaniel Son of Nathaniel Shepard and Mary his
Wife, " 19 September 1731.

1732.

Mary daughter of Nathanael and Elizabeth Adams,	Born	15 April 1732.
William Son of William and Margaret Allen,	"	30 March 1732.
Elizabeth daughter of John and Mary Allen,	"	5 April 1732.
Philip Son of Philip and Lydia Audebert,	"	1 July 1732.
Mary daughter of Jeremiah and Rebekah Allen,	"	4 June 1732.
Isaac Son of Nathanael and Mary Adams,	"	15 February 1732.
Mary daughter of Benjamin and Lydia Barnard,	"	29 January 1731/2.
Sarah daughter of Edward and Abigail Bromfield,	"	20 April 1732.
Abigail daughter of John and Margaret Breck,	"	19 June 1732.
John Son of John and Mary Ann Brown,	"	14 January 1732.
Susanna daughter of John and Elizabeth Bulfinch,	"	29 June 1732.
Benjamin Son of Benjamin and Neezer Balch,	"	4 March 1732.
Deliverance daughter of Caleb and Deliverance Bean,	"	4 July 1732.
Thomas Son of Thomas and Mary Brooks,	"	17 December 1732.
Mary daughter of Belthazer and Mary Bayard,	"	3 July 1732.
Bethia daughter of John and Susanna Bruno,	"	29 August 1732.
Benjamin Son of Hezekiah and Hannah Bill,	"	20 July 1732.
Hannah daughter of Ebenezer and Mary Berry,	"	25 July 1732.
Gideon Son of Gideon and Martha Ball,	"	6 April 1732.
Jeremiah Son of Jeremiah and Hannah Bill,	"	14 September 1732.
John Son of John and Elizabeth Bennet,	"	31 May 1732.
William Son of Increase and Ann Blake,	"	14 September 1732.
Samuel Son of Joseph and Jane Burrell,	"	21 September 1732.
James Son of James and Hephzibah Bradford,	"	26 November 1732.
Alice daughter of Thomas and Susanna Bentley,	"	1 December 1732.
John Son of John and Hannah Bennet,	"	3 December 1732.
Mercy daughter of Edward and Alice Barret,	"	24 December 1732.
Joseph Son of John and Sarah Billings,	"	12 November 1732.
John Welch Son of Richard and Mary Billings,	"	15 February 1732.
Katharine daughter of William and Katharine Bulfinch,	"	27 December 1732.
John Son of John and Sarah Barret,	"	7 April 1732.
Jane daughter of Francis and Jane Borland,	"	24 April 1732.
Benjamin Son of Jonathan and Mary Bowman,	"	29 April 1732.
Elizabeth daughter of Ebenezer and Mary Bridge,	"	2 April 1732.
David Son of Richard and Hannah Barnard,	"	10 April 1732.
Thomas Son of Thomas and Abigail Ballantine,	"	13 April 1732.
Elisha Son of Philip and Mary Bass,	"	6 July 1732.
John Son of James and Abigail Bennet,	"	30 September 1732.
Joseph Son of Joseph and Ruth Bradford,	"	17 February 1732.
Persis daughter of Ebenezer and Mary Bridge,	"	18 March 1732.
Mercy daughter of Alden and Mercy Bass,	"	30 September 1732.
Elizabeth daughter of Samuel and Elizabeth Cutler,	"	13 July 1732.
Sarah daughter of Charles and Mary Coffin,	"	16 May 1732.
Sarah daughter of William and Elizabeth Cunningham,	"	18 October 1732.
William Son of William and Ann Currier,	"	23 October 1732.
Hannah daughter of Ralph and Sarah Carter,	"	31 August 1732.
Clement Son of Clement and Sarah Collins,	"	5 March 1732.
John Son of Charles and Anna Cabbot,	"	13 November 1732.
Katharine daughter of George and Mary Cradock,	"	25 October 1732.
Benjamin Son of John and Mary Crocker,	"	6 February 1732.
Mary daughter of Daniel and Mary Cheever,	"	18 September 1732.

BIRTHS — 1732.

Jonathan Son of John and Hannah Coolidge,	Born	18 February 1732.
Robert Son of Robert and Jane Cole,	"	7 November 1732.
Hannah daughter of Thomas and Hannah Clark,	"	9 February 1732.
Nathanael Son of Jacob and Abiel Chamberlain,	"	27 October 1732.
Nathanael Son of William and Deborah Corbin,	"	11 February 1732.
Abiah daughter of Elisha and Elizabeth Callender,	"	1 June 1732.
John Son of John and Hannah Coverly,	"	8 March 1732.
Mary daughter of John and Mary Cowell,	"	10 July 1732.
Abigail daughter of Philip and Mary Colter,	"	8 April 1732.
Jemima daughter of William and Sarah Cooper,	"	20 April 1732.
Rebekah daughter of James and Sarah Clark,	"	8 June 1732.
Joseph Son of Thomas and Elizabeth Cock,	"	22 March 1732.
Thomas Son of Thomas and Abigail Cannington,	"	23 June 1732.
Hannah daughter of Samuel and Hannah Collins,	"	28 June 1732.
Eunice daughter of Thomas and Eunice Delerew,	"	8 June 1732.
Cornelius Son of Edward and Judith Durant,	"	7 June 1732.
Margaret daughter of Benjamin and Margaret Dyer,	"	4 July 1732.
Eleazer Son of James and Mary Davenport,	"	21 September 1732.
John Son of William and Sarah Downe,	"	2 September 1732.
John Son of Samuel and Susanna Dolbeare,	"	24 September 1732.
Persis daughter of Moses and Persis Dishon,	"	30 September 1732.
Stephen Son of Adam and Susanna Dechezeaux,	"	6 January 1732.
Abigail daughter of Benjamin and Abigail Darling,	"	3 March 1732.
Elizabeth daughter of Elias and Mary Dupee,	"	21 April 1732.
Joseph Son of James and Hannah Dowell,	"	19 May 1732.
Keturah daughter of Samuel and Katharine Davis,	"	25 February 1732.
William Son of Thomas and Elizabeth Dawes,	"	7 March 1732.
Jemima daughter of Thomas and Jemima Debuke,	"	5 May 1732.
Joseph Son of Joseph and Mary Dyer,	"	30 March 1732.
Clark Son of John and Martha Eliot,	"	26 December 1732.
Martha daughter of John and Mary Earle,	"	2 February 1722.
Robert Son of Benjamin and Bathsheba Edwards,	"	18 November 1732.
Jacob Son of Jacob and Mary Emmons,	"	8 November 1732.
Robert Son of Thomas and Deborah Eyre,	"	25 July 1732.
Thomas Son of Thomas and Elizabeth Fleet,	"	10 April 1732.
John Son of John and Hannah Fannah,	"	9 May 1732.
Elizabeth daughter of James and Elizabeth Forder,	"	27 October 1732.
Sarah daughter of John and Sarah Ferry,	"	5 May 1732.
Thomas Son of Thomas and Auna Foxcroft,	"	31 May 1732.
Ebenezer Son of Benjamin and Sarah Floyd,	"	2 April 1732.
Mary daughter of Nathan and Margaret Foster,	"	7 August 1732.
John Son of John and Hannah Fenno,	"	4 May 1732.
Grafton Son of Grafton and Sarah Feveryear,	"	3 September 1732.
Hannah daughter of Benjamin and Elizabeth Fisher,	"	12 October 1732.
Mary daughter of Ephraim and Martha Fenno,	"	29 September 1732.
William Son of Eleazer and Mary Flagg,	"	18 July 1732.
Martha daughter of John and Martha FitzGerrald,	"	16 November 1732.
Elizabeth daughter of Thomas and Ann Foster,	"	1 October 1732.
Benjamin Son of Benjamin and Jerusha Fitch,	"	18 February 1732.
Elizabeth daughter of Samuel and Mary Greenwood,	"	21 December 1732.
Benjamin Son of Isaac and Sarah Gridley,	"	28 January 1732.
Bridget daughter of Nathanael and Rebekah Goodwin,	"	10 September 1732.
John Son of John and Mary Gibson,	"	5 May 1732.
Mary daughter of Joseph and Rebekah Gray,	"	22 March 1732.
Elizabeth daughter of Joseph and Anna Green,	"	17 July 1732.
William Son of Henry and Elizabeth Gibbons,	"	10 October 1732.
Mercy daughter of Charles and Mary Giles,	"	6 September 1732.
William Son of John and Content Gordon,	"	21 October 1732.
John Son of Charles and Ann Grant,	"	18 November 1732.
Mary daughter of Stephen and Mary Greenleaf,	"	20 November 1732.

Hannah daughter of Richard and Hannah Gridley,	Born	1 January 1732.
Edward Son of Caleb-Joseph and Mary Gray,	"	15 June 1732.
Richard Son of Richard and Elizabeth Goodwin,	"	8 May 1732.
Enoch Son of William and Mary Greenleaf,	"	9 July 1732.
Elias Son of Elias and Sarah Girott,	"	23 July 1732.
Jeremiah Son of Jeremiah and Sarah Green,	"	14 February 1732.
Nathanael Son of Samuel and Elizabeth Holland,	"	7 September 1732.
John Son of Daniel and Elizabeth Henshaw,	"	5 December 1732.
Mercy ⎱ Gem. daughters of Samuel and Mary and Lydia ⎰ Hunting,	"	2 September 1732.
Sarah daughter of William and Wilhelmina Haslip,	"	12 October 1732.
Nathanael Son of Samuel and Mary Heath.	"	4 July 1732.
Thomas Son of James and Katherine Hodges,	"	30 June 1732.
Prudence daughter of Jacob and Elizabeth Hurd,	"	11 August 1732.
Shubael Son of George and Abigail Hewes,	"	17 October 1732.
John Son of John and Elizabeth Hill,	"	27 March 1732.
Hannah daughter of Andrew and Dorcas Hall,	"	8 April 1732.
Abraham Son of Nathanael and Abigail Hill,	"	11 May 1732.
Susanna daughter of Samuel and Hannah Harris,	"	8 May 1732.
Elizabeth daughter of William and Elizabeth Hasey,	"	30 May 1732.
Sarah daughter of John and Anna Harris,	"	18 October 1732.
Thomas Son of Abraham and Hannah How,	"	27 October 1732.
Lydia daughter of Zechariah and Lydia Hicks,	"	31 October 1732.
Elizabeth daughter of James and Ann Halsey,	"	18 January 1732.
Samuel Son of Richard and Hannah Hayward,	"	14 March 1732.
Elizabeth ⎱ Gem. daughters of William and Elizabeth and Charity ⎰ beth Healy,	"	16 February 1732.
Mary daughter of Benjamin and Rebekah Hallowell,	"	15 December 1732.
William Son of William and Margaret Jepson,	"	2 January 1732.
Katharine daughter of John and Mary Jones,	"	29 July 1732.
Abigail daughter of Henry and Abigail Jeffry,	"	21 January 1732.
George Son of Robert and Elizabeth Jenkins,	"	9 August 1732.
Ann daughter of James and Ann Jeffs,	"	22 April 1732.
Hannah daughter of Jeremiah and Rebekah Jackson,	"	17 September 1732.
William Son of Thomas and Rachel Johnson,	"	30 December 1732.
Sarah daughter of Christopher and Sarah Kilby,	"	6 April 1732.
Mary daughter of James and Elizabeth Kelly,	"	30 December 1732.
William Son of Solomon and Lydia Kneeland,	"	28 May 1732.
Rebekah daughter of Joseph and Rebekah Lowden,	"	16 May 1732.
Elizabeth daughter of John and Hannah Ludgate,	"	10 August 1732.
Sarah daughter of Ebenezer and Abigail Leadbetter,	"	22 February 1732.
Benjamin Son of Joseph and Elizabeth Leasenby,	"	29 September 1732.
Sarah daughter of Byfield and Sarah Lyde,	"	23 May 1732.
John Piller Son of David and Abigail Lenox,	"	24 December 1732.
Elizabeth daughter of Nicholas and Elizabeth Lash,	"	2 October 1732.
Timothy Son of Edward and Susanna Langdon,	"	17 February 1732.
Elizabeth daughter of Robert and Mary Mines,	"	9 January 1732.
William Son of William and Deborah Mason,	"	14 July 1732.
Matthew Son of James and Margaret May,	"	9 September 1732.
Mary daughter of John and Sarah Morehead,	"	29 January 1732.
John Son of William and Elizabeth Maycock,	"	28 January 1732.
Esther daughter of James and Susanna Melling,	"	20 June 1732.
John Son of John and Jane Milk,	"	4 December 1732.
William Son of Eleazar and Mary Newhall,	"	27 March 1732.
John Son of John and Mary Norvell,	"	21 February 1732.
Ebenezer Son of Thomas and Mary Nowell,	"	6 February 1732.
William Son of Joseph and Lydia Norman,	"	19 January 1732.
William Son of William and Mary Owen,	"	27 March 1732.
Elizabeth daughter of Alexander and Elizabeth Orr,	"	21 April 1732.

BIRTHS — 1732.

Elizabeth daughter of Samuel and Dorcas Parkman,	Born	30 April 1732.
Hannah daughter of David and Hannah Powell,	"	12 May 1732.
Martha daughter of John and Martha Pulling,	"	25 March 1732.
Mehetabel daughter of William and Mehetabel Pratt,	"	6 May 1732.
Joshua Son of Joshua and Susanna Pico,	"	16 July 1732.
Ann daughter of William and Ann Perry,	"	15 July 1732.
Richard Son of Richard and Mary Paty,	"	3 August 1732.
Mary daughter of Benjamin and Margaret Procter,	"	30 August 1732.
Elizabeth daughter of Briantt and Ruth Parott,	"	10 January 1732.
Mary daughter of Richard and Hannah Peircy,	"	5 April 1732.
Abigail daughter of John and Mary Phillips,	"	29 September 1732.
Patience daughter of Henry and Walter Pigeon,	"	30 December 1732.
Samuel Son of Samuel and Rebekah Phillips,	"	22 December 1732.
Rebekah daughter of Samuel and Rebekah Pratt,	"	2 March 1732.
Samuel Son of Nathanael and Abigail Pearse,	"	19 February 1732.
Elizabeth daughter of Caleb and Elizabeth Phillips,	"	23 June 1732.
Jemima daughter of Samuel and Rebekah Paine,	"	18 March 1732.
John Son of William and Ann Phillips,	"	10 March 1732.
Thomas Son of Joseph and Mary Roby,	"	6 April 1732.
Mary daughter of Edward and Elizabeth Rumley,	"	28 May 1732.
Abraham Son of Benjamin and Elizabeth Russell,	"	19 June 1732.
Elizabeth daughter of Skinner and Elizabeth Russell,	"	10 September 1732.
Joseph Son of Thomas and Elizabeth Russell,	"	2 October 1732.
James Son of James and Sarah Raimer,	"	2 February 1732.
Elizabeth daughter of Stephen and Sarah Randall,	"	7 January 1732.
Elias Son of Elias and Mary Robinson,	"	4 March 1732.
Mary daughter of Samuel and Naomi Ridgaway,	"	1 March 1732.
Joseph Son of Joseph and Susanna Shead,	"	17 June 1732.
Ann daughter of William and Ann Scott,	"	3 June 1732.
Sarah daughter of James and Elizabeth Scutt,	"	20 July 1732.
Robert Son of Benjamin and Ann Sanders,	"	15 July 1732.
Sarah daughter of Thomas and Tabitha Stoddard,	"	19 August 1732.
Mary Ann daughter of Andrew and Mary Sigourney,	"	14 August 1732.
John Son of John and Elizabeth Spooner,	"	1 September 1732.
Philippe daughter of Josiah and Philippe Snelling,	"	10 October 1732.
Samuel Son of Samuel and Mary Smith,	"	17 July 1732.
Ann daughter of George and Mary Sharrow,	"	1 January 1732.
Lindal Son of William and Sarah Stoddard,	"	22 November 1732.
Joanna daughter of William and Elizabeth Simpkins,	"	24 December 1732.
John Son of Joseph and Elizabeth Snelling,	"	24 December 1732.
Mary daughter of John and Olive Sturges,	"	14 January 1732.
Isaac Son of Nathanael and Sarah Story,	"	21 January 1732.
Rebekah daughter of Hugh and Rebekah Scott,	"	27 January 1732.
Hannah daughter of Alexander and Hannah Sears,	"	22 February 1732.
Rachel daughter of John and Rachel Sowersby,	"	18 March 1732.
Katharine daughter of Joseph and Mehetabel Scott,	"	15 April 1732.
William Son of John and Mary Smibert,	"	29 January 1732.
Benjamin Son of Benjamin and Elizabeth Snelling,	"	10 April 1732.
Hannah daughter of John and Sarah Sweetser,	"	15 May 1732.
Benjamin Son of Luke and Margaret Stone,	"	4 June 1732.
Eddy daughter of Benjamin and Elizabeth Seward,	"	31 May 1732.
Elisha Son of Elisha and Martha Townsend,	"	12 August 1732.
Benjamin Son of Benjamin and Hannah Thompson,	"	18 July 1732.
James Son of Jonathan and Mary Tarbox,	"	29 May 1732.
David Son of Samuel and Abigail Torrey,	"	7 September 1732.
John Son of Moses and Hannah Tyler,	"	12 November 1732.
Martha daughter of George and Elizabeth Tilley,	"	18 September 1732.
John Son of John and Jane Tudor,	"	21 March 1732.
Sarah daughter of Samuel and Elliphall Tyley,	"	8 November 1732.
Mary daughter of Ebenezer and Mary Torrey,	"	8 April 1732.

Rebekah daughter of John and Rebekah Tilestone, Born 16 April 1732.
Joseph Son of Daniel and Hannah Tucker, " 10 November 1732.
Gilbert Son of Ebenezer and Elizabeth Thornton, " 23 May 1732.
Murford Son of Cornelius and Sarah Thompson, " 28 January 1732.
Lydia daughter of Alexander and Elizabeth Thorp, " 9 January 1732.
Sarah daughter of John and Susanna Tinkum, " 5 December 1732.
Esther daughter of William and Bethiah Torrey, " 16 January 1732.
James Son of John and Elizabeth Ventinon, " 24 May 1732.
Mary daughter of Hugh and Mary Vans, " 21 December 1732.
Elizabeth daughter of Isaac and Elizabeth Vergoose, " 12 February 1732.
John Son of Philip and Dorcas Viscount, " 18 February 1732.
Bellingham Son of Samuel and Hannah Watts, " 30 August 1732.
Thomas Son of Gamaliel and Abigail Wallis, " 10 September 1732.
Joseph Son of Joseph and Priscilla Wakefield, " 13 October 1732.
Mary daughter of Joshua and Elizabeth Winslow, " 23 June 1732.
Sarah daughter of Seward and Sarah Walter, " 30 November 1732.
Kezia daughter of John and Mary West, " 3 February 1732.
Abigail daughter of Francis and Eliza: Whitman, " 4 March 1732.
Ruth daughter of Benjamin and Ruth Wheeler, " 27 March 1732.
Oliver Son of Jacob and Sarah Wendell, " 5 March 1732.
Samuel Son of Timothy and Margaret Winship, " 3 May 1732.
Daniel Son of Samuel and Mary Waterhouse, " 3 March 1732.
Daniel Son of John and Elizabeth Whitney, " 22 July 1732.
Hannah daughter of William and Hannah Young, " 17 March 1732.
Abigail daughter of William Beartell and Elizabeth his Wife " 15 April 1732.
Joseph Son of John Carnes and Sarah his Wife, " 19 November 1732.
Hannah daughter of Ralph Carter and Sarah his Wife, " 31 August 1732.
John Son of John Fenno and Hannah his Wife, " 4 May 1732.
John Son of John Gardner and Mary his Wife, " 9 June 1732.
Sarah daughter of Nathaniel Shepard and Mary his Wife, " 30 January 1732.
William Son of Samuel Torrey and Silence his Wife, " 22 October 1732.

1733.

Margaret daughter of John and Mary Adams. Born 13 April 1733.
Philip Son of Nathanael and Elisabeth Adams, " 21 February 1733.
John Son of Edward and Hannah Ayers, " 12 April 1733.
Timothy Son of Joshua and Elisabeth Atwood, " 21 February 1733.
Stephen Son of Stephen and Elisabeth Avery, " 7 September 1733.
Mary daughter of Zechariah and Lydia Alden, " 6 July 1733.
Sarah daughter of Samuel and Mary Adams, " 18 November 1733.
Sarah daughter of James and Bathsheba Allen. " 7 June 1733.
Sarah daughter of Henry and Deliverance Atkins, " 3 December 1733.
Joseph Son of Nathanael and Mary Adams. " 6 February 1733.
Ann daughter of Benjamin and Ann Babbidge, " 11 November 1733.
Thomas Son of John and Jerusha Baker, " 19 August 1733.
Mary daughter of Benjamin and Mary Brown. " 22 November 1733.
Daniel Son of John and Rebekah Barret, " 25 October 1733.
Sarah daughter of Samuel and Sarah Barber, " 3 December 1733.
John Son of John and Margaret Breck. " 2 February 1733.
Thomas Son of Edward and Abigail Bromfield, " 30 October 1733.
George Son of Francis and Hannah Butler, " 14 January 1733.
Rebekah daughter of Henry and Rachel Baler, " 29 December 1733.
Hannah daughter of Ebenezer and Mary Berry, " 19 March 1733.
Richard Son of Joshua and Sarah Blanchard, " 3 December 1733.
Benjamin Son of Benjamin and Lydia Barnard, " 21 February 1733.
Mary daughter of William and Ann Beer, " 25 January 1733.

BIRTHS — 1733.

Ann daughter of Jonathan and Ann Barnard,	Born	1 September 1733.
William Son of William and Susanna Butler,	"	29 January 1733.
John Son of Robert and Isabella Breck,	"	26 May 1733.
John Son of John and Sarah Bradford,	"	19 May 1733.
John Son of Thomas and Mary Baker,	"	1 June 1733.
William Son of John and Susanna Brown,	"	26 June 1733.
Martha daughter of Benjamin and Martha Bunker,	"	21 September 1733.
Lydia daughter of John and Susanna Blake,	"	10 August 1733.
Sarah daughter of John and Sarah Beacham,	"	29 May 1733.
Mary daughter of Amos and Elizabeth Breed,	"	29 September 1733.
Elizabeth ⎱ Gem. daughters of Samuel and Mary and Mary ⎰ Butler,	"	30 October 1733.
Jerusha daughter of Pyam and Jerusha Blowers,	"	25 July 1733.
Daniel Son of Daniel and Mary Ballard,	"	14 August 1733.
Richard Son of Richard and Mary Buckley,	"	17 October 1733.
Hope daughter of Benjamin and Ruth Borden,	"	14 July 1733.
Abigail daughter of Zephaniah and Mary Basset,	"	2 February 1733.
Hannah daughter of Increase and Ann Blake,	"	9 September 1733.
Eleazer Son of John and Rebekah Compton,	"	7 November 1733.
Rebekah daughter of Gayer and Rebekah Coffin,	"	10 December 1733.
Elizabeth daughter of Samuel and Elizabeth Cravath,	"	8 January 1733.
John Son of John and Ann Chambers,	"	4 February 1733.
William Son of Jonathan and Hannah Chandler,	"	5 March 1733.
Thomas Son of Benjamin and Miriam Clark,	"	24 February 1733.
Abigail daughter of John and Abigail Collson,	"	25 March 1733.
Joseph Son of James and Alice Cox,	"	29 March 1733.
Martha daughter of Nathanael and Martha Cobbit,	"	8 May 1733.
John Son of Joseph and Margaret Clark,	"	1 May 1733.
Hannah daughter of Richard and Elizabeth Clarke,	"	27 February 1733.
Sarah daughter of Isaac and Patience Clark,	"	25 May 1733.
Sarah daughter of John and Sarah Comrin,	"	22 March 1733.
Margaret daughter of Isaac and Hannah Casno,	"	30 May 1733.
Sarah daughter of Charles and Elizabeth Chauncy,	"	22 September 1733.
Joshua Son of Samuel and Elizabeth Checkley,	"	1 July 1733.
James Son of David and Sarah Christie,	"	11 January 1733.
Mary daughter of Alexander and Mary Chamberlain,	"	14 August 1733.
Mary daughter of Henry and Elizabeth Coulton,	"	3 January 1733.
Katharine daughter of Charles and Mary Coffin,	"	3 September 1733.
Jeremiah Son of Benjamin and Elizabeth Cushing	"	24 September 1733.
James Son of James and Hannah Cox,	"	18 September 1733.
Lydia daughter of Joseph and Lydia Carter,	"	26 October 1733.
Mary daughter of William and Martha Dowrick,	"	23 May 1733.
Abigail daughter of Eleazer and Mary Dorby,	"	5 May 1733.
Sarah daughter of James and Mary Dolbeare,	"	13 August 1733.
Elizabeth daughter of Thomas and Elizabeth Davee,	"	23 September 1733.
John Son of John and Abigail Doble,	"	23 September 1733.
Walter Son of Elias and Mary Dupee,	"	26 September 1733.
Abigail daughter of John and Abigail Davenport,	"	20 February 1733.
Roger Son of Roger and Ammi Dench,	"	25 October 1733.
Thomas Son of John and Hannah Diamond,	"	2 April 1733.
Moses Son of Moses and Persis Dishon,	"	8 November 1733.
Jeremiah Son of James and Mary Day,	"	10 May 1733.
Sarah daughter of James and Susanna Dix,	"	10 November 1733.
Thomas Son of Thomas and Eunice Dilarew,	"	22 February 1733.
Nathanael Son of Jonathan and Mary Dwight	"	30 December 1733.
Abigail daughter of James and Mary Dawson,	"	10 March 1733.
Lucy daughter of James and Mary Davenport,	"	17 November 1733.
Elizabeth daughter of William and Lydia Doke,	"	1 February 1733.
Benjamin Son of Benjamin and Elizabeth Egglestone,	"	30 October 1733.

Abigail daughter of John and Abigail Erving,	Born	17 September 1733.
Abigail daughter of Thomas and Abigail Eustus,	"	16 September 1733.
Martha daughter of Edward and Sarah Edes,	"	17 July 1733.
Sarah daughter of Edward and Mary Ellis,	"	22 August 1733.
Benjamin Son of Benjamin and Mary Emmons,	"	15 May 1733.
Alexander Son of Benjamin and Bathsheba Edwards,	"	18 December 1733.
Mary daughter of Brice and Mary Eccles,	"	3 August 1733.
John Son of Joseph and Margaret Fitch,	"	2 October 1733.
Sarah daughter of William and Elizabeth Fairfield,	"	25 July 1733.
Nicholas Son of Nicholas and Hephzibah Fessenden,	"	28 October 1733.
Abigail daughter of Nathan and Margaret Foster,	"	17 March 1733.
Thomas Son of James and Hannah Fosdick,	"	29 May 1733.
Sarah daughter of Eleazer and Mary Flagg,	"	18 July 1733.
John Son of Jonathan and Elizabeth Farnis,	"	3 September 1733.
Samuel Son of William and Margaret Fletcher,	"	7 March 1733.
John Son of William and Mary Fullerton,	"	4 March 1733.
Richard Son of Samuel and Abigail Green,	"	23 April 1733.
John Son of John and Mary Gatchell,	"	28 April 1733.
Elizabeth daughter of Jacob and Mary Green,	"	13 June 1733.
Joseph Son of John and Sarah Greenough,	"	3 May 1733.
Mary daughter of James and Elizabeth Gerreck,	"	14 July 1733.
Sarah daughter of Daniel and Elizabeth Goffe,	"	1733.
Joseph Son of Bartholomew and Sarah Gedney,	"	8 March 1733.
Ann daughter of John and Elizabeth George,	"	10 March 1733.
Phillip Son of Joseph and Martha Goldthwait,	"	27 March 1733.
Nathanael Son of Nathanael and Elizabeth Green,	"	16 August 1733.
Rufus Son of Rufus and Katharine Green,	"	23 August 1733.
Thomas Son of Bickford and Judith Greenleaf,	"	10 September 1733.
William Son of Newman and Elizabeth Greenough,	"	10 March 1733.
John Son of William and Ruth Greenleaf,	"	17 March 1733.
Edward Son of Joseph and Anna Green,	"	18 September 1733.
Ezekiel Son of Ezekiel and Elizabeth Goldthwait,	"	10 January 1733.
Nathanael Son of Ames and Judith Howard,	"	17 June 1733.
Katharine daughter of Peter and Katharine Harratt,	"	27 June 1733.
Abigail daughter of Israel and Abigail Hearsey,	"	27 November 1733.
Mary daughter of John and Mary Henshaw,	"	9 May 1733.
Esther daughter of James and Esther Hill,	"	3 March 1733.
Joseph Son of Joseph and Ann Hudson,	"	18 August 1733.
Elizabeth daughter of Samuel and Elizabeth Henshaw,	"	18 February 1733.
Deborah daughter of Samuel and Deborah Hewes,	"	25 March 1733.
Prudence daughter of Jacob and Elizabeth Hurd,	"	25 August 1733.
Abigail daughter of Samuel and Elizabeth Hood,	"	24 February 1733.
Joseph Son of Stephen and Elizabeth Honiwell,	"	30 September 1733.
Elizabeth daughter of Samuel and Elizabeth Haley,	"	24 April 1733.
Elizabeth daughter of Thomas and Hannah Hill,	"	10 April 1733.
Elizabeth daughter of Joseph and Sarah Henderson,	"	22 April 1733.
Sarah daughter of Abraham and Sarah Harris,	"	20 April 1733.
Elizabeth daughter of Daniel and Elizabeth Henshaw,	"	22 December 1733.
John Son of John and Herris Halden,	"	4 December 1733.
Robert Son of Robert and Sarah Harris,	"	19 February 1733.
Nathanael Son of Nathanael and Abigail Hill,	"	7 December 1733.
Thomas Son of Thomas and Mary Hubbard,	"	6 October 1733.
Susanna daughter of Samuel and Susanna Hill,	"	31 October 1733.
Edward Son of Jacob and Susanna Holyoke,	"	21 December 1733.
Mary daughter of Nathanael and Ann Hodgdon,	"	19 November 1733.
Sage daughter of John and Sarah Hyer,	"	30 January 1733.
Mehetabel daughter of John and Mary Hill,	"	2 February 1733.

Births — 1733.

William Son of Benjamin and Sarah Jepson,	Born	12 April 1733.
Samuel Son of Samuel and Ruth Jackson,	"	14 June 1733.
Sarah daughter of Joseph and Susanna Jackson,	"	5 January 1733.
Solomon Son of Solomon and Ann Jennings,	"	6 June 1733.
Sarah daughter of James and Ann Jeffs,	"	28 December 1733.
Sarah daughter of Philip and Elizabeth Jones,	"	31 December 1733.
Sarah daughter of Joseph and Mary Kneeland,	"	5 March 1733.
Israel Son of Israel and Mehetabel Look,	"	4 November 1733.
Sarah daughter of John and Ruth Leech,	"	29 September 1733.
Thomas Son of Joseph and Elizabeth Leasenby,	"	19 February 1733.
Mary daughter of John and Abigail Low,	"	11 August 1733.
Lydia daughter of Phillip and Lydia Lewis,	"	16 May 1733.
Ephraim Son of Josiah and Elizabeth Langdon,	"	7 August 1733.
William Son of John and Mercy Late,	"	25 March 1733.
Hickman Son of John and Sarah Lambert,	"	11 November 1733.
Margaret daughter of John and Margaret Le Cras,	"	9 November 1733.
Mary daughter of Isaac and Mary Loring,	"	3 September 1733.
Sampson Son of Sampson and Mary Mason,	"	4 November 1733.
Rachel daughter of John and Ann Maylem,	"	1 January 1733.
Elizabeth daughter of Edward and Elizabeth Masters,	"	4 January 1733.
Katharine daughter of William and Katharine Melling,	"	5 January 1733.
Thomas Son of Thomas and Mary Maccollo,	"	13 January 1733.
Samuel Son of John and Elizabeth McLean,	- "	7 August 1733.
Elizabeth daughter of Lewis and Abigail Nations,	"	28 June 1733.
John Son of George and Sarah Norton,	"	1 November 1733.
Hannah daughter of William and Mary Owen,	"	29 March 1733.
William Son of William and Mary Owen,	"	29 March 1733.
Jane daughter of Thomas and Bethiah Phillips,	"	25 September 1733.
Edward Son of John and Hannah Procter,	"	28 August 1733.
Eunice daughter of Thomas and Eunice Paine,	"	30 April 1733.
Samuel Son of Samuel and Dorcas Parkman,	"	23 December 1733.
Elisha Cooke Son of John and Sarah Phillips,	"	21 September 1733.
Joshua Son of Joshua and Susanna Pico,	"	25 December 1733.
Abigail daughter of John and Mary Phillips,	"	14 February 1733.
Mary daughter of Isaac and Agnes Peirce,	"	7 January 1733.
John Son of Samuel and Rebekah Phillips,	"	20 February 1733.
James Son of Joseph and Mary Prince,	"	28 January 1733.
Frances daughter of Eliphalet and Frances Parker,	"	27 August 1733.
Katharine daughter of Edmund and Elizabeth Quincy,	"	30 May 1733.
Thomazin daughter of Simon and Thomazin Rogers,	"	6 September 1733.
Mary daughter of Samuel and Hannah Russell,	"	2 May 1733.
Esther daughter of Benjamin and Priscilla Roberts,	"	18 November 1733.
George Son of Edward and Elizabeth Rumley,	"	24 February 1733.
Mary daughter of Joseph and Mary Roby,	"	7 October 1733.
John Son of Gamaliel and Sarah Rogers,	"	11 January 1733.
Hannah daughter of Andrew and Hannah Symmes,	"	15 June 1733.
Nathanael Son of Nathan and Mary Sargent,	"	31 March 1733.
Peter Son of Moses and Mary Shelly,	"	22 July 1733.
Jabez Son of John and Abigail Salter,	"	23 April 1733.
John Son of Joseph and Mehetabel Scott,	"	7 August 1733.
Ebenezer Son of Ebenezer and Elizabeth Sumner,	"	25 March 1733.
Elizabeth daughter of Arthur and Mercy Stoddard,	"	25 September 1733.
Betty daughter of Henry and Alice Stokes,	"	5 December 1733.
Sarah daughter of John and Elizabeth Scottow,	"	2 January 1733.
Susanna daughter of George and Susanna Sinckler,	"	16 January 1733.
Elizabeth daughter of Benjamin and Hannah Simpson,	"	28 January 1733.
Mary daughter of John and Mary Simpson,	"	12 May 1733.

Lydia daughter of William and Elizabeth Snoden,	Born	16 August 1733.
James Lindal Son of William and Sarah Stoddard.	"	12 November 1733.
John Son of John and Mary Smibert,	"	24 November 1733.
Mary daughter of John and Sarah Sweetser,	"	10 March 1733.
Andrew Son of Andrew and Mary Sigourney,	"	14 February 1733.
Samuel Son of Jonathan and Mary Tarbox,	"	10 March 1733.
James Son of William and Mary Trout,	"	18 March 1733.
Susanna daughter of John and Susanna Tinkum,	"	26 January 1733.
John Son of Morgan and Sarah Thomas,	"	16 April 1733.
James Son of Joshua and Elizabeth Townsend,	"	12 August 1733.
Frances daughter of John and Mary Tyng,	"	19 July 1733.
John Son of John and Mary	"	1 August 1733.
Sarah daughter of Samuel and Abigail Torrey,	"	2 October 1733.
George Son of George and Elizabeth Tilly,	"	7 November 1733.
Joseph Son of Richard and Abigail Trew,	"	5 October 1733.
James Son of Nathanael and Joanna Thwing,	"	15 April 1733.
Ann daughter of Edward and Ann Tyng,	"	22 October 1733.
Thomas Son of William and Mary Trout,	"	15 April 1733.
Davis Son of Davis and Sarah Townsend,	"	26 October 1733.
William Son of Giles and Margaret Tidmarsh,	"	30 May 1733.
Sarah daughter of John and Hannah Teach,	"	28 December 1733.
Sarah daughter of Edward and Elizabeth Tothill,	"	7 January 1733.
Sarah daughter of James and Elizabeth Watts,	"	13 July 1733.
Mary daughter of Owen and Mary Williams,	"	25 July 1733.
Alice daughter of David and Alice Whittemore,	"	25 July 1733.
Mary daughter of John and Hannah Waldo,	"	11 September 1733.
Hannah daughter of James and Elizabeth Willis,	"	18 October 1733.
Lydia daughter of Joseph and Abigail Webb,	"	30 March 1733.
Samuel Son of Samuel and Deborah Webb,	"	21 November 1733.
Eunice daughter of Richard and Eunice Walker,	"	16 November 1733.
John Son of Thomas and Dorothy Wharton,	"	22 November 1733.
Mehetabel daughter of Sendell and Mehetabel Williams.	"	16 January 1733.
Jonathan Son of William and Mary Warner,	"	21 April 1733.
Alice daughter of Samuel and Mary Wheeler,	"	16 April 1733.
Sarah daughter of Thomas and Jane Williston,	"	8 May 1733.
Abigail daughter of Joseph and Martha Wheeler,	"	13 February 1733.
Rebekah daughter of Benjamin and Abigail Wolcut,	"	21 April 1733.
Ebenezer Son of Ebenezer and Susanna Welch,	"	16 April 1733.
Samuel Son of Joshua and Ann Williams,	"	4 June 1733.
Joseph Son of Isaac and Sarah Walker,	"	18 June 1733.
Benedict Son of William and Rebekah Webber,	"	24 June 1733.
Mary daughter of Nathanael and Hannah Warner,	"	5 July 1733.
John Son of James and Rebekah Wimble,	"	15 July 1733.
Sarah daughter of John and Lydia Wise,	"	3 January 1733.
Ann daughter of Thomas and Ann White,	"	10 January 1733.
Sarah daughter of John and Elizabeth Whitney,	"	7 January 1733.
Mary daughter of Joseph and Ruth Whittemore,	"	6 February 1733.
Timothy Son of Elias and Rhoda Whittemore,	"	14 March 1733.
Sarah daughter of Amos and Mary Wood.	"	18 November 1733.
Dorothy daughter of John and Elizabeth Wendell,	"	19 March 1733.
Sarah daughter of Francis and Elizabeth Whitman,	"	28 February 1733.
Katharine daughter of Joshua and Elizabeth Winslow,	"	8 September 1733.
Elizabeth daughter of Samuel and Elizabeth Wentworth,	"	26 September 1733
Thomas Son of Thomas and Mary Walker,	"	8 March 1733.
Henry Son of Henry and Mary Williams,	"	14 March 1733.
Sarah daughter of Samuel and Sarah Warden,	"	15 February 1733.

BIRTHS — 1733-34.

Ann Langdon daughter of Abraham and Amiable York,	Born	9 July 1733.
Richard Son of James and Jane Young,	"	3 June 1733.
Peter Son of William Blin and Elizabeth his Wife,	"	30 October 1733.
John Son of Cord Cordis and Sarah his Wife,	"	28 December 1733.
Mary daughter of Joseph Drinker and Sarah his Wife	"	12 September 1733.
Martha daughter of James Gooch and Hester his Wife	"	27 February 1733.

These two births happened before 1734:
Mary daughter of John and Abigail Hawkins	"	
Anna daughter of Amos and Elizabeth Breed	"	

1734.

Robert Son of Edward and Margaret Allen,	Born	7 April 1734.
Nathanael Son of Nathanael and Elisabeth Ayres,	"	31 August 1734.
John Son of Jeremiah and Rebekah Allen,	"	12 November 1734.
William Son of Philip and Lydia Audebert,	"	13 May 1734.
Benjamin Son of John and Mary Adams,	"	11 January 1734.
Elizabeth daughter of Jonathan and Eliza. Brown	"	21 May 1734.
Sarah daughter of John and Sarah Barret,	"	18 May 1734.
Hannah daughter of Francis and Hannah Butler,	"	17 February 1734.
Jonathan Son of John and Elizabeth Bouve,	"	15 September 1734.
Samuel Son of Richard and Hannah Barnard,	"	July 1734.
William Son of Phillip and Mary Bass,	"	31 May 1734.
Jeremiah Son of John and Elizabeth Bulfinch,	"	4 May 1734.
Robert Son of Robert and Isabella Breck,	"	27 February 1734.
Rachel daughter of Phillip and Elizabeth Bennet,	"	29 April 1734.
John Son of Thomas and Ruth Bill,	"	27 March 1734.
Sarah daughter of John and Katharine Beny,	"	6 July 1734.
Richard Son of John and Sarah Billings,	"	15 July 1734.
Samuel Son of Ebenezer and Mary Bridge,	"	19 June 1734.
Elizabeth daughter of Joseph and Ruth Bradford,	"	14 August 1734.
Elizabeth daughter of Daniel and Abigail Bell,	"	11 August 1734.
James Son of James and Abigail Bennet,	"	18 August 1734.
Elizabeth daughter of Aaron and Bethesda Bordman,	"	16 September 1734.
Susanna daughter of Increase and Ann Blake,	"	14 October 1734.
Elizabeth daughter of Pyam and Jerusha Blowers,	"	30 October 1734.
Beulah daughter of Nathanael and Rebekah Belknap,	"	25 July 1734.
John Son of Anthony and Elizabeth Burrillion,	"	17 December 1734.
Charles Son of Thomas and Mary Brooks,	"	11 June 1734.
Sarah daughter of Josias and Sarah Byles,	"	17 June 1734.
Rebekah daughter of Alden and Mercy Bass,	"	18 April 1734.
Abigail daughter of John and Sarah Bradford,	"	22 June 1734.
Mary daughter of George and Mary Beard,	"	28 June 1734.
Abigail daughter of Daniel and Mary Ballard,	"	17 January 1734.
Caleb Son of Thomas and Susanna Bentley,	"	21 January 1734.
Miriam daughter of Daniel and Miriam Bell,	"	29 January 1734.
Mary daughter of Richard and Mary Billings,	"	4 March 1734.
Elizabeth daughter of John and Mary Ann Brown,	"	10 December 1734.
Richard Son of Richard and Mary Buckley,	"	27 January 1734.
Mather Son of Mather and Anna Byles,	"	12 January 1734.
Desire daughter of John and Susanna Bruno,	"	23 March 1734.
Hannah daughter of John and Hannah Bennet,	"	12 March 1734.
Foster, Son of Edward and Abigail Croff,	"	29 May 1734.
Mary daughter of John and and Mary Crocker,	"	4 June 1734.
Elizabeth daughter of James and Sarah Clark,	"	13 May 1734.
David Son of John and Abigail Collson,	"	2 June 1734.
Owen Son of Daniel and Sarah Coney,	"	14 July 1734.

Charles Son of Charles and Anna Cabbot,	Born	28 August 1734.
Sarah daughter of William and Sarah Clark,	"	20 August 1734.
Mary daughter of John and Hannah Coolidge,	"	13 November 1734.
Mary daughter of Elisha and Elizabeth Callender,	"	14 July 1734.
Mercy daughter of Alexander and Mary Chamberlain,	"	8 December 1734.
Frances daughter of John and Rebekah Compton,	"	23 December 1734.
Sarah daughter of Cord and Sarah Cordis,	"	29 December 1734.
Sarah daughter of Thomas and Hannah Clark,	"	21 January 1734.
Ann daughter of John and Margaret Clark,	"	24 February 1734.
Ann daughter of Samuel and Elizabeth Checkley,	"	14 March 1734.
Elizabeth daughter of Robert and Eleanor Cuming,	"	22 September 1734.
William Son of Richard and Elizabeth Clarke,	"	21 February 1734.
Rebekah daughter of Clement and Sarah Collins,	"	25 September 1734.
Anna daughter of Henry and Elizabeth Coulton,	"	28 September 1734.
Abiel Son of Jacob and Abiel Chamberlain,	"	7 October 1734.
Jeremiah Son of Jeremiah and Ann Cushing,	"	17 April 1734.
Lydia daughter of David and Lydia Cutler,	"	8 May 1734.
Thomas Son of John and Zibiah Cravath,	"	27 May 1734.
Thomas Son of Nathanael and Martha Cobbit,	"	9 October 1734.
Samuel Son of Samuel and Hannah Collens,	"	15 April 1734.
Katharine daughter of James and Katharine Davis,	"	3 August 1734.
Joseph Son of John and Elizabeth Dring,	"	27 April 1734.
David Son of James and Mary Day,	"	21 August 1734.
Grace daughter of Elias and Mary Dupee,	"	19 August 1734.
Joseph Son of Joseph and Mary Dyar,	"	10 September 1734.
Charles Son of Charles and Mary Dupee,	"	18 October 1734.
Sarah daughter of William and Sarah Downe,	"	10 September 1734.
Joseph Son of Brice and Mary Eccles,	"	16 November 1734.
John Son of John and Sarah Ewell,	"	19 July 1734.
Sarah daughter of David and Mary Evans,	"	10 May 1734.
Sarah daughter of Jacob and Mary Emmons,	"	26 September 1734.
William son of John and Abigail Erving,	"	8 September 1734.
Sarah daughter of Thomas and Deborah Eyre,	"	18 April 1734.
Mary daughter of John and Mary Earle,	"	27 November 1734.
John Son of Benjamin and Bathsheba Edwards,	"	4 January 1734.
Nathanael Son of James and Hannah Fosdick,	"	26 November 1734.
Prudence daughter of Joseph and Margaret Fitch,	"	5 March 1734.
John Son of Benjamin and Elizabeth Fisher,	"	24 February 1734.
Elizabeth } Samuel } Gem. of William and Mary Fullerton,	"	24 March 1734.
Mary daughter of Seth and Susanna Foster,	"	18 October 1734.
John Son of Andrew and Sarah Friswell,	"	29 April 1734.
Jerusha daughter of Benjamin and Jerusha Fitch,	"	13 April 1734.
Joseph Son of Ephraim and Martha Fenno,	"	18 May 1734.
Ephraim Son of John and Hannah Fenno,	"	15 June 1734.
Benjamin Son of Benjamin and Mary Frothingham,	"	6 April 1734.
Sarah daughter of Grafton and Sarah Feveryeare,	"	14 August 1734.
John Son of Thomas and Elizabeth Fleet,	"	9 September 1734.
Katharine daughter of Thomas and Anna Foxcroft,	"	21 July 1734.
Daniel Son of Daniel and Hannah Frazer,	"	24 September 1734.
Jonathan Son of David and Elizabeth Frankline,	"	24 October 1734.
Robert Son of Thomas and Anna Greene,	"	25 March 1734.
Grace daughter of Stephen and Eunice Greenleaf,	"	11 April 1734.
Elizabeth daughter of Henry and Elizabeth Gibbon,	"	10 April 1734.
Mary daughter of Thomas and Elizabeth Green,	"	1 May 1734.
Rebekah daughter of John and Mary Getchell,	"	10 February 1734.
Samuel Son of Joseph and Rebekah Gray,	"	30 January 1734.
James Son of Samuel and Abigail Green,	"	3 March 1734.
William Son of Samuel and Elizabeth Grant,	"	23 September 1734.

Births — 1734.

Mary daughter of Rufus and Katharine Green,	Born	27 February 1734.
Nathanael Son of Nathanael and Rebekah Goodwin,	"	28 July 1734.
Rebekah daughter of Thomas and Rebekah Goodwin,	"	25 August 1734.
Mary daughter of Daniel and Elizabeth Goffe	"	5 October 1734.
Sarah daughter of Elias and Sarah Girot,	"	24 May 1734.
Joseph Son of John and Ruth Gridley,	"	8 June 1734.
Samuel Son of Richard and Hannah Gridley,	"	14 June 1734.
George Son of Joseph and Katharine Giddinge,	"	17 June 1734.
Richard Son of John and Sarah Greenough,	"	24 June 1734.
Abigail daughter of Jeremiah and Abigail Gridley,	"	8 August 1734.
Elizabeth daughter of John and Martha Gibbs,	"	16 August 1734.
William Son of Jacob and Susanna Griggs,	"	4 September 1734.
George Son of Richard and Maria (Negro) George,	"	1 May 1734.
Isaac Son of Isaac and Sarah Gridley,	"	27 June 1734.
Elizabeth daughter of Joseph and Anna Green,	"	12 October 1734.
Mary daughter of Joseph and Elizabeth Gooch,	"	30 September 1734.
Edward Son of Bartholomew and Sarah Gedney,	"	8 February 1734.
Elizabeth daughter of Nathanael and Elizabeth Green,	"	25 December 1734.
Elizabeth daughter of Nathanael and Elizabeth Greenwood,	"	18 November 1734.
James Gold Son of Stephen and Mary Greenleaf,	"	1 January 1734.
Solomon Son of George and Abigail Hewes,	"	4 December 1734.
John Son of John and Anna Harris,	"	4 January 1734.
Katharine daughter of Peter and Katharine Harratt,	"	7 January 1734.
Hannah daughter of Samuel and Elizabeth Haley,	"	13 March 1734.
Elizabeth daughter of Samuel and Mary Heath,	"	25 February 1734.
James Son of Israel and Abigail Hearsey,	"	12 March 1734.
Katharine daughter of Benjamin and Mary Hammatt,	"	3 March 1734.
Ann daughter of Joseph and Ann Hudson,	"	4 February 1734.
William Son of Samuel and Mary Hunting,	"	18 March 1734.
Hannah daughter of Thomas and Hannah Hill,	"	16 February 1734.
Sarah daughter of Samuel and Eleanor Hilton,	"	6 June 1734.
Sarah daughter of Jabez and Mary Hatch,	"	21 June 1734.
Jennet daughter of James and Katharine Hodges,	"	23 June 1734.
Elizabeth daughter of William and Wilhelmina Haslip,	"	25 July 1734.
Ann daughter of John and Kezia Harvey,	"	31 August 1734.
Elizabeth daughter of John and Elizabeth Haslet,	"	9 November 1734.
Sarah daughter of Samuel and Elizabeth Holland,	"	29 November 1734.
Joseph Son of John and Mary Jones,	"	26 April 1734.
Thomas Son of Nathaniel and Abigail Jarvis,	"	5 May 1734.
John Son of John and Margaret Jenkins,	"	27 May 1734.
Margaret daughter of Zechariah and Eliza. Johonnot,	"	18 July 1734.
Thomas Son of Thomas and Ann Jackson,	"	30 July 1734.
Henry Son of Peter and Mary Jersey,	"	20 November 1734.
Joseph Son of Joseph and Susanna Jackson,	"	22 December 1734.
Benjamin Son of William and Margaret Jepson,	"	30 December 1734.
John Son of Ebenezer and Bathsheba Kilby,	"	17 September 1734.
William Son of William and Ann Kier,	"	18 December 1734.
Asa Son of Ebenezer and Hannah Kendal,	"	16 March 1734.
Elizabeth daughter of James and Elizabeth Kelley,	"	22 February 1734.
Thomas Son of John and Margarett Keeffe,	"	17 March 1734.
John Son of Richard and Sarah Kent,	"	26 March 1734.
John Son of Ebenezer and Mary Lowell,	"	1 April 1734.
Mary daughter of David and Abigail Lenox,	"	10 January 1734.
Martha daughter of Phillip and Lydia Lewis,	"	21 July 1734.

Sarah daughter of Nicholas and Elizabeth Lash,	Born	24 January 1734.
Elizabeth daughter of Byfield and Sarah Lyde,	"	6 May 1734.
David Son of John and Miriam Lawson	"	8 June 1734.
John } Jacob } Gem. of Isaac and Mary Lewis,	"	6 October 1734.
Thomas Son of Thomas and Mary Lee,	"	9 December 1734.
James Son of Alexander and Mary Marten,	"	14 April 1734.
Rachel daughter of William and Deborah Mason,	"	9 June 1734.
Susanna daughter of David and Susanna Mason,	"	22 June 1734.
Mary daughter of Joseph and Sarah Mather,	"	28 July 1734.
Nicholas Son of Nicholas and Susanna Morris,	"	21 March 1734.
Edward Son of Edward and Jane Moberly,	"	20 June 1734.
Mary daughter of Sampson and Mary Mason,	"	21 March 1734.
Sarah daughter of John and Sarah Morine,	"	22 August 1734.
William Son of William and Sarah Morris,	"	10 November 1734.
John Son of John and Sarah Moorhead,	"	3 September 1734.
Nathanael Son of David and Rachel Matthews,	"	17 February 1734.
James Son of John and Jane Milk,	"	7 March 1734.
Eleazer Son of Eleazar and Mary Newhall,	"	21 January 1734.
Hannah daughter of James and Hannah Nichols,	"	15 March 1734.
Thomas Churchman Son of Thomas and Mary Newman,	"	5 November 1734.
Charles Son of William and Mary Nicholson,	"	16 March 1734.
Rebekah daughter of William and Mary Owen,	"	31 May 1734.
Sarah daughter of Jacob and Mary Parker,	"	24 March 1734.
Freeman Son of Joseph and Sarah Pulsifer,	"	20 March 1734.
Thomas Son of Caleb and Mary Parker,	"	2 January 1734.
Mary daughter of William and Mary Paine,	"	26 February 1734.
Mary daughter of John and Mary Potwine,	"	26 March 1734.
John Son of John and Sarah Parry,	"	1 July 1734.
Sarah daughter of William and Ann Phillips,	"	6 November 1734.
Margaret daughter of Benjamin and Margaret Procter,	"	25 September 1734.
Ann daughter of Benjamin and Ann Pemberton,	"	15 December 1734.
Edward Son of Moses and Elizabeth Peirce,	"	27 April 1734.
Jacob Son of Edmund and Elizabeth Quincy,	"	2 October 1734.
Timothy Son of Elias and Mary Robinson,	"	13 October 1734.
Hannah daughter of Stephen and Sarah Rogers,	"	18 November 1734.
Elizabeth daughter of James and Sarah Raymar,	"	22 November 1734.
Ebenezer Son of Ebenezer and Sarah Rainger,	"	20 September 1734.
Paul Son of Paul and Deborah Rivoire,	"	21 December 1734.
Elizabeth daughter of Samuel and Amy Ridgaway,	"	4 January 1734.
John White Son of Nathaniel and Mary Roberts,	"	7 January 1734.
Mary daughter of Samuel and Abigail Robinson,	"	5 May 1734.
Rachel daughter of John and Elizabeth Read,	"	4 August 1734.
Joseph Son of Benjamin and Elizabeth Russell,	"	8 September 1734.
Mary daughter of Skinner and Elizabeth Russell,	"	5 March 1734.
Hannah daughter of Aaron and Mary Read,	"	13 October 1734.
Jeremiah Condy Son of Thomas and Elizabeth Russell,	"	8 November 1734.
Mary daughter of Stephen and Sarah Randall,	"	10 January 1734.
Patience daughter of Thomas and Tabitha Stoddard,	"	24 February 1733–4.
Joseph Son of Samuel and Mary Smith,	"	23 February 1734.
Mary daughter of Andrew and Hannah Symmes,	"	20 January 1734.
Josiah Son of Nicholas and Martha Salisbury,	"	10 March 1734.
John Son of William and Sarah Stoddard,	"	20 November 1734.
Nathanael Son of John and Mary Smibert,	"	20 January 1734.
Sarah daughter of John and Mary Simpson,	"	20 February 1734.
Jonathan Son of Jonathan and Mary Snelling,	"	28 July 1734.
Benjamin Son of Benjamin and Elizabeth Snelling,	"	24 August 1734.

BIRTHS — 1734. 219

William Son of John and Abigail Stringer,	Born	24 April 1734.
Benjamin Son of Benjamin and Ann Sanderson,	"	16 April 1734.
James Son of Joseph and Susanna Shead,	"	14 July 1734.
James Son of Benjamin and Elizabeth Seward,	"	22 July 1734.
Sarah daughter of Alexander and Anna Sears,	"	17 August 1734.
Humphrey Son of Humphrey and Mary Scarlet,	"	1 September 1734.
Katharine daughter of Thomas and Elizabeth Simpkins,	"	12 October 1734.
William Son of John and Elizabeth Spooner,	"	24 October 1734.
William Son of William and Elizabeth Simpkins,	"	12 December 1734.
Elizabeth daughter of John and Sarah Smallpeice,	"	27 December 1734.
Hannah daughter of Ebenezer and Mary Storer,	"	16 January 1734.
Bartholomew Son of Bartholomew and Mary Sutton,	"	3 January 1734.
Joseph Son of Abraham and Hannah Snelling,	"	15 April 1734.
James Son of John and Sarah Tyler,	"	20 April 1734.
John Son of Nathanael and Joanna Thwing,	"	22 August 1734.
Samuel Son of William and Sarah Tyler,	"	23 August 1734.
William Son of William and Mary Townsend,	"	28 September 1734.
Sarah daughter of Alexander and Elizabeth Thorp,	"	3 November 1734.
Mary daughter of John and Jane Tudor,	"	17 November 1734.
Hannah daughter of Daniel and Hannah Tucker,	"	6 November 1734.
Ebenezer Son of Nathanael and Ruth Thayer,	"	16 July 1734.
Moses Son of Moses and Hannah Tyler,	"	26 November 1734.
John Son of William and Bethia Torrey,	"	14 August 1734.
Edward Son of Edward and Ann Tyng,	"	19 January 1734.
Jeremiah Son of Jeremiah and Hannah Townsend,	"	20 January 1734.
Mary daughter of John and Susanna Tinkum,	"	11 March 1734.
Lucy daughter of John and Mary Tyng,	"	28 November 1734.
Ebenezer Son of Joseph and Joanna Turell,	"	2 March 1734.
Margaret daughter of Giles and Margaret Tidmarsh,	"	1 March 1734.
Ann daughter of John and Rebecca Tillston,	"	2 February 1734.
Matthew Son of Joseph and Priscilla Wakefield,	"	4 August 1734.
John Son of John and Ann Waterhouse,	"	21 July 1734.
Eunice daughter of John and Mary West,	"	2 December 1734.
Sarah daughter of Joseph and Joanna Wood,	"	10 January 1734.
Nathanael Son of Nathanael and Hannah Warner,	"	3 March 1734.
Abigail daughter of Jonathan and Abigail Wheeler,	"	18 August 1734.
Samuel Son of Samuel and Hannah Watts,	"	18 February 1734.
Rebekah daughter of John and Mary Wendell,	"	15 June 1734.
Hezekiah Son of Ebenezer and Susanna Welch,	"	26 August 1734.
Edward Son of Edward and Mary Winter,	"	25 June 1734.
William Son of William and Elizabeth Walter,	"	4 October 1734.
Abigail daughter of Gamaliel and Abigail Wallis,	"	8 April 1734.
William Son of William and Mary Whittemore,	"	4 May 1734.
Ebenezer Son of Benjamin and Joanna West,	"	29 April 1734.
Rebekah daughter of Benjamin and Sarah Whittemore,	"	7 June 1734.
Bellingham Son of Samuel and Hannah Watts,	"	22 May 1734.
Joseph Son of Joseph and Abigail Webb,	"	28 October 1734.
Alice daughter of David and Alice Whittmore,	"	24 December 1734.
Martha ⎱ Gem. daughters of Joshua and Elizabeth Ann ⎰ Winslow,	"	20 January 1734.
Daniel Son of Daniel and Elizabeth Watts,	"	18 February 1734.
Dorothy daughter of Thomas and Dorothy Wharton,	"	27 February 1734.
Mary daughter of Isaac and Sarah Walker,	"	13 February 1734.
Sarah daughter of Thomas and Sarah Williston,	"	24 January 1734.
Nathaniel Son of William and Hannah Young,	"	23 May 1734.
Hannah daughter of Richard Clark and Elizabeth his Wife,	"	27 February 1733-4.

Mary daughter of John Bowden and Patience his Wife,	Born	12 November 1734.
Hannah daughter of John Carnes and Sarah his Wife,	"	28 September 1734.
Elizabeth daughter of Ralph Carter and Sarah his Wife,	"	2 September 1734,
Ephraim Son of John Fenno and Hannah his Wife,	"	15 June 1734.
Elizabeth daughter of John Hill and Elizabeth his Wife,	"	27 May 1734.
Thomas Son of Thomas Jackson and Anne his Wife,	"	30 July 1734.
Mary daughter of Nathaniel Shepard and Mary his Wife,	"	15 July 1734.
Abigail daughter of Samuel Torrey and Silence his Wife,	"	10 January 1734.

1735.

Mary daughter of John and Mary Avery,	Born	13 April 1735.
Hannah daughter of Nathanael and Mary Alden,	"	3 June 1735.
Ann daughter of John and Mary Allen,	"	9 July 1735.
Mary daughter of Henry and Deliverance Atkins,	"	18 September 1735.
Elisabeth daughter of Stephen and Elisabeth Avery,	"	10 February 1735.
Abigail daughter of Samuel and Mary Adams,	"	19 October 1735.
Thomas Son of Thomas and Mehetabel Bolter,	"	23 April 1735.
Gee Son of Thomas and Sarah Bennet,	"	11 July 1735.
Martha daughter of Jonathan and Mary Bowman,	"	21 July 1735.
William Son of John and Jerusha Baker,	"	12 December 1735.
Thomas Son of John and Sarah Bonner,	"	9 August 1735.
Mary daughter of Zephaniah and Mary Basset,	"	2 December 1735.
Joseph Son of Thomas and Mary Baker,	"	19 July 1735.
Elizabeth daughter of Martin and Susanna Brimmer,	"	22 March 1735.
Mary daughter of Samuel and Mary Butler,	"	29 July 1735.
Joseph Son of Joseph and Martha Brandon,	"	29 August 1735.
Caleb Son of Caleb and Dilly Bean,	"	31 July 1735.
Hannah daughter of John and Sarah Billings,	"	16 November 1735.
James Son of Belthazer and Mary Bayard,	"	7 August 1735.
Abigail daughter of John and Susanna Brown,	"	11 December 1735.
Samuel Son of John and Sarah Barret,	"	13 August 1735.
Ann daughter of Robert and Isabella Breck,	"	26 February 1735.
Joseph Son of John and Sarah Becham,	"	4 October 1735.
Josias Son of Josias and Sarah Byles,	"	9 October 1735.
Sarah daughter of Joseph and Mary Birch,	"	18 November 1735.
Nathanael Son of Benjamin and Neezer Balch,	"	7 May 1735.
William Son of Thomas and Elizabeth Brooks,	"	10 November 1735.
John Son of Joseph and Ruth Bradford,	"	29 November 1735.
William Son of Ebenezer and Mary Bridge,	"	13 January 1735.
Nathanael Son of John and Margaret Breck,	"	29 January 1735.
Benjamin Son of Benjamin and Anna Brown,	"	3 November 1735.
Susanna daughter of John and Elizabeth Bulfinch,	"	22 December 1735.
Abigail daughter of Benjamin and Lydia Barnard,	"	20 March 1735.
Joseph } Gem. Sons of Benjamin and Ann Babbidge, Benjamin }		24 March 1735.
Abigail daughter of Elisha and Elizabeth Callender,	"	7 March 1735.
Sarah daughter of David and Sarah Christie,	"	22 October 1735.
John Son of John and Zibiah Cravath,	"	18 February 1735.
Abigail daughter of David and Lydia Cutler,	"	24 March 1735.
Sarah daughter of Daniel and Mary Cheever,	"	2 June 1735.
Timothy Son of Robert and Anna Cutler,	"	14 October 1735.
Phillip Son of Abraham and Ruth Cutler,	"	21 May 1735.
Palfrey Son of Samuel and Hannah Collins,	"	29 July 1735.
Samuel Son of Samuel and Elizabeth Cravath,	"	7 June 1735.
Elizabeth daughter of Thomas and Elizabeth Cock,	"	9 August 1735.

Births — 1735.

Lydia daughter of John and Hannah Coolidge,	Born	27 November 1735.
Ebenezer Son of Ebenezer and Elizabeth Cushing,	"	27 May 1735.
Benjamin Son of William and Elizabeth Cunningham,	"	14 April 1735.
Elizabeth daughter of Richard and Elizabeth Clarke,	"	8 March 1735.
Hannah daughter of Jeremiah and Anna Cushing,	"	5 February 1735.
Peter Son of Peter and Sarah Van Cumber,	"	26 December 1735.
John Son of John and Abigail Collson,	"	31 May 1735.
Dorcas daughter of Gayer and Rebekah Coffin,	"	27 July 1735.
Elizabeth daughter of John and Elizabeth Clark,	"	6 July 1735.
Isabella daughter of Ward and Joanna Cotton,	"	2 July 1735.
William Son of William and Mary Downing,	"	10 September 1735.
Margaret daughter of Joseph and Jane Dowse,	"	2 October 1735.
Samuel Son of Jonathan and Mary Dwight,	"	29 April 1735.
Susanna daughter of Moses and Persis Deshon,	"	22 June 1735.
James Son of James and Mary Davenport,	"	12 June 1735.
Adam Son of Adam and Susanna Dechezeaux,	"	26 June 1735.
Dorothy daughter of Harbottle and Dorothy Dorr,	"	18 August 1735.
Abigail daughter of John and Abigail Doble,	"	14 September 1735.
James Son of James and Mary Dolbeare,	"	20 September 1735.
Sarah daughter of William and Lydia Doke,	"	8 January 1735.
Abigail daughter of James and Mary Dawson,	"	26 January 1735.
Sarah daughter of Story and Sarah Dawes,	"	14 March 1735.
Thomas Son of Thomas and Abigail Eustis,	"	8 August 1735.
John Son of Edward and Sarah Eades,	"	6 September 1735.
Hannah daughter of John and Sarah Eliot,	"	2 October 1735.
Elizabeth daughter of Edward and Mary Ellis,	"	22 March 1735.
Ann daughter of Samuel and Elizabeth Everton,	"	6 February 1735.
Sarah daughter of Joseph and Sarah Edwards,	"	17 March 1735.
Bathsheba daughter of Benjamin and Bathsheba Edwards,	"	23 February 1735.
William Son of David and Mary Evans,	"	10 December 1735.
Sarah daughter of Andrew and Sarah Friswell,	"	8 February 1735.
Abiah daughter of Eleazer and Mary Flagg,	"	21 January 1735.
Joseph Son of Benjamin and Jerusha Fitch,	"	24 August 1735.
Ebenezer Son of Nathan and Margaret Foster,	"	26 April 1735.
Hannah daughter of John and Hannah Fenno,	"	4 February 1735.
Mary daughter of Hopestill and Sarah Foster,	"	4 March 1735.
Sarah daughter of Samuel and Sarah Gooding,	"	12 November 1735.
Sarah daughter of Stephen and Eunice Greenleaf,	"	30 November 1735.
Abraham, Son of Abraham and Mary Gybuat,	"	12 January 1735.
Bethia daughter of John and Sarah Gold,	"	3 February 1735.
Alexander Son of William and Elizabeth Grigg,	"	31 August 1735.
Samuel Son of John and Sarah Greenough,	"	7 September 1735.
Christian daughter of John and Content Gordon,	"	28 September 1735.
Francis Son of Francis and Rachel Gatcombe,	"	18 August 1735.
Francis Son of Thomas and Elizabeth Gouge,	"	15 June 1735.
Elizabeth daughter of Joseph and Katharine Giddinge,	"	13 June 1735.
Sarah daughter of Thomas and Martha Greenough,	"	25 August 1735.
Elizabeth daughter of Ezekiel and Elizabeth Goldthwait,	"	29 August 1735.
John Son of Thomas and Ann Green,	"	7 May 1735.
Newman Son of Newman and Elizabeth Greenough,	"	10 September 1735.
Sarah daughter of Bickford and Judith Greenleaf,	"	29 July 1735.
Pollard Son of Isaac and Sarah Gridley,	"	23 March 1735.
Sarah daughter of Joseph and Elizabeth Gooch,	"	1 December 1735.
Charles Son of Joseph and Anna Green,	"	30 November 1735.
Samuel Son of Joseph and Martha Goldthwait,	"	20 March 1735.
William Son of Samuel and Ann Gibson,	"	1 April 1735.
Ann daughter of Benjamin and Rebekah Hallowell,	"	21 September 1735.

Lydia daughter of Joshua and Lydia Hutton,	Born	17 September 1735.
Sarah daughter of Jacob and Susanna Holyoke,	"	28 September 1735.
William Son of Daniel and Elizabeth Henshaw,	"	20 October 1735.
Jonathan Son of Stephen and Elizabeth Hunniwell,	"	18 November 1735.
Ann daughter of Jacob and Elizabeth Hurd,	"	5 April 1735.
Elizabeth daughter of Amos and Judith Howard,	"	17 November 1735.
Rebekah daughter of Benjamin and Rebekah Hobart,	"	28 January 1735.
Turner Son of James and Esther Hill,	"	27 February 1735.
Samuel Son of William and Elizabeth Healy,	"	12 October 1735.
Mary daughter of Samuel and Elizabeth Henshaw,	"	13 September 1735.
Whiton Son of Whiton and Katharine Harvey,	"	15 November 1735.
Penn Townsend Son of William and Sarah Hickling,	"	5 November 1735.
Mehetabel daughter of Abraham and Mehetabel Holland,	"	21 July 1735.
Elizabeth daughter of William and Sarah Haislup,	"	17 February 1735.
Sarah daughter of Thomas and Ann Jackson,	"	20 August 1735.
Lydia daughter of Samuel and Ruth Jackson,	"	8 November 1735.
William Son of John and Hannah Jones,	"	22 September 1735.
Mary daughter of James and Ann Jeffs,	"	9 February 1735.
James Son of James and Mary Jackson,	"	3 April 1735.
Edward Son of Joseph and Susanna Jackson,	"	1 March 1735.
Abigail daughter of Thomas and Elizabeth Kemble,	"	9 May 1735.
James Son of James and Elizabeth Knap,	"	17 February 1735.
Colford Son of Ebenezer and Mary Lowell,	"	8 January 1735.
Elizabeth daughter of Michael and Abigail Lowell,	"	14 November 1735.
Mary daughter of John and Mercy Late,	"	20 July 1735.
Thomas Son of Phillip and Lydia Lewis,	"	15 November 1735.
Mary daughter of Joseph and Elizabeth Leasenby,	"	3 October 1735.
Joseph Son of Joseph and Rebekah Lowden,	"	12 June 1735.
Nathaniel Byfield Son of Byfield and Sarah Lyde,	"	16 May 1735.
Elizabeth daughter of Joseph and Elizabeth Lewis,	"	24 December 1735.
John Son of John and Abigail Lowe,	"	4 February 1735.
Thomas Son of Jonathan and Mary Lambert,	"	28 January 1735.
Robert Son of Robert and Mary Miers,	"	7 April 1735.
Samuel Son of Samuel and Mary Marshall,	"	16 June 1735.
Deborah daughter of Adam and Deborah Montgomery,	"	18 April 1735.
William Son of Daniel and Eunice Merritt,	"	21 June 1735.
Esther daughter of John and Elizabeth McClelan,	"	11 January 1735.
Edward Son of James and Mary Moore,	"	14 February 1735.
Mary daughter of William and Katharine Mellens,	"	18 March 1735.
Peter Son of Thomas and Mary Newman,	"	29 December 1735.
John Son of Samuel and Mary Neate,	"	23 March 1735.
Mary daughter of John and Mary Norvell,	"	11 February 1735.
Priscilla daughter of Eleazar and Mary Newhall,	"	25 December 1735.
Elizabeth daughter of Peter and Mary Oliver,	"	30 June 1735.
Elizabeth daughter of William and Mary Owen,	"	24 July 1735.
Mary daughter of Andrew and Mary Oliver,	"	20 September 1735.
Jonathan Son of Joseph and Mary Pierce,	"	27 November 1735.
Houghton Son of Isaac and Sarah Perkins,	"	10 February 1735.
Sarah daughter of John and Mary Perry,	"	21 January 1735.
Elizabeth daughter of James and Elizabeth Pitts,	"	5 November 1735.
Elizabeth daughter of Thomas Handiside and Elizabeth Peck,	"	14 February 1735.
Mary ⎱ Gem. daughters of Thomas and Esther Esther ⎰ Porter,	"	4 June 1735.
Nathanael Son of Samuel and Rebekah Phillips,	"	2 June 1735.
Elizabeth daughter of Roger and Elizabeth Price,	"	23 March 1735.
Lucy daughter of Joshua and Susanna Peco,	"	23 June 1735.
William Bowes Son of Samuel and Dorcas Parkman,	"	25 July 1735.

BIRTHS — 1735.

Mary daughter of James and Mary Penniman,	Born	14 July 1735.
Lydia daughter of John and Lydia Procter,	"	13 August 1735.
John Son of John and Ann Phillips,	"	15 September 1735.
Joanna daughter of Benjamin and Margaret Procter,	"	30 September 1735.
John Son of John and Sarah Phillips,	"	5 April 1735.
Susanna daughter of John and Susanna Pinkney,	"	25 March 1735.
Sarah daughter of John and Mary Phillips,	"	7 April 1735.
Hannah daughter of William and Mehetabel Pratt,	"	27 April 1735.
Benjamin Son of Simon and Thomazin Rogers,	"	11 November 1735.
Eleanor daughter of Joseph and Eleanor Ranger,	"	15 December 1735.
Edmund Son of Edmund and Hannah Ranger,	"	9 March 1735.
Mary daughter of Benjamin and Priscilla Roberts,	"	15 December 1735.
Joseph Son of James and Mehetabel Ridgaway,	"	4 April 1735.
Jonathan Son of Joseph and Rachel Roberts,	"	26 March 1735.
Elizabeth daughter of Samuel and Hannah Russell,	"	22 April 1735.
Joanna daughter of Benjamin and Abigail Renken,	"	26 April 1735.
Benjamin Son of Edward and Elizabeth Rumley,	"	8 September 1735.
Jeremiah Son of Jeremiah and Mary Snow,	"	20 April 1735.
Thomas Son of Joseph and Elizabeth Snelling,	"	11 May 1735.
Nathan Son of Nathan and Mary Sargent,	"	4 August 1735.
Samuel Son of Samuel and Hannah Sprague,	"	19 June 1735.
Andrew Son of Andrew and Hannah Symmes,	"	19 March 1735.
Samuel Son of Benjamin and Ann Sanderson,	"	30 December 1735.
Joshua Son of James and Elizabeth Scutt,	"	30 October 1735.
Mary daughter of Andrew and Mary Sigourney,	"	26 November 1735.
Rachel daughter of Henry and Alice Stokes,	"	29 April 1735.
Hannah daughter of John and Sarah Sweetser,	"	15 March 1735.
Sarah daughter of Thomas and Sarah Skinner,	"	13 June 1735.
Samuel Son of Joseph and Susanna Shed,	"	2 October 1735.
Mary daughter of Cornelius and Sarah Thompson,	"	12 May 1735.
William Son of Jonathan and Mary Tarbox,	"	23 August 1735.
Ann daughter of Samuel and Abigail Torrey,	"	31 March 1735.
Thomas Son of Onesiphorus and Judith Tilestone,	"	10 September 1735.
Benjamin Son of Nathanel and Joanna Thwing,	"	5 January 1735.
James Son of Davis and Sarah Townsend,	"	30 August 1735.
Mary daughter of Morgan and Sarah Thomas,	"	2 September 1735.
Elias Son of Elias and Elizabeth Townsend,	"	16 November 1735.
William Son of George and Elisabeth Tilley,	"	12 January 1735.
George Son of Edward and Elizabeth Tothill,	"	13 January 1735.
Richard Son of Joshua and Elizabeth Townsend,	"	4 February 1735.
John Son of John and Rebekah Tilestone,	"	27 February 1735.
Joseph ⎱ Gem. Sons of William and Bethia Benjamin ⎰ Torrey,	"	25 February 1735. 8 February 1735.
Jeremiah Son of Samuel and Deborah Webb,	"	26 February 1735.
Deborah daughter of Joseph and Abigail Webb,	"	13 May 1735.
Edmund Son of John and Elizabeth Wendell,	"	23 August 1735.
Miriam daughter of William and Miriam Williams,	"	6 March 1735.
Seward Son of Seward and Sarah Waters,	"	10 February 1735.
Abraham Son of Benjamin and Sarah Whittemore,	"	2 November 1735.
Abraham Son of Jacob and Sarah Wendell,	"	5 January 1735.
Isaac Son of John and Elizabeth Whitney,	"	4 May 1735.
Joseph Son of Joseph and Martha Wheeler,	"	7 February 1735.
Preston Son of John and Ann Waterhouse,	"	12 March 1735.
Mary daughter of Thomas and Mary Walker,	"	16 March 1735.
Thomas Son of James and Rebekah Wimble,	"	25 August 1735.
Ralph Gulston Son of Samuel and Lucy Waldo,	"	14 April 1735.
Ebenezer Son of Ebenezer and Rebekah Williston,	"	11 September 1735.
John Son of John and Sarah Welch,	"	16 May 1735.
Frances daughter of Isaac and Rebekah White,	"	31 October 1735.
Margaret daughter of James and Margaret Webster,	"	

Abraham Son of Samuel and Mary Wheeler,	Born	17 December 1735.
Rebekah daughter of William and Submit Walton,	"	27 December 1735.
Ann daughter of Gamaliel and Abigail Wallis,	"	16 June 1735.
Robert Son of Robert and Mary Way,	"	17 July 1735.
Mary daughter of Samuel and Mary Waterhouse,	"	30 July 1735.
Nathan Son of Joseph and Ruth Whittmore,	"	16 September 1735.
Sarah daughter of Samuel and Elizabeth Wentworth,	"	19 December 1735.
William Son of James and Jane Young,	"	30 August 1735.
Sarah daughter of William and Hannah Young,	"	1 December 1735.
Robert Son of Youth and Lydia Young,	"	30 January 1735.
William Son of Richard Clark and Elizabeth his Wife,	"	21 February 1734–5.
George Son of William Blin and Elizabeth his Wife,	"	21 July 1735.
Nathaniel Son of Nathaniel Bird and Priscilla his Wife,	"	23 April 1735.
Jerusha daughter of John Carnes and Sarah his Wife,	"	31 December 1735.
Elizabeth daughter of Peter Cade and Elizabeth his Wife,	"	July 1735.
Joseph Son of James Gooch and Hester his Wife,	"	21 October 1735.
Sarah daughter of Thomas Jackson and Anne his Wife,	"	20 August 1735.
Elizabeth daughter of Nathaniel Shepard and Mary his Wife,	"	28 December 1735.
Henry Son of Ebenezer Swan and Rebecca his Wife,	"	26 February 1735.
Owen Son of Owen Williams and Mary his Wife,	"	13 December 1735.

1736.

James Son of James and Bathsheba Allen,	Born	11 August 1736.
John Son of John and Mary Allison,	"	20 July 1736.
Richard Son of Joshua and Elisabeth Atwood,	"	10 October 1736.
Susanna daughter of Jeremiah and Hannah Bill,	"	27 April 1736.
James Son of James and Hephzibah Bradford,	"	11 May 1736.
Jonathan Son of Benjamin and Martha Bunker,	"	29 March 1736.
Samuel Son of Edward and Abigail Bromfield,	"	7 October 1736.
John Son of Jonathan and Elizabeth Brown,	"	16 April 1736.
Dorothy daughter of Samuel and Sarah Barber,	"	16 April 1736.
John Son of Thomas and Mary Brooks,	"	28 April 1736.
John Son of Increase and Ann Blake,	"	22 June 1736.
Henry Son of Ebenezer and Mary Berry,	"	23 May 1736.
Abigail daughter of William and Susanna Butler,	"	19 July 1736.
Samuel Son of Mather and Anna Byles,	"	10 July 1736.
John Son of John and Katharine Beney,	"	31 July 1736.
Jonathan Son of David and Rely Belcher,	"	29 August 1736.
Sarah daughter of John and Sarah Blowers,	"	3 September 1736.
Mary daughter of Thomas and Susanna Bentley,	"	4 November 1736.
Dorcas daughter of Daniel and Mary Ballard,	"	2 December 1736.
Martha daughter of John and Hannah Bennet,	"	23 December 1736.
Deborah daughter of Daniel and Abigail Bell,	"	24 January 1736.
Sarah daughter of Joseph and Ruth Bradford,	"	7 March 1736.
William Son of Belthazer and Mary Bayard,	"	14 March 1736.
Thomas Son of John and Mary Crocker,	"	8 July 1736.
Samuel Son of James and Sarah Clark,	"	26 September 1736.
Lydia daughter of Charles and Mary Coffin,	"	14 August 1736.
Frederick Son of Cord and Sarah Cordis,	"	28 October 1736.
Samuel Son of Samuel and Mary Chandler,	"	28 May 1736.
Ebenezer Son of William and Ann Coffin,	"	21 May 1736.
Mary daughter of Phillip and Mary Coulter,	"	28 June 1736.
Mary daughter of James and Elizabeth Codner,	"	3 April 1736.
Anna daughter of Charles and Anna Cabbot,	"	12 April 1736.

BIRTHS — 1736.

Jonathan Son of Jonathan and Hannah Chandler,	Born	13 April 1736.
Daniel Son of Clement and Sarah Collins,	"	26 May 1736.
Elizabeth daughter of Nathanael and Martha Cobbit,	"	14 January 1736.
Abia daughter of John and Mehetabel Cowley,	"	4 February 1736.
Thomas Son of Josiah and Susanna Cotton,	"	23 July 1736.
James Son of James and Ruth Clark,	"	17 August 1736.
Rebekah daughter of Henry and Elizabeth Coulton,	"	6 September 1736.
Moses Son of John and Abigail Collson,	"	17 June 1736.
William Son of Thomas and Ann Crafts,	"	18 June 1736.
Thomas Son of John and Elizabeth Dring,	"	4 December 1736.
Elizabeth daughter of Samuel and Elizabeth Eliot,	"	28 February 1736.
Hannah daughter of Edward and Hannah Emerson,	"	5 January 1736.
Elizabeth daughter of Brice and Mary Eccles,	"	18 August 1736.
James Son of John and Abigail Erving,	"	4 April 1736.
Mary daughter of Edmund and Rachel Ellis,	"	9 August 1736.
Mary daughter of Jacob and Mary Emmons,	"	19 October 1736.
Ann daughter of William and Elizabeth Fairfield,	"	25 June 1736.
Ebenezer Son of Daniel and Hannah Frazer,	"	30 December 1736.
Hannah daughter of Joseph and Margaret Fitch,	"	19 October 1736.
Zabdiel Son of Benjamin and Jerusha Fitch,	"	29 November 1736.
Margaret daughter of Thomas and Martha Flagg,	"	24 February 1736.
Joseph Son of Joseph and Abigail Flood,	"	5 June 1736.
Joseph Son of Grafton and Sarah Feveryear,	"	16 June 1736.
Sarah daughter of James and Hannah Fosdick,	"	17 July 1736.
Mary daughter of Thomas and Ann Green,	"	6 November 1736.
Dean Son of Dean and Elizabeth Grover,	"	21 November 1736.
Martha daughter of Thomas and Martha Greenough,	"	12 December 1736.
Miles Son of Nathanael and Elizabeth Greenwood,	"	31 December 1736.
William Son of Silvester and Ann Gardiner,	"	13 June 1736.
Benjamin Son of Benjamin and Sarah Goold,	"	30 June 1736.
Ann daughter of John and Elizabeth Grant,	"	14 June 1736.
Sarah daughter of Bartholomew and Sarah Gedney,	"	5 April 1736.
William Son of Thomas and Elizabeth Green,	"	25 October 1736.
Joseph Son of Joseph and Mary Gale,	"	1 March 1736.
Sarah daughter of Joseph and Mary Glidden,	"	25 April 1736.
Susanna daughter of Joseph and Rebekah Gray,	"	25 October 1736.
Sarah daughter of Jeremiah and Abigail Gridley,	"	4 April 1736.
James Son of Samuel and Ann Gibson,	"	23 May 1736.
Ann daughter of Rufus and Katharine Green,	"	19 December 1736.
Joseph Son of Richard and Hannah Gridley,	"	5 November 1736.
Elizabeth daughter of Samuel and Susanna Hill,	"	28 April 1736.
Dorothy daughter of Thomas and Sarah Hawden,	"	17 May 1736.
William Son of John and Mary Hasey,	"	13 May 1736.
Elizabeth daughter of George and Rebekah Hanners,	"	21 May 1736.
Mary daughter of Nathanael and Hephzibah Howard,	"	12 August 1736.
Therase daughter of Samuel and Susanna Hubbard,	"	5 July 1736.
Mary daughter of John and Ann Harris,	"	9 September 1736.
Elizabeth daughter of James and Katharine Hodges,	"	19 June 1736.
Hannah daughter of Zechariah and Lydia Hicks,	"	1 July 1736.
Samuel Son of Samuel and Hannah Hallowell,	"	29 July 1736.
Sarah daughter of George and Mary Hunnewell,	"	23 February 1736.
William Son of John and Elizabeth Haslet,	"	17 February 1736.
Sarah daughter of Joshua and Elizabeth Henshaw,	"	16 January 1736.
Elizabeth daughter of Stephen and Elizabeth Hall,	"	3 January 1736.
Thomas Son of Samuel and Mary Heath,	"	9 January 1736.
Mary daughter of Joseph and Ann Hudson,	"	10 December 1736.
Henry Son of Thomas and Hannah Hill,	"	26 February 1736.
Samuel Son of Samuel and Sarah Hilton,	"	6 November 1736.
Desire daughter of Jabez and Mary Hatch,	"	22 April 1736.

Martha daughter of Richard and Martha Hall,	Born	15 July 1736.
Benjamin Son of John and Margaret Jenkins,	"	4 November 1736.
John Son of Samuel and Ruth Jackson,	"	17 November 1736.
Hannah daughter of John and Hannah Jones,	"	8 September 1736.
Samuel Son of William and Margaret Jepson	"	1 January 1736.
Nathanael Son of Richard and Sarah Kent,	"	24 August 1736.
Sarah daughter of Christopher and Sarah Kilby,	"	15 August 1736.
Solomon Son of Solomon and Lydia Kneeland,	"	8 July 1736.
Ebenezer Son of Ebenezer and Hannah Kendal,	"	5 October 1736.
Benjamin Son of John and Mehetabel Kneeland	"	20 January 1736.
John Son of Joseph and Mary Kneeland,	"	11 October 1736.
William Tyler Son of Thomas and Sarah Kilby,	"	2 January 1736.
Hannah daughter of Nicholas and Elizabeth Lash,	"	5 February 1736.
Nancy daughter of David and Abigail Lenox,	"	23 January 1736.
Thomas Son of Thomas and Deborah Lothrop,	"	6 March 1736.
William Son of John and Elizabeth Lee,	"	8 July 1736.
Edward Son of Phillip and Elizabeth Lewis,	"	7 April 1736.
Richard Son of Richard and Abigail Lane,	"	26 October 1736.
Benjamin Son of Jonathan and Anne Lowder,	"	13 January 1736.
Abigail daughter of Michael and Abigail Lowell,	"	25 December 1736.
John Son of John and Abigail Lovell,	"	17 May 1736.
Isaac Son of Isaac and Mary Lewis,	"	29 March 1736.
Jennet daughter of John and Margaret Moor,	"	2 January 1736.
Samuel Son of Samuel and Hannah Mather,	"	8 February 1736.
John Son of Samuel and Mary Marshall,	"	1 January 1736.
Mary daughter of Zebulun and Anna Norwood,	"	25 July 1736.
John Son of Thomas and Mary Newman,	"	29 December 1736.
James Son of James and Eunice Nicolls,	"	1 April 1736.
William Rand Son of James and Mary Penniman,	"	6 January 1736.
Thomas Son of Thomas and Abigail Poole,	"	7 December 1736.
Hannah daughter of James and Elizabeth Pitts,	"	16 November 1736.
William Lee Son of John and Abigail Perkins,	"	10 February 1736.
Elizabeth ⎱ Gem. daughter of Joseph and Mary Abigail ⎰ Prince,	"	2 March 1736.
William Son of John and Sarah Phillips,	"	30 August 1736.
Joseph Son of Joseph and Sarah Pulcifer,	"	4 February 1736.
Elizabeth daughter of Isaac and Agnes Peirce,	"	8 April 1736.
Sarah daughter of Samuel and Rebekah Pain,	"	4 April 1736.
Sarah daughter of Joseph and Sarah Putnam,	"	17 September 1736.
Mary daughter of John and Mary Peirce,	"	28 October 1736.
Jedidiah Son of Caleb and Mary Parker,	"	18 November 1736.
Mehetabel daughter of John and Sarah Parker,	"	30 September 1736.
Ann daughter of Gillam and Mary Phillips,	"	18 August 1736.
Joseph Son of Samuel and Rebekah Phillips.	"	17 October 1736.
William Son of William and Mary Pain,	"	7 December 1736.
Hannah daughter of Josiah and Hannah Quincy,	"	11 September 1736.
Rachel daughter of Benjamin and Abigail Renken,	"	2 November 1736.
Thomas Son of Nathanael and Mary Roberts,	"	28 January 1736.
Stephen Son of Stephen and Sarah Randall,	"	5 December 1736.
Lydia daughter of Edward and Elizabeth Rumley,	"	20 March 1736.
Frances daughter of Paul and Deborah Rivoire,	"	11 July 1736.
Samuel Son of Samuel and Hannah Ruggles,	"	1 September 1736.
Sarah daughter of James and Sarah Raymar,	"	21 September 1736.
Sarah daughter of Gamaliel and Sarah Rogers,	"	16 September 1736.
Abigail daughter of Samuel and Abigail Sumner,	"	24 August 1736.
Thomas Son of Joseph and Margaret Savell,	"	26 March 1736.
Sarah daughter of John and Mary Salmon,	"	16 September 1736.
Katharine daughter of John and Mary Shepard,	"	7 July 1736.
Mary daughter of Daniel and Mary Sigourney,	"	31 August 1736.
Sarah daughter of Benjamin and Hannah Simpson,	"	1 December 1736.

BIRTHS — 1736.

Edward Son of Thomas and Hannah Shepard,	Born	8 September 1736.
Joseph Son of Joseph and Ann Scott,	"	22 May 1736.
Daniel Son of Arthur and Mercy Stoddard,	"	28 May 1736.
Elizabeth daughter of John and Sarah Smallpiece,	"	28 July 1736.
Mary daughter of Ebenezer and Mary Storer,	"	2 January 1736.
Susanna daughter of Jonathan and Martha Salter,	"	14 December 1736.
Samuel Son of David and Margaret Snoden,	"	23 December 1736.
Katharine daughter of William and Elizabeth Simpkins,	"	9 January 1736.
Thomas Son of Thomas and Deborah Savage,	"	11 December 1736.
Bethia daughter of Daniel and Hannah Tucker,	"	12 July 1736.
Jonathan Son of Edward and Anne Tyng,	"	5 August 1736.
Edward Son of Moses and Hannah Turner,	"	17 August 1736.
John Son of Giles and Margaret Tidmarsh,	"	28 January 1736.
Mary daughter of Timothy and Elizabeth Thornton,	"	2 September 1736.
Mary daughter of Thomas and Bethia Tyler,	"	25 February 1736.
William Son of John and Susanna Tinkum,	"	22 September 1736.
William Son of William and Faith Taylor,	"	12 October 1736.
Ruth daughter of Josiah and Ann Torrey,	"	1 October 1736.
Hannah daughter of Alexander and Elizabeth Thorp,	"	14 October 1736.
Mary daughter of William and Mary Townsend,	"	8 September 1736.
Benjamin Son of Richard and Abigail True,	"	16 November 1736.
Mary daughter of John and Mary Tyng,	"	29 August 1736.
Elizabeth daughter of Joshua and Martha Thornton,	"	3 February 1736.
Marah daughter of Elisha and Martha Townsend,	"	16 February 1736.
Elizabeth daughter of Samuel and Anne Tuttle,	"	5 March 1736.
Nathanael Son of Nathanael and Ruth Thayer,	"	27 April 1736.
Jane daughter of John and Jane Tudor,	"	30 June 1736.
Sarah daughter of James and Rachel Townsend,	"	19 May 1736.
Isaac Son of Isaac and Elizabeth Vergoose,	"	29 July 1736.
John Son of Elijah and Elizabeth Vinall,	"	30 May 1736.
Anna daughter of Ambrose and Anna Vincent,	"	21 June 1736.
Hannah daughter of John and Hannah Wells,	"	29 March 1736.
John Son of Henry and Mary Williams,	"	25 March 1736.
Joseph Son of Joseph and Joanna Woods, at Fort Richmond,	"	22 February 1736.
Elizabeth daughter of John and Elizabeth Whitney,	"	31 July 1736.
William Son of William and Miriam Williams,	"	31 January 1736.
Jacob Son of John and Elizabeth Wendell,	"	19 October 1736.
John Son of William and Elizabeth Wingfield,	"	19 June 1736.
David Son of John and Mary West,	"	9 May 1736.
Nathanael Son of Joseph and Ann Welsh,	"	15 June 1736.
Stephen Son of Allen and Agness Wheppe,	"	26 February 1736.
William Son of Joseph and Martha Wheeler,	"	8 September 1736.
Elizabeth daughter of John and Mary Wendell,	"	30 August 1736.
Mary daughter of William and Mary Warner,	"	23 September 1736.
Sarah daughter of Thomas and Jane Williston,	"	26 September 1736.
Joshua Son of Joshua and Elizabeth Winslow,	"	1 January 1736.
Hannah daughter of Stephen and Hannah Winter,	"	10 January 1736.
Mary daughter of Abraham and Amiable York,	"	21 April 1736.
Elizabeth daughter of Richard Clark and Elizabeth his Wife,	"	8 March 1735–6.
Rebecca daughter of John Bowden and Patience his Wife,	"	13 December 1736.
Mary daughter of Peace Cazneau and Mary his Wife,	"	18 October 1736.
Peter Son of Peter Cade and Elizabeth his Wife,	"	September 1736.
Samuel Son of Samuel Emmes and Abigail his Wife,	"	17 May 1736.
Mary daughter of John Liddell and Sarah his Wife,	"	29 November 1736.

1737.

Alexander Son of Henry and Deliverance Atkins,	Born	14 February 1737.
Samuel Son of Samuel and Mary Butler,	"	21 May 1737.
Sarah daughter of John and Elizabeth Bouve,	"	24 January 1737.
Elizabeth daughter of John and Abigail Breck,	"	1 May 1737.
Elizabeth daughter of John and Susanna Brown,	"	24 December 1737.
John Son of John and Susanna Blake,	"	20 June 1737.
Mary daughter of Benjamin and Mary Ballard,	"	26 November 1737.
Samuel Son of William and Rachel Brown,	"	28 July 1737.
William Son of William and Anne Beer,	"	29 April 1737.
Daniel Son of Daniel and Elizabeth Barker,	"	4 August 1737.
William Son of John and Sarah Billings,	"	13 September 1737.
Henry Son of Ebenezer and Mary Berry,	"	14 August 1737.
Benjamin Son of Ebenezer and Mary Bridge,	"	9 September 1737.
Benjamin Son of Thomas and Mehetabel Bolter,	"	2 September 1737.
Martin Son of Martin and Susanna Brimmer,	"	18 March 1737.
Joanna daughter of Richard and Mary Buckley,	"	15 May 1737.
Elizabeth daughter of Joseph and Mary Ballard,	"	7 February 1737.
Susanna daughter of Benjamin and Deborah Beard,	"	5 October 1737.
William Son of John and Rebecca Barrett,	"	5 July 1737.
William Son of William and Elizabeth Bennet,	"	26 September 1737.
Nathanael Son of Nathanael and Mary Brown,	"	27 September 1737.
John Son of Benjamin and Neezer Balch,	"	16 May 1737.
Jerusha daughter of Pyam and Jerusha Blowers,	"	27 October 1737.
Robinson Son of Caleb and Deliverance Bean,	"	13 November 1737.
Thomas Son of Increase and Ann Blake,	"	14 January 1737.
Sarah daughter of John and Sarah Barret,	"	14 January 1737.
Abraham Son of Joseph and Jane Burrill,	"	25 January 1737.
Davenport Son of Benjamin and Lydia Barnard,	"	24 January 1737.
Ebenezer Son of Jonathan and Elizabeth Brown,	"	9 February 1737.
Henry Son of Henry and Rachel Barlow,	"	29 January 1737.
Mary daughter of Joshua and Sarah Blanchard,	"	12 February 1737.
Elizabeth daughter of Mather and Anna Byles,	"	22 March 1737.
Ursula daughter of Gayer and Rebekah Coffin,	"	7 April 1737.
Abigail daughter of Isaac and Hannah Casno,	"	7 June 1737.
Mary daughter of David and Sarah Christie,	"	8 May 1737.
Abigail daughter of John and Abigail Collson,	"	22 July 1737.
Rebekah daughter of Ebenezer and Rebekah Coburn,	"	14 June 1737.
Obadiah Son of Jonathan and Hannah Chandler,	"	27 August 1737.
Michael Son of Michael and Mary Coutanch,	"	13 August 1737.
John Son of John and Jane Child,	"	17 September 1737.
David Son of John and Rebekah Compton,	"	26 September 1737.
Lydia daughter of John and Hannah Coolidge,	"	3 October 1737.
Deborah daughter of Benjamin and Deborah Colman.	"	11 May 1737.
Abigail daughter of John and Abigail Corney,	"	1 May 1737.
Christopher Son of Benjamin and Miriam Clarke,	"	2 February 1737.
Zibiah daughter of John and Zibiah Cravath,	"	12 February 1737.
John Son of John and Sarah Colman,	"	19 January 1737.
David Son of David and Lydia Cutler,	"	19 March 1737.
Mary daughter of Benjamin and Mary Dorby,	"	4 May 1737.
Isaac Son of Elias and Mary Dupee,	"	31 March 1737.
Katharine daughter of Joseph and Jane Dowse,	"	20 June 1737.
Rebekah daughter of James and Mary Davenport,	"	23 May 1737.
Ezekiel Son of Thomas and Abigail Demerry,	"	1 September 1737.
Katharine daughter of Thomas and Sarah Drowne,	"	4 January 1737.
Dolling Son of Benjamin and Bathsheba Edwards,	"	9 May 1737.
Susanna daughter of Edward and Sarah Edes,	"	14 May 1737.
Sarah daughter of John and Abigail Erving,	"	8 June 1737.

Births — 1737.

Joseph Son of Joseph and Sarah Edwards,	Born	11 November 1737.
Robert Son of Thomas and Deborah Eyre,	"	16 June 1737.
William Son of Thomas and Abigail Eustis,	"	29 July 1737.
Lydia daughter of Peter and Malatiah Farrow,	"	12 September 1737.
Ebenezer Son of Nathan and Margaret Foster,	"	2 May 1737.
John Son of Samuel and Elizabeth Fulton,	"	16 February 1737.
John Son of William and Elizabeth Fairfield,	"	26 December 1737.
David Son of Robert and Mary Gardner,	"	24 January 1737.
Broughton Son of Bartholomew and Sarah Gedney,	"	1 September 1737.
Mary daughter of John and Mary Gibson,	"	28 June 1737.
Hannah daughter of Newman and Elizabeth Greenough,	"	6 September 1737.
John Son of John and Esther Goold,	"	1 September 1737.
Thomas Son of Bickford and Judith Greenleaf,	"	21 May 1737.
Sarah daughter of Joseph and Mary Glidden,	"	28 December 1737.
Timothy Son of John and Martha Gibbs,	"	23 July 1737.
Ann daughter of Henry and Elizabeth Gibbon,	"	20 August 1737.
John Son of James and Elizabeth Gerreck,	"	18 September 1737.
Elizabeth daughter of Stephen and Eunice Greenleaf,	"	2 October 1737.
Samuel Son of Samuel and Ann Gibson,	"	24 August 1737.
John Son of Silvester and Ann Gardiner,	"	4 December 1737.
Mary Duesbury daughter of James and Thomazin Gibson,	"	27 December 1737.
Benjamin Son of Joseph and Martha Goldthwait,	"	6 August 1737.
John Son of Joseph and Elizabeth Gooch,	"	14 April 1737.
Joseph Son of Jacob and Susanna Griggs,	"	2 June 1737.
Freelove daughter of Samuel and Sarah Gooding,	"	12 July 1737.
Mary daughter of John and Mary Gatchell,	"	10 July 1737.
Hannah daughter of John and Elizabeth Grant,	"	23 July 1737.
Thomas Son of Amos and Judith Howard,	"	25 April 1737.
Phebe daughter of Benjamin and Phebe Harrod,	"	16 April 1737.
William Son of John and Elizabeth Helyer,	"	15 April 1737.
Elizabeth daughter of Thomas and Mary Hubbard,	"	21 April 1737.
Richard Bill Son of Joshua and Elizabeth Henshaw,	"	10 June 1737.
Wharton Son of Joshua and Hannah Hill,	"	24 June 1737.
Anna daughter of William and Sarah Hickling,	"	5 January 1737.
Abigail daughter of George and Abigail Hewes,	"	19 July 1737.
Noah Son of Peter and Katharine Harratt,	"	22 September 1737.
Samuel Son of Benjamin and Rebekah Hallowell,	"	16 August 1737.
Thomas ⎱ Gem. Sons of Samuel and Elizabeth Samuel ⎰ Haley,	"	8 April 1737.
Mary daughter of William and Sarah Haislup,	"	6 September 1737.
Francis Son of Francis and Sarah Hunt,	"	7 November 1737.
Jabez Son of Jabez and Mary Hatch,	"	17 February 1737.
Mary daughter of Jacob and Susanna Holyoke,	"	26 January 1737.
Ebenezer Son of William and Abigail Hasey,	"	5 September 1737.
Elizabeth daughter of Daniel and Elizabeth Henshaw,	"	27 September 1737.
Hannah daughter of Samuel and Mary Hunting,	"	16 September 1737.
Susanna daughter of James and Katharine Hodges,	"	4 March 1737.
Samuel Son of Samuel and Elizabeth Henshaw,	"	15 May 1737.
Thomas Son of Thomas and Martha Homans,	"	4 August 1737.
Thomas Son of Abraham and Mehetabel Holland,	"	20 October 1737.
Elizabeth daughter of Richard and Elizabeth Houghton,	"	26 February 1737.
Mary daughter of Phillip and Mary Howell,	"	15 October 1737.
Ebenezer Son of Samuel and Ruth Jackson,	"	28 November 1737.
Clement Son of Joseph and Susanna Jackson,	"	31 May 1737.
Elizabeth daughter of Joseph and Abigail Jackson,	"	15 January 1737.

Abigail daughter of Joseph and Abigail Jones,	Born	19 February 1737.
Martha daughter of John and Hannah Jones,	"	22 July 1737.
Elizabeth daughter of Stephen and Elizabeth Kent,	"	20 March 1737.
Sarah daughter of Henry and Sarah King,	"	8 July 1737.
Mehetabel daughter of John and Mehetabel Kneeland,	"	23 March 1737.
Mary daughter of Thomas and Elizabeth Kemble,	"	2 September 1737.
John Son of Abel and Hannah Kiggell,	"	8 January 1737.
William Son of Christopher and Sarah Kilby,	"	10 October 1737.
Sarah daughter of John and Mary Lee,	"	31 August 1737.
James Son of John and Abigail Lovell,	"	31 October 1737.
Thomas Son of Israel and Mehetabel Look,	"	20 January 1737.
Mary daughter of Joseph and Rebekah Lowden,	"	12 February 1737.
Abigail daughter of Jonathan and Anne Lowder,	"	6 March 1737.
Mary daughter of John and Jane Milk,	"	25 March 1737.
Phillip Son of Phillip and Mary Merrett,	"	31 March 1737.
John Son of David and Susanna Mason,	"	20 April 1737.
Elizabeth daughter of John and Sarah Morine,	"	11 May 1737.
Hannah daughter of Obadiah and Elizabeth Mors,	"	25 March 1737.
Ebenezer Son of Moses and Lydia Mackintosh,	"	20 June 1737.
James Son of James and Elizabeth Morris,	"	12 August 1737.
David Son of David and Sarah Martin,	"	23 August 1737.
John Son of John and Elizabeth McClelan,	"	14 September 1737.
Mary daughter of John and Ann Maylem,	"	12 August 1737.
William Son of William and Katharine Mellens,	"	12 November 1737.
Margaret daughter of James and Margaret Mays,	"	6 March 1737.
Thomas Son of Thomas and Abigail McCollough,	"	21 March 1737.
Jonathan Son of Daniel and Eunice Merritt,	"	20 September 1737.
James Son of James and Hannah Nicholson,	"	16 August 1737.
Eunice daughter of James and Eunice Nicolls,	"	10 March 1737.
John Son of William and Mary Owen,	"	9 April 1737.
Grizzell daughter of Andrew and Mary Oliver,	"	9 May 1737.
Samuel Son of William and Ann Phillips,	"	29 May 1737.
Thomas Son of John and Sarah Phillips,	"	24 August 1737.
Jonah Son of John and Mary Perry,	"	1 February 1737.
Joseph Son of John and Mary Patterson,	"	14 April 1737.
John Son of Caleb and Sarah Pratt,	"	25 December 1737.
Mary daughter of Joseph and Sarah Putman,	"	5 May 1737.
Susanna daughter of Edmund and Esther Perkins,	"	26 July 1737.
William Son of John and Mary Phillips,	"	29 August 1737.
Hannah daughter of Briant and Ruth Parrott,	"	9 January 1737.
Peter Son of Peter and Elizabeth Prescott,	"	15 August 1737.
John Son of Thomas and Elizabeth Russell,	"	12 April 1737.
Sarah daughter of Samuel and Naomi Ridgaway,	"	4 June 1737.
Ruth daughter of William and Ruth Read,	"	13 August 1737.
John Son of James and Sarah Raymar,	"	19 December 1737.
Margaret daughter of John and Margaret Rush,	"	11 November 1737.
John Son of John and Tabitha Ruddock,	"	2 October 1737.
Mary daughter of John and Mary Sorien,	"	15 October 1737.
Elizabeth daughter of Joseph and Susanna Shed,	"	24 August 1737.
Andrew Son of Daniel and Mary Sigourney,	"	11 February 1737.
Abigail daughter of John and Sarah Sweetser,	"	3 March 1737.
Ebenezer Son of Andrew and Hannah Symmes,	"	6 January 1737.
William Son of John and Mary Shepard,	"	17 December 1737.
Richard Son of Richard and Rachel Salter,	"	24 August 1737.
Deborah daughter of John and Mercy Scolley,	"	18 April 1737.
Caleb Son of John and Mary Simpson,	"	6 January 1737.
Benjamin Son of Joseph and Ann Scott,	"	24 January 1737.
John Bentley Son of Aftar and Mercy Stoddard,	"	13 June 1737.
Rebekah daughter of Robert and Lydia Snelling,	"	19 June 1737.

Births — 1737.

Samuel Son of Samuel and Sarah Service,	Born	27 June 1737.
Elizabeth daughter of Joseph and Mary Sherburn,	"	21 July 1737.
Sarah daughter of Nathanael and Joanna Thwing,	"	4 May 1737.
Elizabeth daughter of Edward and Elizabeth Tothill,	"	20 April 1737.
Henry Son of John and Sarah Tyler,	"	20 April 1737.
Joseph Son of Davis and Sarah Townsend,	"	2 December 1737.
Elizabeth daughter of Jonathan and Mary Tarbox,	"	23 May 1737.
Katharine daughter of Nathanael and Ruth Thayer,	"	7 June 1737.
William Son of Edward and Ann Tyng,	"	17 August 1737.
Francis Son of John and Susanna Tinkum,	"	1 November 1737.
Mary daughter of William and Bethia Torrey,	"	20 July 1737.
Susanna daughter of Jonathan and Susanna Vickery,	"	17 August 1737.
Mary daughter of Nathaniel and Mary Viall,	"	19 December 1737.
Mary daughter of Jonathan and Abigail Wheeler,	"	15 August 1737.
Henry Flynt Son of John and Elizabeth Wendell,	"	23 December 1737.
John Son of John and Hannah Wells,	"	3 February 1737.
William Son of William and Rebekah Whitwell,	"	27 December 1737.
Mary daughter of Henry and Mary Williams,	"	12 February 1737.
John Son of Thomas and Mary Walker,	"	12 March 1737.
Mary daughter of Edward and Mary Winter,	"	21 April 1737.
John Hayward Son of Josiah and Sarah Winslow,	"	21 March 1737.
Grace daughter of Joseph and Abigail Webb,	"	14 June 1737.
Ann daughter of Davenport and Sarah Walker,	"	19 January 1737.
Elizabeth daughter of John and Elizabeth West,	"	7 October 1737.
Rebekah daughter of Seward and Sarah Waters,	"	21 July 1737.
Edward Son of Samuel and Hannah Watts,	"	25 July 1737.
David Son of John and Mary West,	"	25 August 1737.
John Son of John and Mary Wendell,	"	29 August 1737.
Gamaliel Son of Gamaliel and Abigail Wallis,	"	16 August 1737.
William Son of Allen and Agness Wheppe,	"	11 November 1737.
John Son of James and Rebekah Wimble,	"	18 November 1737.
Abigail daughter of Nathanael and Hannah Warner,	"	30 August 1737.
Elizabeth daughter of Richard and Eunice Walker,	"	15 April 1737.
Abraham Son of William and Hannah Young,	"	19 May 1737.
William Son of William and Hannah Young,	"	1 October 1737.
Ruth daughter of John Avery and Mary his Wife,	"	26 October 1737.
Nathaniel Son of William Blin and Elizabeth his Wife,	"	21 April 1737.
Jane daughter of John Carnes and Sarah his Wife,	"	13 May 1737.
Aaron Son of Charles Cabot and Anna his Wife,	"	27 December 1737.
Edward Son of Richard Clark and Elizabeth his Wife,	"	30 November 1737.
William Son of James Gooch and Hester his Wife,	"	5 September 1737.
Elizabeth daughter of John Gardner and Mary his Wife,	"	13 October 1737.
Ebenezer Son of Gershom Flagg and Hannah his Wife,	"	30 October 1737.
William Son of John Hill and Elizabeth his Wife,	"	15 April 1737.
Nathaniel Prebble Son of Ebenezer Hayward and Rachel his Wife,	"	22 July 1737.
Elizabeth Frances daughter of Ibroke Hacker and Elizabeth his Wife,	"	25 June 1737.
Martha daughter of John Jones and Hannah his Wife,	"	22 July 1737.
Grace daughter of Thomas Jackson and Anne his Wife,	"	29 May 1737.
Mary daughter of David McLeod and Mary his Wife,	"	23 January 1737.

232   CITY DOCUMENT No. 43.

Katharine daughter of Nathaniel Shepard and Mary
  his wife,   Born   4 April, 1737.
Samuel Stillman was born February 27, 1737, in the City of Philadelphia,
  Province of Pennsylvania.
Ebenezer Son of Samuel Torrey and Silence his
  Wife   Born   9 April 1737.

The following births took place before 1738:
Samuel Son of Edmund and Rachel Ellis,
John Son of John and Martha Gibbs,
John Son of John and Margaret Keeffe,
James Rand Son of James and Mary Penniman, " at Fairfield.
Mehetabel daughter of John and Sarah Parker,

1738.

Samuel Son of Stephen and Elizabeth Avery,	Born	8 December 1738.
John Son of John and Susanna Allen,	"	22 January 1738.
Elizabeth daughter of Thomas and Elizabeth Barnard,	"	29 April 1738.
Mary daughter of Samuel and Sarah Barber,	"	3 May 1738.
Samuel Son of John and Sarah Barrett,	"	18 January 1738.
Martha daughter of John and Sarah Blowers,	"	19 December 1738.
Joseph Son of Joseph and Mary Blake,	"	5 February 1738.
Anna daughter of John and Abigail Breck,	"	19 August 1738.
Daniel Son of Josias and Sarah Byles,	"	31 June 1738.
Elizabeth daughter of Ebenezer and Mary Berry,	"	3 September 1738.
John Son of John and Hannah Brown,	"	12 September 1738.
Rebecca daughter of Robert and Isabella Breck,	"	9 September 1738.
Susanna daughter of John and Mary Ann Brown,	"	7 September 1738.
Hannah daughter of Daniel and Elizabeth Barker,	"	31 August 1738.
Dorothy daughter of Thomas and Susanna Bentley,	"	22 December 1738.
Samuel Son of Belthazer and Mary Bayard,	"	23 March 1738.
Mary daughter of Daniel and Mary Ballard, Junr.	"	23 January 1738.
Joseph Son of Benjamin and Nezer Balch,	"	10 February 1738.
John Son of Samuel and Mary Butler,	"	17 February 1738.
Sarah daughter of Nathanael and Abigail Brown,	"	18 February 1738.
Thomas Son of William and Elizabeth Bennett,	"	21 March 1738.
Ann daughter of Robert and Margaret Cartmill,	"	29 July 1738.
Frederick Son of John and Margaret Clark,	"	2 August 1738.
Susanna daughter of Charles and Mary Coffin,	"	9 August 1738.
Sarah daughter of Phillip and Mary Colter,	"	17 October 1738.
Susanna daughter of John and Susanna Chick,	"	15 April 1738.
Adam Son of John and Abigail Collson,	"	3 August 1738.
John Son of Samuel and Lillian Collop,	"	7 November 1738.
Andrew Son of Paice and Mary Casno.	"	20 December 1738.
Thankful daughter of Ebenezer and Elizabeth Clough,	"	8 January 1738.
Martha daughter of Samuel and Honour Clark,	"	15 January 1738.
John Son of Obadiah and Margaret Cookson,	"	10 April 1738.
Anna daughter of Gayer and Rebekah Coffin,	"	22 January 1738.
Mary daughter of James and Rachel Clough,	"	29 December 1738.
Hannah daughter of James and Alice Cocks,	"	21 February 1738.
William Son of William and Sibbill Clark,	"	23 February 1738.
Sarah daughter of Ebenezer and Rebekah Coburn,	"	19 January 1738.
Samuel Son of Samuel and Mary Chandler,	"	20 February 1738.
Judith daughter of Benjamin and Deborah Colman,	"	8 July 1738.
William Son of Story and Sarah Dawes,	"	16 May 1738.
John Son of John and Elizabeth Daniell,	"	21 May 1738.
Mehetabel ⎰ Gem. daughters of Jonathan and Mary		
Abiah ⎱ Dwight,	"	30 April 1738.
Ann daughter of Elias and Elizabeth Delarue,	"	24 October 1738.

Abigail daughter of William and Lydia Doke,	Born	15 November 1738.
Mary daughter of James and Mary Dodge,	"	27 February 1738.
Thomas Son of Benjamin and Mary Emmons,	"	6 March 1738.
Martha daughter of Benjamin and Elizabeth Egglestone,	"	25 December 1738.
Hannah daughter of Benjamin and Bathsheba Edwards,	"	20 May 1738.
John Son of Jacob and Mary Emmons,	"	11 October 1738.
Thomas Son of Thomas and Abigail Foster, junr.,	"	July 4 1738.
Susanna daughter of Jonathan and Elizabeth Farnum,	"	20 December 1738.
John Son of Benjamin and Jerusha Fitch,	"	14 January 1738.
Andrew Son of Joseph and Abigail Flood,	"	13 May 1738.
Deborah daughter of John and Deborah Fraser,	"	7 June 1738.
Sarah daughter of Richard and Sarah Freeman,	"	29 June 1738.
Rebekah daughter of Charles and Rebekah Florence,	"	10 August 1738.
Thomas Son of Thomas and Martha Flagg,	"	16 September 1738.
Mary daughter of Grafton and Sarah Feveryear,	"	20 May 1738.
Josiah Son of Josiah and Mary Flagg,	"	22 October 1738.
Elizabeth daughter of Thomas and Elizabeth Fleet,	"	23 May 1738.
Nathanael Son of Thomas and Elizabeth Greene,	"	12 April 1738.
James Son of Richard and Elizabeth Goodwin,	"	6 May 1738.
Daniel Son of John and Sarah Greenough,	"	11 July 1738.
John Son of Nathaniel and Elizabeth Greenwood,	"	7 March 1738.
Henry Son of Rufus and Katharine Green,	"	6 July 1738.
Elizabeth daughter of Stephen and Mary Greenleaf,	"	10 December 1738.
Samuel Son of Samuel and Sarah Gray,	"	13 July 1738.
Benjamin Son of Benjamin and Mary Green,	"	16 June 1738.
William Son of Samuel and Mary Greenwood,	"	29 July 1738.
Margaret daughter of Benjamin and Margaret Green,	"	8 October 1738.
Anna daughter of Michael and Mary Geoghegan,	"	1 August 1738.
Jane daughter of Richard and Hannah Gridley,	"	7 July 1738.
Thomas Son of Thomas and Martha Greenough,	"	8 May 1738.
Mary daughter of Joseph and Mary Gale,	"	30 July 1738.
Martha daughter of John and Martha Gibbs,	"	4 August 1738.
John Son of John and Content Gordon,	"	28 October 1738.
Roope Son of Thomas and Abigail Gooding,	"	19 December 1738.
Elizabeth daughter of Caleb Joseph and Mary Gray,	"	11 December 1738.
Elizabeth daughter of Stephen and Eunice Greenleaf,	"	19 January 1738.
John Son of George and Margaret Gray,	"	3 January 1738.
Esther daughter of John and Esther Goold,	"	26 February 1738.
George Broughton Son of Bartho. and Sarah Gedney,	"	21 October 1738.
Ezekiel Son of Ezekiel and Elizabeth Goldthwait,	"	31 March 1738.
Benjamin Mulberry Son of George and Ann Holmes,	"	24 April 1738.
Elizabeth daughter of James and Esther Hill,	"	27 April 1738.
Ann } Gem. daughters of John and Mary Hill, Elizabeth	"	17 May 1738.
Benjamin Son of Samuel and Hannah Hallowell,	"	27 June 1738.
Rachel daughter of Samuel and Elizabeth Haley,	"	1 October 1738.
Mary daughter of George and Mary Hunnewell,	"	2 June 1738.
James Son of James and Anna Hubbart,	"	18 October 1738.
Thomas Dagget Son of Zechariah and Lydia Hicks,	"	16 December 1738.
Elizabeth daughter of John and Elizabeth Hutte,	"	5 February 1738.
John Son of Nathanael and Ann Harris,	"	15 September 1738.
John Son of Benjamin and Phebe Harrod,	"	3 January 1738.
Elisha Son of Francis and Sarah Hunt,	"	6 November 1738.
Richard Son of John and Margaret Jenkins,	"	6 April 1738.
Mary daughter of Peter and Mary Jersey,	"	16 August 1738.
William Son of William and Anna Johnson,	"	2 July 1738.
Sarah daughter of Samuel and Ruth Jackson,	"	12 March 1738.
Henry Son of William and Margaret Jepson,	"	5 February 1738.
Katharine daughter of Christoper and Sarah Kilby,	"	22 February 1738.

Abigail daughter of Stephen and Elizabeth Kent,	Born	12 November 1738.
Mercy daughter of John and Mercy Late,	"	5 May 1738.
Thomas Son of Nicholas and Grace Luce,	"	15 June 1738.
Samuel Son of John and Mary Lee,	"	23 July 1738.
Elizabeth daughter of George and Elizabeth Lewis,	"	16 July 1738.
David Son of David and Rebekah Lupton,	"	4 September 1738.
David Son of David and Abigail Lenox,	"	21 November 1738.
Nicholas Son of Nicholas and Elizabeth Lash,	"	13 March 1738.
Katharine daughter of Francis and Elizabeth Moore,	"	4 August 1738.
Jonas Clarke Son of Stephen and Sarah Minot,	"	20 August 1738.
Stevens Son of David and Susanna Mason,	"	14 January 1738.
William Son of Samuel and Mary Marshall,	"	9 February 1738.
Oliver Son of Belcher and Ann Noyes,	"	6 August 1738.
William Son of William and Mary Nisbitt,	"	18 November 1738.
Mary daughter of Thomas and Mary Newman,	"	3 September 1738.
Samuel Son of Samuel and Mary Neate,	"	28 February 1738.
Ebenezer Son of William and Mary Owen,	"	21 August 1738.
Samuel Son of Dean and Mary Osgood,	"	1 September 1738.
Daniel Son of Peter and Mary Oliver,	"	8 October 1738.
Elisabeth daughter of Andrew and Mary Oliver,	"	7 March 1738.
William Son of Roger and Elizabeth Price,	"	3 April 1738.
Abigail daughter of John and Abigail Perkins,	"	25 March 1738.
John Son of Isaac and Agnes Peirce,	"	19 May 1738.
Samuel Son of Samuel and Abigail Pousley,	"	15 July 1738.
William Son of William and Elizabeth Peirce,	"	9 December 1738.
Mary daughter of John and Mary Phillips,	"	2 September 1738.
Elizabeth daughter of Nathanael and Susanna Procter,	"	29 July 1738.
Samuel Son of John and Hannah Procter,	"	26 September 1738.
Mary daughter of Henry and Mary Price,	"	18 October 1738.
Elizabeth daughter of William and Mary Paine,	"	17 March 1738.
Anna daughter of Thomas and Martha Parker,	"	2 March 1738.
Richard Son of Benjamin and Abigail Renken,	"	10 Octbber 1738.
Samuel Son of Samuel and Hannah Robinson,	"	1 November 1738.
Elizabeth daughter of Nathanael and Mary Roberts,	"	9 December 1738.
Rebecca daughter of Gamaliel and Sarah Rogers,	"	16 November 1738.
Lydia daughter of Samuel and Lydia Rogers,	"	15 September 1738.
Andros Son of Stephen and Sarah Randall,	"	20 February 1738.
John Son of Samuel and Hannah Ruggles,	"	26 May 1738.
Thomas Son of Benjamin and Elizabeth Russell,	"	10 May 1738.
John Son of John and Elizabeth Stevens,	"	11 April 1738.
Elizabeth daughter of Nathan and Mary Sargent,	"	16 September 1738.
Mary daughter of Jeremiah and Mary Snow,	"	26 May 1738.
William Son of Richard and Rachel Salter,	"	23 November 1738.
Mary daughter of Elias and Huldah Sorien,	"	24 October 1738.
George Son of John and Sarah Smallpeice,	"	25 December 1738.
Mary daughter of Nathan and Lydia Safford,	"	27 December 1738.
Mary daughter of John and Mary Salmon,	"	10 February 1738.
John Son of John and Sarah Sale,	"	17 March 1738.
Elizabeth daughter of Andrew and Hannah Symmes,	"	4 March 1738.
Elizabeth daughter of John and Mercy Scolley,	"	15 February 1738.
Richard Son of Daniel and Hannah Tucker,	"	27 March 1738.
Sarah daughter of Moses and Hannah Tyler,	"	21 April 1738.
John Son of Thomas and Sarah Townsend,	"	11 May 1738.
Hannah daughter of John and Hannah Turner,	"	11 May 1738.
Lucy daughter of John and Mary Tyng,	"	15 April 1738.
Mary daughter of John and Elizabeth Turner,	"	30 June 1738.
William Son of Alexander and Elizabeth Thorp,	"	14 July 1738.
Samuel Son of Jonathan and Mary Tarbox,	"	10 November 1738.
Sarah daughter of Thomas and Bethiah Tyler,	"	17 November 1738.

BIRTHS — 1738-39.

Hannah daughter of Edward and Ann Tyng,	Born	25 October 1738.
Samuel Son of William and Bethiah Torrey,	"	7 February 1738.
Josiah Son of Josiah and Ann Torrey,	"	22 May 1738.
Nathanael Son of Nathanael and Ruth Thayer,	"	27 January 1738.
Joanna daughter of Nathanael and Joanna Thwing,	"	28 November 1738.
John Son of William and Faith Taylor,	"	25 April 1738.
Ambrose Son of Ambrose and Anna Vincent,	"	14 September 1738.
Hannah daughter of James and Judith Worth,	"	10 July 1738.
Nathanael Son of Samuel and Mary Wheeler,	"	16 July 1738.
Abraham Son of Thomas and Jane Williston,	"	23 July 1738.
William Son of William and Submit Walton,	"	12 April 1738.
Samuel Son of Samuel and Mary White,	"	16 October 1738.
Francis Breno Son of John and Elizabeth Whitney,	"	1 August 1738.
Grace daughter of Gamaliel and Abigail Wallis,	"	31 October 1738.
Elisha Son of Joseph and Abigail Webb,	"	26 January 1738.
Bennet Son of Joseph and Joanna Woods,	"	27 February 1738.
Henry Son of Francis and Susanna Wells,	"	15 January 1738.
James Son of James and Margaret Webster,	"	9 March 1738.
Stephen Son of Stephen and Hannah Winter,	"	16 February 1738.
Hannah daughter of William and Mary Warner,	"	12 March 1738.
David Son of David Bell and Anna his Wife,	"	5 May 1738.
Benjamin Son of John Carnes and Sarah his Wife,	"	31 August 1738.
Anne daughter of Peter Cade and Elizabeth his Wife,	"	February 1738.
John Son of Ralph Carter and Sarah his Wife,	"	8 October 1738.
Margaret daughter of John Gardner and Mary his Wife,	"	17 March 1738.
Thomas Son of Thomas Jackson and Anne his Wife,	"	6 January 1738.
Sarah daughter of Ebenezer Lowell and Mary his Wife,	"	10 April 1738.
Margaret daughter of Sylvester Mackannawy and Mary his Wife,	"	15 May 1738.
Oliver Son of Belcher Noyes and Ann his Wife,	"	6 August 1738.
Richard Son of Owen Williams and Mary his Wife,	"	6 November 1738.
Benjamin Son of Benjamin Williams and Mary his Wife,	"	19 August 1738.

1739.

James Son of Jeremiah and Elizabeth Allen,	Born	24 July 1739.
Elizabeth daughter of Nathanael and Mary Adams,	"	21 October 1739.
Mary daughter of Henry and Deliverance Atkins,	"	18 September 1739.
John Son of John and Mary Avery,	"	2 September 1739.
John Son of John and Dorcas Brown,	"	25 March 1739.
Benjamin Son of Increase and Ann Blake,	"	9 May 1739.
Pyam Son of Pyam and Jerusha Blowers,	"	16 April 1739.
Ann daughter of Benjamin and Mary Ballard,	"	30 April 1739.
Sarah daughter of William and Sarah Bryant,	"	16 May 1739.
Isabella daughter of Benjamin and Mary Brown,	"	21 May 1739.
Samuel Son of Powning and Sarah Bridgham,	"	21 July 1739.
Sarah daughter of Benjamin and Ann Babbidge,	"	18 April 1739.
Thomas Son of Thomas and Elizabeth Brown,	"	29 July 1739.
Susanna daughter of Joseph and Mary Birch,	"	23 July 1739.
Rowland Son of John and Hannah Bennet,	"	13 May 1739.
Abigail daughter of Abijah and Abigail Brown,	"	2 March 1739.
Ebenezer Son of Thomas and Mehetabel Bolter,	"	22 June 1739.
Mary daughter of John and Sarah Billings,	"	8 October 1739.
James Son of James and Elizabeth Butler,	"	15 February 1739.
Elizabeth daughter of Ebenezer and Mary Berry,	"	11 October 1739.
Alford Son of Alford and Elizabeth Butler,	"	19 October 1739.
Isaiah Son of Edward and Martha Barrett,	"	27 October 1739.
Anna daughter of John and Anna Ballard,	"	18 February 1739.

Herman Son of Martin and Susanna Brimmer,	Born	25 February 1739.
Joseph Son of John and Ruth Barrell,	"	28 February 1739.
Anna daughter of John and Sarah Barrett,	"	8 March 1739.
Gibbins Son of John and Elizabeth Bouve,	"	11 May 1739.
Mehetabel daughter of Joseph and Elizabeth Clough,	"	31 March 1739.
Ellis Son of Joseph and Sarah Clough,	"	28 March 1739.
Rebekah daughter of David and Sarah Christy,	"	5 April 1739.
Mary daughter of Nathanael and Mary Cobbet,	"	18 June 1739.
Lucretia daughter of Anthony and Mary Caverley,	"	1 July 1739.
Lydia daughter of John and Lydia Cullam,	"	20 April 1739.
Samuel Johnson Son of Isaac and Hannah Casno,	"	12 July 1739.
Abigail daughter of William and Elizabeth Cunningham,	"	11 July 1739.
Mercy daughter of Charles and Mary Coffin,	"	4 July 1739.
John Son of John and Katharine Cumming,	"	15 July 1739.
Catharine daughter of Jonathan and Hannah Chandler,	"	18 December 1739.
Lydia daughter of David and Lydia Cutler,	"	20 January 1739.
Ann daughter of John and Ann Chandler,	"	2 March 1739.
Catharine daughter of Cord and Sarah Cordis,	"	18 March 1739.
Fawley Son of John and Elizabeth Daniel,	"	22 June 1739.
Dorothy daughter of Thomas and Sarah Drowne,	"	27 June 1739.
Mehetabel daughter of Jonathan and Mary Dwight,	"	3 September 1739.
Jonathan Son of Joseph and Jane Dowse,	"	22 July 1739.
William Son of William and Elizabeth Dinsdell,	"	3 October 1739.
Ann daughter of James and Mary Davenport,	"	18 May 1739.
Susanna daughter of Thomas and Prudence Delaplace,	"	30 December 1739
Robert Son of John and Elizabeth Davis,	"	19 November 1739.
Katharine daughter of Samuel and Elizabeth Everton,	"	28 April 1739.
John Son of Joseph and Sarah Edwards,	"	23 March 1739.
Thomas Son of Thomas and Sarah Edes,	"	8 November 1739.
Samuel Son of Samuel and Elizabeth Eliot,	"	25 August 1739.
Robert Son of John and Mary Earle,	"	31 January 1739.
Mary daughter of Edward and Sarah Edes,	"	23 March 1739.
Hannah daughter of Seth and Susanna Foster,	"	26 March 1739.
Hannah daughter of Paul and Hannah Farmer,	"	2 August 1739.
Thomas Son of Nathan and Mary Foster,	"	20 August 1739.
Elizabeth daughter of Andrew and Sarah Friswell,	"	29 September 1739.
Mary daughter of Joseph and Margaret Fitch,	"	10 September 1739.
William Son of Jonathan and Elizabeth Farnum,	"	18 December 1739.
Stephen Son of Josiah and Mary Flagg,	"	24 December 1739.
William Son of William and Ann Frost,	"	12 February 1739.
Elizabeth daughter of Hopestill and Sarah Foster,	"	20 February 1739.
Charles Son of Charles and Rebekah Florence,	"	24 October 1739.
Mehetabel daughter of Grafton and Sarah Feveryear,	"	28 February 1739.
Benjamin Son of Benjamin and Margaret Green,	"	31 January 1739.
Samuel Son of Samuel and Sarah Goodwin,	"	20 April 1739.
Scarborough Son of Richard and Hannah Gridley,	"	9 October 1739.
Mary daughter of John and Elizabeth Grant,	"	18 August 1739.
James Son of Silvester and Ann Gardner,	"	9 September 1739.
Huldah daughter of John and Sarah Greenough,	"	23 September 1739.
Sarah daughter of Bartholomew and Sarah Gedney,	"	2 November 1739.
Absalom Son of John and Mary Gatchell,	"	24 September 1739.
Sarah daughter of Ezekiel and Elizabeth Goldthwait,	"	20 March 1739.
John Son of Joseph and Mary Grande,	"	22 October 1739.
Mary daughter of Jonathan and Mary Greenleaf,	"	22 November 1739.

Births — 1739.

Joseph Son of Ebenezer and Abigail Gross,	Born	20 December 1739.
Elizabeth daughter of Rufus and Katharine Greene,	"	3 January 1739.
Mary daughter of Abraham and Mary Gibaut,	"	23 January 1739.
Martha daughter of Joseph and Martha Goldthwait,	"	10 May 1739.
Sarah daughter of Joseph and Ann Hudson,	"	4 May 1739.
Elizur Son of Jacob and Susanna Holyoke,	"	25 September 1739.
Isabella daughter of James and Katharine Hodges,	"	30 May 1739.
Mary Belcher daughter of Daniel and Elizabeth Henshaw,	"	20 June 1739.
Tabitha daughter of Nathanael and Ann Hodgdon,	"	17 June 1739.
Elizabeth daughter of Israel and Abigail Hearsey,	"	11 March 1739.
Ann daughter of Abraham and Mehetabel Holland,	"	17 June 1739.
Martha daughter of George and Abigail Hewes,	"	27 June 1739.
John Son of John and Elizabeth Hutte,	"	17 July 1739.
Josiah Son of Josiah and Mary Holland,	"	13 August 1739.
Abigail daughter of Stephen and Elizabeth Hunniwell,	"	25 July 1739.
Neverson Son of Samuel and Mary Hastings,	"	6 October 1739.
Sarah daughter of William and Sarah Hickling,	"	19 September 1739.
Phillip Son of Phillip and Mary Howell,	"	10 October 1739.
Abigail daughter of John and Ann Harris,	"	20 October 1739.
William Son of John and Mary Hill,	"	27 April 1739.
Ann daughter of George and Ann Holmes,	"	25 December 1739.
Mary daughter of Richard and Elizabeth Houghton,	"	17 August 1739.
Samuel Son of Samuel and Hannah Hallowell,	"	23 February 1739.
Henry Maxwell Son of John and Elizabeth Hill,	"	20 September 1739.
Thomas Son of Leach and Hannah Harris,	"	9 March 1739.
Joseph Son of Abraham and Ann Ingersol,	"	5 August 1739.
William Son of Silence and Hannah Ivory,	"	16 January 1739.
Sarah daughter of Joseph and Susanna Jackson,	"	20 March 1738/9.
Anna daughter of William and Anna Johnson,	"	20 February 1739.
Sarah daughter of Jeffs and Sarah Johnson,	"	14 August 1739.
Nathanael Son of Richard and Sarah Kent,	"	6 April 1739.
Henry Son of Henry and Sarah King,	"	5 April 1739.
Mary daughter of Solomon and Lydia Kneeland,	"	11 April 1739.
Hugh Son of Hugh and Susanna Kennady,	"	6 February 1739.
Katharine daughter of Robert and Katharine Lord,	"	14 April 1739.
Mehetabel daughter of Israel and Mehetabel Look,	"	10 June 1739.
Hannah daughter of James and Hannah Lowden,	"	21 June 1739.
Nicholas Son of Nicholas and Grace Luce,	"	2 September 1739.
Jonathan Son of Jonathan and Ann Lowder,	"	16 December 1739.
John Son of Robert and Rebekah Lovering,	"	17 August 1739.
John Son of John and Mary Larrabee,	"	23 January 1739.
Elizabeth daughter of John and Elizabeth Macklelan,	"	3 August 1739.
Jane daughter of John and Jane Milks,	"	16 September 1739.
Elizabeth daughter of William and Katharine Mellens,	"	23 January 1739.
Ann daughter of Samuel and Ann Maltby,	"	24 January 1739.
Stephen Son of Stephen and Sarah Minot,	"	14 February 1739.
David Son of David and Mary Newhall,	"	21 June 1739.
Mary daughter of James and Hannah Nicholson,	"	14 August 1739.
Alexander Son of James and Eunice Nicol,	"	14 December 1739.
Elizabeth daughter of John and Anna Norton,	"	21 March 1739.
John Son of John and Abigail Perkins,	"	6 July 1739.
Samuel Son of Moses and Jane Prince,	"	29 October 1739.
Mary daughter of William and Atterlanta Prichard,	"	14 March 1739.
Thomas Son of Thomas and Sarah Pooke,	"	27 January 1739.
Sarah daughter of Caleb and Sarah Pratt,	"	17 October 1739.
Benjamin Son of John and Mary Phillips,	"	19 February 1739.
Edward Son of Peter and Elizabeth Prescott,	"	6 October 1739.

Henry Yelverton Son of Rev. Roger and Elizabeth Price,	Born	26 February 1739.
Mehetabel daughter of Joseph and Sarah Putman,	"	1 February 1739.
Mary daughter of John and Sarah Phillips,	"	12 May 1739.
Nathaniel Son of John and Tabitha Ruddock,	"	18 January 1738/9.
Jeremiah Son of Benjamin and Elizabeth Russell,	"	4 May 1739
Elizabeth daughter of Samuel and Lydia Rogers,	"	20 February 1739.
Ann daughter of James and Sarah Raymar,	"	19 July 1739.
William Son of Thomas and Elizabeth Russell,	"	12 September 1739.
Sarah daughter of Benjamin and Priscilla Roberts,	"	11 October 1739.
Elizabeth daughter of William and Elizabeth Raymond,	"	22 May 1739.
John Son of John and Rebekah Robinson,	"	16 October 1739.
Hannah daughter of Ebenezer and Mary Storer,	"	22 May 1739.
William Son of William and Susanna Sloper,	"	1 September 1739.
John Son of Thomas and Deborah Savage,	"	11 June 1739.
Rachel daughter of William and Rachel Swanton,	"	13 April 1739.
John Son of Jonathan and Mary Snelling,	"	3 February 1739.
Daniel Son of Daniel and Mary Sigourney,	"	1 October 1739.
Elizabeth daughter of Simeon and Ruth Skilling,	"	27 January 1739.
Elizabeth daughter of John and Mary Shepard,	"	10 October 1739
Samuel Son of Nicholas and Martha Salisbury,	"	18 November 1739.
Samuel Son of Samuel and Deborah Smith,	"	5 December 1739.
Matthew Son of Alexander and Alice Slowly,	"	24 July 1739.
Samuel Son of Samuel and Abigail Sumner,	"	3 November 1739.
Edward Son of John and Sarah Sale,	"	3 March 1739.
Peter Son of John and Mary Sorien,	"	9 March 1739.
Susanna daughter of John and Sarah Sweetser,	"	2 March 1739.
Thomas Son of Thomas and Sarah Townsend,	"	23 May 1739.
Deborah daughter of Moses and Hannah Tyler,	"	23 July 1739.
Ann daughter of Josiah and Ann Torrey,	"	20 January 1739.
Benjamin Son of John and Hannah Thwing,	"	2 December 1739
Sarah daughter of John and Mary Tyng,	"	19 October 1739
Abigail daughter of William and Faith Taylor,	"	12 December 1739.
James Son of Onesiphorus and Judith Tileston,	"	18 February 1739.
Elisha Son of Elisha and Martha Townsend,	"	11 February 1739.
Sarah daughter of William and Anne Vassall,	"	17 June 1739.
Elizabeth daughter of Samuel and Elizabeth Vaughan,	"	4 January 1739.
Jonathan Son of Jonathan and Susanna Vickery,	"	15 August 1739.
Jemima daughter of Benjamin and Jemima White,	"	25 April 1739.
Samuel Son of Allen and Agness Wheppe,	"	24 June 1739.
Edward Son of Isaac and Sarah Walker,	"	10 October 1739.
Eunice daughter of Gamaliel and Abigail Wallis,	"	19 October 1739.
Ephraim Son of Ephraim and Elizabeth Wheeler,	"	2 March 1739.
Francis Brinno Son of John and Elizabeth Whitney,	"	1 February 1739.
Mary daughter of Joseph and Martha Wheeler,	"	26 January 1739.
David Son of David and Mary Webb,	"	16 December 1739.
Mary daughter of John and Hannah Wells,	"	30 December 1739.
Francis Son of Elisha and Abigail West,	"	13 March 1739.
Lydia daughter of William and Hannah Young,	"	1 March 1739.
Nathaniel Son of John Baker and Jerusha his Wife,	"	17 December 1739.
Deborah daughter of Bejamin Beard and Deborah his Wife,	"	30 July 1739.
Hepzibah daughter of John Carnes and Sarah his Wife,	"	8 January 1739.
George Son of Peter Cade and Elizabeth his Wife,	"	September 1739.
Abigail daughter of Edward Foster and Abigail his Wife,	"	18 December 1739.
James Son of Gershom Flagg and Hannah his Wife,	"	28 October 1739.

BIRTHS — 1739-40.

Samuel Smith Son of Ebenezer Hayward and Rachel his Wife,	Born	23 August 1739.
Mary daughter of Edward Jackson and Dorothy his Wife,	"	16 December 1739.
John Son of Michael Lowell and Abigail his Wife,	"	12 March 1739.
Sarah daughter of William Marshall and Ann his Wife,	"	16 February 1739.
Catharine daughter of Neal McIntyer and Esther his Wife,	"	30 May 1739.
Ann daughter of Caleb Parker and Mary his Wife,	"	20 November 1739.
Mary daughter of Ebenezer Sumner and Elizabeth his Wife,	"	26 March 1739.
John Son of John Underwood and Elizabeth his Wife,	"	14 February 1739.

1740.

Cornelius Son of Richard and Hannah Abbot,	Born	2 April 1740.
Joshua Son of James and Bathsheba Allen,	"	17 November 1740.
Josiah Son of Jonathan and Elizabeth Browne,	"	27 March 1740.
Hannah daughter of John and Margaret Breck,	"	1 May 1740.
Joseph Son of Increase and Ann Blake,	"	5 July 1740.
Emma daughter of John and Sarah Blowers,	"	12 March 1740.
Abigail daughter of Nathaniel and Abigail Brown,	"	8 August 1740.
John Son of Joseph and Mary Blake,	"	27 August 1740.
Mehetabel daughter of John and Content Buttolph,	"	25 March 1740.
Frances daughter of William and Frances Bowen,	"	2 August 1740.
Hugh Son of John and Elizabeth Brown,	"	13 March 1740.
John Son of John and Lydia Bell,	"	24 February 1740
Susanna daughter of James and Susanna Boutineau,	"	22 February 1740.
Samuel Son of Robert and Isabella Breck,	"	18 June 1740.
Christopher Son of William and Susanna Butler,	"	26 July 1740.
Joseph Wadsworth Son of Isaiah and Elizabeth Barrett,	"	19 September 1740.
John Son of Henry and Sarah Blasdell,	"	2 October 1740.
Benjamin Son of John and Susanna Brown,	"	15 November 1740.
Sarah daughter of William and Ann Beers,	"	11 July 1740.
Thomas Son of Richard and Mary Basset,	"	24 November 1740.
Sarah daughter of Daniel and Mary Ballard, Jun.,	"	16 December 1740.
Mary daughter of Mather and Anna Byles,	"	20 December 1740.
Amey daughter of John and Lydia Cullam,	"	7 February 1740.
Benjamin Son of John and Sarah Colman,	"	19 July 1740
Jane daughter of William and Mary Curtis,	"	2 April 1740.
Ebenezer Son of Ebenezer and Elizabeth Clough,	"	20 June 1740.
Archibald Son of Archibald and Sarah Crawford,	"	5 February 1740.
Katharine daughter of James and Christian Clark,	"	10 October 1740.
Elizabeth daughter of John and Katharine Cummins,	"	14 February 1740.
William Son of John and Ann Chambers (born at Medford),		25 May 1740.
Margaret daughter of Obadiah and Margaret Cookson,	"	29 May 1740.
Thomas Son of Thomas and Ann Crafts,	"	13 July 1740.
John Son of Edmund and Jane Condon,	"	14 June 1740.
Ebenezer Son of Ebenezer and Rebecca Coburn,	"	19 June 1740.
Mary daughter of William and Civil Clark,	"	1 November 1740.
Joseph Son of James and Sarah Clark,	"	22 December 1740.
Susanna daughter of John and Deborah Colson,	"	20 January 1740.
Ebenezer Son of Harbottle and Dorothy Dorr,	"	24 July 1740.
Samuel Son of John and Elizabeth Daniel,	"	31 October 1740.
George Son of James and Mary Davenport,	"	9 December 1740.
Ruth daughter of John and Abigail Doble,	"	1 February 1740.

Joanna daughter of James and Mary Dodge,	Born	27 February 1740.
Ann daughter of John and Abigail Erving,	"	20 January 1740.
Joseph Son of Nathan and Mary Foster,	"	5 January 1740.
Eliphalet Son of Benjamin and Jerusha Fitch,	"	5 November 1740.
James Son of Joseph and Abigail Flood,	"	9 October 1740.
Elizabeth daughter of Edward and Jane Fryer,	"	8 July 1740.
Anna daughter of Joshua and Sarah Gee,	"	18 November 1740.
William Son of Thomas and Martha Greenough,	"	2 May 1740.
Elizabeth daughter of Joseph and Mary Gale,	"	18 May 1740.
Sarah daughter of John and Elizabeth Grant,	"	19 September 1740.
Abigail daughter of Samuel and Sarah Gooding,	"	1 October 1740.
Samuel Son of Jonathan and Mary Greenleaf,	"	28 October 1740.
Abigail daughter of Stephen and Mary Greenleaf,	"	18 April 1740.
Edward Son of Samuel and Sarah Gray,	"	26 May 1740.
Bethiah daughter of John and Bethiah Gerrish,	"	28 April 1740.
Ellis Son of Ellis and Sarah Gray,	"	24 June 1740.
Mary daughter of Thomas and Mary Green,	"	2 October 1740.
John Son of Samuel and Ann Gibson,	"	2 April 1740.
Samuel Son of Thomas and Elizabeth Greene,	"	4 October 1740.
Michael Burrell Son of Joseph and Martha Goldthwait,	"	5 January 1740.
Harris Son of Jabez and Mary Hatch,	"	20 October 1740.
Thomas Son of Thomas and Margaret Hutchinson,	"	15 October 1740.
Abigail daughter of Nathaniel and Abigail Howland,	"	24 October 1740.
Thomas Son of Thomas and Mary Hubbard,	"	30 December 1740.
Margaret daughter of Thomas and Hannah Hill,	"	24 May 1740.
Samuel Son of Samuel and Elizabeth Haley,	"	25 June 1740.
John Son of John and Mary Hind,	"	10 January 1740.
Prudence daughter of John and Ann Harris,	"	2 March 1740.
Elisha Son of Francis and Sarah Hunt,	"	6 April 1740.
John Son of Peter and Katharine Harratt,	"	6 April 1740.
Miles Son of Miles and Mary Hubbard,	"	4 September 1740.
Susanna daughter of William and Sarah Hickling,	"	6 February 1740.
Mary daughter of William and Rebecca Homes,	"	5 March 1740.
Mary daughter of John and Margaret Jenkins,	"	11 September 1740.
Joseph Son of Joseph and Abigail Jackson,	"	21 October 1740.
Clement Son of Joseph and Susanna Jackson,	"	8 December 1740.
John Son of Samuel and Ruth Jackson,	"	24 August 1740.
Samuel Son of Jeffs and Sarah Johnson,	"	1 March 1740.
Sarah daughter of Joseph and Mary Kneeland,	"	18 April 1740.
Mary daughter of John and Mehetabel Kneeland,	"	19 October 1740.
Margaret daughter of Hugh and Susanna Kennady,	"	26 February 1740.
Mary daughter of John and Elizabeth Lee,	"	14 April 1740.
Abigail daughter of David and Abigail Lenox,	"	26 January 1740.
Sarah daughter of Robert and Katharine Lord,	"	27 September 1740.
Thomas Son of John and Sarah Macklish,	"	5 April 1740.
Elizabeth daughter of David and Susanna Mason,	"	28 March 1740.
Samuel Son of Samuel and Sarah Makelwain,	"	22 September 1740.
Thomas Dyer Son of Samuel and Ann Maltby,	"	24 December 1740.
Sarah daughter of Benjamin and Sarah Marshall,	"	12 May 1740.
Mary daughter of David and Mary Newhall,	"	7 October 1740.
Jeremiah Jackson Son of James and Hannah Nicholson,	"	2 February 1740.
Dean Son of Dean and Mary Osgood,	"	19 August 1740.
Joseph Son of William and Mary Owen,	"	9 December 1740.
Thomas Son of Thomas and Sarah Oxnard,	"	17 March 1740.
Margaret daughter of Andrew and Mary Oliver,	"	3 July 1740.
Joshua Son of Isaac and Agnes Peirce,	"	25 August 1740.
Bulkely Son of Peter and Elizabeth Prescott,	"	21 September 1740.

BIRTHS — 1740. 241

Sarah daughter of William and Mary Paine,	Born	25 January 1740.
Jonathan Son of William and Elizabeth Peirce,	"	6 January 1740.
Hannah daughter of James and Rachel Pitson,	"	28 February 1740.
Love daughter of John and Lydia Procter,	"	20 December 1740.
William Son of William and Dorcas Page,	"	5 June 1740.
Joseph Son of Samuel and Hannah Ruggles,	"	27 June 1740.
Deborah daughter of James and Deborah Robins,	"	22 February 1740.
Elizabeth daughter of Gamaliel and Sarah Rogers,	"	20 November 1740.
Elizabeth daughter of Benjamin and Elizabeth Russell,	"	16 June 1740.
Edward Son of John and Tabitha Ruddock,	"	18 May 1740.
John Son of John and Margaret Rush,	"	28 April 1740.
Elizabeth daughter of John and Mary Salmon,	"	9 November 1740.
Thomas Son of Andrew and Anna Symmes,	"	3 January 1740.
John Son of William and Elizabeth Simpkins,	"	12 November 1740.
Elizabeth daughter of John and Elizabeth Stevens,	"	16 December 1740.
Andrew Son of Anthony and Mary Sigourney,	"	23 January 1740.
Nathaniel Son of Nathaniel and Martha Simpson,	"	24 February 1740.
John Ronshon Son of Andrew and Mary Sigourney,	"	29 May 1740.
William Son of Thomas and Mary Speakman,	"	30 September 1740.
John Viscount Son of John and Mary Stuart,	"	17 August 1740.
Nathaniel Son of Nathaniel and Alicia Shower,	"	9 February 1740.
Elizabeth daughter of Richard and Rachel Salter,	"	18 May 1740.
Simeon Son of Simeon and Ruth Skilling,	"	29 December 1740.
Martha daughter of Joseph and Elizabeth Scott,	"	22 December 1740
Elizabeth daughter of John and Mary Tyng,	"	23 December 1740.
George Son of John and Sarah Tyler,	"	11 December 1740.
James Son of John and Jane Tudor,	"	19 March 1740.
Lucy daughter of Thomas and Bethiah Tyler,	"	12 September 1740.
William Son of Nathaniel and Joanna Thwing,	"	16 May 1740.
Sarah daughter of Ebenezer and Elizabeth Townsend,	"	14 November 1740.
Mary daughter of John and Rebecca Tillston,	"	8 August 1740.
Mary daughter of Richard and Abigail True,	"	15 July 1740.
Ann daughter of Lewis and Dorothy Vassall,	"	13 July 1740.
James Son of James and Judith Worth,	"	23 March 1740.
William Son of Richard and Abigail Willis,	"	2 October 1740.
Nathaniel Son of Nathaniel and Elizabeth Woodward,	"	4 September 1740.
William Son of Francis and Susanna Wells,	"	22 June 1740.
Mary daughter of Nathaniel and Hannah Warner,	"	16 April 1740.
Samuel Son of William and Rebecca Whitwell,	"	3 April 1740.
John Son of John and Sarah Willett,	"	10 June 1740.
William Son of Joseph and Abigail Webb,	"	26 June 1740.
Samuel Son of Gamaliel and Abigail Wallis,	"	20 December 1740.
Jonathan Son of Sendall and Elizabeth Williams	"	27 November 1740.
Joseph Son of Samuel and Mary Wheeler,	"	5 February 1740.
George Son of Davenport and Sarah Walker,	"	6 January 1740
Susannah daughter of James Boutineau and Susannah his Wife,	"	22 February 1740.
Susanna daughter of Peace Cazneau and Mary his Wife,	"	18 August 1740.
Sarah daughter of Ralph Carter and Sarah his Wife,	"	5 October 1740.
John Son of John Crosley and Susanna his Wife.	"	27 September 1740.
Joseph Lee Son of Richard Clark and Elizabeth his Wife,	"	28 April 1740.
Joseph Son of Samuel Deluceny and Elizabeth his Wife,	"	29 April 1740.
Grace daughter of Robert Four Acre and Susannah his Wife,	"	11 June 1740.

Thomas Son of Thomas Jackson and Anne his Wife, Born 5 October 1740.
Mary daughter of Ebenezer Lowell and Mary his Wife, " 20 February 1740.
David Son of David McLeod and Mary his Wife, " 16 May 1740.
Belcher Son of Belcher Noyes and Ann his Wife, " 29 June 1740.
Hannah daughter of Emanuel Perero and Elizabeth his Wife, " 10 September 1740.
Robert Son of John Smallpeice and Sarah his Wife, " 6 May 1740.
Joseph Son of Samuel Torrey and Silence his Wife, " 9 September 1740.
William Son of Fortescue Vernon and Jane his Wife, " 27 June 1740.

1741.

Hull Son of Richard and Hannah Abbot, Born 14 July 1741.
Ann daughter of Henry and Deliverance Atkins, " 28 June 1741.
Ebenezer Son of Ebenezer and Mary Brown, " 6 July 1741.
William Son of William and Sarah Baker, " 13 June 1741.
Elizabeth daughter of Daniel and Elizabeth Barker, " 8 February 1741.
Mary daughter of Thomas and Mary Brookes, " 29 March 1741.
Benjamin Son of John and Anna Bennett, " 14 April 1741.
William Son of James and Hephzibah Bradford, " 26 May 1741.
Hannah daughter of Samuel and Hannah Brown, " 9 January 1741.
Sampson Salter Son of John and Sarah Blowers, " 10 March 1741.
Mehetabel daughter of Belthazer and Mary Bayard, " 26 April 1741.
William Son of John and Elizabeth Bovey, " 19 April 1741.
Elizabeth daughter of Benjamin and Elizabeth Bailey, " 5 May 1741.
Francis Lindall Son of Francis and Jane Borland, " 2 May 1741.
Elizabeth daughter of Thomas and Elizabeth Browne, " 6 June 1741.
Nathaniel Son of Thomas and Susanna Bently, " 3 September 1741.
Theodore Son of John and Ruth Barrell, " 27 August 1741.
William Son of William and Elizabeth Bennett, " 10 September 1741.
Nathaniel Son of Increase and Ann Blake, " 28 September 1741.
Nathaniel Son of Nathaniel and Elizabeth Breed, " 16 September 1741.
Abigail daughter of Joseph and Mary Birch, " 30 September 1741.
Thomas Son of Samuel and Sarah Barber, " 4 October 1741.
Susanna daughter of John and Sarah Barrett, " 18 October 1741.
Dorothy daughter of Thomas and Susanna Baxter, " 26 December 1741.
Mary daughter of Nathaniel and Abigail Brown, " 19 July 1741.
Elizabeth daughter of John and Zebiah Cravath, " 9 November 1741.
Elizabeth daughter of Andrew and Elizabeth Craigie, " 4 December 1741.
Ebenezer Son of Ebenezer and Rebecca Coburn, " 13 September 1741.
John Son of James and Rachel Clough, " 15 April 1741.
John Son of John and Mehetabel Cowley, " 30 August 1741.
Thomas Son of Cord and Hannah Cordis, " 5 September 1741.
Jerusha daughter of Phillip and Mary Coulter, " 26 November 1741.
Phillip Son of Phillip and Rebecca Cartwright, " 16 December 1741.
Samuel Johnson Son of Isaac and Hannah Cazneau, " 18 January 1741.
Mary daughter of John and Abigail Colson, " 3 September 1741.
David Son of John and Abigail Colson, " 17 January 1741.
John Son of John and Ann Chandler, " 22 March 1741.
Sarah daughter of John and Sarah Dabney, " 11 June 1741.
William Son of William and Margaret Downe, " 17 July 1741.
Shem Son of Thomas and Sarah Drowne, " 10 August 1741.
Elizabeth daughter of Benjamin and Mary Dorby, " 17 September 1741.
Ruth daughter of Samuel and Elizabeth Eliot, " 29 March 1741.
Hannah daughter of Jacob and Mary Emmons, " 21 November 1741.
Sarah daughter of Thomas and Sarah Edes, " 21 November 1741.

BIRTHS — 1741.

Ann daughter of William and Ann Frost,	Born	1 August 1741.
Elizabeth daughter of Grafton and Sarah Feveryear,	"	23 February 1741.
James Son of John and Hannah Fenno,	"	31 May 1741.
Thomas Wait Son of Seth and Susanna Foster,	"	2 May 1741.
John Son of Thomas and Sarah Foster, jr.	"	28 November 1741.
Ann daughter of Patrick and Katharine Gibbins,	"	4 June 1741.
John Son of John and Mary Gatchell,	"	15 June 1741.
Samuel Son of Nathaniel and Elizabeth Greenwood,	"	11 September 1741.
Hannah daughter of Jonathan and Mary Greenleaf,	"	17 December 1741.
Hannah daughter of Benjamin and Mary Green,	"	29 March 1741.
Thomas Son of John and Sarah Greenough,	"	9 July 1741.
Harrison Son of Harrison and Elizabeth Gray,	"	9 August 1741.
John Son of Stephen and Eunice Greenleaf,	"	31 July 1741.
Rebecca daughter of Richard and Hannah Gridley,	"	25 April 1741.
Ann daughter of Silvester and Ann Gardner,	"	21 April 1741.
Alexander Son of Samuel and Sarah Gray,	"	23 February 1741.
Lydia daughter of Hill and Lydia Green,	"	25 December 1741.
Anstis daughter of Stephen and Mary Greenleaf,	"	26 January 1741.
Elizabeth daughter of Samuel and Elizabeth Grant,	"	2 November 1741.
William Son of Rufus and Katharine Greene,	"	13 December 1741.
Sarah daughter of John and Elizabeth Grant,	"	9 December 1741.
Mary daughter of John and Esther Goold,	"	20 January 1741.
Thomas Son of Ezekiel and Elizabeth Goldthwait,	"	22 July 1741.
Mary daughter of Jacob and Susanna Holyoke,	"	3 July 1741.
Micherson Son of Zechariah and Lydia Hicks,	"	6 August 1741.
Mary daughter of James and Hannah Hinks,	"	3 June 1741.
Ann daughter of James and Katharine Hodges,	"	2 May 1741.
Thomas Son of Thomas and Hannah Hill,	"	26 July 1741.
Benjamin Son of Benjamin and Phebe Harrod,	"	4 June 1741.
Sarah daughter of Samuel and Mercy Hunstable,	"	27 November 1741.
Mary daughter of James and Esther Hill,	"	19 April 1741.
William Son of Israel and Tabitha Hearsey,	"	24 October 1741.
Job and Elizabeth } Gem. Children of John and Ann Harris,	"	20 March 1741.
Charlotte daughter of Zechariah and Elizabeth Johonnott,	"	16 August 1741.
Elizabeth daughter of James and Elizabeth Jeffs,	"	5 September 1741.
Susanna daughter of John and Hannah Jones,	"	6 December 1741.
Jacob Son of John and Mary Johnson,	"	17 August 1741.
Elizabeth daughter of William and Anna Johnson,	"	25 December 1741.
Sarah daughter of Joseph and Sarah Johnson,	"	8 February 1741.
Thornton Son of Jeffs and Sarah Johnson,	"	22 March 1741.
Robert Son of Henry and Sarah King,	"	10 August 1741.
Ann daughter of Jonathan and Ann Lowder,	"	22 November 1741.
Ezekiel Son of Ezekiel and Jane Lewis,	"	6 September 1741.
Samuel Son of Samuel and Judith Larrabee,	"	15 January 1741.
Oliver Son of Oliver and Elizabeth Luckis,	"	25 June 1741.
Elizabeth daughter of Israel and Mehetabel Look,	"	14 August 1741.
John Son of John and Sarah Larrabee,	"	11 November 1741.
Elizabeth daughter of John and Hannah Lee,	"	19 September 1741.
Abigail daughter of William and Abigail Maxwell,	"	6 April 1741.
William Son of John and Elizabeth Macklelain,	"	14 May 1741.
Lydia daughter of Daniel and Lydia Merrett,	"	7 September 1741.
Caleb Son of Francis and Abigail Marshall,	"	24 September 1741.
John Son of John and Anna Norton,	"	19 October 1741.
Samuel Son of James and Eunice Nicoll,	"	10 November 1741.
Peter Son of Peter and Mary Oliver,	"	17 June 1741.
Mary daughter of Josiah and Mary Peirce,	"	23 June 1741.
Mary-Anna daughter of John and Mary Phillips,	"	25 July 1741.
Dorcas daughter of William and Dorcas Page,	"	21 February 1741.

Anne daughter of Caleb and Sarah Pratt,	Born	8 April 1741.
Isaac Son of John and Abigail Perkins,	"	4 September 1741.
William Son of Samuel and Rebecca Partridge,	"	12 October 1741.
Ruth daughter of William and Ruth Putman,	"	13 December 1741.
Susanna daughter of Benjamin and Elizabeth Russell,	"	14 August 1741.
Mary daughter of James and Sarah Raymar,	"	9 March 1741.
Joanna daughter of Nathaniel and Mary Roberts,	"	20 April 1741.
William Son of William and Sarah Russell,	"	5 August 1741.
Sarah daughter of William and Elizabeth Raymond,	"	5 December 1741.
Joseph Son of John and Sarah Smallpeice,	"	19 May 1741.
Ebenezer Son of Samuel and Deborah Smith,	"	9 September 1741.
Samuel Son of Samuel and Sarah Smith,	"	23 September 1741.
William Son of William and Patience Sterling,	"	16 October 1741.
James Son of Daniel and Mary Sigourney,	"	22 May 1741.
Ebenezer Son of Holmes and Lucretia Simpson,	"	15 January 1741.
John Son of Andrew and Hannah Symmes,	"	5 February 1741.
Mercy daughter of John and Mercy Scolley,	"	11 September 1741.
Habijah Son of Thomas and Deborah Savage,	"	27 April 1741.
Joseph Son of Johnathan and Mary Snelling,	"	6 December 1741.
Mary daughter of Samuel and Mariah Servis,	"	10 December 1741.
Benjamin Son of Benjamin and Susanna Sault,	"	18 January 1741.
Hannah daughter of John and Sarah Sweetser,	"	20 February 1741.
Jane daughter of John and Mary Salmon,	"	8 February 1741.
Mary daughter of Anthony and Mary Sigourney,	"	23 March 1741.
William Son of Richard and Rachel Salter,	"	8 February 1741.
Susanna daughter of Thomas and Susanna Snow,	"	23 June 1741.
Thomas Son of Joshua and Martha Thornton,	"	25 March 1741.
Mary daughter of Edward and Anne Tyng,	"	2 June 1741.
David Son of Christopher and Sarah Tilden,	"	5 October 1741.
Elizabeth daughter of William and Faith Taylor,	"	20 August 1741.
Joanna daughter of Nathaniel and Joanna Thwing,	"	21 June 1741.
Ebenezer Son of William and Bethiah Torrey,	"	31 January 1741.
Jonathan Son of Jonathan and Mary Tilden,	"	23 March 1741.
Mary daughter of Samuel and Elizabeth Vaughan,	"	28 April 1741.
Lewis Son of Lewis and Dorothy Vassall,	"	16 September 1741.
Samuel Son of Thomas and Jane Williston,	"	3 November 1741.
William Son of William and Rebecca Wardell,	"	25 December 1741.
William } Ebenezer } Gem. Sons of Seward and Sarah Waters,	"	27 January 1741.
James Son of Joseph and Martha Wheeler,	"	19 August 1741.
David Son of Allen and Agness Wheppe,	"	28 July 1741.
John Son of William and Mary Williams,	"	15 October 1741.
William Son of Ephraim and Elizabeth Wheeler,	"	19 October 1741.
Thankful daughter of Samuel and Elizabeth Woods,	"	1 April 1741.
Jacob Son of Sendall and Elizabeth Williams,	"	21 March 1741.
Susanna daughter of John and Elizabeth Whitney,	"	7 June 1741.
William Son of Thomas and Mary Walker,	"	23 May 1741.
Samuel Son of Stephen and Hannah Winter,	"	29 May 1741.
Susanna daughter of Francis and Susanna Wells,	"	29 October 1741.
Benjamin Son of Benjamin Andrews and Hannah his Wife.	"	12 November 1741.
Esther daughter of John Allen and Susanna his Wife,	"	30 August 1741.
Samuel Son of Thomas Barnard and Martha his Wife,	"	25 September 1741.
Edward Son of James Burt and Hannah his Wife,	"	11 November 1741.
Jerusha daughter of John Baker and Jerusha his Wife,	"	16 June 1741.
Richard Son of Richard Cotta and Margery his Wife,	"	8 July 1741.
Mary daughter of Richard Clark and Elizabeth his Wife,	"	17 August 1741.

BIRTHS — 1741-42.

Edward Son of Edward Foster and Abigail his Wife,	Born	25 July 1741.
William Son of Richard Francis and Margaret his Wife,	"	23 May 1741.
Hannah daughter of Gershom Flagg and Hannah his Wife,	"	27 November 1741.
Mary daughter of Samuel Holland and Elizabeth his Wife,	"	22 June 1741.
Susanna daughter of John Jones and Hannah his Wife,	"	6 December 1741.
Ann daughter of William Marshall and Ann his Wife,	"	19 January 1741.
Elizabeth daughter of Ratcliffe and Hagar his Wife (free negroes)	"	13 July 1741.
Thomas Son of Thomas Sherburne and Margaret his Wife,	"	26 January 1741.
John Son of Ephraim Turner and Silence his Wife,	"	22 August 1741.

1742.

Mary daughter of Silas and Mary Atkins,	Born	1 February 1742.
Hannah daughter of Henry and Deliverance Atkins,	"	8 November 1742.
Belcher Son of Mather and Anna Byles,	"	12 July 1742.
Edward Son of Zepheniah and Mary Basset,	"	15 April 1742.
John Son of John and Lois Bryant,	"	19 May 1742.
William Son of Samuel and Elizabeth Ballard,	"	8 June 1742.
Elizabeth daughter of Henry and Elizabeth Berry,	"	9 July 1742.
Sarah daughter of William and Sarah Baker,	"	7 July 1742.
Elizabeth daughter of Joseph and Mary Blake,	"	23 May 1742.
Isaiah Son of Isaiah and Elizabeth Barrett,	"	27 July 1742.
Martin Son of Martin and Susanna Brimmer,	"	12 August 1742.
William Son of Abijah and Abigail Browne,	"	5 September 1742.
Rachel daughter of John and Anna Ballard,	"	30 April 1742.
Richard Son of Richard and Susanna Boar,	"	5 December 1742.
Elizabeth daughter of Benjamin and Ann Babbidge,	"	9 November 1742.
Dorcas daughter of Daniel and Mary Ballard,	"	15 January 1742.
Joseph Son of John and Susanna Brown,	"	15 September 1742.
Elizabeth daughter of John and Sarah Billings,	"	18 October 1742.
Jerusha daughter of Ebenezer and Mary Bridge,	"	8 January 1742.
William Son of William and Prudence Bowles,	"	8 March 1742.
William Son of John and Ruth Barrell,	"	9 January 1742.
Joseph Son of Joseph and Prudence Clark,	"	4 September 1742.
Abigail daughter of William and Civil Clark,	"	7 October 1742.
Benjamin Son of Benjamin and Mary Child,	"	17 November 1742.
John Son of James and Christian Clark,	"	25 April 1742.
William Son of John and Abigail Colson,	"	16 April 1742.
Elizabeth daughter of Ebenezer and Elizabeth Clough,	"	20 May 1742.
Alexander Son of John and Katharine Cummins,	"	26 March 1742.
Deborah daughter of Josiah and Lydia Carter,	"	21 June 1742.
Mary daughter of John and Mehetabel Cowley,	"	7 February 1742.
Samuel Son of Samuel and Mary Cutts,	"	22 February 1742.
Aaron John Son of Aaron and Rebecca Deale,	"	21 June 1742.
Joseph Son of William and Margaret Downe,	"	30 December 1742.
Elizabeth daughter of William and Elizabeth Dinsdale,	"	30 April 1742.
Joseph Son of Joseph and Abiel Dyar,	"	12 June 1742.
Richard Son of Israel and Susanna Ellinwood,	"	7 January 1742.
Edward Son of Edward and Sarah Edes,	"	8 June 1742.
Elizabeth daughter of Nathan and Mary Foster,	"	23 July 1742.

Mary daughter of Benjamin and Jerusha Fitch,	Born	23 September 1742.
Abigail daughter of Samuel and Abigail Goffe,	"	28 June 1742.
Elizabeth daughter of Thomas and Elizabeth Greene,	"	25 October 1742.
Alice daughter of Samuel and Sarah Gooding,	"	28 October 1742.
John Son of John and Bethiah Gerrish,	"	13 October 1742.
Mary daughter of Samuel and Elizabeth Grant,	"	24 January 1742.
Martha daughter of Ezekiel and Elizabeth Goldthwait,	"	5 January 1742.
Sarah daughter of Ellis and Sarah Gray,	"	7 May 1742.
Francis Son of Benjamin and Margaret Green,	"	21 August 1742.
John Son of Thomas and Martha Greenough,	"	4 April 1742.
Mary daughter of Stephen and Eunice Greenleaf,	"	16 March 1742.
William Son of Francis and Sarah Hunt,	"	6 August 1742.
John Son of John and Elizabeth Hutter,	"	5 May 1742.
Mary daughter of Benjamin and Mary Hammett,	"	14 March 1742.
William Son of William and Sarah Hickling,	"	21 May 1742.
Mary daughter of Joseph and Mary How,	"	22 October 1742.
William Son of William and Rebecca Homes,	"	7 May 1742.
Nathaniel Son of Nathaniel and Abigail Howland,	"	5 July 1742.
George Robert Twelves Son of George and Abigail Hewes,	"	25 August 1742.
John Son of John and Sarah Hunt,	"	21 October 1742.
Sarah daughter of George and Ann Holmes,	"	22 June 1742.
Fenton daughter of John and Elizabeth Hill,	"	7 March 1742.
James Son of Daniel and Hannah Ingersoll,	"	1 May 1742.
Daniel Son of Samuel and Ruth Jackson,	"	23 April 1742.
John Son of David and Sarah Jeffries,	"	10 July 1742.
Thomas Son of Adam and Martha Knox,	"	7 April 1742.
Elizabeth daughter of Hugh and Susanna Kennady,	"	9 October 1742.
Paul Son of Moses and Jane Larkin,	"	4 June 1742.
Elizabeth daughter of Robert and Katharine Lord,	"	26 May 1742.
Henry Son of Oliver and Elizabeth Luckis,	"	11 February 1742.
Susanna daughter of Nathaniel and Mary Loring (Junr.),	"	4 March 1742.
Thomas Dyer Son of Samuel and Anne Maltby,	"	17 December 1742.
Abigail daughter of Peter and Hannah Morgan,	"	5 January 1742.
William Son of Stephen and Sarah Minot,	"	7 February 1742.
Thomas Son of Samuel and Sarah Makelwain,	"	12 July 1742.
Abigail daughter of William and Abigail Maxwell,	"	21 June 1742.
Elizabeth daughter of Francis and Abigail Marshall,	"	26 September 1742.
Katharine daughter of James and Hannah Nicholson,	"	17 August 1742.
Jeffery Son of Jeffery a Free Negro and Cloe his Wife, Servant to Robert Auchmuty Esq.	"	18 December 1742.
William Sandford Son of Andrew and Mary Oliver,	"	14 April 1742.
Luce daughter of Charles and Joanna Price,	"	2 February 1742.
Abigail daughter of Caleb and Sarah Pratt,	"	14 January 1742.
Elizabeth daughter of Thomas and Elizabeth Perkins,	"	23 June 1742.
Elizabeth daughter of Joseph and Sarah Putman,	"	14 October 1742.
Elizabeth daughter of Peter and Elizabeth Prescott,	"	2 September 1742.
Josiah Son of Josiah and Mary Peirce.	"	19 October 1742.
Samuel Son of Samuel and Deborah Peirce,	"	4 February 1742.
John Son of William and Atterlanta Pritchard,	"	4 December 1742.
Jonathan Son of Thomas and Elizabeth Russell,	"	22 November 1742.
Samuel Son of Samuel and Lydia Rogers,	"	6 January 1742.
Benjamin Son of Benjamin and Susanna Renken,	"	5 July 1742.
Elizabeth daughter of James and Deborah Robins.	"	21 April 1742
William Son of Samuel and Hannah Ruggles,	"	8 January 1742.
Abiel Son of John and Tabitha Ruddock,	"	23 July 1742.

BIRTHS — 1742.

Anne daughter of Gamaliel and Sarah Rogers,	Born	10 March 1742.
Mary daughter of Nicholas and Martha Salisbury,	"	18 May 1742.
Seth Son of William and Kezia Smith,	"	2 April 1742.
Andrew Son of Andrew and Mary Sigourney,	"	22 May 1742.
Ellen daughter of William and Elizabeth Story,	"	9 May 1742.
Thomas Son of Thomas and Abigail Stoddard,	"	21 June 1742.
Daniel Son of Aftar and Hannah Stoddard,	"	30 June 1742.
John Son of John and Elizabeth Smith,	"	6 February 1742.
Elizabeth daughter of John and Mary Salmon,	"	22 February 1742.
Sibyl daughter of Ebenezer and Mary Storer,	"	6 February 1742.
Samuel Son of Simeon and Ruth Skillin,	"	5 July 1742.
Alexander Son of Thomas and Deborah Savage,	"	17 March 1742.
Mary-Law daughter of John and Mary Shepard,	"	5 August 1742.
Elisheba daughter of Elisha and Martha Townsend,	"	29 May 1742.
Elisabeth daughter of Jonathan and Mary Tarbox,	"	8 September 1742.
Sarah daughter of Christopher and Sarah Tilden,	"	6 March 1742.
Abigail daughter of Richard and Abigail True,	"	6 November 1742.
Abigail daughter of Harvey and Sarah Thomas	"	21 December 1742.
Daniel Son of Nathaniel and Joanna Thwing,	"	3 December 1742.
Bethiah daughter of Thomas and Bethiah Tyler,	"	21 April 1742.
William Son of William and Anne Vassall,	"	12 January 1742.
Elizabeth daughter of John and Elizabeth Wheelwright, Junr.,	"	30 May 1742.
Mary daughter of John and Elizabeth West,	"	31 May 1742.
John Newall Son of Nathaniel and Elizabeth Woodward,	"	6 June 1742.
Nehemiah Son of Joseph and Abigail Webb,	"	31 March 1742.
Benjamin Son of Samuel and Elizabeth Woods,	"	7 February 1742.
Elizabeth daughter of William and Mary Warner,	"	11 March 1742.
Hannah daughter of John Avery and Mary his Wife,	"	10 May 1742.
Content daughter of John Buttolph and Content his Wife,	"	31 May 1742.
William Son of Benjamin Brown and Mary his Wife,	"	22 September 1742.
Benjamin Son of Benjamin Burdick and his Wife,	"	23 May 1742.
Ann daughter of William Curtis and Mary his Wife,	"	10 April 1742.
Elizabeth daughter of Peace Cazneau and Mary his Wife,	"	16 September 1742.
Jane daughter of John Crosley and Susanna his Wife,	"	18 July 1742.
Mary daughter of Jonathan Dakin and Sarah his Wife,	"	6 January 1742.
Ruth daughter of John Decoster and Ruth his Wife,	"	5 December 1742.
Addington Son of James Davenport and Mary his Wife,	"	17 March 1742.
Joshua Snoden Son of Benjamin Emmons and Sarah his Wife	"	5 November 1742.
Mary daughter of Jabez Hatch and Mary his Wife,	"	15 October 1742.
Thomas Son of Thomas Hill and Hannah his Wife,	"	2 February 1742.
Alice daughter of Bagwell Irish and Elizabeth his Wife,	"	8 July 1742.
John Son of Thomas Jackson and Anne his Wife,	"	27 August 1742.
Grace daughter of Nicholas Luce and Grace his Wife,	"	31 March 1742.
Janet daughter of David McLeod and Mary his Wife,	"	30 December 1742.
George Son of George Nowell and Elizabeth his Wife,	"	3 September 1742.
Mary daughter of Edward Page and Rebecca his Wife,	"	20 August 1742.
Ellin daughter of William Story and Elizabeth his Wife,	"	8 May 1742.
William Son of William Skinner and Lydia his Wife,	"	7 February 1742.

Elizabeth daughter of William Sloper and Susanna his Wife,	Born	25 March 1742.
Margaret daughter of Thomas Sherburne and Margaret his Wife,	"	23 June 1742.
Anna daughter of Thomas Shepard and Hannah his Wife,	"	6 July 1742.
Hannah daughter of Moses Tyler and Hannah his Wife,	"	24 June 1742.
Elizabeth daughter of Nathaniel Woodward and Elizabeth his Wife,	"	2 February 1742.
Nathaniel Son of Benjamin Williams and Mary his Wife,	"	1 August 1742.

1743.

Abigail daughter of Joshua and Elizabeth Atwood,	Born	4 August 1743.
Samuel Son of James and Mary Allen,	"	23 August 1743.
Nathaniel Son of Henry and Deliverance Atkins,	"	21 January 1743.
Nathaniel Son of Nathaniel and Abigail Brown,	"	8 January 1743.
Daniel Son of John and Margaret Breck,	"	28 July 1743.
Samuel Son of Mather and Anna Byles,	"	23 March 1743.
Joseph } Isabella } Children of Robert and Isabella Breck,	"	29 February 1743.
William Son of John and Lydia Bell,	"	10 April 1743.
Ellis Gray Son of Increase and Ann Blake,	"	9 September 1743.
Deliverance daughter of Nathaniel and Deliverance Breed,	"	10 August 1743.
Nathaniel Son of Thomas and Susanna Bently,	"	27 August 1743.
Mary daughter of Ebenezer and Mary Brown,	"	15 July 1743.
Dorcas daughter of John and Mary Ann Brown,	"	17 September 1743.
Samuel Son of John and Sarah Barrett,	"	27 March 1743.
Benjamin Son of Benjamin and Abigail Babbidge,	"	26 October 1743.
Elizabeth daughter of Nathaniel and Elizabeth Breed,	"	17 February 1743.
Andrew Son of Andrew and Elizabeth Craigie,	"	7 June 1743.
Abigail daughter of Thomas and Abigail Cox,	"	12 June 1743.
Joseph Son of Seth and Elizabeth Coburn,	"	21 May 1743.
Rebecca daughter of Phillip and Rebecca Cartwright,	"	30 April 1743.
John Son of John and Zebiah Cravath,	"	26 December 1743.
David Son of David and Sarah Christy,	"	13 June 1743.
Mary daughter of John and Mary Cotton,	"	19 January 1743.
Elizabeth daughter of Samuel and Ann Clough,	"	31 July 1743.
Samuel Turell Son of Josiah and Lydia Carter,	"	21 March 1743.
Susanna daughter of Ebenezer and Rebecca Coburn,	"	26 May 1743.
Mary daughter of Benjamin and Hannah Church,	"	18 June 1743.
Thomas Son of Thomas and Sarah Drowne,	"	24 April 1743.
Jonathan Son of Edmund and Elizabeth Dwight,	"	4 June 1743.
James Son of James and Mary Dodge,	"	3 May 1743.
Samuel Son of Robert and Margaret Due (Free Negroes),	"	19 July 1743.
Hannah daughter of William and Lydia Dawes,	"	18 September 1743.
Lydia daughter of Joseph and Abiel Dyar,	"	14 March 1743.
Joseph Son of Edward and Hannah Eayres,	"	11 April 1743.
Henry Son of Benjamin and Elizabeth Egglestone,	"	1 July 1743.
Naomi daughter of Edward and Sarah Edes,	"	24 August 1743.
Andrew Son of Samuel and Elizabeth Eliot,	"	25 May 1743.
Andrew Son of Andrew and Elizabeth Eliot,	"	11 January 1743.
John Son of Thomas and Sarah Edes,	"	30 January 1743.
Thomas Son of Thomas and Martha Flagg,	"	20 July 1743.
Bossenger Son of Thomas and Sarah Foster,	"	3 June 1743.
Abigail daughter of Joseph and Abigail Flood,	"	26 December 1743.
Samuel Son of Benjamin and Jane Gleason,	"	19 April 1743.

BIRTHS — 1743.

Lewis Son of Harrison and Elizabeth Gray,	Born	30 October 1743.
Sarah daughter of Rufus and Katharine Greene,	"	7 December 1743.
Abigail daughter of Stephen and Mary Greenleaf,	"	17 September 1743.
Hannah daughter of Henry and Hannah Gibbon,	"	20 December 1743.
William Son of Thomas and Martha Greenough,	"	19 December 1743.
William Son of Charles and Mary Gyles,	"	14 September 1743.
Hannah daughter of Silvester and Ann Gardner,	"	18 July 1743.
John Son of John and Elizabeth Grant,	"	30 March 1743.
Mary daughter of Josiah and Mary Holland,	"	27 June 1743.
Hannah daughter of Charles and Martha Hendley,	"	27 July 1743.
John Son of William and Sarah Hickling,	"	14 August 1743
Mary daughter of John and Mary Hind,	"	26 June 1743.
Susanna daughter of James and Katharine Hodges,	"	25 March 1743.
Thomas Son of William and Rebecca Homes,	"	16 May 1743.
Zechariah Son of Zechariah and Abigail Hall,	"	15 June 1743.
Jonathan Son of Samuel and Hannah Hallowell,	"	13 April 1743.
Benjamin Son of Benjamin and Mary Howard,	"	9 September 1743.
James Son of James and Esther Hill,	"	5 October 1743.
Rachel daughter of John and Ann Harris,	"	17 October 1743.
Elias Son of Israel and Tabitha Hearsey,	"	5 November 1743.
Benjamin Son of John and Margaret Jenkins,	"	23 April 1743.
Susanna daughter of James and Elizabeth Jeffs,	"	22 June 1743.
Sarah daughter of Joseph and Sarah Johnson,	"	6 June 1743.
Nathaniel Son of Samuel and Ruth Jackson,	"	28 August 1743.
John Son of John and Mary Johnson,	"	24 July 1743.
Mary Anne daughter of John and Mary-Anne Jones,	"	19 January 1743.
Peter Son of Peter and Martha Jenkins,	"	23 September 1743.
Adam Son of Adam and Martha Knox,	"	22 January 1743.
Edward Son of Thomas and Mary Keightly,	"	15 October 1743.
Mary daughter of Robert and Katharine Lord,	"	11 December 1743.
Mary daughter of Jonathan and Ann Lowder,	"	1 August 1743.
Thomas Son of Thomas and Susanna Lawlor,	"	14 January 1743.
Samuel Son of Daniel and Lydia Merrett,	"	17 July 1743.
Sarah daughter of John and Elizabeth Macklelan,	"	14 September 1743.
Christopher Bridge Son of Daniel and Martha Marsh,	"	30 September 1743.
James Son of Samuel and Frances McLaine,	"	19 February 1743.
Mary daughter of Ezekiel and Dorothy Needham,	"	18 August 1743.
Daniel Son of James and Hannah Nicholson,	"	25 February 1743.
William Son of Peter and Mary Oliver,	"	23 May 1743.
Daniel Son of Andrew and Mary Oliver,	"	22 February 1743.
Lydia daughter of Samuel and Rebecca Partridge,	"	7 February 1743.
Thomas Son of John and Abigail Perkins,	"	21 February 1743.
Stephen Son of Stephen and Elizabeth Parker,	"	11 April 1743.
Abigail daughter of Samuel and Dorcas Parkman,	"	6 April 1743.
Thomas Son of William and Mary Pain,	"	23 April 1743.
Eleazer Son of William and Atterlanta Pritchard,	"	30 December 1743.
Hannah daughter of William and Ruth Putman,	"	4 August 1743.
George Son of Moses and Jane Prince,	"	22 July 1743.
Hannah daughter of James and Sarah Raymar,	"	16 February 1743.
Phillip Son of Samuel and Naomi Ridgaway,	"	29 February 1743.
John Son of John and Tabitha Ruddock,	"	9 November 1743.
Ruth daughter of Samuel and Ruth Smalledge,	"	20 July 1743.
Hannah daughter of Aftar and Hannah Stoddard,	"	22 July 1743.
Mary daughter of William and Mary Shepard,	"	1 August 1743.
Patience daughter of James and Rebecca Sherman,	"	10 December 1743.
Deborah daughter of Samuel and Deborah Smith,	"	29 December 1743.
James Son of John and Mercy Scollay,	"	17 August 1743.
Susanna daughter of Anthony and Mary Sigourney,	"	11 January 1743.
Dorcas daughter of John and Sarah Smallpeice,	"	28 September 1743.
Richard Son of Simeon and Ruth Skillin,	"	19 January 1743.

Mary daughter of William and Bethiah Torrey,	Born	23 July 1743.
Rebecca daughter of Richard and Abigail True,	"	19 November 1743.
Susanna daughter of Thomas and Susanna Thompson,	"	19 April 1743.
Michael Son of John and Rebecca Tillston,	"	19 April 1743.
Samuel Son of Samuel and Mercy Tyler,	"	21 February 1743.
Winslow Son of William and Faith Taylor,	"	1 March 1743.
Abigail daughter of Jonathan and Susanna Vickery,	"	16 May 1743.
John Foster Son of Sendall and Elizabeth Williams,	"	12 October 1743.
Elizabeth daughter of Henry and Mary Williams,	"	1 October 1743.
William Son of Gamaliel and Abigail Wallis,	"	25 May 1743.
William Son of William and Mary Wilson,	"	7 May 1743.
John Son of John and Elizabeth Wheelwright, Junr.,	"	3 July 1743.
Nathaniel ⎱ Gem. children of John and Susanna Mary ⎰ Whitley,	"	4 May 1743.
Benjamin Son of Stephen and Hannah Winter,	"	17 June 1743.
Persis daughter of Joseph and Abigail Webb,	"	27 July 1743.
Susanna daughter of John and Elizabeth West,	"	25 November 1743.
Sarah daughter of Francis and Sarah Whitman,	"	8 January 1743.
Elizabeth daughter of Thomas and Isabella Warden,	"	15 March 1743.
Thomas Son of Thomas and Sarah Wade,	"	25 January 1743.
Henry Son of John Andrews and Margaret his Wife,	"	8 March 1743.
John Son of Benjamin Andrews and Hannah his Wife,	"	5 June 1743.
Solomon Son of Joseph Blake and Mary his Wife,	"	22 January 1743.
Judah daughter of Benjamin Bowland and Mary his Wife,	"	22 December 1743.
William Son of John Bovue and Elizabeth his Wife,	"	8 September 1743.
Jane daughter of Thomas Browne and Jane his Wife,	"	12 March 1743.
John Clifton Son of Peter Cade and Elizabeth his wife,	"	9 January 1743.
Jane daughter of John Doane and Jane his Wife,	"	11 May 1743.
Hannah daughter of Benjamin Dolbeare and Hannah his Wife,	"	14 February 1743.
John Son of John Decoster and Ruth his Wife,	"	14 March 1743.
Elizabeth daughter of Edward Fryar and Jane his Wife,	"	22 May 1743.
Gershom Son of Gershom Flagg and Hannah his Wife,	"	1 September 1743.
Frances daughter of John Gore and Frances his Wife,	"	3 February 1743.
Thomas Son of Thomas Goldthwait and Esther his Wife,	"	27 April 1743.
Elizabeth daughter of Jabez Hatch and Mary his Wife,	"	15 February 1743.
Susanna daughter of Benjamin Harrod and Phebe his Wife,	"	10 March 1743.
Jean daughter of Robert Henry and Jean his Wife,	"	9 September 1743.
Elisha Son of Thomas Hutchinson, Esqr., and Margaret his Wife,	"	25 December 1743.
Jonathan Son of Edward Jackson and Dorothy his Wife,	"	5 June 1743.
Mary Ann daughter of John Jones and Mary Ann his Wife,	"	19 January 1743.
Benjamin Son of Joseph Jackson and Abigail his Wife,	"	10 March 1743.
William Son of William Lambert and Judeth his Wife,	"	22 December 1743.

BIRTHS — 1743-44. 251

Nicholas Son of Nicholas Luce and Grace his Wife,	Born	24 May 1743.
Mary Anna daughter of Ezekiel Lewis and Jane his Wife,	"	31 May 1743.
William Son of William Marshall and Ann his Wife,	"	3 May 1743.
Neal Son of Neal McIntyer and Esther his Wife,	"	15 September 1743.
Nathaniel Son of Belcher Noyes and Ann his Wife,	"	20 December 1743.
Eunice daughter of James Nicoll and Eunice his Wife,	"	18 September 1743.
Thomas Son of Thomas Palmer, Esqr., and Mary his Wife,	"	7 August 1743.
John Son of Thomas Handside Peck and his Wife,	"	24 August 1743.
Thomas Son of Thomas Pearson and Susanna his Wife,	"	14 February 1743.
Rebecca daughter of John Ridgaway and Eliza. his Wife,	"	30 September 1743.
Edward Son of Edward Stowe and Meletiah his Wife,	"	13 September 1743.
Gammon Son of Gammon Stevens and Abigail his Wife,	"	16 December 1743.
Thomas Clarke Son of George Searle and Katharine his Wife,	"	6 September 1743.
Elisha Son of William Story and Elizabeth his Wife,	"	3 December 1743.
Sarah daughter of Thomas Sherburne and Margaret his Wife,	"	17 January 1743.
Elizabeth daughter of Andrew Sigourney and Mary his Wife,	"	17 August 1743.
Jane daughter of Fortescue Vernon and Jane his Wife,	"	1 October 1743.
Mary daughter of John Wardell and Susanna his Wife,	"	28 November 1743.
Elizabeth daughter of Joseph Woods and Joanna his Wife,	"	26 May 1743.
Benjamin Son of Benjamin Willis and Ann his Wife,	"	10 January 1743.

1744.

Mary daughter of Nathaniel and Mary Adams,	Born	6 April 1744.
Thornton Son of Samuel and Mary Barrett,	"	4 May 1744.
Peter Son of Peter and Hannah Bourgin,	"	3 August 1744.
Jeremiah Son of Joseph and Sarah Belknap,	"	4 June 1744.
Jeremiah Son of John and Ruth Barrell,	"	6 April 1744.
Martha daughter of John and Sarah Blowers,	"	8 April 1744.
Susanna daughter of Ebenezer and Elizabeth Clough,	"	30 April 1744.
Elizabeth daughter of William and Elizabeth Dinsdale,	"	28 August 1744.
Susanna daughter of Israel and Susanna Ellinwood,	"	8 April 1744.
Nathaniel Son of Henry and Mary Emmes,	"	10 August 1744.
William Son of John and Hannah Fenno,	"	4 May 1744.
Abigail daughter of Nathan and Mary Foster,	"	9 June 1744.
Hopestill Son of Hopestill and Sarah Foster,	"	29 June 1744.
Abigail daughter of Stephen and Eunice Greenleaf,	"	4 July 1744.
Abigail daughter of John and Elizabeth Grant,	"	13 April 1744.
Mary daughter of John and Elizabeth Hutter,	"	27 March 1744.
John Son of Nathaniel and Abigail Howland,	"	21 April 1744.
Joseph Son of Joseph and Mary How,	"	18 July 1744.
Rebecca daughter of Alexander and Thankful Hill,	"	11 July 1744.
John Son of John and Elizabeth Jones,	"	7 July 1744.
Clement Son of Joseph and Susanna Jackson,	"	14 August 1744.

252   CITY DOCUMENT No. 43.

Hannah daughter of John and Hannah Procter,	Born	18 April.1744.
Mary daughter of William and Mary Pitman,	"	13 August 1744.
Joseph Son of Joseph and Sarah Putman,	"	20 August 1744.
James Son of James and Deborah Robins,	"	15 June 1744.
Edward Son of John and Tabitha Ruddock,	"	13 December 1744.
William Son of William and Lydia Skinner,	"	24 June 1744.
Charles Son of Daniel and Mary Sigourney,	"	21 August 1744.
Richard Son of William and Patience Sterling,	"	19 July 1744.
Faith daughter of Samuel-Phillips and Sarah Savage,	"	7 May 1744.
Elizabeth daughter of Oxenbridge and Sarah Thatcher, Junr.,	"	26 March 1744.
Harvey Son of Harvey and Sarah Thomas,	"	14 August 1744.
Samuel Son of Nathaniel and Joanna Thwing,	"	1 June 1744.
Lydia daughter of Joseph Gale and Mary his Wife,	"	2 January 1743/4.
Benjamin Son of Benjamin Austin and Elizabeth his Wife,	"	25 July 1744.
Francis Son of Benjamin Andrews and Hannah his Wife,	"	26 February 1744.
William Son of William Brown and Mindwell his Wife,	"	7 October 1744.
Bethiah daughter of William Baker and Sarah his Wife,	"	30 March 1744.
Susanna daughter of William Breed and Susanna his Wife,	"	2 November 1744.
Ann daughter of John Bowden and Ann his Wife,	"	17 November 1744.
Aaron Son of Aaron Bickford and Mary his Wife,	"	1 December 1744.
James Son of Thomas Burton and Rebecca his Wife,	"	7 June 1744.
Alice daughter of Thomas Bentley and Susanna his Wife,	"	16 February 1744.
Sarah daughter of John Beaver and Sarah his Wife,	"	28 February 1744.
Andrew Son of Martin Brimmer and Susanna his Wife,	"	20 February 1744.
Thankful daughter of Jonathan Browne and Elizabeth his Wife,	"	27 September 1744.
Benjamin Son of Benjamin Babbidge and Abigail his Wife,	"	13 January 1744.
Ruth daughter of Walter Baker and Martha his Wife,	"	15 August 1744.
Ann daughter of Thomas Barnard and Martha his Wife,	"	27 July 1744.
Hannah daughter of John Bell and Lydia his Wife,	"	29 December 1744.
John Son of John Buttolph and Content his Wife,	"	7 September 1744.
Nathaniel Son of Joseph Clarke and Prudence his Wife,	"	9 September 1744.
Elizabeth daughter of David Cutler and Lydia his Wife,	"	28 April 1744.
Gilbert Son of Gilbert Colesworthy and Mary his Wife,	"	23 December 1744.
Seth Storer Son of Seth Coburn and Elizabeth his Wife,	"	29 December 1744.
Ebenezer Son of Ebenezer Coburn and Rebecca his Wife,	"	6 January 1744.
Elizabeth daughter of Pearne Cowell and Elizabeth his Wife,	"	28 July 1744.
Samuel Son of William Clarke and Sybil his Wife.	"	16 October 1744.
Edward Son of Edward Drinker and Sarah his Wife,	"	25 October 1744.
Mary daughter of George Durant and Susanna his Wife,	"	7 December 1744.
Stephen Son of Edward Dumaresq and Mary his Wife,	"	13 November 1744.

Births — 1744.

Anne daughter of John Doane and Jane his Wife,	Born	8 September 1744.
Benjamin Son of Benjamin Dolbeare and Hannah his Wife,	"	21 March 1744.
Esther daughter of James Davenport and Mary his Wife,	"	19 April 1744.
Sarah daughter of Samuel Eliot and Elizabeth his Wife,	"	17 January 1744.
Nathaniel Son of Nathaniel Eaton and Mercy his Wife,	"	24 July 1744.
Hephzibah daughter of Samuel Emmes and Abigail his Wife,	"	19 April 1744.
Joseph Son of William Farrington and Sarah his Wife,	"	30 July 1744.
Thomas Son of John Farmer and Sarah his Wife,	"	2 September 1744.
Ann daughter of Edward Foster and Abigail his Wife,	"	3 February 1744.
Prudence daughter of Joseph Fitch and Ann his Wife,	"	16 December 1744.
Abigail daughter of Richard Francis and Margaret his Wife,	"	1 January 1744.
William Son of William Fletcher and Elizabeth his Wife,	"	10 August 1744.
Martha daughter of Ezekiel Goldthwait and Elizabeth his Wife,	"	15 December 1744.
Edward Son of Harrison Gray and Elizabeth his Wife,	"	30 December 1744.
Edward Son of Edward Gyles and Elizabeth his Wife,	"	8 April 1744.
Moses Son of Samuel Grant and Elizabeth his Wife,	"	6 March 1744.
Hannah daughter of Ellis Gray and Sarah his Wife,	"	18 July 1744.
John Son of Jacob Griggs and Susanna his Wife,	"	27 May 1744.
Mary daughter of Jonathan Greenleaf and Mary his Wife,	"	19 July 1744.
John Son of Shrimpton Hunt and Margaret his Wife,	"	11 January 1744.
Elizabeth daughter of George Holmes and Anne his Wife,	"	27 August 1744.
Sarah daughter of John Hunt and Sarah his Wife,	"	4 February 1744.
Esther daughter of Israel Hearsey and Tabitha his Wife,	"	10 March 1744.
William Son of Cary Harriss and Mehetable his Wife,	"	2 July 1744.
John Son of David Jeffries and Sarah his Wife,	"	5 February 1744.
John Son of John Jenkins and Mary his Wife,	"	8 March 1744.
Ann daughter of Thomas Jackson and Anne his Wife,	"	3 April 1744.
Peter Faneuil Son of John Jones and Mary Ann his Wife,	"	24 January 1744.
Lydia daughter of Robert Logan and Mercy his Wife,	"	16 September 1744.
Elizabeth daughter of Ebenezer Lowell and Mary his Wife,	"	18 August 1744.
Benjamin Son of Oliver Luckis and Elizabeth his Wife,	"	24 November 1744.
Lydia daughter of Samuel Peirce and Deborah his Wife,	"	22 August 1744.
Abigail daughter of Moses Peck and Elizabeth his Wife,	"	17 October 1744.
Joseph Son of John Phillips and Abigail his Wife,	"	29 January 1744.
Diana daughter of William Paine and Mary his Wife,	"	24 February 1744.
Hannah daughter of Robert Pierpoint and Hannah his Wife,	"	12 June 1744.
Mary daughter of Peter Pace and Mary his Wife,	"	1 July 1744.

Edward Son of Edward Page and Rebecca his Wife, Born		25 October 1744.
Daniel Son of Gamaliel Rogers and Ann his Wife,	"	9 October 1744.
Joanna daughter of John Sweetser and Sarah his Wife,	"	30 September 1744.
Elizabeth daughter of After Stoddard and Hannah his Wife,	"	17 December 1744.
Mary daughter of William Simpkins and Elizabeth his Wife,	"	16 November 1744.
John Son of Gammon Stevens and Abigail his Wife,	"	15 January 1744.
Susanna daughter of William Shepard and Margaret his Wife,	"	17 March 1744.
Hannah daughter of Thomas Savage and Deborah his Wife,	"	20 August 1744.
Joanna daughter of Jonathan Tilden and Mary his Wife,	"	30 November 1744.
Elisha Son of Moses Tyler and Hannah his Wife,	"	16 April 1744.
John Gutteridge Son of Jonathan Vickery and Susanna his Wife,	"	14 April 1744.
John Son of Philip White and Elizabeth his Wife,	"	18 September 1744.
Benjamin Son of Isaac Walker and Sarah his Wife,	"	26 October 1744.
Abigail daughter of Josiah Waters and Abigail his Wife,	"	5 June 1744.
Lois daughter of Gamaliel Wallis and Abigail his Wife,	"	29 August 1744.
Joanna daughter of Ebenezer Brown and Mary his Wife,	"	16 October 1744.
John Son of Hercules John Brilsford and Prudence his Wife,	"	19 February 1744.
Benjamin Belcher Son of Isaac Cazneau and Hannah his Wife,	"	18 July 1744.
James Son of Peace Cazneau and Mary his Wife,	"	18 June 1744.
Sarah daughter of John Cullam and Lydia his Wife,	"	2 November 1744.
Catharine daughter of Thomas Goldthwait and Esther his Wife,	"	5 January 1744.
Elizabeth daughter of Joshua Henshaw and Elizabeth his Wife,	"	17 September 1744.
Deborah daughter of Thomas Hill and Hannah his Wife,	"	31 March 1744.
Thomas Son of William Hickling and Sarah his Wife,	"	21 February 1744.
Jonathan Clark Son of Ezekiel Lewis and Jane his Wife,	"	26 January 1744.
Rebecca daughter of William Marshall and Ann his Wife,	"	27 January 1744.
Isabella daughter of David McLeod and Mary his Wife,	"	26 July 1744.
Mary daughter of the Rev. Roger Price and Elizabeth his Wife,	"	10 September 1744.
Daniel Son of Joseph Scot and Elizabeth his Wife,	"	23 August 1744.
Jane daughter of ―― McNeill and ―― his Wife,	"	14 February 1744.
Mary daughter of Peter Cade and Elizabeth his Wife,	"	August 1744.
Joseph Son of Joseph Johnson and Sarah his Wife,	"	5 January 1744.
Mary daughter of John Mellus and Sarah his Wife,	"	25 February 1744.
Susanna daughter of Andrew Sigourney and Mary his Wife,	"	13 October 1744.
Sarah daughter of Thomas Hutchinson Esq. and Margaret his Wife,	"	22 Nov. 1744.
Faith daughter of Samuel Phillips Savage and Sarah his Wife,	"	7 May 1744.

Births — 1744–45.

Jonathan Son of Richard Clark and Elizabeth his Wife, Born 20 May 1744.

The following births took place before 1745, probably all in 1743:

Ann daughter of William and Sarah Waite,	Born	25 April 174 .
Hannah daughter of Nathaniel and Hannah Wardell, Junr.,	"	12 February 174 .
Mary daughter of Nathaniel and Hannah Wardell, Junr.,	"	4 March 174 .
George Davenport Son of Davenport and Sarah Walker,	"	16 March 174 .
Josiah Son of Samuel and Mary Wheeler,	"	13 July 174 .
James Son of James and Phebe Williams,	"	14 May 174 .
Mary daughter of John and Elizabeth Wheelwright.	"	29 June 174 .
Samuel Son of Nathaniel and Elizabeth Woodward,	"	12 August 174 .
Sarah daughter of John and Susanna Wheatley,	"	23 July 174 .
Joseph Son of William and Hannah Young,	"	17 July 174 .
Lydia daughter of William and Hannah Young,	"	20 October 174 .

1745.

Samuel Son of John Andrews and Margaret his Wife,	Born	10 October 1745.
Sarah daughter of Silas Atkins and Mary his Wife,	"	5 October 1745.
Elizabeth daughter of John Allen and Susanna his Wife,	"	22 May 1745.
John Son of John Amiel and Christian his Wife,	"	23 April 1745.
Thomas Son of Thomas Browne and Jane his Wife,	"	25 November 1745.
William Son of John Breck and Margaret his Wife,	"	20 April 1745.
Sivil daughter of Samuel Badcock and Sivil his Wife,	"	28 February 1745.
John Baker Son of Martin Brimmer and Susanna his Wife,	"	6 March 1745.
Jane Keene daughter of David Burnet and Hannah his Wife,	"	30 August 1745.
Benjamin Son of John Ballard and Anna his Wife,	"	15 November 1745.
Elizabeth daughter of John Barrett and Sarah his Wife,	"	27 September 1745.
Mary daughter of Samuel Barrett and Mary his Wife,	"	5 December 1745.
Elizabeth daughter of Isaiah Barrett and Elizabeth his Wife,	"	26 January 1745.
Abigail daughter of Josias Byles junr. and Sarah his Wife.	"	21 November 1745.
George Son of Richard Barrington and Hannah his Wife,	"	1 July 1745.
Anna daughter of Nathaniel Breed and Deliverance his Wife,	"	30 June 1745.
Edward Son of John Barrell and Ruth his Wife,	"	23 May 1745.
Samuel } Gem. Sons of Benjamin Barnard and Jonathan } Elizabeth his Wife,	"	28 July 1745. 17 August 1745.
Mary daughter of Increase Blake and Ann his wife,	"	17 August 1745.
Elizabeth daughter of Richard Billings and Mary his Wife.	"	4 September 1745.
Benjamin Son of Benjamin Bowland and Mary his Wife,	"	1 November 1745.
Susannah Farnum daughter of Richard Clark and Elizabeth his Wife,	"	20 May 1745.
Ann daughter of Samuel Clough and Ann his Wife,	"	7 March 1745.
John Son of John Cullam and Lydia his Wife,	"	24 June 1745.

Susannah daughter of John Crosley and Susanna his Wife,	Born	21 November 1745.
Bethia daughter of Richard Cotta and Margery his Wife,	"	3 May 1745.
Mary daughter of David Cutler and Lydia his Wife,	"	11 September 1745.
Joseph Son of Jonathan Cary and Elizabeth his Wife,	"	8 April 1745.
Lydia daughter of John Clough and Lydia his Wife,	"	15 January 1745.
Jane daughter of James Davenport and Mary his Wife,	"	16 December 1745.
Nathaniel Paine Son of Thomas Drowne and Sarah his Wife,	"	9 May 1745.
William Son of Joseph Dyar and Abia his Wife,	"	27 October 1745.
Thomas Son of Elias Dupee and Mary his Wife,	"	21 December 1745.
William Son of William Dawes and Lydia his Wife,	"	6 April 1745.
Benjamin Son of Benjamin Darby and Mary his Wife,	"	27 January 1745.
Josiah Son of Andrew Eliot and Elizabeth his Wife,	"	31 January 1745.
Ann daughter of Joseph Edwards and Sarah his Wife,	"	12 June 1745.
Ralph Son of Israel Ellinwood and Susanna his Wife,	"	11 September 1745.
Edward Son of Thomas Edes and Sarah his Wife,	"	10 February 1745.
Jane daughter of Edward Fryar and Jane his Wife,	"	23 April 1745.
Samuel Son of John Fenno and Hannah his Wife,	"	1 July 1745.
John Son of William Fletcher and Elizabeth his Wife,	"	30 November 1745.
Elizabeth daughter of Gershom Flagg and Hannah his Wife,	"	13 August 1745.
Mary daughter of Charles Florence and Mary his Wife,	"	10 December 1745.
Samuel Son of Samuel Gooding and Sarah his Wife,	"	6 May 1745.
John Son of John Gore and Frances his Wife,	"	23 April 1745.
Jonathan Son of John Gardner and Sarah his Wife,	"	15 August 1745.
Mary daughter of Benjamin Greene and Mary his Wife,	"	3 November 1745.
Joseph Son of Thomas Greene and Martha his Wife,	"	26 July 1745.
Ellis Son of Ellis Gray and Sarah his Wife,	"	26 February 1745.
Esther daughter of Thomas Goldthwait and Esther his Wife,	"	11 January 1745.
Mehetable daughter of Cary Harriss and Mehetable his Wife,	"	11 March 1745.
Jonathan Son of Benjamin Harrod and Phebe his Wife,	"	27 January 1745.
Margaret daughter of Robert Henry and Jean his Wife,	"	3 September 1745.
Elizabeth daughter of James Hodges and Katharine his Wife.	"	12 May 1745.
Sarah daughter of Ambrose Harris and Sarah his Wife.	"	28 June 1745.
Desire daughter of Jabez Hatch and Mary his Wife,	"	25 August 1745.
Katharine daughter of John Hill and Elizabeth his Wife.	"	25 August 1745.
Mary daughter of Samuel Hallowell and Hannah his Wife,	"	8 February 1745.
Charles Son of Charles Harrison and Anna his Wife,	"	19 August 1745.
Abigail daughter of Joseph How and Mary his Wife,	"	23 March 1745.

BIRTHS — 1745.

Hannah daughter of Joseph Hiller and Hannah his Wife,	Born	2 November 1745.
William Son of Joseph Jackson and Susanna his Wife,	".	23 August 1745.
Elizabeth daughter of Thomas Jackson and Anne his Wife,	"	10 March 1745.
Henry Son of Henry Johnson and Mary his Wife,	"	29 November 1745.
Alice daughter of Hugh Kennedy and Susanna his Wife,	"	28 March 1745.
Elizabeth daughter of Benjamin Kent and Elizabeth his Wife,	"	6 January 1745.
Mary daughter of John Kennedy and Joanna his Wife,	"	17 October 1745.
Mary daughter of John Lefaver and Rebecca his Wife,	"	5 November 1745.
John Son of John Langdon and Mary his Wife,	"	19 November 1745.
Joshua Son of Joshua Loring and Elizabeth his Wife,	"	23 December 1745.
Abigail daughter of Robert Lord and Katharine his Wife,	"	11 November 1745.
Wait daughter of Roger Macknight and Wait his Wife,	"	1 February 1744/5.
Mary daughter of Francis Marshall and Abigail his Wife,	"	26 March 1745.
Diana daughter of William Milbourne and Elizabeth his Wife,	"	9 May 1745.
Thomas Son of Thomas March and Dorcas his Wife,	"	26 May 1745.
Sarah daughter of Jonathan Mountfort and Sarah his Wife,	"	11 May 1745.
Elizabeth daughter of Unite Moseley and Elizabeth his Wife,	"	16 January 1745.
John Son of Neal McIntyer and Esther his Wife,	"	13 August 1745.
Ebenezer Son of Ebenezer Messenger, Junior, and Lydia his Wife,	"	1 November 1745.
John Son of James Nicholl and Eunice his Wife,	"	29 December 1745.
Sarah daughter of John Newell and Sarah his Wife,	"	7 April 1745.
Hubbard Son of Edward Brattle Oliver and Ann his Wife,	"	28 September 1745.
Mary daughter of Daniel Oliver and Bethia his Wife,	"	24 November 1745.
Sarah daughter of Andrew Oliver, Esq., and Mary his Wife,	"	18 September 1745.
Elizabeth daughter of James Pittson and Elizabeth his Wife,	"	17 June 1745.
Benjamin Son of Benjamin Peirce and Abigail his Wife,	"	4 April 1745.
Mary daughter of Nathaniel Parkman and Mary his Wife,	"	28 July 1745.
Joseph Son of Isaac Peirce and Mary his Wife,	"	25 December 1745.
Eliakim Son of Thomas Palmer, Esq., and Mary his Wife,	"	4 February 1745.
Samuel Son of William Pritchard and Atterlanta his Wife,	"	23 October 1745.
Abigail daughter of William Phillips and Abigail his Wife,	"	14 April 1745.
Walter Son of Walter Piper and Miriam his Wife.	"	5 May 1745.
Ann daughter of Jonathan Payson and Ann his Wife,	"	24 June 1745.
Thomas Son of Thomas Perkins and Elizabeth his Wife,	"	30 June 1745.
Sarah daughter of Benjamin Procter and Sarah his Wife,	"	29 September 1745.

Rebecca daughter of Samuel Partridge and Rebecca his Wife,	Born	25 July 1745.
Amos Son of Joshua Parker and Jemima his Wife,	"	12 March 1745.
Elizabeth daughter of William Pitman and Mary his Wife,	"	28 February 1745.
Mary daughter of John Rider and Mary his Wife,	"	18 April 1745.
Susanna daughter of James Raymar and Sarah his Wife,	"	18 October 1745.
Mary daughter of William Rhodes and Mary his Wife,	"	11 December 1745.
Edward Son of Edward Rumley and Abigail his Wife,	"	22 August 1745.
Hannah daughter of Samuel Ruggles and Hannah his Wife,	"	14 June 1745.
Elizabeth Son of William Story and Elizabeth his Wife,	"	9 September 1745.
Hannah daughter of Thomas Sherburne and Margaret his Wife,	"	24 September 1745.
William Son of William Swan and Levinah his Wife,	"	18 March 1745.
John Son of John Scollay and Mercy his Wife,	"	24 May 1745.
Sarah daughter of Nicholas Salisbury and Martha his Wife,	"	15 June 1745.
Elizabeth daughter of John Symmes and Philadelphia his Wife,	"	5 May 1745.
Thomas Son of Francis Shaw and Lydia his Wife,	"	11 December 1745.
Rebecca daughter of James Sherman and Rebecca his wife,	"	12 April 1745.
Katharine daughter of George Searle and Katharine his Wife,	"	22 July 1745.
Peter Son of Anthony Sigourney and Mary his Wife,	"	8 December 1745.
William Son of Samuel Phillips Savage and Sarah his Wife,	"	26 December 1745
Thomas Son of John Tilson and Rebecca his Wife,	"	23 October 1745.
Elizabeth daughter of John Tudor and Jane his Wife,	"	31 March 1745.
Ellis Son of Moses Tyler and Hannah his Wife,	"	16 September 1745.
George Son of Jonathan Tarbox and Mary his Wife,	"	30 August 1745.
Silence ⎱ Gem. of William Todd and Mary his Mary ⎰ Wife,	"	14 April 1745.
Sarah daughter of Oxenbridge Thatcher, jun. and Sarah his Wife.	"	18 November 1745
William Son of Thomas Tyler and Bethia his Wife,	"	13 December 1745.
Abigail daughter of Christopher Tilden and Sarah his Wife,	"	17 April 1745.
Joseph Son of William Taylor and Faith his Wife,	"	16 March 1745
James Son of James Topp and Martha his Wife,	"	16 June 1745.
Abigail daughter of William Torrey and Bethiah his Wife,	"	9 November 1745.
William Son of Ephraim Turner and Silence his Wife,	"	27 February 1745.
Nerias Son of Nerias Vaughan and Mary his Wife.	"	28 November 1745.
Mary daughter of William Vose and Hannah his Wife,	"	11 November 1745.
Mary daughter of Henry Weston and Mary his Wife,	"	4 May 1745.
Francis daughter of Francis Whitman and Sarah his Wife,	"	11 July 1745.
William Son of William White and Rebecca his Wife,	"	24 September 1745.

Births — 1745-46.

Mary daughter of Stephen Winter and Hannah his Wife,	Born	18 October 1745.
John Son of Joseph Webb and Abigail his Wife,	"	13 March 1745.
Abigail daughter of Joseph Woods and Joanna his Wife,	"	27 May 1745.
Rebecca daughter of Gamaliel Wallis and Abigail his Wife,	"	16 September 1745.
Elisha Son of Josiah Waters and Abigail his Wife,	"	31 October 1745.

1746.

Samuel Son of Henry Atkins and Deliverance his Wife,	Born	23 March 1746.
Samuel Son of John Avery and Mary his Wife,	"	1 December 1746.
Joshua Son of Joshua Blanchard and Elizabeth his Wife,	"	13 August 1746.
Norton Son of Hercules John Brilsford and Prudence his Wife,	"	7 May 1746.
Sarah daughter of James Burt and Hannah his Wife,	"	13 January 1746.
Sarah daughter of Joseph Butler and Sarah his Wife,	"	8 May 1746.
John Son of William Bowles and Prudence his Wife,	"	4 June 1746.
Benjamin Son of William Brown and Jemima his Wife,	"	29 September 1746.
Josias Son of Daniel Ballard and Mary his Wife,	"	17 November 1746.
John Son of John Bowden and Ann his Wife,	"	4 July 1746.
Ruth daughter of Thomas Bentley and Susanna his Wife,	"	8 August 1746.
Sarah daughter of Increase Blake and Ann his Wife,	"	18 August 1746.
William Son of Isaac Cazneau and Hannah his Wife,	"	7 October 1746.
William Son of Peace Cazneau and Mary his Wife,	"	14 September 1746.
Thomas Son of Charles Cabot and Anna his Wife.	"	28 August 1746.
William Son of William Codner and Mary his Wife,	"	21 August 1746.
Katharine daughter of Gear Coffin and Rebecca his Wife,	"	4 July 1746.
Prudence daughter of Joseph Clarke and Prudence his Wife,	"	19 October 1746.
Sarah daughter of Benjamin Child and Mary his Wife,	"	9 September 1746.
Mary daughter of Josiah Carter and Lydia his Wife,	"	14 May 1746.
Sarah daughter of Ebenezer Coburn and Rebecca his Wife,	"	17 December 1746.
Jonathan Son of Gilbert Colesworthy and Mary his Wife,	"	5 October 1746.
Isaac Winslow daughter [sic] of Richard Clark and Elizabeth his Wife,	"	27 October 1746.
Elizabeth daughter of Seth Coburn and Elizabeth his Wife,	"	24 May 1746.
Samuel Son of David Cutler and Lydia his Wife,	"	16 October 1746.
Dorothy daughter of Joseph Coit and Dorothy his Wife,	"	28 August 1746.
Hezekiah Barber Son of William Crouch and Eunice his Wife,	"	28 December 1746.
Elizabeth daughter of Jonathan Cary and Elizabeth his Wife,	"	21 November 1746.
Edward Son of Thomas Crafts and Ann his Wife,	"	12 October 1746.
Lydia daughter of William Dawes and Lydia his Wife,	"	10 February 1746.
Mary daughter of John Dixwell and Mary his Wife,	"	15 January 1746.

Isaac Son of Isaac Dafforne and Sarah his Wife,	Born	19 October 1746.
Mary daughter of John DeJersey and Margaret his Wife,	"	1 November 1746.
Mary daughter of Arthur Dunn and Mary his Wife,	"	11 July 1746.
Charles Beighton Son of Charles Deming and Mary his Wife,	"	16 October 1746.
Sarah daughter of Benjamin Dolbeare and Hannah his Wife,	"	12 April 1746.
William Son of William Frost and Anne his Wife,	"	14 April 1746.
John Son of John Farmer and Sarah his Wife,	"	29 May 1746.
Ann daughter of Joseph Fitch and Ann his wife,	"	22 October 1746.
Lewis Son of Lewis Follings and Susanna his Wife,	"	26 September 1746.
John Son of John Grant and Elizabeth his Wife,	"	1 September 1746.
Joseph Son of Samuel Grant and Elizabeth his Wife.	"	22 June 1746.
Sarah daughter of Ezekiel Goldthwait and Elizabeth his Wife,	"	8 November 1746.
Samuel Son of Edward Gyles and Elizabeth his Wife,	"	24 March 1746.
William Son of Joseph Gale and Mary his Wife,	"	26 April 1746.
Sarah daughter of James Hodges and Katharine his Wife,	"	7 October 1746.
James Son of Desire Hawes and Mary his Wife.	"	26 October 1746.
Mary daughter of Jabez Hunt and Hannah his Wife,	"	25 May 1746.
Rebecca daughter of Shrimpton Hunt and Margaret his Wife.	"	10 November 1746.
Thomas Son of John Huttee and Elizabeth his Wife,	"	7 December 1746.
Ebenezer Son of George Hewes and Abigail his Wife,	"	26 November 1746.
John Son of Josiah Holland and Mary his Wife,	"	11 March 1746.
William Son of Jabez Hatch and Mary his Wife,	"	3 July 1746.
Susanna daughter of Israel Hearsey and Tabitha his Wife,	"	17 December 1746.
Mary daughter of William Hickling and Sarah his Wife,	"	8 February 1746.
Peter Son of Samuel Hughes and Elizabeth his Wife,	"	26 December 1746.
Joshua Son of Joshua Henshaw and Elizabeth his Wife,	"	16 February 1746.
Katharine daughter of William Homes and Rebecca his Wife,	"	12 April 1746.
Jonathan Son of Daniel Ingersole and Hannah his Wife.	"	3 March 1746.
William Son of Joseph Jackson and Susanna his Wife,	"	5 September 1746.
George Son of David Jeffries and Sarah his Wife,	"	13 July 1746.
Abigail daughter of Joseph Jackson and Abigail his Wife,	"	26 June 1746.
William Son of John Jones and Mary Ann his Wife,	"	7 June 1746.
Lydia daughter of Samuel Jackson and Ruth his Wife,	"	24 March 1746.
James Son of James Lamb and Desire his Wife,	"	13 August 1746.
Elizabeth daughter of John Loring and Ann Maria his Wife,	"	17 October 1746.
Judith daughter of William Lambert and Judith his Wife,	"	3 May 1746.
William Son of Robert Lovering and Rebecca his Wife,	"	19 October 1746.
Elizabeth daughter of Oliver Luckis and Elizabeth his Wife,	"	11 November 1746.
Timothy Son of John Langdon and Mary his Wife,	"	7 February 1746.
Dorcas daughter of Thomas March and Dorcas his Wife,	"	11 June 1746.
Martha daughter of William Marshall and Ann his Wife,	"	25 April 1746.

Births — 1746.

Elizabeth daughter of Roger Macknight and Wait his Wife,	Born	18 November 1746.
Jonathan Son of Jonathan Mountfort and Sarah his Wife,	"	6 December 1746.
William Son of Arthur McGill and Ann his Wife,	"	3 January 1746.
William Son of William Mcneill and Katharine his Wife,	"	18 August 1746.
Francis Son of Francis Marshall and Abigail his Wife,	"	3 May 1746.
John Son of David McLeod and Mary his Wife,	"	24 April 1746.
Belcher Son of Belcher Noyes and Anna his Wife,	"	25 January 1746.
Mary daughter of John Newell and Sarah his Wife,	"	28 December 1746.
Joseph Son of Joseph Osgood and Margaret his Wife,	"	25 November 1746.
Andrew Son of Peter Oliver and Mary his Wife,	"	15 September 1746.
Hannah daughter of Caleb Pratt and Sarah his Wife,	"	30 April 1746.
Mary daughter of Joseph Palmer and Mary his Wife,	"	18 January 1746.
John Son of Peter Pace and Mary his Wife,	"	24 June 1746.
Rebecca daughter of Edward Page and Rebecca his Wife,	"	10 October 1746.
Moses Son of Walter Piper and Miriam his Wife,	"	7 October 1746.
Ruth daughter of William Page and Dorcas his Wife,	"	10 November 1746.
Elizabeth daughter of Benjamin Procter and Sarah his Wife,	"	23 October 1746.
Sarah daughter of Robert Pierpoint and Hannah his Wife,	"	14 May 1746.
Hannah daughter of Nathaniel Parkman and Mary his Wife,	"	15 December 1746.
William Son of William Phillips and Abigail his Wife,	"	15 July 1746.
Ruth daughter of John Ruddock and Tabitha his Wife,	"	5 March 1745-6.
Mary daughter of James Robins and Deborah his Wife,	"	28 March 1746.
John Son of John Rogers and Mary his Wife,	"	1 March 1746.
Ebenezer Son of Ebenezer Rockwell and Rebecca his Wife,	"	13 August 1746.
Robert Son of Samuel Ruggles and Hannah his Wife,	"	11 February 1746.
Elizabeth daughter of Thomas Sherburne and Margaret his Wife,	"	18 December 1746.
Daniel Son of John Scollay and Mercy his Wife,	"	26 February 1746.
Francis Son of William Skinner and Lydia his Wife,	"	1 January 1746.
James Son of James Sherman and Rebecca his Wife,	"	16 January 1746.
Abigail daughter of Richard Stayner and Abigail his Wife,	"	21 December 1746.
Sarah daughter of John Sims and Philadelphia his Wife,	"	30 January 1746.
Jacob Son of John Sweetser and Sarah his Wife,	"	27 December 1746.
Andrew Son of Andrew Sigourney and Mary his Wife,	"	27 March 1746.
Thomas Son of Jonathan Tilden and Mary his Wife,	"	1 July 1746.
Elizabeth daughter of Thomas Tufton and Elizabeth his Wife,	"	23 January 1746.
Mehetable daughter of Samuel Wheeler and Mary his Wife,	"	27 March 1746.
John Son of Stephen Whiting and Mary his Wife,	"	26 May 1746.
Benjamin Swain Son of Thomas Walker and Abigail his Wife,	"	24 October 1746.
Edward Lloyd Son of Edward Whittemore and Sarah his Wife,	"	13 November 1746.

262   CITY DOCUMENT No. 43.

Nathaniel Son of William White and Rebecca his Wife,	Born	16 February 1746.
Hannah daughter of Abraham Wood and Abiah his Wife,	"	2 April 1746.
John Son of John Wheatley and Susanna his Wife,	"	16 December 1746.
Elizabeth daughter of Philip White and Elizabeth his Wife,	"	12 November 1746.
John Son of Nathaniel Wardell and Hannah his Wife,	"	20 May 1746.

1747.

Hannah daughter of Benjamin Andrews and Hannah his Wife,	Born	31 October 1747.
Jonathan Loring Son of Benja. Austin and Elizabeth his Wife,	"	22 December 1747.
Sarah daughter of Isaiah Barrett and Elizabeth his Wife,	"	13 March 1747.
Hannah daughter of James Burt and Hannah his Wife,	"	13 August 1747.
Jonathan Son of Ebenezer Brown and Mary his Wife,	"	11 February 1747.
Samuel Son of Joshua Blanchard and Elizabeth his Wife,	"	18 June 1747.
Sarah daughter of Ephraim Baker and Mary his Wife,	"	4 June 1747.
Aaron Son of Nathaniel Bull and Tabitha his Wife,	"	26 December 1747.
Deborah daughter of Joshua Barker and Abigail his Wife,	"	22 October 1747.
Martha daughter of Samuel Badcock and Sivil his Wife,	"	14 February 1747.
Mildred daughter of Samuel Bicknel and Mildrid his Wife,	"	29 February 1747.
Benjamin Son of Benjamin Babbidge and Anne his Wife,	"	12 May 1747.
Sarah daughter of Joseph Belknap and Sarah his Wife,	"	1 September 1747.
Sarah daughter of John Ball and Sarah his Wife,	"	4 September 1747.
Mercy daughter of John Bell and Lydia his Wife,	"	30 May 1747.
Mary Ann daughter of James Buck and Mary his Wife,	"	27 October 1747.
Katharine daughter of James Brown and Katharine his Wife,	"	10 January 1747.
John Son of Samuel Clough and Ann his Wife,	"	29 October 1747.
Sarah daughter of Josiah Carter and Lydia his Wife,	"	12 February 1747.
Joan daughter of John Cullam and Lydia his Wife,	"	10 June 1747.
Mary daughter of William Clough and Mary his Wife,	"	23 July 1747.
Mehetable daughter of Seth Coburn and Elizabeth his Wife,	"	18 June 1747.
Mary daughter of Samuel Cowdry and Mary his Wife,	"	3 February 1747.
Thomas Son of Benjamin Dolbeare and Hannah his Wife,	"	24 March 1747.
Susanna daughter of David Drowne and Frances his Wife,	"	26 June 1747.
Mary daughter of James Davenport and Mary his Wife,	"	3 June 1747.
Joseph Son of Joseph Dyer and Abiel his Wife,	"	13 August 1747.

Births — 1747.

John Son of John Dunham and Mary his Wife,	Born	31 October 1747.
Ann daughter of Edward Dumaresq and Mary his Wife,	"	13 December 1747.
Sarah ⎱ Gem. of Thomas Drowne and Sarah his Godfrey ⎰ Wife,	"	26 October 1747.
Edmund Son of Edmund Dwight and Elizabeth his Wife,	"	8 April 1747.
Sarah daughter of James Dodge and Mary his Wife,	"	26 March 1747.
Sarah daughter of Israel Ellingwood and Susanna his Wife,	"	25 August 1747.
Elizabeth daughter of Andrew Eliot and Elizabeth his Wife,	"	4 May 1747.
Susanna daughter of William Edes and Rebecca his Wife,	"	17 January 1747.
John Son of Richard Francis and Margaret his Wife,	"	5 November 1747.
Henry Son of William Fletcher and Elizabeth his Wife,	"	25 April 1747.
Martha daughter of Edward Foster and Martha his Wife,	"	26 May 1747.
Elizabeth daughter of John Fenno and Hannah his Wife,	"	8 July 1747.
William Son of William Farrington and Sarah his Wife,	"	12 October 1747.
Elizabeth daughter of Paul Farmer and Thankful his Wife,	"	2 August 1747.
Sarah daughter of James Foster and Sarah his Wife,	"	25 December 1747.
Joseph Son of Nathan Foster and Mary his Wife,	"	20 March 1747.
Sarah daughter of John Farmer and Sarah his Wife,	"	7 March 1747.
Benjamin Son of Thomas Greene and Martha his Wife,	"	25 August 1747.
William Son of William Green and Elizabeth his Wife,	"	11 August 1747.
Katharine daughter of Ezekiel Goldthwait and Elizabeth his Wife,	"	21 November 1747.
Samuel Son of Joseph Gardner and Hannah his Wife,	"	8 September 1747.
James son of James Gifford and Susanna his Wife,	"	11 December 1747.
William Son of Ellis Gray and Sarah his Wife,	"	13 August 1747.
Mary daughter of William Greenleaf and Mary his Wife,	"	15 March 1747.
Joseph Son of John Grant and Rebecca his Wife,	"	29 June 1747.
Joseph son of Benjamin Harrod and Phebe his Wife,	"	4 November 1747.
Abigail daughter of Edward Hunt and Sarah his Wife,	"	14 February 1747.
Mary daughter of John Hewton and Mary his Wife,	"	2 August 1747.
Roop Son of Ambrose Harris and Sarah his Wife,	"	12 March 1747.
Elizabeth daughter of Thomas Hubbard and Judeth his Wife,	"	29 February 1747.
Rebecca daughter of John Hunt and Sarah his Wife,	"	11 October 1747.
Martha daughter of Nathaniel Howland and Abigail his Wife,	"	21 October 1747.
Joseph Son of Zachariah Hall and Abigail his Wife.	"	1 October 1747.
Mary ⎱ Gem. Daughters of Johnson Jackson and Hannah ⎰ Sarah his Wife,	"	21 November 1747.
Rachel daughter of Isaac Jones and Rachel his Wife,	"	2 November 1747.
Henry Son of Joseph Jackson and Susanna his Wife,	"	19 October 1747.
Ann daughter of Benjamin Kent and Elizabeth his Wife.	"	7 August 1747.
Edward Son of John Kneeland and Abigail his Wife,	"	20 October 1747.

Abigail daughter of Michael Lowell and Abigail his Wife,	Born	6 April 1747.
Elizabeth daughter of Henry Leddel and Elizabeth his Wife,	"	30 March 1747.
Thomas Son of Joshua Loring and Elizabeth his Wife,	"	26 June 1747.
Mary Daughter of William Lambert and Judeth his Wife,	"	22 November 1747.
Ebenezer Son of Ebenezer Leadbetter and Elizabeth his Wife,	"	19 January 1747.
Ruth daughter of James Lamb and Desire his Wife,	"	13 November 1747.
Robert Son of John Larrabee and Sarah his Wife,	"	14 January 1747.
Henry Son of David McLeod and Mary his Wife,	"	2 January 1747.
John Son of John Mellus and Sarah his Wife,	"	21 April 1747.
William Son of Neal McIntyer and Esther his Wife,	"	27 April 1747.
Samuel Son of Francis Marshall and Abigail his Wife,	"	12 May 1747.
Oliver Son of Belcher Noyes and Ann his Wife,	"	19 November 1747.
William Son of David Newhall and Elizabeth his Wife,	"	24 April 1747.
Margaret daughter of Henry Newman and Margaret his Wife,	"	7 June 1747.
Bethia daughter of Daniel Oliver and Bethia his Wife	"	19 July 1747.
William Son of William Pitman and Mary his Wife,	"	6 November 1747.
Hannah daughter of William Phillips and Abigail his Wife,	"	20 July 1747.
Joseph Son of William Pritchard and Atterlanta his Wife,	"	28 February 1747.
Isaac Son of Isaac Peirce and Mary his Wife,	"	17 January 1747.
William Son of William Putnam and Ruth his Wife,	"	5 July 1747.
Elizabeth daughter of John Proctor and Hannah his Wife,	"	10 June 1747.
Benjamin Son of Benjamin Pollard and Margaret his Wife,	"	3 September 1747.
Robert Manyard Son of John Peck and Hester his Wife,	"	1 October 1747.
Isaac Son of Isaac Peirce and Miriam his Wife,	"	23 June 1747.
Elias Son of Elias Parkman and Abigail his Wife,	"	9 December 1747.
John Son of William Paine and Mary his Wife,	"	30 December 1747.
Rebecca daughter of John Ruddock and Tabitha his Wife,	"	16 February 1746/7.
Henry Son of Henry Robie and Elizabeth his Wife,	"	8 April 1747.
Francis Son of James Robins and Deborah his Wife,	"	3 December 1747.
Samuel Son of William Rhodes and Mary his Wife,	"	7 June 1747.
William Son of William Story and Joanna his Wife,	"	17 March 1747.
Samuel Son of Samuel Sloper and Mary his Wife,	"	12 June 1747.
Francis Frederick Son of William Sanders and Anne his Wife,	"	5 November 1747.
Gilbert Warner Son of Thomas Speakman and Mary his Wife,	"	7 November 1747.
Elizabeth daughter of Roger Stayner and Elizabeth his Wife,	"	5 July 1747.
Mary daughter of Nathan Sawyer and Mary his Wife,	"	25 November 1747.
James Son of James Tilton and Joanna his Wife,	"	11 October 1747.
Othniel Son of Othniel Tarr and Sarah his Wife,	"	20 November 1747.
Penelope daughter of Oxenbridge Thatcher junr. and Sarah his Wife,	"	5 October 1747.
Thomas Son of Thomas Tyler and Bethiah his Wife,	"	11 September 1747.

BIRTHS — 1747–48.

Mercy daughter of James Topp and Martha his Wife,	Born	6 May 1747.
Abigail daughter of John Treat and Abigail his Wife,	"	30 December 1747.
Mabel daughter of Shippie Townsend and Mehitable his Wife,	"	28 February 1747.
Deborah daughter of Moses Tyler and Hannah his Wife,	"	15 November 1747.
Joanna daughter of James Thomas and Ruth his Wife,	"	1 July 1747.
William Son of William Vose and Hannah his Wife,	"	22 April 1747.
Mary daughter of William Vintenon and Mary his Wife,	"	29 September 1747.
Elizabeth daughter of Benjamin Wheeler and Elizabeth his Wife,	"	16 April 1747.
Stephen Son of Stephen Whiting and Mary his Wife,	"	23 May 1747.
Elizabeth daughter of Francis Whitman and Sarah his Wife,	"	28 July 1747.
Susanna daughter of John White and Susanna his Wife,	"	28 August 1747.
Samuel Son of Nathaniel Woodward and Elizabeth his Wife,	"	30 October 1747.
Josiah Son of Jonathan Williams and Grace his Wife,	"	31 December 1747.
Sarah daughter of Miles Whitworth and Deborah his Wife,	"	7 March 1747.
Josiah Son of Josiah Waters and Abigail his Wife,	"	28 September 1747.
Joseph Son of Cornwall and Katharine Free Negroes	"	3 August 1747.

1748.

Thomas Son of Thomas Armstrong and Hannah his Wife,	Born	29 December 1748.
Margaret daughter of John Andrews and Margt. his Wife,	"	14 June 1748.
Jemima daughter of William Adams and Jemima his Wife,	"	12 October 1748.
Anne daughter of James Boutineau and Susannah his Wife,	"	18 January 1748.
Joseph Son of Mather Byles and Rebecca his Wife,	"	29 March 1748.
Elizabeth daughter of David Bell and Eliza. his Wife,	"	18 July 1748.
Susanna daughter of Nathaniel Baker and Susanna his Wife,	"	28 June 1748.
Sarah daughter of Joshua Blanchard and Elizabeth his Wife,	"	29 September 1748.
William Son of William Blake and Susanna his Wife,	"	7 September 1748.
Elizabeth daughter of John Bennet and Hannah his Wife,	"	6 October 1748.
Walker Son of Walker Barsto and Mary his Wife,	"	25 January 1748.
Hepzibah daughter of Samuel Barrett and Mary his Wife,	"	1 January 1748.
John Son of John Ball and Sarah his Wife,	"	2 December 1748.
Edward Son of Edward Baker and Hannah his Wife,	"	6 March 1748.
Avis daughter of Barnabas Binney and Avis his Wife,	"	17 August 1748.
Mercy daughter of Jonathan Brown and Elizabeth his Wife,	"	5 February 1748.
Mary daughter of William Codner and Mary his Wife,	"	16 October 1748.

266   CITY DOCUMENT NO. 43.

Pearne Son of Pearne Cowell and Elizabeth his Wife	Born	26 April 1748.
Hannah daughter of Philip Carteret and Rebecca his Wife,	"	16 March 1748.
Mary daughter of Thomas Cushing and Deborah his Wife,	"	30 January 1748.
John Son of Thomas Cole and Elizabeth his Wife,	"	21 December 1748.
Solomon Son of John Cotton and Mary his Wife,	"	21 August 1748.
William Son of William Crombie and Rebecca his Wife,	"	8 November 1748.
Sarah daughter of John Cowdry and Mary his Wife,	"	10 April 1748.
Eunice daughter of William Crouch and Eunice his Wife,	"	18 April 1748
Mary daughter of Gilbert Colesworthy and Mary his Wife,	"	13 December 1748.
Joseph Son of David Cutler and Lydia his Wife,	"	14 January 1748.
Mary daughter of Joseph Clarke and Prudence his Wife,	"	11 August 1748.
Benjamin Son of Benjamin Craddock and Amy his Wife,	"	1 August 1748.
Sarah [daughter of William Clarke and Sybil his Wife,	"	9 October 1748.
William Son of Benjamin Child and Mary his Wife,	"	29 October 1748.
Edward Son of Isaac Cazneau and Hannah his Wife,	"	29 December 1748.
Benjamin Son of Benjamin Dorby and Mary his Wife,	"	25 May 1748.
Mary daughter of George DeRue and Mary his Wife,	"	23 July 1748.
Martha daughter of Arthur Dun and Mary his Wife,	"	8 August 1748.
Samuel Son of Andrew Eliot and Elizabeth his Wife,	"	17 June 1748.
John Son of John Fillis and Elizabeth his Wife,	"	7 December 1748.
Joseph Son of Joseph Fitch (deceased) and Ann his Wife,	"	14 December 1748.
Thomas Waite Son of Seth Foster and Susanna his Wife,	"	22 September 1748.
Edward Son of John Grant and Rebecca his Wife,	"	4 February 1748.
William Son of John Greenough and Sarah his Wife,	"	5 April 1748.
John Son of Thomas Goldthwait and Catharine his Wife,	"	9 July 1748.
Lucretia daughter of Benjamin Greene and Mary his Wife,	"	16 July 1748.
James Son of John Gatchel and Mary his Wife,	"	9 May 1748.
Elizabeth daughter of John Greenleafe and Priscilla his Wife,	"	11 July 1748.
John Son of William Green and Elizabeth his Wife,	"	23 January 1748.
John Son of Alexander Hill and Thankful his Wife,	"	22 July 1748.
Uriah Son of John Huttee and Elizabeth his Wife,	"	19 June 1748.
Margaret daughter of Shrimpton Hunt and Margaret his Wife,	"	8 September 1748.
Sarah daughter of John Hutchinson and Sarah his Wife,	"	2 February 1748.
Richard Tothill Son of Richard Hunt and Mary his Wife,	"	23 February 1748.
Rebecca daughter of Nathaniel Holmes and Rebecca his Wife,	"	22 January 1748.
Mary daughter of Robert Henry and Jean his Wife,	"	28 October 1748.
Samuel Son of Samuel Hughes and Elizabeth his Wife,	"	7 October 1748.
Ephraim Son of William Hickling and Sarah his Wife,	"	7 August 1748.

BIRTHS — 1748.

Ann daughter of Abraham Holland and Abigail his Wife,	Born	26 September 1748.
Samuel Parkman Son of Israel Hearsey and Tabitha his Wife,	"	3 September 1748.
Dorcas daughter of Francis Ingraham and Dorcas his Wife,	"	23 December 1748.
Elizabeth daughter of John Jones and Mary Ann his Wife,	"	8 April 1748.
Katharine daughter of David Jeffries and Sarah his Wife,	"	5 April 1748.
William Son of Joseph Jackson and Abigail his Wife,	"	5 February 1748.
Mary daughter of Henry Johnson and Mary his Wife,	"	8 June 1748.
Abigail daughter of Hugh Kennedy and Susanna his Wife,	"	23 June 1748.
Philip Viburt Son of Mathew Kennedy and Jane his Wife,	"	28 July 1748.
Joseph Son of John Kneeland and Abigail his Wife,	"	30 November 1748.
John Son of John Kneeland jun. and Sarah his Wife,	"	14 October 1748.
Anna daughter of Michael Lowell and Abigail his Wife,	"	8 January 1748.
Sarah daughter of Henry Leddel and Elizabeth his Wife,	"	20 December 1748.
Anna daughter of John Loring and Ann Maria his Wife,	"	24 December 1748.
Robert Son of Robert Lord and Katharine his Wife,	"	29 October 1748.
Mary daughter of Nathaniel Loring and Mary his Wife,	"	4 June 1748.
Miriam daughter of Jonathan Mason and Miriam his Wife,	"	9 September 1748.
Amy Pickerin daughter of John Mellus and Sarah his Wife,	"	27 December 1748.
Daniel Son of William Mcneill and Katharine his Wife,	"	5 April 1748.
Sarah daughter of William Merchant jun. and Sarah his Wife,	"	12 December 1748.
John Son of William Marshall and Ann his Wife,	"	11 January 1748.
Mark Son of Mark Mcklaughlan and Ruth his Wife,	"	21 October 1748.
John Son of James Nicoll and Eunice his Wife,	"	24 May 1748.
Mary daughter of John Newell and Sarah his Wife,	"	30 October 1748.
Jane daughter of James Noble and Jane his Wife,	"	4 July 1748.
Hannah daughter of Henry Newman and Margaret his Wife,	"	14 September 1748.
Susanna daughter of Daniel Oliver and Bethia his Wife,	"	27 January 1748.
Samuel Son of Samuel Osborn and Margaret his Wife,	"	14 April 1748.
William Sanford Son of Andrew Oliver Esq. and Mary his Wife,	"	8 April 1748.
Andrew Son of Andrew Oliver and Susanna his Wife,	"	2 June 1748.
John Son of Joseph Osgood and Margaret his Wife,	"	22 October 1748.
Erasmus Son of Isaac Peirce and Meriam his Wife,	"	22 September 1748.
Sarah daughter of Daniel Pecker and Elizabeth his Wife,	"	2 October 1748.
Joseph Son of James Pierpont and Sarah his Wife,	"	9 January 1748.
William Son of William Pitman and Mary his Wife,	"	6 November 1748.
Henry Son of Peter Pelham and Mary his Wife,	"	14 March 1748.
Sarah daughter of William Phillips and Abigail his Wife,	"	31 August 1748.

Elizabeth daughter of Nathaniel Parkman and Mary his Wife,	Born	30 March 1748.
Benjamin Son of Benjamin Procter and Sarah his Wife,	"	4 March 1748.
Anna daughter of John Perkins and Abigail his Wife,	"	20 April 1748.
Jonathan Son of Edward Page and Rebecca his Wife,	"	8 August 1748.
William Son of Nathaniel Phillips and Ann his Wife,	"	8 August 1748.
Ebenezer Son of John Ruddock and Tabitha his Wife,	"	28 January 1747-8.
Richard Son of Richard Robinson and Sarah his Wife,	"	30 December 1748.
John Son of John Rogers and Mary his Wife,	"	8 January 1748.
Rebecca daughter of John Robinson and Rebecca his Wife,	"	8 May 1748.
William Son of Samuel Russell and Elizabeth his Wife,	"	23 May 1748.
Joseph Son of Henry Roby and Elizabeth his Wife,	"	18 August 1748.
William Son of Thomas Sherburne and Margaret his Wife,	"	16 August 1748.
Joanna daughter of Roger Stainer and Elizabeth his Wife,	"	15 December 1748.
Mary daughter of Michael Stewart and Mary his Wife,	"	4 September 1748.
David Son of David Seabury and Abigail his Wife,	"	24 February 1748.
Benjamin Son of Isaac Smith and Rachel his Wife,	"	3 May 1748.
Grace daughter of John Sims and Philadelphia his Wife,	"	29 July 1748.
John Son of John Sartel and Mary his Wife,	"	3 August 1748.
Francis Son of Francis Shaw and Sarah his Wife,	"	25 August 1748.
Nathaniel Son of John Sweetser and Sarah his Wife,	"	17 October 1748.
John Son of William Skinner and Lydia his Wife,	"	5 December 1748.
Samuel Son of Samuel Phillips Savage and Sarah his Wife,	"	11 August 1748.
John Son of James Sherman and Rebecca his Wife,	"	16 October 1748.
Charles Son of Andrew Sigourney and Mary his Wife,	"	4 March 1748.
James Son of William Blair Townsend and Mary his Wife,	"	7 December 1748.
John Son of George Tilley and Mary his Wife,	"	30 March 1748.
Abigail daughter of Gillam Tailer and Elizabeth his Wife,	"	2 June 1748.
John Son of Jonathan Tarbox and Mary his Wife,	"	14 April 1748.
Joshua Son of William Taylor and Faith his Wife,	"	2 August 1748.
John Son of Fortescue Vernon and Jane his Wife,	"	2 June 1748.
Abigail daughter of William Vose and Hannah his Wife,	"	31 December 1748.
Mary daughter of Richard White and Mary his Wife,	"	20 April 1748.
Thomas Son of Thomas Whiting and Lydia his Wife,	"	3 October 1748.
Elizabeth daughter of Gamaliel Wallis and Abigail his Wife,	"	24 November 1748.
William Son of Stephen Whiting and Mary his Wife,	"	2 March 1748.
Susanna daughter of John Wheatley and Susanna his Wife.	"	14 May 1748.
William Son of Philip White and Elizabeth his Wife,	"	12 June 1748.
Elizabeth daughter of Francis Whitman and Sarah his Wife,	"	7 May 1748.
Rebecca daughter of Davenport Walker and Sarah his Wife,	"	14 February 1748.

1749.

Peter Son of John Amiel and Christian his Wife,	Born	25 October 1749.
Martha daughter of Samuel Austin and Mary his Wife,	"	16 October 1749.
Rebecca daughter of Benja. Austin and Elizabeth his Wife,	"	20 June 1749.
Joseph Son of James Allen and Mary his Wife,	"	13 September 1749.
George Son of Benja. Andrews and Hannah his Wife,	"	31 October 1749.
Mary daughter of Francis Archibald and Anne his Wife,	"	9 May 1749.
Martha daughter of James Burt and Hannah his Wife,	"	9 August 1749.
Sarah daughter of Jeremiah Belknap and Mary his Wife,	"	27 May 1749.
Elizabeth daughter of Joshua Blanchard and Elizabeth his Wife,	"	20 October 1749.
Samuel Son of Samuel Badcock and Sybil his Wife,	"	3 March 1749.
Mehetable daughter of Edward Baker and Hannah his Wife,	"	11 March 1749.
Rachel daughter of John Barnard and Ann his Wife,	"	10 May 1749.
Thomas Son of Cutting Bean and Susanna his Wife,	"	24 June 1749.
Abigail daughter of Philip Breading and Abigail his Wife,	"	6 June 1749.
Stephen Hall Son of Jonathan Binney and Martha his Wife,	"	19 June 1749.
John Son of James Boyce and Mary his Wife,	"	4 June 1749.
Peter Son of James Buck and Mary his Wife,	"	19 September 1749.
Sarah daughter of Thomas Clarke and Jane his Wife,	"	1 August 1749.
Hannah daughter of John Cotton and Mary his Wife,	"	14 January 1749.
Andrew son of Andrew Campbell and Susanna his Wife,	"	22 June 1749.
Thomazin daughter of Thomas Cunningham and Joanna his Wife,	"	19 March 1749.
Elizabeth daughter of Joseph Clarke and Elizabeth his Wife,	"	31 July 1749.
Sarah daughter of Peace Cazneau and Mary his Wife,	"	4 May 1749.
John Son of Seth Coburn and Elizabeth his Wife,	"	5 March 1749.
Lucy daughter of Josiah Carter and Lydia his Wife,	"	6 September 1749.
David Son of John Cullam and Lydia his Wife,	"	6 February 1749.
Nathaniel Son of Barnabas Clark and Hepzibah his Wife,	"	16 August 1749.
Susanna daughter of Samuel Cowdry and Mary his Wife,	"	19 July 1749.
Elizabeth daughter of Samuel Clough and Ann his Wife,	"	15 October 1749.
Thomas Son of John Cunnable and Sarah his Wife.	"	12 December 1749.
Elinor daughter of William Downes Cheever and Elizabeth his Wife,	"	1 February 1749.
William Son of William Crouch and Eunice his Wife,	"	4 February 1749.
Eunice daughter of John Cowdry and Mary his Wife,	"	2 March 1749.
Samuel Son of Thomas Drowne and Sarah his Wife,	"	4 December 1749.
Deborah daughter of John Dobel and Deborah his Wife,	"	17 September 1749.
Addington Son of James Davenport and Mary his Wife,	"	6 February 1749.

John Son of John Douglass and Mary his Wife,	Born	3 March 1749.
Hannah daughter of Benjamin Dolbeare and Hannah his Wife,	"	11 December 1749.
John Son of Joseph Dyer and Abiel his Wife,	"	17 November 1749.
William Son of Thomas Davis and Sarah his Wife,	"	30 November 1749.
Samuel Son of Samuel Dexter and Hannah his Wife,	"	14 March 1749.
John Son of Isaac Dafforne and Sarah his Wife,	"	13 May 1749.
Elizabeth daughter of Edward Dwight and Elizabeth his Wife,	"	24 May 1749.
Ebenezer Son of James Dodge and Mary his Wife,	"	17 July 1749.
William Son of William Edes and Rebecca his Wife,	"	14 August 1749.
Ruth daughter of Andrew Eliot and Elizabeth his Wife,	"	2 October 1749.
Margaret daughter of Joshua Emmes and Margaret his Wife,	"	19 November 1749.
Edward Son of Edward Edwards and Sarah his Wife,	"	20 March 1749.
Edward Son of Edward Fryer and Jane his Wife,	"	20 April 1749.
Thomas Son of John Fenno and Hannah his Wife,	"	19 June 1749.
Dorcas daughter of William Fallass and Charity his Wife,	"	4 August 1749.
James Son of James Foster and Sarah his Wife,	"	30 August 1749.
William Son of William Farmer and Abigail his Wife,	"	23 January 1749.
John Son of John Farmer and Sarah his Wife,	"	16 July 1749.
David Son of Thomas Green and Martha his Wife,	"	20 June 1749.
John Son of John Greenleafe and Priscilla his Wife,	"	31 January 1749.
Elizabeth daughter of William Greenleafe and Mary his Wife,	"	6 March 1749.
Mary daughter of John Hamilton and Elizabeth Eburn his Wife,	"	18 February 1749.
Sarah daughter of Andrew Hall jun. and Sarah his Wife,	"	3 June 1749.
Joseph Son of Nathaniel Howland and Abigail his Wife,	"	30 September 1749.
Simon Ray Son of Thomas Hubbard and Judeth his Wife,	"	19 September 1749.
Dorcas daughter of Israel Hearsey and Tabitha his Wife,	"	16 March 1749.
John Son of Joshua Henshaw and Elizabeth his Wife,	"	7 August 1749.
Ward Son of Benjamin Hallowell and Mary his Wife,	"	22 November 1749.
John Son of John Jones and Mary Ann his Wife,	"	23 April 1749.
Benjamin Son of John Jones and Mary Ann his Wife,	"	24 March 1749.
Hannah daughter of Henry Johnson and Mary his Wife,	"	18 July 1749.
Ann daughter of David Jeffries and Sarah his Wife,	"	8 November 1749.
Susanna daughter of Joseph Jackson and Susanna his Wife,	"	2 September 1749.
Adam Son of Adam Knox and Martha his Wife,	"	10 November 1749.
William Son of Ezekiel Lewis and Jane his Wife,	"	20 March 1749.
Hannah daughter of Charles Lenox and Hannah his Wife,	"	2 September 1749.
Edward Son of John Langdon and Mary his Wife,	"	3 May 1749.
Sarah daughter of Joseph Lee and Sarah his Wife,	"	17 September 1749.
Robert Son of James Lamb and Desire his Wife,	"	17 February 1749.
Thomas Son of David McLeod and Mary his Wife,	"	20 January 1749.

Births — 1749.

Mary daughter of Samuel May and Catharina his Wife,	Born	1 December 1749.
Esther daughter of Neal McIntyer and Esther his Wife,	"	2 July 1749.
Samuel Son of Nathaniel Green Moody and Elizabeth his Wife,	"	27 January 1749.
Elizabeth daughter of Nathaniel Mason and Ruth his Wife,	"	11 October 1749.
Jane daughter of Peter McTagert and Margaret his Wife,	"	12 October 1749.
Andrew Son of Andrew McKenzie and Sarah his Wife,	"	29 October 1749.
Abigail daughter of William Marchant jun. and Sarah his Wife,	"	18 December 1749.
Benjamin Son of David Newhall and Elizabeth his Wife,	"	26 April 1749.
Mary daughter of Joseph Nowell and Mary his Wife,	"	31 August 1749.
Frances daughter of John Nichols and Mary his Wife,	"	19 December 1749.
Ann daughter of Belcher Noyes and Ann his Wife,	"	24 January 1749.
Peter Son of Andrew Oliver Esq. and Mary his Wife,	"	17 September 1749.
Thomas Maynard Son of Thomas Hand: Peck and his Wife,	"	18 July 1749.
Sarah daughter of Moses Peck and Elizabeth his Wife,	"	11 March 1749.
Walter Son of William Perkins and Mary his Wife,	"	24 September 1749.
John Son of Benjamin Proctor and Sarah his Wife,	"	15 October 1749.
Hezekiah Blanchard Son of Job Prince and Elizabeth his Wife,	"	15 August 1749.
Thomas Son of the revd. Roger Price and Elizabeth his Wife,	"	3 February 1749.
Jonathan Son of Benjamin Pollard and Margaret his Wife,	"	19 June 1749.
Samuel Son of Samuel Partridge and Rebecca his Wife,	"	9 June 1749.
Mary daughter of John Procter and Hannah his Wife,	"	14 June 1749.
John Son of Ebenezer Rockwell and Rebecca his Wife,	"	5 August 1749.
Elizabeth daughter of John Ridgaway and Elizabeth his Wife,	"	27 July 1749.
Uriel Son of Uriel Rea and Anne his Wife,	"	11 June 1749.
William Viscount Son of William Randel and Mary his Wife,	"	14 September 1749.
Hannah daughter of Mathew Ross and Hannah his Wife,	"	5 April 1749.
Ann daughter of James Rob and Ann his Wife,	"	7 June 1749.
Richard Son of John Ruddock and Tabitha his Wife,	"	10 November 1749.
James Son of John Scollay and Mercy his Wife,	"	9 June 1749.
Nanny daughter of William Scot and Nanny his Wife,	"	16 October 1749.
John Son of Thomas Spear and Susanna his Wife,	"	13 May 1749.
Isaac Son of William Story and Joanna his Wife,	"	9 September 1749.
Isaac Son of Isaac Smith and Elizabeth his Wife,	"	7 May 1749.
Elizabeth daughter of Samuel Sewall and Elizabeth his Wife,	"	12 March 1749.
Levinah daughter of William Swan and Levinah his Wife,	"	1 August 1749.
Joseph Son of Joseph Storer and Sarah his Wife,	"	19 August 1749.

272   CITY DOCUMENT No. 43.

John Cumins Son of John Salmon and Mary his Wife,	Born	30 April 1749.
Susanna daughter of Richard Stainer and Abigail his Wife,	"	27 June 1749.
Stephen Son of Joseph Scot and Elizabeth his Wife,	"	19 April 1749.
Mary daughter of Samuel Treat and Mary his Wife,	"	8 May 1749.
John Montague Son of James Topp and Martha his Wife,	"	23 August 1749.
Bathsheba daughter of Oxenbridge Thatcher and Sarah his Wife,	"	22 January 1749.
Sarah daughter of Othniel Tarr and Sarah his Wife,	"	18 April 1749.
Eliezer Son of Shippie Townsend and Ann his Wife,	"	29 January 1749.
Thomas son of Jonathan Tilden and Mary his Wife,	"	29 May 1749.
Thomas Coverley Son of Fortescue Vernon and Jane his Wife,	"	24 February 1749.
Lucy daughter of Isaac Winslow and Lucy his Wife,	"	7 October 1749.
Mary daughter of Thomas Walley and Mary his Wife,	"	12 June 1749.
Thomas Son of Nathaniel Woodward and Elizabeth his Wife,	"	3 February 1749.
Joshua Son of Edward Winslow and Jane Isabelle his Wife,	"	20 September 1749.
Elizabeth daughter of Edward Whittemore and Sarah his Wife,	"	7 April 1749.
John Son of Richard Woodward and Susanna his Wife,	"	21 September 1749.
Eunice daughter of Samuel Whitman and Eunice his Wife,	"	19 September 1749.
John Dean Son of Miles Whitworth and Deborah his Wife,	"	26 November 1749.

Of the following entries the last figure is worn away:

Margaret daughter of John Gardner and Margaret his Wife,	"	6 April 174 .
Hannah daughter of Joseph Gardner and Hannah his Wife,	"	29 June 174 .
Elizabeth daughter of Harrison Gray and Elizabeth his Wife,	"	22 June 174 .
John Son of Nicholas Gray and Mary his Wife,	"	13 April 174 .
—— Sears Son of Alexander Hill and Thankful his Wife,	"	? August 174 .

1750.

Katharine daughter of John Andrews and Margaret his Wife,	Born	10 August 1750.
Francis Son of Francis Archibald and Hannah his Wife,	"	19 October 1750.
Jeremiah Son of Jeremiah Allen and Elizabeth his Wife,	"	1 September 1750.
Lydia daughter of Coster Aish and Mary his Wife,	"	4 July 1750.
William Son of William Adams and Jemima his Wife,	"	18 August 1750.
Mary daughter of Mather Byles and Rebecca his Wife,	"	27 June 1750.
Abigail daughter of Joseph Belknap and Sarah his Wife,	"	1 September 1750.
Abigail daughter of William Bowman and Susanna his Wife,	"	23 September 1750.
John Son of John Barrett and Sarah his Wife,	"	9 October 1750.
Nathaniel Son of Nathaniel Baker and Susanna his Wife,	"	21 October 1750.
Margaret daughter of Henry Bromfield and Margaret his Wife,	"	5 October 1750.

BIRTHS — 1750.

Samuel Son of John Bowden and Ann his Wife,	Born	30 November 1750.
Jane daughter of Thomas Clarke and Jane his Wife,	"	21 October 1750.
William Son of John Cotton and Mary his Wife,	"	9 January 1750.
Abraham Son of William Codner and Mary his Wife,	"	18 January 1750.
Mehetable daughter of Josiah Cleveland and Joanna his Wife,	"	22 April 1750.
Sarah daughter of Richard Clark and Elizabeth his Wife,	"	9 April 1750.
Bartholomew Son of Bartholomew Cheever and Hannah his Wife,	"	31 March 1750.
Thomas Son of Thomas Cartwright and Hannah his Wife,	"	8 March 1750.
Margaret daughter of Thomas Cushing and Deborah his Wife,	"	16 July 1750.
Mary daughter of Gier Coffin and Rebecca his Wife,	"	4 April 1750.
William Son of John Cross and Mary his Wife,	"	7 August 1750.
Sarah daughter of David Cutler and Lydia his Wife,	"	24 November 1750.
Elizabeth daughter of James Clark and Ruth his Wife,	"	19 August 1750.
Robert Son of Jacob Davis and Sarah his Wife,	"	24 October 1750.
Katharine daughter of William Darby and Hannah his Wife,	"	19 November 1750.
John Son of John Dobel and Deborah his Wife,	"	27 September 1750.
Edward Son of Thomas Dane and Abigail his Wife,	"	7 July 1750.
Mary daughter of Richard Dana and Lydia his Wife,	"	17 February 1750.
Mary Lawrence daughter of Thomas Delotte and Susanna his Wife,	"	5 February 1750.
Samuel Gillam Son of Samuel Dogget and Katharine his Wife,	"	11 August 1750.
George Son of Lewis Deblois and Elizabeth his Wife,	"	27 October 1750.
Arthur Son of Arthur Dunn and Mary his Wife,	"	14 April 1750.
Lydia daughter of Thomas Emmons and Lydia his Wife,	"	28 July 1750.
Jonathan Welch Son of William Edes and Rebecca his Wife,	"	1 February 1750.
Abigail ⎱ Gem. daughters of Henry Erving and Elizabeth ⎰ Elizabeth his Wife,	"	13 September 1750. 9 June 1750.
John Son of John Edwards and Abigail his Wife,	"	
Mary daughter of Andrew Eliot and Elizabeth his Wife,	"	24 January 1750.
Benjamin (dead) Son of Benjamin Eustis and Elizabeth his Wife,	"	31 August 1750.
John Son of Nathan Foster and Mary his Wife,	"	10 May 1750.
John Son of John Fillis and Elizabeth his Wife,	"	5 June 1750.
William Son of John Fenno and Hannah his Wife,	"	19 December 1750.
Mary daughter of Gershom Flagg and Hannah his Wife,	"	25 October 1750.
David Son of David Flagg and Margaret his Wife,	"	1 July 1750.
Thomas Son of Thomas Goldthwait and Catharine his Wife,	"	4 June 1750.
Francis Son of William Green and Elizabeth his Wife,	"	18 January 1750.
Susanna daughter of Jacob Griggs jun. and Rachel his Wife,	"	3 June 1750.
Sarah daughter of Ezekiel Goldthwait and Elizabeth his Wife,	"	22 February 1750.
Sarah daughter of Benjamin Greene and Mary his Wife,	"	17 December 1750.

Elizabeth daughter of Thomas Griffiths and Dorcas his Wife	Born	18 May 1750.
Mary daughter of John Hutchinson and Sarah his Wife,	"	20 August 1750.
Mary daughter of Nathaniel Holmes and Rebecca his Wife,	"	2 September 1750.
Samuel Son of Alexander Hill and Thankful his Wife,	"	27 July 1750.
Mary daughter of Caleb Hopkins and Mary his Wife,	"	28 July 1750.
Hugh Son of John Hotte and Elizabeth his Wife,	"	4 November 1750.
Benjamin Son of Benjamin Hallowell and Mary his Wife,	"	14 January 1750.
Joseph } Twins and children of Thomas and Judith Hubbard, Deborah }	"	13 December 1750.
Thomas Mitchell Son of Zachariah Hall and Abigail his Wife,	"	16 October 1750.
Shrimpton Son of Shrimpton Hunt and Margaret his Wife,	"	18 January 1750.
William Son of William Hall and Margaret his Wife,	"	4 March 1750.
Mary daughter of Abraham Ingersol and Experience his Wife,	"	18 September 1750.
Jonathan Son of Jonathan Jenkins and Leah his Wife,	"	9 January 1750.
Daniel Son of Daniel Jones and Sarah his Wife,	"	16 August 1750.
Elizabeth daughter of John Jenkins and Prudence his Wife,	"	14 September 1750.
Joseph Son of Joseph Jackson and Miriam his Wife,	"	3 May 1750.
Abigail daughter of John Kneeland and Abigail his Wife,	"	28 April 1750.
Mary daughter of Mathew Kennedy and Jane his Wife,	"	27 July 1750.
Sarah daughter of John Kneeland jun. and Sarah his Wife,	"	18 March 1750.
Susanna daughter of John Langdon and Mary his Wife,	"	15 February 1750.
Mary daughter of James Lamb and Desire his Wife,	"	1 February 1750.
Elizabeth Irish daughter of Ebenezer Leadbetter and Elizabeth his Wife,	"	23 August 1750.
Mary daughter of Michael Lowell and Abigail his Wife,	"	14 January 1750.
Hannah daughter of Nathaniel Loring and Mary his Wife,	"	30 August 1750.
Elizabeth daughter of Jonathan Mason and Miriam his Wife,	"	16 August 1750.
John Son of Roger Macnight and Wait his Wife,	"	5 September 1750.
Elizabeth daughter of Thomas Manning and Esther his Wife,	"	1 November 1750.
Elizabeth daughter of William Merchant jun. and Sarah his Wife,	"	16 November 1750.
Thomas Debuke Son of Mark McKlaughlan and Ruth his Wife,	"	23 December 1750.
Abigail daughter of John Mellus and Sarah his Wife,	"	18 August 1750.
Hannah daughter of Jonathan Mountfort and Sarah his Wife,	"	27 June 1750.
Archibald Son of William McNeill and Katharine his Wife,	"	23 June 1750.
daughter of Peter Mctagert and Margaret his Wife,	"	3 October 1750.
Elizabeth daughter of David Newhall and Elizabeth his Wife,	"	23 June 1750.

BIRTHS — 1750–51.

Elizabeth daughter of Joseph Nowell and Mary his Wife,	Born	30 December 1750.
Elizabeth daughter of John Newhall and Sarah his Wife,	"	13 September 1750.
Anthony Son of Andrew Oliver and Susanna his Wife,	"	26 March 1750.
Daniel Son of Daniel Oliver and Bethia his Wife,	"	30 March 1750.
Daniel Son of Daniel Pecker and Elizabeth his Wife,	"	2 June 1750
John Son of William Paine and Mary his Wife,	"	22 September 1750.
Joseph Pearse Son of Joseph Palmer and Mary his Wife,	"	31 July 1750.
Abiel daughter of Edward Page and Rebecca his Wife,	"	14 November 1750.
John Son of Isaac Peirce and Mary his Wife,	"	28 September 1750.
William Son of William Phillips and Abigail his Wife,	"	30 March 1750.
Mary daughter of John Pusley and Sarah his Wife,	"	23 August 1750.
Sarah daughter of Richard Robinson and Sarah his Wife,	"	17 September 1750.
James Son of John Rogers and Mary his Wife,	"	25 November 1750.
Mary daughter of Alexander Russell and Mary his Wife,	"	29 May 1750.
William Son of Henry Roby and Elizabeth his Wife,	"	22 May 1750.
William Son of Samuel Phillips Savage and Sarah his Wife,	"	14 June 1750.
Mary daughter of Thomas Sherburne and Margaret his Wife,	"	18 February 1750.
Hannah daughter of } Gem. Thomas Savage and Ezekiel Son of } Sarah his Wife,	"	26 August 1750. 26 March 1750.
Thomas Son of Aftar Stoddard and Hannah his Wife,	"	
Joseph Son of Joseph Stevens and Hepzibah his Wife,	"	23 October 1750.
John Son of Francis Shaw and Sarah his Wife,	"	6 July 1750.
Elizabeth daughter of Isaac Smith and Elizabeth his Wife,	"	2 December 1750.
Henry Son of William Skinner and Lydia his Wife,	"	29 September 1750.
Dorothy daughter of Ephraim Turner and Dorothy his Wife,	"	22 September 1750.
William Son of John Tudor and Jane his Wife,	"	28 March 1750.
Mary daughter of William Thomas and Rebecca his Wife,	"	9 June 1750.
Joseph Son of Joseph Turell and Elizabeth his Wife,	"	19 September 1750.
Henry Son of William Thomas and Susanna Eburn his Wife,	"	28 October 1750.
Samuel Son of Samuel Tuffts and Susanna his Wife,	"	13 August 1750.
Richard Son of Richard Woodward and Susanna his Wife,	"	14 November 1750.
Abigail daughter of Joseph Winslow and Mary his Wife,	"	20 January 1750.
Samuel Son of Stephen Whiting and Mary his Wife,		4 December 1750.
Richard Son of Richard White and Mary his Wife,	"	7 January 1750.
Susanna daughter of Jonathan Waldo and Mary his Wife,	"	22 April 1750.
Jonathan Son of Jonathan Williams and Grace his Wife,	"	15 May 1750.

1751.

Samuel Son of Samuel Adams and Elizabeth his Wife,	Born	13 October 1751.
Jonathan Williams Son of Samuel Austin and Mary his Wife,	"	7 April 1751.

John Baxter Son of Barnabas Allen and Mary his Wife,	Born	8 October 1751.
Margaret daughter of John Billings jun. and Mary his Wife,	"	3 February 1750/1.
James Son of James Buck and Mary his Wife,	"	29 December 1751.
Sarah daughter of David Bell and Elizabeth his Wife,	"	17 November 1751.
Joshua Son of Joshua Blanchard and Elizabeth his Wife,	"	5 April 1751.
James Son of James Burt and Hannah his Wife,	"	10 June 1751.
Samuel Son of Jeremiah Belknap and Mary his Wife,	"	28 May 1751.
Nathaniel Son of Nathaniel Barber junr. and Elizabeth his Wife,	"	28 March 1751.
Thomas Son of Thomas Bailey and Sarah his Wife,	"	21 April 1751.
Rebecca daughter of George Brown and Rebecca his Wife,	"	25 June 1751.
Phoebe daughter of John Borland and Anna his Wife,	"	27 October 1751.
John Son of John Barber and Elizabeth his Wife,	"	15 September 1751.
David Son of James Boies and Mary his Wife,	"	10 October 1751.
Henry Son of Henry Bromfield and Margaret his Wife,	"	23 December 1751.
Tabitha daughter of Gear Coffin and Rebecca his Wife,	"	14 July 1751.
William Son of Andrew Campbell and Susanna his Wife,	"	9 December 1751.
Mary daughter of Andrew Craigie and Elizabeth his Wife,	"	13 October 1751.
Edward Scott Son of Seth Coburn and Elizabeth his Wife,	"	1 June 1751.
Thomas Son of Thomas Cole and Elizabeth his Wife,	"	23 May 1751.
Mary daughter of John Cutler and Mary his Wife,	"	2 December 1751.
William Son of William Currier and Ann his Wife,	"	15 October 1751.
Ann daughter of John Cullam and Lydia his Wife,	"	17 June 1751.
Thomas Son of Thomas Cunningham and Hannah his Wife,	"	29 September 1751.
Sarah daughter of Thomas Davis and Sarah his Wife,	"	26 July 1751.
Andrew Son of Samuel Dexter and Hannah his Wife,	"	4 May 1751.
Archibald Son of Archibald Dinmore and Hannah his Wife.	"	27 May 1751.
Grizzel daughter of Benjamin Dolbeare and Hannah his Wife,	"	3 August 1751.
Mary daughter of Thomas Dane and Abigail his Wife,	"	26 August 1751.
Daniel Son of James Dodge and Mary his Wife,	"	21 August 1751.
Lydia daughter of Joseph Dyre and Abiel his Wife,	"	8 October 1751.
Joanna Richards daughter of William Davis and Mary his Wife,	"	5 September 1751.
John Son of John Edwards and Abigail his Wife,	"	19 May 1751.
Benjamin Son of Benjamin Eustis and Elizabeth his Wife.	"	4 September 1751.
John Son of Nathan Foster and Mary his Wife,	"	28 July 1751.
Elizabeth daughter of William Fleet and Elizabeth his Wife,	"	11 May 1751.
Elizabeth daughter of Thomas Goldthwait and Catharine his Wife,	"	23 August 1751.
Sarah daughter of David Greenleafe and Sarah his Wife,	"	27 July 1751.

BIRTHS — 1751.

Sarah daughter of Edward Gouge and Sarah his Wife,	Born	23 November 1751.
Elizabeth daughter of Robert Gould and Elizabeth his Wife,	"	8 August 1751.
Rebecca daughter of Joseph How and Rebecca his Wife,	"	28 August 1751.
James Son of William Hyslop and Mehetable his Wife,	"	18 September 1751.
John Son of John Hutchinson and Sarah his Wife,	"	13 November 1751.
Sarah daughter of Robert Henry and Jean his Wife,	"	7 April 1751.
Richard Bill Son of Joshua Henshaw and Elizabeth his Wife,	"	10 March 1751.
Sarah daughter of William Hickling and Sarah his Wife,	"	11 August 1751.
James Son of William Hyslop and Mehetable his Wife,	"	17 September 1751.
Mary daughter of Samuel Hughes and Elizabeth his Wife,	"	27 August 1751.
James Son of Benjamin Harrod and Phebe his Wife,	"	10 December 1751.
Daniel Son of Daniel Ingersol and Bethia his Wife,	"	21 April 1751.
Sarah daughter of David Jeffries and Sarah his Wife,	"	5 June 1751.
Anna Khun daughter of Jacob Khun and Hannah his Wife,	"	5 July (dec'd) 1751.
Benjamin Son of Benjamin Kent and Elizabeth his Wife,	"	14 May 1751.
Elizabeth daughter of John Kneeland jun. and Sarah his Wife,	"	9 November 1751.
Nancy daughter of James Lamb and Desire his Wife,	"	17 September 1751.
Joseph Royal ⟩ Gem. Sons of Joshua Loring Esq. Benjamin ⟨ and Mary his Wife,	"	4 October 1751.
Sarah Fudge daughter of Daniel Malcom and Ann his Wife,	"	28 September 1751.
Robert Son of Neal McIntyer and Esther his Wife,	"	2 July 1751.
Mehettable daughter of Samuel May and Catharina his Wife,	"	6 August 1751.
Thomas Son of Allan Melvin and Jane his Wife,	"	16 January 1751.
Mary daughter of Thomas March and Mary his Wife,	"	25 October 1751.
Elizabeth daughter of Roger Mcnite and Wait his Wife,	"	14 December 1751.
Ann daughter of John Malcom and Sarah his Wife,	"	17 September 1751.
Mary daughter of Peter Oliver Esq. and Mary his Wife,	"	22 June 1751.
Martha daughter of Andrew Oliver Esq. and Mary his Wife,	"	18 July 1751.
William Son of Hugh Obrian and Margaret his Wife,	"	1 December 1751.
William Son of John Osborn and Jane his Wife,	"	23 November 1751
Daniel Goffe Son of Solomon Phipps and Abigail his Wife,	"	13 July 1751.
Sarah daughter of Nathaniel Parkman and Mary his Wife,	"	24 April 1751.
John Son of John Prince and Esther his Wife,	"	11 July 1751.
Job Son of Job Prince and Elizabeth his Wife,	"	28 September 1751.
Mary daughter of William Phillips and Abigail his Wife,	"	8 October 1751.
Thomas Son of William Pritchard and Atterlante his Wife,	"	31 August 1751.
John Son of William Pitman and Mary his Wife,	"	15 April 1751.
Mathew Son of Mathew Ross and Hannah his Wife,	"	28 October 1751.
Rebecca daughter of Ebenezer Rockwell and Rebecca his Wife,	"	22 September 1751.

Sarah daughter of Henry Rhodes and Sarah his Wife,	Born	4 June 1751.
Thomas Son of Samuel Ruggles and Hannah his Wife,	"	11 July 1751.
Anna daughter of John Rogers and Mary his Wife,	"	10 October 1751.
Catharine daughter of William Rhodes and Mary his Wife,	"	17 October 1751.
James Son of James Rob and Ann his Wife,	"	13 February 1751.
Joseph Son of Samuel Sewall and Elizabeth his Wife,	"	25 August 1751.
Martin Baker Son of Andrew Sigourney and Mary his Wife,	"	3 September 1751.
Ebenezer Son of Ebenezer Stevens and Elizabeth his Wife,	"	12 August 1751.
Anthony Son of Anthony Sigourney and Elizabeth his Wife,	"	12 May 1751.
Arthur Son of Thomas Savage and Sarah his Wife,	"	14 October 1751.
Thomas Son of William Swan and Levinah his Wife,	"	7 August 1751.
William Son of William Scot and Nanny his Wife,	"	4 April 1751.
Susanna daughter of Thomas Spear and Susanna his Wife,	"	21 May 1751.
Thomas Son of James Sherman and Rebecca his Wife,	"	18 August 1751.
John Ruggles Son of Arthur Savage and Rachel his Wife,	"	22 December 1751.
Joseph Son of Joseph Sherburne and Mary his Wife,	"	11 October 1751.
Ruth daughter of Simon Tufts and Ruth his Wife,	"	16 April 1751.
Ann daughter of Shippey Townsend and Ann his Wife,	"	19 August 1751.
William Son of Thomas Tyler and Bethiah his Wife,	"	5 January 1751.
Ambrose Sloper Son of Thomas Uran and Mary his Wife,	"	7 November 1751.
Jacob Son of William Vose and Hannah his Wife,	"	4 December 1751.
Elizabeth daughter of Nathaniel Whittel and Sarah his Wife,	"	26 September 1751.
John Son of Allin Whippe and Agnus his Wife,	"	9 November 1751.
William Son of Francis Whitman and Sarah his Wife,	"	30 May 1751.

1752.

Coster Son of Coster Aish and Mary his Wife,	Born	21 February 1752.
Amos Son of William Adams and Jemima his Wife,	"	21 September 1752.
Benjamin Son of Benja. Austin and Elizabeth his Wife,	"	18 November 1752.
Sarah daughter of Joshua Blanchard and Elizabeth his Wife,	"	13 May 1752.
John Son of Nathaniel Baker and Susanna his Wife,	"	20 October 1752.
John Son of John Burges and Elizabeth his Wife,	"	20 June 1752.
Andrew Son of Andrew Bowman and Martha his Wife,	"	15 April 1752.
Hannah daughter of Josias Byles and Sarah his Wife,	"	14 March 1752.
George Maxwel Son of Nathaniel Barber jun. and Elizabeth his Wife,	"	11 May 1752.
Jeremiah Son of Jeremiah Belknap and Mary his Wife,	"	14 May 1752.
John Son of Samuel Blunt and Hannah his Wife,	"	11 May 1752.
Thomas Stoddard Son of William Boardman and Susanna his Wife,	"	23 March 1752.

BIRTHS — 1752.

John Son of John Bennet and Hannah his Wife,	Born	17 August 1752.
Elizabeth daughter of Samuel Barrett and Mary his Wife,	"	31 January 1752.
Edward Son of John Cotton and Mary his Wife,	"	3 November 1752.
Elizabeth daughter of Seth Coburn and Elizabeth his Wife,	"	1 November 1752.
John and ⎱ Gem. Sons of John Crompston and Elizabeth his Wife, Edward ⎰	"	10 February 1752.
Susanna daughter of Gilbert Colesworthy and Mary his wife,	"	7 May 1752.
Lucy daughter of Richard Clark and Elizabeth his Wife,	"	19 May 1752.
David Son of William Crouch and Eunice his Wife,	"	9 February 1752.
William Son of William Downe Cheever and Elizabeth his Wife,	"	27 July 1752.
Samuel Son of David Cutler and Lydia his Wife,	"	5 October 1752.
Samuel Son of Samuel Downe and Elizabeth his Wife,	"	9 June 1752.
Mary daughter of Thomas Drowne and Sarah his Wife,	"	12 January 1752.
Abigail daughter of William Dawes and Lydia his Wife,	"	27 December 1752.
Joseph Son of William Dall and Elizabeth his Wife,	"	25 May 1752.
John Son of Benjamin Dolbeare and Hannah his Wife,	"	15 June 1752.
Mary daughter of Israel Eaton and Mary his Wife,	"	30 June 1752.
Jane daughter of John Eustis and Elizabeth his Wife,	"	22 March 1752.
Benjamin Son of William Edes and Rebecca his Wife,	"	25 May 1752.
Abigail daughter of William Farmer and Abigail his Wife,	"	29 July 1752.
Elizabeth daughter of John Fenno and Hannah his Wife,	"	13 August 1752.
Joseph Son of Jonas Fitch and Mary his Wife,	"	9 February 1752.
James Son of John Fillis and Elizabeth his Wife,	"	28 November 1752.
Sarah daughter of Daniel Greenleafe and Mary his Wife,	"	18 August 1752.
Mary daughter of William Greenleafe and Mary his Wife,	"	15 May 1752.
David Stoddard Son of Thomas Greenough and Sarah his Wife,	"	31 July 1752.
Daniel Son of Daniel Greenleafe and Sarah his Wife,	"	13 November 1752.
Nathaniel Son of Nathaniel Holmes and Rebecca his Wife,	"	11 March 1752.
Susanna daughter of Nathaniel Howland and Abigail his Wife,	"	9 July 1752.
Ann daughter of John Hutter and Elizabeth his Wife,	"	13 November 1752.
James Son of James Hatch and Mary his Wife,	"	5 February 1752.
Thomas Son of William Hall and Margaret his Wife,	"	8 April 1752.
Elizabeth daughter of Richard Harris and Elizabeth his Wife,	"	12 June 1752.
Thomas Son of Benjamin Hallowell and Mary his Wife,	"	18 July 1752.
Sarah daughter of Alexander Hill and Thankful his Wife,	"	11 August 1752.
Andrew Son of Joshua Henshaw and Elizabeth his Wife,	"	28 May 1752.

Rebekah daughter of William Hickling and Sarah his Wife,	Born	4 December 1752.
William Sanford Son of Thomas Hutchinson Esq. and Margaret his Wife,	"	August 1752.
Gideon Ray Hubbard Son of Thomas and Judith Hubbard,	"	1 September 1752.
Francis Son of Francis Ingraham and Dorcas his Wife,	"	20 December 1752.
Elizabeth daughter of Martin Johnson and Elizabeth his Wife,	"	29 September 1752.
Elizabeth daughter of David Jeffries and Sarah his Wife,	"	27 May 1752.
Daniel Son of Ichabod Jones and Apphia his Wife,	"	28 October 1752.
Philip Son of Philip Lewis and Jane his Wife,	"	26 October 1752.
George Son of George Lecross and Ann his Wife,	"	17 July 1752.
David Colson Son of Unite Moseley and Elizabeth his Wife,	"	17 December 1752.
Daniel Son of Neal McIntyer and Esther his Wife,	"	27 November 1752.
David Son of David Mason and Hannah his Wife,	"	7 August 1752.
William Son of John Mellus and Sarah his Wife,	"	18 June 1752.
William Son of William Marchant and Sarah his Wife,	"	13 April 1752.
Jonathan Son of Jonathan Mason and Miriam his Wife,	"	30 August 1752.
Jonathan Son of Andrew Oliver Esq. and Mary his Wife,	"	18 November 1752.
Benjamin Son of Benjamin Pollard and Margaret his Wife,	"	8 February 1752.
John Son of John Proctor and Susanna his Wife,	"	17 September 1752.
Elizabeth daughter of William Pritchard and Attalante his Wife,	"	29 December 1752.
Elizabeth daughter of Nathaniel Proctor and Elizabeth his Wife.	"	6 October 1752.
Elijah Son of Moses Peck and Elizabeth his Wife,	"	24 November 1752.
Isaac Son of William Pitman and Mary his Wife,	"	28 July 1752.
Thomas Son of Thomas Robson and Elizabeth his Wife,	"	16 November 1752.
Samuel Son of John Ruddock and Tabitha his Wife,	"	29 September 1752.
Elizabeth daughter of Samuel Ridgaway and Elizabeth his Wife,	"	16 May 1752.
John Son of David Scudder and Mary his Wife,	"	4 April 1752.
Elizabeth daughter of David Spear and Sarah his Wife,	"	13 May 1752.
Mary daughter of John Scollay and Mercy his Wife,	"	4 March 1752.
Ebenezer Son of Ebenezer Storer jun. and Elizabeth his Wife,	"	10 August 1752.
Andrew Son of Anthony Sigourney and Elizabeth his Wife,	"	30 November 1752.
Thomas Son of William Sanders and Anne his Wife,	"	31 January 1752.
Sarah daughter of Francis Shaw and Sarah his Wife,	"	14 February 1752.
Elizabeth daughter of Gillam Tailer and Elizabeth his Wife,	"	13 February 1752.
Mary daughter of Jacob Thayer and Mary his Wife,	"	24 July 1752.
John Son of Jonathan Williams and Grace his Wife,	"	2 August 1752.
Sarah daughter of Joseph Winslow and Mary his Wife,	"	7 December 1752.
John Son of John White and Susanna his Wife,	"	5 August 1752.

1753.

Edward Son of Francis Archibald and Anna his Wife,	Born	24 September 1753.
Mary daughter of Robert Allcock and Mary his Wife,	"	4 December 1753.
Christian daughter of John Amiel and Christian his Wife,	"	17 May 1753.
Philip Son of Isaiah Audebert and Sarah his Wife,	"	16 November 1753.
Katharine daughter of Mather Byles and Rebecca his Wife,	"	22 August 1753.
Hannah daughter of Andrew Bowman and Martha his Wife,	"	12 March 1753.
Sarah daughter of John Billings jun and Mary his Wife,	"	10 May 1753.
Elizabeth daughter of Daniel Boyer and Elizabeth his Wife,	"	30 May 1753.
Joseph Lasinby Son of Ebenezer Brown and Elizabeth his Wife,	"	12 September 1753.
Thomas Son of Thomas Bazin and Sarah his Wife,	"	27 October 1753.
Hannah daughter of Edward Baker and Hannah his Wife,	"	9 November 1753.
Sarah daughter of Caleb Blanchard and Haile his Wife,	"	1 December 1753.
Margaret daughter of Moses Collier and Susanna his Wife,	"	22 April 1753.
Thomas Jenner Son of Edward Carnes and Joanna his Wife,	"	18 December 1753.
Sarah daughter of Thomas Carman and Sarah his Wife,	"	23 December 1753.
Timothy Son of Thomas Cartwright and Hannah his Wife,	"	10 February 1753.
Elizabeth daughter of John Cutler and Mary his Wife,	"	16 July 1753.
William Son of William Dall and Elizabeth his Wife,	"	22 December 1753,
Sarah daughter of Lewis Deblois and Elizabeth his Wife,	"	29 December 1753.
Anna daughter of Thomas Dawes and Hannah his Wife,	"	19 May 1753.
Mary daughter of Samuel Dexter and Hannah his Wife,	"	15 August 1753.
Thomas Son of John Dobel and Deborah his Wife,	"	14 July 1753.
Mary daughter of Elijah Doubledee and Mary his Wife,	"	30 November 1753.
John Son of Solomon Davis and Elizabeth his Wife,	"	19 May 1753.
Thomas Son of Thomas Dane and Abigail his Wife,	"	6 August 1753.
Sarah daughter of Adam Dollard and Mary his Wife,	"	7 January 1753.
Ann daughter of Thomas Dawes and Hannah his Wife,	"	19 May 1753.
Thomas son of John Edwards and Abigail his Wife,	"	1 August 1753.
William Son of Benjamin Eustis and Elizabeth his Wife,	"	10 June 1753.
Grizel Apthorp daughter of Greshom Flagg and Hannah his Wife,	"	2 May 1753.
Elizabeth daughter of Jonathan Freeman and Ruth his Wife,	"	18 March 1753.
Ann daughter of William Fleet and Elizabeth his Wife,	"	15 October 1753.

Gardiner Son of Benjamin Greene and Mary his Wife,	Born	23 September 1753.
Mary daughter of Thomas Goldthwait and Catharine his Wife,	"	1 March 1753.
Abigail daughter of Joseph Greenleafe and Abigail his Wife,	"	27 February 1753.
Benjamin Son of Benjamin Gardner and Sarah his Wife,	"	19 December 1753.
Sarah daughter of Robert Gould and Elizabeth his Wife,	"	11 March 1753.
Ann daughter of Richard Humphrys and Ann his Wife,	"	22 January 1753.
Joseph Son of Joseph How and Rebecca his Wife,	"	4 March 1753.
Jane daughter of Shrimpton Hunt and Margaret his Wife,	"	4 May 1753.
Abigail daughter of John Homer and Abigail his Wife,	"	21 August 1753.
Sarah daughter of Benjamin Henderson and Sarah his Wife,	"	2 September 1753.
Elizabeth daughter of Robert Henry and Jean his Wife,	"	27 March 1753.
Sarah daughter of John Haskins and Hannah his Wife,	"	23 April 1753.
William Son of William Hyslop and Mehetable his Wife,	"	6 November 1753.
Benjamin Son of Silence Ivery and Elizabeth his Wife,	"	4 November 1753.
John Son of Joseph Jackson and Abigail his Wife,	"	17 March 1753.
Sarah daughter of Daniel Jones and Sarah his Wife,	"	2 November 1753.
John Son of John Jenkins and Prudence his Wife,	"	29 August 1753.
Fanny daughter of Francis Johonnott and Mary his Wife,	"	5 November 1753.
Thomas Son of Patrick Kinsley and Leah his Wife,	"	12 May 1753.
James Son of Edward King and Mary his Wife,	"	25 July 1753.
Robert Son of Adam Knox and Martha his Wife,	"	10 October 1753.
John Gyles Son of Nathaniel Loring and Mary his Wife,	"	25 March 1753.
Mary daughter of Edward Langdon and Mary his Wife,	"	14 December 1753.
Thomas Son of James Lamb and Desire his Wife,	"	20 November 1753.
Susannah daughter of Daniel Malcom and Ann his Wife,	"	6 September 1753.
Olive daughter of Joseph Morse and Ollive his Wife,	"	8 December 1753.
John Son of John Moloney and Margaret his Wife,	"	30 August 1753.
John Johnson Son of William Moore and Margaret his Wife,	"	23 June 1753.
John Son of John Malcom and Sarah his Wife,	"	25 June 1753.
Margaret ⎱ Gem. daughters of Henry Newman and Mary ⎰ Margaret his Wife,	"	9 April 1753.
Daniel Son of Nathaniel Oliver Esq. and Sarah his Wife,	"	4 April 1753.
John Son of Hugh Obrian and Margaret his Wife,	"	9 September 1753.
Agnes daughter of Isaac Peirce and Miriam his Wife,	"	22 June 1753.
Elizabeth daughter of Job Prince and Elizabeth his Wife,	"	28 May 1753.
Rebecca daughter of John Potter and Sarah his Wife,	"	24 May 1753.
Joseph Son of John Prince and Esther his Wife,	"	24 August 1753.
Patience daughter of John Pigeon and Jane his Wife,	"	14 September 1753.
Isaac Son of Isaac Peirce and Mary his Wife,	"	25 December 1753.

BIRTHS — 1753–54.

Henry Son of Henry Roby and Elizabeth his Wife,	Born	15 April 1753.
Mary daughter of David Scudder and Mary his Wife,	"	1 September 1753.
Benjamin Son of Ebenzer Stevens and Elizabeth his Wife,	"	29 March 1753.
Margaret daughter of William Sloper and Tamson his Wife,	"	2 November 1753.
Mary daughter of Thomas Sherburne and Margaret his Wife,	"	13 April 1753.
Hannah daughter of William Skinner and Lydia his Wife,	"	16 September 1753.
Lydia daughter of William Scott and Nanny his Wife,	"	4 January 1753.
Hannah daughter of Samuel Sewall and Elizabeth his Wife,	"	15 March 1753.
David Son of Shippey Townsend and Ann his Wife,	"	7 January 1753.
Joseph Son of Thomas Uran and Mary his Wife,	"	11 June 1753.
Edward Son of Edward Wentworth and Susanna his Wife,	"	11 April 1753.
Joshua Son of Joshua Winter and Sarah his Wife,	"	7 December 1753.
Robert Son of Robert Williams and Ann his Wife,	"	22 July 1753.
Seth Son of Seth Webber and Sarah his Wife,	"	18 July 1753.
William Brattle Son of John Mico Wendell and Katharine his Wife,	"	14 October 1753.
Charles Son of Charles Willis and Abigail his Wife,	"	27 June 1753.
John Son of John Winslow and Elizabeth his Wife,	"	29 September 1753.
James Son of Menzer and Lettice, free Negroes,	"	6 May 1753.

1754.

John Son of John Andrews and Margaret his Wife,	Born	18 February 1754.
Samuel Son of Samuel Allen and Elizabeth his Wife,	"	28 April 1754.
Nathaniel Son of Silas Atkins and Mary his Wife,	"	13 September 1754.
Mary daughter of Joshua Blanchard and Elizabeth his Wife,	"	19 July 1754.
Jane daughter of Paul Baxter and Theodosia his Wife,	"	13 April 1754.
Ezekiel Son of Samuel Blunt and Hannah his Wife,	"	8 January 1754.
William Son of Edward Brown and Katharine his Wife,	"	2 August 1754.
Mary daughter of Samuel Blodget and Hannah his Wife,	"	1 December 1754.
William Son of William Boardman and Susanna his Wife,	"	3 February 1754.
John Lindal Son of John Borland and Anna his Wife,	"	18 August 1754.
Elizabeth daughter of John Bell and Rachel his Wife,	"	22 September 1754.
Elizabeth daughter of Thomas Blanchard and Margory his Wife,	"	30 October 1754.
Joseph Son of John Cotton and Mary his Wife,	"	23 July 1754.
Alexander Son of Alexander Chamberlain and Elizabeth his Wife,	"	20 March 1754.
John Son of Elias Cattance and Mary his Wife,	"	10 November 1754.
Andrew Son of Andrew Craigie and Elizabeth his Wife,	"	22 February 1754.
Ann daughter of Reuben Chandler and Ann his Wife,	"	24 February 1754.
Thomas Austin Son of William Coffin junr. and Mary his Wife,	"	31 March 1754.
William Son of Samuel Downe and Elizabeth his Wife,	"	12 May 1754.

William Son of William Darracott and Sarah his Wife,	Born	24 April 1754.
Elizabeth daughter of Thomas Drowne and Sarah his Wife,	"	10 November 1754.
Samuel Son of Samuel Deming and Mary his Wife,	"	6 February 1754.
Joseph Son of Noah Dogget and Mary his Wife,	"	16 August 1754.
Hannah daughter of Thomas Dawes and Hannah his Wife,	"	8 July 1754.
Solomon Son of Solomon Davis and Elizabeth his Wife,	"	29 September 1754.
Joseph Son of Joseph Eustis and Ann his Wife,	"	15 April 1754.
Josiah Son of William Edes and Rebekah his Wife,	"	12 April 1754.
Elizabeth daughter of John Eustis and Elizabeth his Wife,	"	15 October 1754.
John Son of Andrew Elliot and Elizabeth his Wife,	"	31 May 1754.
Ruth daughter of Isaac Freeman and Mary his Wife,	"	20 November 1754.
Percivall Son of William Farmer and Abigail his Wife,	"	22 November 1754.
Susanna daughter of William Greenleafe and Mary his Wife,	"	6 February 1754.
Joseph Son of Joseph Greenleafe and Abigail his Wife,	"	28 May 1754.
Catharine daughter of Ezekiel Goldthwait and Elizabeth his Wife,	"	4 March 1754.
Daniel Son of Daniel Henchman and Elizabeth his Wife,	"	6 March 1754.
Rachel daughter of Estick How and Rachel his Wife,	"	25 June 1754.
Mary daughter of James Hatch and Mary his Wife,	"	19 September 1754.
John Son of Joseph How and Rebecca his Wife,	"	14 October 1754.
Elizabeth daughter of Shrimpton Hunt and Margaret his Wife,	"	4 December 1754.
Margaret daughter of Thomas Hutchinson Esq. and Margaret his Wife,	"	14 February 1754.
Judith daughter of Thos. and Judith Hubbard,	"	28 May 1754
Elizabeth daughter of Henderson Inches and Elizabeth his Wife,	"	19 October 1754.
James Son of James Ivers and Hannah his Wife.	"	7 July 1754.
Francis Son of Francis Johonnot and Mary his Wife.	"	20 December 1754.
Ruth daughter of William Jackson and Ruth his Wife,	"	25 February 1754.
Malachy Son of Joseph Jackson and Abigail his Wife,	"	18 November 1754.
Mary daughter of Ichabod Jones and Apphia his Wife,	"	10 December 1754.
George Wiswell Son of George Jeffords and Hannah his Wife,	"	1 March 1754.
John Son of John Kneeland and Abigail his Wife,	"	8 October 1754.
Andrew Son of David Mason and Hannah his Wife,	"	19 August 1754.
Abigail daughter of Samuel May and Abigail his Wife,	"	13 October 1754.
Ebenezer Son of Francis Marshal and Abigail his Wife,	"	27 March 1754.
Benjamin Soper Son of Zerubbabel Marshall and Elizabeth his Wife,	"	21 February 1754.
John Son of John Mager and Abigail his Wife,	"	8 October 1754.
Meriam daughter of Jonathan Mason and Meriam his Wife,	"	16 June 1754.
John Son of John Newhall and Sarah his Wife,	"	10 September 1754.
William Son of Josiah Newhall and Rachel his Wife,	"	17 May 1754.

Births — 1754-55.

Elizabeth daughter of Joseph Nowell and Mary his Wife,	Born	8 February 1754.
Elizabeth daughter of Henry Newman and Margaret his Wife,	"	13 November 1754.
Thomas Son of Andrew Oliver Esq. and Mary his Wife,	"	22 March 1754.
Mary daughter of Andrew Oliver jun. and Mary his Wife,	"	28 April 1754.
Lydia daughter of John Proctor and Mary his Wife,	"	8 September 1754.
Peggy Savage daughter of Benja. Pollard Esq. and Margaret his Wife,	"	27 January 1754.
Thomas Son of Job Prince and Elizabeth his Wife,	"	27 September 1754.
Lydia daughter of John Proctor and Susanna his Wife,	"	8 September 1754.
Samuel Son of Samuel Ridgaway and Elizabeth his Wife,	"	3 August 1754.
John Son of Henry Roby and Elizabeth his Wife,	"	11 August 1754.
Hannah daughter of Isaac Ridgaway and Bridget his Wife,	"	6 June 1754.
John Son of Joseph Sherburne and Mary his Wife,	"	8 November 1754.
Hannah daughter of Andrew Sigourney and Mary his Wife,	"	30 April 1754.
Daniel Son of John Scollay and Mercy his Wife,	"	20 January 1754.
Ebenezer Son of Ebenezer Storer and Elizabeth his Wife,	"	17 February 1754.
Samuel Son of Francis Shaw and Sarah his Wife,	"	2 October 1754.
John Son of William Story and Joanna his Wife,	"	6 August 1754.
Gillam Son of Gillam Tailer and Elizabeth his Wife,	"	5 November 1754.
Thomas Son of Ephraim Turner and Dorothy his Wife,	"	4 December 1754.
Eunice daughter of Samuel Whitman and Eunice his Wife,	"	8 March 1754.
Elizabeth daughter of Jonathan Williams and Grace his Wife,	"	25 March 1754.
Mary daughter of Stephen Whiting and Mary his Wife,	"	7 August 1754.
John Son of Edward Walch and Elizabeth his Wife,	"	22 September 1754.
Sarah daughter of Seth Webber and Sarah his Wife,	"	23 October 1754.
Samuel Son of Samuel Whitwell and Elizabeth his Wife,	"	12 January 1754.
Jonathan Son of Jonathan Waldo and Mary his Wife,	"	25 June 1754.

1755.

Abigail daughter of William Adams and Jemima his Wife,	Born	7 March 1755.
Nathaniel Walker Son of Nathaniel Appleton and Mary his Wife,	"	14 June 1755.
Abraham Son of Robert Alcock and Mary his Wife,	"	2 November 1755.
Daniel Son of Daniel Ballard jun. and Ann his Wife.	"	14 May 1755.
Abigail daughter of John Bennet and Susanna his Wife,	"	8 July 1755.
Anne daughter of Increase Blake and Anne his Wife,	"	9 August 1755.
Elizabeth daughter of Nathaniel Barber and Elizabeth his Wife,	"	20 April 1755.
Mary daughter of Thomas Bazin and Sarah his Wife,	"	16 June 1755.
Mary daughter of John Bryan and Priscilla his Wife.	"	22 June 1755.
Hannah daughter of Samuel Blunt and Hannah his Wife,	"	7 August 1755.

Caleb Son of Caleb Blanchard and Haile his Wife,	Born	15 January 1755.
Elizabeth daughter of Benjamin Brown and Ann his Wife,	"	3 April 1755.
Mary daughter of John Billings jun. and Mary his Wife,	"	24 February 1755.
Margaret daughter of John Cotton and Mary his Wife,	"	26 August 1755.
John Son of Andrew Craigie and Elizabeth his Wife,	"	7 November 1755.
James Son of Dominick Cavenay and Mary his Wife,	"	25 July 1755.
Abigail daughter of John Cross and Mary his Wife,	"	24 April 1755.
Edward Son of Edward Carnes and Joanna his Wife,	"	23 February 1755.
Ann daughter of William Coffin junr. and Mary his Wife,	"	2 July 1755.
William Son of William Crouch and Eunice his Wife,	"	14 November 1755.
James Son of William Dall and Elizabeth his Wife,	"	11 March 1755.
Edward Son of Solomon Davis and Elizabeth his Wife,	"	31 December 1755.
Sarah daughter of Nyott Doubt and Sarah his Wife,	"	29 June 1755.
Sarah daughter of John Dobel and Deborah his Wife,	"	1 July 1755.
Hannah daughter of Archibald Dinmore and Hannah his Wife,	"	21 April 1755.
Nathaniel Son of Nathaniel Dunn and Abigail his Wife,	"	30 May 1755.
Samuel Son of Samuel Doggett and Esther his Wife,	"	16 May 1755.
Anstis daughter of Thomas Dane and Abigail his Wife,	"	1 March 1755.
Samuel Son of William Edes and Rebekah his Wife,	"	23 August 1755.
Mary daughter of John Edwards and Abigail his Wife,	"	15 April 1755.
Benjamin Son of Benjamin Edes and Martha his Wife,	"	8 November 1755.
Sarah daughter of Andrew Eliot and Elizabeth his Wife,	"	3 November 1755.
Jerusha daughter of Israel Eaton and Jerusha his Wife,	"	5 February 1755.
George Son of Benjamin Eustis and Elizabeth his Wife,	"	8 February 1755.
Mary daughter of John Foreakers and Rebecca his Wife,	"	21 July 1755.
Mary daughter of John Fairservice and Mary his Wife,	"	19 November 1755.
John Son of Harrison Gray and Elizabeth his Wife,	"	18 May 1755.
Priscilla daughter of William Greenleafe and Mary his Wife,	"	25 October 1755.
Thomas Son of Joseph Greenleafe and Abigail his Wife,	"	27 May 1755.
Margaret daughter of Ezekiel Goldthwait and Elizabeth his Wife,	"	25 June 1755.
George Son of Alexander Gordon and Jane his Wife,	"	6 August 1755.
Elizabeth daughter of Richard Hunniwell and Sarah his Wife,	"	12 March 1755.
William Son of Samuel Harris and Sarah his Wife,	"	26 February 1755.
Nathaniel Son of Nathaniel Holmes and Rebecca his Wife,	"	20 September 1755.
John Son of John Homer and Abigail his Wife,	"	30 June 1755.
Thomas Hake Son of John Haskins and Hannah his Wife,	"	12 January 1755.
Edward Son of Alexander Hill and Thankful his Wife,	"	21 January 1755.

BIRTHS — 1755.

Phœbe daughter of Benjamin Harrod and Phœbe his Wife,	Born	31 July 1755.
Rebecca daughter of Joseph How and Rebecca his Wife,	"	17 November 1755.
David Son of William Hyslop and Mehetable his Wife,	"	28 December 1755
Dorothy daughter of William Jackson and Ruth his Wife,	"	18 March 1755
Susanna daughter of Francis Johonnot and Mary his Wife,	"	26 November 1755.
Jeremiah Fones Son of John Jenkins and Prudence his Wife,	"	2 June 1755
Ann daughter of Thomas Knox and Mary his Wife,	"	3 October 1755.
Mary daughter of Edward King and Mary his Wife,	"	13 November 1755.
John Son of James Lamb and Desire his Wife,	"	4 May 1755.
Ann daughter of David Low and Sarah his Wife,	"	22 April 1755.
Daniel Son of John Malcom and Sarah his Wife,	"	26 February 1755.
Daniel Son of Daniel Malcom and Ann his Wife,	"	30 October 1755.
Mary daughter of Jonathan Mountfort and Sarah his Wife,	"	16 February 1755.
James Son of Neal McIntyer and Esther his Wife,	"	10 January 1755.
Thomas Son of John Moloney and Margaret his Wife,	"	23 August 1755.
Mercy daughter of Uriah Norcross and Mercy his Wife,	"	31 March 1755.
Mercy daughter of Joseph Nowel and Mary his Wife,	"	17 October 1755.
Brinley Sylvester Son of Andrew Oliver Esq. and Mary his Wife,	"	6 September 1755.
Joshua Son of Benjamin Pollard and Margaret his Wife,	"	13 January 1755.
John Son of John Potter and Mary his Wife,	"	29 March 1755.
William Son of Jonathan Parker and Martha his Wife,	"	29 August 1755.
Susanna daughter of John Proctor and Mary his Wife,	"	16 October 1755.
Edward Son of John Pulling and Jerusha his Wife,	"	30 October 1755.
Martha daughter of Joseph Pyncheon Esq. and Mary his Wife,	"	22 January 1755.
Samuel Son of Samuel Procter and Elizabeth his Wife,	"	13 December 1755.
Turner Son of Isaac Phillips and Preseler his Wife,	"	12 September 1755.
Sarah daughter of William Pitman and Mary his Wife,	"	21 April 1755.
George Son of James Rob	"	16 February 1755.
Joseph Son of Ebenezer Rockwell and Rebecca his Wife,	"	21 April 1755.
Mary daughter of John Rogers and Mary his Wife,	"	4 February 1755.
John Son of Thomas Roberts and Mercy his Wife,	"	7 October 1755.
Andrew Son of Andrew Reed and Mary his Wife,	"	12 December 1755.
Thomas Son of Thomas Savage and Sarah his Wife,	"	25 June 1755.
Joseph Son of David Scudder and Mary his Wife,	"	16 May 1755.
John Son of Ferrers Shirley and Ann his Wife,	"	1 January 1755.
Benjamin Clough Son of Samuel Sumner jun. and Bethia his Wife,	"	14 April 1755.
William Son of Isaac Smith and Elizabeth his Wife,	"	19 June 1755.
Elizabeth daughter of John Soren and Elizabeth his Wife,	"	4 January 1755.
Abigail daughter of David Spear and Sarah his Wife,	"	15 December 1755.
Sarah daughter of Joseph Scott and Freelove his Wife,	"	14 October 1755.
Priscilla daughter of John Scolly and Mercy his Wife,	"	15 August 1755.
Elizabeth daughter of Samuel Torrey and Deborah his Wife,	"	11 September 1755.

Margaret daughter of Thomas Uran and Mary his Wife,	Born	14 April 1755.
Jacob Son of John Mico Wendell and Katharine his Wife,	"	3 March 1755.
Jacob Son of John Welsh and Mary his Wife,	"	23 April 1755.
Josiah Winslow Son of Edward Wentworth and Susanna his Wife,	"	24 March 1755.
Nathaniel Son of Charles Willis and Abigail his Wife,	"	17 February 1755.
Sarah daughter of John Winslow and Elizabeth his Wife,	"	12 April 1755.
Hannah daughter of Isaac Winslow and Lucy his Wife,	"	28 February 1755.

1756.

Anna daughter of Francis Archbald and Anna his Wife,	Born	14 March 1756.
Hailey daughter of Caleb Blanchard and Hailey his Wife,	"	16 December 1756.
Caleb Lyman Son of Nathaniel Barber and Elizabeth his Wife,	"	19 December 1756.
Susanna daughter of William Boardman and Susanna his Wife,	"	25 November 1756.
Samuel Son of Joshua Blanchard and Elizabeth his Wife,	"	29 February 1756.
Benjamin Son of Benjamin Barnard and Elizabeth his Wife,	"	20 June 1756.
John Briggs Son of John Bell and Rachel his Wife,	"	September 1756.
Shute Son of Edward Baker and Hannah his Wife,	"	7 November 1756.
John Son of John Bradford and Margaret his Wife,	"	18 August 1756.
Francis Son of Samuel and Mary Bangs,	"	26 March 1756.
Ann daughter of James Brett and Abigail his Wife,	"	3 January 1756.
Melatiah Son of Melatiah Bourn and Mary his Wife,	"	3 January 1756.
Margery daughter of Thomas Blanchard and Margery his Wife,	"	13 April 1756.
Bethia daughter of Reuben Chandler and Ann his Wife,	"	3 April 1756.
Joanna daughter of Edward Carnes and Joanna his Wife,	"	5 September 1756.
Richard Son of Richard Clark and Elizabeth his Wife,	"	19 May 1756.
John Son of Moses Collier and Susanna his Wife,	"	22 December 1756.
Elizabeth daughter of Thomas Carnes and Elizabeth his Wife,	"	30 September 1756.
Elizabeth daughter of Thomas Daws and Hannah his Wife,	"	22 July 1756.
Rebecka daughter of William Dawes and Lydia his Wife,	"	26 September 1756.
Thomas Son of Ebenezer Dogget and Elizabeth his Wife,	"	19 December 1756.
Bethiah daughter of Noah Dogget and Mary his Wife,	"	22 August 1756.
Grace daughter of John Dobel and Deborah his Wife,	"	1 September 1756.
Ann daughter of Joseph Eustis and Ann his Wife,	"	7 February 1756.
Elizabeth daughter of Henry Evans and Elizabeth his Wife,	"	22 July 1756.
Samuel Son of John Edwards and Abigail his Wife,	"	7 November 1756.
Peter Son of Benj. Edes and Martha his Wife,	"	17 December 1756.
Sarah daughter of John Fisher and Sarah his Wife,	"	20 October 1756.

BIRTHS — 1756.

Jonathan Son of Jonathan Freeman and Ruth his Wife,	Born	18 January 1756.
Eunice daughter of Samuel Franklin and Eunice his Wife,	"	25 November 1756.
Ebenezer Son of Ebenezer Floyd and Mary his Wife,	"	13 December 1756.
William Son of Thomas Greenough and Sarah his Wife	"	29 June 1756.
John Son of John Gill and Ann his Wife,	"	24 December 1756.
Ann daughter of Benjamin Greene and Mary his Wife,	"	28 February 1756.
William Son of Shrimpton Hunt and Margaret his Wife,	"	23 January 1756.
John Son of Ezekiel Hatch and Hannah his Wife,	"	19 March 1756.
Benjamin Son of Benjamin Henderson and Sarah his Wife,	"	30 May 1756.
Samuel Son of Samuel Holbrook and Elizabeth his Wife,	"	9 June 1756.
Elizabeth daughter of William Hall and Margaret his Wife,	"	14 August 1756.
Catharine daughter of Thomas and Judith Hubbard,	"	22 May 1756.
Charles Paxton Son of Nathaniel Hatch and Elizabeth his Wife,	"	27 June 1756.
Hannah daughter of John Haskins and Hannah his Wife,	"	17 December 1756.
Lucy daughter of Benjamin Hallowell and Mary his Wife,	"	28 January 1756.
Sarah daughter of Samuel Harris and Sarah his Wife,	"	22 December 1756.
Hannah daughter of James Ivers and Hannah his Wife,	"	20 March 1756.
Deborah daughter of David Jeffries and Deborah his Wife,	"	10 June 1756.
Mary daughter of Daniel Jones and Sarah his Wife,	"	3 September 1756.
George Stewart Son of Francis Johonnot and Mary his Wife,	"	23 November 1756.
Katharine daughter of Joseph Jackson and Susanna his Wife,	"	25 October 1756.
William Son of James Lamb and Desire his Wife,	"	26 September 1756.
Andrew Son of Roger Mcknight and Wait his Wife,	"	24 December 1756.
Zabiah daughter of Ephraim May and Zabiah his Wife,	"	16 October 1756.
Jonathan Son of Jonathan Mason and Meriam his Wife,	"	12 September 1756.
John Son of John Mackay and Elizabeth his Wife,	"	31 March 1756.
Henry Son of John Mellus and Sarah his Wife,	"	1 April 1756.
Samuel Son of Samuel May and Abigail his Wife,	"	17 February 1756.
Hannah daughter of David Mason and Hannah his Wife,	"	21 December 1756.
Mary daughter of Neal McIntyer and Esther his Wife,	"	9 March 1756.
Eleazer Son of Josiah Newhall and Rachel his Wife,	"	6 January 1756.
Henry Son of Henry Newman and Margaret his Wife,	"	15 April 1756.
Sarah daughter of Job Prince and Elizabeth his Wife,	"	29 March 1756.
Thomas Son of John Prince and Esther his Wife,	"	28 February 1756.
Peter Son of Benjamin Pollard Esq. and Margaret his Wife,	"	1 August 1756.
John Son of John Pigeon and Jane his Wife,	"	9 April 1756.
Hannah ⎱ Gem. daughters of William Phillips and Sarah ⎰ Abigail his Wife,	"	29 November 1756.
Hardy Son of Isaac Peirce and Mary his Wife,	"	20 July 1756.

Margaret daughter of Joseph Pyncheon Esq. and Mary his Wife, Born 13 August 1756.
Elizabeth daughter of James Perkins and Elizabeth his Wife, " 18 January 1756.
Nathan Son of Uriel Rea and Ann his Wife, " 1 April 1756.
Abigail daughter of Samuel Ross and Abigail his Wife, " 6 April 1756.
Anna daughter of David Scudder and Mary his Wife, " 25 December 1756.
Joseph Son of Samuel Phillips Savage and Sarah his Wife, " 14 June 1756.
Thomas Son of Thomas Stanley and Mary his Wife, " 15 January 1756.
Elizabeth daughter of Ebenezer Storer and Elizabeth his Wife, " 23 February 1756.
William Son of Francis Shaw and Sarah his Wife. " 30 March 1756.
Charles Son of William Skinner and Lydia his Wife, " 16 November 1756.
William Son of John Scollay and Mercy his Wife, " 24 November 1756.
Samuel Son of Samuel Simpson and Alice his Wife, " 26 October 1756.
Sarah daughter of William Story and Joanna his Wife, " 28 July 1756.
Sarah daughter of Samuel Sewall and Elizabeth his Wife, " 14 January 1756.
Thomas Son of Oxenbridge Thacher and Sarah his Wife, " 24 October 1756.
Samuel Son of Ephraim Turner and Dorothy his Wife, " 15 July 1756.
Mary daughter of Thomas Uran and Mary his Wife, " 1 November 1756.
Oliver Son of Oliver Wiswall and Margaret his Wife, " 26 February 1756.
William Son of Edward Walch and Elizabeth his Wife, " 21 August 1756.
John Son of Jonathan Williams and Grace his Wife, " 5 April 1756.
Joseph Son of Stephen Whiting and Mary his Wife, " 2 September 1756.
Benjamin Son of Robert Williams jun. and Ann his Wife, " 13 June 1756.
Mary daughter of Isaac Wendell and Mary his Wife, " 16 March 1756.
Katherine daughter of John Mico Wendell and Katherine his Wife,. " 2 April 1756.

1757.

Thomas Son of John Amory and Katharine his Wife. Born 27 September 1757.
Henry Son of John Andrews and Margaret his Wife, " 9 July 1757.
Benja. Fenno Son of William Adams and Jemima his Wife, " 19 November 1757.
Christian daughter of William Andrews and Mary his Wife, " 2 May 1757.
John Son of Thomas Barron and Mercy his Wife, " 9 March 1757.
Sarah daughter of Henry Bromfield and Margaret his Wife, " 1 May 1757.
Nathaniel Son of Nathaniel Baker and Susanna his Wife, " 8 February 1757.
Samuel Son of Samuel Blodget and Hannah his Wife, " 28 August 1757.
Sarah daughter of Josias Byles and Mary his Wife, " 30 September 1757.
Benjamin Son of Benjamin Brown and Ann his Wife, " 30 May 1757.
Richard Son of Richard Billings and Hannah his Wife, " 8 June 1757.

BIRTHS — 1757.

John Son of Jonathan Brown and Elizabeth his Wife,	Born	16 September 1757.
Newcomb Son of Gilbert Colesworthy and Mary his Wife,	"	20 June 1757.
Elizabeth daughter of Benjamin Cudworth and Mary his Wife,	"	25 February 1757.
Bartholomew Son of William Downes Cheever and Elizabeth his Wife,	"	4 July 1757.
Sarah daughter of Reuben Chandler and Ann his Wife,	"	14 July 1757.
Sarah daughter of Thomas Carnes and Elizabeth his Wife,	"	26 September 1757.
Elizabeth daughter of Samuel Downe and Elizabeth his Wife,	"	9 May 1757.
Thomas Son of Thomas Dawes and Hannah his Wife,	"	8 July 1757.
Mary daughter of Samuel Deming and Mary his Wife,	"	26 June 1757.
Edmund Son of Edmund Dolbeare and Sarah his Wife,	"	5 March 1757.
William Son of Samuel Dogget and Esther his Wife,	"	3 April 1757.
Henry Silvester Son of Thomas Dering and Mary his Wife,	"	21 April 1757.
Mary daughter of Solomon Davis and Mary his Wife,	"	4 October 1757.
Mercy daughter of Israel Eaton and Jerusha his Wife,	"	27 May 1757.
Rebekah daughter of William Edes and Rebecca his Wife,	"	14 May 1757.
William Son of John Eustis and Elizabeth his Wife,	"	19 August 1757.
Mary daughter of Robert Edwards and Mary his Wife,	"	22 October 1757.
Abraham Son of Benjamin Eustis and Elizabeth his Wife,	"	26 April 1757.
James Son of John Fenno and Katharine his Wife,	"	5 October 1757.
Elizabeth daughter of Jonathan Freeman and Ruth his Wife,	"	16 October 1757.
Elizabeth daughter of John Fairservice and Mary his Wife,	"	7 April 1757.
David Son of David Gardner and Frances his Wife,	"	28 April 1757.
Sarah daughter of Ezekiel Goldthwait and Elizabeth his Wife,	"	15 October 1757.
Alexander Son of Alexander Gordon and Jane his Wife,	"	21 April 1757.
Sarah daughter of William Greenleaf and Mary his Wife,	"	19 March 1757.
Thomas Son of Shrimpton Hunt and Margaret his Wife,	"	9 March 1757.
Lois daughter of Joseph How and Rebecca his Wife,	"	5 April 1757.
Martha daughter of Naler Hatch and Martha his Wife,	"	11 July 1757.
Samuel Son of Samuel Harris and Ann his Wife,	"	22 July 1757.
Elizabeth daughter of William Hyslop and Mehetable his Wife,	"	5 August 1757.
Elizabeth daughter of Samuel Hewes and Elizabeth his Wife,	"	10 September 1757.
Sarah daughter of Benjamin Hallowell and Mary his Wife,	"	3 January 1757.
Elizabeth daughter of Samuel Holbrook and Elizabeth his Wife,	"	15 June 1757.
Lucy daughter of Silence Ivery and Elizabeth his Wife,	"	24 April 1757.
Elizabeth daughter of Thomas Jarvis and Lydia his Wife,	"	30 August 1757.

Lewis Son of John Jenkins and Prudence his Wife,	Born	10 April 1757.
Andrew Belcher Son of David Jeffries and Deborah his Wife,	"	31 July 1757.
Desire daughter of James Lamb and Desire his Wife,	"	4 October 1757.
Joseph Son of John Langdon and Mary his Wife,	"	30 November 1757.
Joseph Son of Joseph and Mary Loring,	"	20 October 1757.
Agnis daughter of David McLeod and Mary his Wife,	"	18 May 1757.
Sarah daughter of John Malcom and Sarah his Wife,	"	31 January 1757.
Catharina daughter of Samuel May and Abigail his Wife,	"	27 September 1757.
Napthaly Son of Josiah Newhall and Rachel his Wife,	"	24 June 1757.
Mary daughter of Uriah Norcross and Mercy his Wife,	"	22 December 1757.
William Son of Henry Newman and Margaret his Wife,	"	5 June 1757.
William Son of William Owen and Sarah his Wife,	"	13 March 1757.
Elizabeth daughter of James Otis and Ruth his Wife,	"	28 March 1757.
Thomas Fitch Son of Andrew Oliver jun. and Mary his Wife,	"	14 May 1757.
Thomas Son of Thomas Pons and Sarah his Wife.	"	16 May 1757.
Unity daughter of Jonathan Parker and Martha his Wife,	"	26 January 1757.
David Son of John Prince and Esther his Wife,	"	18 September 1757.
Mary ⎱ Gem. daughters of Edward Payne and Re- Sarah ⎰ becca his Wife,	"	1 December 1757.
Rachel ⎱ Gem. daughters of Moses Pitcher and Mary Mary ⎰ his wife,	"	26 November 1757.
Caleb Son of Caleb Prince and Susanna his Wife,	"	28 June 1757.
Briant Son of Benjamin Parrott and Rebecca his Wife,	"	20 January 1757.
Daniel Son of Daniel Parker and Margaret his Wife,	"	20 January 1757.
Sarah daughter of Isaac Phillips and Preseler his Wife,	"	15 December 1757.
Edward Son of Edward Procter and Judith his Wife,	"	4 February 1757.
Elizabeth daughter of Thomas Russel and Onner his Wife,	"	16 April 1757.
Thomas Son of James Rob,	"	5 November 1757.
Sarah daughter of Thomas Savage and Sarah his Wife,	"	7 May 1757.
John Jones Son of John Spooner and Hannah his Wife,	"	14 July 1757.
Samuel Son of Samuel Sewall and Elizabeth his Wife,	"	11 December 1757.
Mary daughter of Isaac Smith and Elizabeth his Wife,	"	28 March 1757.
Sarah daughter of David Spear and Sarah his Wife.	"	24 April 1757.
Abigail daughter of Francis Shaw and Sarah his Wife,	"	5 July 1757.
Ebenezer Son of William Story and Joanna his Wife,	"	7 August 1757.
John Son of John Soren and Elizabeth his Wife,	"	10 July 1757.
John Son of John Torrey and Eleanor his Wife,	"	4 January 1757.
Ann daughter of Shippie Townsend and Ann his Wife,	"	24 August 1757.
John Tudor Son of William Thompson and Jane his Wife,	"	15 October 1757.
Nathaniel Son of James Thwing and Martha his Wife,	"	8 December 1757.
Lydia daughter of Jonathan Trott and Lydia his Wife,	"	5 October 1757.
Timothy Son of Timothy Tileston and Hannah his Wife,	"	18 September 1757.

BIRTHS — 1757-58.

Samuel Son of Samuel Torrey and Deborah his Wife,	Born	14 November 1757.
Richard Son of Thomas Uran and Mary his Wife,	"	16 December 1757.
William Son of Thomas Warner and Sarah his Wife,	"	8 June 1757.
Elizabeth daughter of Matthew West and Elizabeth his Wife,	"	18 April 1757.
John Son of John Welsh and Mary his Wife,	"	2 April 1757.
Samuel Son of Richard White and Mary his Wife,	"	21 July 1757.
George Son of Lindzey George Wallis and Rachel his Wife,	"	19 May 1757.
Seth Son of Seth Webber and Sarah his Wife,	"	19 January 1757.
William Son of John Weare and Catharine his Wife,	"	15 June 1757.
Abigail daughter of Job Wheelwright and Abigail his Wife,	"	5 November 1757.
William Son of Jonathan Williams and Grace his Wife,	"	24 December 1757.
Thomas Son of Oliver Wiswall and Margaret his Wife,	"	4 August 1757.
Samuel Son of Isaac Winslow and Lucy his Wife at Roxbury,	"	9 June 1757.
Lancaster Son of Free negro, Lancaster and Mary his Wife,	"	27 July 1757.

1758.

Ellenor daughter of Jolley Allen and Ellenor his Wife,	Born	1 December 1758.
John Son of Samuel Aves and Rebecca his Wife,	"	19 September 1758.
John Son of Nathaniel Appleton and Rachell his Wife,	"	1 March 1758.
Danforth Son of Benjamin Barnard and Elizabeth his Wife,	"	13 October 1758.
Sarah daughter of William Boardman and Susanna his Wife,	"	22 October 1758.
John Dixwell Son of Joshua Blanchard and Elizabeth his Wife,	"	21 January 1758.
Mary daughter of Caleb Blanchard and Hailey his Wife,	"	15 July 1758.
Letitia daughter of Edward Baker and Hannah his Wife,	"	22 October 1758.
William Son of Increase Blake and Anne his Wife,	"	12 March 1758.
Jane daughter of John Ballard and Martha his Wife,	"	18 March 1758.
Rachel daughter of John Bell and Rachel his Wife,	"	18 July 1758.
Dorothy daughter of Thomas Carnes and Elizabeth his Wife,	"	22 December 1758.
David Son of Edward Carnes and Joanna his Wife.	"	17 July 1758.
Susanna daughter of Moses Collier and Susanna his Wife,	"	20 September 1758.
Elizabeth daughter of William Downe Cheever and Elizabeth his Wife,	"	29 November 1758.
Isaac Son of Isaac Churchill and Sarah his Wife,	"	19 July 1758.
Sarah daughter of George Cross and Sarah his Wife,	"	16 June 1758.
Andrew Son of John Cuningham and Abigail his Wife,	"	12 January 1758.
William Son of William Coffin junr. and Mary his Wife,	"	29 January 1758.
Bethia Cushing daughter of Jonathan Cushing and Bethia his Wife,	"	23 August 1758.
Sarah daughter of William Dall and Elizabeth his Wife,	"	21 April 1758.

Lucy daughter of Thomas Drowne and Sarah his Wife,	Born	24 May 1758.
Sarah daughter of Elijah Doubleday and Mary his Wife,	"	18 August 1758.
William Son of Gilbert Deblois and Ann his Wife,	"	8 October 1758.
Sylvester Son of Thomas Dering and Mary his Wife,	"	27 November 1758.
John Son of John Dobel and Ann his Wife,	"	17 June 1758.
Martha daughter of Benjamin Edes and Martha his Wife,	"	18 August 1758.
Alexander Son of Alexander Edwards and Sarah his Wife,	"	19 March 1758.
Joseph Son of John Edwards and Abigail his Wife,	"	17 April 1758.
John West Son of Trueworthy Folsom and Mary his Wife,	"	1 June 1758.
John Son of John Fairservice and Mary his Wife,	"	5 November 1758.
Hannah daughter of Samuel Franklin and Eunice his Wife,	"	23 December 1758.
Annabella daughter of Alexander Gordon and Jane his Wife,	"	27 April 1758.
James Son of Thomas Green and Ruth his Wife,	"	26 May 1758.
Ann daughter of John Gill and Ann his Wife,	"	24 January 1758.
William Son of William Greenleaf and Mary his Wife,	"	10 July 1758.
Elizabeth daughter of Ezekiel Hatch and Hannah his Wife,	"	22 July 1758.
Caleb Son of Joseph Hall and Abigail his Wife,	"	27 October 1758.
Mary daughter of John Hill and Hannah his Wife,	"	16 January 1758.
Lydia daughter of Nath. Holmes and Rebecca his Wife,	"	17 July 1758.
Katharine daughter of Shrimpton Hunt and Margaret his Wife,	"	30 August 1758.
Martha daughter of Daniel Hubbard and Mary his Wife,	"	13 June 1758.
Elizabeth daughter of John Haldan and Hannah his Wife,	"	9 July 1758.
Samuel Son of Samuel Harris and Sarah his Wife,	"	13 September 1758.
Isaac Son of Isaac Hawse and Sarah his Wife,	"	1 January 1758.
Thomas Son of Thomas and Judith Hubbard,	"	10 January 1758.
Jane daughter of James Ivers and Hannah his Wife,	"	17 March 1758.
Daniel Son of Francis Johonnot and Mary his Wife,	"	21 May 1758.
William Son of Ichabod Jones and Apphia his Wife,	"	4 June 1758.
Lucy daughter of Joseph Jackson and Susanna his Wife,	"	1 November 1758.
Henry Son of Levi Jennings and Bethia his Wife,	"	9 December 1758.
Sarah daughter of Benjamin Kent and Elizabeth his Wife,	"	19 May 1758.
George Son of James Lamb and Desire his Wife,	"	30 November 1758.
Thomas Son of Thomas Leverett and Hannah his Wife,	"	5 January 1758.
Mary daughter of John Lemine and Mary his Wife,	"	6 February 1758.
John Son of John Leverett and Mary his Wife,	"	19 September 1758.
Mary daughter of Alexander Morrison and Mary his Wife,	"	20 April 1758.
Sarah daughter of William Minns and Sarah his Wife,	"	16 January 1758.
Samuel Son of John Mellus and Sarah his Wife,	"	19 May 1758.
Sarah daughter of Richard Mitchel and Prudence his Wife,	"	3 June 1758.
Arthur Son of David Mason and Hannah his Wife,	"	2 September 1758.

Births — 1758-59.

Margarett daughter of Thomas Morton and Mary his Wife,	Born	27 July 1758.
Robert son of Robert Murray and Mary his Wife,	"	24 July 1758.
Elizabeth daughter of Ephraim May and Zabiah his Wife,	"	11 September 1758.
Michael Son of John Malcom and Sarah his Wife,	"	5 October 1758.
Edward Cornwallis Son of Thomas Moncrieffe and Margaret his Wife,	"	16 December 1758.
Samuel Son of Henry Newman and Margaret his Wife,	"	1 December 1758.
John Son of William Owen and Sarah his Wife,	"	1 November 1758.
David Son of David Ochterlony and Catherine his Wife,	"	12 February 1758.
Mary daughter of Samuel Peirson and Elizabeth his Wife,	"	16 January 1758.
James Son of Job Prince and Elizabeth his Wife,	"	20 February 1758.
Susanna daughter of Caleb Prince and Susanna his Wife,	"	24 September 1758.
Christopher Son of Christopher Prince and Mary his Wife,	"	5 October 1758.
Deliverance daughter of Isaac Peirce and Miriam his Wife,	"	11 October 1758.
Sarah daughter of Isaac Peirce and Mary his Wife,	"	24 November 1758.
Samuel Son of Moses Peck and Elizabeth his Wife,	"	30 October 1758.
Samuel Son of Samuel Paine and Bethiah his Wife,	"	20 October 1758.
Elizabeth daughter of Thomas Pelham and Hannah his Wife,	"	2 August 1758.
Hannah daughter of Edward Procter and Judith his Wife,	"	29 June 1758.
John Townsend Son of John Presson and Anna his Wife,	"	11 January 1758.
Isaac Son of Isaac Ridgaway and Bridget his Wife,	"	27 May 1758.
Thomas Son of Thomas Russell and Onner his Wife,	"	28 September 1758.
Jonathan Darby Son of Robert Robins and Mary his Wife,	"	21 April 1758.
James Son of James Stewart and Sarah his Wife,	"	18 April 1758.
David Son of David Spear and Sarah his Wife,	"	21 April 1758.
Benjamin Son of Francis Shaw and Sarah his Wife,	"	4 August 1758.
Benjamin Son of William Scot and Ann his Wife,	"	1 December 1758.
Dorothy daughter of Samuel Sewall and Elizabeth his Wife,	"	23 December 1758.
Henry Son of Samuel Phillips Savage and Sarah his Wife,	"	18 December 1758.
Mary daughter of Ebenezer Storer and Elizabeth his Wife,	"	11 March 1758.
Nathaniel Son of Oxenbridge Thacher and Sarah his Wife,	"	3 January 1758.
Edward Son of Edward Walch and Elizabeth his Wife,	"	7 August 1758.
Joseph Son of Daniel Waldo and Rebecca his Wife,	"	26 April 1758.
George Scot Son of Joshua Winslow and Anna his Wife,	"	14 November 1758.
Ann daughter of Robert Williams and Ann his Wife,	"	1 September 1758.
John Son of John Mico Wendell and Katharine his Wife,	"	8 January 1758.

1759.

Huldah daughter of Francis Archibald and Anna his Wife,	Born	7 June 1759.
Robert Son of Robert Alcock and Mary his Wife,	"	5 April 1759.

John Son of John Amory and Katharine his Wife,	Born	21 June 1759.
John Son of John Barden and Mary his Wife,	"	25 July 1759.
William Son of Joshua Bentley and Elizabeth his Wife,	"	22 June 1759.
Thomas Son of William Barrett and Abigail his Wife,	"	21 March 1759.
Jacob Son of Jacob Bucknam and Lydia his Wife,	"	16 August 1759.
Caleb Son of Samuel Blodget and Hannah his Wife,	"	17 August 1759.
Mary daughter of Thomas Barron and Mercy his Wife,	"	22 February 1759.
Samuel Son of Samuel Bass junr. and Deborah his Wife,	"	8 February 1759.
Elizabeth daughter of William Cordwell and Jemima his Wife,	"	8 February 1759.
Mary daughter of Benjamin Cooper and Rachel his Wife,	"	30 November 1759.
Susanna daughter of John Cuningham and Abigail his Wife,	"	7 August 1759.
Hannah daughter of Thomas Clark and Jane his Wife,	"	8 March 1759.
Sarah daughter of Samuel Downe and Elizabeth his Wife.	"	28 March 1759.
Sarah daughter of Thomas Dimond and Sarah his Wife,	"	10 November 1759.
William Son of Ebenezer Dogget and Elizabeth his Wife,	"	3 August 1759.
Benjamin Son of Edmund Dolbeare and Sarah his Wife,	"	3 October 1759.
Elizabeth daughter of Thomas Davis and Sarah his Wife,	"	2 March 1759.
Nathaniel Son of Nathaniel Dunn and Abigail his Wife,	"	6 November 1759.
Nyott Son of Nyott Doubt and Sarah his Wife,	"	21 April 1759.
Elizabeth daughter of Samuel Dogget and Esther his Wife,	"	22 May 1759.
John Son of Doling Edwards and Rebecca his Wife,	"	14 August 1759.
Abigail daughter of John Edwards and Abigail his Wife,	"	21 May 1759.
Susannah daughter of Andrew Elliot and Elizabeth his Wife,	"	25 February 1759.
Jacob Son of Benjamin Eustis and Elizabeth his Wife,	"	24 July 1759.
James Son of Constant Freeman and Lois his Wife,	"	22 April 1759.
William Brown Son of William Foggo and Mary his Wife,	"	6 February 1759.
Hannah daughter of John Fenno and Katharine his Wife,	"	13 September 1759.
Hugh Mackay Son of Alexander Gordon and Jane his Wife,	"	18 September 1759.
John Hubbard Son of Thomas and Judith Hubbard,	"	22 April 1759.
Deborah daughter of Samuel Hewes and Elizabeth his Wife,	"	14 March 1759
Joseph son of Joseph Hall and Abigail his Wife,	"	2 December 1759.
Elizabeth daughter of Isaac Hawse and Sarah his Wife,	"	9 April 1759.
Robert Son of Samuel Harris and Ann his Wife,	"	7 January 1759.
Lucinda daughter of Elihu Hewes and Elizabeth his Wife, was born at Ipswich,		20 May 1759.
Charles Son of Silence Ivery and Elizabeth his Wife,	"	20 June 1759.
Margaret daughter of Eleazer Johnson and Elizabeth his Wife,	"	1 May 1759.

BIRTHS — 1759.

Thomas Son of Thomas Jarvis and Lydia his Wife, Born	16 September 1759.
Prudence daughter of John Jenkins and Prudence his Wife, "	7 April 1759.
Andrew Son of Francis Johonnot and Mary his Wife, "	21 June 1759.
Eunice Norton daughter of George Kilcup and Eunice his Wife, "	1 December 1759.
Abigail daughter of Thomas Leverett and Hannah his Wife, "	2 January 1759.
William Son of Israel Loring and Mary his Wife, "	11 April 1759.
Mary daughter of John Langdon and Mary his Wife, "	27 June 1759.
Hannah daughter of Jonathan Lord and Sarah his Wife, "	21 July 1759.
James Fudge Son of Daniel Malcom and Ann his Wife, "	21 June 1759.
Susannah daughter of Alexander Morrison and Mary his Wife, "	17 September 1759.
Louisa daughter of Andrew Oliver Esq. and Mary his Wife, "	16 June 1759.
James Son of James Otis and Ruth his Wife, "	July 1759.
Thomas Son of Thomas Oliver and Hephzibah his Wife, "	30 September 1759.
Rebecca daughter of Edward Payne and Rebeckah his Wife, "	25 August 1759.
Ann Maynard daughter of James Perkins and Elizabeth his Wife, "	25 May 1759.
Abigail daughter of Isaac Phillips and Preseler his Wife, "	8 October 1759.
Mary daughter of Daniel Parker and Margaret his Wife, "	25 June 1759.
Samuel Son of Samuel Pearson and Elizabeth his Wife, "	22 February 1759.
William Son of Simeon Polley and Mary his Wife, "	17 June 1759.
Caleb Son of Caleb Parker and Mary his Wife, "	18 August 1759.
Abigail daughter of John Perrin and Abigail his Wife, "	3 September 1759.
Nathaniel Son of Nathaniel Proctor and Elizabeth his Wife, "	12 August 1759.
Richard Son of James Roberts and Elizabeth his Wife, "	5 June 1759.
Mercy daughter of David Scudder and Mary his Wife, "	9 May 1759.
Charlotte daughter of Thomas Tyler and Bethiah his Wife, "	29 October 1759.
Frances daughter of Joseph Tyler and Frances his Wife, "	18 October 1759.
Deborah daughter of Samuel Torrey and Deborah his Wife, "	4 January 1759.
Elizabeth daughter of Joseph Tomson and Susanna his Wife, "	12 August 1759..
Abigail daughter of Jonathan Trott and Lydia his Wife, "	2 September 1759.
Ann daughter of Timothy Tileston and Hannah his Wife, "	28 July 1759.
Joseph Son of Seth Webber and Sarah his Wife, "	30 August 1759.
Anna Green daughter of Joshua Winslow and Anna his Wife, "	29 November 1759.
Isaac Son of Isaac Wendell and Mary his Wife, "	20 March 1759.
Esther daughter of Job Wheelwright and Abigail his Wife, "	24 April 1759.
Isaac Son of Isaac White and Mary his Wife, "	14 June 1759.

John Son of Daniel Waldo and Rebecca his Wife,	Born	1 May 1759.
Ann daughter of Jonathan Williams and Grace his Wife,	"	17 May 1759.
John Son of John Weare and Katharine his Wife,	"	15 February 1759.
Abigail daughter of Charles Willis and Abigail his Wife,	"	1 June 1759.
Elizabeth daughter of Isaac Winslow and Lucy his Wife, born at Roxbury,		12 June 1759

1760.

Rufus Greene Son of John Amory and Katharine his Wife,	Born	20 December 1760.
Ann daughter of Francis Archbald and Anna his Wife,	"	22 July 1760.
Mary daughter of Nathaniel Appleton and Rachell his Wife,	"	20 January 1760.
John Son of William Adams and Jemima his Wife,	"	30 January 1760.
Sarah daughter of Robert Allcock and Mary his Wife,	"	5 December 1760.
Henry Son of Jolley Allen and Ellenor his Wife,	"	11 May 1760.
James Son of Peter Boyer and Susannah his Wife,	"	3 November 1760.
Catharine daughter of Joshua Blanchard and Elizabeth his Wife,	"	29 August 1760.
Edward Son of Edward Blanchard and Sarah his Wife,	"	26 December 1760.
Abigail daughter of James Brett and Abigail his Wife,	"	20 June 1760.
William Son of William Boardman and Susanna his Wife,	"	1 May 1760.
Ann daughter of Benjamin Brown and Ann his Wife,	"	13 January 1760.
William Son of Nathaniel Barber and Elizabeth his Wife,	"	15 November 1760.
William Son of William Barrett and Abigail his Wife,	"	28 August 1760.
John Son of John Coffin * and Isabella his Wife,	"	28 March 1760.
Seth Son of Isaac Churchill and Sarah his Wife,	"	4 June 1760.
Mary daughter of William Coffin and Mary his Wife,	"	29 January 1760.
John Son of Thomas Carnes and Elizabeth his Wife,	"	30 March 1760.
Moses Son of Moses Collier and Susannah his Wife,	"	16 May 1760.
Thomas and Sarah gem: of Gilbert Colesworthy and Mary his Wife,	"	22 January 1760.
Mary Ann daughter of John Downe and Ann his Wife,	"	17 April 1760.
Catharine Maria daughter of Samuel Dexter and Hannah his Wife,	"	11 April 1760.
Lucy the second daughter of Thomas Drowne and Sarah his Wife,	"	5 June 1760.
Mary daughter of Solomon Davis and Mary his Wife,	"	1 October 1760.
Thomas son of Thomas Dakin and Abigail his Wife.	"	9 November 1760.
Eleazer son of Robert Darby and Mary his Wife,	"	28 May 1760.
Bathsheba daughter of Robert Edwards and Mary his Wife,	"	14 July 1760.
John Son of John Edwards and Abigail his Wife,	"	16 August 1760.
James Son of Adam Engster and Mary his Wife,	"	13 January 1760.
Hannah daughter of John Edes and Hannah his Wife,	"	28 December 1760.
John Son of John Fairservice and Mary his Wife,	"	14 July 1760.

*The eleven children of John Coffin, who married Isabella Child 5 Dec. 1758, were recorded in 1841, being "taken from the family bible."

BIRTHS — 1760.

John William Wair Son of John Godbold and Mary his Wife,	Born	10 July 1760.
William yᵉ 2ᵈ Son of William Greenleaf and Mary his Wife,	"	5 February 1760.
Elizabeth daughter of John Gill and Ann his Wife,	"	17 June 1760.
Chancey Son of Thomas Grenough and Sarah his Wife,	"	25 July 1760.
Elizabeth daughter of Samuel Gray and Mary his Wife,	"	July 1760.
Martha Hall daughter of William Gray and Elizabeth his Wife,	"	12 September 1760.
Hannah daughter of Robert Gould and Elizabeth his Wife,	"	25 September 1760.
John Son of John Greenleaf and Ann his Wife,	"	4 March 1760.
John Son of John Hurd and Elizabeth his Wife,	"	7 September 1760.
Timothy Prout Son of Zachariah Hicks and Lydia his Wife,	"	24 May 1760.
Joseph Son of Joseph Hall and Abigail his Wife,	"	2 December 1760.
Elizabeth daughter of Daniel Hubbard and Mary his Wife,	"	17 March 1760.
Mary daughter of Benja. Hendersen and Sarah his Wife,	"	15 April 1760.
Susannah daughter of Edward Jackson and Mary his Wife,	"	24 December 1760.
Sarah daughter of Ichabod Jones and Apphia his Wife,	"	16 January 1760.
Hannah daughter of Levi Jennings and Bethia his Wife,	"	5 November 1760.
Sarah daughter of Nathaniel Kneeland and Sarah his Wife,	"	8 January 1760.
Mary daughter of John Kneeland and Abigail his Wife,	"	8 December 1760.
William Son of John Leverett and Mary his Wife,	"	3 March 1760.
Thomas Son of Thomas Luckis and Mary his Wife,	"	6 February 1760.
Elizabeth daughter of John Langdon and Mary his Wife,	"	13 October 1760.
Hannah daughter of Thomas Leverett and Hannah his Wife,	"	7 November 1760.
Jane daughter of James Lamb and Desire his Wife,	"	18 March 1760.
John Son of John Lemain and Mary his Wife,	"	28 July 1760.
Joseph Son of John Mellus and Sarah his Wife,	"	25 March 1760.
Sarah daughter of Ephraim May and Zabiah his Wife,	"	6 February 1760.
Joseph Son of Samuel May and Abigail his Wife,	"	25 March 1760.
Andrew Son of Neal McIntyer and Esther his Wife,	"	20 June 1760.
Joseph Watts Son of Uriah Norcross and Mercy his Wife,	"	4 August 1760.
Sarah daughter of William Owen and Sarah his Wife,	"	4 May 1760.
Benjamin Lynde Son of Andrew Oliver jun. and Mary his Wife,	"	20 May 1760.
Penelope daughter of Thomas Pelham and Hannah his Wife,	"	6 March 1760.
John Son of Christopher Prince and Mary his Wife,	"	9 January 1760.
Elias son of Daniel Parker and Margaret his Wife,	"	3 June 1760.
Susanna daughter of William Powell and Mary his Wife,	"	16 September 1760.
Nathaniel Son of Samuel Paine and Bethiah his Wife,	"	18 August 1760.
Frances Dandridge daughter of John Peck and Hannah his Wife,	"	17 November 1760.

Elizabeth daughter of Moses Peck and Elizabeth his Wife, Born 24 January 1760.
Samuel Son of John Prince and Esther his Wife, " 13 December 1760.
Eunice daughter of Henry Quincy and Eunice his Wife, " 5 October 1760.
Paul Son of Paul Revere and Sarah his Wife, " 6 January 1760.
Thomas Chancy Son of Isaac Ridgaway and Bridget his Wife, " 26 March 1760.
Mary daughter of Clemment Sumner and Mary his Wife, " 20 December 1760
Sarah daughter of Saml. Phillips Savage and Sarah his Wife, " 27 June 1760.
Ezekiel Son of Thomas Savage and Sarah his Wife, " 17 October 1760.
Katharine daughter of Samuel Sewall and Elizabeth his Wife, " 5 June 1760.
William Son of John Spooner and Hannah his Wife, " 24 March 1760.
Elizabeth daughter of Rev. Samuel Stillman and Hannah his Wife, on James Island, So. Carolina, " 16 May 1760.
William Son of Oxenbridge Thacher and Sarah his Wife, " 30 July 1760.
William Son of William Thompson and Jane his Wife, " 24 July 1760.
Sarah daughter of John Troutbeck and Sarah his Wife, " 28 January 1760.
John Son of Nathaniel Taylor and Sarah his Wife, " 14 April 1760.
Sarah daughter of Samuel Torrey and Deborah his Wife, " 17 May 1760.
Martha daughter of James Thwing and Martha his Wife, " 27 May 1760.
Samuel Son of Edward Walch and Elizabeth his Wife, " 3 October 1760.
Elizabeth daughter of Samuel Webb and Margaret his Wife, " 17 October 1760.
Mary daughter of John Welsh and Mary his Wife, " 9 September 1760.
William Son of Nathaniel Woodward and Elizabeth his Wife, " 12 October 1760.
Elizabeth daughter of John Winslow and Elizabeth his Wife " 14 September 1760.
Nathaniel Brown Son of Jeremiah Webb and Ruth his Wife, " 8 February 1760.
Benjamin Son of Jonathan Williams and Grace his Wife, " 11 July 1760.
Grizel daughter of Isaac Winslow and Lucy his Wife, at Roxbury, " 9 September 1760.

1761.

William Son of William Andrews and Mary his Wife, Born 14 March 1761.
Mary Son [sic] of Samuel and Mary Bangs, " 30 January 1761
Thomas Son of Joshua Blanchard and Elizabeth his Wife, " 2 October 1761.
Anna daughter of Edward Baker and Hannah his Wife, " 16 March 1761.
Elizabeth daughter of Samuel Blodget and Hannah his Wife, " 12 January 1761.
Sarah daughter of Thomas Barron and Mercy his Wife, " 22 September 1761.
Silvanus Son of Melatiah Bourn and Mary his Wife, " 3 August 1761.

BIRTHS — 1761.

John Son of Benjamin Barnard and Elizabeth his Wife,	Born	8 February 1761.
Isaac Son of Isaac Chittinden and Perces his Wife,	"	21 September 1761.
William Son of Benjamin Cooper and Rachel his Wife,	"	20 July 1761.
Jeremiah Cushing Son of Jonathan Cushing and Bethia his Wife,	"	18 March 1761.
Mary daughter of John Champney and Mary his Wife,	"	23 November 1761.
William Son of John and Isabella Coffin,	"	18 February 1761.
Mary Greenleaff daughter of Thomas Davis and Mary his Wife,	"	4 October 1761.
Samuel Son of Samuel Dashwood and Ann his Wife,	"	29 September 1761.
Catharine daughter of Nyott Doubt and Sarah his Wife,	"	16 September 1731.
Samuel Son of Samuel Dexter and Hannah his Wife,	"	14 May 1761.
Sarah daughter of Edmund Dolbear and Sarah his Wife,	"	27 December 1761.
Sarah daughter of Samuel Doggett and Esther his Wife,	"	31 December 1761.
Isaac Son of Isaac Dickman and Mary his Wife,	"	17 April 1761.
George Holmes Son ot John Downe and Ann his Wife,	"	2 August 1761.
Catharine daughter of Benjamin Eustis and Elizabeth his Wife,	"	18 March 1761.
Ephraim Son of Andrew Eliot and Elizabeth his Wife,	"	29 December 1761.
Mary daughter of Israel Eaton and Jerusha his Wife,	"	24 August 1761.
Esther daughter of Benjamin Edes and Martha his Wife,	"	20 January 1761.
William Son of William Fisher and Mary his Wife,	"	28 August 1761.
Sarah daughter of Samuel Franklin and Eunice his Wife,	"	1 August 1761.
James Son of John Fenno and Katharine his Wife.	"	29 August 1761.
Thomas Son of John Fairservice and Mary his Wife,	"	23 July 1761.
Margaret daughter of William Greenleaf and Mary his Wife,	"	22 May 1761.
John Pimm Son of Richard Green and Sarah his Wife,	"	25 August 1761.
Stephen Hall Son of William Gray and Elizabeth his Wife,	"	9 October 1761.
Sarah daughter of Benjamin Gould and Mary his Wife,	"	14 December 1761.
Benjamin Edwards Son of Gray and Bathsheba his Wife,	"	23 April 1761.
James Son of William Gould and Sarah his Wife,	"	13 March 1761.
Benjamin Son of Isaac Hawse and Sarah his Wife,	"	16 February 1761.
Benjamin Son of Benjamin Hallowell jun. and Mary his Wife,	"	1 January 1761.
John Son of William Hill and Rebecca his Wife,	"	29 August 1761.
Amelia daughter of Elihu Hewes and Elizabeth his Wife,	"	11 September 1761.
Joseph Son of Joseph Hall and Abigail his Wife,	"	26 April 1761.
Jacob Son of John Hurd and Elizabeth his Wife,	"	10 October 1761.
Susanna daughter of Thomas and Judith Hubbard.	"	30 January 1761.
William Son of Benjamin Jeffry and Abigail his Wife,	"	3 January 1761.

Sarah daughter of David Jeffries and Deborah his Wife, Born 13 November 1761.
Johnson Son of Joseph Jackson and Susanna his Wife, " 9 March 1761.
Charles Son of Robert Jenkins and Percey his Wife, " 27 February 1761.
James Son of Eleazer Johnson and Elizabeth his Wife. " 18 June 1761.
Abigail daughter of John Leverett and Mary his Wife, " 14 September 1761.
David Son of James Lamb and Desire his Wife, " 14 May 1761.
Alexander Sears Son of Jonathan Lord and Sarah his Wife, " 9 September 1761.
Harrison Son of Thomas Leverett and Hannah his Wife, " 5 November 1761.
William Son of William Lang and Margaret his Wife, " 6 September 1761.
Mary daughter of Samuel Laha and Mercy his Wife, " 26 December 1761.
Mary daughter of Thomas Morton and Mary his Wife, " 22 November 1761.
Sarah daughter of Alexander Morrison and Mary his Wife, " 4 May 1761.
Patty daughter of Moses May and Mary his Wife, " 9 January 1761.
John Son of Samuel May and Abigail his Wife, " 5 December 1761.
Samuel Son of David Mason and Hannah his Wife, " 20 April 1761.
Samuel Son of Job Prince and Elizabeth his Wife, " 2 April 1761.
Mary daughter of Caleb Parker and Mary his Wife, " 3 April 1761.
Mary daughter of Isaac Peirce and Mary his Wife, " 7 April 1761.
Mary daughter of Ebenezer Pratt and Mary his Wife, " 12 September 1761.
Elizabeth daughter of Edward Powers and Elizabeth his Wife, " 13 January 1761.
Isaac Son of Isaac Phillips and Preseler his Wife. " 16 October 1761.
James Son of James Perkins and Elizabeth his Wife, " 30 March 1761.
Simeon Son of Simeon Polley and Mary his Wife, " 29 July 1761.
Hannah daughter of Moses Peck and Elizabeth his Wife, " 25 July 1761.
Mary daughter of Isaac Ridgaway and Bridget his Wife, " 21 September 1761.
Lucy daughter of Samuel Phillips Savage and Sarah his Wife, " 11 November 1761.
Samuel Son of John Stebbens and Martha his Wife, " 5 April 1761.
Josiah Son of David Scudder and Mary his Wife, " 16 February 1761.
Sarah daughter of James Stewart and Sarah his Wife, " 31 August 1761.
Charles Son of Ebenezer Storer and Elizabeth his Wife, " 4 March 1761.
John Tyng Son of Joseph Tyler and Frances his Wife, " 10 December 1761.
Melatiah Stow daughter of Jacob Thayer and Lydia his Wife, " 13 March 1761.
James Son of Timothy Tileston and Hannah his Wife, " 2 October 1761.
Nathaniel Son of Nathaniel Taylor and Sarah his Wife, " 30 September 1761.
Joanna daughter of James Thwing and Martha his Wife, " 15 October 1761.
John Son of John Vinall and Ruth his Wife, " 18 March 1761.
Francis Son of Obadiah Whiston and Priscilla his Wife, " 31 November 1761.

BIRTHS — 1761–62.

Martha daughter of Daniel Waldo and Rebecca his Wife,	Born	14 September 1761.
Samuel Son of Job Wheelwright and Abigail his Wife,	"	3 September 1761.

1762.

Elijah Son of Elijah Adams and Deborah his Wife,	Born	5 April 1762.
Hannah daughter of Jolley Allen and Ellenor his Wife,	"	12 August 1762.
Samuel Son of William Adams and Jemima his Wife,	"	24 June 1762.
Thomas Son of John Amory and Katharine his Wife,	"	9 May 1762.
Luther Son of Robert Breck and Sarah his Wife,	"	15 March 1762.
Jonas Stone Son of Samuel Bass jun. and Deborah his Wife,	"	10 September 1762.
Abigail, daughter of James Bragg and Abigail his Wife,	"	17 April 1762.
Susanna daughter of Peter Boyer and Susannah his Wife,	"	25 February 1762.
William Son of Samuel Blodget and Hannah his Wife,	"	18 December 1762.
John Son of John Brown and Elizabeth his Wife,	"	4 August 1762.
David Farnam Son of Nathaniel Barber and Elizabeth his Wife,	"	10 August 1762.
John Spooner Son of William Barrett and Abigail his Wife,	"	26 July 1762.
Thomas Son of John and Isabella Coffin,	"	5 July 1762.
William Son of William Cordwell and Jemima his Wife,	"	14 August 1762.
Mary daughter of Thomas Carnes and Elizabeth his Wife,	"	30 September 1762.
Ann daughter of Gilbert Colesworthy and Mary his Wife,	"	14 October 1762.
Rooksby daughter of William Coffin and Mary his Wife,	"	19 April 1762.
Sally daughter of Jessee Cox and Ann his Wife,	"	9 December 1762.
Phebe Cushing daughter of Jonathan Cushing and Bethia his Wife,	"	15 November 1762.
John Son of William Dall and Elizabeth his Wife.	"	5 July 1762.
Lewis Son of Lewis Deblois and Elizabeth his Wife,	"	10 April 1762.
Ebenezer Son of Ebenezer Dorr and Abigail his Wife,	"	30 December 1762.
Abigail daughter of Thomas Dakin and Abigail his Wife,	"	20 July 1762.
John Son of John Dyar and Mary his Wife,	"	15 December 1762.
Nathaniel Son of Benjamin Eustis and Elizabeth his Wife,	"	24 November 1762.
Robert Son of Robert Edwards and Mary his Wife,	"	1 October 1762.
Martha daughter of Benjamin Edes and Martha his Wife,	"	22 January 1762.
Lewis Son of John Edwards and Abigail his Wife,	"	14 March 1762.
Daniel Son of William Greenleaf and Mary his Wife,	"	29 September 1762.
Joseph Son of William Gould and Sarah his Wife,	"	25 February 1762.
William Son of William Gray and Elizabeth his Wife,	"	21 November 1762.
Mary daughter of Benjamin Green jun. and Elizabeth his Wife,	"	9 March 1762
George Son of William Groom and Frances his Wife,	"	16 September 1762.
George Son of Benj. Mull: Holmes and Mary his Wife,	"	26 October 1762

Sarah daughter of Ezekiel Hatch and Hannah his Wife,	Born	16 January 1762.
Samuel Son of Samuel Holbrook and Elizabeth his Wife,	"	4 April 1762.
Thomas Son of Jacob Hunt and Sarah his Wife,	"	14 July 1762.
Daniel Son of Daniel Hubbard and Mary his Wife,	"	27 January 1762.
Abigail daughter of Joseph Hall and Abigail his Wife,	"	11 August 1762.
William Hubbard Son of Thomas and Judith Hubbard,	"	12 August 1762.
Mary daughter of Benjamin Hallowell, junr. and Mary his Wife,	"	23 October 1762.
Susannah daughter of Ichabod Jones and Apphia his Wife,	"	22 October 1762.
Caroline daughter of Robert Jenkins and Persis his Wife,	"	18 December 1762.
Samuel Son of John Kneeland and Abigail his Wife,	"	16 August 1762.
Samuel Son of James Lamb and Desire his Wife,	"	24 December 1762.
James Son of William Lang and Margaret his Wife,	"	8 November 1762.
Elizabeth daughter of John Langdon and Mary his Wife,	"	20 July 1762.
John Cravath Son of Ephraim May and Zabiah his Wife,	"	22 August 1762.
John Son of Peter McTaggart and Margaret his Wife,	"	21 May 1762.
Hannah daughter of Uriah Norcross and Mercy his Wife,	"	16 July 1762.
Anna daughter of William Owen and Sarah his Wife,	"	25 July 1762.
Thomas Son of *Thomas Pelham and Hannah his Wife,	"	4 January 1762.
Judith daughter of Edward Procter and Judith his Wife,	"	17 May 1762.
William Payne Son of Edward Payne and Rebeckah his Wife,	"	18 July 1762.
Boylston Son of John Potter and Sarah his Wife,	"	30 June 1762.
Mary daughter of William Powell and Mary his Wife,	"	30 July 1762.
Hannah daughter of Samuel Quincy and Hannah his Wife,	"	24 September 1762.
Henry Son of Henry Quincy and Eunice his Wife,	"	23 March 1762.
Sarah daughter of Paul Revere and Sarah his Wife,	"	3 January 1762.
Abigail daughter of Joseph Ridgway and Abigail his Wife,	"	5 October 1762.
James Son of James Roberts and Elizabeth his Wife,	"	17 February 1762.
Elizabeth daughter of Henry Roby and Sarah his Wife,	"	26 May 1762.
John Son of Isaac Ridgway and Bridget his Wife,	"	18 November 1762.
Elizabeth daughter of Clement Sumner and Mary his Wife,	"	17 November 1762.
Joseph Son of Samuel Sewall and Elizabeth his Wife,	"	9 March 1762.
Francis Son of Francis Tree and Bridget his Wife,	"	12 December 1762.
Jacob Thayer Son of Jacob Thayer and Lydia his Wife,	"	3 October 1762.
William Son of William Taylor and Mary his Wife,	"	13 October 1762.
Elizabeth daughter of Samuel Torrey and Deborah his Wife,	"	29 June 1762.
Richard Gridley Son of James Thompson and Hannah his Wife,	"	12 July 1762.
John Perrigo Son of Joseph Thompson and Susannah his Wife,	"	15 November 1762.
Thomas Son of Thomas Uran and Mary his Wife,	"	1 May 1762.

BIRTHS — 1762–63.

William Son of John Vinall and Ruth his Wife,	Born	29 September 1762.
Martha Fitch daughter of John Mico Wendell and Katharine his Wife,	"	8 October 1762.
William Son of Seth Webber and Sarah his Wife,	"	4 March 1762.
Grace daughter of John Welsh and Mary his Wife,	"	4 October 1762.
John Son of Samuel Webb and Margaret his Wife,	"	14 July 1762.
Phillip Carteret Son of Jeremiah Webb and Ruth his Wife,	"	17 July 1762.
Othelo Son of Samuel, Negro servant to Widow Syrcomb and Sylvia servant of W. Davis,	"	10 July 1762.

1763.

Azor Gale Son of Francis Archbald and Anna his Wife,	Born	4 August 1763.
Jonathan Son of John Amory and Katharine his Wife,	"	1 June 1763.
Thomas Son of Nathaniel Appleton and Rachell his Wife,	"	2 April 1763.
Thomas Son of Thomas Barron and Mercy his Wife,	"	17 November 1763.
Mathew Son of Mathew Bayley and Anna his Wife,	"	16 August 1763.
Susanna Farnam daughter of Nathaniel Barber and Elizabeth his Wife,	"	22 October 1763.
Elizabeth daughter of Daniel Berry and Mary his Wife,	"	16 February 1763.
Abigail daughter of Henry Bromfield and Margaret his Wife,	"	11 April 1763.
Elizabeth daughter of Benjamin Barnard and Elizabeth his Wife,	"	25 February 1763.
Eliz daughter of Henry Bromfield and Hannah his Wife,	"	19 August 1763.
Rebecah daughter of Thomas Brown and Rebeccah his Wife,	"	17 June 1763.
Samuel Son of Jacob Bucknam and Lydia his Wife,	"	16 February 1763.
Mary daughter of Joshua Blanchard and Elizabeth his Wife,	"	27 November 1763.
William Son of Edward Blanchard and Sarah his Wife,	"	29 October 1763.
William Son of William Brown and Mary his Wife,	"	26 October 1763.
Martha daughter of Roland Bennet and Elishaba his Wife,	"	19 April 1763.
Sarah daughter of Benjamin Brown and Ann his Wife,	"	21 May 1763.
Ebenezer Son of William Coffin and Mary his Wife,	"	6 May 1763.
Samuel Son of Benjamin Cooper and Rachel his Wife,	"	30 August 1763.
Anna daughter of Samuel Colesworthy and Mary his Wife,	"	12 September 1763.
Samuel Son of John Cogswell and Abigail his Wife,	"	24 June 1763.
Isabella daughter of John and Isabella Coffin,	"	19 July 1763.
Nathaniel Holmes Son of John Downe and Ann his Wife,	"	1 November 1763.
Samuel Son of Samuel Downe and Elizabeth his Wife,	"	21 February 1763.
Elizabeth daughter of William Dall and Elizabeth his Wife,	"	10 December 1763.
Mary daughter of Joseph Dakin and Mary his Wife,	"	6 October 1763.
Gilbert Son of Lewis Deblois and Elizabeth his Wife,	"	20 December 1763.
Abigail Dunn daughter of Nathaniel Dunn and Abigail his Wife,	"	25 March 1763.
James Son of Henry Dawson and Isabella his Wife,	"	7 April 1763.

Joseph Son of Isaac Dickman and Mercy his Wife. Born	14 June 1763.
Anne daughter of John Edwards and Abigail his Wife, "	31 May 1763.
Esther daughter of Benjamin Edes and Martha his Wife, "	1 September 1763.
George Son of John Fairservice and Mary his Wife, "	21 February 1763.
Katharine daughter of John Fenno and Katharine his Wife, "	2 February 1763.
Mary Brown daughter of William Foggo and Mary his Wife, "	27 September 1763.
Robert Son of Robert Gardner and Hannah his Wife, "	5 November 1763.
John Son of William Greenleaf and Mary his Wife, "	10 September 1763.
Thomas Son of Nathaniel Greene and Anstis his Wife, "	3d March 1763.
Jeremiah Son of Jeremiah Gore and Mary his Wife, "	12 January 1763.
William Son of William Gould and Sarah his Wife, "	9 December 1763.
Martha daughter of Benjamin Green junr. and Elizabeth his Wife, "	9 June 1763.
Rebecca daughter of Ludwick Hill and Mary his Wife, "	18 September 1763.
Mary daughter of Joseph How and Rebecca his Wife, "	4 November 1763.
Rebecca daughter of Joseph Hall and Abigail his Wife, "	17 September 1763.
Mary daughter of William Hill and Rebecca his Wife, "	31 March 1763.
Elliss Son of Benjamin Henderson and Sarah his Wife, "	9 September 1763.
Cyrus ⎱ Gem. children of Elihu Hews and Elizabeth his Wife, " Clarissa ⎰	25 June 1763.
Lucretia daughter of Levi Jennings and Bethia his Wife, "	7 January 1763.
Michael Son of Michael Jordan and Susannah his Wife, "	1 June 1763.
Hannah daughter of William Tyler Kilbey and Jane his Wife, "	16 May 1763.
Mary daughter of John Leverett and Mary his Wife, "	28 July 1763.
Nathaniel Son of John Langdon and Mary his Wife, "	15 September 1763.
Margaret daughter of John Moloney and Margaret his Wife, "	12 January 1763.
Elizabeth daughter of Samuel Minott and Elizabeth his Wife, "	11 August 1763.
Hannah daughter of Alexander Morrison and Mary his Wife, "	25 May 1763.
Sarah daughter of Nicholas Murphy and Elizabeth his Wife, "	11 December 1763.
Grafton Feveryear Son of Isaac Peirce and Mary his Wife, "	12 September 1763.
Sarah daughter of Edward Peirce and Sarah his Wife, "	13 April 1763.
John Son of Samuel Paine and Bethiah his Wife, "	29 May 1763.
Lydia Ranks daughter of John Ranks and Lydia his Wife, "	15 April 1763.
Ebenezer Son of Ebenezer Seaver and Sarah his Wife, "	7 June 1763.
Ruth daughter of David Scudder and Mary his Wife. "	25 January 1763.
Andrew Son of John Spooner and Margaret his Wife, "	14 March 1763.
Jane daughter of Richard Salter and Jane his Wife, "	7 August 1763.
Mary daughter of Bartho. Sutton and Mary his Wife, "	28 August 1763.
Isabella daughter of Thomas Stevenson and Isabella his Wife, "	10 October 1763.

BIRTHS — 1763-64.

Thomas Son of Thomas Shepherd and Rebecca his Wife,	Born	23 October 1763.
Abigail daughter of Timothy Tileston and Hannah his Wife,	"	16 August 1763.
James Son of James Thwing and Martha his Wife,	"	1 June 1763.
John Mason Son of Thomas Tufton and Anna his Wife,	"	8 March 1763.
Abigail daughter of James Thompson and Abigail his Wife,	"	24 June 1763.
William Son of Nathaniel Taylor and Sarah his Wife,	"	19 June 1763.
Ruth daughter of John Vinall and Ruth his Wife,	"	20 November 1763
Obadiah Son of Obadiah Whiston and Priscilla his Wife,	"	31 March 1763.
Edward Son of Oliver Wendell and Mary his Wife,	"	27 May 1763.
Daniel Son of Daniel Waldo and Rebecca his Wife,	"	20 January 1763.
Mary daughter of Stephen Winter and Mary his Wife,	"	21 June 1763.
John Son of John Wells junr. and Betty his Wife,	"	3 December 1763.
William Son of Thomas Wellch and Elizabeth his Wife,	"	26 November 1763.

Isaac Son of Isaac Winslow and Lucy his Wife, born at Roxbury 27 April 1763.

1764.

Sarah daughter of Nathaniel Atwood and Sarah his Wife,	Born	28 January 1764.
Sarah daughter of Gyles Alexander and Mary his Wife,	"	1 August 1764.
Mary daughter of William Andrews and Mary his Wife,	"	3 June 1764.
Henry Barlow Son of Thomas Brown and Rebeccah his Wife,	"	12 July 1764.
Ebenezer Son of Samuel Bass junr. and Deborah his Wife,	"	3 September 1764.
Nathaniel Son of Nathaniel Balch and Mary his Wife,	"	26 February 1764.
John Farnam Son of Nathaniel Barber aud Elizabeth his Wife,	"	3 November 1764.
Daniel Son of William Barrett and Abigail his Wife,	"	20 September 1764.
Macom McNeil Son of Benja. Burdick and Jane his Wife,	"	7 November 1764.
Peter Son of Peter Boyer and Susanna his Wife,	"	29 May 1764.
Mary daughter of Melatiah Bourn and Mary his Wife,	"	18 July 1764.
Meriah Cushman daughter of Jacob Bucknam and Jerusha his Wife,	"	17 July 1764.
John Son of John Badger and Abigail his Wife,	"	3 June 1764.
Elizabeth daughter of John Brown and Elizabeth his Wife,	"	9 September 1764.
Mary daughter of Josiah Carter and Mary his Wife,	"	8 April 1764.
Hannah daughter of Thomas Cartwright and Hannah his Wife,	"	4 August 1764.
John Son of William Cordwell and Jemima his Wife,	"	1 June 1764.
Anna daughter of Thomas Chase and Anna his Wife,	"	20 November 1764.
Samuel Son of Samuel Colesworthy and Mary his Wife,	"	2d October 1764.
Rushton Son of Samuel Dashwood and Ann his Wife,	"	15 March 1764.
John Gardner Son of John Doubleday and Elizabeth his Wife,	"	12 June 1764.
William Story Son of William Daws and Olive his Wife,	"	18 January 1764.

Jacob Dun Son of Nathaniel Dun and Abigail his Wife,	Born	20 June 1764.
William Son of Ebenezer Dorr and Abigail his Wife,	"	4 June 1764.
Thomas Son of Thomas Davis and Sarah his Wife,	"	8 August 1764.
Mary daughter of John Dyer and Mary his Wife,	"	10 September 1764.
Sarah daughter of Thomas Daking and Abigail his Wife,	"	16 December 1764.
John Dorr Son of Edmund Dolbeare and Sarah his Wife,	"	13 March 1764.
William Beers Son of Joseph Eustis and Ann his Wife,	"	23 May 1764.
Elizabeth daughter of Benjamin Eustis and Elizabeth his Wife,	"	8 October 1764.
Lois daughter of Constant Freeman and Lois his Wife,	"	12 August 1764.
Anstis daughter of Nathaniel Greene and Anstis his Wife,	"	5 November 1764.
John Son of John Godfrey and Susanna his Wife,	"	10 June 1764.
Edward Son of William Gray and Elizabeth his Wife,	"	16 July 1764.
Benjamin Son of Benjamin Green jun. and Elizabeth his Wife,	"	20 July 1764.
Mehettable daughter of Samuel Greenleaff and Mehettable his Wife,	"	5 July 1764.
Joshua Son of Joshua Greene and Hannah his Wife,	"	5 October 1764.
Mary daughter of Ezekiel Hatch and Hannah his Wife,	"	16 May 1764.
William Son of William Hearsey and Martha his Wife,	"	19 March 1764.
Thomas Green Son of Daniel Hubbard and Mary his Wife,	"	13 February 1764.
Abiah Holbrook Son of Samuel Holbrook and Elizabeth his Wife,	"	20 January 1764.
William Son of John Hodgson and Cecilia his Wife,	"	6 February 1764.
Sarah daughter of Stephen Hall and Margaret his Wife,	"	21 February 1764.
Samuel Son of Samuel Horn and Mary his Wife,	"	2 May 1764.
Apphia daughter of Ichabod Jones and Apphia his Wife,	"	26 September 1764.
Elizabeth daughter of Byfield Lyde and Elizabeth his Wife,	"	16 September 1764.
Jonathan Son of Jonathan Lord and Sarah his Wife,	"	20 September 1764.
Francis daughter of James Lamb and Desire his Wife,	"	17 January 1764.
Hannah daughter of Samuel Minott and Elizabeth his Wife,	"	31 October 1764.
John Son of John May and Mary his Wife,	"	10 October 1764.
Hannah daughter of William Milward and Hannah his Wife,	"	12 April 1764.
Charlotte daughter of Ephraim May and Zabiah his Wife,	"	14 January 1764.
Susannah daughter of William Pitman and Mary his Wife,	"	11 February 1764.
Thomas Handasyd Son of James Perkins and Elizabeth his Wife,	"	15 December 1764.
Mary daughter of Edward Procter and Judith his Wife,	"	30 January 1764.
John Cox Son of Samuel Pearson and Elizabeth his Wife,	"	6 February 1764.
James Son of Isaac Pierce and Miriam his Wife,	"	7 September 1764.
David Son of Isaac Phillips and Preseler his Wife,	"	28 August 1764.

Bridget daughter of Isaac Ridgway and Bridget his Wife, Born 12 May 1764.
William Son of James Roberts and Elizabeth his Wife, " 27 June 1764.
Mary daughter of Andrew Symmes and Lydia his Wife, " 6 August 1764.
Joseph Son of Clement Sumner and Mary his Wife, " 14 April 1764.
Sarah daughter of Levi Stutson and Mary his Wife, " 17 March 1764.
Elizabeth daughter of James Stuart and Sarah his Wife, " 12 January 1764.
Benjamin Son of Thomas Seward and Sarah his Wife, " 28 June 1764.
David Son of David Spear and Sarah his Wife, " 18 September 1764.
William Son of Thomas Stevenson and Isabella his Wife, " 24 June 1764.
George Son of Ebenezer Storer and Elizabeth his Wife, " 19 August 1764.
Elizabeth daughter of William Taylor and Mary his Wife, " 7 January 1764.
William Son of William Tate and Isabel his Wife, " 11 July 1764.
Deborah daughter of Samuel Torrey and Deborah his Wife, " 16 January 1764.
John Perrigo Son of Joseph Thompson and Susanna his Wife, " 20 September 1764.
Lydia daughter of Jacob Thayer and Lydia his Wife, " 11 November 1764.
Rhoda daughter of Abraham Thayer and Pheby his Wife, " 4 April 1764.
Samuel Son of Nathaniel Tayler and Sarah his Wife, " 8 December 1764.
Elizabeth daughter of John Underwood and Elizabeth his Wife, " 31 March 1764.
Bellingham Son of Bellingham Watts and Hannah his Wife, " 21 March 1764.
Rebecca Elbridge daughter of Daniel Waldo and Rebecca his Wife, " 1 May 1764.
Joseph Son of Joseph Waldo and Martha (Dorchester) his Wife, " 18 June 1764.
Mary daughter of Jeremiah Webb and Ruth his Wife, " 5 January 1764.
Lucy daughter of Ezekiel Walker and Abigail his Wife, " 24 December 1764.

1765.

Elizabeth daughter of Nathaniel Abrahams and Elizabeth his Wife, Born 9 June 1765.
Abigail daughter of John Adams and Abigail his Wife at Braintree, " 14 July 1765.
Rebecca ⎱ Gem. daughters of Joshua Appleton and
Elizabeth ⎰ Mary his Wife, " 24 September 1765.
Jonathan Son of Seth Adams and Ann his Wife, " 13 June 1765.
William Son of John Amory and Katharine his Wife, " 18 April 1765.
Mary daughter of William Adams and Jemima his Wife, " 29 April 1765.
John Welm Son of James Adlington and Anna his Wife, " 8 February 1765.
Sarah daughter of Francis Archbald and Anna his Wife, " 11 May 1765.
Ann daughter of Jolley Allen and Ellenor his Wife, " 19 March 1765.
Anna daughter of Mathew Bayley and Anna his Wife, " 11 March 1765.
William Son of Nathaniel Balch and Mary his Wife, " 11 July 1765.
Moses Son of Moses Bradley and Hannah his Wife, " 19 January 1765.

Mary daughter of Edward Blanchard and Sarah his Wife,	Born	10 January 1765.
Elizabeth daughter of James Brett and Abigail his Wife,	"	13 May 1765.
Sarah daughter of Bartholomew Ballard and Mary his Wife,	"	10 June 1765.
Ann daughter of Edward Burt and Ann his Wife,	"	12 August 1765.
Lydia daughter of Benjamin Barnard and Elizabeth his Wife,	"	2 May 1765.
Mary Daughter of Daniel Berry and Mary his Wife,	"	7 February 1765.
Mary daughter of Peter Boyer and Susanna his Wife,	"	26 September 1765.
Jerusha daughter of Jacob Bucknam and Jerusha his Wife,	"	1 November 1765.
Anna daughter of Thomas Chase and Anna his Wife,	"	10 August 1765.
Grace Stevens daughter of Edward Carnes and Joanna his Wife,	"	26 July 1765.
Thankful daughter of Jessee Cox and Ann his Wife,	"	10 July 1765.
Lucy daughter of Josiah Carter and Mary his Wife,	"	5 September 1765.
John Son of Benjamin Cooper and Rachel his Wife,	"	9 June 1765.
Isaac Son of Benjamin Cooper and Rachel his Wife,	"	9 June 1765.
Joseph Son of Joseph Dakin and Mary his Wife,	"	15 September 1765.
Richard Son of Richard Draper junr. and Ann his Wife,	"	25 September 1765.
Anna daughter of Andrew Eliot and Elizabeth his Wife,	"	27 April 1765.
Elizabeth daughter of Robert Edwards and Mary his Wife,	"	27 February 1765.
Elizabeth daughter of John Fleet and Elizabeth his Wife,	"	12 April 1765.
Jennet daughter of John Fenno and Katharine his Wife,	"	26 May 1765.
Caleb Balch Son of William Foggo and Mary his Wife,	"	6 October 1765.
James Son of William Greanleaf and Mary his Wife,	"	9 June 1765.
Abigail Homer daughter of David Gleason and Abigail his Wife,	"	20 April 1765.
Silvanus Son of Winthrop Gray and Mary his Wife,	"	25 October 1765.
Elizabeth daughter of John Greanleaf and Ann his Wife,	"	15 November 1765.
Mary daughter of William Groom and Frances his Wife,	"	20 November 1765.
Hannah daughter of Robert Gardner and Hannah his Wife,	"	28 November 1765.
Amelia daughter of Samuel Holbrook and Elizabeth his Wife,	"	8 September 1765.
John Son of William Hearsey and Martha his Wife,	"	27 May 1765.
Christian daughter of John Hodgson and Cicilia his Wife,	"	26 September 1765.
William Son of William Homes junr. and Elizabeth his Wife,	"	7 December 1765.
Matilda daughter of Elihu Hewes and Elizabeth his Wife,	"	23 February 1765.
Lydia daughter of William Hubbard and Lydia his Wife,	"	10 July 1765.
John Son of Daniel Hubbard and Mary his Wife,	"	4 December 1765.
Margaret daughter of Stephen Hall and Margaret his Wife,	"	2 May 1765.
Rebecca daughter of Joseph Hall and Abigail his Wife,	"	6 February 1765.

Births — 1765.

Samuel Son of Samuel Hemmenway and Hannah his Wife,	Born	3 September 1765.
Ephraim Son of Joseph Jackson and Susanna his Wife,	"	4 April 1765.
Thomas Son of John Leverett and Mary his Wife,	"	10 July 1765.
Mungo Son of Mungo Mackay and Ruthey his Wife,	"	13 March 1765.
James Son of John Moloney and Margaret his Wife,	"	22 February 1765.
Mary ⎱ Gem. of William Milward and Hannah his Mercy ⎰ Wife,	"	20 August 1765.
Sarah daughter of Samuel Minott and Elizabeth his Wife,	"	18 November 1765.
Elizabeth daughter of Alexander Morrison and Mary his Wife,	"	12 March 1765.
Nathaniel Son of Nathaniel Norton and Sarah his Wife,	"	5 October 1765.
Uriah Son of Uriah Norcross and Mercy his Wife,	"	9 January 1765.
William Son of Uriah Norcross and Mercy his Wife,	"	25 March 1765.
Samuel Ruggles Son of John Neat and Hannah his Wife,	"	11 November 1765.
Nathaniel Son of Nathaniel Oliver Esq. and Sarah his Wife,	"	7 July 1765.
Mary daughter of Nathaniel Pally and Mary his Wife,	"	9 April 1765.
William Son of William Palphry and Susannah his Wife,	"	15 December 1765.
Joshua Son of Samuel Paine and Bethiah his Wife,	"	3 September 1765.
John Son of Simeon Polley and Mary his Wife,	"	4 August 1765.
George Son of Samuel Pearson and Elizabeth his Wife,	"	31 December 1765.
James Son of Isaac Ridgway and Bridget his Wife,	"	30 December 1765.
Benjamin Morgan Son of Rev. Samuel Stillman and Hannah his Wife,	"	13 February 1765.
Elizabeth daughter of David Scudder and Mary his Wife.	"	4 March 1765.
Elizabeth daughter of Thomas Shepherd and Rebecca his Wife,	"	13 March 1765.
Elizabeth daughter of Alexander Smith and Elizabeth his Wife,	"	7 September 1765.
Sarah daughter of Ebenezer Seaver and Sarah his Wife,	"	8 September 1765.
Susannah daughter of Francis Tree and Bridget his Wife,	"	20 January 1765.
William Son of James Thwing and Martha his Wife,	"	10 February 1765.
Katharine daughter of William Tayler and Mary his Wife,	"	16 July 1765.
Isabella daughter of James Thompson and Abigail his Wife,	"	11 March 1765.
Thomas Son of Thomas Valintine and Rebecca his Wife,	"	22 February 1765.
Elizabeth daughter of Daniel Waldo and Rebecca his Wife,	"	24 November 1765.
Joseph Son of Thomas Welch and Elizabeth his Wife,	"	18 July 1765.
Elizabeth daughter of Seth Webber and Sarah his Wife,	"	14 March 1765.
Benjamin Salt Son of Jacob Williams and Margaret his Wife,	"	12 May 1765.

1766.

Rebeccah daughter of Thomas Amory and Elizabeth his Wife,	Born	16 February 1766.
Jolley Son of Jolley Allen and Ellenor his Wife,	"	22 December 1766.
Charlott daughter of Nathaniel Appleton and Rachell his Wife,	"	5 September 1766.
Nathaniel Son of Nathaniel Atwood and Sarah his Wife,	"	3 September 1766.
Francis Son of John Amory and Katharine his Wife,	"	28 December 1766.
Benjamin Son of Benjamin Andrews and Hannah his Wife,	"	25 October 1766.
Susannah daughter of William Bordman and Susannah his Wife	"	5 June 1766.
George Gidney son of Paul Baxter and Hannah his Wife,	"	15 October 1766.
Wilkes Son of Nathaniel Barber and Elizabeth his Wife,	"	16 October 1766.
Mercy daughter of Thomas Barron and Mercy his Wife,	"	20 January 1766.
William Doble Son of Richard Billings and Ruthy his Wife,	"	23 February 1766.
William Son of James Bell and Cerston his Wife,	"	17 May 1766.
Daniel Son of Peter Boyer and Susanna his Wife,	"	10 October 1766.
John Allen Son of Joseph Bradford junior and Elizabeth his Wife,	"	7 June 1766.
Hannah daughter of Moses Bradley and Hannah his Wife,	"	8 September 1766.
Nathaniel Son of John and Isabella Coffin,	"	20 February 1766.
William Son of John Colman and Elizabeth his Wife,	"	14 February 1766.
Samuel Clark Son of Samuel Clark and Sarah his Wife,	"	13 March 1766.
William Son of Jacob Cole and Hannah his Wife,	"	8 August 1766.
Mary Cushing daughter of Jonathan Cushing and Bethia his Wife,	"	21 November 1766.
John Son of Samuel Dashwood and Ann his Wife,	"	1 October 1766.
Abigail daughter of Ebenezer Dorr and Abigail his Wife,	"	7 May 1766.
William } children of William Delarue and Katharine his Wife, Elizabeth }	"	26 May 1766.
Ruth daughter of William Daws and Hannah his Wife,	"	10 July 1766.
Mary daughter of Noah Doggett and Mary his Wife,	"	12 March 1766.
Sarah daughter of Richard Draper jun. and Ann his Wife,	"	12 February 1766.
Elizabeth daughter of John Dyer and Mary his Wife,	"	10 June 1766.
Mary daughter of Thomas Dakin and Abigail his Wife,	"	14 December 1766.
Abigail daughter of Benjamin Edes and Martha his Wife,	"	2 August 1766.
William Son of Jethro Furber and Sarah his Wife,	"	19 May 1766.
John Son of John Fleet and Elizabeth his Wife,	"	29 April 1766.
Rebecca daughter of William Greenleaf and Mary his Wife,	"	27 May 1766.
Mary daughter of Nathaniel Greene and Anstis his Wife,	"	9 March 1766.
Martha daughter of Samuel Greanleaff and Mehettable his Wife,	"	23 May 1766.
Samuel Son of William Hearsey and Martha his Wife,	"	3 November 1766.

Caleb Brooks Son of Joseph Hall and Abigail his Wife,	Born	12 July 1766.
Ebenezer Son of Samuel Hemmenway and Hannah his Wife,	"	5 November 1766.
Samuel Son of Thomas and Judith Hubbard	"	9 June 1766.
Elizabeth daughter of David Loring and Elizabeth his Wife,	"	10 April 1766.
Elizabeth daughter of James Lamb and Desire his Wife,	"	22 September 1766.
Robert Erskin Son of Alexander Morrison and Mary his Wife,	"	31 December 1766.
Elizabeth Harris daughter of Stephen Marson and Elizabeth his Wife,	"	25 March 1766.
Alexander Son of Mungo Mackay and Ruthey his Wife,	"	14 August 1766.
Elizabeth daughter of Robert McElroy and Elizabeth his Wife,	"	23 September 1766.
Joseph Son of Thomas Newell and Elizabeth his Wife,	"	22 November 1766.
Ezekiel Son of Ezekiel Price and Elizabeth his Wife,	"	20 May 1766.
Mary daughter of Thomas Pelham and Hannah his Wife,	"	17 November 1766.
Samuel Son of Samuel Pepper and Sarah his Wife,	"	27 October 1766.
Moses Son of Moses Peck and Elizabeth his Wife,	"	4 July 1766.
Elizabeth daughter of Samuel Procter and Elizabeth his Wife,	"	23 May 1766.
Samuel Son of Job Prince and Elizabeth his Wife,	"	9 March 1766.
Francis Son of Paul Revere and Sarah his Wife,	"	19 February 1766.
Henry Roby Son of Henry Roby and Sarah his Wife,	"	19 February 1766.
Mary daughter of Rev. Samuel Stillman and Hannah his Wife,	"	20 July 1766.
John Son of Habijah Savage and Elizabeth his Wife,	"	18 April 1766.
Martha daughter of John Stebbens and Martha his Wife,	"	21 November 1766.
George Son of George Singleton and Mary his Wife,	"	28 August 1766.
Sarah daughter of Nathan Sawyer and Mary his Wife,	"	27 August 1766.
Susannah daughter of James Stewart and Sarah his Wife,	"	28 February 1766.
Benjamin Son of Thomas Seward and Sarah his Wife,	"	29 June 1766.
John Son of William Tayler and Mary his Wife,	"	12 December 1766.
Rachel daughter of Jacob Thayer and Lydia his Wife,	"	28 March 1766.
Supply Clap Son of James Thwing and Martha his Wife,	"	27 February 1766.
Isabel daughter of William Tate and Isabel his Wife,	"	22 June 1766.
Abraham Son of Abraham Thayer and Pheby his Wife,	"	12 May 1766.
William Son of William Taylor Esq. and Sarah his Wife, at Milton,	"	19 May 1766.
Sarah daughter of Samuel Torrey and Mehettable his Wife,	"	27 August 1766.
Sarah daughter of Thomas Uran and Mary his Wife,	"	10 June 1766.
Jane daughter of William Varnon and Rebecca his Wife,	"	28 August 1766.
Joseph Son of Joseph Winslow and Margaret his Wife,	"	6 October 1766.
Hannah daughter of John White and Susannah his Wife,	"	7 September 1766.
Margaret daughter of Jonathan and Jane Wheeler.	"	31 May 1766.
Samuel Son of Bellingham Watts and Hannah his Wife,	"	16 September 1766.

314 CITY DOCUMENT NO. 43.

Lucy Bradford daughter of Ezekiel Walker and Abigail his Wife,	Born	18 March 1766.
George Son of George D. Walker and Ann his Wife,	"	24 February 1766.
John Son of and Susanna free negroes,	"	4 January 1766.

1767.

Seth Son of Seth Adams and Ann his Wife,	Born	1 April 1767.
Thomas Son of Thomas Amory and Elizabeth his Wife,	"	25 March 1767.
Sarah daughter of William Adams and Rachel his Wife,	"	5 August 1767.
Joseph Son of Gyles Alexander and Mary his Wife,	"	10 March 1767.
John Quincy Son of John Adams and Abigail his Wife, at Braintree,	"	11 July 1767.
Robert Son of James Bell and Cerston his Wife,	"	14 August 1767.
James Son of James Brett and Abigail his Wife,	"	30 June 1767.
Thomas Son of John Bartlett and Tabitha his Wife,	"	14 May 1767.
Margaret daughter of Nathaniel Balch and Mary his Wife,	"	17 May 1767.
Benjamin Son of Mathew Bayley and Anna his Wife,	"	20 March 1767.
John Son of Nicholas Butler and Sarah his Wife,	"	23 February 1767.
Sarah daughter of Melatiah Bourn and Mary his Wife,	"	10 March 1767.
Hannah Peabody daughter of Jacob Bucknam and Jerusha his Wife,	"	11 April 1767.
Mary daughter of Edward Burt and Ann his Wife,	"	4 April 1767.
Henry Son of Daniel Berry and Mary his Wife,	"	2 January 1767.
Samuel Thompson Son of Samuel Belcher and Deborah his Wife,	"	18 April 1767.
Elizabeth daughter of William Bordman and Susannah his Wife,	"	16 July 1767.
Ann daughter of Jessee Cox and Ann his Wife,	"	27 June 1767.
Francis Son of William Coffin and Mary his Wife,	"	20 December 1767.
John Son of Thomas Crafts and Frances his Wife,	"	14 August 1767.
Thomas Bradford Son of Josiah Carter and Mary his Wife,	"	14 March 1767.
Elizabeth daughter of Edward Carnes and Joanna his Wife,	"	10 July 1767.
John Son of Thomas Crafts and Fanney his Wife,	"	14 August 1767.
Thomas Son of Thomas Chase and Anna his Wife,	"	23 June 1767.
Susanna daughter of John and Isabella Coffin,	"	12 February 1767.
Euphame daughter of Archibald Cunningham and Lydia his Wife,	"	30 January 1767.
Mary daughter of Joseph Clark and Mary his Wife,	"	10 August 1767.
Joseph Son of Ebenezer Dorr and Abigail his Wife,	"	3 December 1767.
William Son of Richard Draper junr. and Ann his Wife,	"	28 February 1767.
Sarah daughter of Samuel Doggett and Esther his Wife,	"	1 October 1767.
Henry Son of Noah Doggett and Mary his Wife,	"	15 February 1767.
William Son of Benjamin Edes and Martha his Wife,	"	29 November 1767.
Elizabeth daughter of Samuel Franklin and Eunice his Wife,	"	2 April 1767.
Bossenger Son of Bossenger Foster and Elizabeth his Wife,	"	9 December 1767.
Rebecca Balch daughter of William Foggo and Mary his Wife,	"	4 December 1767.
William Son of John Fairservice and Mary his Wife,	"	24 March 1767.

BIRTHS — 1767.

Elizabeth daughter of John Fenno and Katharine his Wife,	Born	7 February 1767.
Thomas Son of John Greenleaf and Ann his Wife,	"	15 May 1767.
Mary Smith Horn daughter of Samuel Horn and Mary his Wife,	"	2 May 1767.
Julius Son of Elihu Hewes and Elizabeth his Wife,	"	29 July 1767.
Sarah daughter of Nathaniel Howland and Sarah his Wife,	"	20 November 1767.
William Son of William Hubbard and Lydia his Wife,	"	5 December 1767.
John Son of Ezekiel Hatch and Hannah his Wife,	"	August 1767.
Lucretia daughter of Daniel Hubbard and Mary his Wife,	"	18 September 1767.
Katharine daughter of Stephen Hall and Margaret his Wife,	"	11 February 1767.
Mary daughter of Stephen Hill and Mary his Wife,	"	26 July 1767.
Mary daughter of Nathaniel Low and Abigail his Wife,	"	19 November 1767.
Joseph Son of James Lamb and Desire his Wife,	"	2 June 1767.
Margaret daughter of Zaccheus Morton and Rachel his Wife,	"	21 May 1767.
Perring Son of Moses May and Mary his Wife,	"	13 September 1767.
Ruthey daughter of Mungo Mackay and Ruthey his Wife,	"	2 November 1767.
Samuel Son of Samuel Minott and Elizabeth his Wife,	"	5 May 1767.
Elizabeth daughter of Ebenezer Mackintosh and Elizabeth his Wife,	"	12 December 1767.
William Watts Son of William Milward and Hannah his Wife,	"	25 August 1767.
Mary daughter of Robert McElroy and Elizabeth his Wife,	"	30 November 1767.
Mary Deming daughter of Ezekiel Price and Elizabeth his Wife,	"	9 June 1767.
Abigail daughter of Job Prince and Elizabeth his Wife,	"	14 March 1767.
William Howell Son of William Paine junr. and Phœbe his Wife,	"	14 August 1767.
James Son of Isaac Phillips and Preseler his Wife,	"	14 May 1767.
Samuel Son of James Perkins and Elizabeth his Wife,	"	24 May 1767.
William Burroughs Son of Edward Procter and Judith his Wife,	"	24 July 1767.
William Salter Son of Henry Quincy and Eunice his Wife,	"	17 December 1767.
James Carter Son of George Singleton and Mary his Wife,	"	11 August 1767.
John Pool Son of Clement Sumner and Mary his Wife,	"	21 February 1767.
William Son of James Swift and Winefrad his Wife,	"	8 October 1767.
Zachariah Son of Ebenezer Sever and Sarah his Wife,	"	4 February 1767.
Phillip Son of Francis and Bridget Tree his Wife,	"	10 December 1767.
Elisha Son of Elisha Tyler and Dorcas his Wife,	"	3 March 1767.
John Son of John Underwood and Elizabeth his Wife,	"	12 February 1767.
Elizabeth daughter of Thomas Uran and Mary his Wife,	"	15 October 1767.
Joseph Son of Thomas Valintine and Rebecca his Wife,	"	1 February 1767.
Sarah daughter of Thomas Welch and Elizabeth his Wife,	"	15 April 1767.

316   CITY DOCUMENT No. 43.

Hannah daughter of Bellingham Watts and Hannah his Wife,	Born	11 December 1767.
John Jones Son of Joseph Waldo and Martha his Wife,	"	15 September 1767.
Sarah daughter of Daniel Waldo and Rebecca his Wife,	"	22 February 1767.

These two entries stand just before one of 1768:

Thomas Kilby Son of Daniel Jones and Sarah his Wife,	"	
Jane daughter of Daniel Jones and Sarah his Wife,	"	

1768.

Susanna daughter of John Adams and Abigail his Wife,	Born	28 December 1768.
Betsey daughter of Nathaniel Appleton and Rachel his Wife,	"	14 June 1768.
Elizabeth daughter of Thomas Amory and Elizabeth his Wife,	"	2 July 1768.
Joseph Son of Benjamin Andrews and Hannah his Wife,	"	7 February 1768.
Sarah daughter of Nathaniel Atwood and Sarah his Wife,	"	29 April 1768.
Mary daughter of Thomas Brackett and Margaret his Wife,	"	19 January 1768.
Deborah daughter of Samuel Belcher and Deborah his Wife,	"	11 August 1768.
John Hurculus Son of Norton Brailsford and Sarah his Wife,	"	24 August 1768.
Sarah daughter of Henry Bass and Faith his Wife,	"	21 April 1768.
Oliver Cromwell Son of Nathaniel Barber and Elizabeth his Wife,	"	24 August 1768.
Benjamin Son of William Barrett and Abigail his Wife,	"	17 September 1768.
Elizabeth daughter of Thomas Cartwright and Hannah his Wife,	"	13 February 1768.
Mary daughter of Jessee Cox and Ann his Wife,	"	4 November 1768.
John Son of John Coleman and Elizabeth his Wife,	"	13 August 1768.
Francis Holmes Son of John and Isabella Coffin,	"	12 July 1768.
Katharine daughter of Jonathan Durant and Keturah his Wife,	"	10 July 1768.
Sarah daughter of William Daws and Hannah his Wife,	"	23 April 1768.
Thomas Son of John Fleet and Elizabeth his Wife,	"	26 June 1768.
Frances daughter of William Groom and Frances his Wife,	"	13 February 1768.
Winthrop Son of Winthrop Gray and Mary his Wife,	"	7 October 1768.
Mary daughter of Joseph Green and Mary his Wife,	"	20 January 1768.
Robert Son of William Greanleaf and Mary his Wife,	"	16 December 1768.
John Son of William Gray and Elizabeth his Wife,	"	14 February 1768.
David Son of David Gleason and Mary his Wife,	"	26 January 1768.
Mary daughter of Nathan Greene and Mary his Wife,	"	11 July 1768.
Samuel Son of Samuel Greenleafe and Mehettable his Wife,	"	26 July 1768.
John Son of Jacob Gill and Elizabeth his Wife,	"	20 November 1768.
Mary daughter of Samuel Holbrook and Elizabeth his Wife,	"	24 January 1768.
Joshua Son of Joseph Hall and Abigail his Wife,	"	26 July 1768.
Mary daughter of George Hogoneauge and Sarah his Wife,	"	29 November 1768.

BIRTHS — 1768-69.

Edward Son of William Hearsey and Martha his Wife,	Born	2 June 1768.
John Son of Sylvester Kick and Hannah his Wife,	"	5 August 1768.
Sally and Martha daughters of James Lamb and Desire his Wife,	"	17 August 1768.
William Jackson Son of William Mitchel and Lydia his Wife,	"	28 October 1768.
Hannah daughter of John Neat and Hannah his Wife,	"	27 April 1768.
Elisha Son of Nathaniel Norton and Sarah his Wife,	"	10 May 1768.
John Son of William Palfrey and Susannah his Wife,	"	15 October 1768.
Elizabeth daughter of Ezekiel Price and Ruth his Wife,	"	24 August 1768.
Sarah daughter of Samuel Perkins and Sarah his Wife,	"	3 May 1768.
Mary daughter of William Pope and Mary his Wife,	"	3 June 1768.
Samuel Son of Moses Peck and Elizabeth his Wife,	"	21 September 1768.
Mary daughter of Paul Revere and Sarah his Wife,	"	19 March 1768.
Deborah daughter of Paul Revere and Sarah his Wife,	"	8 April 1768.*
Harriot daughter of Rev. Samuel Stillman and Hannah his Wife,	"	20 February 1768.
Jenny daughter of Habijah Savage and Elizabeth his Wife,	"	17 February 1768.
Betsey daughter of Alexander and Elizabeth Smith,	"	16 August 1768.
Elizabeth daughter of Daniel Scott and Margaret his Wife,	"	13 November 1768.
Sarah Martin daughter of Thomas Seward and Sarah his Wife,	"	4 November 1768.
Elizabeth daughter of Ebenezer Sever and Sarah his Wife,	"	1 April 1768.
Lydia daughter of Andrew Symmes and Lydia his Wife,	"	18 December 1768.
Gideon Son of Gideon Snow and Sarah his Wife,	"	28 September 1768.
Mehettable daughter of Samuel and Mehettable Torrey,	"	9 June 1768.
Mary daughter of James Thompson and Abigail his Wife,	"	15 September 1768.
Rhuhamah Son [sic] of Josiah Vose and Ruhamah his Wife,	"	17 October 1768.
Deborah daughter of Nathaniel Waterman and Mercy his Wife,	"	9 January 1768.
John Son of John Winslow and Mary his Wife,	"	13 December 1768.
Jonathan Son of Robert Williams and Ann his Wife,	"	4 August 1768.
Mary daughter of Thomas Welch and Elizabeth his Wife,	"	21 October 1768.
William Son of William Warden and Sarah his Wife,	"	12 December 1768.
Sarah daughter of Oliver Wendell and Mary his Wife,	"	30 October 1768.
Thomas Son of Thomas Walley and Sarah his Wife,	"	2 September 1768.
Joseph Son of Shaper Negro servant to Mr. Oliver Wendell and Molly free Negro,	"	23 July 1768.

1769.

Ann daughter of Thomas Amory and Elizabeth his Wife,	Born	1 August 1769.
Sarah daughter of Jolley Allen and Ellenor his Wife,	"	15 October 1769.

* This is a slip of the pen for 1758.

Hannah daughter of Giles and Mary Alexander,	Born	2 March 1769.
Betsey daughter of Gilbart Aish and Elizabeth his Wife.	"	8 April 1769.
William Andrews Son of William and Mary his Wife,	"	3 January 1769.
Thomas Kidder Son of William Adams and Rachel his Wife,	"	12 June 1769.
Mary daughter of William Bordman and Susannah his Wife,	"	19 December 1769.
Mary daughter of Nathaniel Balch and Mary his Wife,	"	15 May 1769.
Saml. Son of Samll. and Mary Bangs his Wife,	"	7 December 1769.
Elizabeth daughter of Thomas Barron and Mercy his Wife,	"	12 December 1769.
Elizabeth daughter of Moses Belcher Bass and Elizabeth his Wife,	"	25 December 1769.
Rebecah Bennett daughter of Benja. Burdick and Jane his Wife,	"	7 July 1769.
Elizabeth daughter of William Baker junr. and Allice his Wife,	"	5 May 1769.
Sarah daughter of Daniel Berry and Mary his Wife,	"	5 October 1769.
John Son of Benjamin Bass and Mary his Wife,	"	10 June 1769.
Sarah Bound daughter of Edward Burt and Ann his Wife,	"	22 January 1769.
Sarah daughter of Moses Bradley and Hannah his Wife,	"	16 April 1769.
Elizabeth Capen daughter of Hopestill Capen and Patience his wife,	"	18 January 1769.
Margaret daughter of William Coffin and Mary his Wife,	"	16 April 1769.
Fanny daughter of Thomas Crafts and Frances his Wife,	"	2 September 1769.
Sarah daughter of Benjamin Cooper and Rachel his Wife,	"	13 January 1769.
William Tilestone Clap Son of William Clap and Sarah his Wife,	"	13 April 1769.
Joseph Son of Thomas Chase and Anna his Wife,	"	23 March 1769.
Fanney daughter of Thomas Crafts and Fanney his Wife,	"	2 September 1769.
Ann daughter of John and Isabella Coffin,	"	6 August 1769.
William Co junr. Son of William and Hannah Co his Wife,	"	10 September 1769.
Elizabeth daughter of Ebenezer Dorr and Abigail his Wife,	"	9 January 1769.
Hannah daughter of William Dawes and Mehettable his Wife,	"	12 February 1769.
Thomas Son of John Doubleday and Elizabeth his Wife,	"	8 February 1769.
Jane daughter of Noah Dogget and Mary his Wife,	"	27 January 1769.
George Son of George Erving and Lucy his Wife,	"	15 July 1769.
Abigail daughter of Stephen Floyd and Abigail his Wife,	"	14 October 1769.
Nancy daughter of John Farnum and Ann his Wife.	"	30 April 1769.
Nehemiah Son of Constant Freeman and Lois his Wife,	"	25 June 1769.
John Son of John Ferriy and Abigail his Wife,	"	27 August 1769.
Paoli Son of Elihu and Elizabeth Hewes,	"	14 January 1769.
Elizabeth daughter of John Hodgson and Cicilia his Wife,	"	1 January 1769.

BIRTHS — 1769.

Ann daughter of Samuel Holbrook and Elizabeth his Wife,	Born	19 September 1769.
Ruth daughter of Ezekiel Hatch and Hannah his Wife,	"	24 October 1769.
Henry Son of Daniel Hubbard and Mary his Wife,	"	26 October 1769.
Mary daughter of Stephen Hall and Margaret his Wife,	"	11 May 1769.
Elias Son of William Hearsey and Martha his Wife,	"	8 November 1769.
David Son of Samuel Hemmenway and Hannah his Wife,	"	27 July 1769.
John Son of Joseph Hall and Abigail his Wife,	"	4 July 1769.
Nabby daughter of Cuthbert Inglesby and Abigail his Wife,	"	24 January 1769.
Samuel Son of Samuel Jepson and Lydia his Wife,	"	25 August 1769.
Margaret daughter of Ebenezer Love and Dorcas his Wife,	"	2 July 1769.
Abigail daughter of Nathaniel Low and Abigail his Wife,	"	29 September 1769.
Joshua Loring Son of Joseph and Mary Loring,	"	13 January 1769.
Lois daughter of Ephraim May and Zabiah his Wife,	"	7 April 1769.
Sarah daughter of Robert McElroy and Elizabeth his Wife,	"	29 August 1769.
Mary daughter of Samuel Minott and Elizabeth his Wife,	"	14 July 1769.
Paschal Paoli Son of Ebenezer Mackintosh and Elizabeth his Wife,	"	31 March 1769.
Sarah daughter of Mungo Mackay and Ruthey his Wife,	"	4 May 1769.
Nathaniel Son of Uriah Norcross and Mercy his Wife,	"	22 July 1769.
Samuel Son of Edward Procter and Judith his Wife,	"	22 May 1769.
Isaac Son of Samuel Pepper and Sarah his Wife,	"	18 June 1769.
Mary daughter of James Perkins and Elizabeth his Wife,	"	24 May 1769.
Annis daughter of John Pulling and Annis his Wife,	"	27 February 1769.
John Leate Son of John White Roberts and Mercy his Wife,	"	30 July 1769.
Mary daughter of John Roulstone and Mary his Wife,	"	13 January 1769.
Susanna daughter of James Robbins and Susanna his Wife,	"	19 May 1769.
Benjamin Son of Benjamin Richardson and Ann his Wife,	"	26 June 1769.
John Son of George Roulstone and Mary his Wife,	"	26 November 1769.
Sarah Brigdam daughter of James Swift and Winefrad his Wife,	"	11 September 1769.
Sarah daughter of Nehemiah Skillings and Elizabeth his Wife,	"	5 May 1769.
John Son of Nehemiah Somes and Susanna his Wife,	"	17 September 1769.
James Son of James Sullivan and Mehitable his Wife,	"	6 January 1769.
Christopher Son of David Tilden and Joannah his Wife,	"	12 April 1769.
Samuel Son of James Thwing and Martha his Wife,	"	18 January 1769.
John Son of Thomas Uran and Mary his Wife,	"	16 January 1769.
Nathaniel Son of Thomas Valintine and Rebecca his Wife,	"	4 December 1769.
Nathan Coolidge Son of Ezekiel Walker and Abigail his Wife,	"	9 December 1769.
John Son of Thomas Walley and Sarah his Wife,	"	28 September 1769.
Marcy daughter of Nathaniel Waterman and Mercy his Wife,	"	17 November 1769.

Timothy Son of Timothy White and Elizabeth his
Wife, Born 28 March 1769.
Mary daughter of Sharper negro servant to Mr.
O. Wendell and Molly free negro " 19 November 1769.

These two entries stand just before one of 1770:
Susannah daughter of James Otis and Ruth his Wife, "
Mary daughter of James Otis and Ruth his Wife, "

1770.

Jonathan Son of Thomas Amory and Elizabeth his Wife,	Born	7 July 1770.
Rebecca daughter of John Allen and Mary his Wife,	"	16 March 1770.
Charles Son of John Adams and Abigail his Wife,	"	29 May 1770.
Catharine Macaulay daughter of Nathaniel Barber and Elizabeth his Wife,	"	15 April 1770.
Moses Son of Moses Bradley and Hannah his Wife,	"	3 November 1770.
Nathaniel Son of William Barrett and Abigail his Wife,	"	27 February 1770.
Binjamin Gorrish Son of Nathaniel Barrett and Margaret his Wife,	"	11 August 1770.
William Son of William Baker junr. and Allice his Wife,	"	27 August 1770.
Jean daughter of James Baird and Mary his Wife,	"	19 June 1770.
Samuel Son of Samuel Condron and Dorothy his Wife,	"	11 December 1770.
Sarah Cushing daughter of Jonathan Cushing and Bethia his Wife,	"	22 July 1770.
Nathaniel Son of Samuel Colesworthy and Mary his Wife,	"	24 November 1770.
John Son of Ebenezer Dorr and Abigail his Wife,	"	2 October 1770.
Samuel Dyer Son of Nicholas Deering and Lydis his Wife,	"	12 January 1770.
Noah Son of Noah Doggett and Mary his Wife,	"	1 November 1770.
James Son of Thomas Dakin and Abigail his Wife,	"	9 February 1770.
Sarah daughter of Joseph Dakin and Mary his Wife,	"	15 February 1770.
Betsy daughter of Bossenger Foster and Elizabeth his Wife,	"	23 January 1770
Mary daughter of John Fleet and Elizabeth his Wife,	"	27 April 1770
Benjamin Wood Son of Hopestill Foster junr. and Susannah his Wife,	"	14 July 1770.
William Son of William Groom and Frances his Wife,	"	18 March 1770.
Mary Snoden daughter of Samuel Greenleaf and Mehettable his Wife,	"	11 August 1770.
Jenny daughter of James Gambier Esq.	"	30 December 1770.
Stephen Son of Stephen Hill and Mary his Wife,	"	5 March 1770.
Elizabeth Hubbard daughter of Thomas and Judith Hubbard	"	24 May 1770.
Jonathan Son of Jonathan Houghton and Mary his Wife,	"	7 January 1770.
George Whitefield Son of Samuel Holbrook and Elizabeth his Wife,	"	7 October 1770.
Elizabeth daughter of Joseph Hall and Abigail his Wife,	"	20 July 1770.
William Son of Samuel Jepson and Lydia his Wife,	"	20 October 1770.
Martha daughter of James Lamb and Desire his Wife,	"	28 October 1770.
Mary Loring daughter of Joseph and Mary Loring,	"	17 December 1770.
John Foster Son of Israel and Mary Loring	"	10 November 1770.
Eunice daughter of Ephraim May and Zabiah his Wife,	"	21 July 1770.

BIRTHS — 1770-71.

William Son of Mungo Mackay and Ruthey his Wife,	born	24 May 1770.
Sally daughter of John McFadden and Sarah his Wife,	"	30 January 1770.
John Scollay Son of Thomas Osborn and Susannah his Wife,	"	19 September 1770.
Thomas Son of Thomas Popkin and Sarah his Wife,	"	18 March 1770.
John Son of John Pulling and Annis his Wife,	"	29 July 1770.
Edmund Son of Henry Quincy and Eunice his Wife,	"	10 May 1770.
Ann daughter of Benjamin Richardson and Ann his Wife,	"	1 November 1770.
Mary daughter of John White Roberts and Mercy his Wife,	"	13 December 1770.
Elizabeth Greenleaf daughter of John Roulstone and Mary his Wife,	"	14 October 1770.
Elizabeth daughter of Isaac Smith and Elizabeth his Wife,	"	30 January 1770.
Daniel Son of Daniel Scott and Margarett his Wife,	"	2 September 1770.
Mary daughter of Edward Stow and Mary his Wife,	"	6 October 1770.
Betsy daughter of Habijah Savage and Elizabeth his Wife,	"	15 April 1770.
Peter Johonnot Son of Ebenezer Sever and Sarah his Wife,	"	18 October 1770.
Thomas Son of Thomas Seward and Sarah his Wife,	"	26 November 1770.
Peter Chardon Son of John Scott and Judith his Wife,	"	7 May 1770.
Deborah daughter of Rev. Samuel Stillman and Hannah his Wife,	"	15 June 1770.
Isaac Son of Isaac Stokes and Mary his Wife,	"	23 March 1770.
David Son of Gideon Snow and Sarah his Wife,	"	8 December 1770.
John Son of Richard Salter and Jane his Wife,	"	13 April 1770.
Josiah Son of James Thompson and Abigail his Wife,	"	12 March 1770.
Mary daughter of John Underwood and Elizabeth his Wife,	"	24 February 1770.
Benjamin Son of Thomas Uran and Mary his Wife,	"	30 March 1770.
Thomas Son of Josiah Vose and Ruhamah his Wife,	"	11 November 1770.
Martha daughter of Simon Whipple and Mary his Wife,	"	26 August 1770.
Poledore Son of Samuel negro and Sylvia his Wife,	"	6 November 1770.

1771.

John Son of Thomas Amory and Elizabeth his Wife,	born	14 September 1771.
Thomas Son of Thomas Adams and Dianah his Wife,	"	6 September 1771.
Josiah Son of William Adams and Rachel his Wife,	"	5 October 1771.
Sarah daughter of Samuel Andrews and Sarah his Wife,	"	1 February 1771.
Lucy daughter of Enoch Brown and Abigail his Wife,	"	22 January 1771.
Samuel Son of Samuel Breck and Hannah his Wife,	"	17 July 1771.
William Son of William Bowes and Mary his Wife,	"	15 October 1771.
Samuel Son of Samuel Breck and Hannah his Wife,	"	17 July 1771.
Daniel Son of John Colman and Elizabeth his Wife,	"	18 April 1771.
Dudley Son of John Cotton and Mary his Wife,	"	3 January 1771.
John Son of Hopestill Capen and Patience his Wife,	"	25 March 1771.
George Son of Archibald Cunningham and Lydia his Wife,	"	16 February 1771.
James Son of John Coffin and Isabella his Wife,	"	9 June 1771.
John Son of John Campbell and Francis his Wife,	"	15 March 1771.
Nancy daughter of Samuel Dashwood and Ann his Wife,	"	4 June 1771.

William Mears Son of William Dawes and Mehettable his Wife,	born	26 December 1771.
Elizabeth daughter of Benjamin Edes and Martha his Wife,	"	1 January 1771.
Juliana daughter of George Green and Katherine his Wife,	"	10 July 1771.
William Son of Jacob Gill and Elizabeth his Wife,	"	22 June 1771.
Gilbert Harrison Son of Daniel Hubbard and Mary his Wife,	"	2 August 1771.
Mary daughter of William Hearsey aud Martha his Wife,	"	8 April 1771.
George Son of George Hogoneauge and Sarah his Wife,	"	3 February 1771.
Polly daughter of Joseph Harrod and Anna his Wife,	"	11 June 1771.
John Kitridge Son of Joseph Hall and Abigail his Wife,	"	29 November 1771.
Susannah daughter of Stephen Hall and Mary his Wife,	"	24 July 1771.
Charles Son of Samuel Hemmenway and Hannah his Wife,	"	21 April 1771.
Nancy daughter of John Hodgson and Cicilia his Wife,	"	11 March 1771.
Mary daughter of Jonathan Houghton and Mary his Wife,	"	29 July 1771.
Sarah daughter of Henderson Inches and Sarah his Wife,	"	30 January 1771.
Richard Son of Richard Jennys and Sarah his Wife,	"	28 December 1771.
Esther daughter of William Lawrance and Lydia his Wife,	"	16 September 1771.
Clarissa daughter of Ephraim May and Zabiah his Wife,	"	17 August 1771.
Thomas Son of Zaccheus Morton and Rachel his Wife,	"	9 January 1771.
Joanna daughter of Samuel Minott and Elizabeth his Wife,	"	13 March 1771.
Robert Son of Robert McElroy and Elizabeth his Wife,	"	15 April 1771.
Richard Son of Nathaniel Norton and Sarah his Wife,	"	11 March 1771.
Sarah daughter of John Fisk and Lucy Osgood,	"	25 October 1771.
John Avery Son of Ezekiel Price and Ruth his Wife,	"	2 June 1771.
Elizabeth daughter of Moses Peck and Elizabeth his Wife,	"	24 June 1771.
Hannah daughter of Joseph and Ann Peirce,	"	30 September 1771.
Esther daughter of James Perkins and Elizabeth his Wife,	"	28 March 1771.
Abraham Son of Henry Quincy and Eunice his Wife,	"	29 September 1771.
James Son of George Roulstone and Mary his Wife,	"	26 January 1771.
Benjamin Son of Benjamin Roberts and Sarah his Wife,	"	26 March 1771.
Elizabeth Gillam daughter of James Swift and Winefrad his Wife,	"	28 February 1771.
Hannah daughter of Ebenezer Sever and Sarah his Wife,	"	24 September 1771.
Samuel Son of Rev. Samuel Stillman and Hannah his Wife,	"	18 August 1771.
Martha daughter of James Thwing and Martha his Wife,	"	18 July 1771.
Joseph Son of Simon Whipple and Mary his Wife,	"	12 September 1771.
Rebecca daughter of Daniel Waldo and Rebecca his Wife,	"	22 September 1771.

BIRTHS — 1771-72.

Henry Harris Son of Samuel Whitwell and Sarah his Wife,	born	25 July 1771.
Josiah Son of Josiah Waters junr. and Mary his Wife,	"	29 December 1771.
Nathaniel Son of Nathaniel Waterman and Marcy his Wife,	"	22 December 1771.
Sarah daughter of William Warden and Sarah his Wife,	"	31 January 1771.

1772.

John Atkinson Son of Nathaniel Abrahams and Elizabeth his Wife,	born	3 August 1772.
Samuel Son of Seth Adams and Ann his Wife,	"	4 February 1772.
Jeremiah Son of John Allen and Mary his Wife,	"	1 April 1772.
William Rice Son of William Apthorp and Mary his Wife,	"	8 May 1772.
John Son of Samuel Andrews and Sarah his Wife,	"	10 September 1772.
Martha Saunders daughter of Samuel Barret and Elizabeth his Wife,	"	18 February 1772.
Mary McNeil daughter of Benja. Burdick and Jane his Wife,	"	28 May 1772.
Abigail daughter of Jonathan Balch and	"	23 September 1772.
Hannah daughter of Samuel Breck and Hannah his Wife,	"	7 December 1772.
James Son of James Baird and Mary his Wife,	"	4 May 1772.
Hannah daughter of Samuel Breck and Hannah his Wife,	"	7 December 1772.
Smith Freeman Son of William Barrett and Abigail his Wife,	"	13 May 1772.
Benjamin Cushing Son of Jonathan Cushing and Bethia his Wife,	"	22 May 1772.
Nancy daughter of Thomas Crafts and Frances his Wife,	"	8 October 1772.
Jacob Son of Jacob Cole and Hannah his Wife,	"	8 March 1772.
Abigail daughter of Thomas Chase and Elizabeth his Wife,	"	10 June 1772.
John Son of Hopestell Capen and Patience his Wife,	"	20 October 1772.
Jessee Mosely Son of Jessee Cox and Ann his Wife,	"	5 February 1772.
Job Prince Son of Samuel Condron and Dorothy his Wife,	"	31 July 1772.
Hannah daughter of Samuel Danforth and Hannah his Wife,	"	31 January 1772.
Andrew Cunningham Son of Ebenezer Dorr and Abigail his Wife,	"	11 August 1772.
Polly daughter of Joseph Ford and Hannah his Wife,	"	14 August 1772.
James Son of Hopestill Foster junr. and Susannah his Wife,	"	9 February 1772.
John Son of Jeremiah Gore and Hannah his Wife,	"	19 January 1772.
John Son of Stephen Hill and Mary his Wife,	"	30 January 1772.
Hannah daughter of Samuel Hemmenway and Hannah his Wife,	"	3 June 1772.
Jane Tyler daughter of John Lothrop and Mary his Wife,	"	18 December 1772.
Phebe daughter of Nathaniel Low and Abigail his Wife,	"	21 September 1772.
John Son of John Lothrop and Mary his Wife,	"	13 January 1772.
Alexander Son of Alexander Mackay and Ruth his Wife,	"	13 June 1772.
Elizabeth daughter of Mungo Mackay and Ruthey his Wife,	"	27 June 1772.

324   CITY DOCUMENT NO. 43.

William Son of William Marshall and Susanna his
    Wife, born 21 February 1772.
John Son of John McFadden and Sarah his Wife, " 23 January 1772.
Polly daughter of James Robins and Susanna his
    Wife, " 16 March 1772.
Elizabeth daughter of Samuel Ruggles and Elizabeth
    his Wife, " 19 November 1772.
William Son of John White Roberts and Mercy his
    Wife, " 9 March 1772.
Margaret daughter of Daniel Scott and Margaret his
    Wife, " 8 May 1772.
John Son of Rev. Samuel Stillman and Hannah his
    Wife, " 25 August 1772.
Mary Ann daughter of Isaiah Thomas and Mary his
    Wife, " 26 March 1772.
Rebecca daughter of Thomas Uran and Mary his
    Wife, " 22 April 1772.
Benjamin Son of Samuel Whitwell and Sarah his
    Wife, " 21 June 1772.
Sally daughter of Thomas and Sarah Walley, " 25 March 1772.

1773.

Mary daughter of Thomas Amory and Elizabeth his
    Wife, born 9 May 1773.
Mary Thompson daughter of Samuel Belcher and
    Deborah his Wife, " 31 January 1773.
Peggy daughter of William Breck and Margaret his
    Wife, " 5 July 1773.
John Son of William Clap and Sarah his Wife, " 29 January 1773.
Samuel Son of Benjamin Cooper and Rachel his Wife, " 27 March 1773.
Charles Son of John and Isabella Coffin, " 31 April 1773.
Nancy daughter of Samuel Colesworthy and Mary
    his Wife, " 21 January 1773.
Samuel Son of Samuel Danforth and Hannah his
    Wife. " 24 January 1773.
Elizabeth daughter of William Daws and Mary his
    Wife, " 18 August 1773.
Hannah daughter of Samuel Dashwood and Ann his
    Wife. " 19 September 1773.
Rebecca daughter of William Groom and Frances
    his Wife, " 13 February 1773.
Charles Son of Daniel Hubbard and Mary his Wife, " 16 November 1773.
John Son of Jonathan Houghton and Mary his Wife. " 9 October 1773.
John Son of George Hogoneauge and Sarah his
    Wife, " 25 December 1773.
Sally Whitwell daughter of William Holmes and
    Elizabeth his Wife, " 25 September 1773.
Lydia daughter of Samuel Jepson and Lydia his
    Wife. " 31 January 1773.
Henry Loring Son of Jos. and Mary Loring, " 18 February 1773.
William Son of John Lothrop and Mary his Wife, " 25 December 1773.
Seth Downs Son of William Lawrance and Lydia his
    Wife. " 27 September 1773.
Susanna daughter of William Marshall and Susanna
    his Wife, " 18 October 1773.
Frederick Son of John May Esq. and Abigail his
    Wife. " 16 November 1773.
Sarah daughter of John Fisk and Lucy Osgood, " 7 April 1773.
Joseph Son of Joseph Peirce and Anna his Wife, " 8 March 1773.

Births — 1773-74.

Betsy daughter of Ezekiel Price and Ruth his Wife,	born	12 May 1773.
Margaret daughter of James Perkins and Elizabeth his Wife,	"	27 March 1773.
Sarah daughter of John Pulling and Sarah his Wife,	"	19 October 1773.
Andrew Son of George Roulstone and Mary his Wife,	"	5 April 1773.
Jerusha Colter daughter of Thomas Seward and Sarah his Wife,	"	14 July 1773.
Mary daughter of James Thwing and Martha his Wife,	"	21 October 1773.
John Son of Thomas and Sarah Walley,	"	1 December 1773.
Samuel White Son of William and Mary White,	"	1 June 1773.
Elizabeth daughter of Timothy White and Elizabeth his Wife,	"	16 January 1773.
Peter Son of Samuel Negro and Sylvia his Wife,	"	14 November 1773.

1774.

William Son of Thomas Amory and Elizabeth his Wife,	born	11 November 1774.
John Son of Samuel Andrews and Sarah his Wife,	"	15 March 1774.
Betsy daughter of William Adams and Rachel his Wife,	"	4 November 1774.
William Son of Benja. Burdick and Jane his Wife,	"	16 March 1774.
Sarah daughter of Nathaniel Balch and Mary his Wife,	"	5 December 1774.
Jonathan Son of Jonathan Balch and his Wife,	"	7 April 1774.
Margaret daughter of Jessee Cox and Ann his Wife,	"	1 February 1774.
Elizabeth daughter of Hopestill Capen and Patience his Wife,	"	15 October 1774.
Sally daughter of Ebenezer Dorr and Abigail his Wife,	"	26 February 1774.
Thomas Son of Samuel Danforth and Hannah his Wife,	"	31 July 1774.
Elizabeth daughter of Benjamin Edes and Martha his Wife,	"	3 June 1774.
Hannah Goldthwait daughter of Joseph Gowen and Martha his Wife,	"	29 September 1774.
Sarah and Gem daughters of Solomon Hewes and Elizabeth Elizabeth his Wife,	"	20 May 1774.
Samuel Clark Son of Stephen Hill and Mary his Wife,	"	30 June 1774.
Sarah daughter of Samuel Holbrook and Elizabeth his Wife,	"	25 February 1774.
Charles Son of Samuel Hemmenway and Hannah his Wife,	"	17 September 1774.
John Son of Nathaniel Hall and Mary his Wife,	"	18 August 1774.
Jane daughter of John Lothrop and Mary his Wife,	"	26 December 1774.
James Lanman Son of Samuel Lawrance and Mary his Wife,	"	18 August 1774.
Job Son of Mungo Mackay and Ruthey his Wife,	"	31 May 1774.
Peggy daughter of Samuel Minot and Elizabeth his Wife,	"	2 September 1774.
John Son of William Marshall and Susanna his Wife,	"	20 December 1774.
Samuel Burt Son of Samuel Parkman and Sarah his Wife,	"	19 February 1774.
Nehemiah Wright Son of Nehemiah Skillens and Elizabeth his Wife,	"	8 June 1774.
John Son of Dr. John Stedman and Mary his Wife,	"	7 August 1774.

John Beney Son of Francis Southack and Sarah his Wife, born 13 June 1774.
Samuel Son of Thomas Uran and Mary his Wife, " 22 April 1774.
Calvin Son of Calvin White and Mary his Wife, " 22 December 1774.
Ebenezer Son of Ebenezer Woodward and Hannah his Wife, " 24 November 1774.

1775.

Diana daughter of Thomas Adams and Diana his Wife, born 21 January 1775.
Charles Ward Son of William Apthorp and Mary his Wife, " 14 July 1775.
George Washington Son of Nathaniel Appleton and Rachel his Wife, " 27 October 1775.
Ann Easton daughter of Norton Brailsford and Sarah his Wife, " November 1775.
Polly daughter of John Ballard and Mary his Wife, " 8 January 1775.
Catharine daughter of Thomas Crafts and Frances his Wife, " 24 February 1775.
Samuel Son of Benjamin Coates and Mary his Wife, " 8 January 1775.
Samuel Adams Son of Ebenezer Dorr and Abigail his Wife, at Medfield, " 1 July 1775.
Edward Son of William Groom and Frances his Wife, " 15 December 1775.
Joseph Goldthwait Son of Joseph Gowen and Martha his Wife, " 27 November 1775.
Micah Son of Micha Hammond and Elizabeth his Wife, " 21 May 1775.
Polly daughter of Benjamin and Sarah Hall. " 28 January 1775.
Charles Son of Samuel Hemmenway and Hannah his Wife, " 2 October 1775.
Joseph Lewis Son of George Hogoneauge and Sarah his Wife, " 10 September 1775.
William Son of Joseph and Sarah Hudson, " 15 June 1775.
Mary daughter of John Lothrop and Mary his Wife, " 3 December 1775.
John Son of Alexander Morrison and Mary his Wife, " 17 March 1775.
Abigail daughter of John May Esq. and Abigail his Wife, " 27 November 1775.
Charles Son of William Newell and Mary his Wife, " 7 November 1775.
Sarah daughter of Samuel Parkman and Sarah his Wife. " 17 October 1775.
Dolly daughter of Henry Quincy and Eunice his Wife, " 27 September 1775.
Elizabeth daughter of Thomas Robins and Mary his Wife, " 27 January 1775.
Michael Son of George Roulstone and Mary his Wife, " 15 May 1775.
Rebecca daughter of Thomas Uran and Mary his Wife, " 26 December 1775.
Charles Son of Thomas and Sarah Walley, " 6 March 1775.
Polly daughter of William and Mary White, " 17 August 1775.

1776.

Polly Andrews daughter of William and Mary his Wife, born 28 March 1776.
Ebenezer Turell Andrews Son of William and Mary his Wife, " 18 November 1776.
Nabby daughter of Jonathan Balch and his Wife, " 14 March 1776.
Charles Lee Son of Norton Brailsford and Sarah his Wife, " 27 January 1776.

Births — 1776–77.

Caleb Champney Dinsdell Son of Caleb Champney and Sarah his Wife,	born	21 June 1776.
Daniel Son of Solomon Hewes and Elizabeth his Wife,	"	7 February 1776.
Cicilia daughter of John Hodgson and Cicilia his Wife,	"	9 February 1776,
Mary Timmins daughter of Daniel Hubbard and Mary his Wife,	"	26 March 1776.
Elizabeth daughter of John Leighton and Elizabeth his Wife,	"	22 September 1776.
Samuel Son of Samuel May and Abigail his Wife,	"	4 December 1776.
Nabby daughter of Joseph Otis junr. and Abigail his Wife,	"	16 February 1776.
Thomas Son of William and Mehitabel Pierce,	"	10 October 1776.
Mary daughter of Robert Rand and Mary his Wife,	"	14 December 1776.
George Son of Rev. Samuel Stillman and Hannah his Wife,	"	10 April 1776.
Rebecca daughter of Henry Walter Stevens and Luce his Wife,	"	15 June 1776.
Abigail daughter of Samuel Welles and Isabella his Wife,	"	21 August 1776.

1777.

Nathaniel Son of Thomas Amory and Elizabeth his Wife,	born	22 November 1777.
Sarah daughter of William Baker and Alice his Wife,	"	22 February 1777.
Daniel Pecker Son of Samuel Colesworthy and Mary his Wife,	"	24 November 1777.
Elizabeth daughter of Nathaniel Champlain and Eliza his Wife,	"	30 April 1777.
Jane daughter of Thomas Dakin and Jane his wife,	"	24 October 1777.
Israel Putnam Son of William Daws and Mary his Wife,	"	17 May 1777.
Hannah daughter of Isaiah Doane and Hannah his Wife,	"	20 June 1777.
Peter Son of Peter Dolliver and Harriott his Wife,	"	24 November 1777.
Sally Williams daughter of Joseph Gowen and Martha his Wife,	"	11 February 1777.
Benjamin Son of Benjamin and Sarah Hall,	"	24 March 1777.
John Son of Samuel Hemmenway and Hannah his Wife,	"	9 February 1777.
Philip Colter Son of Samuel Rand Harris and Mary his Wife,	"	6 February 1777.
James Son of Jonathan Houghton and Mary his Wife,	"	9 July 1777.
Jane Tyler daughter of John Lothrop and Mary his Wife,	"	5 February 1777.
William Son of William Lawrance and Lydia his Wife,	"	3 February 1777.
John Longley Son of George Longley and Sarah his Wife,	"	17 June 1777.
Nancy daughter of Mungo and Ruth Mackay,	"	15 December 1777.
Frank Johonnot Son of Ebenezer and Susannah Oliver,	"	10 October 1777.
Joseph Son of Joseph Otis junr. and Abigail his Wife,	"	8 July 1777.
Hannah daughter of Samuel Parkman and Sarah his Wife,	"	9 July 1777.
John Son of Daniel Scott and Margaret his Wife,	"	28 September 1777.

Thomas Son of Nehemiah Somes and Betsy his Wife,	born	1 January 1777.
Rebecca daughter of James Thwing and Martha his Wife,	"	23 January 1777.
Richard Son of Benjamin Thompson and Elizabeth his Wife,	"	23 January 1777.
William Son of William White and Mary his Wife,	"	16 April 1777.
Hannah daughter of Ebenezer Woodward and Hannah his Wife,	"	27 June 1777.

1778.

Joshua Son of Joshua Beals and Elizabeth his Wife,	born	16 December 1778.
Deborah Son of Samll. and Mary Bangs,	"	15 January 1778.
Joseph Son of Daniel Ballard and Lucy his Wife,	"	9 November 1778.
Katy daughter of Jonathan Balch and his Wife,	"	31 January 1778.
Daniel Son of Moses Bradley and Hannah his Wife,	"	20 February 1778.
Sarah daughter of James Cary and Sarah his Wife,	"	5 March 1778.
Sullivan Son of Ebenezer Dorr and Abigail his Wife,	"	20 October 1778.
William Son of John Ferriy and Abigial his Wife,	"	15 July 1778.
Richard Son of William Groom and Frances his Wife,	"	29 January 1778.
Joseph Goldthwait Son of Joseph Gowen and Martha his Wife,	"	3 August 1778.
John Ridgway Son of John Bradford Gould and Sarah his Wife,	"	11 August 1778.
Elizabeth Pitson daughter of Micha Hammond and Elizabeth his Wife.	"	25 October 1778.
John Barret daughter of Benjamin Hammet junr. and Mary his Wife,	"	12 July 1778.
John Hunt Hews Son of Solomon Hews and Elizabeth his Wife,	"	2 May 1778.
John Son of Jonathan Harris and Mary his Wife,	"	19 June 1778.
William Son of Bartho. Kneeland and Sarah. his Wife,	"	11 August 1778.
Seth Son of William Lawrance and Lydia his Wife,	"	12 October 1778.
Joseph Son of William Marshall and Susanna his Wife,	"	15 July 1778.
John Son of John May Esq. and Abigail his Wife,	"	4 May 1778.
Sucky McCarty daughter of Ebenezer and Susannah Oliver,	"	26 October 1778.
Elizabeth daughter of Joseph Pitty and Elizabeth his Wife.	"	14 November 1778.
Sally daughter of Nehemiah Somes and Betsy his Wife,	"	9 May 1778.
Ebenezer Son of John Stedman and Mary His Wife,	"	18 August 1778.
Sarah daughter of Henry W. Stevens and Luce his Wife,	"	7 December 1778.
Samuel Hall Son of Thomas and Sarah Walley.	"	12 April 1778.
Samuel Son of Samuel Welles and Isabella his Wife,	"	22 April 1778.
Moses Hazen Son of William White and Mary his Wife,	"	8 November 1778.

1779.

Henry Son of John Andrews and Ruthe his Wife,	born	28 July 1779.
Nathl. Willis Son of Norton Brailsford and Sarah his Wife.	"	22 April 1779.
Margaret daughter of John and Isabella Coffin.	"	18 August 1779.
Thomas Son of Thomas Chapman and Mary his Wife,	"	11 February 1779.

BIRTHS — 1779–80.

Thomas Cole Son of Jonathan Cole and Hannah his Wife,	born	24 December 1779.
Thomas Dennie Son of Thomas and Sarah,	"	2 June 1779.
Thomas Son of Henry Davison and Mary his Wife,	"	28 November 1779.
Henry Son of Ebenezer Dorr and Abigail his Wife,	"	11 December 1779.
Charles Saunders Son of Peter Dolliver and Harriott his Wife,	"	5 September 1779.
Sarah daughter of Samuel and Elizabeth Drowne,	"	22 September 1779.
Isaac Ambrose Son of William Daws and Mary his Wife,	"	3 June 1779.
Harriot daughter of Thomas Flinn and Nancy his Wife,	"	31 January 1779.
Fanny daughter of Matthew Groves and Mary his Wife,	"	19 February 1779.
Henry Son of Henry Gardner and Hannah his Wife,	"	2 August 1779.
Sarah daughter of John Bradford Gould and Sarah his Wife,	"	9 September 1779.
Patty Lewis daughter of Joseph Gowen and Martha his Wife,	"	2 September 1779.
Charles Townsend Son of Daniel Hubbard and Mary his Wife,	"	23 October 1779.
William Son of Benjamin and Sarah Hall	"	29 January 1779.
David Spear Son of John Ingersoll and Sarah his Wife,	"	26 April 1779.
Elizabeth daughter of George Longley and Sarah his Wife,	"	5 April 1779.
Samuel Son of Mungo and Ruth Mackay,	"	15 April 1779.
John Merchant Mayo Son of Simeon Mayo and Martha his Wife,	"	10 July 1779.
Charles Son of Joseph Otis junr. and Abigail his Wife,	"	10 April 1779.
Abigail daughter of Samuel Parkman and Sarah his Wife,	"	14 February 1779.
Elianor Mertino de St. Pry daughter of Bennit Mertino de St. Pry and Elizabeth his Wife,	"	19 August 1779.
Alexander Son of Samuel Pendexter and Mary his Wife,	"	31 August 1779.
Robert Son of Robert Rand and Mary his Wife,	"	22 May 1779.
Mary daughter of George Roulstone and Mary his Wife,	"	15 April 1779.
Hannah daughter of Ebenezer Storer and Hannah his Wife,	"	10 May 1779.
Richard Son of Richard Salter and Jane his Wife,	"	21 September 1779.
Joseph Son of Joseph Tilden and Sarah his Wife,	"	17 June 1779.
William Son of William Tudor and Delia his Wife,	"	28 January 1779.
Hannah daughter of Samuel Welles and Isabella his Wife,	"	8 October 1779.

1780.

Sarah daughter of John Ballard and Mary his Wife,	born	8 December 1780.
Lucy daughter of Daniel Ballard and Lucy his Wife,	"	19 October 1780.
Samuel Williams Son of Jonathan Balch and his Wife,	"	14 March 1780.
Alexander Hodgden Son of Thomas Chapman and Mary his Wife,	"	29 October 1780.
Nancy daughter of Isaiah Doane and Hannah his Wife,	"	1 March 1780.
Polly daughter of Matthew Groves and Mary his Wife,	"	7 September 1780.

Sally Williams daughter of Joseph Gowen and Martha his Wife,	born	24 September 1780.
Elizabeth daughter of John B. Gould and Sarah his Wife,	"	31 December 1780.
Samuel Devens Son of Jonathan Harris and Mary his Wife,	"	1 June 1780.
Charles Hill Son of Abraham and Mary Hunt,	"	28 January 1780.
John Son of William Lawrance and Lydia his Wife,	"	2 August 1780.
Joseph Son of Mungo and Ruth Mackay,	"	15 August 1780.
Marcus Son of Marcus Myars and Elizabeth his Wife,	"	22 September 1780.
Minot Son of Samuel Moody and Hannah his Wife,	"	21 November 1780.
Henry Knox Son of John May Esq. and Abigail his Wife,	"	18 May 1780.
Apphia Freeman daughter of Simeon Mayo and Martha his Wife,	"	1780.
Susanna daughter of Samuel Parkman and Sarah his Wife,	"	4 June 1780.
Nancy daughter of Henry Quincy and Eunice his Wife,	"	6 June 1780.
Ann Gordon daughter of Sampson Reed and Ann his Wife,	"	29 October 1780.
Andrew Son of Samuel Sprague and Joanna his Wife,	"	8 October 1780.
Susanna daughter of Gilbert Warner Speakman and Sarah his Wife,	"	12 February 1780.
Henry Son of John Stedman and Mary his Wife,	"	2 March 1780.
Harriot, daughter of William Sherburn and Mehettable his Wife,	"	14 October 1780.
William Son of Andrew Tukesbury and Susannah his Wife,	"	11 November 1780.
Elizabeth daughter of Benjamin Thompson and Elizabeth his Wife,	"	30 March 1780.
Delia daughter of William Tudor aud Delia his Wife,	"	21 November 1780.

1781.

Sally daughter of Nathaniel Walker Appleton and Sarah his Wife,	born	18 April 1781.
John Son of Joshua Beals and Elizabeth his Wife,	"	23 September 1781.
James Lewis Son of James Bridgham and Martha his Wife,	"	29 August 1781.
Francis Son of Benjamin Brown and Susannah his Wife,	"	17 April 1781.
Samuel Brown Son of Isaiah Doane and Hannah his Wife,	"	9 November 1781.
Lucretia daughter of Ebenezer Dorr and Abigail his Wife,	"	19 June 1781.
Harriott, daughter of Peter Dolliver and Harriott his Wife,	"	6 August 1781.
John Minot Son of Alvan Fosdick and Lydia his Wife,	"	17 June 1781.
Mehitabel daughter of John Greenough and Mehitabel his Wife,	"	3 May 1781.
Hammond Williams Son of Joseph Gowen and Martha his Wife,	"	16 November 1781.
Stephen Son of Stephen Gorham and Mary his Wife,	"	4 February 1781.
Joseph Son of Henry Gardner and Hannah his Wife,	"	16 August 1781.
Sally daughter of Benjamin and Sarah Hall,	"	13 October 1781.
Joseph Son of Samuel Jepson and Lydia his Wife,	"	12 January 1781.
George Son of George Longley and Sarah his Wife,	"	8 March 1781.

BIRTHS — 1781-82.

Hannah daughter of William Marshall and Susanna his Wife,	born	15 December 1781.
Charles Son of Mungo and Ruth Mackay,	"	27 October 1781.
Joseph Son of Joseph Pitty and Elizabeth his Wife,	"	4 April 1781.
Elizabeth Freeman daughter of Henry Prentice and Ruth his Wife,	"	8 January 1781.
Thomas Morton Paine Son of Nathll. Paine and Margaret his Wife,	"	20 December 1781.
Mathew Son of George Roulstone and Mary his Wife,	"	27 February 1781.
Elizabeth daughter of James Robertson and Elizabeth his Wife,	"	12 November 1781.
Elizabeth Simpkins daughter of Robert Rand and Mary his Wife,	"	6 July 1781.
Henry Weeks Son of Henry W. Stevens and Luce his Wife,	"	10 January 1781.
George Son of Samuel Sprague and Joanna his Wife,	"	24 December 1781.
Bryant Parrott Son of Joseph Tilden and Sarah his Wife,	"	24 July 1781.
Jonas Son of Jonas Welsh and Elizabeth his Wife,	"	16 March 1781.
Benjamin Son of Samuel Welles and Isabella his Wife,	"	13 August 1781.

1782.

Benjamin Franklyne Son of Samuel Adams and Catherine his Wife,	born	6 May 1782.
Sally daughter of Jonathan Balch and his Wife,	"	4 April 1782.
Catharine Seward daughter of Thomas Bickford and Elizabeth his Wife,	"	11 July 1782.
John Son of John Ballard and Mary his Wife,	"	10 October 1782.
William Bangs Corcorand Son of William and Francis Corcorand	"	15 January 1782.
Peggy daughter of Thomas Dawes junr. and Margaret his Wife,	"	23 June 1782.
Margaret daughter of Samuel Danforth and Margaret his Wife,	"	21 February 1782.
Grace Williams daughter of Joshua Eaton and Elizabeth his Wife,	"	15 February 1782.
Benjamin Son of Samuel Gardner and Mary his Wife,	"	22 November 1782.
John Son of Joseph Gowen and Martha his Wife,	"	5 December 1782.
Polly daughter of John B. Gould and Sarah his Wife,	"	8 April 1782.
Richard Devens Son of Jonathan Harris and Mary his Wife,	"	8 June 1782.
Elizabeth daughter of John Lothrop and Elizabeth his Wife,	"	18 May 1782.
Polly daughter of Peter Lemercier and Polly his Wife,	"	3 March 1782.
Rebecca daughter of William Lawrance and Lydia his Wife,	"	14 June 1782.
Catharine Cravath daughter of John May Esq. and Abigail his Wife,	"	22 September 1782.
Samuel Son of Marcus Myars and Elizabeth his Wife,	"	8 April 1782.
Martha daughter of Simeon Mayo and Martha his Wife,	"	6 January 1782.
Susanna daughter of Joseph Pitty and Elizabeth his Wife,	"	22 October 1782.

John Son of Samuel Parkman and Sarah his Wife,	born	25 January 1782.
William Cooper Son of Matthew Parke and Judeth his Wife,	"	7 August 1782.
Judy Procter daughter of William and Hannah Shaw,	"	23 April 1782.
Benjamin Son of Benjamin Thompson and Elizabeth his Wife,	"	20 March 1782.
John Henry Son of William Tudor and Delia his Wife,	"	13 April 1782.
William Son of William Trench and Mary his Wife,	"	23 September 1782.
Caliste daughter of Joseph DeValnais and Eunice his Wife,	"	10 September 1782.
Samuel Son of Jonas Welsh and Elizabeth his Wife,	"	30 August 1782.

1783.

Catharine daughter of Samuel Adams and Catharine his Wife,	born	5 November 1783.
Nathaniel Son of Nathaniel Walker Appleton and Sarah his Wife,	"	13 February 1783.
Betsy daughter of Joshua Beals and Elizabeth his Wife,	"	3 October 1783.
William Son of Thomas Stoddard Bordman and Thankful his Wife,	"	17 April 1783.
Joseph Son of John Church and Phebe his Wife,	"	1 March 1783.
Eliza daughter of Isaiah Doane and Hannah his Wife,	"	28 September 1783.
Henry Son of Henry Davison and Mary his Wife,	"	8 January 1783.
Caroline daughter of Peter Dolliver and Harriott his Wife,	"	22 April 1783.
Thomas Son of Thomas Dawes junr. and Margaret his Wife,	"	26 April 1783.
John Son of John and Elizabeth Dyer his Wife,	"	21 January 1783.
Betsy daughter of Joshua Eaton and Elizabeth his Wife,	"	27 August 1783.
Thomas Son of Thomas Flinn and Nancy his Wife,	"	8 January 1783.
Sophia daughter of Nathaniel Gardner and Mary his Wife,	"	1 April 1783.
John Son of Stephen Gorham and Molly his Wife,	"	24 February 1783.
Sophia daughter of Nathaniel Gardner and Mary his Wife,	"	1 April 1783.
Harriot daughter of Edmund Howes and Abigail his Wife,	"	23 August 1783.
Compston Son of Edward C. How and Abigail his Wife,	"	13 March 1783.
John Son of John Ingersoll and Sarah his Wife,	"	17 March 1783.
Samuel Checkley Son of John Lothrop and Elizabeth his Wife,	"	16 August 1783.
Joseph Son of John Lawrance and Elizabeth his Wife,	"	10 August 1783.
Henry Son of Mungo and Ruth Mackay his Wife,	"	1 January 1783.
Simeon Son of Simeon Mayo and Martha his Wife.	"	5 January 1783.
Abigail daughter of James Newhall and Elizabeth his Wife,	"	3 December 1783.
Billings Son of Joseph Otis junr. and Abigail his Wife,	"	11 July 1783.
James Hooper W. Son of James Hooper Whitchurch Owens and Elizabeth his Wife,	"	26 December 1783.
Charles Francis De Guerdy Mertino D. St. Pry Son of Bennit Mertino D. St. Pry and Elizabeth his Wife,	"	28 June 1783.

BIRTHS — 1783–84.

Peggy daughter of Nathaniel Paine and Margaret his Wife,	born	4 May 1783.
Charles Russel Son of Sampson Reed and Ann his Wife,	"	21 May 1783.
Betsy daughter of Ezekiel Russel and Sarah his Wife,	"	20 March 1783.
Katharine daughter of William Sherburne and Mehitable his Wife,	"	24 April 1783.
James Son of Samuel Sprague and Joanna his Wife,	"	16 August 1783.
Frederick Son of William Tudor and Delia his Wife,	"	4 September 1783.
David Son of Ebenezer Woodward and Hannah his Wife,	"	29 November 1783.
Elizabeth daughter of Thomas Wells and Hannah his Wife,	"	25 May 1783.

1784.

James Trecothick Son of Jonathan L. Austin and Hannah his Wife,	born	10 January 1784.
Elizabeth daughter of John Andrews and Ruthe his Wife,	"	2 September 1784.
David Son of Jonathan Balch and his Wife,	"	14 May 1784.
William Son of John Ballard and Mary his Wife,	"	1 December 1784.
Caleb Son of Thomas Stoddard Bordman and Thankful his Wife,	"	6 June 1784.
Abijah Son of Nathan Bond and Joanna his Wife,	"	22 February 1784.
Thomas Roberts Son of John Bromfield and Ann his Wife,	"	8 August 1784.
Joseph Lewis Son of Andrew Cunningham and Polly his Wife,	"	3 October 1784.
Katharine Milledolly daughter of Florence Crowly and Elizabeth his Wife,	"	17 October 1784.
Esther daughter of Rev. John Clarke and his Wife,	"	10 October 1784.
Joshua Chase Son of Joshua and Sarah Chase,	"	27 August 1784.
Amelia daughter of Peter Dolliver and Harriott his Wife,	"	31 December 1784.
William Son of John and Elizabeth Dyer,	"	21 June 1784.
Molly daughter of Matthew Groves and Mary his Wife,	"	18 August 1784.
Charles Son of Jonathan Harris and Mary his Wife,	"	6 May 1784.
Samuel Cooper Son of Joseph Hixon and Abigail his Wife,	"	13 July 1784.
Katharine } Gem: daughters of John Hurd and Elizabeth } Mary his Wife,	"	29 March 1784.
Thomas Son of Jonathan Houghton and Mary (dec'd) his Wife,	"	25 October 1784.
Eugine Sophia daughter of Peter Lemercier and Polly his Wife,	"	9 September 1784.
Ann daughter of John Lothrop and Elizabeth his Wife,	"	24 August 1784.
Nathaniel Gorham Son of John Leighton and Elizabeth his Wife,	"	1 February 1784.
Louis daughter [sic] of David Lewis and Lydia his Wife,	"	18 July 1784.
Sophia daughter of John May Esq. and Abigail his Wife,	"	14 September 1784.
Nancy daughter of John Merchant and Ann his Wife,	"	8 December 1784.
Thomas Son of Thomas Powers and Mary his Wife,	"	17 March 1784.

334 CITY DOCUMENT NO. 43.

Hannah Day daughter of Samuel Pendexter and Mary his Wife,	born	18 May 1784.
Ann Townsend daughter of Walter Perkins and Ann Townsend his Wife,	"	13 December 1784.
Ralph Inman Son of Sampson Reed and Ann his Wife,	"	24 November 1784.
Susannah daughter of Robert Rand and Mary his Wife,	"	23 September 1784.
Lucinda daughter of Barney Smith and Anna his Wife,	"	19 May 1784.
Anna daughter of Samuel Sprague and Joanna his Wife,	"	15 December 1784.
Sally daughter of Benjamin Thompson and Elizabeth his Wife,	"	25 March 1784.
Betsey B. daughter of Jonas Welsh and Elizabeth his Wife,	"	12 June 1784.

1785.

Catharine Noyes daughter of Samuel Adams and Catharine his Wife,	born	29 July 1785.
Henry Son of Dudley Colman and Mary his Wife,	"	12 September 1785.
Isaiah Son of Isaiah Doane and Hannah his Wife,	"	12 July 1785.
Elizabeth daughter of John Dyer and Elizabeth his Wife,	"	7 November 1785.
Emily daughter of Thomas Dawes junr. and Margaret his Wife,	"	29 May 1785.
Anna daughter of John and Anna Margaretta De Nevfville his Wife,	"	7 September 1785.
George Calder Son of Thomas Flinn and Nancy his Wife,	"	8 February 1785.
Benjamin Son of Benjamin Guild and Elizabeth his Wife,	"	8 May 1785.
Polly Bourn daughter of Joseph Gowen and Martha his Wife,	"	4 March 1785.
Elizabeth Loveliss daughter of Richard Green and Sarah his Wife,	"	11 March 1785.
Mary daughter of Stephen Gorham and Molly his Wife (at Exeter, N.H.),	"	1 April 1785.
James Son of Jesse Houghton and Abigail his Wife,	"	30 March 1785.
John Russel Son of John Hurd and Mary his Wife,	"	8 April 1785.
Ann daughter of John Lothrop and Elizabeth his Wife,	"	11 November 1785.
Nancy daughter of John Lawrance and Elizabeth his Wife,	"	12 January 1785.
Fanny daughter of Mungo and Ruth Mackay,	"	20 October 1785.
Apphia daughter of Simeon Mayo and Martha his Wife,	"	12 January 1785.
James Son of James Newhall and Elizabeth his Wife,	"	7 December 1785.
Mary daughter of Samuel Pendexter and Mary his Wife,	"	16 November 1785.
Elizabeth daughter of Samuel Parkman and Sarah his Wife,	"	31 March 1785.
Sukey daughter of Henry Prentiss and Ruth his Wife,	"	3 September 1785.
Ezekiel Cheevers Son of Ezekiel Russell and Sarah his Wife,	"	28 February 1785.
Hosea Son of Hosea Stodder and Luce his Wife,	"	29 March 1785.
William Son of William Scollay and Catharine his Wife,	"	7 September 1785.
Mary daughter of Andrew Tukesbury and Susannah his Wife,	"	24 August 1785.

BIRTHS — 1785-86.

Sarah daughter of Joseph Tilden and Sarah his Wife, born	28 March 1785.
Emma Jane daughter of William Tudor and Delia his Wife, "	10 March 1785.
Mary daughter of ⎱ (Gem) of William White and John Chandler Son ⎰ Mary his Wife, "	9 January 1785.
Elizabeth daughter of Joseph Ward and Prudence his Wife, "	24 December 1785.

1786.

Benjamin Son of John Andrews and Ruthe his Wife, born	9 July 1786.
Benjamin Son of Benjamin Austin and Jane his Wife, "	27 August 1786.
Sukey daughter of Matthew Bayley and Sukey his Wife, "	20 June 1786.
Alexander Son of Jonathan Balch and his Wife, "	9 March 1786.
Thomas Son of Thomas Bickford and Elizabeth his Wife, "	27 March 1786.
Mary daughter of William B. Bradford and Mary Tufts his Wife, "	7 October 1786.
Nathan ⎱ Gem: Sons of Nathan Bond and ⎱ Nathan "	6 June 1786.
Charles ⎰ Joanna his Wife, ⎰ Charles "	8 June 1786.
Nancy daughter of John Ballard and Mary his Wife, "	9 March 1786.
Andrew Son of Andrew Cunningham and Polly his Wife, "	29 October 1786.
John Cathcart Son of Isaac Collins and Abigail his Wife, "	20 September 1786.
William Son of William Donnissen and Mary his Wife, "	5 March 1786.
Gilbert Son of William Deblois and Sarah his Wife, "	24 June 1786.
Andrew Son of John Eliot and Ann his wife, "	15 April 1786.
Betsey daughter of Matthew Groves and Mary his Wife, "	4 November 1786.
Mary daughter of Jonathan Harris and Mary his Wife, "	2 April 1786.
Sally daughter of Jonathan Houghton and Mary his Wife, "	8 September 1786.
Cecile Charlotte daughter of Peter Lemercier and Polly his Wife, "	9 December 1786.
Catharine daughter of Joseph May and Dorothy his Wife, "	30 December 1786.
William Rufus Son of John May Esq. and Abigail his Wife, "	6 December 1786.
Mary Colter Witchurch daughter of James Hooper Witchurch Owens, "	26 January 1786.
Henry Son of Benjamin Russell and Esther his Wife, "	11 April 1786.
Robert Son of Robert Rogerson and Lucy his Wife, "	30 January 1786.
Sophia daughter of William Sherburne and Mehitable his Wife, "	19 November 1786
Lydia daughter of Barney Smith and Anna his Wife, "	13 October 1786.
Peter Geyer Son of Henry W. Stevens and Luce his Wife, "	14 January 1786.
Eliza daughter of Samuel Sprague and Joanna his Wife, "	22 March 1786.
Ruth daughter of Samuel Thwing and Ruth his Wife, "	7 January 1786
David Son of David Tyler and Sarah his Wife, "	12 September 1786.
Arnold Son of Samuel Welles and Isabella his Wife, "	31 August 1786.
Harriot daughter of William White and Mary his Wife, "	31 October 1786.

1787.

Nancey daughter of Samuel Adams and Catharine his Wife,	born	19 July 1787.
Gilbert Son of Hezekiah Blanchard and Esther his Wife,	"	3 August 1787.
Sally daughter of Jonathan Balch and his Wite,	"	17 December 1787.
Royal Son of Nathan Bond and Joanna his Wife,	"	4 September 1787.
Amos Son of John Ballard and Mary his Wife,	"	30 June 1787.
Anna Vassall daughter of Leonard Vassall Borland and Sarah his Wife,	"	26 July 1787.
William Bowes Son of William B. Bradford and Mary his Wife,	"	31 October 1787.
Sophia daughter of Caleb Bingham and Hannah his Wife,	"	7 January 1787.
Elizabeth daughter of William and Susannah Burley,	"	10 September 1787.
John Jones Son of Dudley Colman and Mary his Wife,	"	26 June 1787.
Mary daughter of Isaiah Doane and Hannah his Wife,	"	19 July 1787.
Elizabeth daughter of Henry Davison and Mary his Wife,	"	13 June 1787.
Henry Son of John Dyer and Elizabeth his Wife,	"	16 April 1787.
Hannah daughter of Thomas Dawes junr. and Margaret his Wife,	"	8 January 1787.
Samuel Son of Samuel Eames and Lydia his Wife,	"	14 January 1787.
Hans Benjamin, Son of Hans Gram and Jane his Wife,		13 July 1787.
Henry Gillspie Son of	"	9 October 1787.
Josiah Quincy Son of Benjamin Guild and Elizabeth his Wife,	"	19 March 1787.
Sally daughter of Matthew Groves and Mary his Wife,	"	14 December 1787.
Frances daughter of Stephen Gorham and Molly his Wife,	"	7 June 1787.
Samuel Son of Nathaniel Johnson and Catharine his Wife,	"	17 November 1787.
Dana daughter of David Lewis and Lydia his Wife,	"	25 February 1787.
Lucy daughter of Ozias Morse and Lucy his Wife,	"	28 September 1787.
Phillip Son of Phillip Marett and Elizabeth his Wife,	"	18 September 1787.
Nehemiah Son of Nehemiah and Anna Norcross,	"	19 June 1787.
Mary daughter of Thomas Powers and Mary his Wife,	"	8 March 1787.
William Son of Joseph Pitty and Elizabeth his Wife,	"	25 December 1787.
Betsy daughter of Nathan Peabody and Polly his Wife,	"	21 October 1787.
Judith Cooper daughter of Ezekiel Russell and Sarah his Wife,	"	7 January 1787.
Atherton H. Son of Benjamin Stevens and Hannah his Wife,	"	15 July 1787.
William Son of Joseph Tilden and Sarah his Wife,	"	28 January 1787.
Lucy daughter of Thomas Tileston and Lucy his Wife,	"	3 January 1787.
Harriet daughter of David Tyler and Sarah his Wife,	"	15 December 1787.
Delia daughter of William Tudor and Delia his Wife,	"	8 January 1787.
David Son of Jonas Welsh and Elizabeth his Wife,	"	4 June 1787.
Joseph Son of Joseph Ward and Prudence his Wife,	"	21 August 1787.

BIRTHS — 1787-89.   337

Samuel Adams, Son of Thomas Wells and Hannah his Wife,	born	1 March 1787.
Gem { William Augustus Son of Moses White and Elizabeth Amilia his Wife,	"	9 November 1787.
Esther Augusta daughter of Moses White and Elizabeth Amilia his Wife,	"	9 November 1787.

1788.

Lucretia daughter of Azor G. Archibald and Lucretia his Wife,	born	8 September 1788.
Charles Son of Benjamin Austin and Jane his Wife,	"	6 February 1788.
George Son of Nathan Bond and Joanna his Wife,	"	25 July 1788.
Annis daughter of Matthew Bayley and Sukey his Wife,	"	5 January 1788.
Charles Son of Isaiah Doane and Hannah his Wife,	"	27 December 1788.
Joseph Son of William Donnisson and Mary his Wife,	"	23 December 1788.
Sally Williams daughter of William Deblois and Sarah his Wife,	"	12 May 1788.
Henry Son of Jonathan Harris and Mary his Wife,	"	8 June 1788.
Pitts Son of Pitts Hall and Sarah his Wife,	"	11 April 1788.
Frederick William Son of Joseph Ingraham and Jane his Wife,	"	4 April 1788.
Asa Son of William Lawrance and Lydia his Wife,	"	4 June 1788.
Charles Son of John Lothrop and Elizabeth his Wife,	"	11 November 1788.
Charles Son of Joseph May and Dorothy his Wife,	"	19 March 1788.
Francis Son of Samuel Parkman and Sarah his Wife,	"	3 June 1788.
Delicia Mary daughter of David Poignand and Delicia his Wife,	"	1 April 1788.
George Son of Benjamin Russell and Esther his Wife,	"	3 April 1788.
Sarah daughter of David Spear and Marcy his Wife.	"	20 March 1788.
Lucretia, daughter of Samuel Sprague and Joanna his Wife,	"	21 January 1788.
Jenny Symmes daughter of Fortune Symmes and Jenny his Wife,	"	11 December 1788.
William Pitman, Son of Abraham Wild and Susannah his Wife,	"	27 January 1788.
Isabella Prat, daughter of Samuel Welles and Isabella his Wife,	"	23 April 1788.
John Blair, Son of Ebenezer Woodward and Hannah his Wife,	"	29 January 1788.

1789.

William Son of John Andrews and Ruthy his Wife,	born	5 May 1789.
John Fenno Son of Samuel Adams and Catharine his Wife,	"	23 February 1789.
Eliza, daughter of Benjamin Austin and Jane his Wife,	"	21 November 1789.
Elizabeth daughter of William B. Bradford and Mary his Wife,	"	26 May 1789.
Timothy Son of Thomas Badlington and Mary his Wife,	"	16 September 1789.
Nabby daughter of Jonathan Balch and his Wife,	"	1 June 1789.
Jane daughter of John Bazin and Jane his Wife,	"	24 August 1789.
Harriot daughter of Samll. and Hannah Bangs,	"	21 April 1789.

William Son of William Clap and Sally his Wife,	born	11 November 1789.
John Adams Son of Andrew Cunningham and Polly his Wife,	"	1 February 1789.
Charles Chancy Son of Rev. John Clarke and his Wife,	"	3 April 1789.
Andrew Cunningham Son of Henry Davison and Mary his Wife,	"	5 June 1789.
Sarah Smith daughter of Joseph Dolbear and Elizabeth his Wife,	"	
William Son of Thomas Flinn and Nancy his Wife,	"	9 September 1789.
Nathaniel Lewis Son of Nathaniel Gardner and Mary Anna his Wife,	"	10 April 1789.
Amelia daughter of Stephen Gorham and Molly his Wife,	"	5 April 1789.
John Clark Son of Nathaniel Johnson and Catharine his Wife,	"	11 December 1789.
Nancy daughter of Ozias Morse and Lucy his Wife,	"	7 January 1789.
George Washington Son of John May Esq. and Abigail his Wife,	"	15 October 1789.
Loisa Elizabeth daughter of David Poignand and Delicia his Wife,	"	13 September 1789.
Henry Barney Son of Barney Smith and Nancy his Wife,	"	26 October 1789.
Lydia daughter of Samuel Sprague and Joanna his Wife,	"	22 December 1789.
Thomas Son of Thomas Tileston and Lucy his Wife,	"	15 April 1789.
Elizabeth daughter of Joseph Tilden and Sarah his Wife,	"	8 January 1789.
Sally daughter of David Tyler and Sarah his Wife,	"	9 June 1789.
James Son of William Tudor and Delia his Wife,	"	22 May 1789.
Sally daughter of Jonas Welsh and Elizabeth his Wife,	"	1 February 1789.
Mira Son of Joseph Ward and Prudence his Wife,	"	3 November 1789.

1790.

Susah Lloyd daughter of Leonard Vassall Borland and Sarah his Wife,	born	7 February 1790.
Electa daughter of Caleb Bingham and Hannah his Wife,	"	29 August 1790.
John Son of William B. Bradford and Mary his Wife,	"	19 September 1790.
Matthew Son of Matthew Bayley and Sukey his Wife,	"	7 February 1790.
Benjamin Tufts Son of Hezekiah Blanchard and Esther his Wife,	"	7 March 1790.
Mariah Green Collins daughter of Isaac and Nabby Collins	"	14 November 1790.
Catharine Lippit, daughter of William Donnisson and Mary his Wife.	"	8 December 1790.
James Son of Samuel Eames and Lydia his Wife,	"	30 March 1790.
Susanna daughter of John Fox and Mercy his Wife,	"	6 January 1790.
Patrick Jeffry Wilks Son of Hans Gram and Jane his Wife,	"	23 July 1790.
Mary Ann daughter of Gardner Green and Elizabeth his Wife,	"	19 April 1790.
Mary Ann Gray daughter of Edward and Susanna Gray,	"	27 November 1790.
Hariot Gillspey daughter of	"	23 January 1790.
Frederick Son of Stephen Gorham and Molly his Wife,	"	15 June 1790.

Mary Anna daughter of Nathaniel Gardner and Mary Anna his Wife, born 24 May 1790.
George ⎱ Gem: ⎰ Son and daughter of Jonathan
Harriot ⎰ ⎱ Harris and Mary his Wife, " 16 August 1790.
Susanna Fox daughter of Samuel Laha and Mary his Wife (error), " 10 January 1790.
David Son of David Pratt and Hannah his Wife. " 27 December 1790.
James Son of James Prince and Agniss his Wife, " 15 January 1790.
John Son of Nathan Peabody and Polly his Wife, " 13 December 1790.
Sarah daughter of William and Judith Shaw, " 15 July 1790.
Jonathan Son of Jonathan Stodder and Sibylla his Wife, " 28 June 1790.
Betsy Melvin, daughter of Ebenezer Woodward and Hannah his Wife, " 26 February 1790.
Abraham Son of Abraham Wild and Susannah his Wife, " 5 February 1790.
Thomas Son of Thomas Wells and Hannah his Wife, " 27 March 1790.
Mary daughter of Abel and Chloe Barbadoes, People of Colour, " 1 December 1790.

1791.

Samuel Son of Samuel Adams and Catharine his Wife, born 10 July 1791.
John Son of John and Jane Bazin, " 18 December 1791.
Judith daughter of Abraham Bazin and Mary his wife, " 3 October 1791.
Susan daughter of William and Susannah Burley, " 2 September 1791.
John Son of Samll. and Hannah Bangs, " 2 December 1791.
Hannah Cazneau, daughter of Thomas Brewer and Hannah his Wife, " 21 October 1791.
Charles Son of Andrew Cunningham and Polly his Wife, " 6 April 1791.
Caroline daughter of William and Sally Clap, " 7 November 1791.
Henry Son of Isaiah Doane and Hannah his Wife. " 16 January 1791.
Margaret daughter of John Fox and Mercy his Wife, " 5 February 1791.
Amelia daughter of Stephen Gorham and Molly his Wife, " 22 August 1791.
Francis Son of Jonathan Harris and Mary his Wife, " 13 September 1791.
Daniel Greenleaf Son of Joseph Ingraham and Jane his Wife, " 11 June 1791.
Samuel Son of Nathaniel Johnson and Catharine his Wife, " 2 October 1791.
Henry Son of Zebadiah Johnson and Elizabeth his Wife, " 14 December 1791.
Hannah Ayers daughter of Ozias Morse and Lucy his Wife, " 16 December 1791.
Caroline daughter of James Prince and Agniss his Wife, " 9 March 1791.
Sarah daughter of Thomas Powers and Mary his Wife, " 4 August 1791.
Mary daughter of William and Judith Shaw, " 7 December 1791
John Son of John Sumner and Polly his Wife, " 23 August 1791.
James Son of Fortune Symmes and Jenny his Wife, " 20 October 1791.
Charles Son of Samuel Sprague and Joanna his Wife, " 26 October 1791.
Charles Son of David Tyler and Sarah his Wife, " 17 January 1791.
George Son of Elisha Ticknor and Betsy his Wife. " 1 August 1791.
Henry James Son of William Tudor and Delia his Wife, " 8 April 1791.
John Son of Joseph Tilden and Sarah his Wife, " 12 April 1791.

Augustus William Son of William Warner and Martha his Wife,	born	19 October 1791.
George Williams Son of Robert Williams junr. and his Wife,	"	27 June 1791.
William Son of Abraham Wild and Susannah his Wife,	"	8 December 1791.
Peggy daughter of Edmund Wright and Mary his Wife,	"	23 March 1791.

The following entry stands just before one of 1792:

Sarah Smith daughter of Joseph Dolbear and Elizabebth his Wife, "

1792.

Rufus Son of William B. Bradford and Mary his Wife,	born	7 October 1792.
John Son of Leonard Vassall Borland and Sarah his Wife,	"	19 January 1792.
William Son of Richard Wibort Cooper and Priscilla his Wife,	"	1 May 1792.
Harriet daughter of Revd. John Clarke and his Wife,	"	12 March 1792.
George Son of Isaiah Doane and Hannah his Wife,	"	4 December 1792.
Ann daughter of Joseph Dolbear and Elizabeth his Wife,	"	18 January 1792.
Lydia daughter of Samuel Eames and Lydia his Wife,	"	25 August 1792.
Edward Son of Edward Gray and Susanna his Wife,	"	16 December 1792.
Gardner Son of Gardner Green and Elizabeth his Wife,	"	5 January 1792.
Matilda daughter of Nathaniel Gardiner and Mary Anna his Wife,	"	11 February 1792.
Francis Son of Jonathan Harris and Mary his Wife,	"	2 October 1792.
Caroline Elizabeth daughter of Nathaniel Hancock and Elizabeth his Wife,	"	8 March 1792.
Eliza daughter of Daniel Ingols and Lydia his Wife,	"	1 September 1792.
Hannah Kuhn daughter of Jacob Kuhn and Hannah his Wife,	"	27 August (dead) 1792.
Sally ⎱ Twins Gem: daughters of David Lewis and Lydia ⎰ Lydia his Wife,	"	18 August 1792.
Louisa daughter of Joseph May and Dorothy his Wife,	"	31 December 1792.
John Son of David Pratt and Hannah his Wife,	"	23 August 1792.
Susanna daughter of Nathan Peabody and Polly his Wife,	"	18 December 1792.
Joseph Son of Joseph Peirce junr. and Frances Temple his Wife,	"	9 May 1792.
George Bell Son of David Rick and Bathsheba his Wife,	"	8 September 1792.
George Augustus Son of Robert Rogerson and Lucy his Wife,	"	13 November 1792.
Stephen Son of Stephen Smith and Mary his Wife,	"	19 April 1792.
Sally Brick daughter of Jonathan Stodder and Sibylla his Wife,	"	7 July 1792.
Marcy daughter of David Spear and Marcy his Wife.	"	23 August 1792.
Mary daughter of Edmund Wright and Mary his Wife,	"	15 December 1792.

1793.

Benjamin Son of Benjamin Austin and Jane his Wife,	born	9 April 1793.
Aaron Son of Isaac and Abigail Adams,	"	17 July 1793.
John Son of Ephraim and Sally Bound,	"	25 October 1793.
Catherina Lloyd daughter of Leonard Vassall Borland and Sarah his Wife,	"	12 October 1793.
Mary daughter of Abraham Bazin and Mary his Wife,	"	13 January 1793.
Edward Son of Peter Chardon Brooks and Ann his Wife,	"	22 December 1793.
Eliza daughter of Matthew Bayley and Sukey his Wife,	"	16 December 1793.
Ann daughter of Jonathan Balch and his Wife,	"	23 March 1793.
Stephen Son of John and Jane Bazin,	"	21 April 1793.
Alden Bass Son of Amariah Chapin and Deborah his Wife,	"	13 February 1793.
Mariah daughter of Joseph Cowdin and Mary his Wife,	"	25 January 1793.
Lucretia daughter of Andrew Cunningham and Polly his Wife,	"	29 July 1793.
Sarah Eliza daughter of William Clap and Sally his Wife,	"	14 February 1793.
Mary daughter of John Dyer and Mary his Wife,	"	1 October 1793.
Moses Emanuel Muhemet Von Exter Son of Joachim Van Exter of Hamburgh and Isabella Perkins his Wife, family from St. Eustatia	"	6 February 1793.
John Son of Asa Fuller and Elizabeth his Wife,	"	25 May 1793.
Nathaniel Son of Hans Gram and Jane his Wife,	"	10 July 1793.
Neils Brock Son of Hans Gram and Jane his Wife,	"	10 July 1793.
Benjamin Daniel Son of Gardner Green and Elizabeth his Wife,	"	29 December 1793.
Sally Gardner daughter of Nathaniel and Mary Anna his Wife,	"	28 December 1793.
Thomas Son of Stephen Gorham and Molly his Wife,	"	20 August 1793.
Charlotte daughter of Jonathan Harris and Mary his Wife,	"	23 November 1793.
George Son of Jacob Kuhn and Hannah his Wife,	"	13 Sept. (dead) 1793.
Thomas Son of George Longley and Mary his Wife,	"	31 August 1793.
David Rozel Son of David Poignand and Delicia his Wife,	"	29 January 1793.
Eliza daughter of Thomas Powers and Mary his Wife,	"	24 February 1793.
Robert Edward Son of David Rick and Bathsheba his Wife,	"	5 October 1793.
Francis Son of William and Judith Shaw,	"	26 October 1793.
William Son of Jonathan Stodder and Sibylla his Wife,	"	31 October 1793.
Jeremiah Son of Samuel Sprague and Joanna his Wife,	"	5 November 1793.
Sally daughter of Ebenezer Tileston and Sally his Wife,	"	24 January 1793.
Mary Parker daughter of Joseph Tilden and Sarah his Wife,	"	14 April 1793.
Abraham Gallison Son of Thomas Tannatt and Mary his Wife,	"	30 December 1793.
Charlotty daughter of Jessee Barber Willcox and Bulah his Wife,	"	31 October 1793.

Eleanor daughter of Dudley Walker and Eleanor his Wife, born 4 February 1793.
Mary daughter of Jonathan Wild and Mary his Wife, " 5 November 1793.
Daniel White Son of Daniel Whitney and Dorcas his Wife, " 21 July 1793.
Maria daughter of Ebenezer Woodward and Hannah his Wife, " 14 ? February 1793.

1794.

Humphry Austin Son of Humphrey Alden and Mary his Wife, born 26 September 1794.
Thomas Bulfinch Son of Seth Adams and Elizabeth his Wife, " 26 November 1794.
Samuel Son of Samuel Andrews and Elizabeth his Wife, " 24 December 1794.
Peter Boyer Son of Abraham Bazin and Mary his Wife, " 29 July 1794.
Hephzibah Parker Barber daughter of John Barber and Hephzibah his Wife, " 20 December 1794.
Samuel Son of Richard W. Cooper and Priscilla his Wife, " 13 February 1794.
Joseph Son of Joseph Cowdin and Mary his Wife, " 22 April 1794.
Caroline daughter of Isaiah Doane and Hannah his Wife, " 27 June 1794.
Ellinor daughter of John Dorr and Esther his Wife, " 6 September 1794.
Elizabeth Quincy daughter of William Donnisson and Mary his Wife, " 17 April 1794.
Mary daughter of Samuel Eames and Lydia his Wife, " 20 May 1794.
Mary Allen daughter of Ebenezer Eaton and Mary his Wife, " 19 September 1794.
Elizabeth daughter of Asa Fuller and Elizabeth his Wife. " 6 December 1794.
George ⎰ Gem: Son and daughter of Stephen Gorham and Molly his Wife, " 13 July 1794.
Harriot ⎱
Eliza daughter of John Hofman and Mary his Wife. " 12 September 1794.
Maria daughter of Nathaniel Johnson and Catharine his Wife, " 31 May 1794.
Lydia daughter of George Longley and Mary his Wife, " 27 November 1794.
Joseph Harris Son of Joseph Low and Sarah his Wife, " 2 December 1794.
Fisher Ames Son of   Morse and " 12 December 1794.
Frances daughter of John Peir and Chloe his Wife, " 24 July 1794.
Frances daughter of Joseph Peirce junr. and Frances Temple his Wife, " 17 January 1794.
John Son of Prince Snow and Elizabeth his Wife, " 21 November 1794.
Thomas Stoddard Son of David Spear and Marcy his Wife, " 4 January 1794.
Mary daughter of Ebenezer Tileston and Sally his Wife. " 29 December 1794.
Edmund Son of Edmund Wright and Mary his Wife, " 16 October 1794.
Amos Son of Daniel Whitney and Dorcas his Wife, " 22 September 1794.
Elizabeth daughter of Ezra Waldo Weld and Mary his Wife, " 21 March 1794.

1795.

Mary Ann daughter of Seth Adams and Elizabeth his Wife,	born	3 December 1795.
Elizabeth daughter of Samuel Adams and Catharine his Wife,	"	2 January 1795.
Hannah Trecothick daughter of Benjamin Austin and Jane his Wife,	"	26 June 1795.
Harriot daughter of Isaac Adams and Abigail his Wife,	"	23 September 1795.
Samuel Son of William B. Bradford and Mary his Wife,	"	18 January 1795.
Augusta Elizabeth daughter of Leonard Vassall Borland and Sarah his Wife,	"	12 November 1795.
Gorham Son of Peter Chardon Brooks and Ann his Wife,	"	10 February 1795.
Polly daughter of Matthew Bayley and Sukey his Wife,	"	7 October 1795.
William Barren Son of Andrew Colhoun and Martha his Wife,	"	29 December 1795.
Susan Davis daughter of John Cotton and Susan his Wife,	"	1 October 1795.
Mary Ann daughter of Leon Chappotin and Bridget his Wife,	"	17 April 1795.
Edward Tyler Son of Amariah Chapin and Deborah his Wife (at Dedham),	"	11 July 1795.
Caroline daughter of Isaiah Doane and Hannah his Wife,	"	7 November 1795.
Polly daughter of John Dyer and Mary his Wife,	"	31 December 1795.
Jean Germain Samuel Adams Dennery Son of Jean Baptiste Thomas Dennery and Julie Magdelaine Sophie Forget De St. Germain his Wife,	"	29 March 1795.
William Son of William Fisk and Eunice his Wife,	"	3 February 1795.
John Son of Claude Fortin and Magdeleine L. Amie his Wife,	"	10 March 1795.
Charles Son of Fox and Abigail his Wife,	"	14 September 1795.
Francis Son of *	"	27 May 1795.
Thomas Moor Son of William Greenough and Polly his Wife,	"	24 March 1795.
Eliza daughter of Edward Gray and Susanna his Wife,	"	19 January 1795.
William Parkinson Son of Gardner Green and Elizabeth his Wife,	"	7 September 1795.
Henry Son of Stephen Gorham and Molly his Wife,	"	27 December 1795.
Lucretia daughter of Jonathan Harris and Mary his Wife,	"	8 September 1795.
Stephen Son of Zebulon Hall and Martha his Wife,	"	20 November 1795.
Mary daughter of Joel Johnson and Mary his Wife,	"	11 February 1795.
George Son of George Johnson and Olive his Wife,	"	21 June 1795.
Jacob Son of Jacob Kuhn and Hannah his Wife,	"	3 January (dead) 1795.
George Son of Jacob Kuhn and Hannah his Wife,	"	14 December 1795.
Gilbert Son of David Lewis and Lydia his Wife,	"	9 September 1795.
Hannah daughter of David Pratt and Hannah his Wife,	"	20 April 1795.
Daniel Hews Son of Robert Rogerson and Lucy his Wife,	"	26 April 1795.
William Augustus Son of John M. Stillman and Nancy D. his Wife,	"	24 May 1795.

---

* Perhaps son of Nathaniel and Catharine Johnson.

William Scott Son of Daniel Whitney and Dorcas his Wife, born 30 September 1795.
George Son of Ebenezer and Mary White, " 23 August 1795.
William Meriam Son of Jesse Barber Willcox and Bulah his Wife, " 18 October 1795.
Dudley Son of Dudley Walker and Eleanor his Wife, " 8 February 1795.

1796.

Catharine Willard Amory daughter of John and Catharine Amory, born 24 March 1796.
Harriette daughter of Samuel Adams and Catharine his Wife, " 16 December 1796.
Susanna Buckley daughter of Abraham Bazin and Mary his Wife, " 16 February 1796.
Joseph Son of William B. Bradford and Mary his Wife, " 20 January 1796.
Mary daughter of Andrew Cunningham and Mary his Wife, " 21 February 1796.
Elizabeth Inglish daughter of Richard W. Cooper and Priscilla his Wife, " 26 March 1796.
Julia Ann daughter of John Cushing and Julia his Wife, " 19 May 1796.
Esther daughter of John Dorr and Esther his Wife, " 23 April 1796.
Margaret daughter of Ebenezer Eaton and Mary his Wife, " 3 February 1796.
Thomas, Son of Thomas French and Nancy his Wife, " 16 December 1796.
Hannah daughter of Samuel Fisk junr. and Hannah his Wife, " 14 November 1796.
Mary Anna Lewis daughter of Nathaniel Gardner and Mary Anna his Wife, " 9 April 1796.
Elizabeth daughter of John Gill and Elizabeth his Wife, " 26 March 1796.
Joseph Son of Joseph Hudson and Mary his Wife, " 22 December 1796.
Charlotte daughter of Nathaniel Johnson and Catharine his Wife, " 30 May 1796.
Eliza daughter of Ephraim Jones and Elizabeth his Wife, " 13 September 1796.
Josiah Nottage Son of George Longley and Mary his Wife, " 1 September 1796.
William Henry Son of Ebenezer Moulton and Abigail his Wife, " 18 January 1796.
Ambrose Son of   Morse and " 29 March 1796.
Delia daughter of Joseph Peirce junr. and Frances Temple his Wife, " 16 February 1796.
William Son of William and Lydia Palfrey, " 7 September 1796.
Isaac Son of Isaac Purvere and Catharine his Wife, " 28 July 1796.
William Son of Abraham Staples and Susan his Wife, " 4 October 1796.
Samuel Perkins Spear Son of Samuel Spear and Lydia Henchman his Wife, " 10 December 1796.
Michael Son of Fortune Symmes and Jenny his Wife, " 16 February 1796.
Metelda daughter of Samuel Sprague and Joanna his Wife, " 18 November 1796.
John Son of John M. Stillman and Nancy D. his Wife, " 25 June 1796.
      of Prince Snow and Elizabeth his Wife, " 1 April 1796.

Christopher Son of Christopher Tilden and Elizabeth his Wife, born 12 May 1796.
Eliza daughter of Ebenezer Tileston and Sally his Wife, " 1 October 1796.
Eleanor daughter of Dudley Walker and Eleanor his Wife, " 14 April 1796.

1797.

William Apthorp Adams Son of Seth and Elizabeth his Wife, born 2 July 1797.
Samuel Todd Son of Samuel and Elizabeth Adams his Wife, " 30 March 1797.
Ann Gorham daughter of Peter Chardon Brooks and Ann his Wife, " 19 June 1797.
John How Son of Matthew Bayley and Sukey his Wife, " 13 September 1797.
Charles Son of Andrew Colhoun and Martha his Wife, " 24 June 1797.
Bridget Adeline daughter of Leon Chappotin and Bridget his Wife, " 21 February 1797.
Elizabeth Boyer daughter of Joseph Coolidge junr. and Elizabeth his Wife, " 14 July 1797.
Mary daughter of John Dorr and Esther his Wife, " 22 July 1797.
Simeon Dean Son of Simeon Deane and Martha his Wife, " 29 November 1797.
John Son of John Dyer and Mary his Wife, " 31 March 1797.
William Casneau Son of   Fox and Abigail his Wife, " 26 July 1797.
Lucy White daughter of William Fisk and Eunice his Wife, " 25 March 1797.
George Son of George Green and Mary his Wife, " 8 July 1797.
Elizabeth daughter of Stephen Gorham and Molly his Wife. " 3 December 1797.
Susanna daughter of Edward Gray and Susanna his Wife, " 30 March 1797.
John Buller Son of John Hoffman and Mary his Wife, " 17 February 1797.
Amelia Augusta daughter of Jonathan Harris and Mary his Wife, " 21 August 1797.
Daniel Son of Daniel Ingalls and Lydia his Wife, " 16 June 1797.
Anne daughter of Jacob Kuhn and Hannah his Wife, " 27 March 1797.
John Clark Son of John Lambert and Margaret his Wife, " 15 May 1797.
Sarah Sweetser daughter of Joseph Low and Sarah his Wife, " 23 March 1797.
Nancy daughter of John T. Low and Nancy his Wife, " 17 April 1797.
Samuel Joseph Son of Joseph May and Dorothy his Wife, " 12 September 1797.
Charles Son to Ebenezer and Abigail Moulton. " 12 April 1797.
Edward Son of James O. Neale and Mary his Wife. " 4 July 1797.
Maria daughter of Joseph Peirce and Frances Temple his Wife, " 29 April 1797.
Harriot daughter of Thomas Powers and Mary his Wife, " 18 September 1797.
David Son of David Rick and Bathsheba his Wife, " 15 March 1797.
Isaac Hopkins Son of Isaac Rand the 3d and Jane Vernon his Wife, " 8 September 1797.
George W. Son of John M. Stillman and Nancy D. his Wife, " 19 November 1797.

Mary daughter of Stephen Smith and Mary his Wife,	born	9 April 1797.
Julia Maria daughter of David Spear and Marcy his Wife,	"	14 November 1797.
Harriot daughter of Joseph Tilden and Sarah his Wife,	"	6 April 1797.
Mary daughter of Moses Tyler and Mary his Wife,	"	18 December 1797.
Elizabeth daughter of William Turner and Elizabeth his Wife,	"	30 September 1797.
Edward Niles Son of Nathaniel Thayer and Charlotte his Wife,	"	22 August 1797.
Caroline daughter of Dudley Walker and Eleanor his Wife,	"	26 June 1797.
Catharine Landon daughter of Edmund Wright and Mary his Wife,	"	7 January 1797.

1798.

Peter Chardon Son of Peter Chardon Brooks and Ann his Wife,	born	26 August 1798.
Jacob Bull Son of Joshua and Mary Bull,	"	2 March 1798.
Joseph Son of Nathaniel Butler and Lydia his Wife, (Blacks)	"	22 October 1798.
Margaret Vassall daughter of Leonard Vassall Borland and Sarah his Wife,	"	27 March 1798.
Reuben Son of Reuben Carver and his Wife,	"	8 June 1798.
Solomon Son of John Cotton and Susan his Wife,	"	26 March 1798.
Sally Lewis daughter of Andrew Cunningham and Mary his Wife,	"	16 April 1798.
Mary Keith daughter of John Cushing and Julia his Wife,	"	14 April 1798.
William Son of John D. Dyer and Mary his Wife,	"	4 August 1798.
John Brazer Son of Ezra Davis and Mary his Wife,	"	16 October 1798.
Fanny daughter of Asa Fuller and Eliza his Wife,	"	7 October 1798.
Sally daughter of William Grenough and Polly his Wife,	"	8 September 1798.
John Son of John Gill and Elizabeth his Wife,	"	28 November 1798.
Elizabeth daughter of John Grew and Mary his Wife,	"	2 April 1798.
John Son of Edward Gray and Susanna his Wife,	"	5 December 1798.
Nathaniel junr. Son of Nathaniel Gardner and Mary Anna his Wife,	"	7 January 1798.
Caroline daughter of Jonathan Harris and Mary his Wife,	"	2 October 1798.
Martha Beal daughter of Zebulon Hall and Martha his Wife,	"	4 February 1798.
Nathaniel Son of Nathaniel Johnson and Catharine his Wife,	"	26 February 1798.
Adaline daughter of John Jutau and Mary his Wife,	"	24 September 1798.
Anna daughter of Atkins Lumbard and Anna his Wife,	"	24 December 1798.
Thomas Richardson Son of John Lambert and Margaret his Wife,	"	20 November 1798.
Elizabeth Sewall daughter of Joseph May and Dorothy his Wife,	"	5 December 1798.
Susannah daughter of Ozias Morse and Lucy his Wife,	"	24 November 1798.
Robert Jenkins Son of William and Lydia Palfrey,	"	27 December 1798.
Benjamin Williams Son of John Leate Roberts and Elizabeth his Wife,	"	8 June 1798.

BIRTHS — 1798-99.   347

Nancy daughter of Fortune Symmes and Jenny his Wife,   born   26 November 1798.
Edward Sprague Son of Samuel Swett and Esther his Wife,   "   8 January 1798.
Clerissa daughter of Samuel Sprague and Joanna his Wife,   "   17 June 1798.
Elizabeth daughter of Christopher Tilden and Elizabeth his Wife,   "   16 January 1798.
Sukey daughter of Ebenezer Tileston and Sally his Wife,   "   12 August 1798.
Elizabeth Ruggles daughter of John Whitney and Clarissa his Wife,   "   27 March 1798.
Nancy daughter of Obadiah Wright and Nancy his Wife,   "   19 May 1798.
William Son of William Wymann and Elizabeth his Wife,   "   19 January 1798.
William Son of William Wyman and Elizabeth his Wife,   "   18 January 1798.

1799.

Ann Lowder daughter of Samuel Adams and Elizabeth his Wife,   born   11 February 1799.
Elizabeth daughter of Samuel Andrews and Elizabeth his Wife,   "   25 September 1799
Sidney Son of Peter Chardon Brooks and Ann his Wife,   "   7 October 1799.
Andrew Hamilton Son of Andrew Colhoun and Martha his Wife,   "   30 March 1799.
John Son of John Cotton and Susan his Wife,   "   28 November 1799.
William Sheffield Son of Amariah Chapin and Deborah his Wife at Roxbury,   "   9 February 1799.
John White Son of John D. Dyer and Mary his Wife,   "   29 March 1799.
John Clark Son of William Emerson and Ruth his Wife,   "   22 November 1799.
Eliza daughter of Josep Eaton and Hannah his Wife,   "   9 January 1799.
Harriet daughter of William Fisk and Eunice his Wife,   "   3 January 1799.
John Coolidge Son of Ebenezer Farley and Lydia his Wife,   "   17 April 1799.
John Bradley Son of Joseph Hudson and Mary his Wife,   "   6 March 1799.
Francis Son of Daniel Ingols and Lydia his Wife,   "   3 April 1799.
Joseph Wentworth Son of Joseph Ingraham and Sarah his Wife,   "   13 November 1799.
Ephraim Son of Ephraim Jones and Elizabeth his Wife,   "   10 April 1799.
John Foster Son of Joseph Low and Sarah his Wife,   "   16 January 1799.
Nathl. Hall Son of Joseph Loring junr. and Susan his Wife,   "   17 December 1799.
Esbel Crosby daughter of John T. Low and Nancy his Wife,   "   19 March 1799.
Hannah Tucksbury daughter of John Leeman and Elizabeth his Wife,   "   9 May 1799.
William Son of Thomas Mills and Susannah his Wife,   "   2 February 1799.
Harriot Orne daughter of Perkins Nicholas and Bridget his Wife,   "   3 July 1799.
Marcus Tullius Son of Joseph Peirce junr. and Frances Temple his Wife,   "   17 May 1799.

Henry Son of Thomas Powers and Mary his Wife,	born	26 April 1799.
Caleb Hopkins Son of Isaac Rand the 3d and Jane Vernon his Wife,	"	13 March 1799.
Samuel Son of John M. Stillman and Nancy D. his Wife,	"	2 September 1799.
Charles Harrison Sprague Son of Samuel Swett and Esther his Wife,	"	17 October 1799.
of Prince Snow and Elizabeth his Wife,	"	28 December 1799.
William B. Son of Christopher Tilden and Elizabeth his Wife,	"	5 August 1799.
Sally daughter of Elisha and Hannah Tower,	"	1 December 1799.
Williams, Son of William Turner and Elizabeth his Wife,	"	27 February 1799.
Sarah daughter of Jesse Barber Willcox and Bulah his Wife,	"	29 January 1799.
William Parkhurst Son of John Whitney and Clarissa his Wife,	"	9 July 1799.

1800.

Sally Welch daughter of Isaac Adams and Abigail his Wife,	born	29 October 1800.
Theophilus Son of Ebenezer Little Boyd and Sarah his Wife,	"	9 January 1800.
Caroline daughter of Asa Bullard and Abigail his Wife,	"	21 September 1800.
Charlotta Gray daughter of Peter Chardon Brooks and Ann his Wife,	"	4 November 1800.
Caleb Champney Son of Ammi Cutter junr. and Elizabeth his Wife,	"	3 March 1800.
Susannah daughter of Andrew Colhoun and Martha his Wife,	"	17 October 1800.
Thomas Kilham Son of John D. Dyer and Mary his Wife,	"	4 September 1800.
John Son of John Dorr and Esther his Wife,	"	29 May 1800.
Charlotte ⎱ Gem. daughters of Joseph Eaton and Caroline ⎰ Hannah his Wife,	"	27 June (dead) 1800.
Ann daughter of Thomas French and Nancy his Wife,	"	6 February 1800.
Frederick Augustus Son of Ebenezer Farley and Lydia his Wife,	"	25 June 1800.
Mary Ann daughter of William Fisk and Eunice his Wife,	"	10 September 1800.
Mehitable daughter of David Greenough and Betsy his Wife,	"	21 July (dead) 1800.
Charles Son of Zebulon Hall and Martha his Wife,	"	9 November 1800.
Mary White daughter of Joseph Hudson and Mary his Wife,	"	4 December 1800.
Emily Burnap daughter of Micah and Rachel Holt,	"	19 July 1800.
Phaline daughter of John Jutau and Mary his Wife,	"	9 February 1800.
James Son of John T. Low and Nancy his Wife,	"	5 May 1800.
Lucrana daughter of Nehemiah Lovell and Rhoda his Wife,	"	21 March 1800.
Ephraim Ward Son of Joseph Low and Sarah his Wife,	"	22 May 1800.
Abigail daughter of Joseph May and Dorothy his Wife,	"	8 October 1800.
Constant Freeman Son of Thomas Mills and Susannah his Wife,	"	2 November 1800.

BIRTHS — 1800–1801. 349

Elizabeth daughter of David Pratt and Hannah his Wife,	born	5 June 1800.
James Lloyd Son of Isaac Rand the 3d and Jane Vernon,	"	6 October 1800.
Susan daughter of David Spear and Marcy his Wife,	"	5 July 1800.
Mary daughter of Samuel Sprague and Joanna his Wife,	"	1 May 1800.
George L. Son of John and Annah Stanhope in Newport, R.I.,	"	10 December 1800.
Caroline daughter of Joseph Tilden and Sarah his Wife,	"	21 May 1800.
George Richards Minot Son of Nathaniel Thayer and Charlotte his Wife,	"	6 November 1800.
Susannah daughter of John Whitney and Clarissa his Wife,	"	18 November 1800.
Frances Ruggles daughter of Obadiah Wright and Nancy his Wife,	"	15 August 1800.
Otis Son of John Willcocks and Sally his Wife,	"	20 February 1800.

1801.

Samuel Stillman Son of Amos Atherton and Hannah his Wife,	born	29 October 1801.
Joseph Simonds Son of Samuel Adams and Elizabeth his Wife,	"	6 April 1801.
Nancy Newell daughter of Wilks Barber and Nancy his Wife,	"	6 August 1801.
Edward How Son of Matthew Bayley and Sukey his Wife,	"	1 August 1801.
Thomas Perkins Son of Reuben Carver and his Wife,	"	16 November 1801.
Nathan Davis Son of John Cotton and Susan his Wife,	"	16 January 1801.
James Son of Andrew Cunningham and Polly his Wife,	"	27 April 1801.
Sally daughter of John Dorr and Esther his Wife,	"	13 September 1801.
William Son of William Emmerson and Ruth his Wife,	"	31 July 1801.
Edward Son of Fox and Abigail his Wife,	"	16 September 1801.
Joanna Burdick daughter of Hans Gram and Jane his Wife,	"	2 June 1801.
Susanna daughter of Edward Gray and Susanna his Wife,	"	10 June 1801.
John Son of David Greenough and Betsy his Wife,	"	19 November 1801.
George Clark Johnston Son of Nathaniel Johnston and Catharine his Wife,	"	6 January 1801.
Jacob Son of Jacob Kuhn and Catharine his Wife,	"	23 April 1801.
Catharine Sweetser daughter of Joseph Low and Catharine Sweetser his Wife,	"	18 October 1801.
Mary Ann daughter of Lazarus Lovell and Silvia his Wife,	"	24 February 1801.
Caroline daughter of Giles Lodge and Abigail H. his Wife,	"	25 May 1801.
Ann daughter of James Miller and Harriot his Wife,	"	16 July 1801.
Thomas Fairbanks Son of Samuel Morse and Elizabeth his Wife,	"	2 May 1801.
Mary Ann daughter of Perkins Nichols and Bridget his Wife,	"	20 February 1801.
Constantius Son of Joseph Peirce junr. and Frances Temple his Wife,	"	9 May 1801.

350   CITY DOCUMENT No. 43.

Margaret Skillin daughter of William and Lydia Palfrey,	born	30 March 1801.
Frederick Son of John M. Stillman and Nancy D. his Wife,	"	16 July 1801.
Martha Ann daughter of William Turner and Elizabeth his Wife,	"	10 July 1801.
Thomas Son of Edmund Wright and Mary his Wife (died August 27),	"	30 June 1801.

1802.

George Son of Samuel Andrews and Elizabeth his Wife,	born	2 April 1802.
Cleopas Son of Ebenezer Little Boyd and Sarah his Wife,	"	5 February 1802.
Eunice Shute daughter of Enos Blake and Sarah his Wife,	"	17 February 1802.
Frederick William Son of Joseph Bridge and Sally his Wife,	"	17 April 1802.
Henry Son of Andrew Colhoun and Martha his Wife,		26 October 1802.
George Lewis Son of George Aug. Cushing and Hannah his Wife,	"	20 July 1802.
Henry D. Son of Jonathan Dunton and Susannah his Wife,	"	29 March 1802.
William Son of Thomas French and Nancy his Wife,	"	20 February 1802.
Caroline daughter of William Fisk and Eunice his Wife,	"	10 January 1802.
Harriott daughter of Joseph Hudson and Mary his Wife,	"	6 March 1802.
Elizabeth B. Ingols daughter of Daniel Ingols and Lydia his Wife,	"	31 August 1802.
Henry Son of Ephraim Jones and Elizabeth his Wife,	"	15 March 1802.
Mary Walley daughter of Giles Lodge and Abigail H. his Wife,	"	15 August 1802.
Mary Hall daughter of Joseph Loring and Susan his Wife,	"	1 February 1802.
Charles Stimson Son of John Lambert and Margaret his Wife,	"	15 December 1802.
John Son of John Leman and Elizabeth his Wife,	"	5 December 1802.
Charles Son of Ozias Morse and Lucy his Wife,	"	21 May 1802.
Edward Henry Son of Perkins Nichols and Bridget his Wife,	"	24 September 1802.
Mary Ann daughter of Ebenezer Parker and Sally his wife,	"	2 June 1802.
John Ingersol Son of David Spear and Marcy his Wife,	"	12 October 1802.
Mary Ann daughter of John and Annah Stanhope in Newport, R.I.,	"	7 March 1802.
Faney daughter of Ebenezer Tileston and Sally his Wife,	"	11 January 1802.
Elisha Son of Elisha and Hannah Tower,	"	25 January 1802.
Frederick Nathaniel Son of Nathaniel Thayer and Charlotte his Wife,	"	30 July 1802.
Clarissa daughter of John Whitney and Clarissa his Wife,	"	27 March 1802.
Eliza Leach daughter of George Wattson and Eliza his Wife,	"	22 March 1802.
Hezekiah Son of William Wyman and Elizabeth his Wife,	"	26 May 1802.
Isaac Son of Isaac Winslow and Margaret his Wife,	"	18 February 1802.

1803.

Elizabeth daughter of Samuel Adams and Elizabeth his Wife,	born	13 August 1803.
Mary daughter of Isaac Adams and Abigail his Wife,	"	6 September 1803.
Alfred Helton Son of Joseph Bridge and Sally his Wife,	"	1 August 1803.
Joseph Henry Son of Joseph Burge and Sarah his Wife,	"	12 August 1803.
Benjamin Son of Matthew Bayley and Sukey his Wife,	"	8 February 1803.
Sarah Grant, daughter of Cornelius Coolidge and Sarah his Wife,	"	3 February 1803.
Eliza D. daughter of Jonathan Dunton and Susannah his Wife,	"	31 December 1803.
Abigail Cunningham daughter of John Dorr and Esther his Wife,	"	4 April 1803.
Joseph D. Bass Son of Joseph Eaton and Hannah his Wife,	"	25 January 1803.
Ralph Waldo Son of William Emmerson and Ruth his Wife,	"	25 May 1803.
George Son of Fox and Abigail his Wife,	"	19 July 1803.
Frederick Turell Son of Edward Gray and Susanna his Wife,	"	5 December 1803.
Laura Ann daughter of David Greenough and Betsy his Wife,	"	6 November 1803.
Lydia daughter of Zebulon Hall and Martha his Wife,	"	25 October 1803.
Samuel Bradley Son of Joseph Hudson and Mary his Wife,	"	31 August 1803.
Sarah Winslow daughter of Joseph Ingraham and Sarah his Wife,	"	19 March 1803.
Catharine daughter of Nathaniel Johnston and Catharine his Wife,	"	20 March 1803.
Abigail Harris daughter of Giles Lodge and Abigail H. his Wife,	"	20 November 1803.
Abigail daughter of John Livingston and Abigail his Wife,	"	20 January 1803.
Thomas Son of Thomas Mills and Susannah his Wife,	"	31 July 1803.
Sidney Bradford Son of Samuel Morse and Elizabeth his Wife,	"	5 May 1803.
James Son of James W. Miller and Harriot his Wife,	"	22 February 1803.
Isaac Son of Joseph Peirce junr. and Frances Temple his Wife,	"	21 January 1803.
William Son of Josiah Purvere and Catharine his Wife,	"	9 January 1803.
Elizabeth Cazneau daughter of William and Lydia Palfrey,	"	17 March 1803.
William Ames Son of William Stackpole and Nancy his Wife,	"	14 August 1803.
Eliza Paine daughter of Prince Snow and Elizabeth his Wife,	"	2 August 1803.
Nancey daughter of Ebenezer Tileston and Sally his Wife,	"	2 December 1803.
Andrew English Son of William Turner and Elizabeth his Wife,	"	9 November 1803.
Lucia Marston daughter of George Watson and Eliza his Wife,	"	9 June 1803.

Edward Son of Isaac Winslow and Margaret his
Wife, born 7 November 1803.
William Son of Israel Whitney and Phebe his Wife, " 15 November 1803.
William Son of Derby Vassell and Lucy his Wife
(all Blacks), " 30 January 1803

1804.

Kezia daughter of Isaac Adams and Abigail his
Wife, born 7 September 1804.
Joanna daughter of Ebenezer Little Boyd and Sarah
his Wife, " 4 February 1804.
Ward Chipman Son of Peter Chardon Brooks and
Ann his Wife, " 21 April 1804.
Elizabeth Shute daughter of Enos Blake and Sarah
his Wife, " 17 August 1804.
William Son of William Bicknell and Martha his
Wife, " 23 May 1804.
Cornelius Francis Son of Cornelius Coolidge and
Sarah his Wife, " 18 July 1804.
Simeon Howard Son of Andrew Colhoun and Martha
his Wife, " 15 August 1804.
Francis Son of Andrew Cunningham and Polly his
Wife, " 9 March 1804.
Lemuel junr. Son of Lemuel and Mercy Colbourn, " 25 July 1804.
Joseph Son of John Dorr and Esther his Wife, " 21 April 1804.
Thomas Son of Samuel Eames and Lydia his Wife, " 25 April 1804.
Edwin Son of Joseph Eaton and Hannah his Wife, " 17 October 1804.
Charles Son of Thomas French and Nancy his Wife, " 12 December 1804.
Samuel Son of William Fisk and Eunice his Wife, " 11 August 1804.
Frances Catharine daughter of Daniel Ingalls and
Lydia his Wife, " 17 December 1804.
George Hall Son of Joseph Loring and Susan his
Wife, " 11 January 1804.
Abba Bradshaw daughter of Henry Morgan and Abby
his Wife, " 30 January 1804.
Harriot daughter of James Miller and Harriot his
Wife, " 1 November 1804.
Laura daughter of Joseph Peirce junr. and Frances
his Wife, " 28 April 1804.
Albert Son of Ebenezer Parker and Sally his Wife, " 10 May 1804.
Luisa Caroline Matilda daughter of John Stoughton
Spain's Consul and Ann Margaret Stoughton, " 12 March 1804.
Hannah daughter of Elisha and Hannah Tower, " 30 August 1804.
Charlotte May daughter of Nathaniel Thayer and
Charlotte his Wife, " 5 March 1804.

1805.

Susannah daughter of Ebenezer Little Boyd and
Sarah his Wife, born 21 December 1805.
Sarah Amey daughter of Joseph Burge and Sarah
his Wife, " 21 November 1805.
Samuel Gale Son of Matthew Bayley and Sukey his
Wife, " 19 April 1805.
Horatio S. Son of Montgomery R. Bartlett and
Esther his Wife, " 20 May 1805.
Caroline daughter of Ammi Cutter junr. and Hannah
his Wife, " 8 January 1805.
Lemuel 2d Son of Lemuel and Mercy Colbourn, " 22 August 1805.
Katharine H. daughter of William Dinsmore and
Katharine his Wife, " 8 August 1805.

Births — 1805-1806.

George Barber Son of John Davis and Thankful his Wife,	born	13 January 1805.
Edward Bliss Son of William Emmerson and Ruth his Wife,	"	17 April 1805.
Hannah Dench daughter of John Fairbanks and Hannah his Wife,	"	2 June 1805.
Horatio Son of David Greenough and Elizabeth his Wife,	"	6 September 1805.
Mary Sumner daughter of Joseph Ingraham and Sarah his Wife,	"	31 August 1805.
Sarah Mason, daughter of Nathaniel Johnston and Catharine his Wife,	"	10 April 1805.
Giles Henry Son of Giles Lodge and Abigail H. his Wife,	"	13 March 1805.
Sarah Elizabeth daughter of Samuel Morse and Elizabeth his Wife,	"	11 May 1805.
Cazneau Son of William and Lydia Palfrey,	"	11 August 1805.
John Son of John and Annah Stanhope,	"	9 September 1805.
William Son of Prince Snow and Elizabeth his Wife,	"	22 July 1805
Catharine daughter of John Shaw and Catharine his Wife,	"	14 November 1805.
Sarah Miller daughter of Nathaniel Thayer and Charlotte his Wife,	"	26 November 1805.
Samuel Son of Vose and his Wife,	"	24 August 1805.
William Son of Derby Vassell and Lucy his Wife (Blacks),	"	21 April 1805.
Eliza daughter of Emery Wheeler and Nancy his Wife,	"	2 November 1805.
William Henry Son of Isaac Winslow and Margaret his Wife,	"	26 August 1805.
Eliza daughter of Israel Whitney and Phebe his Wife,	"	9 April 1805.

Each of these entries stands just after one of 1805:

Sarah O. B. daughter of Henry E. Morgan and Abby E. his Wife,	"	1 July.
Mary Emeline daughter of Emmorold Wheer and Nancy his wife,	"	

1806.

Sarah Ann daughter of Stephen Adams and Patty his Wife,	born	27 June 1806.
Abigail Brown daughter of Peter Chardon Brooks and Ann his Wife,	"	23 January 1806.
Enos Son of Enos Blake and Sarah his Wife,	"	1 December 1806.
Ann Boylston daughter of Andrew Cunningham and Polly his Wife,	"	24 November 1806.
Lawson Son of Dench and his Wife,	"	24 August 1806.
John Son of Samuel Eames and Lydia his Wife,	"	14 May 1806.
Eliza daughter of Zacheas Fuller and Salley his Wife,	"	24 July 1806.
John Warland Son of Jason Howe and Mary his Wife,	"	30 October 1806.
John Ellerton Son of Giles Lodge and Abigail Harris his Wife,	"	13 April 1806.
Edward Son of John Lambert and Margaret his Wife,	"	29 October 1806.
Ann Poor daughter of Ezekiel Little and Mehittable his Wife,	"	21 November 1806.

354   CITY DOCUMENT NO. 43.

Ebenezer Son of Ebenezer Parker and Sally his Wife,	born	7 September 1806.
Thomas John Son of Daniel Raynard and Margaret his Wife,	"	7 August 1806.
Francis Son of Derby Vassell and Lucy his Wife (Blacks),	"	9 November 1806.
Henry Son of Israel Whitney and Phebe his Wife,	"	15 September 1806.
Margaret Stackpole daughter of Francis Welch and Margaret his Wife,	"	1 October 1806.
Caleb Strong the 8 Son of Benjamin Whitman and Hannah his Wife,	"	12 April 1806.

1807.

Amos Gould Son of Amos Atherton and Hannah his Wife,	born	5 February 1807.
Benjamin Son of Isaac Adams and Abigail his Wife,	"	18 January 1807.
Elisha Tyler Son of Lemuel Colbourn and Mercy his Wife,	"	26 March 1807.
William Hart Son of William and Sally Dyer,	"	31 March 1807.
Robert Bulkley Son of William Emmerson and Ruth his Wife,	"	11 April 1807.
George Thomas Son of Joseph Eaton and Hannah his Wife,	"	4 August 1807.
John Phillips Son of John Fairbanks and Hannah his Wife,	"	26 March 1807.
Sarah Love daughter of Joseph Hudson and Mary his Wife,	"	12 May 1807.
Catharine S W. Low daughter of Joseph Low and Catharine his Wife,	"	25 June 1807.
John Ellerton Son of Giles Lodge and Abigail H. his Wife,	"	26 November 1807.
Sidney Bradford Son of Samuel Morss and Elizabeth his Wife,	"	21 March 1807.
William Reed Son of James Miller and Harriot his Wife,	"	13 January 1807.
Elizabeth Sewall daughter of Samuel Salisbury and Nancy his Wife,	"	July 1807.
Harriot daughter of John Shaw and Cathrine his Wife,	"	3 October 1807.
Nathaniel Howard Son of Nathaniel Thayer and Charlotte his Wife,	"	27 December 1807.
Samuel Abbot Son of Samuel Tufts junr. and Mary his Wife,	"	28 June 1807.

1808.

William Pelham Son of William Blagrove and Nancy his Wife,	born	18 May 1808.
Caroline Augusta daughter of Joseph Bridge and Sally (dead) his Wife,	"	25 June 1808
Mercy Maria daughter of Lemuel Colbourn and Mary his Wife,	"	15 November 1808.
Charles Chauncy Son of William Emmerson and Ruth his Wife,	"	27 November 1808.
Hannah daughter of Benjamin I. Gun and Hannah his Wife,	"	28 March 1808.
Richard Gay Son of Richard Hasting and Margaret his Wife,	"	9 September 1808.
Henry Bradshaw Son of Henry Morgan and Abigail Edes his Wife,	"	6 September 1808.

BIRTHS — 1809-17.

Lydia Elizabeth Parker daughter of Nathl. Johnston and Catharine his Wife, Hilsborough, County of Hilsborough, N.H., born 28 August 1808.
Harry Parsons Son of Ephraim Smith and Catherine his Wife, " 24 June 1808.
John Appleton Son of John Swett and Alice his Wife, " 3 December 1808.
Ann daughter of John and Annah Stanhope, ' 9 April 1808.
John Winslow ye 9 Son of Benjamin Whitman and Hannah his Wife, " 10 February 1808.
Francis Wm. Son of Francis Welch and Margaret his Wife, " 5 November 1808.

1809.

Charlotte Maria daughter of Joseph Burge and Sarah his Wife, born 6 June 1809.
George Son of Giles Lodge and Abigail H. his Wife, " 2 April 1809.
Samuel Francis Greenough Son of John Francis Newton and Abigail his Wife, " 10 February 1809.

1810.

Lucy Maria daughter of John Francis and Abigail Newton, born 2 August 1810.
Jane daughter of John Shaw and Catharine his Wife, " 27 April 1810.
Sally Campbell daughter of Derby Vassall and Lucy his Wife (Blacks), " 18 March 1810.

1811.

David Washington Son of David and Sarah Spear at Templeton, County of Worcester, born 22 February 1811.

1812.

Hannah Eliza daughter of Lemuel Colbourn and Mary his Wife, born 18 March 1812.

1813.

Sarah daughter of David Spear and Sarah his Wife at Templeton, County of Worcester, born 3 October 1813.

1814.

Richard Chardon Son of Derby Vassall and Lucy his Wife (Blacks), born 13 September 1814.

1817.

Margaret daughter of John and Annah Stanhope, born 1 November 1817.

Edward Son of John and Annah Stanhope in Providence, R.I., " 31 January 18—.

The following births unfortunately missed their proper places:

Mary daughter of William Bown and Eliza. his Wife, born	29 March 1702.
Sarah daughter of Lewis Boucher and Sarah his Wife, "	6 October 1706.
Hannah daughter of Joseph Johnson and Anna his Wife, "	30 March 1707.
Rebekah daughter of William and Rebekah Walker, "	14 December 1707.
Jane daughter of Grove Hirst and Eliza. his Wife, "	4 September 1709.
Martha daughter of John and Rachel Petel, "	17 November 1709.
John Son of Josiah Claik and Sarah his Wife, "	21 October 1710.
Isaac Son of Isaac and Abigail Webb, "	15 June 1710.
Eliza. daughter of John Davis and Eliza. his Wife. "	28 June 1711.
Nathanll. Son of Nicholas Dun and Deborah his Wife, "	11 May 1711.
Prudence daughter of Capt. Samll. Keeling and Eliza. his Wife, "	13 October 1711.
John Son of Timothy Robinson and Dorothy his Wife, "	29 March 1711.
John Son of John Rawlings and Love his Wife, "	27 August 1711.
Robert Son of Robert Harley and Eleanor his Wife, "	15 August 1715.
Lydia daughter of Anthony and Amaritta (Free Negros), "	30 April 1715.
Sarah daughter of Thomas Prince and Deborah his Wife, "	16 July 1728.

INDEX OF NAMES.

INDEX OF NAMES.

Abbott, 12, 26, 40, 54, 73, 103, 239, 242.
Abrahams, 309, 323.
Adams, 5, 12, 13, 19, 26, 32, 39, 40, 46, 52, 54, 66, 73, 80, 88, 95, 103, 111, 119, 126, 127, 134, 142, 148, 149, 153, 163, 168, 174, 179, 184, 190, 195, 196, 200, 206, 210, 215, 220, 235, 251, 265, 272, 275, 278, 285, 290, 298, 303, 309, 314, 316, 318, 320, 321, 323, 325, 326, 331, 332, 334, 336, 337, 339, 341, 342, 343, 344, 345, 347, 348, 349, 351, 352, 353, 354.
Addison, 163, 174.
Adkins, 12, 26, 40, 73, 119, 142.
Adlington, 309.
Aekin, 190, 200.
Ager, 39.
Aires, } 46, 111, 142, 153, 158, 163, 168, 174,
Ayers, } 179, 190, 210, 215.
Ayres, }
Aish, 272. 278, 318.
Akin, 153, 163.
Alcock, } 80, 95, 281, 285, 295, 298.
Allcock, }
Alden, 1, 5, 11, 12, 26, 40, 52, 54, 66, 73, 134, 153, 163, 168, 179, 190, 195, 200, 210, 220, 342.
Alexander, } 80, 96, 307, 314, 318.
Allexander, }
Alford, 5, 18, 66, 88, 103.
Alkin, 66, 80.
Allen, 1, 5, 11, 12, 26, 32, 39, 40, 45, 46, 59, 66, 73, 80, 87, 88, 95, 111, 127, 134, 142, 158, 168, 174, 179, 190, 196, 206, 210, 215, 220, 224, 232, 235, 239, 244, 248, 255, 262, 272, 276, 283, 293, 298, 303, 309, 312, 317, 320, 323.
Alley, 54.
Allin, 149, 153, 168.
Allison, 224.
Alman, 142.
Ambros, 1.
Amiel, 255, 269, 281.
Amory, 153, 158, 168, 174, 184, 290, 296, 298, 303, 305, 309, 312, 314, 316, 317, 320, 321, 324, 325, 327, 344.
Anderson, 80, 184.
Andrews, 134, 153, 158, 168, 179, 244, 250, 252, 255, 262, 265, 269, 272, 283, 290, 300, 307, 312, 316, 318, 321, 323, 325, 326, 328, 333, 335, 337, 342, 347, 350.
Androse, 5, 39.
Angeir, }
Anger, } 59, 95, 119, 134.
Angier, }
Anthony, 103, 158, 174, 184.
Antram, 39, 46, 54.
Appleton, 174, 285, 293, 298, 305, 309, 312, 316, 326, 330, 332.
Apthorp, 323, 326.
Archbald, } 111, 142, 158, 163, 269, 272, 281,
Archibald, } 288, 295, 298, 305, 309, 337.
Armitage, 72.
Armstrong, 1, 39, 134, 265.
Arnall, 142.
Arthur, 103.
Aspinall, 26.
Aston, 179.
Atherton, 349, 354.
Atkins, 168, 179, 190, 200, 210, 220, 228, 235, 242, 245, 248, 255, 259, 283.
Atwood, 5, 80, 103, 158, 168, 179, 190, 200, 210, 224, 248, 307, 312, 316.
Auchmuty, 246.
Audebart, } 163, 206, 215, 281.
Audebert, }
Audling, 5, 18.
Audlington, 158, 168, 174.
Austin, 252, 262, 269, 275, 278, 333, 335, 337, 341, 343.
Avery, 190, 210, 220, 231, 232, 235, 247, 259.
Aves, 293.
Avis, } 1, 25, 39, 46, 59, 80, 111, 168, 179, 190,
Avise, } 200.

Babbage, }
Babbidge, } 1, 159, 168, 196, 210, 220, 235, 245,
Babbridge, } 248, 252, 262.
Babel, } 46, 54, 73, 81.
Babell, }
Bacon, 154, 159, 169, 179.
Badcock, 128, 142, 255, 262, 269.
Badger, 1, 307.
Badlington, 337.
Bagnald, } 110, 112, 133, 142, 159, 174, 185.
Bagnall, }
Bailey, }
Baily, } 5, 20, 96, 111, 127, 128, 135, 142, 149,
Baley, } 242, 276, 305, 309, 314, 335, 337,
Bayley, } 338, 341, 343, 345, 349, 351, 352.
Baird, 320, 323.
Baker, 19, 26, 33, 40, 47, 54, 59, 66, 80, 81, 88, 96, 103, 112, 119, 127, 135, 142, 149, 153, 154, 169, 179, 190, 201, 210, 211, 220, 238, 242, 244, 245, 252, 262, 265, 269, 272, 278, 281, 288, 290, 293, 300, 318, 320, 327.
Balch, 89, 104, 111, 127, 140, 141, 154, 158, 164, 169, 174, 180, 185, 190, 206, 220, 228, 232, 307, 309, 314, 318, 323, 325, 326, 328, 329, 331, 333, 335, 336, 337, 341.
Baler, 210.
Ball, 13, 26, 60, 88, 120, 149, 158, 169, 180, 206, 262, 265.
Ballantine }
Ballentine, } 33, 81, 103, 112, 142, 163, 206.
Ballintine, }
Ballard, 33, 40, 60, 73, 81, 89, 103, 120, 142, 163, 185, 211, 215, 224, 228, 232, 235, 239, 245, 255, 259, 285, 293, 310, 326, 328, 329, 331, 333, 335, 336.
Balston, 196.
Bamus, 127.
Bangs, 288, 300, 318, 328, 337, 339.
Bancks, } 135, 142, 149, 153, 158, 159, 174, 191,
Banks, } 201.
Banister, } 33, 46, 53, 66.
Bannister, }
Bant, 5.
Barber, 81, 96, 134, 149, 154, 158, 159, 163, 169, 185, 210, 224, 232, 242, 276, 278, 285, 288, 298, 303, 305, 307, 312, 316, 320, 342, 349.
Barbeteau, 185.
Barbour, 13, 26, 33, 60.
Barden. 296.
Barer, 128.
Bargier, 96, 119, 135.
Barker, 164, 228, 232, 242, 262.
Barkes, 163.

Barlow, 196, 228.
Barnard, } 25, 40, 47, 54, 60, 66, 73, 88, 96, 103,
Barnerd, } 104, 111, 127, 142, 148, 154, 159,
164, 174, 184, 185, 191, 196, 206,
210, 211, 215, 220, 228, 232, 244,
252, 255, 269, 288, 293, 301, 305,
310.
Barnardo, } 13, 20, 33, 47.
Bernardo, }
Barnes, 1, 13, 19, 20, 33, 45, 54, 66, 73, 74, 96,
103, 112, 128, 135, 168, 179, 185.
Barnet, 5.
Barr, 26, 54.
Barrat, } 1, 13, 20, 32, 33, 45, 47, 54, 60, 66,
Barret, } 87, 88, 110, 120, 128, 149, 154, 159,
Barrett, } 174, 185, 201, 206, 210, 215, 220, 228,
232, 235, 236, 239, 242, 245, 248, 251,
255, 262, 265, 272, 279, 296, 298, 303,
307, 316, 320, 223.
Barrel, } 13, 20, 47, 60, 159, 190, 236, 242, 245,
Barrell, } 251, 255.
Barrick, } 174, 185, 201.
Barwick, }
Barrington, 89, 159, 255
Barron, 169, 190, 201, 290, 296, 300, 305, 312,
318.
Barsto, }
Barstow, } 13, 111, 127, 142, 154, 169, 185, 196,
Beairsto, } 265.
Bearstow, }
Barter, 102, 110, 119, 127, 185.
Bartlett, 314, 352.
Barto, 169, 180, 190.
Barton, 89, 103, 120, 135, 149, 163, 174, 185.
Bason, 5, 20, 33.
Bass, 127, 142, 154, 163, 164, 174, 180, 185,
196, 201, 206, 215, 296, 303, 307, 316,
318.
Basset, 211, 220, 239, 245.
Bath, 59.
Batt, 13, 26, 40, 54.
Baxter, 169, 174, 242, 283, 312.
Bayard, 196, 206, 220, 224, 232, 242.
Baynam, 20.
Bazin, 281, 285, 337, 339, 341, 342, 344.
Beacham, } 149, 159, 185, 196, 211, 220.
Becham, }
Beal, 60, 73, 103, 120, 127, 142, 158, 180.
Beals, 328, 330, 332.
Bean, 111, 185, 196, 206, 220, 228, 269.
Beard, 89, 103, 120, 215, 228, 238.
Beardmore, 119.
Beartell, 168, 179, 200, 210.
Beath, 103, 190.
Beaton, 80.
Beauchamp, 13, 163, 179.
Beaudri, } 142, 154, 201.
Beaudry, }
Beaver, 252.
Bedel, 127, 148, 159.
Bedlington, 112, 128.
Bedson, 185, 190.
Beech, 66.
Beer, 13, 26, 45, 88, 96, 148, 154, 159, 169, 180,
196, 200, 210, 228.
Beers, 60, 74, 239.
Beetle, 103.
Beighton, 120, 135, 164, 169.
Belcher, 5, 20, 40, 47, 59, 66, 81, 88, 96, 119,
126, 135, 149, 153, 154, 169, 174, 179,
180, 185, 191, 196, 200, 201, 224, 314,
316, 324.
Belitho, 174.
Belknap, 18, 33, 47, 54, 60, 66, 73, 81, 88, 103,
112, 134, 143, 149, 154, 158, 163, 169,
179, 180, 196, 215, 251, 262, 269, 272,
276, 278.
Bell, 47, 66, 73, 81, 88, 96, 119, 133, 149, 154,
164, 179, 191, 200, 215, 224, 235, 239,
248, 252, 262, 265, 276, 283, 288, 293,
312, 314.
Beney, }
Beny, } 179, 196, 201, 215, 224.
Binny, }

Bennet, } 5, 6, 26, 46, 66, 169, 174, 180, 190,
Bennett, } 206, 215, 220, 224, 228, 232, 235,
242, 265, 279, 285, 305.
Benning, 39, 59, 66.
Bennington, 81.
Benson, 81.
Bentley, } 169, 174, 185, 196, 206, 215, 224, 232,
Bently, } 242, 248, 252, 259, 296.
Berry, 6, 12, 20, 40, 47, 54, 66, 73, 169, 180, 185,
196, 206, 210, 224, 228, 232, 235, 245,
305, 310, 314, 318.
Best, 164, 179.
Bethune, } 102, 110, 120, 133, 135, 148, 153,
Betune, } 163, 185, 196.
Betterly, 158.
Beuteno, } 60, 66, 88, 103, 112, 128, 149, 154,
Boutineau, } 163, 174, 239, 241, 265.
Bickford, 40, 252, 331, 335.
Bicknel, 262.
Bicknell, 352.
Biles, } 5, 13, 25, 33, 45, 47, 60, 81, 104, 120,
Byles, } 135, 158, 215, 220, 224, 228, 232, 239,
245, 248, 255, 265, 272, 278, 281, 290.
Bill, 1, 6, 19, 26, 38, 54, 60, 66, 73, 80, 81, 89,
96, 111, 159, 169, 179, 185, 190, 201, 206,
215, 224.
Billings, } 12, 74, 133, 142, 154, 180, 190, 196,
Billins, } 201, 206, 215, 220, 228, 235, 245,
255, 276, 281, 286, 290, 312.
Bingham, 336, 338.
Binney, 265, 269.
Birch, 13, 89, 191, 220, 235, 242.
Bird, 74, 88, 102, 118, 120, 158, 169, 224.
Birsell, 135.
Biscon, 4, 12.
Bish, 154.
Bissell, 169.
Bisset, 133.
Bissit, 111.
Black, 185.
Blackman, 88, 112.
Blagrove, 354.
Blague, } 1, 13, 40, 73.
Blaque, }
Blake, 33, 46, 60, 73, 88, 96, 111, 135, 149, 158,
168, 169, 174, 185, 190, 196, 201, 206,
211, 215, 224, 228, 232, 235, 239, 242,
245, 248, 250, 255, 259, 265, 285, 293,
350, 352, 353.
Blanchard, } 103, 120, 127, 133, 142, 154, 159,
Blancherd, } 163, 169, 180, 190, 210, 228, 259,
262, 265, 269, 276, 278, 281, 283,
286, 288, 293, 298, 300, 305, 310,
336, 338.
Blare, 81.
Blasdell, 239.
Blatchford, 20.
Bleigh, }
Bligh, } 66, 74, 81, 103, 134, 154.
Bly, }
Blin, } 12, 26, 60, 164, 168, 185, 205, 215, 224,
Blyn, } 231.
Blith, 60.
Blodget, 283, 290, 296, 300, 303.
Blowers, 153, 164, 211, 215, 224, 228, 232, 235,
239, 242, 251.
Blunt, 278, 283, 285.
Blyth, 46.
Boar, 245.
Boardman, } 215, 278, 283, 288, 293, 298, 312,
Bordman, } 314, 318, 332, 333.
Bodely, 96.
Bodoin, }
Bodwain, }
Bodwin, } 52, 54, 66, 74, 89, 103, 174.
Boudoin, }
Bowdine, }
Bowdoin, }
Boies, 276.
Boiderson, 103, 111, 127, 149, 154, 168, 180.
Bolter, 220, 228, 235.
Boman, } 26, 54, 104, 112, 127, 149, 154, 169,
Bowman, } 174, 185, 196, 206, 220, 272, 278,
281.

Index of Names. 361

Bomer, 38, 73.
Bond, 174, 180, 185, 196, 333, 335, 336, 337.
Bougarden, } 81, 96, 112, 130.
Bongardon,
Bonner, 135, 201, 220.
Boon, 26, 33, 96, 111, 127, 134, 149, 154, 169.
Borden, 211.
Borland, 185, 206, 242, 276, 283, 336, 338, 340, 341, 343, 346.
Bostick, 95, 111, 119.
Bosworth, 112.
Boucher, 19, 119, 356.
Bound, 341.
Bourgin, 251.
Bourn, 288, 300, 307, 314.
Bouve, }
Bovey, } 164, 169, 180, 215, 228, 236, 242, 250.
Bovue, }
Bowd, 158.
Bowden, 220, 227, 252, 259, 273.
Bowen, 6, 25, 26, 168, 180, 239.
Bowes, } 1, 13, 40, 60, 321.
Bows,
Bowland, 250, 255.
Bowles, 245, 259.
Bown, 356.
Boyce, } 96, 120, 269.
Boyec,
Boyd, 66, 348, 350, 352.
Boyer, 174, 180, 190, 195, 201, 281, 298, 303, 307, 310, 312.
Boylston, } 1, 40, 60, 66, 80, 94, 193, 112, 119,
Boylstone, } 127, 141, 142, 149, 154, 164, 169, 180.
Boynton, 158, 190.
Brackenbery, 5.
Bracket, } 13, 26, 54, 316.
Brackett,
Brackinbury, 1.
Braddick, 111.
Bradfield, 96.
Bradford, 5, 33, 47, 127, 135, 148, 154, 158, 163, 174, 185, 191, 196, 201, 206, 211, 215, 220, 224, 242, 288, 312, 335, 336, 337, 338, 340, 343, 244.
Bradley, 309, 312, 318, 320, 328.
Brugg, 303.
Brailsford, 316, 326, 328.
Brame, 1.
Bramley, 74, 104.
Brandon, 164, 185, 220.
Bray, 164,
Bread, 134.
Breading, 269.
Breck, 180, 185, 196, 206, 210, 211, 215, 220, 228, 232, 239, 248, 255, 303, 321, 323, 324.
Breed, 60, 88, 120, 149, 158, 168, 174, 211, 215, 242, 248, 252, 255.
Brentall, 5.
Brentnel, 54, 96.
Brett, 73, 89, 135, 288, 298, 310, 314.
Brewer, 26, 40, 54, 66, 163, 169, 339.
Brewster, 46, 65, 66, 74, 103, 120, 142, 149.
Briant, } 54, 81, 89, 96, 142, 235, 245.
Bryant,
Brick, 33, 47, 54, 73, 88.
Bricksey, 163, 179, 185.
Bridg, } 1, 13, 18, 26, 52, 53, 60, 73, 87, 88, 103,
Bridge, } 112, 127, 144, 158, 174, 185, 200, 206, 215, 220, 228, 245, 350, 351, 354.
Bridger, 33.
Bridgham, 5, 13, 20, 23, 38, 40, 45, 53, 65, 72, 74, 80, 81, 96, 111, 112, 158, 163, 168, 190, 191, 196, 235, 330.
Bridgwater, 40.
Briggs, 1, 20, 33, 47, 60, 66, 81, 96, 111, 128, 142, 190.
Brightman, 1, 5, 32, 103, 111, 112, 133, 148.
Brileford, 103, 120, 159, 254, 259.
Brimmer, 180, 190, 201, 220, 228, 236, 245, 252, 255.
Brintnall, 185.

Brisco, } 1, 33, 54, 66, 89.
Briscow,
Britt, 159.
Britton, 52.
Broccus, 18, 25.
Brock, 33, 45, 54, 60, 73, 89, 103, 163.
Bromfield, } 1, 159, 168, 180, 190, 191, 196, 206,
Brumfield, } 210, 224, 272, 276, 290, 305, 333.
Bronsdon, 54, 66, 81, 95, 102, 111, 127, 141, 148, 149, 154.
Bronton, } 119, 128, 142, 154, 159, 174.
Brunton,
Brookes, } 47, 74, 135, 143, 159, 174, 201, 206,
Brooks, } 215, 220, 224, 242, 341, 343, 345, 346, 347, 348, 352, 353.
Brown, } 1, 4, 6, 13, 20, 33, 40, 47, 52, 54, 65,
Browne, } 66, 73, 74, 81, 89, 94, 96, 111, 127, 128, 135, 142, 149, 153, 154, 158, 159, 163, 168, 169, 174, 180, 185, 190, 191, 196, 206, 210, 211, 215, 220, 224, 228, 232, 235, 239, 242, 245, 247, 248, 250, 252, 254, 255, 259, 262, 265, 276, 281, 283, 286, 290, 291, 298, 303, 305, 307, 321, 330.
Brownsoley, 164.
Bruff, 5.
Bruno, 196, 206, 215.
Bryan, 285.
Bucanan, }
Bucannan, }
Buccanan, } 1, 13, 26, 47, 54, 169, 180.
Buchannon, }
Buck, 262, 269, 276.
Bucker, 154.
Buckland, 13, 47.
Buckley, 1, 54, 66, 96, 111, 135, 190, 196, 201, 211, 215, 228.
Bucknam, 296, 305, 307, 310, 314.
Bulfinch, 1, 20, 33, 58, 81, 96, 135, 164, 168, 180, 185, 196, 196, 200, 206, 215, 220.
Bulkley, 81, 149, 163.
Bull, 66, 80, 96, 118, 127, 149, 158, 262, 346.
Bullard, 348.
Bulman, 5.
Bumsted, 54, 66.
Bumsteed, 33, 40.
Bunker, 196, 201, 211, 224.
Burbanck, } 20, 26, 40.
Burbank,
Burbeck, 96, 111, 159.
Burch, 5, 40, 54.
Burdick, 247, 307, 318, 323, 325.
Burgaine, 81.
Burge, 351, 352, 353.
Burges, 73, 81, 96, 111, 119, 127, 135, 142, 154, 163, 278.
Burgone, 135.
Burley, 336, 339.
Burnel, } 33, 47, 54, 60, 73, 79, 89, 96, 103,
Burnell, } 112, 135.
Burnet, 1, 13, 33, 47, 255.
Burrel, }
Burrell, } 5, 26, 33, 128, 135, 169, 196, 206, 228.
Burrill, }
Burrillion, 215.
Burrington, 13.
Burt, 112, 127, 142, 154, 159, 163, 174, 190, 201, 244, 259, 262, 669, 276, 310, 314, 318.
Burton, 252.
Bushel, 103.
Bushnel, 73, 81, 96, 112, 127, 149.
Busso, 190.
Butcher, 26. 60, 80.
Butler, 1, 26, 40, 46, 54, 60, 65, 66, 74, 80, 89, 94, 95, 103, 118, 120, 128, 134, 142, 154, 190, 196, 210, 211, 215, 220, 224, 228, 232, 235, 239, 259, 314.
Butt, 13.
Buttolph, 1, 20, 26, 40, 73, 81, 96, 112, 128, 135, 154, 169, 239, 247, 252.
Button, 196.

Cabbot, Cabot, } 27, 34, 48, 206, 216, 224, 231, 259.
Cade, 224, 227, 235, 238, 250, 254.
Calef, Calefe, } 14, 27, 55, 67, 74, 82, 102, 113, 140, 154, 164, 201.
Callender, 20, 33, 55, 87, 112, 149, 154, 164, 174, 186, 197, 207, 216, 220.
Calley, 96.
Calwel, 135.
Camden, 27.
Campball, Campbell, } 27, 269, 276, 321.
Candish, 127.
Canner, 120.
Cannington, 191, 201, 207.
Cannon, 20, 67, 97, 186, 191.
Capen, 169, 318, 321, 323, 325.
Capril, 12, 25, 46, 59, 128, 143.
Carew, 6, 27.
Carey, Cary, } 13, 20, 59, 72, 89, 104, 120, 133, 150, 159, 256, 259, 328.
Carlisle, 180.
Carman, 281.
Carnel, 169.
Carnes, 159, 164, 175, 186, 191, 196, 205, 210, 220, 224, 231, 235, 238, 281, 286, 288, 291, 293, 298, 303, 310, 314.
Carpenter, 11.
Carpinter, 104.
Carter, 4, 143, 164, 170, 174, 185, 186, 191, 196, 201, 206, 210, 211, 220, 235, 241, 245, 248, 259, 262, 269, 307, 310, 314.
Carteret, 266.
Cartmill, 232.
Cartwright, 201, 242, 248, 273, 281, 307, 316.
Carvat, Cravat, Cravath, } 1, 11, 20, 33, 47, 81, 211, 216, 220, 228, 242, 248.
Carver, 25, 45, 346, 349.
Casno, Cazneau, Cusno, } 180, 191, 201, 211, 227, 228, 232, 236, 241, 242, 247, 254, 259, 266, 269.
Castle, 1, 13.
Cattance, 283.
Cauverly, Couverly, Coverly, } 59, 73, 89, 97, 113, 149, 201, 207.
Cavenay, 286.
Caverley, 236.
Cawdry, 185.
Center, 67, 82, 104, 120.
Cerlile, 13, 35.
Chace, Chase, } 135, 307, 310, 314, 318, 323, 333.
Chafen, 6.
Chaille, 201.
Chamberlain, Chamberlin, Chamberline. } 1, 13, 27, 40, 55, 67, 82, 89, 97, 104, 112, 113, 135, 149, 185, 197, 207, 211, 216, 283.
Chambers, 180, 191, 201, 211, 239.
Chamlet. 6, 20, 34.
Champlain, 327.
Champlin, 27, 47, 60, 67, 82, 104, 120, 159.
Champney, 27, 47, 89, 301, 327.
Chancey, Chauncey, Chauncy, } 6, 27, 41, 61, 191, 201, 211.
Chandler, 120, 170, 180, 201, 211, 224, 225, 228, 232, 236, 242, 283, 288, 291.
Channing, 94, 97, 120.
Chanter, 112.
Chapin, 150, 341, 343, 347.
Chapman, 328, 329.
Chappotin, 343, 345.
Charnock, 6, 26, 34, 47, 66, 81, 89, 104, 120, 128, 154, 175, 180.
Checkley, 150, 154, 159, 164, 169, 174, 186, 191, 197, 211, 216.
Cheever, Chever, } 13, 143, 154, 164, 174, 191, 206, 220, 263, 273, 279, 291, 293.
Chenevard, 170, 175.
Chick, 113, 128, 154, 175, 185, 232.
Child, 95, 112, 197, 228, 245, 259, 266, 298.

Chittinden, 301.
Christie, Christy, } 128, 211, 220, 228, 236, 248.
Chub, Chubb, } 20, 40, 66, 201.
Church, 248, 332.
Churchill, 293, 298.
Chute, 89, 97, 112.
Clagget, 104.
Clampit, 18.
Clap, 318, 324, 338, 339, 341.
Clark, Clarke, } 6, 14, 20, 26, 27, 34, 40, 45, 47, 53, 55, 59, 60, 67, 74, 81, 82, 89, 95, 97, 104, 112, 113, 120, 128, 135, 143, 150, 154, 159, 164, 169, 175, 186, 191, 196, 197, 201, 207, 211, 215, 216, 219, 221, 224, 225, 227, 228, 231, 232, 239, 241, 244, 245, 252, 255, 259, 266, 269, 273, 279, 288, 296, 312, 314, 353, 338, 340, 356.
Claxton, 104.
Clear, 1, 82, 97.
Cleasby, 104.
Cleer, 14, 41, 65.
Cleley, 164.
Clemans, 127, 150, 154.
Cleveland, 273.
Clewley, Cluley, } 74, 82, 97, 120, 141, 149, 154, 164, 175, 180, 191.
Clough, 6, 13, 14, 26, 27, 40, 45, 47, 60, 67, 74, 89, 97, 104, 112, 113, 135, 135, 140, 149, 150, 159, 164, 169, 180, 185, 191, 197, 201, 232, 236, 239, 242, 245, 248, 251, 255, 256, 262, 269.
Co, 318.
Coates, 326.
Cobbet, Cobbett, Cobbit, } 150, 169, 191, 201, 211, 216, 225, 236.
Coburn, 228, 232, 239, 242, 248, 252, 259, 262, 269, 276, 279.
Cock, 12, 27, 48, 53, 65, 74, 81, 89, 97, 112, 120, 126, 135, 141, 143, 150, 159, 175, 185, 201, 207, 220.
Cocks, Cox, } 1, 6, 26, 41, 60, 112, 164, 174, 175, 180, 186, 191, 197, 201, 211, 232, 248, 303, 310, 314, 316, 323, 325.
Codner, 14, 27, 41, 60, 74, 97, 191, 197, 201, 224, 259, 265, 273.
Coes, 34.
Coffin, 126, 141, 159, 169, 170, 175, 180, 185, 191, 196, 206, 211, 221, 224, 228, 232, 236, 239, 273, 276, 283, 286, 293, 298, 301, 303, 305, 312, 314, 316, 318, 321, 324, 328.
Cogswell, 305.
Colt, Coyt, } 97, 126, 135, 149, 164, 174, 186, 196, 259.
Colbey, 191.
Colbourn, 352, 354, 355.
Cole, 12, 120, 128, 148, 169, 180, 191, 207, 266, 276, 312, 323, 329.
Colefix, 48.
Coleman, Colman, } 1, 20, 27, 47, 52, 55, 67, 89, 228, 232, 239, 312, 316, 321, 334, 336.
Coleson, Colison, Colson, } 34, 47, 60, 80, 87, 97, 119, 135, 201, 211, 215, 221, 225, 228, 232, 239, 212, 245.
Colesworthy, Colsworthy, Colworthy, } 27, 46, 73, 81, 104, 113, 135, 149, 159, 175, 180, 191, 252, 259, 266, 279, 291, 298, 303, 305, 307, 320, 324, 327.
ColLoun, 343, 345, 347, 348, 350, 352.
Collegal, 135.
Collens, Collings, Collins, } 5, 6, 24, 26, 27, 41, 47, 55, 58, 60, 78, 81, 89, 126, 154, 169, 170, 180, 197, 201, 206, 207, 216, 220, 225, 335, 338.
Collier, 281, 288, 293, 298.
Collis, 112.
Collop, 232.
Colter, 207, 232.
Comer, 27.

INDEX OF NAMES. 363

Compton, 143, 154, 169, 180, 191, 201, 211, 216, 228.
Comrin, 211.
Condey, } 47, 55, 74, 89, 97, 110, 112, 113, 143,
Condy, } 164, 169, 180.
Condon, 239.
Condron, 320, 323.
Coney, 1, 2, 39, 60, 74, 81, 97, 112, 134, 143, 154, 164, 175, 185, 215.
Conibal,
Conniball,
Cunnaball,
Cunnable, } 6, 20, 74, 82, 96, 112, 128, 154,
Cunneball, } 159, 169, 180, 191, 269.
Cunnibal,
Cunniball,
Coningham, } 1, 12, 13. 104, 120, 141, 143,
Cuningham, } 150, 154, 159, 164, 169, 175,
Cunningham, } 180, 185, 191, 201, 206, 221, 236, 269, 276, 293, 296, 314, 321, 333, 335, 338, 339, 341, 344, 346, 349, 352, 353.
Cook, 1, 18, 20, 33, 34, 47, 60, 89, 128, 135, 180.
Cookson, 40, 47, 55, 61, 74, 87, 113, 232, 239.
Cooledge, } 89, 104, 120, 134, 149, 180, 186, 196,
Coolidge, } 207, 216, 221, 228, 345, 351, 352.
Coombs, 164, 180, 191.
Cooper, 6, 27, 33, 67, 112, 143, 149, 159, 169, 180, 191, 197, 201, 207, 296, 301, 305, 310, 318, 324, 340, 342, 344.
Copeland, 164, 174.
Copp, 6, 14, 25, 27, 40, 45, 55, 60, 97, 159, 191.
Corbin, 185, 196, 207.
Corcorand, 311.
Cordis, 215, 216, 224, 236, 242.
Cordwell, 296, 303, 307.
Corney, 228.
Cornwall, 150.
Corragall, 112.
Corser, 27, 60, 74.
Coser, 47, 89, 112.
Cotta, 13, 20, 38, 47, 60, 74, 97, 244, 256.
Cotton, 10, 221, 225, 218, 266. 269, 273, 279, 283, 286, 321, 343, 346, 347, 349.
Coulter, 224, 242.
Coulton, 201, 211, 216, 225.
Coutanch, 228.
Covell, 150, 154, 169.
Cowdery, } 6, 159, 164, 180, 197, 262, 266, 269.
Cowdry, }
Cowdin, 341, 342.
Cowel, } 6, 20, 34, 47, 60, 74, 89, 110, 126, 148,
Cowell, } 154, 164, 169, 174, 180, 186, 191, 196, 207, 252, 266.
Cowley, 225, 242, 245.
Craddock, } 149, 159, 164, 169, 180, 185, 196,
Cradock, } 206, 266.
Crafts, 113, 191, 201, 225, 239, 259, 314, 318, 323, 326.
Crage,
Craig, } 6, 20, 27, 55.
Craige,
Craigie, 242, 248, 276, 283, 286.
Crane, 112.
Cranston, 143, *159.
Crawford, 239.
Crawley, 164.
Creese, 1, 11, 25, 40.
Crehore, 180.
Crocker, 135, 186, 196, 206, 215, 224.
Croff, 215.
Crombie, 266.
Crompston, 279.
Cronenshelt, } 32, 40, 59.
Cronenshilt, }
Crosley, 241, 247, 256.
Cross, 65, 67, 110, 120, 180, 273, 286, 293.
Crouch, 67, 133, 143, 154, 164, 186, 259, 266, 269, 279, 286.
Crow, 1, 6, 33.
Crowel, 94, 102.
Crowly, 333.

Cruff, 13, 143, 150.
Cruft, 112, 170, 191.
Crump, 67.
Cudworth, 291.
Cullam, 236, 239, 254, 255, 262, 269, 276.
Cullever, 13.
Cumber, 221.
Cuming, 216.
Cumming, 236.
Cummins, 143, 239, 245.
Currier, 201, 206, 276.
Curtis, 239, 247.
Cushing, 1, 6, 14, 27, 33, 66, 164, 175, 180, 185, 186, 191, 196, 201, 211, 216, 221, 266, 273, 293, 301, 303, 312, 320, 323, 344, 346, 350.
Cussens, 180, 196.
Cutler, 20, 33, 45, 47, 55, 60, 206, 216, 220, 228, 236, 252, 256, 259, 266, 273, 276, 279, 281.
Cutt, 186.
Cutter, 348, 352.
Cutting, 180, 201.
Cutts, 180, 245.

Dabney, 242.
Dacon, 191.
Dafforne, 260, 270.
Dagget, } 105, 136, 150, 170.
Daggett, }
Dakin, } 247, 298, 303, 305, 308, 310, 312,
Daking, } 320, 327.
Dall, 279, 281, 286, 293, 303, 305.
Dana, 273.
Dane, 273, 276, 281, 286.
Danforth, 323, 324, 325, 331.
Daniel, } 2, 14, 55, 61, 82, 97, 133, 150, 170,
Daniell, } 181, 191, 202, 232, 236, 239.
Darbey, } 6, 21, 41, 48, 61, 74, 104, 121, 256,
Darby, } 273, 298.
Darling, 201, 207.
Darracott, 284.
Dashwood, 301, 307, 312, 321, 324.
Dason, 2, 6, 136.
Daubigny, 159.
Davee, 211.
Davenport, 6, 14, 21, 27, 48, 61, 82, 97, 119, 127, 141, 154, 164, 165, 170, 181, 191, 207, 211, 221, 228, 236, 239, 247, 253, 256, 262, 269.
Davie, 113.
Davis, } 6, 12, 48, 74, 82, 89, 90, 97, 104, 113,
Davise, } 121, 128, 140, 143, 155, 175, 191,
Daviss, } 197, 207, 216, 236, 270, 273, 276, 281, 284, 286, 291, 296, 298, 301, 305, 308, 346, 353, 356.
Davison, 329, 332, 336, 338.
Dawbt, 159, 170, 181, 191.
Dawes, } 24, 34, 41, 55, 61, 74, 82, 90, 113,
Daws, } 126, 140, 141, 155, 164, 197, 202, 207, 221, 232, 248, 256, 259, 279, 281, 284, 288, 291, 307, 312, 316, 318, 322, 324, 327, 329, 331, 332, 334, 336.
Dawson, 150, 159, 181, 186, 197, 211, 221, 305.
Day, 170, 181, 191, 202, 211, 216.
Deale, 245.
Deall, 119, 154, 164.
Dean, } 164, 170, 345.
Deane, }
Dear, 181.
Deblois, 273, 281, 294, 303, 305, 335, 337.
Debuke, 90, 104, 113, 128, 150, 159, 175, 181, 186, 207.
Dechezeaux, 207, 221.
Decoster, 61, 155, 170, 186, 247, 250.
Deering, } 90, 105, 121, 143, 154, 164, 175, 186,
Dering, } 291, 294, 320.
De Jersey, 260.
Delaplace, 236.
Delarue, }
Delerew, } 207, 211, 232, 312.
Dilarew, }
De Latour, 104.

Delaway,
Dellway, { 67, 72, 82, 90, 97, 105, 136, 159,
Dillaway,   170, 175.
Dilloway,
Delis, 164.
Delotte, 273.
Deluceny, 241.
Delver, 6.
Demerry, } 2, 14, 67, 82, 97, 104, 113, 136, 150,
Demcry, } 228.
Deming,   } 39, 65, 82, 104, 110, 120, 128, 136,
Demming, }   150, 159, 165, 175, 181, 260, 284,
              291.
Dench, 164, 211, 353.
De Neufville, 334.
Denizot, 143.
Denmark, 27.
Dennery, 343.
Dennie, 329.
Dennis, }
Dennise, { 11, 53, 55, 67, 90, 105.
De Rue, 266.
Deshon, } 207, 211, 221.
Dishon, }
De Valnais, 332.
Deverage, 191.
Dexter, 270, 276, 281, 298, 301.
Diamond, }
Dimond, { 55, 74, 89, 211, 296.
Dickers, 128.
Dickman, 301, 306.
Dike, }
Dyke, { 74, 89, 113.
Dillorock, 7.
Dinley, 27.
Dinmore, 276, 286.
Dinsdale, }
Dinsdell, { 14, 82, 236, 245, 251.
Dinsmore, 352.
Ditchfeeld, 74, 89, 104.
Dix, 211.
Dixwel, } 61, 97, 113, 143, 259.
Dixwell, }
Doan, } 104, 121, 136, 150, 165, 250, 253, 327,
Doane, }   329, 330, 332, 334, 336, 337, 339,
Done. }   340, 342, 343.
Dobel, } 211, 221, 239, 269, 273, 281, 286, 288,
Doble, {   294.
Docke, } 136, 143, 164, 175, 186, 201, 211, 221,
Doke, }   233.
Dokes, }
Dodd, 186.
Dodge, 165, 175, 233, 240, 248, 263, 270, 276.
Dogget, } 273, 284, 286, 288, 291, 296, 301,
Doggett, } 312, 314, 318, 320.
Dolbear, } 7, 14, 27, 34, 48, 55, 67, 74, 82, 90,
Dolbeare, }   104, 207, 211, 221, 250, 253, 260,
Dolbeer, }   262, 270, 276, 279, 291, 296, 301,
              308, 338, 340.
Dollard, 291.
Dolliver, 327, 329, 330, 332, 333.
Donnisen,   } 335, 337, 338, 342.
Donnisson, }
Dopson, 11.
Dorby, 155, 175, 186, 202, 211, 228, 242,
        266.
Dorothy, 104, 120, 150.
Dorr, 186, 2 1, 239, 303, 308, 312, 314, 318,
        320, 323, 325, 326, 328, 329, 330, 342,
        344, 345, 348, 349, 351, 352.
Dorrel, { 58, 65, 150.
Dorrell, }
Dorrington, 164, 170, 186, 202.
Doubleday, }
Doubledce, { 6, 175, 186, 191, 202, 281, 294,
Dubleday, } 307, 318.
Doubt, 286, 296, 301.
Douglas, }
Douglass, { 143, 164, 202, 270.
Douglas, 94.
Dowden, 2.
Dowding, 14, 21, 27, 48, 61, 82.
Dowel, { 128, 143, 159, 164, 170, 181, 192, 207.
Dowell, }

Down, } 104, 126, 133, 136, 150, 159, 164, 170,
Downe, {   175, 186, 197, 207, 216, 242, 245,
           279, 283, 291, 296, 298, 301, 305.
Downing, 48, 74, 221.
Dowrick, 211.
Dowse, 221, 228, 236.
Draper, 2, 14, 34, 48, 61, 180, 310, 312, 314.
Dresser, 90, 104, 143.
Dring, 201, 216, 225.
Drinker, 215, 252.
Drown,   } 2, 27, 41, 55, 89, 97, 105, 121, 136,
Drownd, }   150, 159, 170, 175, 186, 228, 236,
Drowne, }   242, 248, 256, 262, 263, 269, 279,
             284, 294, 298, 329.
Ducker, 202.
Dudley, 34, 39, 46, 48, 53, 59, 61, 72.
Dumaresq, 252, 263.
Dun, { 95, 110, 118, 121, 260, 266, 273, 286,
Dunn, { 296, 305, 308, 356.
Dunbarr, 113.
Duncan, 89, 104, 121, 155.
Dunham, 263.
Dunton, 159, 350, 351.
Dupee, 74, 82, 97, 102, 105, 119, 120, 126, 128,
        135, 143, 165, 175, 181, 186, 191, 197,
        201, 202, 207, 211, 216, 228, 256.
Durant, 14, 104, 110, 113, 128, 136, 141, 150,
         159, 164, 175, 186, 197, 207, 252, 316.
Duray, 175.
Durgee, } 143, 150, 159, 175, 186.
Durgy, }
Durham, 14.
Dutch, 82, 90, 113.
Dwight, 34, 55, 202, 211, 221, 232, 236, 248,
         263, 270.
Dyar, } 2, 14, 20, 27, 48, 55, 128, 143, 150, 175,
Dyer, }   191, 197, 202, 207, 216, 245, 248, 256,
Dyre, }   262, 270, 276, 303, 308, 312, 332, 333,
          334, 336, 341, 343, 345, 346, 347, 349,
          354.

Eades, } 34, 48, 61, 75, 97, 110, 128, 192, 202,
Eads, }   212, 221, 228, 236, 242, 245, 248,
Edes, }   256, 263, 270, 273, 279, 284, 286,
           288, 291, 294, 298, 301, 303, 306,
           312, 314, 322, 325.
Eales, 121.
Eals, 144.
Eames, 21, 336, 338, 340, 342, 352, 353.
Earl, { 7, 19, 21, 34, 143, 160, 170, 186, 197,
Earle, { 207, 216, 236.
East, 90.
Eastabrook, 175, 186, 197.
Eastwick, { 28, 34, 175.
Eustwicke, }
Eaton, 28, 38, 48, 80, 110, 128, 150, 155, 253,
        279, 286, 291, 301, 3 1, 332, 342, 344,
        347, 348, 351, 352, 354.
Eayres, 248.
Eccles, 192, 197, 202, 212, 216, 225.
Eddey, }
Eddy, { 95, 113, 128, 150, 159, 181.
Edey, }
Edgar, 302.
Edmands, }
Edmonds, { 82, 90, 150, 155, 170, 181.
Edmunds, }
Edwards, 2, 7, 12, 21, 28, 34, 48, 52, 82, 121,
         165, 170, 181, 192, 197, 207, 212,
         216, 221, 228, 229, 233, 236, 256,
         270, 273, 276, 281, 286, 288, 291,
         294, 296, 258, 304, 306, 310.
Egglestone, }
Egleston,   { 2, 21, 202, 211, 233, 248.
Ela, 7, 32.
Eles, 113.
Eliot, { 2, 41, 55, 75, 90, 94, 97, 105, 129, 150,
Elliot, { 155, 160, 170, 181, 186, 197, 207, 221,
           225, 236, 242, 248, 253, 2 6, 263, 266,
           270, 273, 284, 286, 296, 301, 310, 335.
Ellery, 82, 121, 143, 181.
Ellet, 75, 113, 128.
Ellingwood, } 245, 251, 256, 263.
Ellnwood,   }

INDEX OF NAMES. 365

Ellis, 2, 11, 32, 39, 53, 65, 88, 90, 97, 113, 155, 165, 175, 181, 197, 202, 212, 221, 225, 232.
Ellisit, 41.
Elliston, 19.
Emerson, } 67, 82, 202, 225, 347, 349, 351,
Emmerson, } 353, 354.
Emorson,
Emmes, } 7, 41, 105, 113, 121, 129, 141, 143, 175,
Emms, } 181, 186, 197, 227, 251, 253, 270.
Emmons, } 2, 34, 186, 192, 202, 207, 212, 216,
Emons, } 225, 233, 242, 247, 273.
Endecot, } 14, 21, 155, 160, 170, 186, 202.
Endicot,
Endicott,
English, 2.
Engs, 14, 32, 38, 48, 155.
Engster, 298.
Ennes, 155.
Enstone, 105, 128.
Epes, 67, 87.
Erskin, 121.
Erskine, 143.
Erving, 181, 192, 197, 202, 212, 216, 225, 228, 240, 273, 318.
Eustas, } 2, 4, 14, 18, 25, 28, 34, 41, 48, 55, 59,
Eustes, } 67, 82, 97, 105, 121, 128, 136, 140,
Eustice, } 143, 150, 155, 160, 170, 181, 192,
Eustis, } 197, 202, 212, 221, 229, 273, 276,
Eustise, } 279, 281, 284, 286, 288, 291, 290,
Eustus, } 301, 303, 308.
Evans, 7, 61, 170, 175, 186, 192, 202, 216, 221, 238.
Everard, 2, 14.
Everden, 148.
Everton, 221, 236.
Ewell, 216.
Exter, Von, 341.
Eyeres, 129.
Eyre, 119, 148, 155, 160, 165, 175, 186, 197, 207, 216, 229.
Eyres, 2.

Fadree, 41, 82.
Fadroe, 97.
Fagen, 82.
Fairbanks, 353, 354.
Fairfield, 111, 134, 141, 148, 186, 192, 202, 212, 225, 229.
Fairservice, 286, 291, 294, 298, 301, 306, 314.
Fairweather, } 75, 105, 113, 121, 136, 144, 148,
Fairwether, } 155, 165, 175, 186, 197.
Fallass, 270.
Falmouth, 113.
Fannah, 207.
Fare, 39, 75, 113.
Farley, 347, 348.
Farmer, 97, 129, 136, 144, 181, 192, 202, 236, 253, 260, 266, 270, 279, 284.
Farnam, } 61, 75, 95, 97, 105, 121, 129, 144,
Farnum, } 155, 165, 170, 181, 233, 236, 318.
Farnis, 212.
Farrindine, 90.
Farrington, 150, 160, 253, 263.
Farro, 121.
Farrow, 229.
Fator, 129.
Fauks, 75.
Faulkner, 18.
Fax, 61.
Felt, 102, 113.
Fenno, 48, 55, 61, 82, 105, 121, 129, 136, 175, 181, 207, 210, 216, 220, 221, 243, 251, 256, 264, 270, 273, 279, 291, 296, 301, 306, 310, 315.
Fenwick, 41.
Ferrington, 129.
Ferriy, 318, 323.
Ferry, 7, 297.
Fessenden, 212.
Fethergill, 61, 90.
Feveryear, } 183, 192, 202, 207, 216, 225, 233,
Feveryeare, } 236, 243.
Fife, 121, 136, 144.

Fifield, 165.
Fillis, 266, 273, 279.
Fine, 160, 170.
Fisher, 41, 48, 61, 129, 170, 175, 186, 207, 216, 283, 301.
Fisk, 90, 97, 343, 344, 345, 347, 348, 350, 352.
Fitch, 2, 21, 28, 41, 61, 136, 144, 150, 155, 160, 165, 170, 175, 181, 186, 192, 202, 207, 212, 216, 221, 225, 233, 236, 240, 246, 253, 260, 266, 279.
Fitz Gerrald, 207.
Flagg, 39, 41, 46, 59, 72, 79, 82, 105, 170, 186, 197, 207, 212, 221, 225, 231, 233, 236, 238, 245, 248, 250, 256, 273, 281.
Flecher, } 75, 82, 129, 144, 155, 160, 165, 170,
Fletcher, } 175, 181, 186, 192, 197, 212, 253, 256, 263.
Fleet, 113, 134, 148, 165, 181, 192, 207, 216, 233, 276, 281, 310, 312, 316, 320.
Flegg, 18.
Fleming, 105, 129, 144.
Flinn, 829, 332, 334, 338.
Flood, 2, 7, 14, 21, 28, 34, 41, 48, 55, 61, 67, 75, 97, 113, 160, 181, 225, 233, 240, 248.
Florence, 67, 82, 98, 121, 140, 155, 192, 233, 236, 256.
Floyd, 21, 28, 82, 192, 202, 207, 289, 318.
Flyn, 155, 160, 170, 181.
Flynt, 48.
Foxgo, 296, 306, 310, 314.
Follings, 260.
Follis, 155.
Folliss, 144.
Folsom, 294.
Forbes, 197.
Forbish, 134.
Ford, 323.
Forder, 207.
Foreakers, 286.
Forest, } 136, 150, 155, 175.
Forrist,
Forsyth, 150, 160, 202.
Fortin, 343.
Fosdick, 197, 202, 212, 216, 225, 330.
Foster, 7, 21, 28, 41, 48, 55, 67, 75, 82, 90, 98, 105, 113, 121, 129, 136, 148, 150, 155, 160, 165, 170, 175, 181, 192, 197, 202, 207, 212, 216, 221, 229, 233, 236, 238, 240, 243, 245, 248, 251, 253, 263, 266, 270, 273, 276, 314, 320, 323.
Fothergill, 170.
Four Acre, 241.
Fowle, 160, 165, 175, 181, 192.
Fox, 41, 59, 75, 338, 339, 343, 345, 349, 351.
Foxcroft, 2, 140, 150, 165, 175, 186, 197, 207, 2, 6.
Foy, } 7, 113, 121, 129, 144, 150, 155, 160, 170,
Foye, } 175.
Francis, 105, 245, 253, 263.
Francisc, 67.
Franckling, } 7, 11, 21, 28, 34, 46, 55, 67, 82,
Franklin, } 97, 111, 136, 144, 150, 170,
Frankline, } 175, 192, 216, 289, 294, 301,
Frankling, } 314.
Franklyn,
Frank, 111, 126.
Fraser, }
Frazer, } 144, 216, 225, 233.
Frazier,
Frathingham, 48.
Frederick, } 97, 129, 150.
Fredrick,
Freeman, 7, 18, 34, 41, 75, 82, 97, 121, 233, 281, 284, 289, 291, 296, 308, 318.
French, 344, 348, 350, 352.
Friend, 181.
Friswell, 216, 221, 236.
Frost, 105, 236, 243, 260.
Frothingham, 216.
Fryar, 250, 256.
Fryer, 240, 270.
Fullarton, } 18, 21, 113, 129, 140, 181, 192, 202,
Fullerton, } 212, 216.
Fuller, 136, 341, 342, 346, 353.

Fulton, 229.
Furber, 312.
Fyfield, 2, 155, 160, 170.

Gainger, 136.
Gale, 7, 75, 165, 176, 181, 225, 233, 240, 252, 260.
Gallop, 2, 19, 34, 48, 61, 68.
Galpin, 160, 171.
Gambier, 320.
Gandy, 187.
Gardener, ⎫ 2, 7, 21, 28, 61, 68, 75, 90, 98, 113,
Gardiner, ⎬ 121, 136, 155, 200, 210, 225, 229,
Gardner,   ⎭ 231, 235, 236, 243, 249, 256, 263, 272, 282, 291, 306, 310, 329, 330, 331, 332, 338, 339, 340, 341, 344, 346.
Garret, 35, 144.
Gatchel, ⎫
Gatchell, ⎬ 7, 21, 34, 55, 67, 165, 197, 212, 216, 229, 236, 243, 266.
Getchell, ⎭
Gatcombe, 155, 160, 170, 187, 221.
Gaud, 56, 144.
Gedney, 150, 165, 170, 176, 186, 197, 212, 217, 225, 229, 233, 236.
Gee, 15, 28, 45, 61, 82, 90, 105, 165, 170, 176, 240.
Gellings, ⎫
Gillings, ⎬ 2, 14, 28, 55.
Gendall, 160, 170.
Geoghegan, 233.
George, 121, 136, 155, 170, 186, 212.
Gerard, 28.
Gerat, 14.
German, 12, 28.
Gerrick, 155, 160, 171, 192, 212, 229.
Gerrish, 2, 14, 28, 34, 48, 61, 68, 75, 80, 89, 90, 94, 98, 105, 121, 136, 144, 150, 155, 160, 187, 240, 246.
Gibaut, 237.
Gibbins, ⎫
Gibbon, ⎬ 170, 176, 186, 187, 192, 197, 207, 216, 229, 243, 249.
Gibbons, ⎭
Gibbs, 7, 15, 202, 217, 229, 232, 233.
Gibson, ⎫ 2, 14, 21, 28, 41, 52, 61, 67, 75, 98,
Gipson, ⎬ 113, 207, 221, 225, 229, 240.
Giddens, ⎫
Giddings, ⎬ 34, 48, 61, 83.
Giddinge, 217, 221.
Gifford, 263.
Gilbert, 7, 15, 25, 34, 48, 56, 129.
Gilcrist, 114.
Giles, ⎫ 2, 11, 21, 28, 34, 61, 98, 121, 129, 144,
Gyles, ⎬ 150, 155, 165, 171, 181, 187, 192, 197, 207, 219, 253, 260.
Gill, 2, 11, 18, 28, 105, 121, 133, 144, 202, 239, 294, 299, 316, 322, 344, 346.
Gillspey, 338.
Gillspie, 336.
Gilmore, 7.
Girot, ⎫
Girott, ⎬ 197, 208, 217.
Glass, 21, 75.
Glazier, 59.
Gleason, 248, 310, 316.
Glidden, ⎫
Glydden, ⎬ 175, 187, 197, 202, 225, 229.
Godbold, 299.
Goddard, 25, 41, 48, 61, 75, 83, 90, 150, 170, 186.
Godfrey, 7, 28, 34, 48, 165, 175, 308.
Goff, ⎫ 4, 34, 48, 56, 58, 61, 65, 67, 75, 82,
Goffe, ⎬ 105, 119, 144, 165, 170, 181, 192, 202, 212, 217, 246.
Gold, 7, 12, 28, 221.
Golden, 7, 18.
Golding, 28, 41.
Goldthwait, ⎫ 7, 21, 28, 41, 56, 72, 75, 105,
Goldthwaite, ⎬ 121, 197, 202, 212, 221, 229, 233, 236, 237, 240, 243, 246, 250, 253, 254, 256, 260, 263, 266, 273, 276, 282, 284, 286, 291.
Gooch, 2, 114, 136, 165, 181, 186, 205, 215, 217, 221, 224, 229, 231.

Goodale, 83, 98.
Gooding, 2, 221, 229, 233, 240, 246, 256.
Goodwill, 121, 150.
Goodwin, 2, 14, 21, 34, 41, 48, 52, 61, 114, 136, 141, 150, 155, 165, 170, 175, 176, 192, 197, 202, 203, 207, 208, 217, 233, 236.
Goold, 2, 41, 61, 67, 83, 136, 144, 225, 229, 233, 243.
Goose, 25.
Gordon, 207, 221, 233, 286, 291, 294, 296.
Gore, 75, 90, 105, 129, 155, 230, 256, 306, 323.
Gorham, 330, 332, 334, 336, 338, 339, 341, 342, 343, 345.
Gosears, ⎫
Gusier, ⎬ 61, 90, 105, 114, 129.
Gussear, ⎭
Gussire,
Gouge, 160, 165, 176, 192, 221, 277.
Gould, 160, 277, 282, 299, 301, 303, 306, 328, 329, 330, 331.
Gowen, 83, 90, 129, 325, 326, 327, 328, 329, 330, 331, 334.
Grace, 202.
Grafton, 171, 197.
Grainger, 110.
Gram, 336, 338, 341, 349.
Grande, 236.
Grangier, 121.
Grant, 39, 41, 56 68, 119, 129, 136, 186, 202, 207, 216, 225, 229, 236, 240, 243, 246, 249, 251, 253, 260, 263, 266.
Grater, 129, 150, 170, 181.
Graves, 129.
Gray, ⎫ 7, 15, 21, 32, 41, 48, 53, 56, 65, 67, 68,
Grey, ⎬ 79 90, 105, 113, 121, 129, 136, 148, 150, 160, 170, 176, 187, 192, 197, 202, 207, 208, 216, 225, 233, 240, 243, 246, 249, 253, 256, 264, 272, 286, 299, 301, 303, 308, 310, 316, 338, 340, 343, 345, 346, 349, 351.
Graham,   ⎫
Grayham, ⎬ 98, 150, 171.
Greenleaf, ⎫ 35, 55, 61, 67, 75, 79, 80, 83, 88,
Greanleaff, ⎬ 98, 105, 113, 114, 129, 136,
Greenleaf, ⎬ 144, 155, 160, 171, 176, 181,
Greenleafe, ⎬ 186, 192, 197, 202, 207, 208,
Greenleaff, ⎬ 212, 216, 217, 221, 229, 233,
Greenleiffe. ⎬ 236, 240, 243, 245, 249, 251,
Greenlief, ⎬ 253, 263, 266, 270, 276, 279,
Greenliefe, ⎬ 282, 284, 286, 291, 294, 299,
Greenlieffe,⎭ 301, 303, 306, 308, 310, 312, 315, 316, 320.
Grecian, 133.
Greecion, 114.
Green, ⎫ 2, 4, 7, 15, 21, 25, 28, 32, 34, 41, 46,
Greene, ⎬ 48, 53, 55, 56, 59, 61, 67, 68, 72, 75, 83, 90, 93, 150, 160, 170, 181, 186, 187, 192, 197, 202, 203, 207, 208, 212, 216, 217, 221, 225, 233, 236, 237, 240, 243, 246, 249, 256, 263, 266, 270, 273, 282 289, 294, 301, 303, 306, 308, 12, 316, 322, 334, 338, 340, 341, 343, 345.
Greenough, ⎫ 12, 25, 39, 55, 67, 75, 98, 165,
Grenough, ⎬ 175, 181, 191, 202, 212, 217, 221, 225, 229, 233, 246, 240, 243, 246, 249, 266, 279, 289, 299, 330, 343, 346, 348, 349, 351, 352.
Greenwood, 2, 14, 39, 55, 65, 68, 79, 133, 134, 144, 155, 176, 181, 192, 202, 207, 217, 225, 233, 243.
Grew, 346.
Gribble, 83.
Grice, 2, 14, 21, 34, 56, 67, 75, 83, 98.
Gridley, ⎫ 11, 21, 56, 68, 202, 207, 208, 217,
Gridly, ⎬ 221, 225, 233, 236, 243.
Griffin, 197.
Griffith, 192.
Griffiths, 274.
Grigg, 186, 192, 221.
Griggs, 181, 192, 217, 229, 253, 273.
Grimes, 144.

INDEX OF NAMES. 367

Groom, 303, 310, 316, 320, 324, 326, 328.
Gross, 237.
Grouard, 165.
Grover, 83, 102, 111, 127, 187, 225.
Groves, 329, 333, 335, 336.
Grozier, 165, 176, 186.
Grubb, 67.
Gruzller, 192.
Guild, 334, 336.
Guille, 14, 21.
Gun. 354.
Gunison, } 113, 121, 170.
Gunnison, }
Gurrin, 98.
Guteridge, }
Gutradge, } 7, 21, 41, 48, 75, 82, 90.
Gutrage, }
Gutridge, }
Guy, 14.
Gwin, 2, 12, 28, 45, 48, 56.
Gybnat, 221.

Habersham, } 15, 68, 91, 95, 106, 129.
Haversham, }
Hacker, 231.
Haisley, }
Hasely, } 91, 106, 114, 129, 144, 151, 155.
Hasley, }
Hazely, }
Haislup, 222, 229.
Halaway, } 8, 15, 28, 39, 49.
Hallaway, }
Haldan, 294.
Halden, 212.
Hale, 29.
Haley, 46, 59, 68, 79, 95, 110, 114, 130, 137, 155, 165, 176, 187, 193, 203, 212, 217, 229, 233, 240.
Hall, 35, 56, 83, 91, 106, 114, 129, 165, 171, 181, 182, 198, 208, 225, 226, 249, 263, 270, 274, 279, 289, 294, 296, 299, 301, 304, 306, 308, 310, 313, 315, 316, 319, 320, 322, 325, 326, 327, 329, 330, 337, 343, 346, 348, 351.
Hallowell, 160, 165, 176, 187, 198, 208, 221 225, 229, 233, 237, 249, 256, 270, 274, 279, 289, 291, 301 304.
Halsey, 4, 11, 12, 25, 29, 129, 137, 165, 176, 208.
Hambleton, 29.
Hamelton, 42, 56, 75.
Hamilton, 270.
Hammatt, 217.
Hammet, 328.
Hammett, 246.
Hammoud, 198, 326, 328.
Hancock, 114, 340.
Hannah, 2, 15, 21, 28, 42.
Hanners, 151, 155, 165, 176, 187, 198, 225.
Hanserd, 203.
Hardcastle, 193.
Harding, 192, 203.
Harey, 171.
Harley, 68, 90, 160, 165, 176, 187, 198, 356.
Haro, 198.
Harper, 137, 193.
Harratt, 176, 182, 198, 212, 217, 229, 240.
Harris, } 28, 59, 72, 83, 87, 90, 98, 106, 107,
Harrise, } 114, 121, 126, 129, 130, 134, 136,
Harriss, } 137, 144, 148, 150, 151, 160, 171, 176, 182, 187, 192, 193, 198, 203, 208, 212, 217, 225, 233, 237, 240, 243, 249, 253, 256, 263, 279, 286, 289, 291, 294, 296, 327, 328, 330, 331, 333, 335, 337, 339, 340, 341, 343, 345, 346.
Harrison, 105, 256.
Harrod, 53, 229, 233, 243, 250, 256, 263, 277, 287, 322.
Harsum, 192, 203.
Hart, 68, 106, 137, 165, 176, 181, 193, 198.
Hartgrove, 35, 42.
Hartley, 192, 203.
Hartshorn, 160.

Harvey, 155, 165, 176, 182, 193, 203, 217, 2 22.
Harwood, 4, 22, 90, 98, 114, 122, 129, 144, 151, 171, 176.
Hasey, } 15, 35, 42, 49, 62, 68, 83, 90, 106, 114,
Hasie, } 129, 134, 151, 181, 182, 203, 208, 225, 229.
Haskins, 282, 286, 289.
Haslet, 217, 225.
Haslip, 203, 208, 217.
Hasting, 354.
Hastings, 171, 181, 237.
Hatch, 90, 217, 225, 229, 240, 247, 250, 256, 260, 279, 284, 289, 291, 294, 304, 308, 315, 319.
Haugh, 2, 12, 56, 68, 95.
Haukins, 49.
Hauksworth, 5, 18, 35.
Hawden, 245.
Hawes, } 260, 294, 296, 301.
Hawse, }
Hawke, 176.
Hawkins, 215.
Haies, }
Haise, } 49, 62, 76, 98, 114, 130, 165.
Hayes, }
Hay, 8, 21.
Hayward, 160, 171, 182, 187, 195, 198, 203, 208, 231, 239.
Haywood, 83, 145.
Head, } 49, 61, 181.
Hed, }
Healey, } 83, 106, 145, 176, 181, 187, 198, 208,
Healy, } 222.
Hearsey, 212, 217, 237, 243, 249, 253, 260, 267, 270, 308, 310, 312, 317, 319, 322.
Heath, 2, 15, 130, 151, 155, 165, 171, 176, 187, 198, 208, 217, 225.
Heaton, 176.
Hedge, 187.
Hedman, 129, 145.
Hekew, 129.
Helyer, } 90, 98, 119, 122, 136, 141, 151, 155,
Hillier, } 160, 165, 176, 187, 193, 229.
Heminway, } 42, 72, 76, 311, 313, 319, 322,
Hemmenway, } 323, 325, 326, 327.
Hencha, } 8, 21, 35, 42, 56, 75, 105, 165, 176,
Hensha, } 181, 187, 193, 198, 208, 212, 222,
Henshaw, } 225, 229, 237, 254, 260, 270, 277, 279.
Henchlee, 145.
Henchman, 68, 75, 83, 98, 284.
Hender, 145.
Hendersen, } 130, 137, 141, 148, 160, 171, 176,
Henderson, } 212, 282, 289, 299, 306.
Hendley, 249.
Henley, 7, 140, 151, 160, 171, 198.
Henry, 250, 256, 266, 277, 282.
Hern, 155.
Herridge, 29, 42.
Hetchbon, } 22, 42, 56, 62, 75, 91.
Hetchbone, }
Hewes, } 6, 15, 22, 28, 105, 121, 193, 198, 208,
Hews, } 212, 217, 229, 237, 246, 260, 291, 296, 301, 306, 310, 315, 318, 325, 327, 328.
Hewton, 263.
Heydon, 68.
Hickling, 222, 229, 237, 240, 246, 249, 254, 260, 266, 277, 280.
Hicks, 208, 225, 233, 243, 299.
Hikinbotham, 83.
Hill, 2, 28, 35, 68, 76, 144, 145, 155, 165, 171, 176, 181, 187, 192, 193, 198, 203, 208, 212, 217, 220, 222, 225, 229, 231, 233, 237, 240, 243, 246, 247, 249, 251, 254, 256, 266, 272, 274, 279, 286, 294, 301, 306, 315, 320, 323, 325.
Hiller, 257.
Hilton, 217, 225.
Hincks, 75.
Hind, 240, 249.
Hines, 130.
Hinks, 243.
Hirst, 25, 35, 46, 56, 88, 102, 356.

Hisket, 21, 28, 90.
Hixou, 333.
Hoar, 83.
Hobart, 222.
Hobbie, 11, 15, 52, 59, 75.
Hobbs, 19, 28, 29, 35, 62, 98, 114, 122, 151 192, 203.
Hodgdon, } 15, 28, 35, 42, 56, 171, 203, 212,
Hodgsdon, } 237.
Hodsdon, }
Hodges, 187, 192, 198, 208, 217, 225, 229, 237, 243, 249, 256, 260.
Hodgson, 308, 310, 318, 322, 327.
Hoffman, 345.
Hofman, 242.
Hogg, 160, 181.
Hoxoneauge, 316, 322, 324, 326.
Holberton, 49, 68, 83.
Holbrook, 98, 121, 129, 140, 145, 165, 289, 291, 304, 308, 310, 316, 319, 320, 325.
Holland, 22, 28, 35, 49, 56, 62, 68, 75, 83, 90, 98, 105, 114, 130, 144, 171, 176, 181, 187, 198, 208, 217, 222, 229, 237, 245, 249, 260, 267.
Hollowell, 2.
Holmes, } 2, 15, 22, 32, 35, 56, 72, 76, 90, 114,
Homes, } 233, 237, 240, 246, 249, 253, 260, 266, 274, 279, 286, 294, 303, 310, 324.
Holt, 348.
Holyoke, 171. 176, 187, 203, 212, 222, 229, 237, 243.
Homans, 229.
Homer, 8, 22, 42, 121, 151, 181, 182, 282, 286.
Honiwell, }
Hunewell, } 2, 42, 182, 193, 203, 212, 222,
Hunnewell, } 225, 233, 237, 286.
Hunniwell, }
Hunnowell, }
Hood, 4, 8, 18, 32, 35, 49, 52, 62, 84, 90, 110, 114, 122, 148, 151, 165, 176, 187, 193, 212.
Hook, 49, 83.
Hooton, 144, 151, 160, 171, 182, 193, 203.
Hopkins, 145, 155, 160, 176, 187, 192, 203, 274.
Horn, 308, 315.
Horsman, 76.
Horton, 28, 35, 49, 68, 83, 90, 114.
Hotte, }
Hutte, } 233, 237, 246, 251, 260, 266, 274,
Huttee, } 279.
Hutter, }
Hough, 165, 171, 182, 187, 193.
Houghton, 229, 237, 320, 322, 324, 327, 333, 334, 335.
How, } 42, 56, 68, 83, 91, 98, 102, 114, 133,
Howe, } 161, 171, 198, 208, 246, 251, 256, 277, 282, 284, 287, 291, 306, 332, 353.
Howard, 129, 136, 151, 160, 171. 176, 181, 182, 187, 193, 198, 203, 212, 222, 225, 229, 240.
Howel, } 62, 68, 80, 83, 87, 91, 98, 105, 106,
Howell, } 122, 203, 229, 237.
Howes, 332.
Howland, 240, 246, 251, 263, 270, 279, 315.
Hubbard, } 15, 35, 49, 65, 83, 106, 122, 130,
Hubbart, } 134, 148, 151, 155, 165, 171,
Hubbert, } 176, 181, 187, 192, 198, 203,
Hubburd, } 212, 225, 229, 233, 240, 263, 270, 274, 280, 284, 289, 294, 296, 299, 301, 304, 308, 310, 313, 315, 319, 320, 322, 324, 327, 329.
Huddiball, 106.
Hudson, 7, 8, 21, 35, 49, 62, 76, 83, 98, 114, 122, 136, 212, 217, 225, 237, 326, 344, 347, 348, 350, 351, 254.
Huges, 105, 137.
Huggins, 2.
Hughes, } 8, 25, 42, 260, 266, 277.
Hughs, }
Humble, 137.
Humphry, 75.
Humphryes, } 91, 114, 145, 282.
Humphrys, }

Hunlock, 56.
Hunstable, 106, 243.
Hunt, 2, 28, 35, 49, 68, 72, 80, 83, 90, 91, 98, 106, 114, 118, 122, 130, 144, 151, 155, 160. 165, 171, 203, 229, 233, 240, 246, 253, 260, 261, 266, 274, 282, 284, 289, 291, 294, 304, 330.
Hunting, 2, 122, 129, 151, 160, 176, 187, 198, 208, 217, 229.
Hurd, 171, 181, 193, 198, 208, 212, 222, 299, 301, 333, 334.
Hurst, 19, 25, 35, 46, 49, 56, 61, 68, 145.
Huston, 165, 171, 181, 193.
Hutchins, 114.
Hutchinson, 29, 56, 59, 62, 68, 76, 80, 87, 90, 91, 98, 106, 121, 122, 130, 145, 155, 160, 165, 176, 193, 203, 240, 250, 254, 266, 274, 277, 280, 284.
Hutton, 68, 98, 222.
Hyer, 182, 193, 203, 212
Hyslop, 277, 282, 287, 291.

Inches, 130, 137, 165, 176, 284, 322.
Indecot, } 15, 22, 29, 35, 42, 59, 84, 106, 155.
Indicott, }
Ingalls, }
Ingles, } 5, 18, 106, 340, 345, 347, 350, 352.
Ingolls, }
Ingols, }
Ingersol, }
Ingersole, } 237, 246, 260, 274, 277, 329, 332.
Ingersoll, }
Ingerson, 62, 76.
Inggs, } 111, 126, 144.
Inngs, }
Ingham, 155, 160, 176.
Inglesby, 319.
Ingolsbee, 29.
Ingraham, 102. 267, 280, 337, 339, 347, 351, 353.
Ingram, 15, 29, 45, 49, 56.
Ireland, 42, 68, 84, 144.
Irish, 247.
Ivers, 284, 289, 294.
Ivery, } 15, 237, 282, 291, 296.
Ivory, }

Jackson, 3, 8, 15, 18, 29, 35, 42, 49, 52, 56, 62, 65, 76, 84, 98, 102, 106, 122, 160, 165, 182, 187, 198, 203, 208, 213, 217, 220, 222, 224, 226, 229, 231, 233, 245, 237, 239, 240, 242, 246, 247, 249, 250, 251, 253, 257, 260, 263, 267, 270, 274, 282, 284, 287, 289, 294, 299, 302, 311.
Jacobs, 22.
Jager, }
Jagger, } 84, 91, 114, 156.
Jngor, }
Jalla, 98.
Jameson, 76.
Jandine, 193.
Janvering, 182.
Jarvis, } 8, 49, 111, 114, 156, 160, 165, 176,
Jarvise, } 187, 193, 198, 203, 217, 291, 297.
Jeffers, 62.
Jeffery, } 15, 62, 76, 193, 208, 301.
Jeffry, }
Jefferyes, } 49, 102, 137, 246, 253, 260, 267, 270,
Jeffries, } 277, 280, 289, 292, 302.
Jeffords, 284.
Jeffs, 193, 208, 213, 222, 243, 249.
Jemeson, 68.
Jenkins, 12, 65, 68, 88, 98, 99, 114, 122, 133, 137, 144, 151, 160, 171, 182, 187, 198, 203, 208, 217, 226, 233, 240, 249, 253, 274, 282, 287, 292, 297, 302, 304.
Jenners, 3.
Jennings, 213, 294, 299, 306.
Jennys, 322.
Jent, 49, 56, 76, 91, 98, 122, 130, 165, 193.
Jepson, 8, 39, 56, 68, 73, 114, 182, 187, 198, 208, 213, 217, 226, 233, 319, 320, 324, 330.

Index of Names. 369

Jerros, 193.
Jersey, 217, 233.
Jersey, De, 260.
Jesse, 2, 11, 15, 29, 35.
Jewel, 56, 76.
Joans, 22.
Joguet, 99.
Johnnot,
Johonnot,
Johonnott,
Johonot, } 3, 25, 35, 42, 165, 171, 182, 193, 203, 217, 243, 282, 284, 287, 289, 294, 297.
Johnson, 8, 18, 25, 42, 49, 130, 151, 156, 203, 208, 233, 237, 240, 243, 249, 254, 257, 267, 270, 280, 296, 302, 336, 338, 339, 342, 343, 344, 346, 356.
Johnston, 349, 351, 354, 355.
Jones, 2, 15, 29, 42, 56, 62, 76, 98, 106, 137, 176, 193, 203, 208, 213, 217, 222, 226, 230, 231, 243, 245, 249, 250, 251, 253, 260, 263, 267, 270, 274, 280, 282, 284, 289, 294, 299, 304, 308, 316, 344, 347, 350.
Jordan, 306.
Josling, 106, 122.
Joyner, 130.
Jutau, 346, 348.

Kally, 84.
Katen, 114, 145.
Keeffe, 217, 232.
Keeling, 39, 59, 356.
Keen, 76, 88, 111.
Keightly, 249.
Kelbey,
Kilbee,
Kilbey,
Kilby, } 8, 15, 35, 42, 56, 76, 84, 106, 114, 141, 156, 166, 176, 182, 187, 193, 203, 208, 217, 226, 230, 233, 306.
Kelder, 145.
Kelley,
Kelly, } 62, 198, 208, 217.
Kelton, 3, 156, 171.
Kemball,
Kemball,
Kemble,
Kemboll, } 8, 15, 22, 42, 62, 68, 73, 91, 94, 102, 203, 222, 230.
Kimbal,
Kempton, 42, 59, 72, 84, 126, 133, 148.
Kendal, 17, 226.
Kency,
Kenney,
Kenny, } 35, 52, 62, 68, 76, 80, 94, 102, 114, 126, 137, 140, 151.
Kennady,
Kennedy, } 237, 240, 246, 257, 267, 274.
Kenner, 106.
Kenrick, 99.
Kent, 3, 18, 84, 106, 122, 160, 161, 166, 176, 187, 203, 217, 226, 230, 234, 237, 257, 263, 277, 294.
Kenton, 156, 166, 177.
Kettel,
Kettle,
Kittle, } 3, 8, 35, 49, 52, 62.
Key, 99.
Khun,
Kuhn, } 277, 340, 341, 343, 345, 349.
Kick, 317.
Kier, 217.
Kiggell, 230.
Kilcup, 3, 15, 49, 91, 114, 187, 203, 297.
Killigrew, 160, 171.
Killworth, 156, 160, 176.
King, 8, 35, 46, 56, 62, 69, 76, 91, 122, 130, 137, 148, 176, 230, 237, 243, 282, 287.
Kingsley, 35.
Kingsly, 76.
Kingston, 84, 114, 137, 145, 161, 176, 187.
Kinsley, 282.
Kirby, 76, 84.
Kittyng, 160.
Knap, 222.
Kneeland, 4, 15, 42, 49, 62, 68, 114, 141, 151, 156, 160, 161, 166, 171, 176, 177, 182, 193, 198, 203, 208, 213, 226, 230, 217, 240, 263, 267, 274, 277, 251, 299, 304, 328.

Knight, 99, 122, 130, 145.
Knot, 4.
Knox, 161, 182, 193, 246, 249, 270, 282, 287.

Labbe, 62.
Labbee, 88.
Lablond, 3, 22, 29, 39, 65.
Laha, 302, 349.
Lake, 182.
Lamark, 69.
Lamarkin, 91, 107.
Lamb, 260, 264, 270, 274, 277, 282, 287, 289, 292, 294, 299, 302, 304, 308, 313, 315, 317, 320.
Lambert, 137, 156, 166, 188, 198, 213, 222, 250, 260, 264, 345, 346, 350, 353.
Lamoth, 187.
Lampson, 177.
Lamson, 122, 137.
Landen, 188.
Lander, 198, 203.
Landman, 127, 134, 151.
Landon, 29, 107.
Lane, 53, 73, 226.
Lang, 302, 304.
Langdon, 8, 25, 91, 99, 106, 122, 137, 151, 156, 166, 182, 208, 213, 257, 260, 270, 274, 282, 292, 297, 299, 304, 306.
Langley, 22, 35, 69, 84.
Langsford,
Lanksford, } 137, 156, 161, 171.
Lansted, 177.
Lappington, 193.
Lark, 156.
Larkin, 22, 25, 42, 56, 62, 246.
Larrabee,
Larraby, } 91, 156, 171, 177, 187, 237, 243, 264.
Lerabee,
Lash, 22, 35, 182, 198, 208, 218, 226, 234.
Lataile, 126.
Late, 177, 187, 198, 213, 222, 234.
Lathrop,
Lothrop, } 62, 69, 187, 226, 323, 324, 325, 326, 327, 331, 332, 333, 334, 337.
Lathe,
Leath,
Leathe, } 130, 145, 156, 177, 182.
Latour, De, 104.
Laughame, 62.
Lawler, 145.
Lawlor, 249.
Lawrance, 322, 324, 325, 327, 328, 330, 331, 332, 334, 337.
Lawrence, 122, 137, 177, 187.
Lawson, 3, 15, 29, 126, 130, 137, 157, 161, 218.
Lax, 15.
Layton, 91.
Leach, 8, 35, 49, 84, 106, 137, 151, 161, 198.
Leech } 213.
Leadbetter, 91, 122, 141, 171, 208, 264, 274.
Leasenby,
Leasonbee, } 8, 137, 151, 156, 166, 171, 177, 182, 187, 193, 208, 213, 222.
Leatherbee,
Letherbee, } 84, 91, 106, 107, 122, 137.
Lebrit, 188.
Lechmere,
Leechmer, } 69, 84, 99, 122, 130, 141, 156, 166.
LeCras, 203, 213.
Lecross, 280.
Le Dane, 192, 203.
Leddel, 264, 267.
Lee, 8, 16, 29, 42, 49, 62, 76, 80, 84, 99, 106, 115, 130, 156, 166, 182, 188, 193, 218, 226, 230, 234, 240, 243, 270.
Leeman, 347.
Lefaver, 257.
Legeree, 99.
Legg, 76, 91.
Leighton, 69, 84, 327, 333.
Lemain, 299.
Leman, 122, 350.
Lemercer,
Lemercier,
Le Mercier, } 138, 145, 151, 161, 166, 177, 182, 331, 333, 335.
Lemine, 294.

Lemon, 29.
Lendall, }
Lindall, } 42, 49, 62, 69, 76.
Lyndal,
Lyndall,
Lenix, } 76, 91, 130, 156, 161, 171, 188, 203,
Lenox, } 208, 217, 226, 234, 240, 270.
Leonard, 182.
Leveret, } 16, 29, 35, 115, 177, 187, 198, 203,
Leverett, } 294, 297, 299, 302, 306, 311.
Leverit,
Lewis, } 22, 35, 42, 49, 56, 69, 84, 95, 99, 115,
Lewise, } 122, 130, 137, 151, 156, 161, 166,
171, 177, 182, 187, 188, 198, 203,
213, 217, 218, 222, 226, 234, 243,
251, 254, 270, 280, 333, 336, 340,
343.
Leworthy, 161.
Leyton, 106.
Liddell, 227.
Lillie, 29, 42, 177, 187, 198.
Lillo, 161.
Linfield, 137, 151.
Linton, 166, 177.
Lisk, 137.
Liswell, 193.
Little, 177, 353.
Livermore, 137, 187.
Livingston, 351.
Lobdale, 42, 69.
Lobdell, 3.
Lobden, 106.
Lodge, 349, 350, 351, 353, 354, 355.
Logan, 137, 253.
Long 76.
Longley, 327, 329, 330, 341, 342, 344.
Loobey, 115, 130.
Look, 42, 193, 203, 213, 230, 237, 243.
Lord, 237, 240, 246, 249, 257, 267, 297, 302,
308.
Lorey, 45, 69.
Loreing, } 3, 8, 16, 22, 29, 35, 43, 49, 56, 69,
Loring, } 84, 91, 99, 106, 115, 122, 137, 151,
177, 213, 216, 257, 260, 264, 267,
274, 277, 282, 292, 297, 313, 319,
320, 324, 347, 350, 352.
Love, 22, 35, 43, 65, 145, 319.
Lovel, } 69, 84, 106, 226, 230, 348, 349.
Lovell,
Lovering, 237, 260.
Low, } 138, 193, 213, 222, 287, 315, 319, 323,
Lowe, } 342, 345, 347, 348, 349, 354.
Lowden, 3, 16, 22, 29, 42, 65, 76, 95, 106, 198,
208, 222, 230, 237.
Lowder, 43, 49, 65, 76, 91, 106, 122, 145, 148,
151, 156, 187, 226, 230, 237, 243,
249.
Lowel, } 8, 22, 62, 69, 217, 222, 226, 235, 239,
Lowell, } 242, 253, 264, 267, 274.
Lowle,
Lowler, 62.
Lowrey, } 15, 193, 203.
Lowry,
Loyd, 39, 95.
Luce, 161, 166, 234, 237, 247, 251.
Luckey, 137.
Luckis, 106, 115, 156, 166, 177, 193, 243, 246,
253, 260, 299.
Ludgate, 198, 208.
Lugar, 177.
Lumbard, 346.
Lumley, 29, 35, 49.
Lupton, 151, 166, 171, 203, 234.
Lyd, 122.
Lyde, 8, 29, 49, 137, 171, 188, 198, 208, 218,
222, 308.
Lym, 56.
Lymon, 106.
Lynch, 177, 198.
Lyon, 114, 122, 141.

Maccarty, } 8, 16, 110, 122, 138, 151, 156, 166.
Mackartey,
McChune, 188, 193.

Maccollo, 204, 213.
Macklelain, }
Macklelan, } 222, 230, 237, 243, 249.
McClelan,
McCullough, } 204, 330.
McCuloch,
Macdaniel, 84, 92, 107.
McElroy, 313, 315, 319, 322.
McFadden, 321, 324.
McGill, 261.
McIntyer, 239, 251, 257, 264, 271, 277, 280,
287, 289, 299.
Mack, 141, 151.
Mackannawy, 235.
Mackay, 289, 311, 313, 315, 319, 321, 323, 325,
327, 329, 330, 331, 332, 334.
Mackinley, 133.
Mackintosh, 230, 315, 319.
McKenzie, 271.
Macknight, }
Macnight, } 257, 261, 274, 277, 289.
McKnight,
Mcnite,
Mcklaughlan, 267, 274.
McLaine, } 156, 193, 213, 249.
McLean,
Macklish, 240.
Macklowd, } 53, 84, 231, 242, 247, 254, 261,
Maclowd, } 264, 270, 292.
McLeod,
McNeill, 254, 261, 267, 274.
McTagert, } 271, 274, 304.
McTaggart,
Mackue, 16.
Mager, 284.
Malcum.
Maycom, } 3, 9, 22, 30, 53, 63, 77.
Maycome,
Maier, }
Maire, } 84, 107, 130, 145.
Mayer,
Mair, 123.
Maison, 36.
Makelwain, 240, 246.
Malcom, 277, 282, 287, 292, 295, 297.
Mallard, } 62, 91, 107, 123.
Mallerd,
Mallet, 73, 91, 107, 122, 138.
Maltby, 237, 240, 246.
Man, 84, 92, 99, 107, 123, 134, 148.
Manley, 22, 39.
Mannakin, 29.
Manning, 182, 274.
Manson, 53.
Marbbell, 3.
March, 257, 260, 277.
Marchant, 271, 280.
Marett, 336.
Marine, 203.
Marion, } 8, 22, 36, 84, 99, 107, 123, 130, 141,
Marrion, } 151, 156, 166, 172, 182, 188, 193,
198.
Mark, 182, 198.
Markes, 156, 161, 166, 177, 188.
Marlow, 25.
Marret, 25, 46, 69.
Marriner, 19, 36, 43, 53, 62.
Marriott, 36.
Marsh, 249.
Marshal, } 3, 8, 16, 22, 32, 36, 43, 50, 57, 62,
Marshall, } 69, 76, 79, 84, 92, 107, 127, 141,
151, 161, 171, 172, 177, 188, 222,
226, 234, 239, 240, 243, 245, 246,
251, 254, 257, 260, 261, 264, 267,
284, 324, 325, 328, 331.
Marson, 313.
Martain,
Marten, } 16, 22, 43, 57, 77, 99, 107, 115, 119,
Martin, } 130, 138, 151, 161, 177, 188, 193,
Martine, } 199, 218, 230.
Martyn,
Marvel, 62, 91, 151, 161.
Mascarane, 123.
Mascareen, 145.

INDEX OF NAMES. 371

Mason, 8, 16, 22, 36 50, 62, 76, 77, 111, 115, 141, 151, 161, 171, 177, 182, 188, 199, 204, 208, 213, 218, 230, 234, 240, 267, 271, 274, 280, 284, 289, 294, 302.
Masters, 99, 115, 182, 188, 213.
Mather, 29, 46, 53, 177, 193, 218, 226.
Mathews, Matthews, } 91, 171, 188, 218.
Mattock, Mattox, } 3, 16, 92, 99, 141, 151, 182, 204.
Mauer, 145.
Maurice, 115, 123.
Maverick, Maverik, } 76, 99, 115, 130, 141, 151, 156, 161, 166, 172, 188, 198.
Maxfield, 177.
Maxwel, Maxwell, } 16, 30, 50, 62, 77, 151, 161, 171, 188, 205, 243, 246.
May, 45, 148, 166, 208, 271, 277, 284, 289, 292, 295, 299, 302, 304, 308, 315, 319, 320, 322, 324, 326, 327, 328, 330, 331, 333, 335, 337, 338, 340, 345, 346, 348.
Maycock, 161, 166, 177, 193, 198, 204, 208.
Maylem, 3, 22, 177, 213, 230.
Mayn, 91.
Mayo, 329, 330, 331, 332, 334.
Mays, 230.
Meda, 145.
Meers, 5, 22, 29, 107, 122, 130, 141.
Melikin, 204.
Melladge, 49.
Mellage, 84.
Mellendy, 193.
Mellens, 16, 30, 50, 63, 91, 122, 222, 230, 237.
Mellican, 138.
Mellikin, 193.
Melling, 145, 151, 161, 172, 188, 198, 208, 213.
Mellington, 188.
Mellish, 193, 204.
Mellus, 254, 264, 267, 274, 280, 289, 294, 299.
Melvel, 156, 166.
Melven, 95, 102, 115.
Melvin, 130, 141, 277.
Menzies, Minzies, Minzies, } 36, 57, 84, 99, 115, 138, 156, 166, 171.
Merchant, 99, 115, 130, 145, 156, 171, 182, 267, 274, 333.
Merefeeld, Merefield, Meriefeeld, Merrefield, Merrifield, Meryfeeld. } 29, 50, 57, 69, 84, 91, 99, 107, 123, 145.
Mero. 43, 69, 91, 123.
Merret, Merrett, Merrit. } 19, 73, 99, 182, 198, 204, 222, 230, 243, 249.
Meriit.
Mertino de St. Pry, 329, 332.
Messenger, Messinger, } 151, 161, 188, 257.
Meyer, 188, 204
Milbourne, 257.
Milburn, 156.
Miles, 16, 36, 43.
Milk, 57, 69, 208, 218, 230.
Milks, 237.
Millar, Miller, } 3, 9, 29, 57, 84, 92, 115, 123, 130, 138, 151, 156, 161, 177, 182, 349, 351, 352, 354.
Millner, 151, 156, 171.
Mills, 91, 115, 130, 138, 151, 161, 172, 177, 182, 188, 204, 347, 348, 351.
Milton, 92, 99, 198.
Milward, 308, 311, 315.
Mines, 208.
Minner, 43.
Minns, 294.
Minot, Minott, } 25, 234, 237, 246, 306, 308, 311, 315, 319, 322, 325.
Miers, Mires, } 8, 53, 69, 72, 92, 107, 156, 166, 222.
Mireck, 123.

Mitchel, Mitchell, } 62, 126, 130, 145, 156, 177, 193, 294, 317.
Moberly, 166, 172, 188, 218.
Mogerage, 8.
Mollens, 3.
Molles, 3.
Moloney, 282, 287, 306, 311.
Monck, 3.
Moncrieffe, 295.
Montgomery, 222.
Moody, 271, 330.
Moor, Moore, More, } 8, 43, 50, 57, 62, 77, 84, 91, 102, 115, 123, 138, 156, 161, 177, 188, 193, 198, 204, 222, 226, 234, 282.
Moorhead, Morehead, } 204, 208, 218.
Morey, 87, 92.
Morgan, 57, 69, 91, 107, 115, 141, 246, 352, 353, 354.
Morine, 218, 230.
Morrel, Morrell, } 57, 69, 87.
Morris, Morrise, Morrise, } 8, 16, 29, 43, 57, 62, 76, 92, 107, 130, 182, 218, 230.
Morrison, 198, 294, 297, 302, 306, 311, 313, 326.
Mors, Morse, Morss, } 16, 22, 36, 69, 72, 79, 119, 134, 148, 156, 166, 182, 230, 282, 336, 338, 339, 342, 344, 346, 349, 350, 351, 353, 354.
Mortemore, 18, 29.
Mortimer, 166, 177, 204.
Morton, 115, 295, 302, 315, 322.
Moseley, 257, 280.
Mossen, 145.
Mould, 11, 19, 29, 123.
Moulds, 138.
Moulin, 65, 73, 88, 102, 127, 141.
Moulton, 344, 345.
Mountfor, Mountfort, } 3, 16, 29, 35, 36, 43, 53, 59, 69, 91, 95, 99, 123, 130, 138, 156, 166, 177, 257, 261, 274, 287.
Mulbery, 172, 182.
Mullens, 76.
Mundan, Munden, } 77, 102, 115, 130, 145, 156, 166.
Murphy, 306.
Murray, 295.
Myars, 330, 331.
Myngs, 9.

Narramore, 119, 145, 156.
Nash, 77.
Nason, 204.
Nations, 213.
Nazaro, Nazro, } 72, 85, 115.
Neal, Neale, } 156, 117, 182, 193, 194, 204, 345.
Neat, Neate, } 85, 222, 234, 311, 317.
Neatby, 156, 172, 182, 188, 204.
Needham, 3, 9, 30, 36, 43, 50, 63, 249.
Nevfville, De, 334.
Newcomb, 150, 156, 166, 177, 199.
Newdigate, 3.
Newel, Newell, } 3, 16, 36, 85, 99, 115, 156, 161, 166, 172, 182, 257, 261, 267, 313, 326.
Newhall, 193, 199, 208, 218, 222, 237, 240, 264, 271, 274, 275, 284, 289, 292, 332, 334.
Newman, 166, 218, 222, 226, 234, 264, 267, 282, 285, 289, 292, 295.
Newton, 99, 123, 166, 355.
Nicholas, 347.
Nicnoll, Nicol, Nicoll, } 237, 243, 251, 257, 267.
Nicholls, Nichols, Nicolls, } 23, 36, 50, 63, 72, 85, 99, 107, 110, 123, 156, 161, 177, 182, 188, 218, 226, 230, 271, 349, 350.
Nicholson, 22, 39, 43, 50, 57, 63, 69, 77, 166, 177, 182, 188, 218, 230, 237, 240, 246, 249.
Nisbitt, 234.
Noakes, 3.

Noaks, 25.
Noble, 134, 267.
Nolan, 107.
Norcross, 287, 292, 299, 304, 311, 319, 336.
Norman, 72, 85, 99, 123, 131, 188, 204, 208.
Normand, 11.
Norris, } 19, 36, 69, 115.
Norrise,
North, 23, 99.
Northey, 22, 32, 50, 63.
Norton, 25, 39, 43, 53, 63, 172, 182, 193, 213, 237, 243, 311, 317, 322.
Norvell, 204, 208, 222.
Norwood, 22, 226.
Nowel, } 22, 30, 36, 50, 57, 138, 145, 156, 166,
Nowell, } 177, 188, 204, 208, 247, 271, 275, 285, 287.
Noyee, } 9, 22, 30, 36, 50, 63, 69, 85, 92, 107,
Noyse, } 115, 131, 148, 234, 235, 242, 251, 261, 264, 271.
Nutt, 194.

Obins, 172.
Oborn, 16, 50.
Obrian, 277. 282.
Ochterlony, 295.
Odltng, 59.
Ofing, 16.
Oglesbee, 30, 107.
Okes, 63, 69.
Olvier, 3, 23, 43, 69, 77, 85, 87, 88, 92, 99, 102, 107, 110, 123, 133, 138, 152, 161, 172, 194, 199, 204, 222, 230, 234, 240, 243, 246, 249, 257, 261, 264, 267, 271, 275, 277, 280, 282, 285, 287, 292, 297, 299, 311, 327, 328.
Orainge, }
Orange, } 25, 39, 53, 69, 77, 85, 99, 107, 115.
Orrange, }
Orio, 9.
Ormond, 152, 172.
Orn, } 63, 77, 85, 99, 115, 131, 151.
Orne, }
Orno, 115.
Orr, 208.
Orrock, 188.
Osborn, } 16, 107, 118, 126, 131, 145, 156,
Osborne, } 161, 166, 182, 199, 267, 277, 321.
Osgood, 234, 240, 261, 267, 322, 324.
Otis, 292, 297, 320, 327, 329, 332.
Oulton, 102, 110.
Owen, 177, 182, 188, 199, 208, 213, 218, 222, 230, 234, 240, 292, 295, 299, 304.
Owens, 332, 335.
Oxenden, 188.
Oxman, 123.
Oxnard, 240.

Pace, 253, 261.
Packanet, 102, 116, 123
Packer, 36.
Padon, 107.
Page, } 85, 92, 108, 123, 138, 152, 161, 172,
Paige, } 178, 199, 241, 243, 247, 254, 261, 268, 275.
Pain, } 9, 16, 30, 43, 50, 199, 204, 209, 213,
Paine, } 218, 226, 234, 241, 249, 253, 264, 275, 295, 299, 306, 311, 315, 331, 333.
Palfrey, } 25, 43, 46, 57, 63, 70, 85, 99, 116,
Palfry, } 123, 138, 152, 166, 172, 194, 311,
Palphry, } 317, 344, 346, 350, 351, 353.
Pally, 311.
Palmer, 12, 25, 32, 59, 65, 70, 77, 108, 110, 115, 156, 251, 257, 261, 275.
Papillion, } 138, 152, 156.
Papillon,
Papoon, 172, 188, 199.
Parke, 332.
Parker, 3, 9, 23, 30, 32, 36, 43, 50, 57, 63, 70, 85, 99, 110, 116, 123, 138, 146, 188, 204, 213, 218, 226, 232, 234, 239, 249, 258, 287, 292, 297, 299, 302, 350, 352, 354.

Parkman, 23, 70, 85, 92, 100, 115, 116, 131, 146, 152, 161, 166, 172, 177, 183, 194, 190, 209, 213, 222, 249, 257, 261, 264, 268, 277, 325, 326, 327, 329, 330, 332, 334, 337.
Parnel, 146.
Parott, } 77, 92, 108, 123, 141, 146, 177, 199,
Parrot, } 209, 230, 292.
Parrott, }
Parry, 16, 218.
Parsons, 77, 115.
Parteridg, } 85, 107, 244, 249, 258, 271.
Parteridge, }
Partridge, }
Pason, } 100, 116, 131, 134, 146, 172, 183, 199,
Payson, } 204, 257.
Pateshall, }
Patishall, } 85, 99, 115, 146, 156, 166, 172, 183.
Patteshall, }
Pattenson, 50.
Patterson, 230.
Patteson, 70.
Paty, 209.
Pauling, 9.
Paxton, 19, 32, 53.
Payn, } 3, 50, 59, 63, 70, 73, 80, 85, 88, 92, 99,
Payne, } 102, 111, 115, 119, 131, 134, 146, 148, 152, 162, 166, 292, 297, 304.
Peabody, 336, 539, 340.
Peak, 108, 123.
Peaice, } 19, 23, 36, 63, 70, 92, 141, 152, 161,
Pearse, } 172, 177, 182, 199, 209.
Pearson, } 9, 16, 36, 39, 50, 63, 85, 146, 166, 183,
Peirson, } 188, 204, 251, 295, 297, 308, 311.
Peat, } 123, 146, 177, 204.
Peet, }
Peck, 9, 23, 77, 85, 108, 123, 138, 148, 152, 172, 182, 222, 251, 253, 264, 271, 280, 295, 299, 300, 302, 313, 317, 322.
Pecker, 63, 70, 77, 92, 107, 108, 123, 152, 161, 182, 204, 267, 275.
Peco, 222.
Peek, 85, 131.
Peeker, 146.
Peir, 342.
Peirce, } 9, 36, 57, 63, 70, 85, 92, 95, 100, 108,
Peirse, } 116, 123, 131, 133, 138, 152, 156, 157, 161, 162, 166, 183, 188, 194, 199, 204, 213, 218, 226, 234, 240, 241, 243, 246, 253, 257, 264, 267, 275, 282, 289, 295, 302, 3 6, 322, 324, 340, 342, 344, 345, 347, 349, 351. 352.
Peircy, 194, 209.
Pelham, 194, 267, 295, 299, 304. 313.
Pell, 80, 92 100, 131, 183, 188, 194
Pemberton, 16, 23, 25, 32, 36, 46, 50, 59, 63, 92, 95, 108, 127, 138, 141, 152, 161, 162, 166, 172, 188, 218.
Pendexter, 329, 334.
Peneman, } 70, 85, 92, 99. 115, 124, 138, 146,
Penneman, } 156, 223, 226, 232.
Penniman, }
Pepper, 313, 319.
Pepple, 194.
Peream, 16, 30, 43.
Pereno, 108.
Perero, 242.
Pereyo, } 69, 77, 92.
Perrewoy, }
Perizo, 177.
Perkins, } 3, 9, 23, 25, 36, 45, 50, 57, 70, 72,
Pirkins, } 77, 100, 116, 131, 161, 222, 226, 230, 234, 237, 244, 246, 249, 268, 271, 290, 297, 302, 308, 315, 317, 319, 322, 325, 334.
Perram, 30, 77.
Perrin, 297.
Perry, 36, 50, 57, 70, 188, 209, 222, 230.
Petail, }
Petaule, }
Petel, } 16, 23, 30, 43, 50, 88, 99, 119, 356.
Petell, }
Pettel, }

INDEX OF NAMES. 373

Pettey, 92.
Phelps, 30, 65.
Philips, 3.
Phillips, 9, 16, 23, 30, 70, 77, 85, 107, 138, 146, 152, 161, 172, 177, 183, 194, 199, 204, 209, 213, 218, 222, 223, 226, 230, 234, 237, 238, 243, 253, 257, 261, 264, 267, 268, 275, 277, 287, 289, 292, 297, 302, 308, 315.
Phippen, 9.
Phippeny, 57.
Phipps, 277.
Pickerin, } 95, 102, 107, 123.
Pickering,
Pickman, 50, 70, 92, 131,
Pico, 161, 209, 213.
Pierce, 222, 308, 327.
Pierpoint, } 253, 261, 267.
Pierpont,
Pigeou, 172, 209, 282, 289.
Pike, 50, 68, 77, 146, 156.
Pilkinson, 3.
Pinckney, } 177, 194, 204, 223.
Pinkney,
Piper, 257, 261.
Pitcher, 43, 50, 85, 107, 138, 292.
Pitman, 16, 116, 131, 145, 188, 252, 258, 264, 267, 277, 280, 287, 308.
Pits, } 3, 23, 36, 43, 50, 63, 70, 92, 99, 116,
Pitts, } 157, 161, 172, 183, 222, 226.
Pitty, 328, 331, 336.
Pitson, } 131, 241, 257.
Pittson,
Plaisted, } 9, 16, 30, 43, 53, 63, 70, 77, 92, 108,
Plasted, } 123, 138, 152, 172, 177.
Plasteed,
Plats, } 3, 23, 50.
Platts,
Play, 65.
Plummer, 116.
Poignand, 337, 338, 341.
Pollard, 264, 271, 280, 285, 287, 289.
Polley, 297, 302, 311.
Pons, 242.
Pooke, 237.
Pool, } 131, 141, 226.
Poole,
Pope, 317.
Popkin, 321.
Porter, 3, 9, 23, 36, 43, 50, 57, 63, 70, 85, 92, 99, 123, 131, 146, 222.
Potter, 85, 100, 116, 138, 157, 282, 287, 304.
Potts, 63, 116.
Potwine, 157, 166, 177, 188, 194, 204, 218.
Poumery, } 85, 107, 123, 156, 199.
Pumery,
Pousley, } 108, 123, 146, 162, 177, 188, 199,
Powsley, } 234.
Powel, } 32, 152, 161, 166, 172, 183, 199, 209,
Powell, } 299, 304.
Powers, 302, 333, 336, 339, 341, 345, 348.
Pranket, 50.
Prat, } 3, 23, 77, 92, 108, 115, 116, 123, 145,
Pratt, } 146, 161, 162, 172, 178, 183, 194, 209, 223, 230, 237, 244, 246, 261, 302, 339, 340, 343, 349.
Preble, 102.
Preeson, 107.
Prentice, 351.
Prentiss, 334.
Presbee, 23.
Presbery, 77.
Prescott, 230, 237, 240, 246.
Presson, 295.
Preston, 70.
Price, 19, 92, 100, 123, 183, 204, 222, 234, 238, 246, 254, 271, 313, 315, 317, 322, 325.
Prichard, } 156, 237, 246, 249, 257, 264, 277,
Pritchard } 280.
Prince, 116, 126, 138, 146, 152, 161, 162, 172, 182, 183, 204, 213, 226, 237, 249, 271, 277, 282, 285, 289, 292, 295, 299, 300, 302, 313, 315, 339, 356.
Prindle, 9, 119, 146.

Pritchet, 145.
Procter, } 3, 9, 23, 36, 43, 53, 63, 85, 100, 108,
Proctor, } 131, 152, 157, 161, 166, 172, 177, 188, 194, 199, 209, 213, 218, 223, 234, 241, 252, 257, 261, 264, 268, 271, 280, 285, 287, 292, 295, 297, 304, 308, 313, 315, 319.
Prout, 36, 50, 63, 70, 85, 108, 118, 134, 141, 148, 152, 161, 172.
Pulcifer, }
Pulsefer, } 57, 70, 77, 124, 218, 226.
Pulsifer,
Pullen, 30, 36, 77.
Pulling, 209, 287, 319, 321, 325.
Pulman, 146.
Purington, } 3, 77, 116.
Purrington,
Pursley, 57.
Purvere, 344, 351.
Pusley, 275.
Putman, 230, 238, 244, 246, 249, 252.
Putnam, 226, 264.
Pyncheon, 287, 290.

Quakee, 9.
Quincy, 172, 178, 183, 188, 194, 213, 218, 226, 300, 304, 315, 321, 322, 326, 330.

Rachel, 131, 146, 162.
Radmore, 23.
Raimer, }
Raymar, } 45, 70, 85, 204, 209, 218, 226, 230,
Raymer, } 238, 244, 249, 258.
Raymor,
Rainger, } 172, 183, 188, 218, 223.
Ranger,
Ramme, 183.
Ramsdale, 70.
Ramsdel, 85.
Rand, 30, 45, 57, 63, 70, 72, 77, 86, 93, 100, 108, 110, 116, 119, 131, 138, 152, 162, 172, 183, 188, 327, 329, 331, 334, 345, 348, 349.
Randall, }
Randel, } 3, 11, 36, 85, 100, 194, 199, 209, 218,
Randol, } 226, 234, 271.
Randoll,
Ranks, 306.
Ransford, 3, 37, 188.
Ransted, 183, 194.
Rawlings, 63, 88, 100, 110, 124, 172, 356.
Rawson, 126, 138.
Ray, 199.
Rayman, 146.
Raymond, 238, 244.
Raynard, 354.
Rayner, 30, 88, 102.
Rea, 271, 290.
Read, } 23, 37, 44, 57, 63, 65, 77, 95, 124, 178.
Reed, } 194, 199, 218, 230, 287, 330, 333, 334,
Readin, }
Reading, } 93, 108, 119, 183.
Redin,
Record, 53, 73.
Reddock, 57.
Redduck, 50.
Redworth, 108.
Reeves, 124.
Renalds, 138.
Renalls, 131.
Reneauf, 178.
Reneuf, 37.
Renken, 223, 226, 234, 246.
Rennolls, 12, 30.
Renolds, 43.
Revere, 300, 304, 313, 317.
Reynolds, 152.
Rhodes, } 146, 152, 178, 183, 199, 258, 264, 278.
Rodes,
Rich, 43, 57, 77, 85, 93.
Richards, 3, 23, 30, 32, 43, 44, 78, 124, 134, 152, 183.
Richardson, 3, 16, 30, 93, 100, 116, 167, 183, 188, 194, 204, 319, 321.

Richbee, 100.
Rick, 340, 341, 345.
Ricks, 111, 124, 127, 141, 152, 162.
Rider, 258.
Ridgaway, } 172, 178, 183, 194, 199, 204, 209,
Ridgway, } 218, 223, 230, 249, 251, 271, 280, 285, 295, 300, 302, 304, 309, 311.
Ridley, 43.
Right, 93, 108.
Righton, 70.
Rillow, 172.
Ripener, } 70, 72, 93.
Ripner, }
Rivoire, 204, 218, 226.
Roach, 157, 172.
Rob, 271, 278, 287, 292.
Robbins, } 241, 246, 252, 261, 264, 295, 319,
Robins, } 324, 326.
Robbinson, } 23, 37, 39, 43, 45, 51, 57, 63, 78,
Robinson, } 93, 100, 108, 116, 124, 131, 138, 146, 152, 157, 167, 172, 178, 188, 209, 218, 234, 238, 268, 275, 356.
Roberts, 9, 16, 30, 37, 50, 86, 116, 124, 131, 138, 146, 152, 157, 166, 167, 178, 188, 189, 194, 199, 204, 213, 218, 223, 226, 234, 238, 244, 287, 297, 304, 309, 319, 321, 322, 324, 346.
Robertson, 331.
Robey, } 9, 19, 30, 139, 149, 152, 157, 167, 172,
Robie, } 183, 188, 209, 213, 264, 268, 275,
Roby, } 283, 285, 304, 313.
Robson, 280.
Rockwell, 261, 271, 277, 287.
Rogers, 30, 70, 119, 124, 131, 134, 138, 146, 148, 157, 162, 167, 172, 178, 183, 188, 194, 199, 204, 213, 218, 223, 226, 234, 238, 241, 246, 247, 254, 261, 268, 275, 278, 287.
Rogerson, 335, 340, 343.
Rolandson, 167.
Rolfe, 148, 152, 162, 194.
Rolison, }
Rolliston, }
Rolston, } 57, 70, 85, 108, 319, 321, 322, 325,
Rolstone, } 326, 329, 331.
Roulstone, }
Rowlston, }
Rollanson, 131.
Rosey, 78.
Ross, 57, 70, 80, 271, 277, 290.
Rouse, 43, 50, 78, 108, 124, 146.
Row, 124.
Rowel, 16, 77, 100, 116.
Rowell, 30, 37, 44, 63.
Rowles, 57.
Royal, } 16, 36, 102, 152, 162, 167, 178.
Royall, }
Rubey, 152, 162.
Ruck, 9, 16, 43, 57, 63, 77, 78, 85, 95, 108, 116, 152.
Ruddock, 85, 95, 230, 238, 241, 246, 249, 252, 261, 264, 268, 271, 280.
Rue, De, 266.
Ruggles, 3, 16, 19. 25, 30, 43, 44, 50, 51, 57, 77, 85, 100, 183, 199, 226, 234, 241, 246, 258, 261, 278, 324.
Rumbley, } 146, 152, 162, 172, 194, 209, 213,
Rumley, } 223, 226, 258.
Rush, 230, 241.
Russell, } 9, 16, 23, 36, 37, 43, 50, 63, 78, 100,
Russel, } 102, 119, 146, 152, 166, 172, 178,
Russell, } 183, 188, 199, 204, 209, 213, 218, 223, 230, 234, 238, 241, 244, 246, 268, 275, 292, 295, 333, 334, 335, 336, 337.

Sables, 10, 24, 37, 51.
Sacome, }
Seacom, } 23, 44, 53, 78.
Seacomb, }
Safford, 234.
Sale, 93, 100, 131, 139, 157, 162, 183, 234, 238.

Salisbury, } 58, 173, 183, 194, 205, 218, 238,
Salsbury, } 247, 258, 354.
Salmon, 51, 78, 93, 226, 234, 241, 244, 247, 272.
Salter, 51, 70, 78, 86, 93, 100, 108, 109, 110, 116, 119, 124, 134, 139, 147, 152, 162, 167, 172, 173, 178, 183, 194, 199, 204, 213, 227, 230, 234, 241, 244, 306, 321, 329.
Sampson, } 109, 189, 194, 204.
Samson, }
Sanders, } 3, 30, 51, 64, 78, 93, 101, 124, 139,
Saunders, } 147, 152, 157, 167, 178, 183, 189, 194, 209, 264, 280.
Sanderson, 4, 25, 58, 199, 219, 223.
Sandey, 10.
Sargent, 31, 37, 53, 124, 194, 199, 213, 223, 234.
Sartel, 268.
Sarvice, }
Service, } 78, 93, 116, 132, 231, 244.
Servis, }
Satly, 78.
Sault, 244.
Sautley, 95.
Savage, 4, 10, 23, 31, 32, 51, 58, 71, 108, 125, 131, 204, 227, 238, 244, 247, 252, 254, 258, 268, 275, 278, 287, 290, 292, 295, 300, 302, 313, 317, 321.
Savell, }
Savil, } 44, 70, 71, 78, 86, 101, 124, 183, 204, 226.
Savil, }
Sawyer, 264, 313.
Saxton, 116.
Scarlet, 139, 219.
Scollay, } 17, 31, 37, 58, 70, 86, 100, 124, 134,
Scolley, } 146, 230, 234, 244, 249, 258, 261,
Scolly, } 271, 280, 285, 287, 290, 334.
Scot, } 37, 45, 78, 80, 95, 108, 109, 124, 132,
Scott, } 139, 147, 152, 157, 162, 173, 183, 189, 199, 200, 209, 213, 227, 230, 241, 254, 271, 272, 278, 283, 287, 295, 317, 321, 324. 327.
Scottow, 10, 178, 194, 204, 213.
Scrivener, 157.
Scudder, 280, 283, 287, 290, 297, 302, 306, 311.
Scut, } 116, 153, 162, 209, 223.
Scutt, }
Seabury, 268.
Seares, }
Sears, } 9, 23, 78, 93, 109, 131, 146, 147, 162,
Seers, } 172, 183, 194, 209, 219.
Searle, 251, 258.
Seaver, } 306, 311, 315, 317, 321, 322.
Sever, }
Segarnee, } 19, 32, 46, 65, 80, 95, 110, 125,
Sigernee, } 139, 209, 214, 223, 226, 230, 238,
Sigorney, } 241, 244, 247, 249, 251, 252, 254,
Sigourney, } 258, 261, 268, 278, 280, 285.
Selly, 23.
Sentall, 72.
Sentel, 124.
Sentell, 86.
Sewall, } 10, 31, 108, 141, 147, 162, 173, 271,
Sewel, } 278, 283, 290, 292, 295, 300, 304.
Seward, 9, 37, 58, 178, 189, 199, 209, 219, 309, 313, 317, 321, 325.
Shaler, 124, 147.
Shaller, 178.
Sharp, 9, 17, 31, 39, 44, 46, 64, 71, 78, 86, 95, 101, 204.
Sharrow, 209.
Shattuck, 64, 71, 86.
Shaw, 4, 37, 51, 64, 100, 109, 124, 131, 132, 152, 157, 167, 199, 258, 268, 275, 280, 285, 290, 292, 295, 332, 339, 341, 353, 354, 355.
Shead, } 178, 189, 199, 209, 219, 223, 230.
Shed, }
Sheaf, } 78, 93, 108, 124, 134, 148, 157, 183,
Sheafe, } 194, 204.
Shelly, 213.
Shepard, 206, 210, 220, 224, 226, 227, 230, 232, 238, 247, 248, 249, 254.
Shepcot, 71.
Shepherd, 307, 311.

Shepreeve, 30, 37, 51, 71, 86, 117.
Sherar, 10, 19.
Sherburn, } 231, 245, 248, 251, 258, 261, 268,
Sherburne, } 275, 278, 283, 285, 330, 333, 335.
Sherlock, 93, 116.
Sherman, 249, 258, 261, 268, 278.
Sherrar, 44.
Sherrard, 3.
Sherren, 4.
Sherrer, 183.
Shipman, 149.
Shirley, 287.
Shoot, } 3, 23, 31, 131.
Shute, }
Shore, 19, 78, 86, 152.
Short, 44, 58, 80, 110.
Shower, 241.
Shrimpton, 19, 31.
Signac, 24, 31.
Sill, 17, 37.
Simkins, } 4, 17, 23, 71, 100, 178, 189, 199,
Simpkins, } 205, 209, 219, 227, 241, 254.
Simpson, } 3, 4, 9, 10, 17, 23, 31, 35, 37, 44, 51,
Simson, } 64, 70, 80, 86 93, 95, 100, 109, 110, 124, 132, 147, 157, 167, 172, 183, 194, 199, 204, 213, 218, 226, 230, 241, 244, 290.
Sims, } 45, 146, 152, 157, 167, 189, 194, 199,
Symmes, } 213, 218, 223, 230, 234, 241, 244,
Syms, } 258, 261, 268, 309, 317, 337, 339, 344, 347.
Sinckler, } 109, 124, 213.
Binkler, }
Singleton, 313, 315.
Sirey, 19, 51.
Skeppell, 23.
Skilleus, 325.
Skillin, } 238, 241, 247, 249.
Skilling, }
Skillings, 319.
Skinner, 9, 23, 44, 51, 59, 71, 93, 172, 183, 189, 223, 247, 252, 261, 268, 275, 283, 290.
Sleeper, 132.
Slegg, 17.
Blocomb, }
Slocome, } 37, 51, 64, 78, 100, 117, 139, 157.
Slocum, }
Slocume. }
Sloper, 238, 248, 264, 283.
Slowly, 238.
Smallage, } 71, 86, 100, 109, 117, 147, 157,
Smalledge, } 183, 189, 194, 249.
Smalleye, }
Smallpeace, } 3, 31, 44, 58, 70, 86, 100, 109,
Smallpeice, } 124, 194, 204, 219, 227, 234,
Smallpiece, } 242, 244, 249.
Smalpeice, }
Smibert, 205, 209, 214, 218.
Smith, 3, 4. 9, 10, 11, 17, 19, 24, 31, 37, 44, 51, 58, 59, 64, 71, 72, 78, 86, 93, 108, 116, 117, 124, 131, 132, 134, 139, 141, 146, 147, 149, 152, 157, 162, 167, 183, 189, 194, 199, 204, 209, 218, 238, 244, 247, 249, 268, 271, 275, 287, 2)2, 311, 317, 321, 334, 335, 338, 340, 346, 355.
Smithson, 4.
Snelling, 9, 10, 24, 31, 44, 57, 71, 86, 109, 132, 139, 152, 162, 173, 178, 183, 189, 194, 1 '', 204, 205, 209, 218, 219, 223, 2 30, 238, 244.
Snoden, 86, 167, 183, 199, 214, 227.
Snoman, 93.
Snoton. 3, 23, 64.
Snow, 223, 234, 244, 317, 321, 342, 344, 348, 351, 353.
Snowton, 10, 39, 51.
Solle, 4.
Somers, 173.
Somes, 319, 328.
Scper, 4, 17, 31, 64, 78.
Soren, 287, 292.
Sorieu, 46, 65, 230, 234, 238.

Southack, } 3, 16, 31, 37, 71, 93, 326.
Southsick, }
Souther, 116, 124, 139, 152, 162, 178, 195.
Sowersby, 189, 209.
Speakman, 241, 264, 330.
Spear, 271, 278, 280, 287, 292, 295, 309, 337, 340, 342, 344, 346, 349, 350, 355.
Spencer, 17, 23, 31, 37, 44, 53, 58, 71, 100, 124.
Spike, 78.
Spiller, 93, 124, 146.
Spooner, 189, 199, 209, 219, 292, 300, 306.
Sprague, 57, 64, 152, 162, 173, 223, 330, 331, 333, 334, 335, 337, 338, 339, 341, 344, 347, 349.
Squire, 39.
Stacey, 23, 37, 152, 162.
Stackpole. 351.
Stainer, 268, 272.
Stanbridge, 108, 162, 167, 183.
Stanhope, 349, 350, 353, 355.
Staniford, 51.
Stanley, 290.
Stanney, 125, 157, 178, 189, 204.
Staples, 108, 344.
Starkey, 157.
Starkie, 139.
Starling, 139.
Starr, 100.
Stayner, 261, 264.
Stearns, 173.
Stebbens, } 100, 116, 117, 125, 139, 302, 313.
Stebbins, }
Stedmau, 325, 328, 330.
Steel, 65, 80, 87, 100, 117, 119, 139, 147, 152, 157, 162, 178.
Stephens, } 3, 10, 17, 24, 37, 44, 58, 64, 70, 78,
Stevens, } 93, 109, 116, 117, 126, 139, 152, 167, 178, 199, 234, 241, 251, 254, 275, 278, 283, 327, 328, 331, 335, 336.
Sterling, 244, 252.
Sterns, 189.
Stesson, 147.
Stevenson, 306, 309.
Stewart, } 78, 117, 167, 241, 268, 295, 302, 309,
Stuart. } 313
Stillman, 232, 300, 311, 313, 317, 321, 322, 324, 327, 343, 344, 345, 348, 350.
Stocker, 111, 124, 139, 152, 162, 178.
Stoddar, } 17, 30, 51, 109, 124, 132, 139, 146,
Stoddard, } 162, 167, 172, 173, 183, 194, 199, 209, 213, 214, 218, 227, 230, 247, 249, 254, 275.
Stodder, 334, 334, 340, 341.
Stokes, 213, 223, 321.
Stone, 10, 17, 37, 152, 157, 173, 178, 183, 189, 199, 209.
Storar, } 86, 109, 157, 167, 172, 173, 178, 194,
Storer, } 219, 227, 2 38, 247, 271, 280, 285, 290, 295, 302, 309, 329.
Storey, } 10, 17, 44, 51, 93, 102, 116, 125, 126,
Story, } 131, 139, 146, 152, 167, 178, 189, 194, 209, 247, 251, 258, 264, 271, 285, 290, 292.
Stoughton, 302.
Stow, 321.
Stowe, 251.
Stratton. 3, 17, 37, 167.
Street, 109, 132.
Stride, 124, 199.
Striger, 110.
Stringer, 139, 178, 189, 219.
Stroag, 70, 86, 108, 178, 199.
Stroud, 178.
Studson, } 10, 31, 44, 131, 139, 157, 167, 173,
Stutson, } 18, 309.
Sturges, 183, 194, 209.
Sullivan, 319.
Sumner, 10, 17, 37, 51, 64, 78, 167, 178, 189, 2 19, 204, 213, 226, 238, 239, 287, 300, 304, 309, 315, 339.
Sunderland. 23, 31. 51.
Sutton, 178, 153, 194, 219, 306.

Swain, Swaine, } 17, 31, 194.
Swan, 224, 258, 271, 278.
Swaiton, 117, 132, 147, 238.
Swasey, 95.
Sweetaer, Sweetsir, Swicher, Switser, } 4, 23, 31, 37, 64, 178, 189, 199, 209, 214, 223, 230, 238, 244, 254, 261, 268.
Swett, 347, 348, 355.
Swift, 315, 319, 322.
Syrcomb, 305.
Taller, Tayler, } 109, 132, 268, 280, 285, 309, 311, 313.
Talbut, 125.
Tannatt, 341.
Tapper, 139, 167, 178.
Tarbox, 167, 178, 184, 195, 200, 209, 214, 223, 231, 234, 247, 258, 268.
Tarr, 264, 272.
Tate, 309, 313.
Tay, 24.
Taylor, 5, 17, 31, 93, 117, 139, 149, 157, 167, 178, 227, 235, 238, 244, 250, 258, 268, 300, 302, 304, 307, 309, 313.
Teach, 214.
Teague, 162, 173.
Teer, 157.
Tekel, 117.
Tely, 10.
Temlet, 147.
Temple, 157.
Tenney, Tenny, } 157, 162, 173, 195.
Tew, 51, 86.
Thacher, Thatcher, } 125, 139, 252, 258, 264, 272, 290, 295, 300.
Thare, Thayer, } 44, 51, 71, 78, 86, 101, 153, 173, 219, 227, 231, 255, 280, 302, 304, 309, 313, 346, 349, 350, 352, 353, 354.
Thomas, 10, 17, 37, 44, 58, 64, 71, 86, 93, 101, 109, 117, 132, 139, 147, 153, 157, 167, 173, 183, 184, 195, 214, 223, 247, 252, 265, 275, 324.
Thompson, Thomson, Tomson, } 10, 38, 51, 58, 71, 93, 117, 125, 132, 153, 167, 178, 189, 195, 205, 209, 210, 223, 250, 292, 297, 300, 304, 307, 309, 311, 317, 321, 328, 330, 332, 334.
Thorald, Thorold, } 19, 31, 162.
Thorn, 71, 93, 109, 117, 125, 157, 162, 173.
Thorning, 4.
Thornton, 11, 125, 132, 153, 157, 162, 167, 178, 184, 189, 195, 205, 210, 227, 244.
Thorp, 195, 205, 210, 219, 227, 254.
Thurber, 38.
Thwing, Twing, } 4, 24, 78, 93, 109, 117, 125, 147, 153, 162, 167, 173, 184, 189, 195, 205, 214, 219, 223, 231, 235, 238, 241, 244, 247, 252, 292, 300, 302, 307, 311, 315, 319, 322, 325, 328, 335.
Ticknor, 339.
Tidmarsh, 214, 219, 227.
Tilburt, 101.
Tilden, 244, 247, 254, 258, 261, 272, 319, 329, 331, 335, 336, 338, 339, 341, 345, 346, 347, 348, 349.
Tiler, Tyler, } 4, 10, 17, 31, 78, 93, 117, 125, 132, 139, 147, 153, 157, 162, 167, 173, 178, 184, 189, 195, 200, 205, 209, 219, 227, 231, 234, 238, 241, 247, 248, 250, 254, 258, 264, 265, 278, 297, 302, 315, 335, 336, 338, 339, 346.
Tileston, Tilestone, Tilleston, } 58, 78, 117, 210, 219, 223, 238, 241, 250, 292, 297, 302, 307, 336, 338, 341, 342, 345, 347, 350, 351.
Tilley, Tyley, } 86, 94, 117, 132, 139, 147, 157, 162, 167, 173, 184, 189, 209.
Tillet, 101.
Tilley, Tilly, } 184, 195, 200, 209, 214, 223, 268.
Tilson, 258.

Tilton, 264.
Timberlake, Timber Lake, } 71, 93, 102, 132, 147, 157.
Tinkum, 173, 205, 210, 214, 219, 227, 231.
Todd, 153, 162, 258.
Tolman, 38, 59, 117, 132, 147.
Tomlin, 11, 37.
Too, 17.
Topp, 258, 265, 272.
Torey, 117.
Torrey, Torry, } 4, 10, 24, 32, 45, 51, 184, 190, 195, 200, 205, 209, 210, 214, 219, 220, 223, 227, 231, 232, 235, 238, 242, 244, 250, 258, 287, 292, 293, 297, 300, 304, 309, 313, 317.
Tothill, 195, 205, 214, 223, 231.
Tout, 184.
Tower, 195, 348, 350, 352.
Townesend, Townsend, } 4, 5, 17, 19, 24, 31, 37, 38, 44, 51, 58, 64, 71, 78, 86, 93, 101, 109, 117, 125, 132, 139, 147, 162, 167, 173, 178, 189, 200, 205, 209, 214, 219, 223, 227, 231, 244, 234, 241, 247, 265, 268, 272, 278, 283, 292.
Towzer, 178.
Trarice, 17.
Trask, 64, 78, 86.
Treat, 102, 117, 147, 265, 272.
Trebeo, 132.
Trebou, 147.
Trecothick, 167.
Tree, 304, 311, 315.
Treludia, 189.
Trench, 117, 139, 147, 167, 332.
Trisot, 117.
Trott, 73, 93, 184, 189, 195, 200, 292, 297.
Trout, 139, 157, 184, 189, 214.
Troutbeck, 300.
Trow, 173, 184.
Trew, True, } 200, 214, 227, 241, 247, 250.
Tucker, 53, 65, 78, 101, 109, 117, 200, 210, 219, 227, 234.
Tudor, 209, 219, 227, 241, 258, 275, 329, 330, 332, 333, 335, 336, 338, 339.
Tuell, 153.
Tuffts, Tufts, } 275, 278, 354.
Tuften, Tufton, } 93, 117, 132, 261, 307.
Tukesbury, 330, 334.
Turel, Turell, } 10, 102, 132, 147, 153, 162, 167, 178, 183, 189, 195, 200, 205, 219, 275.
Turner, 17, 31, 44, 58, 86, 117, 227, 234, 245, 258, 275, 285, 290, 346, 348, 350, 351.
Tuttle, 51, 64, 78, 86, 87, 93, 101, 117, 132, 153, 157, 162, 167, 173, 178, 184, 189, 227.
Tyhurst, 32, 46.
Tyng, 214, 219, 227, 231, 234, 235, 238, 251, 244.

Underwood, 31, 178, 195, 205, 239, 309, 315, 321.
Updike, 10.
Uran, Urann, } 102, 119, 125, 140, 153, 157, 162, 167, 178, 278, 283, 288, 290, 293, 304, 313, 315, 319, 321, 324, 326.
Uter, 38.

Vail, 162, 173.
Valentine, Valintine, Vallentine, } 17, 24, 88, 110, 125, 311, 315, 319.
Valnais, De, 332.
Vamus, 132.
Vaneps, 125.
Vans, 184, 195, 200, 210.
Vardy, 200, 205.
Varney, 24, 44, 51, 59, 64, 71, 72, 79, 86, 101, 125.
Varnon, 313.
Vassall, 238, 241, 244, 247.
Vaughan, 4, 147, 157, 238, 244, 258.

INDEX OF NAMES. 377

Veach, 4.
Velvin, 126, 147.
Venner, 178, 184, 195.
Venteman, 4, 25, 44, 86.
Venteno, 101.
Ventinon, Vintenon, } 189, 200, 210, 265.
Vergoose, Virgoose, } 58, 210, 227.
Verin, 4.
Vering, 31, 125.
Vernon, 242, 251, 268, 272.
Vial, Viall, } 10, 64, 79, 125, 162, 173, 184, 189, 231.
Vibert, 44.
Vickers, 24, 139.
Vickery, 231, 238, 250, 254.
Viler, 10.
Vinall, 134, 141, 173, 189, 227, 302, 305, 307.
Vincent, 31, 39, 51, 53, 227, 235.
Vingus, 184.
Viscount, 210.
Vittery, 147.
Viven, 44.
Von Exter, 341.
Vose, 258, 265, 268, 278, 317, 321, 353.
Vrling, Vryling, } 31, 38, 71, 79.
Vryland, 51, 101.

Wacombe, Wacome, Waycomb, } 10, 18, 72, 80, 94, 110.
Wade, 250.
Wadland, 184.
Wadlin, 200.
Wadling, 24, 44, 58.
Wadsworth, 10, 44, 148.
Wager, 101.
Waine, 81, 64, 94.
Wainright, Wainwright, } 94, 118, 168.
Waite, 117, 119, 153, 163, 195, 255.
Wakefeeld, Wakefeild, Wakefield, } 10, 18, 24, 32, 34, 45, 52, 53, 64, 65, 71, 79, 86, 117, 126, 133, 140, 148, 153, 158, 167, 184, 190, 200, 210, 219.
Waker, 11, 117.
Walch, 285, 290, 295, 300.
Walcott, Wolcut, } 158, 179, 205, 214.
Walden, 163.
Waldering, 125.
Waldo, Woldo, } 4, 19, 32, 38, 58, 64, 79, 80, 94, 109, 117, 119, 133, 140, 149, 157, 158, 163, 167, 168, 178, 184, 189, 214, 223, 27), 285, 295, 298, 303, 307, 309. 311, 316, 322.
Waldron, 158, 168, 179.
Walker, 17, 24, 31, 38, 44, 52, 58, 71, 72, 73, 88, 94, 117, 118, 133, 140, 148, 173, 184, 189, 200, 205, 214, 219, 223, 231, 238, 241, 244, 254, 255, 261, 268, 309, 314, 319, 342, 344, 345, 346, 356.
Walley, 118, 141, 149, 158, 163, 173, 272, 317, 319, 324, 325, 326, 328.
Wallice, Wallis, Wallise, } 11, 25, 45, 58, 65, 85, 117, 140, 153, 210, 219, 224, 231, 235, 238, 241, 250, 254, 259, 268, 293.
Walter, 59, 86, 118, 125, 157, 158, 163, 173, 179, 189, 200, 210, 219.
Walton, 224, 235.
Ward, 335, 336, 338.
Wardall, Wardel, Wardell, Wardwel, Wardwell, } 10, 24, 52, 79, 87, 88, 95, 102, 110, 131, 149, 173, 244, 251, 255, 252.
Warden, 94, 126, 140, 153, 158, 168, 173, 179, 190, 195, 214, 250, 317, 323.
Ware, 190.
Warham, 178, 190, 200.

Warner, 153, 168, 173, 184, 190, 200, 205, 214, 219, 227, 231, 235, 241, 247, 293, 340.
Warrick, Warwick, } 64, 79, 94, 118, 134, 158, 179.
Wass, 80.
Waterhouse, 190, 200, 210, 219, 223, 224.
Waterman, 317, 319, 323.
Waters, Watters, } 11, 18, 38, 45, 51, 94, 109, 118, 133, 158, 168, 223, 231, 244, 254, 259, 265, 323.
Watkins, 4, 132, 162, 189.
Watson, Wattson, } 79, 125, 173, 350, 351.
Watts, 86, 95, 111, 125, 132, 133, 148, 168, 179, 184, 195, 205, 210, 214, 219, 231, 309, 313, 316.
Way, 4, 184, 195, 224.
Wear, Weare, } 52, 64, 87, 293, 298.
Weavor, 32, 45.
Webb, 11, 52, 58, 64, 94, 101, 109, 118, 140, 153, 158, 162, 163, 168, 179, 184, 195, 205, 214, 219, 223, 231, 235, 238, 241, 247, 250, 259, 300, 305, 309, 356.
Webber, 24, 38, 39, 51, 53, 80, 94, 95, 132, 133, 153, 173, 214, 283, 285, 293, 297, 305, 311.
Weber, 4.
Webster, 12, 19, 24, 45, 53, 72, 94, 95, 118, 126, 147, 153, 163, 168, 179, 184, 195, 223, 235.
Wedford, 195.
Weeler, 10, 87, 101.
Weems, 133.
Welch, Welich, } 12, 32, 64, 79, 87, 94, 101, 133, 148, 158, 163, 173, 184, 195, 214, 219, 223, 307, 311, 315, 317, 354, 355.
Weld, 342.
Welland, 71, 79, 101, 125, 140, 153, 168, 179, 184.
Welles, Wells, } 4, 11, 18, 38, 168, 184, 200, 227, 231, 239, 241, 244, 307, 327, 328, 321, 331, 333, 331, 337, 339.
Welsh, 227, 288, 293, 300, 305, 331, 332, 334, 336, 338.
Welsteed, 79.
Wems, 148.
Wendall, Wendell, } 110, 125, 133, 149, 157, 162, 173, 179, 184, 189, 195, 200, 205, 210, 214, 219, 223, 227, 231, 283, 288, 290, 295, 297, 305, 307, 317, 320.
Wentworth, 101, 118, 214, 224, 283, 288.
West, 178, 195, 205, 210, 219, 227, 231, 238, 247, 250, 293.
Weston, 258.
Weyman, 179.
Wharton, 4, 11, 125, 214, 219.
Wheatley, 255, 262, 268.
Wheeler, Wheler, } 5, 17, 24, 38, 52, 53, 64, 79, 87, 94, 118, 140, 153, 168, 173, 179, 184, 189, 190, 200, 205, 210, 214, 219, 223, 224, 227, 231, 235, 238, 241, 244, 255, 261, 255, 313, 353.
Wheelwright, 118, 140, 153, 179, 189, 195, 227, 250, 255, 293, 297, 303.
Wheer for Wheeler, 353.
Wheppe, 227, 231, 238, 244.
Whetcomb, 52, 72, 87, 109, 132.
Whippe, 278.
Whipple, 321, 822.
Whiston, 302, 307.
Whitaker, 148, 184, 189, 200.
White, 4, 11, 17, 19, 24, 38, 44, 45, 46, 53, 58, 65, 71, 72, 79, 87, 94, 101, 109, 118, 125, 126, 132, 133, 140, 141, 148, 149, 153, 157, 158, 162, 163, 173, 179, 184, 189, 190, 195, 205, 214, 223, 235, 238, 254, 258, 262, 265, 268, 275, 280, 293, 297, 313, 320, 325, 326, 328, 335, 337, 344.
Whitehead, Whitehed, } 101, 126, 147.

Whitell, 140.
Whitemore, 101, 110, 118, 125, 133.
Whitford, 87.
Whiting, 261, 265, 268, 275, 285, 290.
Whitley, 250.
Whitman, 10, 32, 118, 141, 158, 163, 168, 173, 184, 210, 214, 250, 258, 265, 268, 272, 278, 285, 354, 355.
Whitney, 189, 195, 200. 210, 214, 223, 227, 235, 238, 244, 342, 344, 347, 348, 349, 350, 352, 353, 354.
Whittel, 278.
Whittemore,) 149, 153, 163, 167, 168, 173,
Whittimore,) 178, 184, 189, 195, 200, 205, 214, 219, 223, 261, 272.
Whittmore, 219, 224.
Whitwel,) 102, 126, 140, 231, 241, 285, 323,
Whitwell,) 324.
Whitworth, 265, 272.
Wiat,)
Wyat,)
Wyate, } 11, 64, 87, 101, 125.
Wyatt,)
Wiborn, 4, 117.
Wier,)
Wire,)
Wyer, } 4, 17, 38, 53, 94, 118, 205.
Wyre,)
Wilcot, 79.
Wild, 51, 87, 101, 118, 133, 148, 158, 337, 339, 340, 342.
Wildey, 94.
Wilkins, 12, 24.
Wilkinson, 109, 140.
Willard, 5, 11, 18, 24, 32, 38, 45, 125, 133, 141, 153, 163.
Willcocks,) 341, 344, 348, 349.
Willcox,)
Willet,) 11, 31, 39, 52, 64, 87, 101, 118, 133,
Willett,) 168, 173, 179, 241.
Williams, 11, 18, 19, 24, 31, 38, 44, 45, 52, 58, 64, 65, 71, 72, 79, 86, 87, 94, 101, 109, 110, 118, 119, 125, 126, 140, 141, 147, 158, 163, 173, 179, 184, 189, 195, 200, 205, 214, 223, 224, 227, 231, 245, 241, 244, 248, 250, 255, 265, 275, 280, 283, 285, 290, 293, 295, 298, 300, 311, 317, 340.
Willis,) 38, 58, 71, 79, 87, 94, 101, 110, 118,
Willise, } 125, 132, 140, 153, 189, 190, 205,
Williss,) 214, 241, 251, 283, 288, 298.
Williston, 4, 18, 31, 52, 71, 87, 109, 125, 141, 158, 167, 179, 184, 200, 205, 214, 219, 223, 227. 245, 244.
Wilson, 17, 18, 31, 32, 45, 52, 58, 86, 126, 147, 153, 157, 250.

Wimble, 167, 179, 214, 223, 231.
Winburn, 45.
Winchister, 109, 118, 132.
Wincoll, 179.
Windsor, 179, 195.
Wing, 38, 51, 109, 118, 140, 148, 163, 200.
Wingfield, 205, 227.
Winnock, 173, 179, 184.
Winship, 210.
Winslow, 4, 12, 24, 38, 52, 64, 87, 158, 168, 173, 195, 200, 210, 214, 219, 227, 231, 272, 275, 280, 283, 288, 293, 295, 297, 298, 300, 307, 313, 317, 350, 352, 353.
Winsor, 4.
Winter, 118, 141, 163, 219, 227, 231, 235, 244, 250, 259, 283, 307.
Winthrop, 24, 32, 52, 58, 65, 79, 94, 101, 118, 125, 153, 162, 168.
Wise, 173, 214.
Wiswall, 148, 157, 173, 205, 290, 293.
Wood, 101, 102, 190, 214, 219, 262.
Woodhery,) 101, 117, 125, 163, 184.
Woodberry,)
Wooden, 148.
Woods, 110, 125, 140, 227, 235, 244, 247, 251, 259.
Woodward, 79, 94, 109, 241, 247, 248, 255, 265, 272, 275, 300, 326, 328, 333, 337, 339, 342.
Woodwel, 94.
Woody, 25.
Woolfe, 148.
Wootton, 205.
Wormwall,) 10, 31, 38, 64.
Wormwell,)
Worth, 79, 118, 235, 241.
Worthylake,) 12, 24, 52, 71, 94, 118.
Worthyleg,)
Wright, 12, 17, 45, 118, 140, 147, 148, 157, 158, 168, 205, 340, 342, 346, 347, 349, 350.
Wroe, 162, 189, 195, 205.
Wyborn, 18, 44.
Wyman,) 347, 350.
Wymann,)

Yates, 101, 118.
Yeals, 133, 148.
Yeamans, 153.
York, 179, 190, 200, 215, 227.
Young, 18, 65, 87, 110, 118, 126, 133, 140, 148, 153, 163, 168, 174, 179, 184, 190, 195, 200, 205, 210, 215, 219, 224, 231, 238, 253.
Youngman, 72. 101, 119, 133, 149, 153, 163, 174, 179.

NEGROES.

Abel Barbadoes, 339.
Chloe Barbadoes, 339.
Richard Bordman, 40.
Ann Boidman, 40.
Samuel Bow, 5.
Eliner Bow, 5.
Nathaniel Butler, 346.
Lydia Butler, 346.
Robert Due, 248.
Margaret Due, 248.
Ned Edwards, 2.
Margaret Edwards, 2.
Richard George, 217.
Maria George, 217.
Thomas Quaquo, 102.
Thomas Simit, 102.
Robert Soco or Socow, 107, 131.
Fidella Soco or Socow, 107, 131.
Exeter Turner, 45, 51.
Lucy Turner, 45, 51.
Derby Vassell, 352, 353, 354, 355.

Lucy Vassell, 352, 353, 354, 355.

Amaritta, 126, 356.
Anthony, 126, 356.
Boston, 6, 20, 29, 57.
Charles, 92.
Cloe, 246.
Cornwall, 265.
Dinah, 130.
Hagar, 190, 206, 245.
Hager, 4.
Jane, 6, 20, 39, 57.
Jeffery, 246.
John, 314.
Joseph, 317.
Katharine, 265.
Lancaster, 293.
Lettice, 283
Maudlin, 92.
Menzer, 283.
Molly, 317, 320.

Nancy, 115.
Nanney, 107.
Onesimus, 190, 206.
Othelo, 305.
Patience, 130.
Peter, 325.
Poledore, 321.
Ratcliffe, 245.

Richard, 4.
Samuel, 305, 321, 325.
Shaper, or Sharper, 317, 320.
Sisley, 130.
Susanna, 314.
Sylvia, 305, 321, 325.
Tobey, 130.
Wanlip, 115.

www.ingramcontent.com/pod-product-compliance
Lightning Source LLC
Chambersburg PA
CBHW051803230426
43672CB00012B/2614